A DIGEST

OF THE

LAW OF EVIDENCE

BY

SIR JAMES FITZJAMES STEPHEN, Bart., K. C. S. I., D. C. L.

FORMERLY A JUDGE OF THE HIGH COURT OF JUSTICE, QUEEN'S
BENCH DIVISION; HONORARY FELLOW OF
TRINITY COLLEGE, CAMBRIDGE

SECOND AMERICAN EDITION

(FROM THE SIXTH ENGLISH EDITION)

WITH ANNOTATIONS AND REFERENCES TO AMERICAN CASES

BY

GEORGE CHASE, LL.B.

PROFESSOR OF LAW IN THE NEW YORK LAW SCHOOL, NEW YORK CITY,
AND DEAN OF THE FACULTY

NEW YORK
PRINTED FOR THE EDITOR
1907

EDITOR'S NOTE TO FIRST AMERICAN EDITION.

THE merits of "Stephen's Digest" are too well known to need repetition. It has been accepted in this country, as well as in England, as a standard treatise upon the subject of Evidence. The editor has sought in this edition to increase its usefulness for American lawyers and students of law by fully annotating it, so as to exhibit the general principles of the American Law of Evidence in accordance with the latest and best decisions. The contents of the original work are preserved without change, except that, in a few instances, articles stating special provisions of English statutes have been transferred to the foot-notes or to the Appendix. These transfers are always clearly indicated wherever made. But no omissions have been made, and the editor's additions are always indicated by being enclosed between brackets. It will, therefore, be easy to distinguish between the original articles and notes and those of this edition. The extent of correspondence or difference between the English and the American law is thus made clearly manifest.

The American cases cited by the editor are considerably more numerous than the English citations of Mr. Stephen; this has seemed necessary in order that the book might satisfactorily exhibit the Law of Evidence for the different States and Territories, and thus be serviceable in all parts of the country.

A new and more complete index will be found in this edition.

G. C.

NEW YORK, October, 1885.

EDITOR'S NOTE TO SECOND AMERICAN EDITION.

THIS edition incorporates such additions and changes in the text of the work as were made by Mr. Stephen in the last English edition which was published before his death.

The annotations which set forth the American law have been

thoroughly revised and largely re-written. Some important topics
have thus received fuller treatment than was given to them in
the former edition. In the twelve years that have elapsed since
that edition appeared several thousand cases have been published
in the American reports, bearing upon the subject of Evidence.
These have been carefully examined, and are extensively cited
in the notes, so as to exhibit the law upon this subject in its latest
development. Many new Illustrations have also been added.

As in the former edition, whatever I have added to the original
English work is inclosed in brackets.

I have received many gratifying assurances from lawyers and
law-students that my former edition has been found by them
very helpful, both in study and in practice. I trust this edition
will be even more so. I can truly agree with Mr. Stephen in
saying (see page xv, *infra*), that "the labor bestowed upon the
work has been in an inverse ratio to its size."

G. C.

New York, January, 1898.

PREFACE TO THE SIXTH ENGLISH EDITION.

I HAVE referred in this edition to the cases decided and statutes passed since the publication of its predecessor and down to
the end of 1892. The law has hardly been altered at all since
the book was first published. Short as it is, I believe it will be
found to contain practically the whole of the law on the subject.

J. F. STEPHEN.

CONTENTS.

PART I.

RELEVANCY.

CHAPTER I.—PRELIMINARY.

CHAPTER II.—OF FACTS IN ISSUE AND RELEVANT TO THE ISSUE.

CHAPTER III.—OCCURRENCES SIMILAR TO BUT UNCONNECTED WITH THE FACTS IN ISSUE, IRRELEVANT EXCEPT IN CERTAIN CASES.

CHAPTER IV.—HEARSAY IRRELEVANT EXCEPT IN CERTAIN CASES.

SECTION I.—Hearsay when relevant.

PART II.

ON PROOF.

PART III.

PRODUCTION AND EFFECT OF EVIDENCE.

INTRODUCTION.

In the years 1870-1871 I drew what afterwards became the Indian Evidence Act (Act 1 of 1872). This Act began by repealing (with a few exceptions) the whole of the Law of Evidence then in force in India, and proceeded to re-enact it in the form of a code of 167 sections, which has been in operation in India since Sept., 1872. I am informed that it is generally understood, and has required little judicial commentary or exposition.

In the autumn of 1872 Lord Coleridge (then Attorney-General) employed me to draw a similar code for England. I did so in the course of the winter, and we settled it in frequent consultations. It was ready to be introduced early in the Session of 1873. Lord Coleridge made various attempts to bring it forward, but he could not succeed till the very last day of the Session. He said a few words on the subject on the 5th August, 1873, just before Parliament was prorogued. The Bill was thus never made public, though I believe it was ordered to be printed.

It was drawn on the model of the Indian Evidence Act, and contained a complete system of law upon the subject of Evidence.

The present work is founded upon this Bill, though it differs from it in various respects. Lord Coleridge's Bill proposed a variety of amendments of the existing law. These are omitted in the present work, which is intended to represent the existing law exactly as it stands. The Bill, of course, was in the ordinary form of an Act of Parliament. In the book I have allowed myself more freedom of expression, though I have spared no pains to make my statements precise and complete.

In December, 1875, at the request of the Council of Legal Education, I undertook the duties of Professor of Common Law, at the Inns of Court, and I chose the Law of Evidence for the subject of

my first course of lectures. It appeared to me that the draft Bill
which I had prepared for Lord Coleridge supplied the materials
for such a statement of the law as would enable students to obtain
a precise and systematic acquaintance with it in a moderate space
of time, and without a degree of labor disproportionate to its importance in relation to other branches of the law. No such work,
so far as I know, exists; for all the existing books on the Law of
Evidence are written on the usual model of English law-books,
which, as a general rule, aim at being collections, more or less
complete, of all the authorities upon a given subject, to which a
judge would listen in an argument in court. Such works often
become, under the hands of successive editors, the repositories of
an extraordinary amount of research, but they seem to me to have
the effect of making the attainment by direct study of a real
knowledge of the law, or of any branch of it as a whole, almost
impossible. The enormous mass of detail and illustration which
they contain, and the habit into which their writers naturally fall,
of introducing into them everything which has any sort of connection, however remote, with the main subject, make these books
useless for purposes of study, though they may increase their utility
as works of reference. The enormous size and length of the standard works of reference is a proof of this. They consist of thousands
of pages and refer to many thousand cases. When we remember
that the Law of Evidence forms only one branch of the Law of
Procedure, and that the Substantive Law which regulates rights
and duties ought to be treated independently of it, it becomes
obvious that if a lawyer is to have anything better than a familiarity
with indexes, he must gain his knowledge in some other way than
from existing books. No doubt such knowledge is to be gained.
Experience gives by degrees, in favorable cases, a comprehensive
acquaintance with the principles of the law with which a prac-
titioner is conversant. He gets to see that it is shorter and simpler
than it looks, and to understand that the innumerable cases which
at first sight appear to constitute the law, are really no more than

illustrations of a comparatively small number of principles; but those who have gained knowledge of this kind have usually no opportunity to impart it to others. Moreover, they acquire it very slowly, and with needless labor themselves, and though knowledge so acquired is often specially vivid and well remembered, it is often fragmentary, and the possession of it not unfrequently renders those who have it sceptical as to the possibility, and even as to the expediency, of producing anything more systematic and complete.

The circumstances already mentioned led me to put into a systematic form such knowledge of the subject as I had acquired. This work is the result. The labor bestowed upon it has, I may say, been in an inverse ratio to its size. My object in it has been to separate the subject of evidence from other branches of the law with which it has commonly been mixed up; to reduce it into a compact systematic form, distributed according to the natural division of the subject-matter; and to compress into precise definite rules, illustrated by examples, such cases and statutes as properly relate to the subject-matter so limited and arranged. I have attempted, in short, to make a digest of the law, which, if it were thought desirable, might be used in the preparation of a code, and which will, I hope, be useful, not only to professional students, but to every one who takes an intelligent interest in a part of the law of his country bearing directly on every kind of investigation into questions of fact, as well as on every branch of litigation.

The Law of Evidence is composed of two elements, namely, first, an enormous number of cases, almost all of which have been decided in the course of the last 100 or 150 years, and which have already been collected and classified in various ways by a succession of text writers, from Gilbert and Peake to Taylor and Roscoe; secondly, a comparatively small number of Acts of Parliament which have been passed in the course of the last thirty or forty years, and have effected a highly beneficial revolution in the law as it was when it attracted the denunciations of Bentham. Writers on the Law of Evidence usually refer to statutes by the hundred, but the Acts of Parliament which really relate to the subject are but few. A detailed account of this matter will be found at the end of the volume, in Note XLVIII.

The arrangement of this book is the same as that of the Indian Evidence Act, and is based upon the distinction between relevancy and proof, that is, between the question, What facts may be proved? and the question, How must a fact be proved, assuming that proof of it may be given? The neglect of this distinction, which is concealed by the ambiguity of the word evidence (a word which sometimes means testimony and at other times relevancy) has thrown the whole subject into confusion, and has made what is really plain enough appear almost incomprehensible.

In my Introduction to the Indian Evidence Act published in 1872, and in speeches made in the Indian Legislative Council, I entered fully upon this matter. It will be sufficient here to notice shortly the principle on which the arrangement of the subject is based, and the manner in which the book has been arranged in consequence.

The great bulk of the Law of Evidence consists of negative rules declaring what, as the expression runs, is not evidence.

The doctrine that all the facts in issue and relevant to the issue, and no others, may be proved, is the unexpressed principle which forms the center of and gives unity to all these express negative rules. To me these rules always appeared to form a hopeless mass of confusion, which might be remembered by a great effort, but could not be understood as a whole, or reduced to a system, until it occurred to me to ask the question, What is this evidence which you tell me hearsay is not? The expression "hearsay is not evidence" seemed to assume that I knew by the light of nature what evidence was, but I perceived at last that that was just what I did not know. I found that I was in the position of a person who, having never seen a cat, is instructed about them in this fashion: "Lions are not cats, nor are tigers nor leopards, though you might be inclined to think they were." Show me a cat to begin with, and I at once understand both what is meant by saying that a lion is not a cat, and why it is possible to call him one. Tell me what evidence is, and I shall be able to understand why you say that this and that class of facts are not evidence. The question "What is evidence?" gradually disclosed the ambiguity of the word. To describe a matter of fact as "evidence" in the sense of testimony is obviously nonsense. No one wants to be told that hearsay, whatever else it is, is not testimony. What then does the phrase mean? The only possible answer is: It means that the one fact either is or else is not considered by the person using the expression to furnish a premise or part of a premise from which the existence of the other is a necessary or probable inference,—in other words, that the one fact is or is not relevant to the other. When the inquiry is pushed further, and the nature of relevancy has to be considered in itself, and apart from legal rules about it, we are led to inductive logic, which shows that the judicial evidence is only one case of the general problem of science—namely, inferring the unknown from the known. As far as the logical theory of the matter is concerned, this is an ultimate answer. The logical theory was cleared up by Mr. Mill. Bentham and some other[1] writers had more or less discussed the connection of logic with the rules of evidence. But I am not aware that it occurred to any one before I published my 'Introduction to the Indian Evidence Act' to point out in detail the very close resemblance which exists between Mr. Mill's theory and the existing state of the law.

The law has been worked out by degrees by many generations of judges who perceived more or less distinctly the principle on which it ought to be founded. The rules established by them no doubt treat as relevant some facts which cannot perhaps be said to be so. More frequently they treat as irrelevant facts which are really

---

[1] See, *e.g.*, that able and interesting book 'An Essay on Circumstantial Evidence,' by the late Mr. Wills, father of Mr. Justice Wills, Q. C. Chief Baron Gilbert's work on the Law of Evidence is founded on Locke's 'Essay,' much as my work is founded on Mill's 'Logic.'

relevant, but exceptions excepted, all their rules are reducible to the principle that facts in issue or relevant to the issue, and no others, may be proved.

The following outline of the contents of this work will show how, in arranging it, I have applied this principle.

All law may be divided into Substantive Law, by which rights, duties, and liabilities are defined, and the Law of Procedure by which the Substantive Law is applied to particular cases.

The Law of Evidence is that part of the Law of Procedure which, with a view to ascertain individual rights and liabilities in particular cases, decides :

I. What facts may, and what may not be proved in such cases ;

II. What sort of evidence must be given of a fact which may be proved;

III. By whom and in what manner the evidence must be produced by which any fact is to be proved.

I. The facts which may be proved are facts in issue, or facts relevant to the issue.

Facts in issue are those facts upon the existence of which the right or liability to be ascertained in the proceeding depends.

Facts relevant to the issue are facts from the existence of which inferences as to the existence of the facts in issue may be drawn.

A fact is relevant to another fact when the existence of the one can be shown to be the cause or one of the causes, or the effect or one of the effects, of the existence of the other, or when the existence of the one, either alone or together with other facts, renders the existence of the other highly probable, or improbable, according to the common course of events.

Four classes of facts, which in common life would usually be regarded as falling within this definition of relevancy, are excluded from it by the Law of Evidence except in certain cases :

1. Facts similar to, but not specifically connected with, each other. (*Res inter alios actæ.*)

2. The fact that a person not called as a witness has asserted the existence of any fact. (*Hearsay.*)

3. The fact that any person is of opinion that a fact exists. (*Opinion.*)

4. The fact that a person's character is such as to render conduct imputed to him probable or improbable. (*Character.*)

To each of those four exclusive rules there are, however, important exceptions, which are defined by the Law of Evidence.

II. As to the manner in which a fact in issue or relevant fact must be proved.

Some facts need not be proved at all, because the Court will take judicial notice of them, if they are relevant to the issue.

Every fact which requires proof must be proved either by oral or by documentary evidence.

Every fact, except (speaking generally) the contents of a document, must be proved by oral evidence. Oral evidence must in every case be direct, that is to say, it must consist of an assertion by the person who gives it that he directly perceived the fact to the existence of which he testifies.

Documentary evidence is either primary or secondary. Primary evidence is the document itself produced in court for inspection.

Secondary evidence varies according to the nature of the document. In the case of private documents a copy of the document, or an oral account of its contents, is secondary evidence. In the case of some public documents, examined or certified copies, or exemplifications, must or may be produced in the absence of the documents themselves.

Whenever any public or private transaction has been reduced to a documentary form, the document in which it is recorded becomes exclusive evidence of that transaction, and its contents cannot, except in certain cases expressly defined, be varied by oral evidence, though secondary evidence may be given of the contents of the document.

III. As to the person by whom, and the manner in which the proof of a particular fact must be made.

When a fact is to be proved, evidence must be given of it by the person upon whom the burden of proving it is imposed, either by the nature of the issue or by any legal presumption, unless the fact is one which the party is estopped from proving by his own representations, or by his conduct, or by his relation to the opposite party.

The witnesses by whom a fact is to be proved must be competent. With very few exceptions, every one is now a competent witness in all cases. Competent witnesses, however, are not in all cases compelled or even permitted to testify.

The evidence must be given upon oath, or in certain excepted cases without oath. The witnesses must be first examined in chief, then cross-examined, and then re-examined. Their credit may be tested in certain ways, and the answers which they give to questions affecting their credit may be contradicted in certain cases and not in others.

This brief statement will show what I regard as constituting the Law of Evidence, properly so called. My view of it excludes many things which are often regarded as forming part of it. The principal subjects thus omitted are as follows :—

I regard the question, What may be proved under particular issues? (which many writers treat as part of the Law of Evidence) as belonging partly to the subject of pleading, and partly to each of the different branches into which the Substantive Law may be divided.

A is indicted for murder, and pleads Not Guilty. This plea puts in issue, amongst other things, the presence of any state of mind describable as malice aforethought, and all matters of justification or extenuation.

Starkie and Roscoe treat these subjects at full length, as supplying answers to the question, What can be proved under an issue of Not Guilty on an indictment for murder? Mr. Taylor does not go so far as this; but a great part of his book is based upon a similar principle of classification. Thus chapters i. and ii. of Part II. are rather a treatise on pleading than a treatise on evidence.

Again, I have dealt very shortly with the whole subject of presumptions. My reason is that they also appear to me to belong to different branches of the Substantive Law, and to be unintelligible;

except in connection with them. Take for instance the presumption that every one knows the law. The real meaning of this is that, speaking generally, ignorance of the law is not taken as an excuse for breaking it. This rule cannot be properly appreciated if it is treated as a part of the Law of Evidence. It belongs to the Criminal Law. In the same way numerous presumptions as to rights of property (in particular easements and incorporeal hereditaments) belong not to the Law of Evidence but to the Law of Real Property. The only presumptions which, in my opinion, ought to find a place in the Law of Evidence, are those which relate to facts merely as facts, and apart from the particular rights which they constitute. Thus the rule, that a man not heard of for seven years is presumed to be dead, might be equally applicable to a dispute as to the validity of a marriage, an action of ejectment by a reversioner against a tenant *pur auter vie*, the admissibility of a declaration against interest, and many other subjects. After careful consideration, I have put a few presumptions of this kind into a chapter on the subject, and have passed over the rest as belonging to different branches of the Substantive Law.

Practice, again, appears to me to differ in kind from the Law of Evidence. The rules which point out the manner in which the attendance of witnesses is to be procured, evidence is to be taken on commission, depositions are to be authenticated and forwarded to the proper officers, interrogatories are to be administered, &c., have little to do with the general principles which regulate the relevancy and proof of matters of fact. Their proper place would be found in codes of civil and criminal procedure. I have however noticed a fe' of the most important of these matters.

A similar remark applies to a great mass of provisions as to the proof of certain particulars. Under the head of "Public Documents," Mr. Taylor gives amongst other things a list of all, or most, of the statutory provisions which render certificates or certified copies admissible in particular cases.

To take an illustration at random, section 1458 begins thus: "The registration of medical practitioners under the Medical Act of 1858, may be proved by a copy of the 'Medical Register,' for the time being, purporting," &c. I do not wish for a moment to undervalue the practical utility of such information, or the industry displayed in collecting it; but such a provision as this appears to me to belong not to the Law of Evidence, but to the law relating to medical men. It is matter rather for an index or schedule than for a legal treatise, intended to be studied, understood, and borne in mind in practice.

On several other points the distinction between the Law of Evidence and other branches of the law is more difficult to trace. For instance, the law of estoppel, and the law relating to the interpretation of written instruments, both run into the Law of Evidence. I have tried to draw the line in the case of estoppels by dealing with estoppels *in pais* only, to the exclusion of estoppels by deed and by matter of record, which must be pleaded as such; and in regard to the law of written instruments by stating those rules only which seemed to me to bear directly on the question whether a document can be supplemented or explained by oral evidence.

The result is no doubt to make the statement of the law much shorter than is usual. I hope, however, that competent judges will find that, as far as it goes, the statement is both full and correct. As to brevity, I may say, in the words of Lord Mansfield:—"The law does not consist of particular cases, but of general principles which are illustrated and explained by these cases." [1]

Every one will express somewhat differently the principles which he draws from a number of illustrations, and this is one source of that quality of our law which those who dislike it describe as vagueness and uncertainty, and those who like it as elasticity. I dislike the quality in question, and I used to think that it would be an improvement if the law were once for all enacted in a distinct form by the Legislature, and were definitely altered from time to time as occasion required. For many years I did my utmost to get others to take the same view of the subject, but I am now convinced by

---

[1] *R. v. Bembridge*, 3 Doug. 332.

experience that the unwillingness of the Legislature to undertake such an operation proceeds from a want of confidence in its power to deal with such subjects, which is neither unnatural nor unfounded. It would be as impossible to get in Parliament a really satisfactory discussion of a Bill codifying the Law of Evidence as to get a committee of the whole House to paint a picture. It would, I am equally well satisfied, be quite as difficult at present to get Parliament to delegate its powers to persons capable of exercising them properly. In the meanwhile the Courts can decide only upon cases as they actually occur, and generations may pass before a doubt is set at rest by a judicial decision expressly in point. Hence, if anything considerable is to be done towards the reduction of the law to a system, it must, at present at least, be done by private writers.

Legislation proper is, under favorable conditions, the best way of making the law, but if that is not to be had, indirect legislation, the influence on the law of judges and legal writers who deduce, from a mass of precedents, such principles and rules as appear to them to be suggested by the great bulk of the authorities, and to be in themselves rational and convenient, is very much better than none at all. It has, indeed, special advantages, which this is not the place to insist upon. I do not think the law can be in a less creditable condition than that of an enormous mass of isolated decisions, and statutes assuming unstated principles; cases and statutes alike being accessible only by elaborate indexes. I insist upon this because I am well aware of the prejudice which exists against all attempts to state the law simply, and of the rooted belief which exists in the minds of many lawyers that all general propositions of law must be misleading, and delusive, and that law books are useless except as indexes. An ancient maxim says "*Omnis definitio in jure periculosa.*" Lord Coke wrote, "It is ever good to rely upon the books at large; for many times *compendia sunt dispendia*, and *Melius est petere fontes quam sectari rivulos.*" Mr. Smith chose this expression as the motto of his 'Leading Cases,' and the sentiment which it embodies has exercised immense influence over our law. It has not perhaps been sufficiently observed that when Coke wrote, the "books at large," namely the 'Year Books' and a very few more modern reports, contained probably about as much matter as two, or at most three, years of the reports published by the Council of Law Reporting; and that the *compendia* (such books, say, as Fitzherbert's 'Abridgment') were merely abridgments of the cases in the 'Year Books' classified in the roughest possible manner, and much inferior both in extent and arrangement to such a book as Fisher's 'Digest.'[1]

In our own days it appears to me that the true *fontes* are not to be found in reported cases, but in the rules and principles which such cases imply, and that the cases themselves are the *rivuli*, the following of which is a *dispendium*. My attempt in this work has been emphatically *petere fontes*, to reduce an important branch of the law to the form of a connected system of intelligible rules and principles.

Should the undertaking be favorably received by the profession and the public, I hope to apply the same process to some other branches of the law; for the more I study and practice it, the more firmly am I convinced of the excellence of its substance and the defects of its form. Our earlier writers, from Coke to Blackstone, fell into the error of asserting the excellence of its substance in an exaggerated strain, whilst they showed much insensibility to defects, both of substance and form, which in their time were grievous and glaring. Bentham seems to me in many points to have fallen into the converse error. He was too keen and bitter a critic to recognise the substantial merits of the system which he attacked; and it is obvious to me that he had not that mastery of the law itself which is unattainable by mere theoretical study, even if the student is, as

---

[1] Since the beginning of 1865 the Council has published eighty-six volumes of Reports. The Year Books from 1307–1535, 228 years, would fill not more than twenty-five such volumes. There are also ten volumes of Statutes since 1865 (May, 1876). There are now (Feb., 1877) at least ninety-three volumes of Reports and eleven volumes of Statutes. There are now 154 volumes of Reports and twenty-three of Statutes (1887).

Bentham certainly was, a man of talent, approaching closely to genius.

During the last generation or more Bentham's influence has to some extent declined, partly because some of his books are like exploded shells, buried under the ruins which they have made, and partly because under the influence of some of the most distinguished of living authors, great attention has been directed to legal history, and in particular to the study of Roman Law. It would be difficult to exaggerate the value of these studies, but their nature and use are liable to be misunderstood. This history of the Roman Law no doubt throws great light on the history of our own; and the comparison of the two great bodies of law, under one or the other of which the laws of the civilized world may be classified, cannot fail to be instructive; but the history of bygone institutions is valuable mainly because it enables us to understand, and so to improve existing institutions. It would be a complete mistake to suppose either that the Roman Law is in substance wiser than our own, or that in point of arrangement and method the Institutes and the Digest are anything but warnings. The pseudo-philosophy of the Institutes, and the confusion of the Digest, are, to my mind, infinitely more objectionable than the absence of arrangement and of all general theories, good or bad, which distinguish the Law of England.

However this may be, I trust the present work will show that the law of England on the subject to which it refers is full of sagacity and practical experience, and is capable of being thrown into a form at once plain, short, and systematic.

I wish, in conclusion, to direct attention to the manner in which I have dealt with such parts of the Statute Law as are embodied in this work. I have given, not the very words of the enactments referred to, but what I understand to be their effect, though in doing so I have deviated as little as possible from the actual words employed. I have done this in order to make it easier to study the subject as a whole. Every Act of Parliament which relates to the Law of Evidence assumes the existence of the unwritten law. It cannot, therefore, be fully understood, nor can its relation to other parts of the law be appreciated, till the unwritten law has been written down so that the provisions of particular statutes may take their places as parts of it. When this is done, the Statute Law itself admits of, and even requires, very great abridgment. In many cases the result of a number of separate enactments may be stated in a line or two. For instance, the old Common Law as to the incompetency of certain classes of witnesses was removed by parts of six different Acts of Parliament,—the net result of which is given in five short Articles (106–110).

So, too, the doctrine of incompetency for peculiar or defective religious belief has been removed by many different enactments the effect of which is shown in one Article (123).

The various enactments relating to documentary evidence (see Chap. X.) appear to me to become easy to follow and to appreciate, when they are put in their proper places in a general scheme of the law, and arranged according to their subject-matter. By rejecting every part of an Act of Parliament except the actual operative words which constitute its addition to the law, and by setting it (so to speak) in a definite statement of the unwritten law of which it assumes the existence, it is possible to combine brevity with substantial accuracy and fulness of statement to an extent which would surprise those who are acquainted with Acts of Parliament only as they stand in the Statute Book.[1] At the same time I should warn any one who may use this book for the purposes of actual practice in or out of court, that he would do well to refer to the very words of the statutes embodied in it. It is very possible that, in stating their effect instead of their actual words, I may have given in some particulars a mistaken view of their meaning.

Such are the means by which I have endeavored to make a state-

---

[1] Twenty Articles of this work represent all that is material in the ten Acts of Parliament, containing sixty-six sections, which have been passed on the subject to which it refers. For the detailed proof of this, see Note XLVIII. [Appendix].

ment of the Law of Evidence which will enable not only students of law, but I hope any intelligent person who cares enough about the subject to study attentively what I have written, to obtain from it a knowledge of that subject at once comprehensive and exact,—a knowledge which would enable him to follow in an intelligent manner the proceedings of Courts of Justice, and which would enable him to study cases and use text-books of the common kind with readiness and ease. I do not say more than this. I have not attempted to follow the matter out into its minute ramifications, and I have avoided reference to what after all are little more than matters of curiosity. I think, however, that any one who makes himself thoroughly acquainted with the contents of this book, will know fully and accurately all the leading principles and rules of evidence which occur in actual practice.

If I am entitled to generalise at all from my own experience, I think that even those who are already well acquainted with the subject will find that they understand the relations of its different parts, and therefore the parts themselves more completely than they otherwise would, by being enabled to take them in at one view, and to consider them in their relation to each other.

TABLE OF CASES CITED.

LIST OF ABBREVIATIONS.

(ENGLISH AND IRISH REPORTS, ETC.)

A. & E...................Adolphus & Ellis's Reports.
A. C...................⎫
App. Cas..............⎬Appeal Cases.
Atk...................Atkyn's Reports.

B & A.................⎫
B. & Ald..............⎬Barnewall & Alderson's Reports.
B. & Ad...............Barnewall & Adolphus's Reports.
B. & B................Broderip & Bingham's Reports.
B. & C................Barnewall & Cresswell's Reports.
B. & S................Best & Smith's Reports.
Beav..................Beavan's Reports.
Bell,.................Bell's Crown Cases.
Best,.................Best on Evidence, 6th ed.
Bing.................Bingham's Reports.
Bing. N. C............Bingham's New Cases.
Bligh, N. S...........Bligh's House of Lords' Reports, New Series.
B. & P...............Bosanquet & Puller's Reports.
Br. P. C..............Brown's Parliamentary Cases.
B. N. P...............⎫
Buller, N. P..........⎬Buller's Nisi Prius.
Burr..................Burrows' Reports.

C. A..................Court of Appeal.
Camp..................Campbell's Reports.
C. & F...............Clark & Finnelly's Reports.
C & J.................Crompton & Jervis's Reports.
C. & K...............Carrington & Kirwan's Reports.
C & M.................Carrington & Marshman's Reports.
C. & P...............Carrington & Paine's Reports.
C. B..................Common Bench Reports.
C. B. (N. S.).........Common Bench Reports, New Series.
Ch. App..............Chancery Appeals.
Ch. D................⎫
Ch. Div..............⎬Chancery Division.
C. C. R..............Crown Cases Reserved.
C. M. & R............Crompton, Meeson, & Roscoe's Reports.
Cowp..................Cowper's Reports.
Cox,..................Cox's Crown Cases.
C. P.................Common Pleas ; Common Pleas Reports
C. P. D..............⎫
C. P. Div............⎬Common Pleas Division.

D. & B.......................Dearsley & Bell's Crown Cases.
Dears..........................Dearsley's Crown Cases.
De G. & J ....De Gex & Jones's Reports.
De G. M. & G.................De Gex, Macnaghten, & Gordon's Reports.
De G. & S.....................De Gex & Smale's Reports.
Den. C. C.....................Denison's Crown Cases.
Doug..........................Douglas's Reports.
Dru. & War...................Drury & Warren's Reports.

Ea............................East's Reports
East, P. C.....................East's Pleas of the Crown.
E. & B.........................Ellis & Blackburn's Reports.
E. & E. ....Ellis & Ellis's Reports.
E. & I. App.....................English & Irish Appeals.
Esp...........................Espinasse's Reports.
Ex............................Exchequer Reports.
Ex. D.........................⎱
Ex. Div.......................⎰ Exchequer Division.

F. & F.........................Foster & Finlason's Reports.

Godb...........................Godbolt's Reports.

Hale, P. C.....................Hale's Pleas of the Crown.
Hare............................Hare's Reports.
H. Bl.........................H. Blackstone's Reports.
H. L. ....House of Lords Reports.
H. & C.........................Hurlstone & Coltman's Reports.
H. & N.........................Hurlstone & Norman's Reports.
H. L. C........................House of Lords Cases.

Ir. Cir. Rep. ....Irish Circuit Reports.
Ir. Eq. Rep....................Irish Equity Reports.

Jac. & Wal....................Jacob & Walker's Reports.
Jebb, C. C....................Jebb's Criminal Cases (Ireland).

L. & C.........................Leigh & Cave's Crown Cases.
Leach,........................Leach's Crown Cases.
L. J. Ch.......................Law Journal, Chancery.
L. J. Eq.......................Law Journal, Equity.
L. J. M. C....................Law Journal, Magistrates' Cases.
L. J. N. S.....................Law Journal, New Series.
L. J. Q. B....................Law Journal, Queen's Bench.
L. R...........................Law Reports. (See Q. B., Q. B. D., C. P., C. P. D., Ex., Ex. D., etc.)

Madd..........................Maddock's Reports.
Man. & R.....................Manning & Ryland's Reports.
McNally, Ev..................McNally's Rules of Evidence.
M. & G.........................Manning & Granger's Reports.
M. & M........................Moody & Malkin's Reports.

M. & S. .... Maule & Selwyn's Reports.
M. & W. .... Meeson & Welsby's Reports.
Moody, ...
Moo. C. C. ....}Moody's Crown Cases.
M. & R. ....
Mo. & Ro. ....}Moody & Robinson's Reports.
Moo. P. C. .... Moore's Privy Council Reports.

P. .... Probate Court.
P. D. .... Probate Division.
P. & D. .... Probate & Divorce.
Pea. .... Peake's Reports.
Ph. Ev. .... Phillips on Evidence, 10th ed.
Phill. ....Phillips' Reports.

Q. B. .... Queen's Bench; Queen's Bench Reports.
Q. B. D. .... Queen's Bench Division.

Rep. .... Coke's Reports.
R. N. P. .... Roscoe's Nisi Prius, 13th ed.
R. & R. .... Russell & Ryan's Crown Cases.
Roscoe, Cr. Ev .... Roscoe's Criminal Evidence.
Russ. Cri. ....
Russ. on Crimes. ....}Russell on Crimes, 4th ed.
R. & M .... Russell & Mylne's Reports.
Ry. & Mo. .... Ryan & Moody's Nisi Prius Reports.

Sc. App. .... Scotch Appeals.
Selw. N. P. .... Selwyn's Nisi Prius.
Sim .... Simon's Reports.
Sim. (N. S.). .... Simon's Reports, New Series.
Sim. & Stu. .... Simon & Stuart's Reports.
S. L. C. ....
Smith, L. C. ....}Smith's Leading Cases, 7th ed.
Stark. .... Starkie's Reports.
Stark. Ev. .... Starkie on Evidence, 4th ed.
S. & T. ....
Sw. & Tr. ....}Swabey & Tristram's Reports.
S. T., or St. Tri. .... State Trials.
Story's Eq. Juris. .... Story on Equity Jurisprudence.

T. E. .... Taylor on Evidence, 6th ed.
T. R. .... Term Reports.
Tau. .... Taunton's Reports.

Ves .... Vesey's Reports.
Vin. Abr. .... Viner's Abridgment.

Wig. Ext. Ev .... Wigram on Extrinsic Evidence.
Wills' Circ. Ev..... .. .. Wills on Circumstantial Evidence.

[AMERICAN REPORTS, ETC.]

(The abbreviations of the names of the several States, being well understood, are omitted.)

Abb. Dec .... Abbott's Decisions, Court of Appeals, N. Y.
Abb. N. C. .... Abbott's New Cases, N. Y.
Abb. Pr. .... Abbott's Practice Reports, N. Y.
Abb. Pr. (N. S.). ....   "   "   "   " New Series.
Alb. L. J .... Albany Law Journal, N. Y.
Allen, ... Allen's Reports, Mass.
Am. Dec. .... American Decisions (cases from all States).
Am. Law Reg. N. S. .... American Law Register, New Series.
Am. Law Rev. .... American Law Review.
Anth. N. P .... Anthon's Nisi Prius Reports, N. Y.
App. D. C. .... Appeal Cases, Court of Appeals, District of Columbia.
App. Div. (N. Y.). .... Appellate Division Reports, Supreme Court, N. Y.
Atl. R. .... Atlantic Reporter.

Barb ....Barbour's Reports, Supreme Court, N. Y.
Barb. Ch .... Barbour's Chancery Reports, N. Y.
Baxt .... Baxter's Reports, Tenn.
Ben. .... Benedict's Reports, U. S. District Court.
Binn. .... Binney's Reports, Pa.
Bishop, Cr. L. .... Bishop on Criminal Law.
Bishop, Cr. Pro. .... Bishop on Criminal Procedure.
Bishop, M. D. & S. .... Bishop on Marriage, Divorce, and Separation.
Biss .... Bissell's Reports, U. S. Circuit Court.
Black, ... Black's Reports, U. S. Supreme Court.
Blackf .... Blackford's Reports, Ind.
Blatch. .... Blatchford's Reports, U. S. Circuit Court.
B. Mon .... Ben Monroe's Reports, Ky.
Bos .... Bosworth's Reports, Superior Court, N. Y.
Br. Purd. Dig .... Brightly's Purdon's Digest of Statutes, Pa.
Bump's Fed. Pro .... Bump on Federal Procedure.
Bush, ... Bush's Reports, Ky.

Cai. .... Caine's Reports, N. Y.
Cf. .... *Confer*, compare.
Cinc. .... Cincinnati Reports, Ohio.
Connol. .... Connoly's Reports, Surrogate Courts, N. Y.
Cow. .... Cowen's Reports, N. Y.
Cr. .... Cranch's Reports, U. S. Supreme Court.
Cr. C. C. .... Cranch's U. S. Circuit Court Reports.
Ct. of Cl. .... Court of Claims Reports, U. S.
Cush. .... Cushing's Reports, Mass.

Daly, ... Daly's Reports, Court of Common Pleas, N. Y.
Daniel, Neg. Inst. .... Daniel on Negotiable Instruments.
Deady, ... Deady's Reports, U. S. Circuit Court.
Del. Ch .... Delaware Chancery Reports.
Dem .... Demarest's Reports, Surrogate Courts, N. Y.
Den .... Denio's Reports, N Y.

Dill............................Dillon's Reports, U. S. Circuit Court.
Disney,........................Disney's Reports, Superior Court, Ohio.
Duer,..........................Duer's Reports, Superior Court, N. Y.

E. D. Sm ....E. D. Smith's Reports, Court of Common Pleas, N. Y.
Edm. Sel. Cas.................Edmond's Select Cases, N. Y.
Edw. Ch.......................Edwards' Chancery Reports, N. Y.

F. R...........................Federal Reporter, U. S. Circuit and District Courts.

G. & J.........................Gill & Johnson's Reports, Md.
Gilm ....Gilman's Reports, Ill.
Gr. Ev.........................Greenleaf on Evidence.
Gratt ....Grattan's Reports, Va.
Gray,..........................Gray's Reports, Mass.

Hill,...........................Hill's Reports, N. Y.
Hilt............................Hilton's Reports, Court of Common Pleas, N. Y.
Houst..........................Houston's Criminal Cases, Del.
How. Pr........................Howard's Practice Reports, N. Y.
How. St ....Howell's General Statutes of Michigan.
How. (U. S.)...................Howard's Reports, U. S. Supreme Court.
Humph ....Humphrey's Reports, Tenn.
Hun,...........................Hun's Reports, Supreme Court, N. Y.

Ill. App ....Illinois Appeals Reports.
Ind. App.......................Indiana Appeals Reports.

J. & Sp........................Jones & Spencer's Reports, Superior Court, N. Y.
Johns..........................Johnson's Reports, N. Y.
Johns. Cas.....................Johnson's Cases, N. Y.
Johns. Ch......................Johnson's Chancery Reports, N. Y.

Kent's Comm....................Kent's Commentaries on American Law.
Keyes,.........................Keyes' Reports, Court of Appeals, N. Y.

La. Ann ....Louisiana Annual Reports.
Lans...........................Lansing's Reports, Supreme Court, N. Y.
Lea,...........................Lea's Reports, Tenn.
Lowell,........................Lowell's Reports, U. S. District Court.

McArth.........................McArthur's Reports, Supreme Court, D. C.
McCrary,.......................McCrary's Reports, U. S. Circuit Court.
McL............................McLean's Reports, U. S. Circuit Court.
Mackey,........................Mackey's Reports, District of Columbia.
Md. Ch.........................Maryland Chancery Reports.
Met............................Metcalf's Reports, Mass.
Mill, (S. Car)................Mill's Reports, S. Car.
Mills, Em. Dom.................Mills on Eminent Domain.
Misc...........................Miscellaneous Reports, N. Y.
Mo. App ....Missouri Appeals Reports.
Munf. ....Munford's Reports, Va.

N..............................Note.
N. J. Eq.......................New Jersey Equity Reports.

N. J. L. ....New Jersey Law Reports.
N. J. Rev.....................New Jersey Revision of Statutes.
N. S........................ .....New Series.
N. Y. Civ. Pro. R. ....N. Y. Civil Procedure Reports.
N. Y. Code Civ. Pro.........New York Code of Civil Procedure.
N. Y. Code Cr. Pro...........New York Code of Criminal Procedure.
N. Y. Pen. Code ....New York Penal Code.
N. Y. S. ....New York Supplement.
N. Y. St. R....................New York State Reporter.

O. C. C............... ....Ohio Circuit Courts Reports.
O. St.........................Ohio State Reports.

Pai..........................Paige's Chancery Reports, N. Y.
Park. Cr.....................Parker's Criminal Reports, N. Y.
Pet..........................Peters' Reports, U. S. Supreme Court.
Pet C. C...................Peters' U. S. Circuit Court Reports.
Phila.................. .....Philadelphia Reports, Pa.
Pub. St ....Public Statutes.
Pick.........................Pickering's Reports, Mass.

R. S. ....Revised Statutes.
Redf.........................Redfield's Reports, Surrogate Courts, N. Y.
Rev. St......................Revised Statutes.
Rob........................Robertson's Reports, Superior Court, N. Y.

S. ....∴.Section.
S. C. ....Same Case.
S P. . .. .Same Principle.
S. & R......................Sergeant & Rawle's Reports, Pa.
Sandf ....Sandford's Reports, Superior Court, N. Y.
Sandf. Ch..................Sandford's Chancery Reports, N. Y.
Sawy ....Sawyer's Reports, U. S. Circuit Court.
Scam.......................Scammon's Reports, Ill.
Sumn ....Sumner's Reports, U. S. Circuit Court.

Tenn. (Ch.).................Tennessee Chancery Reports.
Tex. App....................Texas Criminal Appeals Reports.
T. & C..................... .Thompson & Cook's Reports, Supreme Court. N. Y
Tucker,.....................Tucker's Reports, Surrogate Courts, N. Y.

W. D........................Weekly Digest, N. Y.
W. & S........... ....Watts and Sergeant's Reports, Pa.
Wall........................Wallace's Reports, U. S. Supreme Court.
Wash. C. C................Washington's U. S. Circuit Court Reports.
Washb. R. P..............Washburn on Real Property.
Watts,......................Watts' Reports, Pa.
Wend.......................Wendell's Reports, N. Y.
Wh. Cr. Ev.................Wharton on Criminal Evidence, 9th ed.
Wh. Ev....................Wharton on Evidence.
Whart........... ....Wharton's Reports, Pa.
Wheat......................Wheaton's Reports, U. S. Supreme Court.
Woods,................,,.....Woods' Reports, U. S. Circuit Court.

A DIGEST

OF

THE LAW OF EVIDENCE.

PART I.

RELEVANCY.

CHAPTER I.

PRELIMINARY.

ARTICLE 1.*

DEFINITION OF TERMS.

IN this book the following words and expressions are used in the following senses, unless a different intention appears from the context:

"Judge" includes all persons authorized to take evidence, either by law or by the consent of the parties.

"Fact" includes the fact that any mental condition of which any person is conscious exists.[1]

"Document" means any substance having any matter expressed or described upon it by marks capable of being read.

"Evidence"[2] means—

---

* See Note I. [Appendix].

[1] [But, besides "including" what is here stated as to "mental conditions," the word "fact" is used throughout this book in its ordinary signification, as denoting acts, events, occurrences, etc.]

[2] [*Evidence* is the means or medium of proof, while *proof* is the effect or result of evidence (*People* v. *Beckwith*, 108 N. Y. 67, 73). *Demonstrative evidence* is such as establishes a fact conclusively,

(1) Statements made by witnesses in court under a legal sanction, in relation to matters of fact under inquiry;

such statements are called oral evidence:[1]

(2) Documents produced for the inspection of the court or judge;

such documents are called documentary evidence.

"Conclusive proof" means evidence upon the production of which, or a fact upon the proof of which, the judge

---

beyond doubt; *moral evidence* is evidence by which the truth of a matter may be established to a confident belief or conviction, though not excluding possible doubt (*Babcock* v. *Fitchburg R. Co.*, 140 N. Y. 308, 311). *Competent evidence* is that which is fit and appropriate in its nature as a means of proof; *satisfactory* or *sufficient evidence*, that amount or weight of evidence which is adapted to convince a reasonable mind. The judge or court decides whether evidence is competent or admissible, and, therefore, primarily, whether such facts are sufficiently proved as must exist to render it admissible; the jury, in jury trials, decide as to the weight or sufficiency of the evidence bearing on the point in issue (*Comm.* v. *Robinson*, 146 Mass. 571; *Deal* v. *State*, 140 Ind. 354). *Cumulative evidence* is, strictly speaking, evidence of the same general character to the same point; but it is sometimes used with the same meaning as *corroborative evidence*, which is additional evidence, of whatever kind, tending to the same conclusion (*Boggess* v. *Read*, 83 Ia. 548; *Grogan* v. *Chesapeake, etc. R. Co.*, 39 W. Va. 415; *Wynne* v. *Newman*, 75 Va. 811; *Keeler* v. *Jacobs*, 87 Wis. 545; *Waller* v. *Graves*, 20 Ct. 305; *People* v. *Superior Ct.*, 10 Wend. 285). *Direct evidence* is that given by witnesses who testify their actual knowledge of the fact to be proved (see Art. 62, *infra*); *circumstantial evidence* is evidence of facts and circumstances from which the existence of the particular fact to be established may be legitimately deduced or inferred (*Comm.* v. *Webster*, 5 Cush. 295; *People* v. *Anthony*, 56 Cal. 397; *Gannon* v. *People*, 127 Ill. 507; *People* v. *Harris*, 136 N. Y. 423; *State* v. *Rome*, 64 Ct. 329). Rules of evidence may be changed by the legislature, if vested rights are not thereby destroyed. *Howard* v. *Moot*, 64 N. Y. 262; *People* v. *Cannon*, 139 N. Y. 32; *Meadowcroft* v. *People*, 163 Ill. 56; *Pennsylvania Co.* v. *McCann*, 54 O. St. 10; *Larson* v. *Dickey*, 39 Neb. 463.]

[1] [They are also called "testimony." *Dibble* v. *Dimmick*, 143 N. Y. 549, 554.]

is bound by law to regard some fact as proved, and to exclude evidence intended to disprove it.[1]

"A presumption" means a rule of law that courts and judges shall draw a particular inference from a particular fact, or from particular evidence, unless and until the truth of such inference is disproved.[1]

The expression "facts in issue" means—

(1) All facts which, by the form of the pleadings in any action, are affirmed on one side and denied on the other:

(2) In actions in which there are no pleadings, or in which the form of the pleadings is such that distinct issues are not joined between the parties, all facts from the establishment of which the existence, non-existence, nature, or extent of any right, liability, or disability asserted or denied in any such case would by law follow.

The word "relevant" means that any two facts to which it is applied are so related to each other that according to the common course of events one either taken by itself or in connection with other facts proves or renders probable the past, present, or future existence or non-existence of the other.[2]

---

[1][What is here called "conclusive proof" is termed by Mr. Greenleaf and some other writers a "conclusive presumption of law," while what is here called a "presumption" is termed by them a "disputable presumption of law." (Gr. Ev. i. §§ 14-46). For illustrations of "conclusive proof," see *post*, Articles 40-44, 98; of "presumptions," see Articles 85-89, 94, 95, 99-101; see also *Ulrich v. Ulrich*, 136 N. Y. 120.]

[2][See Note I, Appendix; *Plumb v. Curtis*, 66 Ct. 154; *Insurance Co. v. Weide*, 11 Wall. 438, 440; *Comm. v. Abbott*, 130 Mass. 472; *Comm. v. Jeffries*, 7 Allen, 548, 563; *Rodgers v. Stophel*, 32 Pa. 111; *Nickerson v. Gould*, 82 Me. 512; *Darling v. Westmoreland*, 52 N. H. 401. It is to be observed that the author uses the expression, "deemed to be relevant," in many of the following Articles to apply not only to evidence which has true logical relevancy as here defined, but also to evidence which, not being logically relevant, is nevertheless declared admissible by law as a means of proof. And so the expression "deemed to be irrelevant," is applied to evidence, which, though it may be logically relevant, is yet deemed in law inadmissible.]

CHAPTER II.

OF FACTS IN ISSUE AND RELEVANT TO THE ISSUE

ARTICLE 2.*

FACTS IN ISSUE AND FACTS RELEVANT TO THE ISSUE MAY BE PROVED.

EVIDENCE may be given in any proceeding of any fact in issue,

and of any fact relevant[1] to any fact in issue unless it is hereinafter declared to be deemed to be irrelevant,

and of any fact hereinafter declared to be deemed to be relevant to the issue, whether it is or is not relevant thereto.[2]

Provided that the judge may exclude evidence of facts which, though relevant or deemed to be relevant to the issue, appear to him too remote to be material under all the circumstances of the case.[3]

---

* See Note II. [Appendix].

[1] [*Schmidt* v. *Packard*, 132 Ind. 398. Evidence which is pertinent to the issue is admissible, though it may have been improperly, or even unlawfully, obtained; as *e. g.*, documents or articles of property which have been wrongfully taken from a man's room or house (*Comm.* v. *Tibbetts*, 157 Mass. 519; *State* v. *Mathers*, 64 Vt. 101; *State* v. *Burroughs*, 72 Me. 479; *Trask* v. *People*, 151 Ill. 523; *State* v. *Pomeroy*, 130 Mo. 489; *State* v. *Griswold*, 67 Ct. 290; *Shields* v. *State*, 104 Ala. 35); so if evidence is obtained by writing decoy letters. *Andrews* v. *U. S.*, 162 U. S. 420.]

[2] [Facts which are not relevant are often called "collateral facts," and it is a commonly stated rule that evidence of collateral facts is not admissible. *McLoghlin* v. *Mohawk, etc. Bk.*, 139 N. Y. 514; *Eaton* v. *Telegraph Co.*, 68 Me. 63; *Moore* v. *Richmond*, 85 Va. 538.]

[3] [As to the exclusion of evidence for remoteness, see Illustrations (*b*)

Illustrations.

(*a*) A is indicted for the murder of B, and pleads not guilty.
The following facts may be in issue :—The fact that A killed B ;
...ct that at the time when A killed B he was prevented by disease
...nowing right from wrong :[1] the fact that A had received from
provocation as would reduce his offense to manslaughter.[2]

fact that A was at a distant place at the time of the murder
be relevant to the issue ;[3] the fact that A had a good character
be deemed to be relevant ;[4] the fact that C on his deathbed
...d that C and not A murdered B would be deemed not to be
...nt.[5]

The question is, whether A had sufficient mental capacity to
...te a deed at the time when it was executed.
...idence of A's mental condition a year afterwards may be ex-
...ed, in the discretion of the trial judge, as too remote.][6]

(*c*) [The question is, whether the death of A, a fireman upon a
locomotive, was due to the negligence of the railroad company in
allowing a culvert to become obstructed whereby the water overflowed
and washed away the soil under the track.

(*c*) (*d*) ; also *Nicholson* v. *Waful*, 70 N. Y. 604 ; *Kennedy* v. *People*, 39
N. Y. 245, 254 ; *Ockershausen* v. *Durant*, 141 Mass. 338 ; *People* v. *Niles*,
44 Mich. 606 ; *People* v. *Hendrickson*, 53 Mich. 525 ; *Packard* v.
Bergen R. Co., 54 N. J. L. 553 ; *Mansfield Coal Co.* v. *McEnery*, 91
Pa. 185 ; *Amoskeag Co.* v. *Head*, 59 N. H. 332. But evidence which
has a legitimate tendency, though slight, to prove a fact in issue, is
admissible, unless it be deemed too slight and therefore remote.
Nickerson v. *Gould*, 82 Me. 512 ; *Huntsman* v. *Nichols*, 116 Mass.
521 ; *Comm.* v. *Abbott*, 130 Mass. 472 ; *Johnson* v. *Comm.*, 115 Pa. 369 ;
Ryan v. *People*, 79 N. Y. 593 ; see Articles 9 and 10.]

[1] [*Moett* v. *People*, 85 N. Y. 373 ; *State* v. *Hoyt*, 47 Ct. 518 ; *Nevling*
v. *Comm.*, 98 Pa. 322 ; see Art. 95, Illustration (*ce*).]

[2] [Bishop Cr. L. ii. §§ 701–719 ; see *Shufflin* v. *People*, 62 N. Y. 229.]

[3] [See Art. 95, Illustration (*ce*), and note.]

[4] [*Stover* v. *People*, 56 N. Y. 315 ; *Remsen* v. *People*, 43 N. Y. 6 ;
Comm. v. *Webster*, 5 Cush. 295 ; *Hamilton* v. *People*, 29 Mich. 195 ;
see Art. 56.]

[5] [So a letter of C, stating that he committed the murder, would be
deemed not to be relevant. *Greenfield* v. *People*, 85 N. Y. 75 ; see
Art. 14, Illustration (*f*), *post.*]

[6] [*White* v. *Graves*, 107 Mass. 325 ; *Wright* v. *Wright*, 139 Mass
177.]

Evidence that the same culvert was obstructed by logs and an accumulation of mud and brush at a date three years after the injury to A, was deemed inadmissible.][1]

(*d*) [The question is, whether an injury to A, a railway passenger, was caused by the negligence of the railroad company in having its bridge too narrow for the safe passage of the car in which A was riding.

Evidence that this bridge (a wooden one) was replaced by a new iron bridge a few months afterwards, which afforded a wider space for the passage of cars, was deemed too remote.][2]

ARTICLE 3.

RELEVANCY OF FACTS FORMING PART OF THE SAME TRANSACTION AS THE FACTS IN ISSUE.

A transaction is a group of facts so connected together as to be referred to by a single legal name, as a crime, a contract, a wrong, or any other subject of inquiry which may be in issue.

Every fact which is part of the same transaction as the facts in issue is deemed to be relevant to the facts in issue, although it may not be actually in issue, and although if it were not part of the same transaction it might be excluded as hearsay.[3]

---

[1] [*Stoher* v. *St. Louis, etc. R. Co.*, 91 Mo. 509.]

[2] [*Dale* v. *Delaware, etc. R. Co.*, 73 N. Y. 468.]

[3] [This rule is embraced in the doctrine which is commonly called in the law of evidence the doctrine of *res gestæ*. (See Gr. Ev. i. § 108). This, briefly stated, is that evidence of acts or declarations forming part of the *res gestæ* (*i. e.*, "transaction," or "act to be proved") so as to explain or qualify it, is admissible when such "transaction" or "act" forms the fact in issue or is deemed relevant thereto (*Waldele* v. *N. Y. C. R. Co.*, 95 N. Y. 274 ; *Lander* v. *People*, 104 Ill. 248 ; *Norwich Co.* v. *Flint*, 13 Wall. 3 ; *Steamboat Co.* v. *Brockett*, 121 U. S. 637 ; *Springfield, etc. R. Co.* v. *Welsch*, 155 Ill. 511 ; *Comm.* v. *Densmore*, 12 Allen, 535 ; *Elkins* v. *McKean*, 79 Pa. 493). These acts or declarations so connected with the *res gestæ* are deemed relevant,

Whether any particular fact is or is not part of the same transaction as the facts in issue is a question of law upon which no principle has been stated by authority and on which single judges have given different decisions.[1]

---

because they serve to show its nature, purpose, occasion, or object, to explain its origin or significance, to exhibit the relations of the parties concerned therein, etc. (Id.; *People* v. *Davis*, 56 N. Y. 95, 102; *Eighmy* v. *People*, 79 N. Y. 546; *Deveney* v. *Baxter*, 157 Mass. 9). But declarations which are subsequent to the transaction, being a narrative of it as a past event, or otherwise forming no constituent part of it, are not admissible; and the same is true of declarations which are antecedent to the transaction and so form no part thereof (*Wood* v. *State*, 92 Ind. 269; *Martin* v. *N. Y., etc. R. Co.*, 103 N. Y. 626; *Vicksburg, etc. R. Co.* v. *O'Brien*, 119 U. S. 99; *Estell* v. *State*, 51 N. J. L. 182; *Durkee* v. *Cent. Pac. R. Co.*, 69 Cal. 533; *Montag* v. *People*, 141 Ill. 75; *Hall* v. *State*, 132 Ind. 317; *State* v. *Kennade*, 121 Mo. 405; see *Comm.* v. *Crowley*, 165 Mass. 569; *Bigley* v. *Williams*, 80 Pa. 107). But declarations may form part of the *res gestæ*, though made, not by parties to the action, but by bystanders (Illustration (*a*); *Castner* v. *Sliker*, 33 N. J. L. 95 & 507; *Walter* v. *Gernant*, 13 Pa. 515; *Ordway* v. *Sanders*, 58 N. H. 132; *Morton* v. *State*, 91 Tenn. 437; *State* v. *Kaiser*, 124 Mo. 651; *Metr. R. Co.* v. *Collins*, 1 App. D. C. 383; *Baker* v. *Gausin*, 76 Ind. 317). Declarations made by a party in his own favor are admissible, if they form part of the *res gestæ* (*Chase* v. *Chase*, 66 N. H. 588; *Pinney* v. *Jones*, 64 Ct. 545).

This general doctrine also includes the rule stated *post* at the beginning of Article 8, and is usually deemed to embrace the cases considered under Article 4 ("Acts of Conspirators"), Article 17 (so far as the declarations of agents and partners are concerned), Article 27 ("Declarations made in course of business," etc.), and also certain cases included under Article 9 (see Illustration *c*) and Article 11 (see Illustrations *k, l,* and *m*). Sometimes also other cases are included under this general principle. Gr. Ev. i. §§108–123; see *post*, Note V. Appendix.]

[1] [The author has added this paragraph to the text since the decision in England in Bedingfield's case (see Illustration *b*). In some American decisions an attempt has been made to express a definite rule upon the subject, but it is stated in so vague and general a form as to be difficult of application. Thus it is said, "The general rule is that declarations, to become a part of the *res gestæ*, must accompany the

When a question as to the ownership of land depends on the application to it of a particular presumption capable of being rebutted, the fact that it does not apply to other

---

act which they are supposed to characterize and must so harmonize with it as to be obviously one transaction" (*Moore* v. *Meacham*, 10 N. Y. 207, 210; *Enos* v. *Tuttle*, 3 Ct. 250). It is often stated that acts or declarations, to form part of the *res gestæ*, must be "contemporaneous" or "concomitant" with it (Gr. Ev. i. § 110), and Bedingfield's case shows that this rule is applied in England very strictly.   In this country also numerous decisions are found applying the rule strictly, and holding that declarations made "immediately after" an act or occurrence to which they relate are not admissible in evidence (Illustration (*ca*); *People* v. *Wong Ark*, 96 Cal. 125; *Williamson* v. *Cambridge R. Co.*, 144 Mass. 148; *Sullivan* v. *Oregon R. Co.*, 12 Or. 392; *Cleveland, etc. R. Co.* v. *Mara*, 26 O. St. 185; *Rockwell* v. *Taylor*, 41 Ct. 55); while, on the other hand, many cases hold it to be sufficient if the acts or declarations occur *at* or *near* the time of the main transaction, if they are so closely near, and are of such a character, that they may properly be regarded as directly occasioned or evoked by such transaction, and not by any supervening cause or motive (Illustration (*cb*) and cases cited; *Insurance Co.* v. *Mosley*, 8 Wall. 397; *Hunter* v. *State*, 40 N. J. L. 495; *Hanover R. Co.* v. *Coyle*, 55 Pa. 396; *International, etc. R. Co.* v. *Anderson*, 82 Tex. 516; *State* v. *Horan*, 32 Minn. 394; *State* v. *Driscoll*, 72 Ia. 583; *State* v. *Harris*, 45 La. Ann. 842; *Ohio, etc. R. Co.* v. *Stein*, 133 Ind. 243; *Christianson* v. *Pioneer Co.*, 92 Wis. 649; *Cleveland* v. *Newsom*, 45 Mich. 62; *McLeod* v. *Ginther*, 80 Ky. 399; and see *Lund* v. *Tyngsborough*, 9 Cush. 36. The subject is fully discussed in *Waldele* v. *N. Y. C. R. Co.*, 95 N. Y. 274).

This disagreement among the authorities is, however, to a considerable extent, more seeming than real, because in some kinds of cases an interested or designing or otherwise improper motive is apt to spring into activity more speedily than in other cases, and, therefore, declarations, attributable to it, may require, in principle, to be excluded, though made immediately after the transaction (Illustration (*ca*); *Metr. R. Co.* v. *Collins*, 1 App. D. C. 383). And again, immediately ensuing statements may be in the nature of narrative or explanation, and so be deemed no part of the transaction (see p. 12, n. 1, *post*). But, nevertheless, there is still a noteworthy conflict of opinion in applying the doctrine of *res gestæ*. See the diverse opinions in *Vicksburg, etc. R. Co.* v. *O'Brien* 119 U. S. 99, and in *Barber* v. *St. Louis, etc. R. Co.*, 126 Mo. 143.]

neighboring pieces of land similarly situated is deemed to be relevant.[1]

Illustrations.

(a) The question was, whether A murdered B by shooting him.

The fact that a witness in the room with B, when he was shot, saw a man with a gun in his hand pass a window opening into the room in which B was shot, and thereupon exclaimed, "There's butcher!" (a name by which A was known), was allowed to be proved by Lord Campbell, L. C. J.[2]

---

[1] [Gr. Ev. i. §53 a.]

[2] *R. v. Fowkes,* Leicester Spring Assizes, 1856. Ex relatione O'Brien, Serjt.

In the report of this case in the *Times* for March 8, 1856, the evidence of the witnesses on this point is thus given:—

"*William Fowkes:* My father got up (? went to) the window, and opened it and shoved the shutter back. He waited there about three minutes. It was moonlight, the moon about the full. He closed the window but not the shutter. My father was returning to the sofa when I heard a crash at the window. I turned to look and hooted 'There's butcher.' I saw his face at the window, but did not see him plain. He was standing still outside. I aren't able to tell who it was, not certainly. I could not tell his size. While I was hooting the gun went off. I hooted very loud. He was close to the shutter or thereabouts. It was only open about eight inches. *Lord Campbell:* Did you see the face of the man? *Witness:* Yes, it was moonlight at the time. I have a belief that it was the butcher. I believe it was. I now believe it from what I then saw. I heard the gun go off when he went away. We heard him run by the window through the garden towards the park."

Upon cross-examination the witness said that he saw the face when he hooted and heard the report at the same moment. The report adds, "The statement of this witness was confirmed by Cooper, the policeman (who was in the room at the time), except that Cooper saw nothing when William Fowkes hooted 'there's butcher at the window!'" He stated he had not time to look before the gun went off. In this case the evidence as to W. Fowkes' statement could not be admissible on the ground that what he said was in the prisoner's presence, as the window was shut when he spoke. It is also obvious that the fact that he said at the time "there's butcher" was far more likely to impress the jury than the fact that he was at the trial uncertain whether the person he saw was the butcher, though he was dis-

(*b*) The question was, whether A cut B's throat, or whether B cut it herself.

A statement made by B when running out of the room in which her throat was cut. immediately after it had been cut was not allowed to be proved by Cockburn, L. C. J.[1]

(*c*) The question was, whether A committed manslaughter on B by carelessly driving over him.

A statement made by B as to the cause of his accident as soon as he was picked up was allowed to be proved by Park, J., Gurney,

---

posed to think so. [Cases closely resembling *R.* v. *Fowkes* are: *Dismukes* v. *State*, 83 Ala. 287 ; *State* v. *Schmidt*, 73 Ia. 469 ; *Lander* v. *People*, 104 Ill. 248 ; *State* v. *Duncan*, 116 Mo. 288 ; *State* v. *Desroches*, 48 La. Ann. 428 ; *State* v. *Biggerstaff*, 17 Mont. 510.]

[1] *R.* v. *Bedingfield*, Suffolk Assizes, 1879, [14 Cox, 341]. The propriety of this decision was the subject of two pamphlets, one by W. Pitt Taylor, who denied, the other by the Lord Chief Justice, who maintained it. [In a similar American case the declarations were held admissible (*Von Pollnitz* v. *State*, 92 Ga. 16 ; cf. *People* v. *Ah Lee*, 60 Cal. 85). In Massachusetts it has been held that where a person was stabbed and said to a person who reached him within about twenty seconds after the injury, " I'm stabbed ; I'm gone ; Dan Hackett stabbed me," these words were admissible on the trial of his assailant for murder, as part of the *res gestæ* (*Comm.* v. *Hackett*, 2 Allen, 136 ; see *Comm.* v. *M'Pike*, 3 Cush. 181 ; *People* v. *Simpson*, 48 Mich. 474 ; *Waldele* v. *N. Y. C. R. Co.*, 95 N. Y. 278). But declarations by the wounded man, made a few minutes after the fatal injury, so as to be a narrative or explanation of what had happened, are not admissible (*Parker* v. *State*, 136 Ind. 284 ; see *State* v. *Deuble*, 74 Ia. 509 ; *State* v. *Pomeroy*, 25 Kan. 349). In *Kirby* v. *Comm.*, 77 Va. 681, however, the wounded man ran eighty feet, and then exclaimed, about two minutes after the injury, " I am shot ; William Kirby has shot me," and these statements were held to be part of the *res gestæ* and admissible. In *State* v. *Murphy*, 16 R. I. 528, statements made by the injured man ten or fifteen minutes after the injury were held admissible ; few cases, however, have gone to this length. (Cf. *State* v. *Martin*, 124 Mo. 514 ; *Comm.* v. *Werntz*, 161 Pa. 591 ; *Jones* v. *Comm.*, 86 Va. 740 ; *Jones* v. *State*, 71 Ind. 66 ; *Louisville, etc. R. Co.* v. *Pearson*, 97 Ala. 211 ; *State* v. *Brown*, 28 Or. 147).

For a valuable discussion of Bedingfield's case and of the general doctrine of *res gestæ*, see American Law Review, xiv. 817, xv. 1 and 71. The writer thinks the evidence should have been admitted in this case. Id. xv. 89.]

B., and Patteson, J., though it was not a dying declaration within Article 26.[1]

(ca) [The question is, whether A was injured through the negligent driving by B's servant of a car drawn by horses. The driver, as he was getting off the car and out of the crowd which had gathered, directly after the accident, was asked why he did not stop the car and replied that the brake was out of order. This statement of his was not allowed to be proved. " The alleged wrong was complete and the driver was only endeavoring to account for what he had done. He was manifestly excusing himself and throwing the blame on his principals."][2]

(cb) [A sues B (a railroad company) to recover damages for injuries suffered by him, through B's alleged negligence, in falling upon the platform at a station, while he was alighting from a train.

Declarations by A as to the cause of his injuries, made by him immediately after the train left the station and while he lay upon the platform where he fell, were allowed to be proved.][3]

(cc) [The question was, whether A, a physician, committed the crime of killing B (a woman) by the use of means to procure an abortion upon B's person.

A statement made by B after returning home from A's office of what A had done and said to her there was not allowed to be proved.][4]

(cd) [The question was, whether A was negligent in jumping from the vehicle of B (a carrier of passengers) when the vehicle was apparently in a position of imminent danger.

---

[1] *R.* v. *Foster*, 6 C. & P. 325; [cf. *Lahey* v. *Ottman & Co.*, 73 Hun, 61.]

[2] [*Luby* v. *Hudson River R. Co.*, 17 N. Y. 131; *Lane* v. *Bryant*, 9 Gray, 245.]

[3] [*Pennsylvania R. Co.* v. *Lyons*, 129 Pa. 113. But statements by an injured person as to the cause of injury, which were not made until he had been removed a short distance from the place of the injury and a doctor obtained, were deemed not admissible (*Merkle* v. *Bennington*, 58 Mich. 156; see *Chicago, etc. R. Co.*, v. *Becker*, 128 Ill. 545; *Eastman* v. *Boston, etc. R. Co.*, 165 Mass. 342). In Indiana, similar statements made before removal from the place of injury and within two minutes of its occurrence were held admissible. *Louisville, etc. R. Co.* v. *Buck*, 116 Ind. 566; see *Leahey* v. *Cass Ave., etc. R. Co.*, 97 Mo. 165; *Mo. Pac. R. Co.* v. *Baier*, 37 Neb. 235.]

[4] [*People* v. *Davis*, 56 N. Y. 95; *Maine* v. *People*, 9 Hun, 113; cf. *People* v. *Murphy*, 101 N. Y. 126; *Mutcha* v. *Pierce*, 49 Wis. 231.]

The acts of other passengers in jumping from the vehicle at the same time were allowed to be proved.]¹

(d) The question is, whether A, the owner of one side of a river, owns the entire bed of it or only half the bed at a particular spot. The fact that he owns the entire bed a little lower down than the spot in question is deemed to be relevant.²

(e) The question is, whether a piece of land by the roadside belongs to the lord of the manor or to the owner of the adjacent land. The fact that the lord of the manor owned other parts of the slip of land by the side of the same road is deemed to be relevant.³

ARTICLE 4.*

ACTS OF CONSPIRATORS.

When two or more persons conspire together to commit any offence or actionable wrong,⁴ everything said, done, or written by any one of them in the execution or further-ance of their common purpose, is deemed to be so said, done, or written by every one, and is deemed to be a relevant fact as against each of them;⁵ but statements

---

* See Note III. [Appendix].

¹ [*Twomley* v. *C. P. N. R. Co.*, 69 N. Y. 158 ; *Kleiber* v. *People's R. Co.*, 107 Mo. 240 ; *Mitchell* v. *So. Pac. R. Co.*, 87 Cal. 62.]

² *Jones* v. *Williams*, 2 M. & W. 326.

³ *Doe* v. *Kemp*, 7 Bing. 332 ; 2 Bing. N. C. 102.

⁴ [Evidence admissible under this Article is not limited to in-dictments for the crime of conspiracy, distinctively so-called (*Ctune* v. *U. S.*, 159 U. S. 590), but is competent in all cases, civil and criminal, where two or more persons have combined to do an unlaw-ful act ; as *e. g.*, where the trial is for murder, forgery, larceny, or other crime (*Goins* v. *State*, 46 O. St. 457 ; *People* v. *Parker*, 67 Mich. 222 ; *People* v. *Davis*, 56 N. Y. 95), or where the proceeding is of a civil nature, as for wrongful acts done with intent to defraud creditors, etc. *Knower* v. *Cadden Clothing Co.*, 57 Ct. 202 ; *Lowe* v. *Dalrymple*, 117 Pa. 564 ; *Gumberg* v. *Treusch*, 103 Mich. 543; *Beeler* v. *Webb*, 113 Ill. 436 ; *Cuyler* v. *McCartney*, 40 N. Y. 221.]

⁵ [The reason for the admission of this evidence is that such acts

made by individual conspirators as to measures taken in the execution or furtherance of any such common purpose are not deemed to be relevant as such as against any conspirators, except those by whom or in whose presence such statements are made.[1] Evidence of acts or statements deemed to be relevant under this Article may not be given until the judge is satisfied that, apart from them, there are *prima facie* grounds for believing in the existence of the conspiracy to which they relate.[2]

---

and declarations form part of the *res gestæ* (*Dewey* v. *Moyer,* 72 N. Y. 70; *Comm.* v. *Scott,* 123 Mass. 222; *Nudd* v. *Burrows,* 91 U. S. 426; *Hartman* v. *Diller,* 62 Pa. 37; *Lincoln* v. *Claftin,* 7 Wall. 132; see Art. 3, and notes). Acts or declarations not done or made in furtherance of the common design are not admissible (*Garnsey* v. *Rhodes,* 138 N. Y. 461; *State* v. *McGee,* 81 Ia. 17). It is immaterial at what time any one entered into the conspiracy; he is deemed a party to all acts done by any of the other conspirators before or afterwards, in furtherance of the common design. Gr. Ev. i. § 111; *State* v. *Crab,* 121 Mo. 554; *Ochs* v. *People,* 124 Ill. 399; *U. S.* v. *Johnson,* 26 F. R. 682; *Bonner* v. *State,* 107 Ala. 97.]

[1] [Thus statements made by a co-conspirator, after the conspiracy has ended, as a narrative of past acts or measures taken, are not deemed to be relevant, not forming part of the *res gestæ* (*People* v. *McQuade,* 110 N. Y. 284; *N. Y. Guaranty Co.* v. *Gleason,* 78 N. Y. 503; *Heine* v. *Comm.,* 91 Pa. 145; *Moore* v. *Shields,* 121 Ind. 267; *Samples* v. *State,* 121 Ill. 547; *State* v. *Larkin,* 49 N. H. 39). Confessions or declarations made by one after the conspiracy is ended can only be received as evidence against himself and not against his associates (*Comm.* v. *Ingraham,* 7 Gray, 46; *State* v. *Johnson,* 40 Kan. 266; *State* v. *Minton,* 116 Mo. 605; *Sparf* v. *U. S.,* 156 U. S. 51, 56; *State* v. *Arnold,* 48 Ia. 566; *People* v. *Arnold,* 46 Mich. 268; *People* v. *Aleck,* 61 Cal. 137; see Art. 21, *post*), unless they are made in the presence of any of the other conspirators, when they may be provable under the rule stated on p. 25, *post,* n. 1.]

[2] [*Ormsby* v. *People,* 53 N. Y. 472; *Miller* v. *Dayton,* 57 Ia. 423; *Knower* v. *Cadden Clothing Co.,* 57 Ct. 202; *People* v. *Parker,* 67 Mich. 222; *Phœnix Ins. Co.* v. *Moog,* 78 Ala. 284. But the declarations of an alleged conspirator are not admissible to prove the existence of the conspiracy (*Solomon* v. *Kirkwood,* 55 Mich. 256). The judge may, however, in his discretion admit evidence of the acts and declarations

Illustrations.

(a) The question is, whether A and B conspired together to cause certain imported goods to be passed through the custom-house on payment of too small an amount of duty.

The fact that A made in a book a false entry, necessary to be made in that book in order to carry out the fraud, is deemed to be a relevant fact as against B.

The fact that A made an entry on the counterfoil of his cheque-book showing that he had shared the proceeds of the fraud with B, is deemed not to be a relevant fact as against B.[1]

(b) The question is, whether A committed high treason by imagining the king's death ; the overt act charged is that he presided over an organized political agitation calculated to produce a rebellion, and directed by a central committee through local committees.

The facts that meetings were held, speeches delivered, and papers circulated in different parts of the country, in a manner likely to produce rebellion by, and by the direction of, persons shown to have acted in concert with A, are deemed to be relevant facts as against A, though he was not present at those transactions, and took no part in them personally.

An account given by one of the conspirators in a letter to a friend, of his own proceedings in the matter, not intended to further the common object, and not brought to A's notice, is deemed not to be relevant as against A.[2]

---

of one alleged conspirator, which are alleged to have been done or made in furtherance of the conspiracy, upon condition that proof of the conspiracy be supplied during the trial ; but this should, in general, only be allowed in urgent cases (*Place* v. *Minster,* 65 N. Y. 89 ; *People* v. *Fehrenbach,* 102 Cal. 394 ; *State* v. *Flanders,* 118 Mo. 227 ; *State* v. *Grant,* 86 Ia. 216 ; *Hamilton* v. *People,* 29 Mich. 195). The existence of the conspiracy may be proved by circumstantial evidence as well as by showing by direct evidence an actual preconcerted agreement ; as by proving acts and declarations indicating that the parties were all acting with a common design. *People* v. *Peckens,* 153 N. Y. 576 ; *Comm.* v. *Smith,* 163 Mass. 411 ; *People* v. *Arnold,* 46 Mich. 268 ; *Lowe* v. *Dalrymple,* 117 Pa. 564 ; *Ochs* v. *People,* 124 Ill. 399 ; *People* v. *Bentley,* 75 Cal. 407 ; *Primmer* v. *Primmer,* 75 Ia. 415 ; see *Strout* v. *Packard,* 76 Me. 148.]

[1] *R.* v. *Blake,* 6 Q. B. 137-140.

[2] *R.* v. *Hardy,* 24 S. T. *passim,* but see particularly 451-453.

Article 5.*

When the existence of any right of property, or of any right over property is in question, every fact which constitutes the title of the person claiming the right, or which shows that he, or any person through whom he claims, was in possession of the property, and every fact which constitutes an exercise of the right, or which shows that its exercise was disputed, or which is inconsistent with its existence or renders its existence improbable, is deemed to be relevant.[1]

Illustrations.

(a) The question is, whether A has a right of fishery in a river.

An ancient *inquisitio post mortem* finding the existence of a right of fishery in A's ancestors, licenses to fish granted by his ancestors, and the fact that the licensees fished under them, are deemed to be relevant.[2]

(b) The question is, whether A owns land.

The fact that A's ancestors granted leases of it is deemed to be relevant.[3]

(c) The question is, whether there is a public right of way over A's land.

The facts that persons were in the habit of using the way, that they

---

* See Note IV. [Appendix]; see also Art. 88 as to proof of ancient deeds.

[1] [*Hosford* v. *Ballard*, 39 N. Y. 147; *Cagger* v. *Lansing*, 64 N. Y. 417; *Miller* v. *L. I. R. Co.*, 71 N. Y. 380; *Fletcher* v. *Fuller*, 120 U. S. 534; *Anderson* v. *McCormick*, 129 Ill. 308; *Boston* v. *Richardson*, 105 Mass. 351; *Gloucester* v. *Gaffney*, 8 Allen, 11; *Berry* v. *Raddin*. 11 Allen, 577; *Sailor* v. *Hertzogg*, 10 Pa. 296. In proving facts of ancient date to establish title, evidence may be received which would be inadmissible as to facts within the memory of living witnesses. *Bogardus* v. *Trinity Church*, 4 Sandf. Ch. 633; *Goodwin* v. *Jack*, 62 Me. 414.]

[2] *Rogers* v. *Allen*, 1 Camp. 309.

[3] *Doe* v. *Pulman*, 3 Q. B. 622, 623, 626 (citing *Duke of Bedford* v. *Lopes*). The document produced to show the lease was a counterpart

were turned back, that the road was stopped up, that the road was repaired at the public expense, and A's title-deeds showing that for a length of time, reaching beyond the time when the road was said to have been used, no one had power to dedicate it to the public, are all deemed to be relevant.[1]

(*d*) The question is, whether A has a several fishery in a river. The proceedings in a possessory suit in the Irish Court of Chancery by the plaintiff's predecessor in title, and a decree in that suit quieting the plaintiff's predecessor in his title, is relevant, as showing possession and enjoyment of the fishery at the time of the suit.[2]

ARTICLE 6.

CUSTOMS.

When the existence of any custom is in question, every fact is deemed to be relevant which shows how, in particular instances, the custom was understood and acted upon by the parties then interested.

Illustrations.

(*a*) The question is, whether, by the custom of borough-English as prevailing in the manor of C, A is heir to B.

The fact that other persons, being tenants of the manor, inherited from ancestors standing in the same or similar relations to them as that in which A stood to B, is deemed to be relevant.[3]

---

signed by the lessee. See *post*, Art. 64. [See *Osgood* v. *Coates*, 1 Allen, 77.]

[1] Common practice. As to the title-deeds, *Brough* v. *Lord Scarsdale*, Derby Summer Assizes, 1865. In this case it was shown by a series of family settlements that for more than a century no one had had a legal right to dedicate a certain footpath to the public.

[2] *Neill* v. *Duke of Devonshire*, L. R. 8 App. Cas. 135 ; see especially p. 147.

[3] *Muggleton* v. *Barnett*, 1 H. & N. 282; and see *Johnstone* v. *Lord Spencer*, 30 Ch. D. 581. It was held in this case that a custom might be shown by uniform practice which was not mentioned in any customal court roll or other record. For a late case of evidence of a

(*b*) The question was, whether, by the custom of the country, a tenant-farmer, not prohibited by his lease from doing so, might pick and sell surface flints, minerals being reserved by his lease. The fact that, under similar provisions in leases of neighboring farms flints were taken and sold, is deemed to be relevant.[1]

ARTICLE 7.

MOTIVE, PREPARATION, SUBSEQUENT CONDUCT, EXPLANATORY STATEMENTS.

When there is a question whether any act was done by any person, the following facts are deemed to be relevant, that is to say—

any fact which supplies a motive for such an act,[2] or which constitutes preparation for it ;[3]

---

custom of trade, see *Ex parte Powell, in re Matthews*, 1 Ch. D. 501. [As to proof of a usage of trade or business, see *Dickinson* v. *Poughkeepsie*, 75 N. Y. 65; *Mills* v. *Hallock*, 2 Edw. Ch. 652; *Haskins* v. *Warren*, 115 Mass. 514; *Chateaugay Iron Co.* v. *Blake*, 144 U. S. 476; *Adams* v. *Pittsburgh Ins. Co.*, 95 Pa. 348. Such a custom may be proved by one witness (*Robinson* v. *U. S.*, 13 Wall. 363; *Bissell* v. *Campbell*, 54 N. Y. 353). As to other customs, see *Smith* v. *Floyd*, 18 Barb. 522; *Ocean Beach Ass'n* v. *Brinley*, 34 N. J. Eq. 438; *Ulmer* v. *Farnsworth*, 80 Me. 500.]

[1] *Tucker* v. *Linger*, 21 Ch. D. 18; and see p. 37.

[2] [Illustrations (*a*) and (*ab*). *Murphy* v. *People*, 63 N. Y. 590; *Wright* v. *Nostrand*, 94 N. Y. 31; *Comm.* v. *Bradford*, 126 Mass. 42; *Comm.* v. *Hudson*, 97 Mass. 565; *Ettinger* v. *Comm.*, 98 Pa. 338; *Scott* v. *People*, 141 Ill. 195; *State* v. *Lentz*, 45 Minn. 177; *Benson* v. *State*, 119 Ind. 488. But the evidence to show motive must not be too remote (*Comm.* v. *Abbott*, 130 Mass. 472). Evidence of motive is admissible, though it tends also to prove the commission of another crime than the one charged (Illustration (*ac*); *Pontius* v. *People*, 82 N. Y. 339; *State* v. *Palmer*, 65 N. H. 216; *People* v. *Lane*, 101 Cal. 513; see p. 35, *post*, note 1). A person may, however, be convicted of crime, though the evidence discloses no motive for his act. *People* v. *Johnson*, 139 N. Y. 358; *Johnson* v. *U. S.*, 157 U. S. 320; *Comm.* v. *Buccieri*, 153 Pa. 535.]

[3] Illustrations (*b*) and (*bc*). [See *Walsh* v. *People*, 88 N. Y. 458;

any subsequent conduct of such person apparently
influenced by the doing of the act, and any act done

People v. *Scott,* 153 N. Y. 40; *Comm.* v. *Choate,* 105 Mass. 451. In
trials for homicide, or for assaults with homicidal intent, evidence of
antecedent *threats* or of *expressions of ill-will,* made *by the defendant*
against the person killed or injured, is admissible (*Comm.* v. *Goodwin,*
14 Gray, 55; *State* v. *Hoyt,* 46 Ct. 330; *State* v. *Cole,* 63 Ia. 695; *People*
v. *Jones,* 99 N. Y. 667; *Comm.* v. *Holmes,* 157 Mass. 233); and so in
other cases of forcible injury (*Jewett* v. *Banning,* 21 N. Y. 27; *Caverno*
v. *Jones,* 61 N. H. 623; *State* v. *Fry,* 67 Ia. 475); but threats made by
a person other than the defendant against the person injured are not
provable, being *res inter alios acta* (*State* v. *Beaudet,* 53 Ct. 536); in
trials for arson, the defendant's prior threats to burn the property may
be proved (*State* v. *Day,* 79 Me. 120; *People* v. *Eaton,* 59 Mich. 559;
Comm. v. *Crowe,* 165 Mass. 140).

In cases of homicide, where it appears that the deceased was or may
have been the aggressor, so as to cause the defendant to act in self-
defence, evidence is received in many States of *threats made by the
deceased* against the defendant, even though the defendant had not
heard of such threats (*Wiggins* v. *People,* 93 U. S. 465; *Stokes* v.
People, 53 N. Y. 164; *Roberts* v. *State,* 68 Ala. 156; *Turpin* v. *State,*
55 Md. 462; *State* v. *Harrod,* 102 Mo. 590; *Prine* v. *State,* 73 Miss.
838; *State* v. *Evans,* 33 W. Va. 417; *People* v. *Thomson,* 92 Cal. 506);
so *a fortiori,* if such threats had been made known to the defendant
(*State* v. *Woodson,* 41 Ia. 425; *Wood* v. *State,* 92 Ind. 269; *Lewis* v.
Comm., 78 Va. 732; cf. *Vann* v. *State,* 83 Ga. 44); so in trials for
assault with intent to murder, a similar rule applies (*Leverich* v. *State,*
105 Ind. 277; *State* v. *Scott,* 24 Kan. 68); but generally in other cases
than those of self-defence, such evidence of threats is not admitted
(*State* v. *Elliott,* 45 Ia. 486; *People* v. *Campbell,* 59 Cal. 243).

So in like trials, evidence of the *violent and quarrelsome character
of the deceased* or person injured is received when the circumstances indicate that the defendant was acting in self-defence (*Abbott*
v. *People,* 86 N. Y. 460; *Upthegrove* v. *State,* 37 O. St. 662; *State* v.
Graham, 61 Ia. 608; *Comm.* v. *Straesser,* 153 Pa. 451; *Smith* v. *U. S.,*
161 U. S. 85; *Cannon* v. *People,* 141 Ill. 270; *Knight* v. *Smythe,* 57
Vt. 529; *Galbraith* v. *Fleming,* 60 Mich. 403; *State* v. *Downs,* 91 Mo.
19; see *Comm.* v. *Barnacle,* 134 Mass. 215). The evidence in such
cases must be of *general reputation* for violence, etc., and not of
specific acts of violence. *People* v. *Druse,* 103 N. Y. 655; *Alexander*
v. *Comm.,* 105 Pa. 1; *Harrison* v. *Comm.,* 79 Va. 374; but see *People*
v. *Harris,* 97 Mich. 87.]

in consequence of it by or by the authority of that person.[1]

Illustrations.

(*a*) The question is, whether A murdered B.

The facts that, at the instigation of A, B murdered C twenty-five years before B's murder, and that A at or before that time used expressions showing malice against C, are deemed to be relevant, as showing a motive on A's part to murder B.[2]

(*ab*) [The question is, whether A murdered B.

The fact that A had been living in adultery with B's wife is deemed to be relevant, as showing motive.[3]

The fact that B had been personally pressing A for payment of a debt which A had no means to pay is deemed to be relevant, for a like reason.][4]

(*ac*) [A is indicted and tried for the murder of his eldest daughter by drowning her.

Evidence tending to prove that A caused the deaths of his wife and youngest daughter by drowning at about the same time, and also showing that he married another woman immediately afterwards, is deemed to be relevant, as tending to prove that his motive was, by putting his wife and children out of existence, to enable him to enter into this second marriage.][5]

---

[1] Illustrations (*c*), (*d*) and (*e*). [See *Harrington* v. *Keteltas*, 92 N.Y. 40; *Morris* v. *French*, 106 Mass. 326; *Banfield* v. *Whipple*, 10 Allen, 27; *People* v. *Ah Fook*, 64 Cal. 380.]

[2] *R.* v. *Clewes*, 4 C. & P. 221. [See *Sayres* v. *Comm.*, 88 Pa. 291; *McCue* v. *Comm.*, 78 id. 185; *State* v. *Dickson*, 78 Mo. 438. In *Goodwin* v. *State*, 96 Ind. 550 (a trial for murder) threats made by the defendant thirty years before against the deceased were allowed to be proved; and so as to threats made thirteen years before and repeated in later years (*State* v. *Glahn*, 97 Mo. 679; see *Pulliam* v. *State*, 88 Ala. 1). But the jury may consider the remoteness of such evidence in determining its weight.]

[3] [*Comm.* v. *Ferrigan*, 44 Pa. 386; see *Comm.* v. *Choate*, 105 Mass. 458; *People* v. *Scott*, 153 N.Y. 40; *Pierson* v. *People*, 79 N.Y. 424; *State* v. *Reed*, 53 Kan. 767; *Pate* v. *State*, 94 Ala. 14.]

[4] [*Comm.* v. *Webster*, 5 Cush. 295; see 97 Mass. 566.]

[5] [*Hawes* v. *State*, 88 Ala. 37; cf. *People* v. *Craig*, 111 Cal. 460.]

(*b*) The question is, whether A committed a crime.

The fact that A procured the instruments with which the crime was committed is deemed to be relevant.[1]

(*bc*) [A, B, and C are tried for the murder of D.

The facts that at the time of the alleged crime these persons were members of a secret society, organized for the commission of crimes of violence against person and property, and for the protection of one another from detection and punishment, and that on the night before the murder they met together and planned its commission, are deemed to be relevant.][2]

(*c*) A is accused of a crime.

The facts that, either before or at the time of, or after the alleged crime, A caused circumstances to exist tending to give to the facts of the case an appearance favorable to himself, or that he destroyed or concealed things or papers, or prevented the presence or procured the absence of persons who might have been witnesses, or suborned persons to give false evidence, are deemed to be relevant.[3]

(*d*) The question is, whether A committed a crime.

The facts that, after the commission of the alleged crime, he absconded, or was in possession of property or the proceeds of property acquired by the crime, or attempted to conceal things which were or might have been used in committing it, and the manner in which he conducted himself when statements on the subject were made in his presence and hearing, are deemed to be relevant.[4]

---

[1] *R.* v. *Palmer* (*passim*); reported in Stephen's General View of the Crim. Law of England. [*Comm.* v. *Blair*, 126 Mass. 40; *People* v. *Hope*, 62 Cal. 291; *Colt* v. *People*, 1 Park. Cr. 611; see *La Beau* v. *People*, 6 id. 371, 34 N. Y. 223.]

[2] [*Hester* v. *Comm.*, 85 Pa. 139; *McManus* v. *Comm.*, 91 id. 57; *Spies* v. *People*, 122 Ill. 1, the noted dynamite bomb case in Chicago.]

[3] *R.* v. *Patch*, Wills' Circ. Ev. 230; *R.* v. *Palmer, ub. sup.* (*passim*). [Thus the concealment of an accused person to avoid arrest may be shown (*Comm.* v. *Tolliver*, 119 Mass. 312; *Ryan* v. *People*, 79 N. Y. 593); the act of writing letters to fasten the crime on others (*Gardiner* v. *People*, 6 Park. Cr. 157), or to keep a witness away from the trial (*Adams* v. *People*, 9 Hun, 89); the bribing of witnesses to leave the State (*State* v. *Nocton*, 121 Mo. 537); the alteration of documents to conceal a fraud (*State* v. *Jamison*, 74 Ia. 613). As to suborning witnesses, see *Donohue* v. *People*, 56 N. Y. 208; *Murray* v. *Chase*, 134 Mass. 92; *Snell* v. *Bray*, 56 Wis. 156.]

[4] Common practice. [Thus an accused person's flight may be

(e) The question is, whether A suffered damage in a railway accident.

The fact that A conspired with B, C, and D to suborn false witnesses in support of his case is deemed to be relevant,[1] as conduct subsequent to a fact in issue tending to show that it had not happened.

ARTICLE 8.*

STATEMENTS ACCOMPANYING ACTS, COMPLAINTS, STATEMENTS IN PRESENCE OF A PERSON.

Whenever any act may be proved, statements accompanying and explaining that act made by or to the person doing it may be proved, if they are necessary to understand it.[2]

---

* See Note V. [Appendix ; also Art. 3, note].

shown, not as creating a legal presumption of guilt, but as having a tendency to establish his guilt (*Allen* v. *U. S.*, 164 U. S. 492 ; *Comm.* v. *Boroschino*, 176 Pa. 103 ; *People* v. *Ross*, 115 Cal. 233 ; *Comm.* v. *Annis*, 15 Gray, 197 ; *People* v. *Ogle*, 104 N. Y. 511 ; *Fox* v. *People*, 95 Ill. 71) ; his attempt to avoid or escape arrest or to escape from jail (*Jamison* v. *People*, 145 Ill. 357 ; *Comm.* v. *Brigham*, 147 Mass. 414 ; *State* v. *Jackson*, 95 Mo. 623 ; *State* v. *Stevens*, 67 Ia. 557) ; his advice to an accomplice to escape (*People* v. *Rathbun*, 21 Wend. 509) ; his possession of property obtained by the crime (*Stover* v. *People*, 56 N. Y. 315 ; *Linsday* v. *People*, 63 N. Y. 143 ; *Comm.* v. *Parmenter*, 101 Mass. 211 ; *Brown* v. *Comm.*, 76 Pa. 319) ; his acts in disposal of such property (*Foster* v. *People*, 63 N. Y. 619) ; his giving a false account of himself when arrested (*Comm.* v. *Goodwin*, 14 Gray, 55 ; *People* v. *Conroy*, 97 N. Y. 62, 80) ; his conduct after the crime was committed. *Greenfield* v. *People*, 85 N. Y. 75 ; *People* v. *Welsh*, 63 Cal. 167 ; and see *Ruloff's case*, 11 Abb. Pr. (N. S.) 245.]

[1] *Moriarty* v. *London, Chatham and Dover Ry. Co.*, L. R. 5 Q. B. 314 ; compare *Gery* v. *Redman*, 1 Q. B. D. 161. [*Egan* v. *Bowker*, 5 Allen, 449 ; *Heslop* v. *Heslop*, 82 Pa. 537 ; *Gulerette* v. *McKinley*, 27 Hun, 320 ; *Lyons* v. *Lawrence*, 12 Ill. App. 531. So as to bribing a juror. *Hastings* v. *Stetson*, 130 Mass. 76 ; *Taylor* v. *Gilman*, 60 N. H. 506 ; see p 22, note 3, *supra*.]

[2] Illustrations (a), (ab), (ac), (b) and (ba). Other statements made by such persons are relevant or not according to the rules as to state-

In criminal cases [of rape] the conduct of the person
against whom the offence is said to have been committed,
and in particular the fact that soon after the offence
[she] made a complaint to persons to whom [she] would
naturally complain, are deemed to be relevant ;[1] but the
terms of the complaint itself seem to be deemed to be
irrelevant.

.ments hereinafter contained. See Ch. IV. *post.* [*Aylesford Peerage
Case*, L. R. 11 App. Cas. 1 ; *Swift* v. *Life Ins. Co.*, 63 N. Y. 186, 190 ;
Kingsford v. *Hood*, 105 Mass. 495 ; *Place* v. *Gould*, 123 Mass. 347 ;
Merkel's Appeal, 89 Pa. 340.]

[1] Illustration (*c*). [The form in which this rule is stated by Mr.
Stephen makes it applicable to all criminal cases (he omits the words
"of rape" and has "he" for "she" in the fourth line), but the
rule is regarded in this country as one peculiar to cases of *rape*,
and it is at least questionable whether it applies to other crimes even
under English law. There appear to be only two English decisions
extending the rule to other crimes than rape, and they are both *nisi
prius* cases and of slight value. (This subject is fully discussed in the
Am. Law Rev., xiv. 829-838 ; and see *Haynes* v. *Comm.*, 28 Gratt. 942.)
Still the doctrine of *res gestæ*, as applied to other crimes, is sometimes
extended so far as to make the analogy to cases of rape a noticeable
one (see *Driscoll* v. *People*, 47 Mich. 413) ; and in some States an
analogous rule is applied, under statutes, to bastardy cases (*Benton* v.
Starr, 58 Ct. 285 ; *Reed* v. *Haskins*, 116 Mass. 198).

This rule, as applied to cases of rape (or an attempt to commit rape),
is fully supported by American decisions (*Baccio* v. *People*, 41 N. Y.
265 ; *People* v. *O'Sullivan*, 104 N. Y. 481 ; *State* v. *Ivins*, 36 N. J. L.
233 ; *State* v. *Cook*, 92 Ia. 483 ; *Cross* v. *State*, 132 Ind. 65 ; *State* v.
Carroll, 67 Vt. 477 ; *Stevens* v. *People*, 158 Ill. 111 ; *Parker* v. *State*,
67 Md. 329 ; *Lee* v. *State*, 74 Wis. 45 ; *People* v. *Stewart*, 97 Cal. 238).
In these cases evidence of the particulars or details of the complaint
was held not admissible, and such is the general American rule ; but
in some States such evidence is admitted (*State* v. *Kinney*, 44 Ct. 153 ;
Burt v. *State*, 23 O. St. 394 ; *Hill* v. *State*, 5 Lea, 725), and by a recent
decision this is now the English rule (*R.* v. *Lillyman*, [1896] 2 Q. B.
167). Some cases, however, say that the particulars are provable only
when the person so complaining is a girl of tender years (*Hannon* v.
State, 70 Wis. 448 ; see *People* v. *Gage*, 62 Mich. 271).

Though, in general, the complaint must be made "*soon* after" the
offence, yet if a longer delay in making it be adequately explained,

When a person's conduct is in issue, or is deemed to be relevant to the issue, statements made in his presence and hearing by which his conduct is likely to have been affected, are deemed to be relevant.'

---

as *e. g.*, if the delay be due to threats made by the perpetrator of the wrong, to duress, to lack of suitable opportunity to complain, etc., the fact of making complaint (and also the particulars in States admitting such evidence) may still be proved ; and especially is this true where the injury was done to a child.   Thus a delay of several days, and in some States even of several weeks or months, when thus explained, has been held not to exclude the evidence (*State* v. *Reid*, 39 Minn. 277 ; *People* v. *Duncan*, 104 Mich. 303 ; *Dunn* v. *State*, 45 O. St. 249 ; *People* v. *Terwilliger*, 74 Hun, 310, 142 N. Y. 629 ; *State* v. *Byrne*, 47 Ct. 465 ; *State* v. *Wilkins*, 66 Vt. 1 ; *Jackson* v. *State*, 91 Wis. 253). In such cases, however, the lapse of time may be considered by the jury as affecting the weight of the evidence. (Id.)

The making of a complaint is generally said to be admissible, not as constituting part of the *res gestæ*, but as a fact corroborative of the testimony of the complainant (Gr. Ev. iii. § 213 ; *Baccio* v. *People*, 41 N. Y. 265, 268 ; *State* v. *Mitchell*, 68 Ia. 116 ; *R.* v. *Lillyman*, [1896] 2 Q. B. 167 ; Am. Law Rev., xiv. 832 ; see the cases *supra*). Hence, if she does not testify, the evidence is not received, and that too, even though she is incompetent to testify (*Hornbeck* v. *State*, 35 O. St. 277 ; *State* v. *Meyers*, 46 Neb. 152). Some American decisions hold, however, that complaints made "immediately after" the commission of the wrong are admissible as part of the *res gestæ* (*People* v. *Gage*, 62 Mich. 271 ; *McMurrin* v. *Rigby*, 80 Ia. 322 ; *Snowden* v. *U. S.*, 2 App. D. C. 89 ; see Note V., Appendix).

The particulars of the complaint may be elicited on cross-examination of the complainant, or may be proved to confirm her testimony after it has been impeached.   *State* v. *Jones*, 61 Mo. 232 ; *Barnett* v. *State*, 83 Ala. 40 ; *State* v. *Langford*, 45 La. Ann. 1177.]

[1] *R.* v. *Edmunds*, 6 C. & P. 164 ; *Neil* v. *Jakle*, 2 C. & K. 709. [Illustration (*d*). This is because tacit acquiescence in such statements may be deemed an admission of their truth (*Proctor* v. *Old Colony R. Co.*, 154 Mass. 251 ; *Johnson* v. *Day*, 78 Me. 224 ; *Jewett* v. *Banning*, 21 N. Y. 27). The rule applies when the statements made impute a crime, as well as in other cases (*Kelley* v. *People*, 55 N. Y. 565 ; *Comm.* v. *Galavan*, 9 Allen, 271 ; *Ettinger* v. *Comm.*, 98 Pa. 338 ; *State* v. *Reed*, 62 Me. 129 ; *Watt* v. *People*, 126 Ill. 9 ; *Conway* v. *State*, 118 Ind. 482 ; see Art. 21, note, *post*) ; but it does not apply if the person be in-

Illustrations.

(*a*) The question is, whether A committed an act of bankruptcy, by departing the realm with intent to defraud his creditors.

Letters written during his absence from the realm, indicating such an intention, are deemed to be relevant facts.[1]

(*ab*) [The question is, whether a written paper which A destroyed was his will, and what was his intent in destroying it.

Statements made by A at the time of destruction that the paper was his will and giving his reasons for the act were deemed to be relevant. But statements made after the destruction were deemed not to be relevant.][2]

(*ac*) [The question is, whether a person is domiciled in the town of B.

Statements made by him, accompanying his removal from B to the city of C, that he intended to make his home in C, are deemed to be relevant.][3]

---

capable of hearing or understanding the statements, though these are made in his presence (*Lanergan* v. *People*, 39 N. Y. 39 ; *Wright* v. *Maseras*, 56 Barb. 521 ; *Martin* v. *Capital Ins. Co.*, 85 Ia. 643 ; *Tufts* v. *Charlestown*, 4 Gray, 537 ; *Comm.* v. *Sliney*, 126 Mass. 49). So if the statements are made in a judicial proceeding, silence does not admit their truth, since there is no opportunity to respond (*People* v. *Willett*, 92 N. Y. 29 ; *Collier* v. *Dick*, 111 Ala. 263 ; *State* v. *Mullins*, 101 Mo. 514 ; *State* v. *Boyle*, 13 R. I. 537 ; *Johnson* v. *Holliday*, 79 Ind. 151 ; but see *Blanchard* v. *Hodgkins*, 62 Me. 119). Nor does "silence give consent," if the circumstances are such as would not naturally call for a reply or explanation (*Drury* v. *Hervey*, 126 Mass. 519; *People* v. *Koerner*, 154 N. Y. 355 ; *Fry* v. *Stowers*, 92 Va. 13 ; *Peck* v. *Ryan*, 110 Ala. 336 ; *People* v. *Larubia*, 140 N. Y. 87 ; *Pierce's Admr.* v. *Pierce*, 66 Vt. 369 ; cf. *Hoffmann* v. *Hoffmann's Excr.*, 126 Mo. 486). If a reply is actually made in any case, it is admissible in evidence with the statement. *Comm.* v. *Trefethen*, 157 Mass. 180 ; *People* v. *Driscoll*, 107 N. Y. 414 ; *State* v. *Rogers*, 108 Mo. 202.]

[1] *Rawson* v. *Haigh*, 2 Bing. 99 ; *Bateman* v. *Bailey*, 5 T. R. 512.

[2] [*Eighmy* v. *People*, 79 N. Y. 546 ; *Waterman* v. *Whitney*, 11 N. Y. 157.]

[3] [*Viles* v. *Waltham*, 157 Mass. 542 ; *Fulham* v. *Howe*, 62 Vt. 386 ; *Deer Isle* v. *Winterport*, 87 Me. 37 ; *Roberts' Will*, 8 Pai. 519 ; cf. *Chicago, etc. R. Co.* v. *Chancellor*, 165 Ill. 438. So where a person on leaving home and in going elsewhere to stay or live, states his reasons for so doing, such declarations are admissible, being part of the *res gestæ* (*Johnson* v. *Sherwin*, 3 Gray, 374 ; *Hunter* v. *State*, 40 N. J. L.

(*b*) The question is, whether A was sane.

The fact that he acted upon a letter received by him is part of the facts in issue. The contents of the letter so acted upon are deemed to be relevant, as statements accompanying and explaining such conduct.[1]

(*ba*) [The question is, whether B is liable for the malicious prosecution of A.

The information as to A's guilt upon which B relied in instituting the prosecution is deemed to be relevant, as tending to show whether A had probable cause for the prosecution and was or was not actuated by malice.][2]

(*c*) The question is, whether A was ravished.

The fact that, shortly after the alleged rape, she made a complaint relating to the crime, and the circumstances under which it was made, are deemed to be relevant, but not (it seems) the terms of the complaint itself.[3]

The fact that, without making a complaint, she said that she had been ravished, is not deemed to be relevant as conduct under this Article, though it might be deemed to be relevant (*e.g.*) as a dying declaration under Article 26.

(*d*) [The question is, whether A committed arson.

The fact that at the fire or soon afterwards A's son said to him, " What did you want to set this afire for ? " and that he made no reply, is deemed to be relevant.][4]

495; *Rudd* v. *Rounds*, 64 Vt. 432; *Cattison* v. *Cattison*, 22 Pa. 275; *Robinson* v. *State*, 57 Md. 14; cf. *Mutual Life Ins. Co.* v. *Hillmon*, 145 U. S. 285). So replies given at the house of an absent defendant to the sheriff, who is attempting to serve process upon him, are admissible to show whether he can be found or is evading service. *Buswell* v. *Lincks*, 8 Daly, 518; Gr. Ev. i. § 101.]

[1] *Wright* v. *Doe* d. *Tatham*, 7 A. & E. 324-5 (per Denman, C. J.). [See *Barber's Appeal*, 63 Ct. 393; *Foster's Excrs.* v. *Dickerson*, 64 Vt. 233.]

[2] [*Fitzgibbon* v. *Brown*, 43 Me. 169; *Dwain* v. *Descalso*, 66 Cal. 415. So as to actions for false imprisonment. *Neall* v. *Hart*, 115 Pa. 347; *Perryman* v. *Lister*, L. R. 4 E. & I. App. 521.]

[3] *R.* v. *Walker*, 2 M. & R. 212. See Note V., Appendix. [In England now evidence is received of the particulars of the complaint. *R.* v. *Lillyman*, [1896] 2 Q. B. 167.]

[4] [*Comm.* v. *Brailey*, 134 Mass. 527; see *Brown* v. *State*, 32 Tex. App. 119.]

ARTICLE 9.

Facts necessary to be known to explain or introduce a fact in issue or relevant or deemed to be relevant to the issue, or which support or rebut an inference suggested by any such fact, or which establish the identity of any thing or person whose identity is in issue or is, or is deemed to be, relevant to the issue, or which fix the time or place at which any such fact happened, or which show that any document produced is genuine or otherwise, or which show the relation of the parties by whom any such fact was transacted, or which afforded an opportunity for its occurrence or transaction, or which are necessary to be known in order to show the relevancy of other facts, are deemed to be relevant in so far as they are necessary for those purposes respectively.[1]

Illustrations.

(*a*) The question is, whether a writing published by A of B is libelous or not.

The position and relations of the parties at the time when the libel

---

[1] [As to evidence of identity, see *Udderzook* v. *Comm.*, 76 Pa. 340; *Johnson* v. *Comm.*, 115 Id. 369; *Comm.* v. *Campbell*, 155 Mass. 537; *State* v. *Witham*, 72 Me. 531; of the relations of the parties, *Meltzger* v. *Doll*, 91 N. Y. 365; *Craig's Appeal*, 77 Pa. 448; *Siberry* v. *State*, 133 Ind. 677; *Roach* v. *Caldbeck*, 64 Vt. 593; to support or rebut an inference suggested by other facts in evidence, *State* v. *Adamson*, 43 Minn. 196; *O'Brien* v. *Comm.*, 89 Ky. 354; *Morris* v. *Spofford*, 127 Mass. 85. For other cases of relevant evidence under this Article, see *Pontius* v. *People*, 82 N. Y. 339, 350; *Bronner* v. *Frauenthal*, 37 N. Y. 166; *Quincey* v. *White*, 63 N. Y. 370, 380; *Comm.* v. *Annis*, 15 Gray, 197; *Comm.* v. *Williams*, 105 Mass. 62; *People* v. *Whitson*, 43 Mich. 421; *Wagenseller* v. *Simmers*, 97 Pa. 465; for cases of irrelevant evidence, see *Barnes* v. *Keene*, 132 N. Y. 13; *Phil. R. Co.* v. *Henrice*, 92 Pa. 431; *Thompson* v. *Bowie*, 4 Wall. 463; *Graves* v *Jacobs*, 8 Allen, 141.]

was published may be deemed to be relevant facts as introductory to the facts in issue.

The particulars of a dispute between A and B about a matter unconnected with the alleged libel are not deemed to be relevant under this Article, though the fact that there was a dispute may be deemed to be relevant if it affected the relations between A and B.[1]

(*b*) The question is, whether A wrote an anonymous letter, threatening B, and requiring B to meet the writer at a certain time and place to satisfy his demands.

The fact that A met B at that time and place is deemed to be relevant, as conduct subsequent to and affected by a fact in issue.

The fact that A had a reason, unconnected with the letter, for being at that time at that place, is deemed to be relevant, as rebutting the inference suggested by his presence.[2]

(*c*) A is tried for a riot, and is proved to have marched at the head of a mob. The cries of the mob are deemed to be relevant, as explanatory of the nature of the transaction.[3]

(*d*) The question is, whether a deed was forged. It purports to be made in the reign of Philip and Mary, and enumerates King Philip's titles.

The fact that, at the alleged date of the deed, Acts of State and other records were drawn with a different set of titles, is deemed to be relevant.[4]

(*e*) The question is, whether A poisoned B. Habits of B known to A, which would afford A an opportunity to administer the poison, are deemed to be relevant facts.[5]

(*f*) The question is, whether A made a will under undue influence.

---

[1] Common practice.

[2] *R.* v. *Barnard,* 19 St. Tri. 815, &c. [S. P. *Hoar* v. *Abbott,* 146 Mass. 290; *Schlemmer* v. *State,* 51 N. J. L. 23; *People* v. *Dixon,* 94 Cal. 255; *Prindle* v. *Glover,* 4 Ct. 266; *Comm.* v. *Brady,* 7 Gray, 320.]

[3] *R.* v. *Lord George Gordon,* 21 St. Tri. 520. [See *Stone* v. *Segur,* 11 Allen, 568; *Goins* v. *State,* 46 O. St. 457; *Comm.* v. *Ratcliffe,* 130 Mass. 36; *Alexander* v. *U. S.,* 138 U. S. 353; *McRae* v. *State,* 71 Ga. 96.]

[4] *Lady Ivy's Case,* 10 St. Tri. 615.

[5] *R.* v. *Donellan,* Wills' Circ. Ev. 192; and see my "History of the Criminal Law," 111, 371. [Cf. *McMeed* v. *Comm.,* 114 Pa. 300; *People* v. *Buchanan,* 145 N. Y. 1.]

His way of life and relations with the persons said to have influenced him unduly, are deemed to be relevant facts.[1]

(*g*) [The question is, whether A, an infant child, who was killed while on his way from England to this country, was domiciled in New York State at the time of his death.

The fact that his father, having resided in England, had lived in New York several months prior to A's death, and had come there for the purpose of making his home and living in that State, is deemed to be relevant.][2]

(*h*) [The question is, whether a gold watch, chain, and locket, sold to a wife, are necessaries, for which the husband should pay.

The fact that the husband wore diamonds, and kept a fast horse, and had paid for silk dresses worn by her, is deemed to be relevant.][3]

(*i*) [The question is, whether A was employed by B.

Conduct of A during the term of such employment, inconsistent with the theory of such employment, is deemed to be a relevant fact.][4]

(*j*) [The question is, whether A has survived his partner B.

Evidence that a person having the same name as B has died at the place of B's residence, is deemed to be relevant.][5]

(*k*) [The question is, whether A has been appropriating his employer's property.

The fact that for several years A has been living far beyond his apparent means is deemed to be relevant, as tending to confirm other evidence of dishonesty in taking the employer's property.][6]

(*l*) [The question is, whether A murdered B.

Evidence is relevant which tends to identify a body found six months after B's disappearance as that of B by showing similarity in the color of the hair, in the size of the body, in the appearance of the teeth, etc.

----

[1] *Boyse* v. *Rossborough*, 6 H. L. C. 42-58. [*Horn* v. *Pullman*, 72 N. Y. 269; *Coit* v. *Patchen*, 77 N. Y. 533; *May* v. *Bradlee*, 127 Mass. 414; *Spratt* v. *Spratt*, 76 Mich. 384; *Frew* v. *Clarke*, 80 Pa. 170; *Griffith* v. *Diffenderfer*, 50 Md. 466; *Kenyon* v. *Ashbridge*, 35 Pa. 157.]

[2] [*Kennedy* v. *Ryall*, 67 N. Y. 379.]

[3] [*Raynes* v. *Bennett*, 114 Mass. 424.]

[4] [*Miller* v. *Irish*, 63 N. Y. 652.]

[5] [*Daby* v. *Ericsson*, 45 N. Y. 786. Identity of name is, in general, *prima facie* evidence of identity of person. See Art. 101, note.]

[6] [*Hackett* v. *King*, 8 Allen, 144; *Martin* v. *State*, 104 Ala. 71; see *N. Y. etc. Ferry Co.* v. *Moore*, 1 N. Y. St. R. 374, 102 N. Y. 667; *Boston & W. R. Co.* v. *Dana*, 1 Gray, 83.]

Evidence of the following facts is also deemed relevant .—that blood-stains were found on boards where an accomplice of A testified the body of B had been placed ; that these stains were of human blood ; that A had B's watch in his possession a few months after B's dis-appearance; that the accomplice was absent from home on the night when, as he swore, he aided A in removing the body to another place; that A was seen on this night to ride in the direction of this place.]¹

(*m*) [A, having suffered injury from the defective condition of a highway, machine, structure, etc., sues B (the city in which the high-way lies, or the owner of the machine, etc.), claiming that such defect and the consequent injury are attributable to B's negligence.

Evidence that after the injury happened to A, the defect was repaired by B, is deemed not to be relevant for the purpose of prov-ing that B was negligent, as alleged, *before* the injury.]²

(*n*) [The question is, whether A, a physician, has been guilty of mal-practice and neglect.

The fact that A has not presented any bill or asked any pay for his services is deemed not to be relevant.]³

(*o*) [The question is, whether a credit for goods sold was given to the defendant or his son.

Evidence that the son had no property at the time of the sale, and was entirely irresponsible, is deemed not to be relevant.]⁴

---

¹ [*Linsday* v. *People*, 63 N. Y. 143 ; see *Greenfield* v. *People*, 85 N. Y. 75 ; *People* v. *Beckwith*, 108 N. Y. 67 ; *People* v. *Johnson*, 140 N. Y. 350 ; *State* v. *Ward*, 61 Vt. 153 ; *People* v. *Sanders*, 114 Cal. 216 ; *Comm.* v. *Dorsey*, 103 Mass. 412.]

² [*Corcoran* v. *Peekskill*, 108 N. Y. 151 ; *Morse* v. *Minneapolis, etc. R. Co.*, 30 Minn. 465 ; *Nalley* v. *Hartford Carpet Co.*, 51 Ct. 524 ; *Langworthy* v. *Green Township*, 88 Mich. 207 ; *Lang* v. *Sanger*, 76 Wis. 71 ; *Terre Haute, etc. R. Co.* v. *Clem*, 123 Ind. 15 ; *Shinners* v. *Proprietors*, 154 Mass. 168 ; *Columbia R. Co.* v. *Hawthorne*, 144 U. S. 202 ; *Sappenfield* v. *Main St. R. Co.*, 91 Cal. 48. In some States, however, such evidence is deemed competent as an implied ad-mission of prior negligence. (Id.)]

³ [*Baird* v. *Gillett*, 47 N. Y. 186 ; cf. *McBride* v. *Grand Rapids*, 49 Mich. 239 ; *Barnes* v. *Keene*, 132 N. Y. 13.]

⁴ [*Green* v. *Disbrow*, 56 N. Y. 334 ; but see *Lee* v. *Wheeler*, 11 Gray, 236 ; cf. *Buswell Trimmer Co.* v. *Case*, 144 Mass. 350 ; *Canaday* v. *Krum*, 83 N. Y. 67, 73 ; *McLoghlin* v. *Mohawk, etc. Bk.*, 139 N. Y. 514, 524.]

(*p*) [The question is, whether A, the maker of a promissory note, paid it shortly before he died.

Evidence that for a year before his death he had been hopelessly insolvent, and had had great difficulty in procuring means to meet his obligations, is deemed not to be relevant. " It is common for both solvent and insolvent men to pay some of their debts and to leave some unpaid."][1]

(*q*) [The question is, whether an executor is liable to pay a note of long standing, signed by his testator.

Evidence that the testator was in the habit of paying his debts promptly, or that another person had agreed to pay them for him, or that he made a list of his debts in which this note was not included, is deemed not to be relevant for the purpose of proving that the note has already been paid.][2]

(*r*) [The question is, whether A is the father of B, a young child.

Evidence that B resembles A, or counter-evidence to show non-resemblance, is deemed not to be relevant.[3] But, by some decisions, B may be exhibited to the jury to enable them to judge, from its resemblance or non-resemblance to A, whether A is its father.][4]

---

[1] [*Xenia Bk.* v. *Stewart*, 114 U. S. 224 ; but see *Atwood* v. *Scott*, 99 Mass. 177 ; cf. *Bean* v. *Tonnele*, 94 N. Y. 381.]

[2] [*Abercrombie* v. *Sheldon*, 8 Allen, 532 ; cf. *Martin* v. *Shannon*, 92 Ia. 374 ; *Burke* v. *Kaley*, 138 Mass. 464 ; *Carroll* v. *Deimel*, 95 N. Y. 252.]

[3] [*Young* v. *Makepeace*, 103 Mass. 50 ; *Jones* v. *Jones*, 45 Md. 144 ; *Eddy* v. *Gray*, 4 Allen, 435 ; cf. *People* v. *Carney*, 29 Hun, 47 ; but see *Paulk* v. *State*, 52 Ala. 427.]

[4] [*Gaunt* v. *State*, 50 N. J. L. 490 ; *Scott* v. *Donovan*, 153 Mass. 378 ; *Crow* v. *Jordon*, 49 O. St. 655 ; *Gilmanton* v. *Ham*, 38 N. H. 108 ; contra, *Reits* v. *State*, 33 Ind. 187 ; *Clark* v. *Bradstreet*, 80 Me. 454 ; *Hanawalt* v. *State*, 64 Wis. 84 ; *Robnett* v. *People*, 16 Ill. App. 299. In Iowa it has been held that a child two years and one month old might be exhibited to the jury (*State* v. *Smith*, 54 Ia. 104), but not a child three months old, because at such an age its features would be too immature (*State* v. *Danforth*, 48 Ia. 43). A photograph of the alleged father has been admitted in evidence, after his death, for the purpose of comparison with the child, the latter being old enough to have sufficiently developed features. *Shorten* v *Judd*, 56 Kan. 43 ; see *Farrell* v. *Weitz*, 160 Mass. 288 ; cf. *McKenna* v. *Paper Co.*, 176 Pa. 309, where photographs were compared with each other in order to ascertain a person's identity.]

(s) [The question is, whether A is insane.

The fact that his father, mother, or other blood relation is or has been insane, is deemed to be relevant.][1]

---

[1] [*State* v. *Hoyt*, 47 Ct. 518 ; *Prentis* v. *Bates*, 93 Mich. 234 ; *Baxter* v *Abbott*, 7 Gray, 71 ; *Shaeffer* v. *State*, 61 Ark. 241 ; *Walsh* v. *People*, 88 N. Y. 458. But as to some kinds of insanity, it may be necessary to prove them to be inheritable in order to make such evidence competent ; so held as to melancholia from intemperance. *Reichenbach* v. *Ruddach*, 127 Pa. 564.]

CHAPTER III.

OCCURRENCES SIMILAR TO BUT UNCONNECTED WITH THE FACTS IN ISSUE, IRRELEVANT EXCEPT IN CERTAIN CASES.

ARTICLE 10.*

SIMILAR BUT UNCONNECTED FACTS.

A FACT which renders the existence or non-existence of any fact in issue probable by reason of its general resemblance thereto, and not by reason of its being connected therewith in any of the ways specified in Articles 3–9, both inclusive, is deemed not to be relevant to such fact,[1] except in the cases specially excepted in this chapter.

---

* See Note VI. [Appendix].

[1] [*Barney* v. *Rickard*, 157 U. S. 352 ; *Wise* v. *Ackerman*, 76 Md. 375. But where the question is as to the cause of a certain occurrence, the fact that similar occurrences have, under like conditions, been produced by a particular cause is deemed to be relevant (*Evans* v. *Keystone Gas Co.*, 148 N. Y. 112 ; *Rockford Gas Light Co.* v. *Ernst*, 68 Ill. App. 300) ; and where the question is whether a certain state of things existed at a given time, the fact that a cause was in operation which, under like conditions, constantly produced such a result, is deemed to be relevant (*Upham* v. *Salem*, 162 Mass. 483). So the quality of an act or thing, as prudent or negligent, safe or dangerous, etc., may be exhibited, by showing that under like conditions it has produced similar favorable or injurious results, as in the case in question (see Illustrations *h* to *m*). This rule is analogous to that stated in Article 12, *post.* But if the conditions are not substantially the same in all cases, the evidence is not relevant. *Morse* v. *Minn. etc. R. Co.*, 30 Minn. 465 ; *Hunt* v. *Lowell Gas Co.*, 8 Allen, 169 ; *Cleveland, etc. R. Co.* v. *Newell*, 104 Ind. 264 ; *Bloomington* v. *Legg*, 151 Ill. 9 ; *Shepard* v. *Hill*, 151 Mass. 540 ; *Randolph* v. *Bloomfield*, 77 Ia. 50 ; *Brewing Co.* v. *Bauer*, 50 O. St. 560 ; *Griffin* v. *Auburn*, 58 N. H. 121 ; *Hodgkins* v. *Chappell*, 128 Mass. 197 ; cf. *State* v. *Flint*, 60 Vt. 304.]

Illustrations.

(*a*) The question is, whether A committed a crime.

The fact that he formerly committed another crime of the same sort, and had a tendency to commit such crimes, is deemed to be irrelevant.[1]

(*ab*) [A is indicted and brought to trial for the robbery of a bank-key from the janitor of the bank.

Evidence of a burglary committed on the bank immediately after the taking of the key, of the breaking open of the safe and the larceny of the valuables therein, is deemed to be relevant; also that defendant had for two years been engaged in a conspiracy to rob the bank, and had made two prior attempts to carry out this purpose.][2]

(*b*) The question is, whether A, a brewer, sold good beer to B, a publican. The fact that A sold good beer to C, D, and E, other pub-

---

[1] *R.* v. *Cole*, 1 Ph. Ev. 508 (said to have been decided by all the Judges in Mich. Term, 1810). [*People* v. *Sharp*, 107 N. Y. 427 ; *People* v. *McLaughlin*, 150 N. Y. 365, 386 ; *Jordan* v. *Osgood*, 109 Mass. 457 ; *Costelo* v. *Crowell*, 139 Mass. 588 ; *Jansen* v. *People*, 159 Ill. 440 ; *Boyd* v. *U. S.*, 142 U. S. 450 ; *Shaffner* v. *Comm.*, 72 Pa. 60. But the commission of another crime may be shown, if it supplies a motive or constitutes preparation for the commission of the one in question (*Pierson* v. *People*, 79 N. Y. 424 ; *Comm.* v. *Choate*, 105 Mass. 451, 458 ; *Painter* v. *People*, 147 Ill. 444 ; *People* v. *Harris*, 136 N. Y. 423 ; *McConkey* v. *Comm.*, 101 Pa. 416 ; *State* v. *Kline*, 54 Ia. 183 ; see Illustration (*ab*) ; also Art. 7, *supra*) ; or if it tends to prove any fact constituting an element of the crime charged (*Weed* v. *People*, 56 N. Y. 628) ; or if the different crimes form parts of one general scheme or transaction and exhibit the same general purpose (Illustration (*ab*) ; *People* v. *Murphy*, 135 N. Y. 450 ; *Scott* v. *People*, 141 Ill. 195 ; *Comm.* v. *Scott*, 123 Mass. 222 ; *Brown* v. *Comm.*, 76 Pa. 319 ; *Pa. Co. for Insurance* v. *Phila. etc. R. Co.*, 153 Pa. 160 ; *State* v. *Lee*, 91 Ia. 499 ; *People* v. *Mead*, 50 Mich. 228 ; *People* v. *Smith*, 106 Cal. 73 ; *Halleck* v. *State*, 65 Wis. 147) ; and in other like cases (see *Comm.* v. *Jackson*, 132 Mass. 16, 19 ; *Goersen* v. *Comm.*, 99 Pa. 388). Thus former attempts to commit the same crime may be proved to show criminal intent, the identity of the actor, etc. (*Comm.* v. *Bradford*, 126 Mass. 42 ; *State* v. *Nugent*, 71 Mo. 136 ; *Nicholas' Case*, 91 Va. 741 ; *People* v. *O'Sullivan*, 104 N. Y. 481). These latter cases fall properly under Arts. 11 and 12, *post*. The whole subject is well discussed in *Farris* v. *People*, 129 Ill. 521 and *People* v. *Sharp*, 107 N. Y. 427.]

[2] [*Hope* v. *People*, 83 N. Y. 418.]

licans, is deemed to be irrelevant,[1] (unless it is shown that the beer sold to all is of the same brewing).[2]

(c) [The question is, whether certain shovel-handles sold by A to B were of good quality.

Evidence that shovel-handles sold by A to another party at the same time were of good quality, is deemed to be relevant, if accompanied by evidence that the handles sold to both purchasers were of the same kind and quality.][3]

(d) [The question is, whether A, having killed a person at night, knew him to be an officer of the law.

The fact that there was a lighted street-lamp near by is relevant, as tending to show that A could see the official uniform. But to prove the amount of light cast by the lamp on this night, evidence showing the amount of light cast by the same lamp on a night four months afterwards is irrelevant, (the conditions not being shown to be the same).][4]

(e) [The question is, whether A has a right to travel on a railroad ticket after the time limited therein for its use, without the payment of fare.

The fact that he has at other times purchased similar tickets and used them after the time specified, without being required to pay fare, is irrelevant.][5]

(f) [The question is, what is the value of a certain vessel.

Evidence to prove the value of other vessels with which she might be compared is irrelevant.][6]

---

[1] *Holcombe* v. *Hewson*, 2 Camp. 391; [cf. *Lake* v. *Clark*, 97 Mass. 346.]

[2] See Illustrations to Article 3; [see *Comm.* v. *Goodman*, 97 Mass. 117; *Luetgert* v. *Volker*, 153 Ill. 385.]

[3] [*Ames* v. *Quimby*, 106 U. S. 342; cf. *Albany, etc. Co.* v. *Lundberg*, 121 U. S. 451; *Pike* v. *Fay*, 101 Mass. 134; *Thill's Sons* v. *Perkins Lamp Co.*, 63 Ct. 478.]

[4] [*Yates* v. *People*, 32 N. Y. 509; see *King* v. *N. Y. Central, etc. R. Co.*, 72 N. Y. 610; *Fillo* v. *Jones*, 2 Abb. Dec. 121; *Stone* v. *Ins. Co.*, 71 Mich. 81.]

[5] [*Hill* v. *Syracuse, etc. R. Co.*, 63 N. Y. 101; cf. *Harris* v. *Howard*, 56 Vt. 695; *Dana* v. *Nat. Bk. of Republic*, 132 Mass. 156.]

[6] [*Blanchard* v. *Steamboat Co.*, 59 N. Y. 292; *Gouge* v. *Roberts*, 53 N. Y. 619; *Huntington* v. *Attrill*, 118 N. Y. 635; but see *Berney* v. *Dinsmore*, 141 Mass. 42; *Carr* v. *Moore*, 41 N. H. 131. But in Massachusetts and some other States the value of land may be proved by

(*g*) [The question is, whether a servant was negligent on a particular occasion.

Evidence that he was negligent on previous occasions is irrelevant; but if the question were whether the master was negligent in retaining in his employ a careless and incompetent servant, evidence of the servant's prior acts of negligence to the master's knowledge, would be relevant.][1]

(*h*) [The question is, what sum A is entitled to receive from B, as compensation for services rendered by A as B's attorney, agent, or servant.

Evidence as to what compensation has been paid to other persons by B for similar services is deemed not to be relevant.][2]

(*i*) [The question is, whether A is hired by his employer B by the week or by the year.

Evidence that other employees of B are hired by the year is deemed to be irrelevant.][3]

(*j*) [The question is, whether A, having been injured by slipping

---

showing the prices received upon sales of other lands of like description in the vicinity at times not too remote (*Haven* v. *County Commrs.*, 155 Mass. 467; *St. Louis, etc. R. Co.* v. *Clark*, 121 Mo. 169; *Laing* v. *United N. J. R. Co.*, 54 N. J. L. 576; *Elmore* v. *Johnson*, 143 Ill. 513; *Mayor of Baltimore* v. *Smith Co.*, 80 Md. 458; *Washburn* v. *Milwaukee R. Co.*, 59 Wis. 364). The contrary rule, however, prevails in some States (*Matter of Thompson*, 127 N. Y. 463; *Becker* v. *Phila. etc. R. Co.*, 177 Pa. 252; Mills, Em. Domain, §170; cf. *Kerr* v. *So. Park Commrs.*, 117 U. S. 379; *Witmark* v. *N. Y. Elev. R. Co.*, 149 N. Y. 393). What was paid for property when it was bought is some evidence of its present value. *In re Johnston*, 144 N. Y. 563; *Kendrick* v. *Beard*, 90 Mich. 589.]

[1] [*Baulec* v. *N. Y. etc. R. Co.*, 59 N. Y. 356; *Whittaker* v. *Delaware, etc. R. Co.*, 126 N. Y. 544; *Western Stone Co.* v. *Whalen*, 151 Ill. 472; *Baltimore Elevator Co.* v. *Neal*, 65 Md. 438; *Grube* v. *Mo. Pac. R. Co.*, 98 Mo. 330; cf. *Connors* v. *Morton*, 160 Mass. 333; *Michigan Cent. R. Co.* v. *Gilbert*, 46 Mich. 176; contra, *State* v. *Railroad Co.*, 52 N. H. 528; see p. 46, n. 3, *post;* also Arts. 12, 57, and notes.]

[2] [*Playford* v. *Hutchinson*, 135 Pa. 426; *Seurer* v. *Horst*, 31 Minn. 479; *Linn* v. *Gilman*, 46 Mich. 628; *Bonynge* v. *Field*, 81 N. Y. 159; cf. *Newhall* v. *Appleton*, 102 N. Y. 133.]

[3] [*Lichtenhein* v. *Fisher*, 6 App. Div. (N. Y.) 385; *Schneider* v. *Hill*, 19 Misc. 56.]

and falling upon a sidewalk, can recover damages from the city for its alleged neglect to keep the walk in a safe condition.

The fact that other persons slipped and fell upon the same walk, while its condition remained the same as when A fell, is relevant to show that it was unsafe for use at the time of his fall.][1]

(*k*) [The question is, whether the act or structure of A, which frightened B's horse, was one which was calculated to render the use of the highway with horses dangerous.

Evidence that other horses of ordinary steadiness were frightened by the same act or structure, or one of the same kind under like circumstances, is relevant.][2]

(*l*) [The question is, whether a loom-attachment will work successfully on a certain loom.

The fact that it works successfully on another loom of substantially the same construction, is relevant.][3]

(*m*) [A, having been injured in using (as he lawfully might, as cus-

---

[1] [*District of Col.* v. *Armes*, 107 U. S. 519; *Quinlan* v. *Utica*, 11 Hun, 217, 74 N. Y. 603; *Magee* v. *Troy*, 48 Hun, 383, 119 N. Y. 640; *Gillrie* v. *Lockport*, 122 N. Y. 403; *Lombar* v. *East Tawas*, 86 Mich. 14; *Topeka* v. *Sherwood*, 39 Kan. 690; *Cook* v. *New Durham*, 64 N. H. 419; *Phelps* v. *Winona, etc. R. Co.*, 37 Minn. 485; *Birmingham R. Co.* v. *Alexander*, 93 Ala. 133; *Golden* v. *Clinton*, 54 Mo. App. 100; *Rowlands* v. *Elgin*, 66 Ill. App. 66; cf. *Fraser* v. *Schroeder*, 163 Ill. 459; *Kent* v. *Lincoln*, 32 Vt. 591. But some cases are to the contrary (*Phillips* v. *Willow*, 70 Wis. 6; *Moore* v. *Richmond*, 85 Va. 538; *Bremner* v. *Newcastle*, 83 Me. 415).

Evidence that other persons had been injured at the same place has also been received to show that the city had notice of the defect. *City of Goshen* v. *England*, 119 Ind. 368; *Alberts* v. *Vernon*, 96 Mich. 549; *Chicago* v. *Powers*, 42 Ill. 169; *Ashtabula* v. *Bartram*, 3 O. C. C. 640.]

[2] [*Crocker* v. *McGregor*, 76 Me. 282; *Bemis* v. *Temple*, 162 Mass. 342; *Harrell* v. *Albemarle, etc. R. Co.*, 110 N. C. 215; *Gordon* v. *Boston & M. R. Co.*, 58 N. H. 396; *House* v. *Metcalf*, 27 Ct. 631; cf. *Lewis* v. *Eastern R. Co.*, 60 N. H. 187; *Brown* v. *Eastern, etc. R. Co.*, 22 Q. B. D. 391; *Piollet* v. *Simmers*, 106 Pa. 95; contra, *Cleveland, etc. R. Co.* v. *Wynant*, 114 Ind. 525; *Bloor* v. *Delafield*, 69 Wis. 273.]

[3] [*Brierly* v. *Davoll Mills*, 128 Mass. 291; cf. *Locke* v. *Express, etc. Co.*, 71 Mich. 263; *Boyer* v. *Rhinehart*, 17 N. Y. S. 346, 137 N. Y. 564; *Tremblay* v. *Harnden*, 162 Mass. 383; *Bradley* v. *Hartford, etc. Ins. Co.*, 19 F. R. 246.]

tomer, passenger, traveler, etc.) B's appliance, machine, structure. etc., claims that the injury is due to B's negligence in not having said appliance, machine, structure, etc., in reasonably safe condition for use. Evidence, introduced in B's behalf, that many others had for a long time used the same thing (or an identical thing or things) in the same condition, and that no similar injury had ever occurred, is deemed to be relevant. Such evidence tends to show that the appliance, machine, structure, etc., is such as a reasonably prudent person, exercising reasonable diligence, would properly consider safe for the purposes for which it was designed.][1]

(*n*) [A sues B (a city, village, railway company, bridge company, etc.) to recover damages for an injury alleged to have been sustained through a defect in a highway, railway track, bridge, etc., which defect is alleged to be due to B's neglect or default. A submits no evidence as to the condition of the way, track, bridge, etc., at the precise place where the injury is alleged to have occurred, but offers evidence that the same was defective or dangerous in the immediate vicinity of this place. Such evidence is deemed to be relevant, if it is proved, or if the circumstances of the case justify the conclusion, that the condition of the place where the injury occurred and of the place to which the evidence relates was substantially the same.[2]

A also submits evidence to show what was the condition of the place

---

[1] [*Field* v. *Davis*, 27 Kan. 400 (grain elevator); *Doyle* v. *St. Paul, etc. R. Co.*, 42 Minn. 79; *McGrell* v. *Buffalo Office Bldg. Co.*, 153 N. Y. 265 (passenger elevator); *Frobisher* v. *Fifth Ave. Co.*, 151 N. Y. 431 (omnibus); *Lafflin* v. *Buffalo, etc. R. Co.*, 106 N. Y. 136 (platform of railway station); *Loftus* v. *Union Ferry Co.*, 84 N. Y. 455 (ferry float); *Cleveland* v. *N. J. Steamboat Co.*, 68 N. Y. 306 (steamboat); cf. *Calkins* v. *Hartford*, 33 Ct. 57 (sidewalk); to the contrary are *Hodges* v. *Bearse*, 129 Ill. 87 (elevator); *Langworthy* v. *Green T'p*, 88 Mich. 207 (highway); *Branch* v. *Libbey*, 78 Me. 321 (highway).]

[2] [*Barrett* v. *Hammond*, 87 Wis. 654; *Vicksburg, etc. R. Co.* v. *Putnam*, 118 U. S. 545; *Nashville, etc. R. Co.* v. *Johnson*, 15 Lea, 677 (condition of railway track shown for 100 yards on either side); *Ohio Valley R. Co.* v. *Watson*, 93 Ky. 654; *Fort Wayne* v. *Combs*, 107 Ind. 75 (break in sewer 100 feet distant); *Sidekum* v. *Washburn, etc. R. Co.*, 93 Mo. 400 (railway track, 1½ miles held too far distant and evidence rejected); *Campbell* v. *Kalamazoo*, 80 Mich. 655 (plank walk, condition near by proved). Evidence of this kind is, also, generally received to show *notice* of the condition of the way, track, bridge, etc., to the municipality, railroad company, etc., in order to establish its

where the injury occurred some time before the injury or some time after the injury, as tending to show what was its condition at the time of the injury. This evidence is deemed to be relevant, if it is also proved, or if the circumstances justify the conclusion, that the condition of the place has continued without change during the interval.][1]

(*o*) [The question is, whether a fire was caused by sparks and coals from a locomotive of a railroad company.

The fact that passing locomotives of similar construction have on other occasions, not too remote, caused fires at or near the place in question by scattering sparks and coals, is deemed to be relevant ; so also is the fact that they have thus repeatedly scattered sparks and coals, though no actual fires were thereby caused, since such a cause may have occasioned fire in this instance, though not in others. But preliminary evidence should be given excluding the probability that the fire in question originated from another source.][2]

---

negligence in not having made repairs at the place of the injury. *Girard* v. *Kalamazoo*, 92 Mich. 610 ; *McConnell* v. *Osage*, 80 Ia. 293 ; *Shaw* v. *Sun Prairie*, 74 Wis. 105 ; *Shelbyville* v. *Brant*, 61 Ill. App. 153 ; *McGuire* v. *Ogdensburgh, etc. R. Co.*, 18 N. Y. S. 313.]

[1] [*Jessup* v. *Osceola Co.*, 92 Ia. 178 (condition of bridge shown "a few days after ") ; *Bloomington* v. *Osterlee*, 139 Ill. 120 (two weeks after) ; *Swadley* v. *Mo. Pac. R. Co.*, 118 Mo. 268 ; *Stewart* v. *Everts*, 76 Wis. 35 (six months after) ; *Sullivan* v. *Syracuse*, 77 Hun, 440 (three days after) ; *McCulloch* v. *Dobson*, 133 N. Y. 114 (a few months) ; *Hunt* v. *City of Dubuque*, 96 Ia. 314 (one year before) ; but evidence to show the condition of a railway track one or more years afterwards has been rejected as too remote (*Stoher* v. *Mo. Pac. R. Co.*, 91 Mo. 509). So where the conditions have changed, the evidence is rejected, even though the interval be short. *Woodcock* v. *Worcester*, 138 Mass. 268 (a week before).]

[2] [*Field* v. *N. Y. C. R. Co.*, 32 N. Y. 339 ; *Crist* v. *Erie R. Co.*, 58 N. Y. 638 ; *Grand Trunk R. Co.* v. *Richardson*, 91 U. S. 454 ; *Boyce* v. *Cheshire R. Co.*, 43 N. H. 627 ; *Ky. Cent. R. Co.* v. *Barrow*, 89 Ky. 638 ; *Steele* v. *Pacific, etc. R. Co.*, 74 Cal. 323 ; *Campbell* v. *Mo. Pac. R. Co.*, 121 Mo. 340 ; see *Atchison, etc. R. Co.* v. *Stanford*, 12 Kan. 354 ; *Albert* v. *Nor. Central R. Co.*, 98 Pa. 316. In some of these cases it is also said that evidence of this kind may show a habit of negligence in running the trains. The last sentence of the Illustration states a rule declared by the New York cases, (and see *Wiley* v. *West Jersey R. Co.*, 44 N. J. L. 247 ; *Johnson* v. *Chicago, etc. R. Co.*, 77 Ia. 666).

So where it is claimed that the fire was set by a particular engine,

(*p*) [The question is, whether a fire causing the destruction of a certain building by night was of incendiary origin.

The fact that an attempt was made on the same night to set fire to a neighboring building by the use of similar means is relevant.][1]   .

(*q*) [The question is, whether the foundering of a vessel, while she is being towed by a tug, is caused by her being overladen and unseaworthy, or is due to the reckless and improper rate of speed at which she is towed.

The fact that she has been frequently towed in safety with as heavy or heavier loads and at as high a rate of speed is deemed to be relevant, as tending to show that negligence in towing must have caused the disaster. The fact that she has repeatedly foundered while being carefully towed is deemed to be relevant, as indicating that her own improper condition must have occasioned the loss.][2]

(*r*) [The question is, whether the sickness of A, a seaman, while he was upon a ship at sea of which B was master, was due to B's neglect in failing to furnish suitable provisions and anti-scorbutics.

Evidence of the similar sickness of others of the crew about the same time was deemed to be relevant, on account of the similarity of the conditions and circumstances affecting all the crew.][3]

---

evidence tending to show that other fires were set by the same engine about the same time is admissible (*Haseltine* v. *Concord R. Co.*, 64 N. H. 545; *Patton* v. *St. Louis, etc. R. Co.*, 87 Mo. 117; *Lanning* v. *Chicago, etc. R. Co.*, 68 Ia. 502; *Brighthope R. Co.* v. *Rogers*, 76 Va. 443; *Loring* v. *Worcester, etc. R. Co.*, 131 Mass. 469). In some States, moreover, if the plaintiff identifies a particular engine as being the alleged cause of the fire, evidence as to other engines is in such a case inadmissible. *Henderson* v. *Philadelphia, etc. R. Co.*, 144 Pa. 461; *Gibbons* v. *Wisconsin, etc. R. Co.*, 58 Wis. 335; *Inman* v. *Elberton R. Co.*, 90 Ga. 663; but see *Thatcher* v. *Me. Cent. R. Co.*, 85 Me. 502, and cases *supra*.]

. [1] [*Faucett* v. *Nicholls*, 64 N. Y. 377; *State* v. *Thompson*, 97 N. C. 496; see *Comm.* v. *Gauvin*, 143 Mass. 134; *Landell* v. *Hotchkiss*, 1 T. & C. 580; *Mead* v. *Husted*, 49 Ct. 336.]

[2] [*Baird* v. *Daly*, 68 N. Y. 547; see *Wilson* v. *Granby*, 47 Ct. 59; *Beatrice Gas Co.* v. *Thomas*, 41 Neb. 662; *Weldon* v. *Harlem R. Co.*, 5 Bos 576.]

[3] [*Baxter* v. *Doe*, 142 Mass. 558; *Shea* v. *Glendale Co.*, 162 Mass. 463. But to prove the intoxication of A, it is not competent to prove that B, who had been with him and had drunk the same kinds and amount of liquor, was intoxicated. *Comm.* v. *Cleary*, 135 Pa. 64.]

ARTICLE 11.*

ACTS SHOWING INTENTION, GOOD FAITH, ETC.

When there is a question whether a person said or did something, the fact that he said or did something of the same sort on a different occasion may be proved, if it shows the existence on the occasion in question of any intention, knowledge, good or bad faith, malice, or other state of mind, or of any state of body or bodily feeling, the existence of which is in issue, or is or is deemed to be relevant to the issue;[1] but such acts or words may not be proved merely in order to show that the person so acting or speaking was likely on the occasion in question to act in a similar manner.[2]

---

* See Note VI. [Appendix].

[1] [This rule is fully considered and its proper limitations stated in *Mayer v. People*, 80 N. Y. 364; *Comm. v. Jackson*, 132 Mass. 16; *State v. Kelley*, 65 Vt. 531. See also Gr. Ev. i. §53; *People v. Dimick*, 107 N. Y. 13; *N. Y. Mutual Life Ins. Co. v. Armstrong*, 117 U. S. 591; *State v. Jamison*, 74 Ia. 613; *Butler v. Watkins*, 13 Wall. 456; *Tarbox v. State*, 38 O. St. 581; *State v. Wentworth*, 37 N. H. 196; p. 35, *ante*, note 1.]

[2] [At this point Mr. Stephens adds the following rule derived from an English statute (34 and 35 Vict. c. 112, s. 19): "Where proceedings are taken against any person for having received goods, knowing them to be stolen, or for having in his possession stolen property, the fact that there was found in the possession of such person other property stolen within the preceding period of twelve months, is deemed to be relevant to the question whether he knew the property to be stolen which forms the subject of the proceedings taken against him. If, in the case of such proceedings as aforesaid, evidence has been given that the stolen property has been found in the possession of the person proceeded against, the fact that such person has within five years immediately preceding been convicted of any offence involving fraud or dishonesty, is deemed to be relevant for the purpose of proving that the person accused knew the property which was proved to be in his possession to have been stolen, and may be proved at any

Illustrations.

(*a*) A is charged with receiving two pieces of silk from B, knowing them to have been stolen by him from C.

The facts that A received from B many other articles stolen by him from C in the course of several months, and that A pledged all of them, are deemed to be relevant to the fact that A knew that the two pieces of silk were stolen by B from C.[1]

(*b*) A is charged with uttering, on the 12th December, 1854, a counterfeit crown piece, knowing it to be counterfeit.

The facts that A uttered another counterfeit crown piece on the 11th December, 1854, and a counterfeit shilling on the 4th January, 1855, are deemed to be relevant to show A's knowledge that the crown piece uttered on the 12th was counterfeit.[2]

---

stage of the proceedings; provided that not less than seven days' notice in writing has been given to the person accused that proof is intended to be given of such previous conviction. The fact that the prisoner was within twelve. months in possession of other stolen property than that to which the charge applies is not deemed to be relevant, unless such property was found in his possession at or soon after the time when the proceedings against him were taken. (*R.* v. *Carter*, 12 Q. B. D. 522; and see *R.* v. *Drage*, 14 Cox, 85.)" This enactment, he says, overrules, to a strictly limited extent, *R.* v. *Oddy*, 2 Den. C. C. 264, and practically supersedes *R.* v. *Dunn*, 1 Moo. C. C. 150, and *R.* v. *Davis*, 6 C. & P. 177.

In this country such cases are governed by the general common law rule.   See Illustrations and cases cited.]

[1] *Dunn's Case*, 1 Moo. C. C. 146. [S. P. *Copperman* v. *People*, 56 N. Y. 591; *Coleman* v. *People*, 58 N. Y. 555; *State* v. *Ward*, 49 Ct. 429; *Comm.* v. *Johnson*, 133 Pa. 293; *Shriedley* v. *State*, 23 O. St. 130; see *People* v. *McClure*, 148 N. Y. 95.   But the fact that A received property on other occasions from other persons than B, knowing it to have been stolen, is deemed not to be relevant. *Coleman* v. *People*, 55 N. Y. 81.]

[2] *R.* v. *Forster*, Dears. 456; and see *R.* v. *Weeks*, L. & C. 18. [See *Comm.* v. *Bigelow*, 8 Met. 235; *Comm.* v. *Price*, 10 Gray, 472; *Stalker* v. *State*, 9 Ct. 341 ; *People* v. *Dibble*, 3 Abb. Dec. 518.

So upon a trial for forgery or uttering forged instruments, evidence of other recent forgeries or utterings by the defendant is admissible to show guilty knowledge or intent. *People* v. *Everhardt*, 104 N. Y. 591; *Comm.* v. *Russell*, 156 Mass. 196; *Anson* v. *People*, 148 Ill. 494; *People* v. *Baird*, 105 Cal. 126; *People* v. *Kemp*, 76 Mich. 410.]

(c) A is charged with attempting to obtain money by false pretences, by trying to pledge to B a worthless ring as a diamond ring.

The facts that, two days before, A tried, on two separate occasions, to obtain money from C and D respectively, by a similar assertion as to the same or a similar ring, and that on another occasion on the same day he obtained a sum of money from E by pledging as a gold chain a chain which was only gilt, are deemed to be relevant, as showing his knowledge of the quality of the ring.[1]

(d) A is charged with obtaining money from B by falsely pretending that Z had authorized him to do so.

The fact that on a different occasion A obtained money from C by a similar false pretence is deemed to be irrelevant,[2] as A's knowledge that he had no authority from Z on the second occasion had no connection with his knowledge that he had no authority from Z on the first occasion.

(e) A sues B for damage done by a dog of B's, which B knew to be ferocious.

The facts that the dog had previously bitten X, Y, and Z, and that they had made complaints to B, are deemed to be relevant.[3]

(f) The question is, whether A, the acceptor of a bill of exchange, knew that the name of the payee was fictitious.

The fact that A had accepted other bills drawn in the same manner before they could have been transmitted to him by the payee, if the

---

[1] R. v. Francis, L. R. 2 C. C. R. 128. The case of R. v. Cooper, 1 Q. B. D. (C. C. R.) 19, is similar to R. v. Francis, and perhaps stronger. [S. P. Mayer v. People, 80 N. Y. 364; Comm. v. Coe, 115 Mass. 481; State v. Bayne, 88 Mo. 604; see People v. Henssler, 48 Mich. 49. Evidence of this kind is also relevant in civil actions to prove guilty knowledge or fraudulent purpose. Hall v. Naylor, 18 N. Y. 588; Beuerlien v. O'Leary, 149 N. Y. 33; Lincoln v. Claflin, 7 Wall. 132; Hovey v. Grant, 52 N. H. 569; Lockwood v. Doane, 107 Ill. 235.]

[2] R. v. Holt, Bell, C. C. 280; and see R. v. Francis, ub. sup. p. 130. [Comm. v. Jackson, 132 Mass. 16; Strong v. State, 86 Ind. 208; Jackson v. People, 126 Ill. 139; cf. Huganir v. Cotter, 92 Wis. 1; but see People v. Shulman, 80 N. Y. 373.]

[3] See cases collected in Roscoe's Nisi Prius, 739. [Evans v. McDermott, 49 N. J. L. 163; Graham v. Payne, 122 Ind. 403; Reynolds v. Hussey, 64 N. H. 64; see Godeau v. Blood, 52 Vt. 251; Muller v. McKesson, 73 N. Y. 195. So evidence of the general repute of the

payee had been a real person, is deemed to be relevant, as showing that A knew that the payee was a fictitious person.[1]

(g) A sues B for a malicious libel. Defamatory statements made by B regarding A for ten years before those in respect of which the action is brought are deemed to be relevant to show malice.[2]

(ga) [The question is, whether A committed adultery with B.

The fact that on other occasions, not too remote, these persons had committed adultery is deemed to be relevant, to show the existence of an adulterous disposition; but not to show the commission of the particular act in question.][3]

---

dog in the neighborhood, as being vicious and dangerous, is competent, as tending to raise an inference that the owner knew of such propensity. *Cameron* v. *Bryan*, 89 Ia. 214; *Fake* v. *Addicks*, 45 Minn. 37.]

[1] *Gibson* v. *Hunter*, 2 H. Bl. 288.

[2] *Barrett* v. *Long*, 3 H. L. C. 395, 414. [*Evening Journal Ass'n* v. *McDermott*, 44 N. J. L. 430; *Comm.* v. *Place*, 153 Pa. 314; *Beneway* v. *Thorp*, 77 Mich. 181; *Fredrickson* v. *Johnson*, 60 Minn. 337; *Austin* v. *Remington*, 46 Ct. 116; *Freeman* v. *Sanderson*, 123 Ind. 264; *Cruikshank* v. *Gordon*, 118 N. Y. 178. It is generally held that the charges proved to show malice must be substantially similar to the one in question, and that they may have been made either before it was published or afterwards (Id.; *Comm.* v. *Damon*, 136 Mass. 441, 448; *Conant* v. *Leslie*, 85 Me. 257; *Brown* v. *Barnes*, 39 Mich. 211; *Cavanaugh* v. *Austin*, 42 Vt. 576; *Howard* v. *Sexton*, 4 N. Y. 157). In some States they may be proved though made after suit brought (*Chamberlain* v. *Vance*, 51 Cal. 75; *Larrabee* v. *Minnesota Tribune Co.*, 36 Minn. 141; *Post Pub. Co.* v. *Hallam*, 59 F. R. 530; *Knapp* v. *Smith*, 55 Vt. 311), but not in others (*Daly* v. *Byrne*, 77 N. Y. 182; but see *Turton* v. *N. Y. Recorder Co.*, 144 N. Y. 144, 150). By some decisions, also, enhanced damages are recoverable in the same action for the repeated charges (*Leonard* v. *Pope*, 27 Mich. 145; cf. *Hints* v. *Graupner*, 138 Ill. 158; *Alpin* v. *Morton*, 21 O. St. 536); but in most States damages are only obtainable for the particular charge sued upon, while the evidence of repetitions is deemed competent to show the degree of malice in such charge. *Ward* v. *Dick*, 47 Ct. 300; *Clark* v. *Brown*, 116 Mass. 504; *Enos* v. *Enos*, 135 N. Y. 609.]

[3] [*Brooks* v. *Brooks*, 145 Mass. 574; *Thayer* v. *Thayer*, 101 id. 111; *State* v. *Williams*, 76 Me. 480; *Comm.* v. *Bell*, 166 Pa. 405; *People* v. *Patterson*, 102 Cal. 239; *People* v. *Skutt*, 96 Mich. 449; *State* v. *Potter*, 52 Vt. 33; *State* v. *Markins*, 95 Ind. 464; *State* v. *Briggs*, 68 Ia. 416; *State* v. *Young*, 99 Mo. 284.]

(*h*) A is sued by B for fraudulently representing to B that C was solvent, whereby B, being induced to trust C, who was insolvent, suffered loss.

The fact that, at the time when A represented C to be solvent, C was to A's knowledge supposed to be solvent by his neighbors and by persons dealing with him, is deemed to be relevant, as showing that A made the representation in good faith.[1]

(*i*) A is sued by B for the price of work done by B, by the order of C, a contractor, upon a house, of which A is owner.

A's defence is that B's contract was with C.

The fact that A paid C for the work in question is deemed to be relevant, as proving that A did, in good faith, make over to C the management of the work in question, so that C was in a position to contract with B on C's own account, and not as agent for A.[2]

(*j*) A is accused of stealing property which he had found, and the question is, whether he meant to steal it when he took possession of it.

The fact that public notice of the loss of the property had been given in the place where A was, and in such a manner that A knew or probably might have known of it, is deemed to be relevant, as showing that A did not, when he took possession of it, in good faith believe that the real owner of the property could not be found.[3]

(*k*) The question is, whether A is entitled to damages from B, the seducer of A's wife.

The fact that A's wife wrote affectionate letters to A before the adultery was committed, is deemed to be relevant, as show-

---

[1] *Sheen* v. *Bumpstead*, 2 H. & C. 193. [See *Slingerland* v. *Bennett*, 6 T. & C. 446; *Larkin* v. *Hapgood*, 56 Vt. 597; *Gordon* v. *Ritenour*, 87 Mo. 54; *Killam* v. *Peirce*, 153 Mass. 502; *West* v. *St. Paul Nat. Bk.*, 54 Minn. 466; *Whitcher* v. *Shattuck*, 3 Allen, 319; cf. *Bliss* v. *Johnson*, 162 Mass. 323.]

[2] *Gerish* v. *Charlier*, 1 C. B. 13. [See *Moody* v. *Tenney*, 3 Allen, 327; *Regan* v. *Dickinson*, 105 Mass. 112.]

[3] This Illustration is adapted from *Preston's Case*, 2 Den. C. C. 353, but the misdirection given in that case is set right. As to the relevancy of the fact, see in particular Lord Campbell's remark on p. 359. [Cf. *State* v. *Flint*, 60 Vt. 304; *Woods* v. *Montevallo, etc. Co.*, 84 Ala. 560; *Stallings* v. *State*, 33 Ala. 425. So in order to prove that a master knew of his servant's incompetency, it may be shown that the servant had a general reputation for incompetency in the community. *Driscoll* v. *Fall River*, 163 Mass. 105; *Western Stone Co.* v. *Whalen*, 151 Ill. 472; *Grube* v. *Mo. Pac. R. Co.*, 98 Mo. 330; see p. 160, note, *post.*]

ing the terms on which they lived and the damage which A sustained.[1]

(*l*) The question is, whether A's death was caused by poison.

Statements made by A before his illness as to his state of health, and during his illness as to his symptoms, are deemed to be relevant facts.[2]

---

[1] *Trelawney* v. *Coleman*, 1 B. & A. 90. [Gr. Ev. i. § 102; *Palmer* v. *Crook*, 7 Gray, 418; *Perry* v. *Lovejoy*, 49 Mich. 529; *Harter* v. *Crill*, 33 Barb. 283; *Long* v. *Booe*, 106 Ala. 570; *Fratini* v. *Caslini*, 66 Vt. 273; *Holtz* v. *Dick*, 42 O. St. 23; *Horner* v. *Yance*, 93 Wis. 352; see *Edgell* v. *Francis*, 66 Mich. 303. So, in general, declarations of a person, whether oral or written, expressing *present mental feeling, state of mind*, or *intention*, are admissible in evidence, when his mental state, intention, etc., is a distinct material fact to be proved. Gr. Ev. i. § 102; *Mutual Life Ins. Co.* v. *Hillmon*, 145 U. S. 285; *Comm.* v. *Trefethen*, 157 Mass. 180; *Deer Isle* v. *Winterport*, 87 Me. 37; *Smith* v. *Nat. Benefit Society*, 123 N. Y. 85; but see *State* v. *Fitzgerald*, 130 Mo. 407.]

[2] *R.* v. *Palmer*. See my "Gen. View of Crim. Law," pp. 363, 377, (evidence of Dr. Savage and Mr. Stephens). [Gr. Ev. i. § 102. It is a general rule that expressions of *present bodily pain or suffering* or *symptoms of illness* are admissible as part of the *res gestæ*, and, whether made to physicians or to other persons, may be proved by those who heard them (*Northern Pac. R. Co.* v. *Urlin*, 158 U. S. 271; and see cases *infra*); but statements as to *past* sufferings, or as to the *past* cause of the injury or of the suffering, are not admissible (*Insurance Co.* v. *Mosley*, 8 Wall. 397; *State* v. *Fournier*, 68 Vt. 262; *Globe Ins. Co.* v. *Gerisch*, 163 Ill. 625; *Keller* v. *Gilman*, 93 Wis. 9; *Girard* v. *Kalamazoo*, 92 Mich. 610; *Carthage Co.* v. *Andrews*, 102 Ind. 138; *Atchison, etc. R. Co.* v. *Johns*, 36 Kan. 769; *Comm.* v. *Jardine*, 143 Mass. 567; *Ashland* v. *Marlborough*, 99 id. 47; *Wilson* v. *Granby*, 47 Ct. 59; *Lichtenwallner* v. *Laubach*, 105 Pa. 366; see p. 8, note 3, *ante*). Statements of present bodily feelings have in some States been held admissible, though made *after suit brought*, especially if made to an attending physician with a view to medical advice or treatment (*Cleveland, etc. R. Co.* v. *Newell*, 104 Ind. 264; *Hatch* v. *Fuller*, 131 Mass. 574); but not, if they were made to a physician for the sole purpose of enabling him to testify as a witness on the trial (*Abbott* v. *Heath*, 84 Wis. 314; *Jones* v. *Portland*, 88 Mich. 598; but see *Cleveland, etc. R. Co.* v. *Newell*, supra; *Matteson* v. *N. Y. Cent. R. Co.*, 35 N. Y. 487). Some cases even assert (mainly, however, as *dicta*) that statements made to a physician for medical treatment may be proved, though

(*m*) The question is, what was the state of A's health at the time when an insurance on her life was effected by B.

Statements made by A as to the state of her health at or near the time in question are deemed to be relevant facts.[1]

(*n*) The question is, whether A, the captain of a ship, knew that a port was blockaded.

The fact that the blockade was notified in the Gazette is deemed to be relevant.[2]

(*o*) [The question is, whether a testator, in making his will, was controlled by undue influence.

Statements made by him on prior occasions as to his testamentary intentions in the disposition of his property are deemed to be relevant, as showing his cherished purposes and state of mind when the will was made; if such statements are consistent with the provisions of the will, they tend to rebut charges of undue influence, otherwise to confirm them. But statements of the testator to show the *fact* of undue influence are deemed not to be relevant.][3]

---

they relate to *past* (as well as present) feelings and symptoms (*Roosa* v. *Boston Loan Co.*, 132 Mass. 439; *Cleveland, etc. R. Co.* v. *Newell*, 104 Ind. 264); but it is held otherwise in New York (*Davidson* v. *Cornell*, 132 N. Y. 228).

In New York a more limited rule prevails, and while evidence may be given of an injured person's groans, screams, and exclamations showing present pain, yet his mere declarations, made some time after the injury, that he is then suffering pain, are not competent, unless they are made to a physician for the purpose of treatment. *Roche* v. *Brooklyn, etc. R. Co.*, 105 N. Y. 294; *Davidson* v. *Cornell*, 132 N. Y. 228; S. P. *Atlanta R. Co.* v. *Walker*, 93 Ga. 462; cf. *Comm.* v. *Leach*, 156 Mass. 99; contra, *Board of Commrs.* v. *Leggett*, 115 Ind. 544.]

[1] *Aveson* v. *Lord Kinnaird*, 6 Ea. 188. [See *Swift* v. *Life Ins. Co.*, 63 N. Y. 186; *Edington* v. *Life Ins. Co.*, 67 N. Y. 185; *Dilleber* v. *Life Ins. Co.*, 69 N. Y. 256. By these New York cases the statements of the assured, if made at a time prior to, and not remote from the application, are deemed relevant to show his *knowledge* of his physical condition. See also *Kelsey* v. *Universal, etc. Ins. Co.*, 35 Ct. 225; *State* v. *Gedicke*, 43 N. J. L. 86; and cases cited under last Illustration.]

[2] *Harrat* v. *Wise*, 9 B. & C. 712.

[3] [*Neel* v. *Potter*, 40 Pa. 483; *Marx* v. *McGlynn*, 88 N. Y. 357; *Haines* v. *Hayden*, 95 Mich. 332; *Goodbar* v. *Lidikey*, 136 Ind. 1; *In re Calkins*, 112 Cal. 296; *Hill* v. *Bahrns*, 158 Ill. 314; *Gardner* v.

Article 12.*

FACTS SHOWING SYSTEM.

When there is a question whether an act was accidental or intentional, the fact that such act formed part of a series of similar occurrences, in each of which the person doing the act was concerned, is deemed to be relevant.[1]

---

* See Note VI. [Appendix].

Frieze, 16 R. I. 640; *Thompson* v. *Ish,* 99 Mo. 160; *Moore* v. *Mc Donald,* 68 Md. 321; *Potter* v. *Baldwin,* 133 Mass. 427; *Dye* v. *Young,* 55 Ia. 433; see *Jones* v. *McLellan,* 76 Me. 49; *Herster* v. *Herster,* 122 Pa. 239. So subsequent statements or acts may be shown which indicate the state of mind when the will was made (*Shailer* v. *Bumstead,* 99 Mass. 112; *Waterman* v. *Whitney,* 11 N. Y. 157). And in general, evidence of the testator's acts or declarations may be given, which show his mental peculiarities, settled convictions, deeply rooted feelings or purposes, or any enduring state of mind, as they existed at the making of the will (*Shailer* v. *Bumstead,* supra). So as to making a deed (*Howe* v. *Howe,* 99 Mass. 88), or a lease (*Sherman* v. *Wilder,* 106 Mass. 537), or a gift (*Lane* v. *Moore,* 151 Mass. 87; *Sherman* v. *Sherman,* 75 Ia. 136; *Meriden Bk.* v. *Wellington,* 64 Ct. 553; *Ridden* v. *Thrall,* 125 N. Y. 572; see *Converse* v. *Wales,* 4 Allen, 512).

Similar evidence may be receivable in criminal cases to show the state of the prisoner's mind when the crime was committed. *Comm.* v. *Pomeroy,* 117 Mass. 144; *Comm.* v. *Burlington,* 136 id. 435; *People* v. *Sessions,* 58 Mich. 594, 601.]

[1] [*State* v. *Lapage,* 57 N. H. 245, 294; *Comm.* v. *Robinson,* 146 Mass. 571; *Hawes* v. *State,* 88 Ala. 37, 67; *State* v. *Kelley,* 65 Vt. 531; *People* v. *Murphy,* 135 N. Y. 450; *State* v. *Stice,* 88 Ia. 27; *Dawson* v. *State,* 32 Tex. App. 535; *People* v. *Shulman,* 80 N. Y. 373; *Comm.* v. *Bradford,* 126 Mass. 42; *Goersen* v. *Comm.,* 99 Pa. 388, 106 id. 477; *Hope* v. *People,* 83 N. Y. 418; see *Comm.* v. *Choate,* 105 Mass. 451; *Swan* v. *Comm.,* 104 Pa. 218; *Dayton* v. *Monroe,* 47 Mich. 193; *Haynes* v. *Christian,* 30 Mo. App. 198; and pp. 34, 35, *ante,* and notes.

So a party's system or course of business may be proved to show whether he has exercised due diligence on a particular occasion (*Holly* v. *Boston Gas Co.,* 8 Gray, 123; *Fuller* v. *Naugatuck R. Co.,* 21 Ct. 557; *Wallace* v. *Central Vt. R. Co.,* 138 N. Y. 302; see *Coates* v.

Illustrations.

(*a*) A is accused of setting fire to his house in order to obtain money for which it is insured.

The facts that A had previously lived in two other houses successively, each of which he insured, in each of which a fire occurred, and

---

Burlington, etc. R. Co., 62 Ia. 486; *Bailey* v. *Rome, etc. R. Co.*, 139 N. Y. 302); and the usual practice of others in the same business or employment under like circumstances may be shown, to indicate whether ordinary care has been used in a special instance (*Maynard* v. *Buck*, 100 Mass. 40; *Cook* v. *Champlain, etc. Co.*, 1 Den. 91; *Jarvis* v. *Brooklyn R. Co.*, 16 N. Y. S. 96, 133 N. Y. 623; *Case* v. *Perew*, 46 Hun, 57, 122 N. Y. 665; *Holland* v. *Tenn. Coal Co.*, 91 Ala. 444; *Myers* v. *Hudson Iron Co.*, 150 Mass. 125, 138; *Daley* v. *Amer. Printing Co.*, 152 id. 581; *Reese* v. *Hershey*, 163 Pa. 253; *Doyle* v. *St. Paul, etc. R. Co.*, 42 Minn. 79; *Whitsett* v. *Chicago, etc. R. Co.*, 67 Ia. 150; *Railway Co.* v. *Manchester Mills*, 88 Tenn. 653; cf. *Veginan* v. *Morse*, 160 Mass. 143; but see *Grand Trunk R. Co.* v. *Richardson*, 91 U. S. 454; *Chicago, etc. R. Co.* v. *Clark*, 108 Ill. 113; *Bassett* v. *Shares*, 63 Ct. 39; *Lake Erie, etc. R. Co.* v. *Mugg*, 132 Ind. 168; *Southern Kansas R. Co.* v. *Robbins*, 43 Kan. 145).

With the cases under this Article may be compared those in which a system of conduct or action, as shown by a series of similar acts, is proved, in order to establish the habit of a person or animal, the character of a house, etc. (See *Baulec* v. *N. Y. etc. R. Co.*, 59 N. Y. 356; *Lanpher* v. *Clark*, 149 N. Y. 472; *Comm.* v. *Meany*, 151 Mass. 55; *Beard* v. *State*, 71 Md. 275; *Cameron* v. *Bryan*, 89 Ia. 214). Thus the vicious habit of a horse for shying, balking, etc., may be shown by proving cases of like misbehavior, both before and after the act in question (*Maggi* v. *Cutts*, 123 Mass. 535; *Kennon* v. *Gilmer*, 131 U. S. 22; *Chamberlain* v. *Enfield*, 43 N. H. 356; cf. *Whitney* v. *Leominster*, 136 Mass. 25). And evidence of a person's repeated acts of drunkenness may be admitted, to prove habitual drunkenness (*Comm.* v. *Ryan*, 134 Mass. 223; *Comm.* v. *McNamee*, 112 Mass. 285; *Wright* v. *Crawfordsville*, 142 Ind. 636; *McGill* v. *McGill*, 19 Fla. 341). So sales of liquor to different persons at different times may be proved to show that the seller is in the business of liquor selling (*State* v. *Welch*, 64 N. H. 525). But a habit of lying cannot be proved by evidence of lies told on other occasions (*Comm.* v. *Kennon*, 130 Mass. 39). In New Hampshire, evidence of prior acts of negligence of the same kind by a person is received, as tending to show his negligence on a particular occasion (*Parkinson* v. *Nashua, etc. R. Co.*, 61 N. H. 416);

that after each of those fires A received payment from a different insurance office, are deemed to be relevant, as tending to show that the fires were not accidental.[1]

(*b*) A is employed to pay the wages of B's laborers, and it is A's duty to make entries in a book showing the amounts paid by him. He makes an entry showing that on a particular occasion he paid more than he really did pay.

The question is, whether this false entry was accidental or intentional.

The fact that for a period of two years A made other similar false

---

but in most States this doctrine is denied (see Art. 10, Illustration (*g*); *Robinson* v. *F. & W. R. Co.*, 7 Gray, 92 ; *Brennan* v. *Friendship*, 67 Wis. 223). So in that State, on the question at what speed an engineer drove a railway train at a certain time and place, evidence of the speed at which he drove the same train at the same place on other days may be admitted (*State* v. *B. & M. R. Co.*, 58 N. H. 410 ; S. P. *Hall* v. *Brown*, id. 93 ; cf. *Shaber* v. *St. Paul, etc. R. Co.*, 28 Minn. 103). But it is elsewhere held that to prove care on a particular occasion, the party's habit of being careful cannot be shown (*McDonald* v. *Savoy*, 110 Mass. 49 ; *Chase* v. *Maine Cent. R. Co.*, 77 Me. 62 ; *Morris* v. *East Haven*, 41 Ct. 252 ; *Wooster* v. *Broadway, etc. R. Co.*, 72 Hun, 197 ; but see *Dorman* v. *Kane*, 5 Allen, 38 ; *Toledo, etc. R. Co.* v. *Bailey*, 145 Ill. 159) ; nor can the fact of gambling on a certain occasion, when intoxicated, be proved by showing a habit so to do (*Thompson* v. *Bowie*, 4 Wall. 463 ; cf. *McMahon* v. *Harrison*, 6 N. Y. 443 ; *Triplett* v. *Goff's Admr.*, 83 Va. 784) ; nor drunkenness on a particular occasion by showing a habit of intemperance (*Comm.* v. *Werling*, 164 Pa. 559) ; nor the taking of usury on one occasion by showing prior acts of taking usury. *Ross* v. *Ackerman*, 46 N. Y. 210.]

[1] *R.* v. *Gray*, 4 F. & F. 1102. I acted on this case in *R.* v *Stanley*, Liverpool Summer Assizes, 1882, but I greatly doubt its authority. The objection to the admission of such evidence is that it may practically involve the trial of several distinct charges at once, as it would be hard to exclude evidence to show that the other fires were accidental. [Cf., as tending to support *R.* v. *Gray*, *Hoxie* v. *Home Ins. Co.*, 32 Ct. 21 ; *Whitmore* v. *Supreme Lodge Knights*, 100 Mo. 36 ; *Comm.* v. *McCarthy*, 119 Mass. 354 ; *People* v. *Dimick*, 107 N. Y. 13. But evidence of other fires in defendant's buildings has been rejected, when they occurred from five to eleven years before the fire in question. *State* v. *Raymond*, 53 N. J. L. 260.]

entries in the same book, the false entry being in each case in favor of A, is deemed to be relevant.[1]

(c) The question is, whether the administration of poison to A, by Z, his wife, in September, 1848, was accidental or intentional.

The facts that B, C, and D (A's three sons), had the same poison administered to them in December, 1848, March, 1849, and April, 1849, and that the meals of all four were prepared by Z, are deemed to be relevant, though Z was indicted separately for murdering A, B, and C, and attempting to murder D.[2]

(ca) [The question is, whether A and his wife intentionally caused the death of an infant child, which they had received from its mother for adoption upon the payment of a small sum of money, the body of the child having been found buried in their grounds.

The facts that the defendants had received several other infants from their mothers for adoption, on like terms, and that the bodies of a number of infants had been found buried in a similar manner in the gardens of several houses which they had occupied, are deemed to be relevant.][3]

(cb) [The question is, whether the firing of a pistol by A at B, inflicting a serious wound, was accidental or willful.

Evidence that A had fired his pistol at two other persons the day before was deemed to be relevant to show that the act was willful.][4]

(d) A promises to lend money to B on the security of a policy of insurance which B agrees to effect in an insurance company of his choosing. B pays the first premium to the company, but A refuses to lend the money except upon terms which he intends B to reject, and which B rejects accordingly.

---

[1] *R.* v. *Richardson*, 2 F. & F. 343. [See *Lang* v. *State*, 97 Ala. 41; *Ossipee* v. *Grant*, 59 N. H. 70; *Funk* v. *Ely*, 45 Pa. 444; for a case of forgery, see *Rankin* v. *Blackwell*, 2 Johns. Cas. 198.]

[2] *R.* v. *Geering*, 18 L. J. M. C. 215; cf. *R.* v. *Garner*, 3 F. & F. 681. These cases were discussed in *R.* v. *Neill* (or *Cream*), tried at the Central Criminal Court in October, 1892, when Hawkins, J., admitted evidence of subsequent administrations of strychnine by the prisoner to persons other than and unconnected with the woman of whose murder the prisoner was then convicted. [See *Zoldoske* v. *State*, 82 Wis. 580; *Goersen* v. *Comm.*, 99 Pa. 388, 106 id. 477; *People* v. *Foley*, 64 Mich. 148; *Weyman* v. *People*, 4 Hun, 511, 518, 62 N. Y. 623; *R.* v. *Flannagan*, 15 Cox, 403.]

[3] [*Makin* v. *Attorney General*, [1894] A. C. 57.]

[4] [*State* v. *McDonald*, 14 R. I. 270.]

The fact that A and the insurance company have been engaged in similar transactions is deemed to be relevant to the question whether the receipt of the money by the company was fraudulent.[1]

Article 13.*

EXISTENCE OF COURSE OF BUSINESS, WHEN DEEMED TO BE RELEVANT.

When there is a question whether a particular act was done, the existence of any course of office or business according to which it naturally would have been done, is a relevant fact.[2]

When there is a question whether a particular person held a particular public office, the fact that he acted in that office is deemed to be relevant.[3]

When the question is whether one person acted as agent for another on a particular occasion, the fact that he so. acted on other occasions is deemed to be relevant.[4]

Illustrations.

(a) The question is, whether a letter was sent on a given day. The post-mark upon it is deemed to be a relevant fact.[5]

(b) The question is, whether a particular letter was dispatched.

---

* See Note VII. [Appendix].

[1] *Blake v. Albion Life Assurance Society*, 4 C. P. D. 94.

[2] [Gr. Ev. i. §§ 38, 40; *People v. Oyer and Terminer Court*, 83 N. Y. 436; *Twogood v. Mayor*, 102 N. Y. 216; *Beakes v. Da Cunha*, 126 N. Y. 293; *Dunlop v. United States*, 165 U. S. 486; *State v. Taylor*, 126 Mo. 531; *Knickerbocker Ins. Co. v. Pendleton*, 115 U. S. 339; *Comm. v. Kimball*, 108 Mass. 473; *Hall v. Brown*, 58 N. H. 93.]

[3] 1 Ph. Ev. 449; R. N. P. 46; T. E. s. 139; [see Art. 90, *post*, last paragraph.]

[4] [*Olcott v. Tioga R. Co.*, 27 N. Y. 546; *Beattie v. Delaware, etc. R. Co.*, 90 N. Y. 643; *Gallinger v. Lake Shore Co.*, 67 Wis. 529; *Kent v. Tyson*, 20 N. H. 121; *Thurber v. Anderson*, 88 Ill. 167; Kent's Comm. ii. 615. But it is said that an agency to commit crimes cannot be proved by evidence of prior like crimes committed by one as agent. *People v. McLaughlin*, 150 N. Y. 365, 391.]

[5] *R. v. Canning*, 19 S. T. 370. [*United States v. Williams*, 3 F. R

The facts that all letters put in a certain place were, in the common course of business, carried to the post, and that that particular letter was put in that place, are deemed to be relevant.[1]

(c) The question is, whether a particular letter reached A.

The facts that it was posted in due course, properly addressed, and was not returned through the Dead Letter Office, are deemed to be relevant.[2]

(d) The facts stated in Illustration (d) to the last Article are deemed to be relevant to the question whether A was agent to the company.[3]

484; *United States* v. *Noelke*, 17 Blatch. 554. But there is no presumption that the date of the post-mark was the day of depositing the letter. *Shelburne Falls Bk.* v. *Townsley*, 102 Mass. 177; see *Price* v. *McGoldrick*, 2 Abb. N. C. 69.]

[1] *Hetherington* v. *Kemp*, 4 Camp. 193; and see *Skilbeck* v. *Garbett*, 7 Q. B. 846, and *Trotter* v. *Maclean*, 13 Ch. Div. 574. [See *Howard* v. *Daly*, 61 N. Y. 362; *Swampscott Co.* v. *Rice*, 159 Mass. 404; *Dix* v. *Atkins*, 128 Mass. 43; *Whitney Works* v. *Moore*, 61 Vt. 230; *Hall* v. *Brown*, 58 N. H. 93, 97; cf. *Hastings* v. *Brooklyn Ins. Co.*, 138 N. Y. 473.]

[2] *Warren* v. *Warren*, 1 C. M. & R. 250; *Woodcock* v. *Houldsworth*, 16 M. & W. 124. Many cases on this subject are collected in Roscoe's *Nisi Prius*, pp. 374-5. [*Hedden* v. *Roberts*, 134 Mass. 38; *Rosenthal* v. *Walker*, 111 U. S. 185; *Folsom* v. *Cook*, 115 Pa. 539; *Sabre* v. *Smith*, 62 N. H. 663; *McFarland* v. *Accident Ass'n*, 124 Mo. 204; cf. *Ellison* v. *Lindsley*, 33 N. J. Eq. 258, note. This is only *prima facie* evidence that the letter was received, not a conclusive presumption of law (*Huntley* v. *Whittier*, 105 Mass. 391; *Schutz* v. *Jordan*, 141 U. S. 213; *Harrington* v. *Hickman*, 148 Pa. 405; *Austin* v. *Holland*, 69 N. Y. 571; cf. *Marston* v. *Bigelow*, 150 Mass. 45). The same rule applies to telegrams. *U. S.* v. *Babcock*, 3 Dill. 571; *Oregon Steamship Co.* v. *Otis*, 100 N. Y. 446; *Eppinger* v. *Scott*, 112 Cal. 369.]

[3] *Blake* v. *Albion Life Assurance Society*, 4 C. P. D. 94.

CHAPTER IV.

HEARSAY IRRELEVANT EXCEPT IN CERTAIN CASES.

ARTICLE 14.*

HEARSAY AND THE CONTENTS OF DOCUMENTS IRRELEVANT.

(*a*) THE fact that a statement was made by a person not called as a witness, and

(*b*) the fact that a statement is contained or recorded in any book, document, or record whatever, proof of which is not admissible on other grounds,

are respectively deemed to be irrelevant to the truth of the matter stated, except (as regards (*a*)) in the cases contained in the first section of this chapter ; [1]

and except (as regards (*b*)) in the cases contained in the second section of this chapter.

Illustrations.

(*a*) A declaration by a deceased attesting witness to a deed that he had forged it, is deemed to be irrelevant to the question of its validity.[2]

---

* See Note VIII. [Appendix].

[1] It is important to observe the distinction between the principles which regulate the admissibility of the statements contained in a document and those which regulate the manner in which they must be proved. On this subject see the whole of Part II. [As to the general rule that hearsay evidence is excluded, see *Stephens* v. *Vroman*, 16 N. Y. 381 ; *Felska* v. *N. Y. Central R. Co.*, 152 N. Y. 339 ; *Farrell* v. *Weitz*, 160 Mass. 288 ; *Wallace* v. *Story*, 139 Mass. 115 ; *Hollister* v. *Cordero*, 76 Cal. 649.]

[2] *Stobart* v. *Dryden*, 1 M. & W. 615. [Some American decisions deny the doctrine of this case (*Boylan* v. *Meeker*, 28 N. J. L. 274, 295 ;

(*b*) The question is, whether A was born at a certain time and place. The fact that a public body for a public purpose stated that he was born at that time and place is deemed to be irrelevant, the circumstances not being such as to bring the case within the provisions of Article 34.[1]

(*c*) [The question is, whether A, a person on trial for larceny, was absent from the State at a particular date.

The police sergeant of a city in the State may not testify that a police officer reported to him on that date that he had seen A in the street that night.][2]

(*d*) [A sues a railroad company to recover damages for personal injuries caused by the defendant's negligence.

A written statement made by a physician while he was treating A for these injuries, in which he set forth the nature of the injuries and their effect upon A's bodily and mental condition, is deemed to be hearsay evidence and therefore inadmissible.][3]

(*e*) [A sues B to recover for services rendered as attorney and counselor at law in arguing a case for B before an appellate court.

The report of said case in the published reports of said court is deemed incompetent to show that A did so appear and argue the case.][4]

(*f*) [A is tried for the murder of B.

A statement by C that he murdered B is deemed to be irrelevant.][5]

Otterson v. *Hofford*, 36 id. 129 ; *Neely* v. *Neely*, 17 Pa. 227 ; cf. *Losee* v. *Losee*, 2 Hill, 609; *In re Hesdra*, 119 N. Y. 615) ; but others follow it (*Sewall* v. *Robbins*, 139 Mass. 164 ; *U. S.* v. *Boyd*, 8 App. D. C. 440 ; *Boardman* v. *Woodman*, 47 N. H. 120 ; see also Gr. Ev. i. § 126). That the declarations of other deceased witnesses may be rejected as hearsay, see *Gray* v. *Goodrich*, 7 Johns. 95 ; *Spatz* v. *Lyons*, 55 Barb. 476.]

[1] *Sturla* v. *Freccia*, L. R. 5 App. Cas. 623.

[2] [*Comm.* v. *Ricker*, 131 Mass. 581.]

[3] [*Vicksburg, etc. R. Co.* v. *O'Brien*, 119 U. S. 99. But such statement might be used by the physician as a witness to refresh his recollection. Id. ; cf. *Russell* v. *Hudson River R. Co.*, 17 N. Y. 134 ; *Armstrong* v. *Ackley*, 71 Ia. 76 ; *Weaver* v. *Bromley*, 65 Mich. 212.]

[4] [*Roraback* v. *Pennsylvania Co.*, 58 Ct. 292.]

[5] [*State* v. *Beaudet*, 53 Ct. 536, 545 ; *State* v. *Gee*, 92 N. C. 756 ; *Munshower* v. *State*, 55 Md. 11 ; *Kelly* v. *State*, 82 Ga. 441 ; see p. 7, note 5, *ante*.]

SECTION I.

HEARSAY, WHEN RELEVANT.

ARTICLE 15.*

ADMISSIONS DEFINED.

An admission is a statement, oral or written, suggesting any inference as to any fact in issue or relevant or deemed to be relevant to any such fact, made by or on behalf of any party to any proceeding.[1] Every admission is (subject to the rules hereinafter stated) deemed to be a

---

* See Note IX. [Appendix].

[1] [It is an important rule that if part of a statement made by a party be relevant against him as an admission, other parts of the same statement which in any way qualify or explain such admission are also relevant, though they are in such party's favor (Gr. Ev. i. § 201 ; *Grattan* v. *Metropolitan Ins. Co.*, 92 N. Y. 274 ; *Gildersleeve* v. *Landon*, 73 N. Y. 609 ; *Insurance Co.* v. *Newton*, 22 Wall. 32 ; *Vanneter* v. *Crossman*, 42 Mich. 465 ; *Farley* v. *Rodocanachi*, 100 Mass. 427 ; *Hunter* v. *Pherson*, 89 Me. 71 ; as to letters, see *Simmons* v. *Haas*, 56 Md. 153). But other portions of the same conversation or statement, which do not explain or affect the part which is unfavorable to the declarant, are not admissible (*Platner* v. *Platner*, 78 N. Y. 90) ; nor are independent declarations admissible which are made by a party in his own favor (*Downs* v. *N. Y. C. R. Co.*, 47 N. Y. 83 ; *Corder* v. *Corder*, 124 Ill. 229 ; *Taylor* v. *Brown*, 65 Md. 366 ; *Royal* v. *Chandler*, 79 Me. 265 ; *Tolbert* v. *Burke*, 89 Mich. 132), unless they form part of the *res gestæ* (*Brown* v. *Kenyon*, 108 Ind. 283 ; see Art. 3, notes). But a party giving evidence of the opposing party's admissions may also disprove those parts of the same statement which are in the other party's favor, but are nevertheless receivable in evidence (*Mott* v. *Consumers' Ice Co.*, 73 N. Y. 543).

Oral admissions may be proved by any witness who heard them (*Hartley* v. *Weideman*, 175 Pa. 309) ; if he cannot remember the exact words, he may testify to the substance of the admission (Gr. Ev. i. § 191 ; *Kittredge* v. *Russell*, 114 Mass. 67).

Admissions may also be implied from acts and conduct (Gr. Ev. i. §§ 195–199 ; *Hayes* v. *Kelley*, 116 Mass. 300 ; *Greenfield Bk.* v. *Crafts*, 2 Allen, 269 ; *Wesner* v. *Stein*, 97 Pa. 322 ; *Lefever* v. *Johnson*, 79 Ind.

relevant fact as against the person by or on whose behalf it is made, but not in his favor unless it is, or is deemed to be, relevant for some other reason.

554; *Foster* v. *Persch*, 68 N. Y. 400). Thus, if an account rendered be not objected to within a reasonable time, it is deemed to be admitted by the party charged to be *prima facie* correct (*Wiggins* v. *Burkham*, 10 Wall. 129; *Samson* v. *Freedman*, 102 N. Y. 699). Tender of money to a claimant is an admission of liability to the amount of the tender (*Rainwater* v. *Hummel*, 79 Ia. 571; *Wilson* v. *Doran*, 110 N. Y. 101). The act of a landlord in making repairs after an injury is an admission that it is his duty, rather than that of the tenant (*Readman* v. *Conway*, 126 Mass. 374). So if a partner has access to the books of the firm, the book-entries therein are admissible against him (*Fairchild* v. *Fairchild*, 64 N. Y. 471; *Topliff* v. *Jackson*, 12 Gray, 565). But failure to answer a letter is not generally deemed an admission of the truth of its contents (*Wiedemann* v. *Walpole*, [1891] 2 Q. B. 534; *Thomas* v. *Gage*, 141 N. Y. 506; *Razor* v. *Razor*, 149 Ill. 621; *Fearing* v. *Kimball*, 4 Allen, 125; cf. *Oregon Steamship Co.* v. *Otis*, 100 N. Y. 446; *Hays* v. *Morgan*, 87 Ind. 231; *Murphy* v. *Gates*, 81 Wis. 370). As to other admissions by acquiescence, see Art. 8, *ante*, last paragraph.

Admissions made incidentally or indirectly are competent evidence as well as those made directly (Gr. Ev. i. § 194; *Harrington* v. *Gable*, 81 Pa. 406; see Art. 17, Illustration *g*). Admissions made in a pleading, sworn to by a party, are admissible against him in another action (*Cook* v. *Barr*, 44 N. Y. 156; *Elliott* v. *Hayden*, 104 Mass. 180; *Folger* v. *Boyington*, 67 Wis. 447), though only made upon information and belief (*Pope* v. *Ellis*, 115 U. S. 363; cf. *Mayor of N. Y.* v. *Fay*, 53 Hun, 553). And the same is true of a pleading not so sworn to, if the admissions therein were derived from the instructions of the party, or were otherwise authorized or adopted by him (*Johnson* v. *Russell*, 144 Mass. 409; *Rockland* v. *Farnsworth*, 89 Me. 481; *Vogel* v. *Osborne*, 32 Minn. 167); *aliter*, if they were merely the suggestions of the attorney (Id.; *Dennie* v. *Williams*, 135 Mass. 28; *Delaware Co.* v. *Diebold Co.*, 133 U. S. 473; *Duff* v. *Duff*, 71 Cal. 513). But some authorities admit former pleadings as evidence of admissions without insisting so rigorously upon these distinctions (*Coward* v. *Clanton*, 79 Cal. 23; *Raridan* v. *Cent. Iowa R. Co.*, 69 Ia. 527; *Lamar* v. *Pearre*, 90 Ga. 377). Admissions may also be made in affidavits or depositions, or in evidence given in a former proceeding, etc. (*Whiton* v. *Snyder*, 88 N. Y. 299; *Comm.* v. *Reynolds*, 122 Mass. 454; *Phenix Ins. Co.* v. *Clark*, 58 N. H. 164; *Bogie* v. *Nolan*, 96 Mo. 85). Admissions made simply for

Article 16.*

Admissions may be made on behalf of the real party to any proceeding—

By any nominal party to that proceeding ; [1]

---

* See Note X. [Appendix].

one trial cannot be used in another (*McKinney* v. *Salem*, 77 Ind. 213), but the rule is otherwise, if they are made without such limitation (*Holley* v. *Young*, 68 Me. 215; *Owen* v. *Cawley*, 36 N. Y. 600; *Perry* v. *Simpson, etc. Co.*, 40 Ct. 313; *Central Branch, etc. R. Co.* v. *Shoup*, 28 Kan. 394; *Ex parte Hayes*, 92 Ala. 120).

Evidence of oral admissions, though competent, is in general not conclusive, and may need to be received with great caution (Gr. Ev. i. §§ 199, 200; *Jones* v. *Knauss*, 31 N. J. Eq. 609; *Haven* v. *Markstrum*, 67 Wis. 493; *Allen* v. *Kirk*, 81 Ia. 658; *Miller* v. *Rowan*, 108 Ala. 98). Still, if deliberately made and clearly proved, they may be of much weight (Id.). Admissions may, in proper cases, be explained and shown to be incorrect, or to have been made by mistake or inadvertence (*Davis* v. *McCrocklin*, 34 Kan. 218; *Stowe* v. *Bishop*, 58 Vt. 498; *Knobloch* v. *Mueller*, 123 Ill. 554; *Dale* v. *Gilbert*, 128 N. Y. 625, 628; cf. *Brooks* v. *Belfast, etc. R. Co.*, 72 Me. 365). But admissions are conclusive when they amount to estoppels (Gr. Ev. i. §§ 204-208; *Halloran* v. *Halloran*, 137 Ill. 100) ; and admissions made in pleading and not obviated by amendment, are conclusive in the same case (*Tisdale* v. *Pres. of D. & H. Co.*, 116 N. Y. 416; *Peckham Iron Co.* v. *Harper*, 41 O. St. 100; see Art. 60). But if the law allows a party to plead several pleas, the admissions in one plea cannot be used against him in another. *Glenn* v. *Sumner*, 132 U. S. 152.]

[1] [Mr. Stephen illustrates this rule by saying that the admissions of an assignor of a chose in action, who is the nominal plaintiff in an action brought for the benefit of his assignee, are admissible against the latter. But in New York and many other States of this country the assignee sues in his own name, and there is, therefore, no ground for receiving the admissions of the assignor made after the assignment ; they are therefore excluded (*Van Gelder* v. *Van Gelder*, 81 N. Y. 625). And evidence of such admissions has been generally rejected in this country, even when the rule prevailed that the assignee must sue in the assignor's name (*Wing* v. *Bishop*, 3 Allen, 456; *Butler* v. *Millett*, 47 Me. 492; *Sargeant* v. *Sargeant*, 18 Vt. 371; *Dazey* v.

By any person who, though not a party to the proceeding, has a substantial interest in the event ;[1]

By any one who is privy in law,[2] in blood,[3] or in estate[4]
to any party to the proceeding, on behalf of that party.

Mills, 5 Gilm. (Ill.) 67 ; *Frear* v. *Evertson*, 20 Johns. 142 ; cf. *Fay* v.
Guynon, 131 Mass. 31). But the admissions of the assignee, made
after a valid assignment, are relevant against him.]

[1] [Gr. Ev. i. § 180 ; *Fickett* v. *Swift*, 41 Me. 65 ; *Bigelow* v. *Foss*, 59
Me. 162 ; *Barber's Adm'r* v. *Bennett*, 60 Vt. 662 ; *Benjamin* v. *Smith*,
4 Wend. 332, 335, 12 Wend. 404, 407 ; see *Taylor* v. *Grand Trunk R.
Co.*, 48 N. H. 304. But the declarations of a person who is not a party
to the record nor a witness are not received to show that he is the
real party in interest (*Ryan* v. *Merriam*, 4 Allen, 77).

Under this head is sometimes placed the rule that in an action
against a sheriff for the misconduct of his deputy the admissions of
the deputy are receivable, on the ground that he is the real party in
interest (Gr. Ev. i. § 180, note). But in some States it is held that such
declarations are only receivable when they accompanied the deputy's
official acts, and therefore formed part of the *res gestæ*. *Barker* v.
Binninger, 14 N. Y. 270 ; *Stewart* v. *Wells*, 6 Barb. 79.]

[2] [Thus the admissions of an intestate are receivable against his administrator (*Brown* v. *Mailler*, 12 N. Y. 118 ; *Fellows* v. *Smith*, 130
Mass. 378 ; *Clouser* v. *Ruckman*, 104 Ind. 588) ; and of testator against
executor (*Hurlbut* v. *Hurlbut*, 128 N. Y. 420 ; *Childs* v. *Jordan*, 106
Mass. 321). So in an action by a widow for dower, admissions made
by her husband while living are deemed to be relevant against her.
Van Duyne v. *Thayre*, 14 Wend. 233.]

[3] [Admissions made by an ancestor are receivable against his heirs.
Spaulding v. *Hallenbeck*, 35 N. Y. 204 ; *Enders* v. *Sternbergh*, 2 Abb.
Dec. 31 ; *Davis* v. *Melson*, 66 Ia. 715 ; *McSweeney* v. *McMillen*, 96
Ind. 298.]

[4] [Admissions by a grantor of land are relevant against his grantee ;
of a landlord against his tenant ; of devisor against devisee ; of any
owner of land against those who subsequently derive title from or
through him (*Chadwick* v. *Fonner*, 69 N. Y. 404 ; *New Jersey Zinc Co.*
v. *Lehigh Zinc Co.*, 59 N. J. L. 189 ; *Potter* v. *Waite*, 55 Ct. 236 ;
Simpson v. *Dix*, 131 Mass. 179 ; *Pickering* v. *Reynolds*, 119 Mass. 111).
But the admissions of a tenant for life or years will not bind the reversioner (*Fitzgerald* v. *Brennan*, 57 Ct. 511). As to personal property,
see p. 63, *post*, note.

Not only those declarations by an owner of land, or by one claiming

A statement made by a party to a proceeding may be an admission whenever it is made,[1] unless it is made by a person suing or sued in a representative character only,

---

title, which are in disparagement of his title, are admissible against the declarant or persons in privity with him (see *Bowen* v. *Chase*, 98 U. S. 254; *Dooley* v. *Baynes*, 86 Va. 644), but also those statements made by him while in possession, which show the character of his possession and by what title he claims (*Pitts* v. *Wilder*, 1 N. Y. 525; *Moore* v. *Hamilton*, 44 N. Y. 666; *Creighton* v. *Hoppis*, 99 Ind. 369; *Smith* v. *Putnam*, 62 N. H. 369; *Hale* v. *Rich*, 48 Vt. 217; *Hale* v. *Silloway*, 1 Allen, 21): as *e. g.*, to show that he held under adverse claim of title (*Morss* v. *Salisbury*, 48 N. Y. 636; *Susq. etc. R. Co.* v. *Quick*, 68 Pa. 189; *Mississippi Co.* v. *Vowels*, 101 Mo. 225); or as the tenant or agent of a particular person (*Gibney* v. *Marchay*, 34 N. Y. 301; *Garber* v. *Doersom*, 117 Pa. 162; *Lucy* v. *Tenn. etc. R. Co.*, 92 Ala. 246); or to show the extent of occupation or boundary (*Abeel* v. *Van Gelder*, 36 N. Y. 513; *Wood* v. *Fiske*, 62 N. H. 173; *Flagg* v. *Mason*, 141 Mass. 64; *Sharp* v. *Blankenship*, 79 Cal. 411). Such evidence comes properly under the doctrine of *res gestæ*, and by some decisions such statements are held admissible, though they were, when made, in the declarant's own favor (Gr. Ev. I. § 109; see *ante*, Art. 3, notes; *Bennett* v. *Camp*, 54 Vt. 36; *Sheaffer* v. *Eakman*, 56 Pa. 144; *McConnell* v. *Hannah*, 96 Ind. 102; contra, *Morrill* v. *Titcomb*, 8 Allen, 100; in *Roebke* v. *Andrews*, 26 Wis. 311, the question is fully discussed, *pro* and *con*; cf. *Lampe* v. *Kennedy*, 60 Wis. 110; the same question arises as to personal property. Id.; *Maus* v. *Bome*, 123 Ind. 522). But declarations of an owner in possession of land will not be received in place of record evidence, nor to destroy a record title. *Gibney* v. *Marchay*, supra; *Dodge* v. *Trust Co.*, 93 U. S. 379; *Hancock Ins. Co.* v. *Moore*, 34 Mich. 41; but see *Loomis* v. *Wadhams*, 8 Gray, 557.]

[1] [*Cook* v. *Barr*, 44 N. Y. 156; *Williams* v. *Sergeant*, 46 N. Y. 481; *Wiggin* v. *B. & A. R. Co.*, 120 Mass. 201; *Hatch* v. *Brown*, 63 Me. 410; *Duncan* v. *Lawrence*, 24 Pa. 154; cf. *Shailer* v. *Bumstead*, 99 Mass. 112, 127. So if one be substituted as a party after suit brought, his admissions are receivable (*Wadsworth* v. *Williams*, 100 Mass. 126). The admissions of a party to a suit against the validity of the claim sued upon have been held competent evidence, though made before he became owner of the claim (*Barber's Adm'r* v. *Bennett*, 60 Vt. 662; *Taylor* v. *Grand Trunk R. Co.*, 48 N. H. 304; cf. *Fitzgerald* v. *Weston*, 52 Wis. 354). But statements of a party which merely raise a suspicion or conjecture as to the existence of an alleged fact

in which case (it seems) it must be made whilst the person making it sustains that character.[1]

A statement made by a person interested in a proceeding, or by a privy to any party thereto, is not an admission, unless it is made during the continuance of the interest which entitles him to make it.[2]

---

cannot constitute an admission of its truth. *People* v. *Corey*, 148 N. Y. 476.]

[1] [Gr. Ev. i. § 179; *Lamar* v. *Micou*, 112 U. S. 452. Thus the declarations of an executor or administrator are not competent as admissions, unless made after his appointment and while he was acting in that capacity and representing the estate (*Church* v. *Howard*, 79 N. Y. 415; *Brooks* v. *Goss*, 61 Me. 307; *Webster* v. *Le Compte*, 74 Md. 249; see *Heywood* v. *Heywood*, 10 Allen, 105). But if he sues or is sued in an individual capacity, his admissions made at other times are receivable (see *Whiton* v. *Snyder*, 88 N. Y. 299). And his admissions made as party in one suit are receivable against him as party in another (*Phillipps* v. *Middlesex*, 127 Mass. 262).

Admissions made by a guardian will not be allowed by the courts to prejudice the rights of his ward. *Buffalo Loan, etc. Co.* v. *Knights Templar Ass'n*, 126 N. Y. 450; *Cooper* v. *Mayhew*, 40 Mich. 528.]

[2] [Thus declarations by a grantor or mortgagor of land, which were made before he acquired or after he parted with his title or interest, are not receivable as admissions against his grantee or mortgagee (*Hutchins* v. *Hutchins*, 98 N. Y. 56; *Chase* v. *Horton*, 143 Mass. 118; *Ruckman* v. *Cory*, 129 U. S. 387; *McLaughlin* v. *McLaughlin*, 91 Pa. 462; *Miller* v. *Cook*, 135 Ill. 190); nor those of an assignor of chattels or *choses* in action against the assignee, when they were made after the assignment and transfer of possession (*Coyne* v. *Weaver*, 84 N. Y. 386; *Burnham* v. *Brennan*, 74 N. Y. 597; *Roberts* v. *Medbery*, 132 Mass. 100; *Winchester, etc. Co.* v. *Creary*, 116 U. S. 161; *Ohio Coal Co.* v. *Davenport*, 37 O. St. 194; *Turner* v. *Hardin*, 80 Ia. 691). But if a transferor of land or chattels remains in possession, his declarations characterizing that possession are generally deemed competent, under the doctrine of *res gestæ* (*Pier* v. *Duff*, 63 Pa. 59; *Robbins* v. *Spencer*, 140 Ind. 483; *Loos* v. *Wilkinson*, 110 N. Y. 195; *Merriam* v. *Swensen*, 42 Minn. 383; *Roberts* v. *Medbery*, supra; see *Williams* v. *Williams*, 142 N. Y. 156). In some States the declarations of an assignor of personal property, made while he remains in continuous possession of it after the assignment, are receivable to show fraud as to creditors (*Adams* v. *Davidson*, 10 N. Y. 309; *Tilson* v. *Terwilliger*, 56 N. Y. 273; *Murch* v. *Swensen*,

Illustrations.

(*a*) The assignee of a bond sues the obligor in the name of the obligee.

---

40 Minn. 421 ; *Boyd* v. *Jones,* 60 Mo. 454 ; *Smith* v. *Boyer,* 29 Neb. 76; *Dodge* v. *Goodell,* 16 R. I. 48; *Kirby* v. *Masten,* 70 N. C. 540; cf. *Loos* v. *Wilkinson,* 110 N. Y. 195); and the same rule has been applied to declarations of grantors of land (*Osgood* v. *Eaton,* 63 N. H. 355; *U. S.* v. *Griswold,* 8 F. R. 556; *Byrd* v. *Jones,* 84 Ala. 336; cf. *Williams* v. *Williams,* 142 N. Y. 156; *Hart* v. *Randolph,* 142 Ill. 521; *McCormicks* v. *Williams,* 56 Ia. 143). But the declarations of a grantor of realty or assignor of personalty, made after the transfer of possession, cannot be received for the same purpose (*Holbrook* v. *Holbrook,* 113 Mass. 74; *Flannery* v. *Van Tassel,* 131 N. Y. 639), unless there be a conspiracy between the parties to defraud creditors and such declarations are made in pursuance of the conspiracy (Id.; *Cuyler* v. *McCartney,* 40 N. Y. 221; *Souder* v. *Schechterly,* 91 Pa. 83; *Jones* v. *Simpson,* 116 U. S. 609; *Daniels* v. *McGinnis,* 97 Ind. 549; see Art. 4).

The admissions of an assignor of a chattel or *chose* in action, made while he had ownership and possession, are in many States held competent against his assignee (*Hanchett* v. *Kimbark,* 118 Ill. 121; *Taylor* v. *Hess,* 57 Minn. 96; *Merrick* v. *Parkman,* 18 Me. 407; *Alger* v. *Andrews,* 47 Vt. 238; *Magee* v. *Raiguel,* 64 Pa. 110; *Bond* v. *Fitzpatrick,* 4 Gray, 89; *Randegger* v. *Ehrhardt,* 51 Ill. 101; *aliter,* as to commercial paper negotiated before maturity); but the rule is sometimes limited by important qualifications (*Coit* v. *Howd,* 1 Gray, 547). This rule is like that applied to real estate (see p. 60, note 4, *ante*). But in New York, while the rule as to realty is accepted, a different rule is applied to personalty, and it is held that the declarations of the assignor, though made *before* the assignment, are not admissible against an assignee *for value* or for the benefit of creditors (*Paige* v. *Cagwin,* 7 Hill, 361; *Von Sachs* v. *Kretz,* 72 N. Y. 548, 554; *Bush* v. *Roberts,* 111 N. Y. 278), unless they were made in pursuance of a fraudulent conspiracy between the parties, or in fraudulent sales where the vendor remains in continuous possession, etc. (*Flannery* v. *Van Tassel,* 127 N. Y. 631). The same rule is adopted by the U. S. Supreme Court (*Dodge* v. *Trust Co.,* 93 U. S. 379; S. P. *Deasey* v. *Thurman,* 1 Ida. 775). But against other assignees, not acquiring title for value (as an executor, etc.), such declarations of the assignor are competent (*Von Sachs* v. *Kretz,* supra). And an assignor's declarations may be proved as part of the *res gestæ,* even as against a holder for value, if they were made *at the time* of the transfer and serve to qualify the title. *Benjamin* v. *Rogers,* 126 N. Y. 60.]

An admission on the part of the obligee that the money due has been paid is deemed to be relevant on behalf of the defendant.[1]

(b) An admission by the assignee of the bond in the last Illustration would also be deemed to be relevant on behalf of the defendant.

(ba) [The question is, whether a horse was sold to the defendant by the plaintiff for $500, or was entrusted to him as a bailee.

The defendant upon seeing an entry made in the plaintiff's book of account immediately after the transaction, charging him with $500 as the price of the horse, admitted its accuracy; this admission is deemed to be relevant against him.][2]

(bb) [A sues B to recover the possession of land. A claims under C and B claims under D. Declarations made by D while in possession of the land that C was the owner are admissible against B.][3]

(bc) [The admissions of a holder of a promissory note after maturity, made while he held it, are deemed to be relevant against a subsequent holder.][4]

(c) A statement made by a person before he becomes the assignee of a bankrupt is not deemed to be relevant as an admission by him in a proceeding by him as such assignee.[5]

(d) Statements made by a person as to a bill of which he had been the holder are deemed not to be relevant as against the holder, if they are made after he has negotiated the bill.[6]

(e) [A sues B to recover his salary for services rendered as foreman of B's tannery.

A witness X testifies that B had declared to him that he had discharged A and that he was to pay A $400 a year; and that in the same conversation B said that A got drunk, was absent and neglected his business, and that on that account he had discharged him. These qualifying statements were admitted in evidence in connection with the admission.][7]

---

[1] See *Moriarty* v. *L. C. & D. Co.*, L. R. 5 Q. B. 320; [see p. 59, note 1, *ante*.]

[2] [*Tanner* v. *Parshall*, 4 Abb. Dec. 356.]

[3] [*Simpson* v. *Dix*, 131 Mass. 179.]

[4] [*Bond* v. *Fitzpatrick*, 4 Gray, 89; *Kane* v. *Torbitt*, 23 Ill. App. 311; contra, *Clews* v. *Kehr*, 90 N. Y. 633.]

[5] *Fenwick* v. *Thornton*, M. & M. 51 (by Lord Tenterden). In *Smith* v. *Morgan*, 2 M. & R. 257, Tindal, C. J., decided exactly the reverse.

[6] *Pocock* v. *Billing*, 2 Bing. 269.

[7] [*Bearss* v. *Copley*, 10 N. Y. 93; see *Rouse* v. *Whited*, 25 N. Y. 170. But the fact that the whole statement is admissible does not require the same weight to be given to every part of it. Id.]

ARTICLE 17.*

ADMISSIONS BY AGENTS AND PERSONS JOINTLY INTERESTED WITH
PARTIES.

Admissions may be made by agents authorized to make
them either expressly or by the conduct of their principals; but a statement made by an agent is not an admission merely because if made by the principal himself
it would have been one.[1]

---

* See Note XI. [Appendix].

[1] [Illustrations (a), (ab), (c) and (d). The admission of an agent, in
order to be competent evidence against his principal, must relate to,
and be made in connection with, some act done in the course of his
agency, so as to form part of the *res gestæ* (*Anderson* v. *Rome, etc. R.
Co.*, 54 N. Y. 334; *Manhattan Ins. Co.* v. *Forty-second St. etc. R. Co.*,
139 N. Y. 146; *Goetz* v. *Bank of Kansas City*, 119 U. S. 551; *Xenia Bk.*
v. *Stewart*, 114 U.S. 224; *Lane* v. *B. & A. R. Co.*, 112 Mass. 455; *Giberson* v. *Patterson Mills Co.*, 174 Pa. 369; *Ohio, etc. R. Co.* v. *Stein*, 133
Ind. 243; *Ayres* v. *Hubbard*, 71 Mich. 594). Or else they must be expressly authorized (*White* v. *Miller*, 71 N. Y. 118, 136). But an agent's
declarations are not admissible to prove his own authority (*Stringham*
v. *St. Nicholas Ins. Co.*, 4 Abb. Dec. 315; *Baltimore, etc. Ass'n* v.
Post, 122 Pa. 579; *Swanstrom* v. *Improvement Co.*, 91 Mich. 367).

A wife's declarations are competent against her husband when she
makes them as his agent, within this rule; and so of a husband's admissions as against his wife. The marital relation does not of itself
establish the agency, but it must be otherwise shown to exist; it may
be express or implied (Gr. Ev. i. § 185; *Lay Grae* v. *Peterson*, 2
Sandf. 338; *Deck* v. *Johnson*, 1 Abb. Dec. 497; *Rose* v. *Chapman*, 44
Mich. 312; *Phelps* v. *James*, 86 Ia. 399; *Goodrich* v. *Tracy*, 43 Vt. 314;
see *McGregor* v. *Wait*, 10 Gray, 72; *Wright* v. *Towle*, 67 Mich. 255).

The admissions of a member or officer of an aggregate corporation,
who is not a party to the action, are not competent evidence against
the corporation, unless made within this rule while he was acting as
its authorized agent (*Soper* v. *Buffalo, etc. R. Co.*, 19 Barb. 310; N. Y.
Code Civ. Pro. § 839; *Truesdell* v. *Chumar*, 75 Hun, 416; *Allegheny
Co. Workhouse* v. *Moore*, 95 Pa. 408; 2 How. St. (Mich.) § 7512). So
the admissions of an inhabitant of a municipal corporation are not, in
this country, competent evidence against the corporation; and so of
the admissions of a public officer, unless made while he is acting as

A report made by an agent to a principal is not an admission which can be proved by a third person.[1]

Partners and joint contractors are each other's agents for the purpose of making admissions against each other in relation to partnership transactions or joint contracts.[2]

---

agent of the municipality, and as part of the *res gesta*. *Smyth* v. *Bangor*, 72 Me. 249 ; *Weeks* v. *Needham*, 156 Mass. 289; *Gray* v. *Rollinsford*, 58 N. H. 253 ; *Petition of Landaff*, 34 N. H. 163.]

[1] *Re Devala Co.*, 22 Ch. Div. 593 ; [cf. *Insurance Co. of N. America* v. *Guardiola*, 129 U. S. 642.]

[2] [Illustrations (*e*) and (*f*). This is a well-settled rule as to the admissions of a partner made during the existence of the partnership (*Union Nat. Bk.* v. *Underhill*, 102 N. Y. 336; *Van Keuren* v. *Parmelee*, 2 N. Y. 512; *Smith* v. *Collins*, 115 Mass. 388; *Western Assurance Co.* v. *Towle*, 65 Wis. 247; *Griffin* v. *Stearns*, 44 N. H. 498; *Slipp* v. *Hartley*, 50 Minn. 118; *Ruckman* v. *Decker*, 23 N. J. Eq. 283). The existence of the partnership, however, must be first shown, and the admissions of one alleged partner are not competent against others to prove them to be partners, though each one's admissions are receivable against himself to show him to be a partner (*Robins* v. *Warden*, 111 Mass. 244 ; *McNeilan's Estate*, 167 Pa. 472; *Bundy* v. *Bruce*, 61 Vt. 619 ; *Armstrong* v. *Potter*, 103 Mich. 409 ; *Vannoy* v. *Klein*, 122 Ind. 416 ; *Greenwood* v. *Sias*, 21 Hun, 391 ; *Pleasants* v. *Fant*, 22 Wall. 116). One partner cannot confess judgment against another, even for a partnership debt (*McCleery* v. *Thompson*, 130 Pa. 443 ; *Hall* v. *Lanning*, 91 U. S. 160, 170).

Different rules prevail in different States as to whether the admissions of one partner, made after a dissolution of the firm, shall be receivable against the others. In some States they are admissible against the others, when made in regard to past debts or transactions of the firm, but not so as to create new contracts or obligations (*Gay* v. *Bowen*, 8 Met. 100 ; *Buxton* v. *Edwards*, 134 Mass. 567, 579 ; *Hinkley* v. *Gilligan*, 34 Me. 101 ; *Rich* v. *Flanders*, 39 N. H. 304, 339 ; cf. *Feigley* v. *Whitaker*, 22 O. St. 606 ; *Davis* v. *Poland*, 92 Va. 225) ; and they are also competent in some States to arrest and start anew the running of the Statute of Limitations as to a partnership debt which is not yet barred (*Merritt* v. *Day*, 38 N. J. L. 32 ; *Bissell* v. *Adams*, 35 Ct. 299 ; *McClurg* v. *Howard*, 45 Mo. 365). But in New York admissions by one as to dealings of the firm before dissolution are not competent against the others, nor will his admissions affect the running of the Statute of Limitations except as to himself (*Baker* v. *Stackpole*, 9 Cow. 420 ; *Van Keuren* v. *Parmelee*, supra) ; though if

Barristers and solicitors are the agents of their clients for the purpose of making admissions whilst engaged in the actual management of the cause, either in court or in correspondence relating thereto; but statements made

---

one is authorized to act as agent in the business of winding up, the declarations which he makes in the course of his agency are competent against all (*Nichols* v. *White*, 85 N. Y. 531). When a partner retires, the remaining members cannot bind him by their admissions (*Pringle* v. *Leverich*, 97 N. Y. 181). Some other States have adopted similar rules (*Bell* v. *Morrison*, 1 Pet. 351 ; *Cronkhite* v. *Herrin*, 15 F. R. 888 ; *Wilson* v. *Waugh*, 101 Pa. 233 ; *Gates* v. *Fisk*, 45 Mich. 522 ; *Conkey* v. *Barbour*, 22 Ind. 196; *Nat. Bk. of Commerce* v. *Meader*, 40 Minn. 325 ; *Maxey* v. *Strong*, 53 Miss. 280; see Parsons on Partnership, pp. 184–197).

As respects creditors who have had dealings with the firm but to whom no notice of dissolution has been given, part payments by one partner after dissolution will prevent the bar of the Statute of Limitations as to the other partners (*Davison* v. *Sherburne*, 57 Minn. 355 ; *Buxton* v. *Edwards*, 134 Mass. 355 ; *Tappan* v. *Kimball*, 30 N. H. 136 ; *Gates* v. *Fisk*, 45 Mich. 522).

So in some States the admissions of one joint debtor or contractor are received against the others, and will also arrest and start anew the running of the Statute of Limitations as respects all, except so far as the statutes cited below (see p. 69, note 2) modify this rule (*Dennie* v. *Williams*, 135 Mass. 28 ; *Shepley* v. *Waterhouse*, 22 Me. 497 ; *Clark* v. *Sigourney*, 17 Ct. 510; *Woonsocket Inst.* v. *Ballou*, 16 R. I. 351 ; *Schindel* v. *Gates*, 46 Md. 604 ; *Block* v. *Dorman*, 51 Mo. 31 ; see *Parker* v. *Butterworth*, 46 N. J. L. 244). In other States a contrary or modified doctrine is held (*Campbell* v. *Brown*, 86 N. C. 376 ; see *Kallenbach* v. *Dickinson*, 100 Ill. 427, which enumerates the States having the diverse rules, and cites many leading cases). Thus it is held in a number of the States that one cannot bind the others so as to affect their defence that the claim is barred, but can only bind himself (*Shoemaker* v. *Benedict*, 11 N. Y. 176 ; *Bush* v. *Stowell*, 71 Pa. 208 ; *Clark* v. *Burn*, 86 id. 502 ; *Hance* v. *Hair*, 25 O. St. 349 ; *Willoughby* v. *Irish*, 35 Minn. 63 ; *Steele* v. *Souder*, 20 Kan. 39 ; *Miller* v. *Miller*, 4 McArth. 109). In New York it is well settled that a joint debtor or joint contractor has no authority to bind his associate, unless he is the agent or in some other way the representative of such person (*Wallis* v. *Randall*, 81 N. Y. 164 ; *Lewis* v. *Woodworth*, 2 N. Y. 512 ; *McMullen* v. *Rafferty*, 89 N. Y. 456 ; see *Rogers* v. *Anderson*, 40 Mich. 290). The rule in any State as to joint debtors is much the

by a barrister or solicitor on other occasions are not admissions merely because they would be admissions if
made by the client himself.[1]

---

same as to partners after dissolution ; so, also, it is held in most States
that the admissions of one such partner or debtor, made after the
claim is already barred, will not revive it against the others. *Newman* v. *McComas*, 43 Md. 70; *Parker* v. *Butterworth*, 46 N. J. L. 244;
Harris v. *Odeal*, 39 Mo. App. 270; *Davis* v. *Poland*, 92 Va. 225;
Bates on Partnership, ii. 703.]

[1] [Illustrations (*g*) and (*k*). This rule is generally applicable in this
country to attorneys and counsellors; the admissions may be oral or
written (Gr. Ev. i. § 186; *Lewis* v. *Sumner*, 13 Met. 269; *Loomis* v. *N. Y.
etc. R. Co.*, 159 Mass. 39; *Ohlquest* v. *Farwell*, 71 Ia. 231; *Isabelle* v.
Iron Cliffs Co., 57 Mich. 120; *Nichols* v. *Jones*, 32 Mo. App. 657; *Ohio,
etc. R. Co.* v. *Rooker*, 134 Ind. 343; *Oliver* v. *Bennett*, 65 N. Y. 559;
Rogers v. *Greenwood*, 14 Minn. 333). So the "stipulations" of attorneys
in relation to the conduct of the cause are, in general, binding upon
their clients (*Bray* v. *Doheny*, 39 Minn. 355; *Garrett* v. *Hanshue*, 53
O. St. 482; *Ex parte Hayes*, 92 Ala. 120; *Townsend* v. *Masterson Co.*,
15 N. Y. 587); it is common practice to require that stipulations shall
be in writing (*State* v. *Stewart*, 74 Ia. 336; *People* v. *Stephens*, 52 N. Y.
306). A plaintiff may be nonsuited on admissions contained in his
attorney's opening speech (*Oscanyan* v. *Arms Co.*, 103 U. S. 261;
Ferson v. *Wilcox*, 19 Minn. 449; *Clews* v. *N. Y. Banking Ass'n*, 105
N. Y. 398; *Evans* v. *Montgomery*, 95 Mich. 497; cf. *Converse* v.
Sickles, 146 N. Y. 200). As to unsolemn admissions, or those made
in casual conversation, etc., which are not usually allowed to be
proved against the client, see *Rockwell* v. *Taylor*, 41 Ct. 55; *McKeen*
v. *Gammon*, 33 Me. 187; *Douglass* v. *Mitchell's Excr.*, 35 Pa. 441;
Treadway v. *S. C. etc. R. Co.*, 40 Ia. 526; *Pickert* v. *Hair*, 146 Mass.
1; *Fay* v. *Hebbard*, 42 Hun, 490. As to admissions made by an
attorney on a former trial, or contained in the pleadings, see the
cases cited in the preceding Article (p. 58, *ante*). An admission made
by counsel may be withdrawn by permission of the court (*Sullivan* v.
Eddy, 154 Ill. 199). In this country it is the general rule that an attorney cannot compromise or settle a suit without his client's consent
(*Mandeville* v. *Reynolds*, 68 N. Y. 528; *Dalton* v. *West End, etc. R.
Co.*, 159 Mass. 221; *State* v. *Clifford*, 124 Mo. 492; *Eaton* v. *Knowles*,
61 Mich. 625; *Brockley* v. *Brockley*, 122 Pa. 1; *Wetherbee* v. *Fitch*,
117 Ill. 67). Sometimes, however, an attorney's compromise, if fair
and reasonable, has been sustained, though made without such consent (*Whipple* v. *Whitman*, 13 R. I. 512). English law allows counsel

The fact that two persons have a common interest in the same subject-matter does not entitle them to make admissions respecting it as against each other.[1]

In cases in which actions founded on a simple contract have been barred by the Statute of Limitations no joint contractor or his personal representative loses the benefit of such statute, by reason only of any written acknowledgment or promise made or signed by (or by the agent duly authorized to make such acknowledgment or promise of) any other or others of them (or by reason only of payment of any principal, interest, or other money, by any other or others of them).[2]

---

to make compromises. *Mathews* v. *Munster*, 20 Q. B. D. 141; *Lewis's* v. *Lewis*, 45 Ch. D. 281.]

[1] [Illustration (*i*). Gr. Ev. i. § 176. Thus the admission of one executor or administrator is not competent against his co-executor or co-administrator to establish a demand against the estate of the deceased, nor is it receivable against heirs or devisees (*Church* v. *Howard*, 79 N. Y. 415, 418; *Davis* v. *Gallagher*, 124 N. Y. 487); nor the admission of one devisee or legatee against another (*Clark* v. *Morrison*, 25 Pa. 453; *La Bau* v. *Vanderbilt*, 3 Redf. 384; *McMillan* v. *McDill*, 110 Ill. 47; *Shailer* v. *Bumstead*, 99 Mass. 112, 127); nor of one tenant in common against another (*Dan* v. *Brown*, 4 Cow. 483; *Pier* v. *Duff*, 63 Pa. 59); nor, generally, of one defendant in a tort action against another, unless made as part of the *res gestæ*, as in conspiracy (*Carpenter* v. *Shelden*, 5 Sandf. 77; *Wilson* v. *O'Day*, 5 Daly, 354; cf. *Edgerton* v. *Wolf*, 6 Gray, 453; see Art. 4). As to the admissions of a *cestui que trust*, see *Warren* v. *Carey*, 145 Mass. 78.]

[2] 9 Geo. IV. c. 14, s. 1. The first set of words in parenthesis was added by 19 & 20 Vict. c. 97, s. 13; the second set by s. 14 of the same Act. The language is slightly altered. [Similar statutes have been passed in several States of this country (Mass. Pub. St. c. 197, s. 17; N. J. Rev., p. 595, s. 10; Maine Rev. St. c. 82, ss. 98, 100; *Faulkner* v. *Bailey*, 123 Mass. 588; *Bailey* v. *Corliss*, 51 Vt. 366; *Gates* v. *Fisk*, 45 Mich. 522; *Bottles* v. *Miller*, 112 Ind. 584; *Nat. Bk. of Delavan* v. *Cotton*, 53 Wis. 31). In New York and some other States a similar common law rule prevails; but in a number of the States the contrary rule of the English common law prevails, which was established by *Whitcomb* v. *Whiting*. See pp. 66–68, *ante*, note; also Illustration (*f*), *post*.]

A principal, as such, is not the agent of his surety for the purpose of making admissions as to the matters for which the surety gives security.[1]

Illustrations.

(a) The question is, whether a parcel, for the loss of which a railway company is sued, was stolen by one of their servants. Statements made by the station master to a police officer, suggesting that the parcel had been stolen by a porter, are deemed to be relevant, as against the railway, as admissions by an agent.[2]

(ab) [In an action against a railroad company for an injury sustained by plaintiff from a collision of trains caused by a misplaced switch, the statements of a brakeman, made after the disaster, that he opened the switch, were offered in evidence against the company. They were held not admissible, not having been made as part of the *res gestæ*.][3]

(b) A allows his wife to carry on the business of his shop in his absence. A statement by her that he owes money for goods supplied to the shop is deemed to be relevant against him as an admission by an agent.[4]

(c) A sends his servant, B, to sell a horse. What B says at the time of the sale, and as part of the contract of sale, is deemed to be a relevant fact as against A, but what B says upon the subject at some different time is not deemed to be relevant as against A,[5] (though it might have been deemed to be relevant if said by A himself).

---

[1] [Illustration (*j*). Gr. Ev. i. § 187; *Hatch* v. *Elkins*, 65 N. Y. 489; *Rae* v. *Beach*, 76 N. Y. 164; *Wells* v. *Kavanagh*, 70 Ia. 519; *Lewis* v. *Lee Co.*, 73 Ala. 148; *Chelmsford Co.* v. *Demarest*, 7 Gray, 1. But declarations of the principal are admissible when forming part of the *res gestæ*. Id.; *Bank of Brighton* v. *Smith*, 12 Allen, 243; see *Agricultural Ins. Co.* v. *Keeler*, 44 Ct. 161; *Bissell* v. *Saxton*, 66 N. Y. 55.]

[2] *Kirkstall Brewery* v. *Furness Ry.*, L. R. 9 Q. B. 468. [See *Green* v. *B. & L. R. Co.*, 128 Mass. 221; *B. & M. R. Co.* v. *Ordway*, 140 Mass. 510; *Atchison, etc. R. Co.* v. *Wilkinson*, 55 Kan. 83; *B. & O. R. Co.* v. *Campbell*, 36 O. St. 647; *Steamboat Co.* v. *Brockett*, 121 U. S. 637; cf. *Hoag* v. *Lamont*, 60 N. Y. 96.]

[3] [*Patterson* v. *Wabash, etc. R. Co.*, 54 Mich. 91; see Art. 3, Illustration (*ca*), *ante*.]

[4] *Clifford* v. *Burton*, 1 Bing. 199; [*Riley* v. *Suydam*, 4 Barb. 222; see *State* v. *Lemon*, 92 N. C. 790.]

[5] *Helyear* v. *Hawke*, 5 Esp. 72; [see *Wait* v. *Borne*, 123 N. Y. 592.]

(*d*) The question is, whether a ship remained at a port for an unreasonable time. Letters from the plaintiff's agent to the plaintiff containing statements which would have been admissions if made by the plaintiff himself are deemed to be irrelevant as against him.[1]

(*e*) A, B, and C sue D as partners upon an alleged contract respecting the shipment of bark. An admission by A that the bark was his exclusive property and not the property of the firm is deemed to be relevant as against B and C.[2]

(*f*) A, B, C, and D make a joint and several promissory note. Either can make admissions about it as against the rest.[3]

(*g*) The question is, whether A accepted a bill of exchange. A notice to produce the bill signed by A's solicitor and describing the bill as having been accepted by A is deemed to be a relevant fact.[4]

(*h*) The question is, whether a debt to A, the plaintiff, was due from B, the defendant, or from C. A statement made by A's solicitor to B's solicitor in common conversation that the debt was due from C is deemed not to be relevant against A.[5]

(*i*) One co-part-owner of a ship cannot, as such, make admissions against another as to the part of the ship in which they have a common interest, even if he is co-partner with that other as to other parts of the ship.[6]

(*j*) A is surety for B, a clerk. B being dismissed makes statements as to sums of money which he has received and not accounted for. These statements are not deemed to be relevant as against A, as admissions.[7]

---

[1] *Langhorn* v. *Allnutt*, 4 Tau. 511.

[2] *Lucas* v. *De La Cour*, 1 M. & S. 249. [Cf. *Brahe* v. *Kimball*, 5 Sandf. 237; *Harding* v. *Butler*, 156 Mass. 34; but see *Williams* v. *Lewis*, 115 Ind. 45.]

[3] *Whitcomb* v. *Whiting*, 1 S. L. C. 644. [The decision in this case was that the acknowledgment of one of the drawers of a joint and several note took it out of the Statute of Limitations as against the others. This case is followed in some States of this country, rejected in others. *Kallenbach* v. *Dickinson*, 100 Ill. 427; *Murdock* v. *Waterman*, 145 N. Y. 55, 63; see p. 67, *ante*, note.]

[4] *Holt* v. *Squire*, Ry. & Mo. 282.

[5] *Petch* v. *Lyon*, 9 Q. B. 147; [*Saunders* v. *McCarthy*, 8 Allen, 43.]

[6] *Jaggers* v. *Binning*, 1 Stark. 64. [*The New Orleans*, 106 U. S. 13; *McLellan* v. *Cox*, 36 Me. 95; see *Smith* v. *Aldrich*, 12 Allen, 553.]

[7] *Smith* v. *Whippingham*, 6 C. & P. 78. See also *Evans* v. *Beattie*, 5 Esp. 26; *Bacon* v. *Chesney*, 1 Stark. 192; *Caermarthen R. Co.* v. *Manchester R. Co.*, L. R. 8 C. P. 685.

ARTICLE 18.*

ADMISSIONS BY STRANGERS.

Statements by strangers to a proceeding are not relevant as against the parties,[1] except in the cases hereinafter mentioned.

In actions against sheriffs for not executing process against debtors, statements of the debtor admitting his debt to be due to the execution creditor are deemed to be relevant as against the sheriff.[2]

In actions by the trustees of bankrupts an admission by the bankrupt of the petitioning creditor's debt is deemed to be relevant as against the defendant.[3]

ARTICLE 19.†

ADMISSION BY PERSON REFERRED TO BY PARTY.

When a party to any proceeding expressly refers to any other person for information in reference to a matter in

---

* See Note XII. [Appendix].   † See Note XIII. [Appendix].

[1] *Coole* v. *Braham*, 3 Ex. 183. [*Nelson* v. *Flint*, 166 U. S. 276; *Brown* v. *Mailler*, 12 N. Y. 118; *Happy* v. *Mosher*, 48 N. Y. 313; *Lyon* v. *Manning*, 133 Mass. 439; *Wilson* v. *Bowden*, 113 id. 422; *Montgomery* v. *Brush*, 121 Ill. 513. But statements made by a stranger in the presence and hearing of a party, and naturally calling for a reply, may be deemed admissions of the party if he keeps silent; see *ante*, p. 25, note 1.]

[2] *Kempland* v. *Macaulay*, Peake, 95 ; *Williams* v. *Bridges*, 2 Stark. 42 ; [*Hart* v. *Stevenson*, 25 Ct. 499 ; *Pugh* v. *M'Rae*, 2 Ala. 393.]

[3] *Jarrett* v. *Leonard*, 2 M. & S. 265, (adapted to the new law of bankruptcy). [This rule as thus stated is peculiarly applicable to English practice. But in New York it is held that the declarations of a bankrupt, made before the bankruptcy, are competent against his assignee in bankruptcy, to establish or support a claim against the bankrupt's estate. *Von Sachs* v. *Kretz*, 72 N. Y. 548; see *Holt* v. *Walker*, 26 Me. 107 ; *Carnes* v. *White*, 15 Gray, 378; *Wellington* v. *Jackson*, 121 Mass. 157 ; *In re Clark*, 9 Blatch. 379.]

dispute, the statements of that other person may be admissions as against the person who refers to him.[1]

Illustration.

The question is, whether A delivered goods to B. B says, " If C "
(the carman) " will say that he delivered the goods, I will pay for
them." C's answer may as against B be an admission.[2]

ARTICLE 20.[*]

ADMISSIONS MADE WITHOUT PREJUDICE.

No admission is deemed to be relevant in any civil action
if it is made either upon an express condition that evidence of it is not to be given,[3] or under circumstances
from which the judge infers that the parties agreed to-

---

[*] See Note XIV. [Appendix].

[1] [Gr. Ev. i. § 182 ; *Gott* v. *Dinsmore*, 111 Mass. 45 ; *Wehle* v. *Spel-
man*, 1 Hun, 634, 4 T. & C. 649 ; *Chadsey* v. *Greene*, 24 Ct. 562 ;
Chapman v. *Twitchell*, 37 Me. 59 ; *Folsom* v. *Batchelder*, 22 N. H.
47 ; *Beebe* v. *Knapp*, 28 Mich. 53 ; cf. *Adler-Goldman Co.* v. *Adams
Exp. Co.*, 53 Mo. App. 284. But the statements of the referee are
only admissible when they relate to the subject-matter of the reference (*Duval* v. *Covenhover*, 4 Wend. 561 ; *Lambert* v. *People*, 76 N. Y.
220 ; *Allen* v. *Killinger*, 8 Wall. 480), and when he was referred to
in such a way as to show an intention to give him authority like that
of an agent to make admissions (*Rosenbury* v. *Angell*, 6 Mich. 508 ;
Proctor v. *Old Colony R. Co.*, 154 Mass. 251). Statements made by
the referee before the reference are also not admissible (*Cohn* v.
Goldman, 76 N. Y. 284).

If persons speaking different languages communicate by an interpreter, his version of their words may be proved as their own declarations (Gr. Ev. i. § 183 ; *Comm.* v. *Vose*, 157 Mass. 393 ; *Wright* v.
Maseras, 56 Barb. 521 ; *Miller* v. *Lathrop*, 50 Minn. 91). But evidence of statements made by an interpreter that a party had made
admissions to him is hearsay and inadmissible. *Territory* v. *Big
Knot*, 6 Mont. 242.]

[2] *Daniel* v. *Pitt*, 1 Camp. 366, n.; see, too, *R.* v. *Mallory*, 13 Q. B. D.
33. This is a weaker illustration than *Daniel* v. *Pitt.*

[3] *Cory* v. *Bretton*, 4 C. & P. 462 ; [*Copeland* v. *Taylor*, 99 Mass. 613.]

gether that evidence of it should not be given,[1] or if it
was made under duress.[2]

Illustrations.

(*a*) [A sued B to recover a debt for services rendered. B denied
the indebtedness. A year after the action was begun B wrote this
letter to A : "Dear Sir : To save cost and stop further litigation, I am
willing to send you my check for fifty dollars in full liquidation of
your claim." On the trial this letter was held not receivable in evidence against B as an admission.][3]

(*b*) [A sued B in trover for a colt. Both were brought together by
friends, that they might talk over and settle the case. During the

---

[1] *Paddock* v. *Forester,* 3 M. & G. 918. [Under this rule statements
incorporating the express qualification that they shall be "without
prejudice" are deemed not to be relevant as admissions (*Walker* v.
Wilsher, 23 Q. B. D. 335 ; *Perkins* v. *Concord R. Co.,* 44 N. H. 223).
So statements made as offers to compromise a claim, or to "buy peace,"
as it is termed, are not competent evidence as admissions (Illustration
(*a*) ; Gr. Ev. i. § 192 ; *Draper* v. *Hatfield,* 124 Mass. 53 ; *Home Ins.
Co.* v. *Baltimore, etc. Co.,* 93 U. S. 527 ; *Tennant* v. *Dudley,* 144 N. Y.
504 ; *Slingerland* v. *Norton,* 58 Hun, 578 ; *Montgomery* v. *Allen,* 84
Mich. 656 ; *Louisville, etc. R. Co.* v. *Wright,* 115 Ind. 378). They are
equivalent to statements "without prejudice" (*West* v. *Smith,* 101
U. S. 263, 273 ; *Reynolds* v. *Manning,* 15 Md. 510 ; *White* v. *Old
Dominion St'p Co.,* 102 N. Y. 660). But an admission of an independent fact is relevant, though made during a negotiation for compromise (Illustration (*b*); *Bartlett* v. *Tarbox,* 1 Abb. Dec. 120 ; *Durgin*
v. *Somers,* 117 Mass. 55 ; *Arthur* v. *James,* 28 Pa. 236 ; *Doon* v. *Ravey,*
49 Vt. 293 ; *Beaudette* v. *Gagne,* 87 Me. 534 ; *Manistee Nat. Bk.* v.
Seymour, 64 Mich. 59 ; *Broschart* v. *Tuttle,* 59 Ct. 1 ; *Colburn* v. *Groton,* 66 N. H. 151 ; *Binford* v. *Young,* 115 Ind. 174 ; cf. *Brice* v. *Bauer,*
108 N. Y. 428). This is the general American rule.]

[2] *Stockfleth* v. *De Tastet,* per Ellenborough, C. J., 4 Camp. 11. [But
admissions made by a party, while testifying as witness in a prior suit,
are relevant against him ; the legal constraint to testify is not deemed
"duress" under this rule (Gr. Ev. i. § 193 ; see Art. 15, *ante,* note ;
Tooker v. *Gonner,* 2 Hilt. 71).
A court of equity will sometimes restrain the use of admissions
obtained by fraud and duress. *Callender* v. *Callender,* 53 How. Pr.
364.]

[3] [*Smith* v. *Satterlee,* 130 N. Y. 677.]

conversation A said he would be glad to have the colt, to which B replied, "I sold the colt about four weeks after I got it." Then A said, "I demanded the colt, you recollect?" and B answered, "Yes." No settlement being effected, these declarations were held admissible against B on the trial, as admissions that he had sold the property, and that a demand for it had been made upon him.][1]

ARTICLE 21.

CONFESSIONS DEFINED.

A confession is an admission made at any time by a person charged with a crime, stating or suggesting the inference that he committed that crime.[2]   Confessions,

---

[1] [*Dickinson* v. *Dickinson*, 9 Met. 471.]

[2] [The word "confession" denotes an acknowledgment of guilt. Acknowledgments of other matters of fact in a criminal case are termed "admissions" (Gr. Ev. i. § 170; *People* v. *Hickman*, 113 Cal. 80, 86; *Fletcher* v. *State*, 90 Ga. 468; *Taylor* v. *State*, 37 Neb. 788; *State* v. *Heidenreich*, 29 Or. 381).

Confessions may not only be made expressly, but may also be implied from a person's keeping silence when he is charged with a crime under such circumstances that he would naturally reply (*Sparf* v. *United States*, 156 U. S. 51; *Comm.* v. *McCabe*, 163 Mass. 98; *Richards* v. *State*, 82 Wis. 172; see Art. 8, *ante*, last paragraph, and note). This is true in some States, even though he be under arrest at the time (*Kelley* v. *People*, 55 N. Y. 565; *Murphy* v. *State*, 36 O. St. 628; *Ackerson* v. *People*, 124 Ill. 563; cf. *Ettinger* v. *Comm.*, 98 Pa. 338; contra, *Comm.* v. *McDermott*, 123 Mass. 440; *State* v. *Howard*, 102 Mo. 142).

It is a general rule that an extra-judicial confession (*i. e.*, one made out of court) is not sufficient to sustain a conviction, unless corroborated by additional proof of the *corpus delicti* (Gr. Ev. i. § 217; *People* v. *Hennessy*, 15 Wend. 147; N. Y. Code Cr. Pro. § 395; *Campbell* v. *People*, 159 Ill. 9; *People* v. *Simonsen*, 107 Cal. 345; *Ryan* v. *State*, 100 Ala. 94; *State* v. *Walker*, 98 Mo. 95; *Gray* v. *Comm.*, 101 Pa. 380; *People* v. *Lane*, 49 Mich. 340; *Blackburn* v. *State*, 23 O. St. 146; *State* v. *Knowles*, 48 Ia. 598). It is also an important rule that the whole of a confession is to be taken together, so that the prisoner may have the benefit of all qualifying or exculpatory statements incorporated therein (Gr. Ev. i. § 218; *State* v. *McDonnell*, 32 Vt. 491; *Morehead* v.

if voluntary, are deemed to be relevant facts as against
the persons who make them only.[1]

ARTICLE 22.*

CONFESSION CAUSED BY INDUCEMENT, THREAT, OR PROMISE,
WHEN IRRELEVANT IN CRIMINAL PROCEEDING.

No confession is deemed to be voluntary if it appears
to the judge to have been caused by any inducement,

---

* See Note XV. [Appendix].

State, 34 O. St. 212 ; *Corbett* v. *State*, 31 Ala. 329 ; see *People* v.
Ruloff, 3 Park. Cr. 401). But part of a conversation may be proved,
if it amounts to a confession which is substantially complete (*Comm.*
v. *Pitsinger*, 110 Mass. 101 ; *Levison* v. *State*, 54 Ala. 520). Facts
which explain or qualify a confession, or show it to be untrue in
whole or in part, may be adduced in evidence by the defendant
(*State* v. *Hutchinson*, 60 Ia. 478 ; *People* v. *Fox*, 121 N. Y. 449).

Judicial confessions will warrant a conviction without corroborative
proof of the *corpus delicti* (*State* v. *Lamb*, 28 Mo. 218 ; *Dantz* v. *State*,
87 Ind. 398) ; as *e. g.*, upon a plea of " guilty " in cases either of felony
or misdemeanor (*Hallinger* v. *Davis*, 146 U. S. 314 ; *Green* v. *Comm.*,
12 Allen, 155 ; *Comm.* v. *Brown*, 150 Mass. 331 ; *Craig* v. *State*, 49 O.
St. 415 ; *People* v. *Lennox*, 67 Cal. 113), or a plea of *non volo contendere*
(*Comm.* v. *Holstine*, 132 Pa. 357). But the court may permit a plea of
"guilty" to be withdrawn, when it is due to the prisoner's ignorance
weakness or fears, to deception or duress practiced upon him, or other
like causes (*Myers* v. *State*, 115 Ind. 554 ; *Gardner* v. *People*, 106 Ill.
76 ; *State* v. *Stephens*, 71 Mo. 535 ; *U. S.* v. *Bayaud*, 21 Blatch. 217).
A plea so withdrawn cannot afterwards be proved against the prisoner
as a confession (*People* v. *Ryan*, 82 Cal. 617). In New York no conviction may be had upon a plea of guilty in cases punishable with
death. N. Y. Code Cr. Pro. § 332.]

[1] [Thus the confession of one of two or more defendants in a criminal
case, not made in the presence of the others, is evidence against himself only, and not against the others (*Sparf* v. *United States*, 156 U.
S. 51 ; *Comm.* v. *Ingraham*, 7 Gray, 46 ; *State* v. *Albert*, 73 Mo. 347 ;
People v. *Stevens*, 47 Mich. 411 ; *Fife* v. *Comm.*, 29 Pa. 429 ; *Ackerson*
v. *People*, 124 Ill. 563). As to the declarations of conspirators, see
Art. 4, *ante*.]

threat, or promise, proceeding from a person in authority, and having reference to the charge against the accused person, whether addressed to him directly or brought to his knowledge indirectly;[1]

and if (in the opinion of the judge)[2] such inducement, threat, or promise, gave the accused person reasonable

---

[1] [The admissibility of confessions is to be determined by the judge, their weight by the jury (*Willett* v. *People*, 27 Hun, 469 ; *Comm.* v. *Culver*, 126 Mass. 464 ; *Palmer* v. *State*, 136 Ind. 393 ; *State* v. *Kinder*, 96 Mo. 548 ; *State* v. *Holden*, 42 Minn. 350 ; *Biscoe* v. *State*, 67 Md. 6 ; *Lefevre* v. *State*, 50 O. St. 584 ; and cases *infra*). But in some States, as in England, when a confession is offered in evidence, the burden of proof is on the prosecutor to show it to be voluntary (*Bradford* v. *State*, 104 Ala. 68 ; *Wrye* v. *State*, 95 Ga. 467 ; *Nicholson* v. *State*, 38 Md. 140 ; *People* v. *Soto*, 49 Cal. 67 ; *Thompson* v. *Comm.*, 20 Gratt. 724 ; *R.* v. *Thompson*, [1893] 2 Q. B. 12). In other States it is considered *prima facie* voluntary, but the defendant may object to its being admitted in evidence and show it to have been improperly obtained and so cause its exclusion (*Comm.* v. *Sego*, 125 Mass. 210 ; *Comm.* v. *Culver*, supra ; *Rufer* v. *State*, 25 O. St. 464 ; *State* v. *Meyers*, 99 Mo. 107 ; *People* v. *Barker*, 60 Mich. 277 ; *State* v. *Davis*, 34 La. Ann. 351 ; cf. *People* v. *Fox*, 121 N. Y. 448). In some States, moreover, when the evidence is conflicting whether a confession is voluntary or not, the question may be left to the jury, with instructions to disregard the confession if they find it to be involuntary. *Comm.* v. *Preece*, 140 Mass. 276 ; *Burdge* v. *State*, 53 O. St. 512 ; *Wilson* v. *U. S.*, 162 U. S. 613 ; contra, *Ellis* v. *State*, 65 Miss. 44.]

[2] It is not easy to reconcile the cases on this subject. In *R.* v. *Baldry*, decided in 1852 (2 Den. C. C. 430), the constable told the prisoner that he need not say anything to criminate himself, but that what he did say would be taken down and used as evidence against him. It was held that this was not an inducement, though there were earlier cases which treated it as such. In *R.* v. *Jarvis*, L. R. 1 C. C. R. 96, the following was held not to be an inducement : " I think it is right I should tell you that, besides being in the presence of my brother and myself " (prisoner's master), " you are in the presence of two officers of the police ; and I should advise you that to any question that may be put to you, you will answer truthfully, so that if you have committed a fault you may not add to it by stating what is untrue. Take care. We know more than you think we know." So in *R.* v. *Reeve*, L. R. 1 C. C. R. 362, where the words were, " You had better, as

grounds for supposing that by making a confession he
would gain some advantage or avoid some evil in reference
to the proceedings against him.[1]

---

good boys, tell the truth," the confession was held admissible. In *R. v.
Fennell*, 7 Q. B. D. 147, the prosecutor, in the presence of the police
inspector, said to the prisoner: "The inspector tells me you are making
housebreaking implements ; if that is so, you had better tell the truth,
it may be better for you ;" these words were held to exclude the confession which followed. There are later cases (unreported) which
follow these. [See Illustrations (*aa*) and (*ab*) ; *Comm. v. Preece*, 140
Mass. 276 ; *State v. Anderson*, 96 Mo. 241 ; *Ross v. State*, 67 Md. 286 ;
Kelly v. State, 72 Ala. 244 ; *Bram v. U. S.*, 168 U. S. 532.]

[1] [*People v. Phillips*, 42 N. Y. 200 ; *Comm. v. Curtis*, 97 Mass. 574 ;
Fife v. Comm., 29 Pa. 429 ; *Flagg v. People*, 40 Mich. 706 ; *Robinson
v. State*, 159 Ill. 115 ; *State v. Jones*, 54 Mo. 478. But a confession
made to a person in authority, even though obtained by his inducements, solicitations, or inquiries, is deemed to be voluntary, if no inducements, threats, or promises are used which are calculated to
excite hope or fear in respect to the proceedings against the prisoner
(Illustration (*ac*) ; *Comm. v. Sego*, 125 Mass. 210 ; *People v. Wentz*, 37
N. Y. 303 ; *State v. Fortner*, 43 Ia. 494 ; *Comm. v. Morey*, 1 Gray, 461 ;
Fife v. Comm., supra) ; and the same is true if improper threats or
promises are made, but it satisfactorily appears that the confession
was not induced thereby (*Bartley v. People*, 156 Ill. 234). So confessions made by the prisoner while in custody are competent, if the
officer use no such improper inducements or threats (*People v. Cox*,
80 N. Y. 501 ; *Pierce v. U. S.*, 160 U. S. 535 ; *McQueen v. State*, 94
Ala. 50 ; *Comm. v. Cuffee*, 108 Mass. 285 ; *Comm. v. Mosler*, 4 Pa. 264;
People v. Eckman, 72 Cal. 582), and that, too, even if the prisoner be
in irons and expecting to die from the effects of poison (*State v. Gorham*, 67 Vt. 365 ; cf. *Sparf v. U. S.*, 156 U. S. 51) ; and the same rule
applies even though the arrest be illegal (*Balbo v. People*, 80 N. Y.
484). The fact that confessions are made under actual fear does not
make them involuntary, if this fear were not excited by inducements
or threats of the kind which this Article describes (*Comm. v. Smith*,
119 Mass. 305). So the hope of immunity (no promise of immunity
having been made) will not render a confession inadmissible (*State
v. Griffin*, 48 La. Ann. 1409 ; *Comm. v. Sego*, 125 Mass. 210, 213).

If an accomplice agrees to turn State's evidence, upon a promise
that he shall not be prosecuted, and thereupon makes a confession
but afterwards refuses to testify, his confession may be proved against

A confession is not involuntary, only because it appears to have been caused by the exhortations of a person in authority to make it as a matter of religious duty,[1] or by an inducement collateral to the proceeding,[2] or by inducements held out by a person not in authority.[3]

---

him (*Comm.* v. *Knapp,* 10 Pick. 477; *U. S.* v. *Hins,* 35 F. R. 272; *State* v. *Moran,* 15 Or. 262; but see *Neeley* v. *State,* 27 Tex. App. 324).

In some States these common law rules are changed by statute. Thus in New York it is now provided that a confession, whether made in judicial proceedings or to a private person, can be given in evidence, unless made under the influence of fear produced by threats, or upon a stipulation of the district attorney not to prosecute therefor; but there must be additional proof of the commission of the crime to warrant conviction (Code Cr. Pro. § 395; *People* v. *McCallan,* 103 N. Y. 588; *People* v. *Deacons,* 109 N. Y. 374; cf. *Benson* v. *State,* 119 Ind. 488). But cases decided in New York before this statute are cited herein, since they well illustrate the common law rule.]

[1] [Illustration (*b*); cf. *Comm.* v. *Drake,* 15 Mass. 161.]

[2] [Illustration (*c*); *State* v. *Tatro,* 50 Vt. 483; *People* v. *Cox,* 80 N. Y. 501; *State* v. *Wentworth,* 37 N. H. 196; *State* v. *Hopkirk,* 84 Mo. 278; *Stone* v. *State,* 105 Ala. 60, 69.]

[3] [It is also the general rule in this country that confessions obtained by the inducements of favor or threats of harm, held out by a person *not in authority as respects the prosecution,* are admissible (*U. S.* v. *Stone,* 8 F. R. 232; *Smith* v. *Comm.,* 10 Gratt. 734; *Shifflet* v. *Comm.,* 14 Id. 652; *Young* v. *Comm.,* 8 Bush (Ky.), 366; *State* v. *Holden,* 42 Minn. 350; *State* v. *Morgan,* 35 W. Va. 260; *State* v. *Patterson,* 73 Mo. 695; cf. *Ulrich* v. *People,* 39 Mich. 245; *State* v. *Potter,* 18 Ct. 166; see next note). Promises or threats made by a third person in the presence of one in authority and with his apparent sanction may, however, be regarded as made by the person in authority (Id.). But in a few States confessions are excluded which are obtained by threats of harm or promises of favor held out by any one connected with the prosecution, or by a person who may be fairly supposed by the accused to have power to secure the benefit promised or the harm threatened (*Murphy* v. *State,* 63 Ala. 1; *Spears* v. *State,* 2 O. St. 583; *Miller* v. *State,* 94 Ga. 1, 12; *Beggarly* v. *State,* 8 Baxt. 520; cf. *Comm.* v. *Tuckerman,* 10 Gray, 173, 190; *Gregg* v. *State,* 106 Ala. 44; *People* v. *Wolcott,* 51 Mich. 612). Moreover, confessions extorted by mob violence, or by like forcible means, are excluded, though the persons using such means have no authority as respects the prosecution. *Mil-*

The prosecutor, officers of justice having the prisoner in custody, magistrates, and other persons in similar positions, are persons in authority.[1] The master of the prisoner is not as such a person in authority, if the crime of which the person making the confession is accused was not committed against him.[2]

A confession is deemed to be voluntary if (in the opinion of the judge) it is shown to have been made after the complete removal of the impression produced by any inducement, threat, or promise which would otherwise render it involuntary.[3]

Facts discovered in consequence of confessions improperly obtained, and so much of such confessions as distinctly relate to such facts, may be proved.[4]

Illustrations.

(*a*) The question is, whether A murdered B.

A handbill issued by the Secretary of State, promising a reward and pardon to any accomplice who would confess, is brought to the

---

ler v. *People*, 39 Ill. 457; *Young v. State*, 68 Ala. 569; *Williams v. State*, 72 Miss. 117; *State v. Resells*, 34 La. Ann. 381.]

[1] [*People v. Ward*, 15 Wend. 231; *Wolf v. Comm.*, 30 Gratt. 833; *State v. Brockman*, 46 Mo. 566; *Rector v. Comm.*, 80 Ky. 468; *U. S. v. Pocklington*, 2 Cr. C. C. 293; *State v. Staley*, 14 Minn. 105; and cases cited in last note and in note 1, on p. 78. A private detective has been held not to be a person in authority. *Early v. Comm.*, 86 Va. 921; *U. S. v. Stone*, 8 F. R. 232.]

[2] [*Smith v. Comm.*, 10 Gratt. 734; cf. *Comm. v. Sego*, 125 Mass. 210.]

[3] [The removal of the impression must be *complete*. Illustration (*e*); *Ward v. People*, 3 Hill, 395; *Comm. v. Howe*, 132 Mass. 250; *Thompson v. Comm.*, 20 Gratt. 724; *State v. Brown*, 73 Mo. 631; *Rizzolo v. Comm.*, 126 Pa. 54; cf. *Comm. v. Cullen*, 111 Mass. 435; *People v. Barker*, 60 Mich. 277.]

[4] [Illustration (*f*); *Duffy v. People*, 26 N. Y. 588; *People v. Hoy Yen*, 34 Cal. 176; *Comm. v. James*, 99 Mass. 438; *Pressley v. State*, 111 Ala. 34; *State v. Winston*, 116 N. C. 990; *State v. Mortimer*, 20 Kan. 93; *Laros v. Comm.*, 84 Pa. 200; see *Murphy v. People*, 63 N. Y. 590. Some of these cases seem to adopt a more restricted rule than that of

knowledge of A, who, under the influence of the hope of pardon, makes a confession. This confession is not voluntary.[1]

(aa) [A, having been committed to jail on a charge of murder, the committing magistrate visits him and tells him that "it would be better for him to tell the truth and have no more trouble about it." He also tells A that he can make him no promises. Thereupon A makes a confession. The confession is not voluntary, and is therefore inadmissible.][2]

(ab) [A, in prison on a charge of murder, sent for the sheriff to come and see him and asked the sheriff if it would be best to tell the truth about it. The sheriff replied that it was always best for him, or for any one else, to tell the truth about anything. The sheriff also said, "If you are going to tell the straight truth, I will listen to it and want to hear it ; and if you are not going to tell the truth, I don't want to hear it." A then made a confession. The confession is voluntary.][3]

(ac) [A, a boy fourteen years old, was arrested by two police officers on a charge of murder. Having searched him, stripped him of his clothing, and put him in a cell, they took him out of the cell at night and questioned him for two hours, without warning him of his right not to answer, or offering him opportunity to consult friends or counsel. Answers made by him tending to show his guilt were deemed voluntary confessions, as the officers had made no promises of favor or threats of harm.][4]

(b) A being charged with the murder of B, the chaplain of the gaol reads the Commination Service to A, and exhorts him upon religious grounds to confess his sins. A, in consequence, makes a confession. This confession is voluntary.[5]

---

the text, as to admitting proof of words of confession, though they all hold that the "facts discovered" may be proved.]

[1] *R.* v. *Boswell,* C. & M. 584.

[2] [*Biscoe* v. *State,* 67 Md. 6; S. P. *Comm.* v. *Nott,* 135 Mass. 269; *Comm.* v. *Myers,* 160 Mass. 530; *People* v. *Phillips,* 42 N. Y. 200; *State* v. *Walker,* 34 Vt. 296; *State* v. *York,* 37 N. H. 175; *People* v. *Thompson,* 84 Cal. 598.]

[3] [*Maull* v. *State,* 95 Ala. 1 ; cf. *Comm.* v. *Morey,* 1 Gray, 461 ; *Heldt* v. *State,* 20 Neb. 492.]

[4] [*Comm.* v. *Cuffee,* 108 Mass. 285.]

[5] *R.* v. *Gilham,* 1 Moo. C. C. 186. In this case the exhortation was that the accused man should confess "to God," but it seems from parts of the case that he was urged also to confess to man "to repair any injury done to the laws of his country." According to the practice at

(*c*) The gaoler promises to allow A, who is accused of a crime, to see his wife, if he will tell where the property is. A does so. This is a voluntary confession.[1]

(*d*) A is accused of child murder. Her mistress holds out an inducement to her to confess, and she makes a confession. This is a voluntary confession, because her mistress is not a person in authority.[2]

(*e*) A is accused of the murder of B. C, a magistrate, tries to induce A to confess by promising to try to get him a pardon if he does so. The Secretary of State informs C that no pardon can be granted, and this is communicated to A. After that A makes a statement. This is a voluntary confession.[3]

(*f*) A, accused of burglary, makes a confession to a policeman under an inducement which prevents it from being voluntary. Part of it is that A had thrown a lantern into a certain pond. The fact that he said so, and that the lantern was found in the pond in consequence, may be proved.[4]

ARTICLE 23.*

CONFESSIONS MADE UPON OATH, ETC.

Evidence amounting to a confession may be used as such against the person who gives it, although it was given upon oath, and although the proceeding in which it was given had reference to the same subject-matter as the proceeding in which it is to be proved, and although the witness might have refused to answer the questions

---

* See Note XVI. [Appendix].

that time, no reasons are given for the judgment. The principle seems to be that a man is not likely to tell a falsehood in such cases from religious motives. The case is sometimes cited as an authority for the proposition that a clergyman may be compelled to reveal confessions made to him professionally. It has nothing to do with the subject.

[1] *R*. v. *Lloyd*, 6 C. & P. 393.

[2] *R*. v. *Moore*, 2 Den. C. C. 522.

[3] *R*. v. *Clewes*, 4 C. & P. 221.

[4] *R*. v. *Gould*, 9 C. & P. 364. This is not consistent, so far as the proof of the words goes, with *R*. v. *Warwickshall*, 1 Leach, 263.

put to him;[1] but if, after refusing to answer any such question, the witness is improperly compelled to answer it, his answer is not a voluntary confession.[2]

Illustrations.

(*a*) The answers given by a bankrupt in his examination may be used against him in a prosecution for offences against the law of bankruptcy.[3]

(*b*) A is charged with maliciously wounding B.

Before the magistrates A appeared as a witness for C, who was charged with the same offence. A's deposition may be used against him on his own trial.[4]

(*ba*) [A is tried for burglary. On a former trial of the same case A voluntarily became a witness in his own behalf. Answers given

---

[1] [*Comm.* v. *Bradford*, 126 Mass. 42; *State* v. *Glahn*, 97 Mo. 679; *People* v. *Mitchell*, 94 Cal. 550; *State* v. *Witham*, 72 Me. 531. On the trial of a person for crime, testimony voluntarily given by him under oath in a prior action or proceeding, and amounting to a confession, is receivable (*Dickerson* v. *State*, 48 Wis. 288; *Alston* v. *State*, 41 Tex. 39). So confessions contained in a voluntary affidavit are admissible (*Behler* v. *State*, 112 Ind. 140). But it is provided in some States by statute that on the preliminary examination of a prisoner before a committing magistrate, he shall not be put under oath; if, therefore, he is compelled to take an oath and then makes a confession, such confession is inadmissible (Gr. Ev. i. §§ 224-229; N. Y. Code Cr. Pro. § 198; *Hendrickson* v. *People*, 10 N. Y. 9, 27, 30; *People* v. *Mondon*, 103 N. Y. 211; *Comm.* v. *Harman*, 4 Pa. 269; N. C. Code, § 1145; *State* v. *Matthews*, 66 N. C. 106; see *Wilson* v. *U. S.*, 162 U. S. 613, 623; *U. S.* v. *Duffy*, 1 Cr. C. C. 164; *People* v. *Kelley*, 47 Cal. 125). In other States he may, at his own option, testify under oath at such an examination; if, therefore, he does so testify and makes confessions, they are admissible against him on his subsequent trial. *State* v. *Glass*, 50 Wis. 218; *Jackson* v. *State*, 39 O. St. 37; *State* v. *Miller*, 35 Kan. 328; cf. *Comm.* v. *Clark*, 130 Pa. 641.]

[2] *R.* v. *Garbett*, 1 Den. C. C. 236. See also *R.* v. *Owen*, 20 Q. B. D. 829, as explained in *R.* v. *Paul*, 25 Q. B. D. 202. [Gr. Ev. i. § 451; *Hendrickson* v. *People*, 10 N. Y. 9, 27, 31; see Art. 120, note, *post.*]

[3] *R.* v. *Scott*, 1 D. & B. 47; *R.* v. *Robinson*, L. R. 1 C. C. R. 80; *R.* v. *Widdop*, L. R. 2 C. C. R. 5. [So as to testimony before a fire inquest. *Comm.* v. *Wesley*, 166 Mass. 248.]

[4] *R.* v. *Chidley & Cummins*, 8 Cox, 365; [see *People* v. *Thayer*, 1 Park. Cr. 595.]

by him upon cross-examination on this former trial, and tending to
show his guilt, may be proved against him.] [1]

(c) [A is tried for the murder of B.

Statements made by A under oath at the coroner's inquest upon
·he body of B are competent evidence against him, though he knew
ᵥhen he made the statements that he was suspected of the crime; [2]
Dut not, if at the time he was *under arrest* for the crime, and was
taken before the coroner and put under oath without his own consent
or request.] [3]

ARTICLE 24.

CONFESSION MADE UNDER A PROMISE OF SECRECY.

If a confession is otherwise relevant, it does not become
irrelevant, merely because it was made under a promise
of secrecy, [4] or in consequence of a deception practised on
the accused person for the purpose of obtaining it, [5] or

---

[1] [*State* v. *Eddings*, 71 Mo. 545.]

[2] [*Teachout* v. *People*, 41 N. Y. 7; *State* v. *Gilman*, 51 Me. 206;
People v. *Martinez*, 66 Cal. 278; *Wilson* v. *State*, 110 Ala. 1; *Newton*
v. *State*, 21 Fla. 53; see *Williams* v. *Comm.*, 29 Pa. 102; *State* v.
Coffee, 56 Ct. 399; *Mack* v. *State*, 48 Wis. 271; *State* v. *Taylor*, 36
Kan. 329. Some States, however, exclude confessions made under
such circumstances. *State* v. *Young*, 119 Mo. 495; *State* v. *Senn*,
32 S. Car. 392; *Wood* v. *State*, 22 Tex. App. 431; *State* v. *Hobbs*, 37
W. Va. 812.]

[3] [*People* v. *Mondon*, 103 N. Y. 211; *Farkas* v. *State*, 60 Miss. 847;
Lyons v. *People*, 137 Ill. 602. So as to statements made before the
grand jury by the prisoner while under arrest (*State* v. *Clifford*, 86
Ia. 550). If, however, a prisoner *voluntarily* appears before a coroner
and testifies under oath, confessions so made are provable against
him. Id.; *People* v. *Chapleau*, 121 N. Y. 266; see *State* v. *Wisdom*,
119 Mo. 539.]

[4] [*State* v. *Squires*, 48 N. H. 364.]

[5] [Illustration (a); *People* v. *Wentz*, 37 N. Y. 303, 305, 306; *Price* v.
State, 18 O. St. 418; *State* v. *Phelps*, 74 Mo. 128; *Hardy* v. *United
States*, 3 App. D. C. 35; *Stone* v. *State*, 105 Ala. 60; *Wigginton* v.
Comm., 92 Ky. 282; *State* v. *Staley*, 14 Minn. 105. Hope of immunity
aroused by taking advantage of the prisoner's superstition does not
exclude his confession. *State* v. *Harrison*, 115 N. C. 707.]

when he was drunk,[1] or because it was made in answer
to questions which he need not have answered, whatever
may have been the form of those questions,[2] or because
he was not warned that he was not bound to make such
confession, and that evidence of it might be given against
him.[3]

Illustration.

(a) [A is indicted for the murder of B. A detective, with the connivance of the prosecuting attorney, has himself arrested and indicted
on a fictitious charge of forgery, and, while imprisoned in jail on this
charge, ingratiates himself in the confidence of A, and by this means
obtains confessions from the latter as to the murder of B. These
confessions may be proved against A.] [4]

---

[1] [*Comm.* v. *Howe*, 9 Gray, 110; *Jefferds* v. *People*, 5 Park. Cr. 522;
People v. *Fox*, 121 N. Y. 449; *State* v. *Grear*, 28 Minn. 426; *People*
v. *Ramires*, 56 Cal. 533; *State* v. *Feltes*, 51 Ia. 495; *Williams* v. *State*,
12 Lea, 211; *White* v. *State*, 32 Tex. App. 625; *Eskridge* v. *State*, 25
Ala. 30. The intoxication affects the *credibility*, not the *competency*,
of the evidence; if it be extreme, the jury may give the confession
little or no weight (Id.). Words spoken in sleep are not admissible
as a confession (*People* v. *Robinson*, 19 Cal. 41); but where it was
doubtful whether the accused was asleep or awake, his words were
allowed to go to the jury (*State* v. *Morgan*, 35 W. Va. 260). A confession made by a prisoner in a prayer that was overheard was allowed
to be proved. *Woolfolk* v. *State*, 85 Ga. 69, 101.]

[2] [*People* v. *Wentz*, 37 N. Y. 303, 306; *Comm.* v. *Cuffee*, 108 Mass.
285.]

[3] Cases collected and referred to in 1 Ph. Ev. 420, and T. E. s. 804.
See, too, Joy, ss. iii., iv., v. [*Wilson* v. *United States*, 162 U. S. 613,
623; *Comm.* v. *Cuffee*, 108 Mass. 285. Such a warning is, however,
sometimes given, though not required, and is important evidence,
tending to show that the confession was voluntary (*State* v. *Gilman*,
51 Me. 206; *People* v. *Simpson*, 48 Mich. 474; *People* v. *Chapleau*, 121
N. Y. 266); and sometimes, upon a preliminary examination before
a committing magistrate, it is required by statute. N. Y. Code Cr.
Pro. § 196; N. C. Code, § 1146; *State* v. *Rogers*, 112 N. C. 874; *State*
v. *Hatcher*, 29 Or. 309; *Coffee* v. *State*, 25 Fla. 501; *Salas* v. *State*,
31 Tex. App. 485.]

[4] [*State* v. *Brooks*, 92 Mo. 542; *Burton* v. *State*, 107 Ala 108; *Heldt*
v. *State*, 20 Neb. 492]

ARTICLE 25.

STATEMENTS BY DECEASED PERSONS, WHEN DEEMED TO BE
RELEVANT.

Statements, written or oral, of facts in issue or relevant or deemed to be relevant to the issue are deemed
to be relevant, if the person who made the statement is
dead, in the cases, and on the conditions, specified in
Articles 26–31, both inclusive.[1]   In each of those Articles
the word "declaration" means such a statement as is
herein mentioned, and the word "declarant" means a
dead person by whom such a statement was made in his
lifetime.

ARTICLE 26.*

DYING DECLARATION AS TO CAUSE OF DEATH.

A declaration made by the declarant as to the cause of
his death, or as to any of the circumstances of the transaction which resulted in his death,[2] is deemed to be
relevant

---

* See Note XVII. [Appendix].

[1] [See *Putnam* v. *Fisher*, 52 Vt. 191.]

[2] [Gr. Ev. i. § 156 ; *State* v. *Mace*, 118 N. C. 1244 ; *Sullivan* v. *State*,
102 Ala. 135.   But such declarations are not competent evidence of
prior or subsequent occurrences, as *e. g.*, of antecedent threats (*State*
v. *Wood*, 53 Vt. 560 ; *Hackett* v. *People*, 54 Barb. 370; *Jones* v. *State*,
71 Ind. 66 ; *People* v. *Fong Ah Sing*, 64 Cal. 253), nor of matters of
opinion, but only of *facts* to which declarant would be competent to
testify as a witness (Gr. Ev. i. § 159; *Boyle* v. *State*, 105 Ind. 469;
People v. *Lanagan*, 81 Cal. 142; *State* v. *Baldwin*, 79 Ia. 714;
State v. *Chambers*, 87 Mo. 406 ; *People* v. *Shaw*, 3 Hun, 272, 63 N. Y.
36).   Dying declarations are admissible in favor of the defendant, as
well as against him (*Mattox* v. *U. S.*, 146 U. S. 140 ; *People* v. *Knapp*,
26 Mich. 112 ; but see *Moeck* v. *People*, 100 Ill. 242).   Though made in
answer to leading questions, or obtained by solicitation, or expressed
by signs instead of words, they are still competent evidence (*Maine*
v. *People*, 9 Hun, 113; *Comm.* v. *Casey*, 11 Cush. 417; *State* v. *Foot
You*, 24 Or. 61 ; *Jones* v. *State*, 71 Ind. 66).   The constitutional provision that the accused shall be confronted with the witnesses against

only in trials for the murder or manslaughter of the declarant;[1]

and only when the declarant is shown, to the satisfaction of the judge,[2] to have been in actual danger of death, and to have given up all hope of recovery at the time when his declaration was made.[3]

---

him does not exclude evidence of dying declarations. *Brown* v. *Comm.*, 73 Pa. 321, 328; *State* v. *Dickinson*, 41 Wis. 299; *Comm.* v. *Carey*, 12 Cush. 246; *Robbins* v. *State*, 8 O. St. 131.]

[1] [*People* v. *Davis*, 56 N. Y. 95; *Kilpatrick* v. *Comm.*, 31 Pa. 198; *Scott* v. *People*, 63 Ill. 508; *Puryear* v. *Comm.*, 83 Va. 15; and other cases under this Article.   Thus such evidence is not received in *civil actions* (*Wilson* v. *Boerem*, 15 Johns. 286; *Thayer* v. *Lombard*, 165 Mass. 174; *Hood* v. *Pioneer Co.*, 95 Ala. 461), and that too, though they be actions for injury causing death (*Daily* v. *N. Y. etc. R. Co.*, 32 Ct. 356; *Waldele* v. *N. Y. C. R. Co.*, 19 Hun, 69; *Marshall* v. *Chicago, etc. R. Co.*, 48 Ill. 475); nor is it received in other criminal cases than those of homicide (Illustration (*b*); *Johnson* v. *State*, 50 Ala. 456). But sometimes these rules are changed by statute.   See p. 90, note 2, *post.*]

[2] [Gr. Ev. i. § 160; *State* v. *Nocton*, 121 Mo. 537; *People* v. *Smith*, 104 N. Y. 491; *State* v. *Baldwin*, 79 Ia. 714; *Westbrook* v. *People*, 126 Ill. 81.   The person offering the declarations in evidence must show that they were made under the sense of impending death.   This may be shown by the declarant's own statements, by his acts indicating a sense that death is near, and by other attendant circumstances (Illustrations (*ab*), (*ac*); Gr. Ev. i. § 158; *People* v. *Simpson*, 48 Mich. 474; *Kehoe* v. *Comm.*, 85 Pa. 127; *Westbrook* v. *People*, 126 Ill. 81; *State* v. *Nelson*, 101 Mo. 464; *State* v. *Baldwin*, 79 Ia. 714; *State* v. *Swift*, 57 Ct. 496).   Thus the fact that he received extreme unction has been admitted in evidence as bearing upon this question (*Carver* v. *United States*, 164 U. S. 694).   It is discretionary with the trial court whether this preliminary evidence shall be given in the presence of the jury.   *People* v. *Smith*, 104 N. Y. 491; *Doles* v. *State*, 97 Ind. 555; *State* v. *Furney*, 41 Kan. 115; cf. *North* v. *People*, 139 Ill. 81.]

[3] [*Brotherton* v. *People*, 75 N. Y. 159; *Allison* v. *Comm.*, 99 Pa. 17; *State* v. *Johnson*, 118 Mo. 491; *Simons* v. *People*, 150 Ill. 66; *Hale* v. *Comm.*, 89 Va. 171; *Comm.* v. *Brewer*, 164 Mass. 577; and cases *supra.*   Even a faint hope of recovery excludes the declarations (*People* v. *Gray*, 61 Cal. 164; *Comm.* v. *Roberts*, 108 Mass. 296).   If hope be expressed, but afterwards, when hope is gone, declarations are made, they are competent (*Small* v. *Comm.*, 91 Pa. 304; *State* v.

Such a declaration is not irrelevant merely because it
was intended to be made as a deposition before a magistrate, but is irregular.[1]

Evans, 124 Mo. 397; *Johnson* v. *State,* 102 Ala. 1; *Mockabee* v. *Comm.,*
78 Ky. 380; cf. *Carver* v. *United States,* 160 U. S. 553). And it has
been held that declarations made when there was no hope are
admissible, though the dying person lingered several days, and during
this time expressed some hope (*Swisher* v. *Comm.,* 26 Gratt. 963;
State v. *Kilgore,* 70 Mo. 546; *State* v. *Reed,* 53 Kan. 767).

It is not necessary that the declarant should die immediately. In
one case he died fourteen days after making the statement (*Jones* v.
State, 71 Ind. 66), in others, seventeen days (*Comm.* v. *Cooper,* 5 Allen,
495; *Lowry* v. *State,* 12 Lea, 142), and in one case, four months
(*State* v. *Craine,* 120 N. C. 601).

The sense of impending death is deemed equivalent to the sanction
of an oath. Hence dying declarations made by persons disqualified
to act as witnesses in court are not competent, as *e. g.,* atheists (*Donnelly* v. *State,* 26 N. J. L. 463 and 601); but *aliter* in States where their
disability to testify has been removed (*People* v. *Chin Mook Sow,* 51
Cal. 597; *State* v. *Elliott,* 45 Ia. 486; see Art. 107, note, *post*). So the
declarations of very young children are not received (Gr. Ev. i. § 157),
or of a person who would be incompetent as a witness from mental
debility (*Mitchell* v. *State,* 71 Ga. 128, 146; cf. *Comm.* v. *Straesser,*
153 Pa. 451). As to the contradiction of dying declarations, see Art.
135, *post.*

Though dying declarations are deemed to have a sanction equal to
that of an oath, yet they are not of the same value and weight as the
direct evidence of a witness subject to cross-examination. *People* v.
Kraft, 148 N. Y. 631; cf. *State* v. *Reed,* 137 Mo. 125.]

[1][*People* v. *Knapp,* 1 Edm. Sel. Cas. 177. If the declarations be reduced to writing by a bystander, but are not read over to the dying
person, nor signed by him, parol evidence of the declarations is competent (*Allison* v. *Comm.,* 99 Pa. 17; *State* v. *Sullivan,* 51 Ia. 142;
Darby v. *State,* 92 Ala. 9); but the writing is not, though it may be
used to refresh memory (*State* v. *Fraunburg,* 40 Ia. 555). So parol
evidence was received when the memorandum was lost (*State* v.
Patterson, 45 Vt. 308). Where the writing was read over to decedent
and signed by him, it was held competent evidence, though it was not
so taken as to constitute a deposition (*State* v. *Kindle,* 47 O. St. 358;
People v. *Bemmerly,* 87 Cal. 117; *Jones* v. *State,* 71 Ind. 66); and
where it was subscribed and sworn to by him, but was inadmissible as
a deposition, its use to refresh recollection was held allowable (*Comm.*

Illustrations.

(*a*) The question is, whether A has murdered B.

B makes a statement to the effect that A murdered him.

B, at the time of making the statement, has no hope of recovery, though his doctor had such hopes, and B lives ten days after making the statement. The statement is deemed to be relevant.[1]

B, at the time of making the statement (which is written down), says something, which is taken down thus : " I make the above statement with the fear of death before me, and with no hope of recovery." B, on the statement being read over, corrects this to "with no hope *at present* of my recovery." B dies thirteen hours afterwards. The statement is deemed to be irrelevant.[2]

(*ab*) [A woman had been shot in the head, and the surgeon attending her had told her that she was liable to die at any moment ; that an operation which he would perform would be the only chance for her recovery. He asked her if she expected to get well, and she said : "No, I do not expect to get well, but I would like to get well." She then said that A was the person who shot her. On the trial of A for murder, this statement was held inadmissible.][3]

(*ac*) [The question is, whether A has murdered B.

B, having received a very dangerous wound in the neck, severing the jugular vein, raised the cry of "murder," and then, bleeding profusely, fell upon his bed. X, hearing the alarm, came quickly to the room, when B cried out that he had been stabbed, that he had been murdered, that his throat had been cut. X asked him who did it, and B answered: "A, your bookkeeper." B died about an hour and a

v. *Haney*, 127 Mass. 455; cf. *State* v. *Whitson*, 111 N. C. 695). Some cases, however, have held that the writing, if signed by the decedent, is the primary evidence, and that unless the absence of the writing is accounted for, parol evidence will not be received (Gr. Ev. i. § 161 ; *Boulden* v. *State*, 102 Ala. 78 ; *Turner* v. *State*, 89 Tenn. 548 ; *Saylor* v. *Comm.*, 97 Ky. 184).

Oral declarations may be testified to by any one who heard and remembers them, and he is only required to state their substance (*Comm.* v. *Haney*, supra ; *Montgomery* v. *State*, 11 O. 424 ; *Starkey* v. *People*, 17 Ill. 17); but they must be substantially complete. Gr. Ev. i. § 159; *State* v. *Patterson*, 45 Vt. 308.]

[1] *R.* v. *Mosley*, 1 Moo. C. C. 97 ; [cf. *People* v. *Grunzig*, 1 Park. Cr. 299.]
[2] *R.* v. *Jenkins*, L. R. 1 C. C. R. 187 ; [cf. *People* v. *Evans*, 40 Hun, 492 ; *People* v. *Hodgdon*, 55 Cal. 72 ; *Jackson* v. *Comm.*, 19 Gratt. 656.]
[3] [*Peak* v. *State*, 50 N. J. L. 179; cf. *Young* v. *State*, 95 Ala. 4.]

half afterwards. On the trial of A it was held that X might testify to this statement made by B.][1]

(*b*) The question is, whether A administered drugs to a woman with intent to procure abortion. The woman makes a statement which would have been admissible had A been on his trial for murder. The statement is deemed to be irrelevant[2]

(*c*) The question is, whether A murdered B. A dying declaration by C that he (C) murdered B is deemed to be irrelevant.[3]

(*d*) The question is, whether A murdered B.

B makes a statement before a magistrate on oath, and makes her mark to it, and the magistrate signs it, but not in the presence of A, so that her statement was not a deposition within the statute then in force. B, at the time when the statement was made, was in a dying state, and had no hope of recovery. The statement is deemed to be relevant.[4]

ARTICLE 27.*

DECLARATIONS MADE IN THE COURSE OF BUSINESS OR PROFESSIONAL DUTY.

A declaration is deemed to be relevant when it was made by the declarant in the ordinary course of business, and in the discharge of professional duty,[5] at or near the

---

* See Note XVIII. [Appendix].

[1] [*Donnelly* v. *State*, 26 N. J. L. 463 and 601.]

[2] *R.* v. *Hind*, Bell, 253, following *R.* v. *Hutchinson*, 2 B. & C. 608, n., quoted in a note to *R.* v. *Mead*. [*People* v. *Davis*, 56 N. Y. 95; *State* v. *Harper*, 35 O. St. 78; *Railing* v. *Comm.*, 110 Pa. 100. *Aliter*, upon a trial for murder or manslaughter, caused by an attempt to procure an abortion (*State* v. *Dickinson*, 41 Wis. 299; *State* v. *Leeper*, 70 Ia. 748; cf. *Montgomery* v. *State*, 80 Ind. 338). Now, however, in some States, by statute, dying declarations of the woman are admissible in a trial for an attempt to procure an abortion. N. Y. Rev. St. (Birdseye's 2d ed.) i. 6; Laws of Mass. of 1889, c. 100; *Comm.* v. *Bishop*, 165 Mass. 148.]

[3] *Gray's Case*, Ir. Cir. Rep. 76; [*People* v. *Hall*, 94 Cal. 595; *Davis* v. *Comm.*, 95 Ky. 19; *West* v. *State*, 76 Ala. 98.]

[4] *R.* v. *Woodcock*, 1 East, P.C. 356. In this case, Eyre, C. B., is said to have left to the jury the question, whether the deceased was not in fact under the apprehension of death. 1 Leach, 504. The case was decided in 1789. It is now settled that the question is for the judge.

[5] *Doe* v. *Turford*, 3 B. & Ad. 890. [Gr. Ev. i. §§ 115-120; *Chaffee* v. *U. S.*, 18 Wall. 516; *Fisher* v. *Mayor*, 67 N. Y. 73, 77; *Skipworth* v. *Deyell*, 83 Hun, 307; *Kennedy* v. *Doyle*, 10 Allen, 161; *Wheeler* v.

time when the matter stated occurred, and of his own knowledge.[1]

Walker, 45 N. H. 355; *Macomb* v *Wilkinson*, 83 Mich. 486; *Reynolds* v. *Sumner*, 126 Ill. 58; *Culver* v. *Marks*, 122 Ind. 554; *Sands* v. *Hammell*, 108 Ala. 624; *Laird* v. *Campbell*, 100 Pa. 159; *State* v. *Phair*, 48 Vt. 366. Thus the books or registers of a deceased notary are admissible to prove his acts as to the presentment, demand, and notice of non-payment of negotiable paper (*Halliday* v. *Martinet*, 20 Johns. 168; *Porter* v. *Judson*, 1 Gray, 175; *Nicholls* v. *Webb*, 8 Wheat. 326; see N. Y. Code Civ. Pro. §§ 924, 962); and so as to entries of the deceased clerk of a notary (*Gawtry* v. *Doane*, 51 N. Y. 84). So entries made by merchants' clerks, bank tellers or messengers, or by other persons, as attorneys, physicians, etc., in the ordinary course of business and of professional duty as part of the *res gestæ*, are competent after their death (*Leland* v. *Cameron*, 31 N. Y. 115; *Johnson* v. *Cowdrey*, 19 N. Y. S. 678; *Sheldon* v. *Benham*, 4 Hill, 129; *Arms* v. *Middleton*, 23 Barb. 571; *Hedrick* v. *Hughes*, 15 Wall. 123). In some States such evidence is admissible though the book entries may have been in favor of the person making them (*Lassone* v. *Boston, etc. R. Co.*, 66 N. H. 345; *Augusta* v. *Windsor*, 19 Me. 317; cf. *Donovan* v. *Boston, etc. R. Co.*, 158 Mass. 450). The handwriting of the deceased person should be proved (*Chaffee* v. *U. S.*, 18 Wall. 516; *Hoover* v. *Gehr*, 62 Pa. 136; *Chenango Bridge Co.* v. *Lewis*, 63 Barb. 111). In some States such evidence is also admitted if the person making the entries has become insane (*Union Bk.* v. *Knapp*, 3 Pick. 96), or has gone to parts unknown (*New Haven, etc. Co.* v. *Goodwin*, 42 Ct. 230; *Reynolds* v. *Manning*, 15 Md. 510; see *Chaffee* v. *U. S.*, supra), or is out of the State (*Heiskell* v. *Rollins*, 82 Md. 14; *McDonald* v. *Carnes*, 90 Ala. 147; *Rigby* v. *Logan*, 45 S. Car. 651; *Bridgewater* v. *Roxbury*, 54 Ct. 213; *Hay* v. *Kramer*, 2 W. & S. 137). In New York, however, if the clerk, etc., is out of the State, his deposition must be taken (*Brewster* v. *Doane*, 2 Hill, 537; *Fisher* v. *Mayor*, 67 N. Y. 73; but see Code Civ. Pro. § 924). But it is a general rule that if he is alive and within the State, he should be made a witness and authenticate the entries (*Ocean Bk.* v. *Carll*, 55 N. Y. 440; *Nelson* v. *Mayor of N. Y.*, 131 N. Y. 4; *Bartholomew* v. *Farwell*, 41 Ct. 107; *Briggs* v. *Rafferty*, 14 Gray, 525; *House* v. *Beak*, 141 Ill. 290). As to what is a sufficient authentication, see *Bank of Monroe* v. *Culver*, 2 Hill, 531; *Moots* v. *State*, 21 O. St. 653; *Anderson* v. *Edwards*, 123 Mass. 273. As to the admissibility of entries or memoranda, not made in the regular course of business, see Art. 136, note; *Taylor* v. *Chicago, etc. R. Co.*, 80 Ia. 431.]

[1] [It is a general rule in this country that entries *made by a party*

Such declarations are deemed to be irrelevant, except
so far as they relate to the matter which the declarant
stated in the ordinary course of his business or duty, or

---

himself in his own books of account, in the regular course of business,
are admissible in his own favor, when properly authenticated, as evidence of goods sold and delivered, of services rendered, and sometimes of other matters. But different modes of authentication are
prescribed in different States. Thus in New York it must be shown
by the party offering the books that they are the regular books of
account; that there had been regular dealings between the parties,
resulting in more than a single charge; that he kept no clerk; that
some of the articles charged have been delivered, or some items of
service rendered; and that other persons dealing with him have settled their accounts by his books and found them accurate (*Vosburgh*
v. *Thayer*, 12 Johns. 461; *West* v. *Van Tuyl*, 119 N. Y. 620; *Dooley*
v. *Moan*, 57 Hun, 535). This rule also prevails in Illinois (*House* v.
Beak, 141 Ill. 290). As to the meaning of "clerk" under the rule, see
McGoldrick v. *Traphagen*, 88 N. Y. 334; *Atwood* v. *Barney*, 80 Hun,
1; *Smith* v. *Smith*, 13 App. Div. (N. Y.) 207; as to a physician's books,
see *Knight* v. *Cunnington*, 6 Hun, 100; *Davis* v. *Seaman*, 64 Hun, 572.
But such entries are not admissible to sustain a charge for money lent
(*Low* v. *Payne*, 4 N. Y. 247), but only for sales and dealings in the
ordinary course of business (*Griesheimer* v. *Tanenbaum*, 124 N. Y.
650); books or entries relating to cash items or dealings between the
parties are not admissible (*Smith* v. *Rents*, 131 N. Y. 169). The fact
that parties are now competent witnesses does not exclude their books
as evidence (*Stroud* v. *Tilton*, 4 Abb. Dec. 324).

Book entries by a party *against* his interest are relevant as admissions (*Adams* v. *Olin*, 61 Hun, 318; *Griggs* v. *Day*, 136 N. Y. 152).

In many of the States the party's suppletory oath (or that of his executor or administrator if the party be dead) is required to authenticate
his own book entries which are in his own favor, but there are diverse
rules as to the matters which may be proved by such entries. Generally, however, they are received to prove items of work done and goods
sold and delivered, when the entries have been made in the regular
course of business (*Pratt* v. *White*, 132 Mass. 477; *Kaiser* v. *Alexander*, 144 Mass. 71; *Oberg* v. *Breen*, 50 N. J. L. 145; *Lyman* v.
Bechtel, 55 Ia. 437; *Corr* v. *Sellers*, 100 Pa. 169; *Smith* v. *Law*, 47
Ct. 431). As to the effect of making parties competent witnesses, see
Nichols v. *Haynes*, 78 Pa. 174; *Montague* v. *Dougan*, 68 Mich. 98.
The rules in the different States are stated in the note to *Price* v.
Torrington, S. L. C. (Am. Ed.) (See *Miller* v. *Shay*, 145 Mass. 162;

if they do not appear to be made by a person duly authorized to make them.[1]

Illustrations.

(*a*) The question is, whether A delivered certain beer to B.

The fact that a deceased drayman of A's, on the evening of the
delivery, made an entry to that effect in a book kept for the purpose,
in the ordinary course of business, is deemed to be relevant.[2]

Countryman v. *Bunker*, 101 Mich. 218 and note; *Stallings* v. *Gott-
schalk*, 77 Md. 429; *Hooper* v. *Taylor*, 39 Me. 224; *Anchor Milling
Co.* v. *Walsh*, 108 Mo. 277; *White* v. *Whitney*, 82 Cal. 163; *Schettler*
v. *Jones*, 20 Wis. 433; *Karr* v. *Stivers*, 34 Ia. 123; *Wells' Adm'r* v.
Ayers, 84 Va. 341.)

The book to be produced in evidence is the *book of original entries*
(*Woolsey* v. *Bohn*, 41 Minn. 235; *Stetson* v. *Wolcott*, 15 Gray, 545).
If this be a ledger, it will be competent (*Hoover* v. *Gehr*, 62 Pa. 136;
Swain v. *Cheney*, 41 N. H. 232; *Faxon* v. *Hollis*, 13 Mass. 427); but
not where the ledger is used for posting entries originally made in
another book (*Vilmar* v. *Schall*, 3 J. & Sp. 67; *Fitzgerald* v. *McCarty*,
55 Ia. 702; *Huston's Estate*, 167 Pa. 217). Sometimes day-book and
ledger are taken together as the book of original entries (*McGoldrick*
v. *Traphagen*, 88 N. Y. 334; *Bonnell* v. *Mawha*, 37 N. J. L. 198).

Sometimes entries or memoranda are first made upon a slate or
paper, and afterwards transcribed into the regular account books.
Where this is done on the same day or within two or three days, as
a common business practice, the books are generally admitted in
evidence (*Stroud* v. *Tilton*, 4 Abb. Dec. 324; *McGoldrick* v. *Traphagen*, 88 N. Y. 334; *Van Wie* v. *Loomis*, 77 Hun, 399; *Nichols* v.
Vinson, 9 Houst. 274; *Chisholm* v. *Beaman Co.*, 160 Ill. 101; *Hoover*
v. *Gehr*, 62 Pa. 136; *Barker* v. *Haskell*, 9 Cush. 218). But sometimes
they have been admitted after a much longer interval (*Hall* v. *Glidden*,
39 Me. 445, two to four weeks; *Redlich* v. *Bauerlee*, 98 Ill. 134, four
weeks). But in *Forsythe* v. *Norcross*, 5 Watts, 432, a six days' interval was held too long (cf. *Rumsey* v. *N. Y. etc. Telephone Co.*, 49 N. J.
L. 322). As to the mode of proof when the party is dead or insane,
see *Hoover* v. *Gehr*, 62 Pa. 136; *Pratt* v. *White*, 132 Mass. 477; *Holbrook* v. *Gay*, 6 Cush. 215.]

[1] [*Skipworth* v. *Deyell*, 83 Hun, 307; *Riley* v. *Boehm*, 167 Mass. 183;
Fulton's Estate, 178 Pa. 78; *Burley* v. *German-American Bk.*, 111 U.
S. 216; and cases *supra*.]

[2] *Price* v. *Torrington*, 1 S. L. C. 328, 7th ed.

(*b*) The question is, what were the contents of a letter not produced after notice.

A copy entered immediately after the letter was written, in a book kept for that purpose, by a deceased clerk, is deemed to be relevant.[1]

(*c*) The question is, whether A was arrested at Paddington, or in South Molton Street.

A certificate annexed to the writ by a deceased sheriff's officer, and returned by him to the sheriff, is deemed to be relevant so far as it relates to the fact of the arrest; but irrelevant so far as it relates to the place where the arrest took place.[2]

(*d*) The course of business was for A, a workman in a coal-pit, to tell B, the foreman, what coals were sold, and for B (who could not write) to get C to make entries in a book accordingly.

The entries (A and B being dead) are deemed to be irrelevant, because B, for whom they were made, did not know them to be true.[3]

(*e*) The question is, what is A's age. A statement by the incumbent in a register of baptisms that he was baptized on a given day is deemed to be relevant. A statement in the same register that he was born on a given day is deemed to be irrelevant, because it was not the incumbent's duty to make it.[4]

---

[1] *Pritt* v. *Fairclough*, 3 Camp. 305.

[2] *Chambers* v. *Bernasconi*, 1 C. M. & R. 347 ; see, too, *Smith* v. *Blakey*, L. R. 2 Q. B. 326.

[3] *Brain* v. *Preece*, 11 M. & W. 773. [S. P. *Gould* v. *Conway*, 59 Barb. 355 ; *Kent* v. *Garvin*, 1 Gray, 148 ; *Chaffee* v. *U. S.*, 18 Wall. 516, 543 ; *Hoffman* v. *N. Y. C. R. Co.*, 14 J. & Sp. 526, 87 N. Y. 25 ; *Thomas* v. *Price*, 30 Md. 483. Entries made in the usual course of business upon information communicated by others have, however, been held competent, when their correctness is authenticated by the testimony of those who made such reports and entries, or by other satisfactory proof. *Payne* v. *Hodge*, 7 Hun, 612, 71 N. Y. 598 ; *Mayor of N. Y.* v. *Second Ave. R. Co.*, 102 N. Y. 572 ; *Chisholm* v. *Beaman Co.*, 160 Ill. 101 ; *Chicago Lumbering Co.* v. *Hewitt*, 64 F. R. 314 ; *Harwood* v. *Mulry*, 8 Gray, 250 ; *Smith* v. *Law*, 47 Ct. 431 ; cf. *Chateaugay Iron Co.* v. *Blake*, 144 U. S. 476 ; *Cobb* v. *Wells*, 124 N. Y. 77 ; *Powers* v. *Savin*, 64 Hun, 560, 139 N. Y. 652.]

[4] *R.* v. *Clapham*, 4 C. & P. 29. [*Durfee* v. *Abbott*, 61 Mich. 471 ; *Whitcher* v. *McLaughlin*, 115 Mass. 167 ; *Blackburn* v. *Crawfords*, 3 Wall. 175 ; *Weaver* v. *Leiman*, 52 Md. 708 ; *Sitler* v. *Gehr*, 105 Pa. 577 ; see *Hunt* v. *Order of Friends*, 64 Mich. 671. So as to a register of marriages (*Maxwell* v. *Chapman*, 8 Barb. 579); and a hospital

(*f*) The question is, whether A was married. Proceedings in a college book, which ought to have been, but was not, signed by the registrar of the college, were held to be irrelevant.[1]

ARTICLE 28.*

DECLARATIONS AGAINST INTEREST.

A declaration is deemed to be relevant if the declarant had peculiar means of knowing the matter stated, if he had no interest to misrepresent it, and if it was opposed to his pecuniary or proprietary interest.[2] The whole of any such declaration, and of any other statement referred to in it, is deemed to be relevant, although matters may be stated which were not against the pecuniary or pro-

---

* See Note XIX. [Appendix].

record. *Townsend* v. *Pepperell*, 99 Mass. 40 ; see *Butler* v. *St. Louis Ins. Co.*, 45 Ia. 93.]

[1] *Fox* v. *Bearblock*, 17 Ch. Div. 429.

[2] These are almost the exact words of Bayley, J., in *Gleadow* v. *Atkin*, 1 C. & M. 423. The interest must not be too remote. *Smith* v. *Blakey*, L. R. 2 Q. B. 326. [Gr. Ev. i. §§ 147–155; *Lyon* v. *Ricker*, 141 N. Y. 225; *Chenango Bridge Co.* v. *Paige*, 83 N. Y. 178, 192; *Brennan* v. *Hall*, 131 N. Y. 160; *Taylor* v. *Gould*, 57 Pa. 152; *Hobensack* v. *Hallman*, 17 id. 154, 158; *Hart* v. *Kendall*, 82 Ala. 144; *Bartlett* v. *Patton*, 33 W. Va. 71; *Lamar* v. *Pearre*, 90 Ga. 377; *Scott Co.* v. *Fluke*, 34 Ia. 317; *Zimmerman* v. *Bloom*, 43 Minn. 163; *Dean* v. *Wilkerson*, 126 Ind. 338; cf. *Lassone* v. *Boston, etc. R. Co.*, 66 N. H. 345; *Chase* v. *Smith*, 5 Vt. 556; *Bird* v. *Hueston*, 10 O. St. 418. The doctrine is also recognized in *dicta* in *Comm.* v. *Densmore*, 12 Allen, 537; *Dwight* v. *Brown*, 9 Ct. 83, 92. The declarant must be dead (Id.; *Trammell* v. *Hudmon*, 78 Ala. 222). The statement in *Lawrence* v. *Kimball*, 1 Met. 527, that the rule applies only to written entries or statements, and not to oral declarations, is contrary to the weight of authority. *R.* v. *Exeter*, L. R. 4 Q. B. 341; *County of Mahaska* v. *Ingalls*, 16 Ia. 81; *White* v. *Chouteau*, 10 Barb. 202; *Baker* v. *Taylor*, 54 Minn. 71.]

prietary interest of the declarant;[1] but statements, not
referred to in, or necessary to explain such declarations, are not deemed to be relevant merely because
they were made at the same time or recorded in the
same place.[2]

A declaration may be against the pecuniary interest of
the person who makes it, if part of it charges him with a
liability, though other parts of the book or document in
which it occurs may discharge him from such liability in
whole or in part, and (it seems) though there may be no
proof other than the statement itself either of such liability or of its discharge in whole or in part.[3]

A statement made by a declarant holding a limited
interest in any property and opposed to such interest is
deemed to be relevant only as against those who claim
under him, and not as against the reversioner.[4]

An indorsement or memorandum of a payment made
upon any promissory note, bill of exchange, or other
writing, by or on behalf of the party to whom such payment was made, is not sufficient proof of such payment
to take the case out of the operation of the Statutes of
Limitation;[5] but any such declaration made in any other
form by, or by the direction of, the person to whom the
payment was made is, when such person is dead, sufficient proof for the purpose aforesaid.[6]

Any indorsement or memorandum to the effect above
mentioned made upon any bond or other specialty by
a deceased person, is regarded as a declaration against

---

[1] [*Livingston* v. *Arnoux*, 56 N. Y. 507 ; *Elsworth* v. *Muldoon*, 15
Abb. Pr. (N. S.) 440, 448.]

[2] Illustrations (*a*), (*b*) and (*c*).

[3] Illustrations (*d*) and (*e*).

[4] Illustration (*g*); see Lord Campbell's judgment in case quoted,
p. 177.

[5] 9 Geo. IV. c. 14, s. 3.

[6] *Bradley* v. *James*, 13 C. B. 822. *Newbould* v. *Smith*, 29 Ch. Div.

the proprietary interest of the declarant for the purpose above mentioned, if it is shown to have been made at the time when it purports to have been made;[1] but it is uncertain whether the date of such indorsement or memorandum may be presumed to be correct without independent evidence.[2]

Statements of relevant facts opposed to any other than the pecuniary or proprietary interest of the declarant are not deemed to be relevant as such.[3]

877, seems scarcely consistent with this. It was a decision of North, J. On appeal, 33 Ch. Div. 138, the court expressed no opinion on the admissibility of the entry rejected by North, J.

[1] 3 & 4 Will. IV. c. 42, which is the Statute of Limitations relating to specialties, has no provision similar to 9 Geo. IV. c. 14, s. 3. Hence, in this case the ordinary rule is unaltered.

[2] See the question discussed in 1 Ph. Ev. 302-5, and T. E. ss. 625-9, and see Article 85. [The general rule in this country, independently of statute, is that an indorsement on a bond, bill, note, etc., made by the obligee or promisee, without the privity of the debtor, cannot be admitted as evidence of payment in favor of the party making such indorsement, unless it be shown that it was made at a time when its operation would be against the interest of the party making it,—that is, before the statute has barred the claim. The date of the indorsement is not sufficient to show this, but there must be independent evidence to this point. But it is not necessary that the declarant be dead, in order that the indorsement be received in evidence. Indorsements by the debtor, or with his consent and privity, are competent. (*Mills* v. *Davis*, 113 N. Y. 243; *In re Kellogg*, 104 N. Y. 648; *Runner's Appeal*, 121 Pa. 649; *Coon's Appeal*, 52 Ct. 186; *Haver* v. *Schwyhart*, 39 Mo. App. 303; *Hamilton* v. *Coffin*, 45 Kan. 556; *Curtis* v. *Daughdrill*, 71 Ala. 590; *Clough* v. *McDaniel*, 58 N. H. 201; *White* v. *Beaman*, 85 N. C. 3; *Clark* v. *Burn*, 86 Pa. 502.) Sometimes a similar rule is established by statute (*Young* v. *Perkins*, 29 Minn. 173).

A number of the States have statutes similar to the present English statute (9 Geo. IV. c. 14), stated in the text. Mass. Pub. St. c. 197, s. 16; Me. Rev. St. c. 81, s. 100; *Libby* v. *Brown*, 78 Me. 492; *Rogers* v. *Anderson*, 40 Mich. 290; N. J. Rev. p. 596; Ind. Rev. St. s. 303; Wis. Rev. St. s. 4247.]

[3] Illustration (*h*). [*United States* v. *Mulholland*, 50 F. R. 413; *Maine* v. *People*, 9 Hun, 113.]

Illustrations.

(*a*) The question is, whether a person was born on a particular day.

An entry in the book of a deceased man-midwife in these words is deemed to be relevant :[1]

> "W. Fowden, Junr.'s wife,
> Filius circa hor. 3 post merid. natus H.
> W. Fowden, Junr.,
> App. 22, filius natus,
> Wife, £1 6*s.* 1*d.*
> Pd. 25 Oct., 1768."

(*b*) The question is, whether a certain custom exists in a part of a parish.

The following entries in the parish books, signed by deceased church-wardens, are deemed to be relevant :—

"It is our ancient custom thus to proportion church-lay. The chapelry of Haworth pay one-fifth, etc."

Followed by—

"Received of Haworth, who this year disputed this our ancient custom, but after we had sued him, paid it accordingly,—£8, and £1 for costs."[2]

(*c*) The question is, whether a gate on certain land, the property of which is in dispute, was repaired by A.

An account by a deceased steward, in which he charges A with the expense of repairing the gate, is deemed to be irrelevant, though it would have been deemed to be relevant if it had appeared that A admitted the charge.[3]

(*d*) The question is, whether A received rent for certain land.

A deceased steward's account, charging himself with the receipt of such rent for A, is deemed to be relevant, although the balance of the whole account is in favor of the steward.[4]

(*e*) The question is, whether certain repairs were done at A's expense.

A bill for doing them, receipted by a deceased carpenter, is deemed to be $\left\{ \begin{matrix} \text{relevant,}[5] \\ \text{irrelevant,}[6] \end{matrix} \right\}$ there being no other evidence either that the repairs were done or that the money was paid.

---

[1] *Higham* v. *Ridgway,* 2 S. L. C. 318, 7th ed.
[2] *Stead* v. *Heaton,* 4 T. R. 669.
[3] *Doe* v. *Beviss,* 7 C. B. 456.
[4] *Williams* v. *Graves,* 8 C. & P. 592.
[5] *R.* v. *Heyford,* note to *Higham* v. *Ridgway,* 2 S. L. C. 333, 7th ed.
[6] *Doe* v. *Vowles,* 1 Mo. & Ro. 261. In *Taylor* v. *Witham,* 3 Ch. Div.

(*f*) The question is, whether A (deceased) gained a settlement in the parish of B by renting a tenement.

A statement made by A, whilst in possession of a house, that he had paid rent for it, is deemed to be relevant, because it reduces the interest which would otherwise be inferred from the fact of A's possession.[1]

(*g*) The question is, whether there is a right of common over a certain field.

A statement by A, a deceased tenant for a term of the land in question, that he had no such right, is deemed to be relevant as against his successors in the term, but not as against the owner of the field.[2]

(*h*) The question is, whether A was lawfully married to B.

A statement by a deceased clergyman that he performed the marriage under circumstances which would have rendered him liable to a criminal prosecution is not deemed to be relevant as a statement against interest.[3]

ARTICLE 29.

DECLARATIONS BY TESTATORS AS TO CONTENTS OF WILL.

The declarations of a deceased testator as to his testamentary intentions, and as to the contents of his will, are deemed to be relevant

when his will has been lost, and when there is a question as to what were its contents;[4] and

---

605, Jessel, M. R., followed *R.* v. *Heyford*, and dissented from *Doe* v. *Vowles*.

[1] *R.* v. *Exeter*, L. R. 4 Q. B. 341.

[2] *Papendick* v. *Bridgewater*, 5 E. & B. 166. [See *Lyon* v. *Ricker*, 141 N. Y. 225 ; *Lamar* v. *Pearre*, 90 Ga. 377.]

[3] *Sussex Peerage Case*, 11 C. & F. 108.

[4] [*In re Page*, 118 Ill. 576; *Southworth* v. *Adams*, 11 Biss. 256; *McDonald* v. *McDonald*, 142 Ind. 55; *In re Lambie*, 97 Mich. 49; *Valentine's Will*, 93 Wis. 45; *Pickens* v. *Davis*, 134 Mass. 252; *In re Johnson's Will*, 40 Ct. 587; *Collagan* v. *Burns*, 57 Me. 449; *Behrens* v. *Behrens*, 47 O. St. 323; *Byers* v. *Hoppe*, 61 Md. 206; *Apperson* v. *Dowdy*, 82 Va. 776; *Harris* v. *Knight*, L. R. 15 P. D. 170; cf. *Mutual Life Ins. Co.* v. *Hillmon*, 145 U. S. 285, 298; *Gardner* v. *Gardner*, 177 Pa. 218. It is provided in New York by statute that in an action to

when the question is whether an existing will is genuine or was improperly obtained ;[1] and

when the question is whether any and which of more existing documents than one constitute his will.[2]

In all these cases it is immaterial whether the declarations were made before or after the making or loss of the will.[3]

ARTICLE 30.*

DECLARATIONS AS TO PUBLIC AND GENERAL RIGHTS.

Declarations are deemed to be relevant (subject to the third condition mentioned in the next Article) when they

---

* See Note XX. [Appendix]. Also see *Weeks* v. *Sparke*, 1 M. & S. 679; *Crease* v. *Barrett*, 1 C. M. & R. 917. Article 5 has much in common with this Article. Lord Blackburn's judgment in *Neill* v. *Duke of Devonshire*, 8 App. Cas. 186-7, especially explains the law.

---

establish a lost or destroyed will, or in an application to have it admitted to probate, its provisions must be proved by at least two credible witnesses, a correct copy or draft being equal to one witness (Code Civ. Pro. §§ 1865, 2621 ; *Everitt* v. *Everitt*, 41 Barb. 385). That evidence of the testator's declarations as to its contents may be received in such cases, see *Hatch* v. *Sigman*, 1 Demarest, 519. But in certain proceedings of other kinds it is held that proof by one witness is sufficient. *Harris* v. *Harris*, 26 N. Y. 433 ; *Upton* v. *Bernstein*, 73 Hun, 516.]

[1] [See Art. 11, Illustration (*o*); *Taylor Will Case*, 10 Abb. Pr. (N. S.) 300 ; *Crispell* v. *Dubois*, 4 Barb. 393 ; *Hoppe* v. *Byers*, 60 Md. 381 ; cf. *Beadles* v. *Alexander*, 9 Baxt. 604 ; *Boylan* v. *Meeker*, 28 N. J. L. 274.]

[2] [*Valentine's Will*, 93 Wis. 45. In New York it is essential to the valid execution of a will that the testator declare to the attesting witnesses that it is his last will and testament (2 R. S. * 63, s. 38). This is called the "publication" of the will. Evidence of such declarations is accordingly receivable upon a proceeding for the admission of the will to probate. Or his assent to such declarations, when made for him by others in his presence, may be enough (*Gilbert* v. *Knox*, 52 N. Y. 125 ; *Lane* v. *Lane*, 95 N. Y. 494). And similar evidence is received in other States. *Elkinton* v. *Brick*, 44 N. J. Eq. 154 ; *Denny* v. *Pinney*, 60 Vt. 524 ; *Estate of Johnson*, 57 Cal. 529.]

[3] *Sugden* v. *St. Leonards*, L. R. 1 P. D. (C. A.) 154. [This is cited by

relate to the existence of any public or general right or custom or matter of public or general interest.¹ But declarations as to particular facts from which the existence of any such public or general right or custom or

---

the author as authority for the whole Article.] In questions between the heir and the legatee or devisee, such statements would probably be relevant as admissions by a privy in law, estate, or blood (*Gould* v. *Lakes*, L. R. 6 P. D. 1 ; *Doe* v. *Palmer*, 16 Q. B. 747). The decision in this last case at p. 757, followed by *Quick* v. *Quick*, 3 Sw. & Tr. 442, is overruled by *Sugden* v. *St. Leonards*. [Since the decision of *Sugden* v. *St. Leonards*, it has been questioned in the English House of Lords whether post-testamentary declarations of a testator as to the contents of his will should be deemed admissible. *Woodward* v. *Goulstone*, 11 App. Cas. 469 ; cf. *Atkinson* v. *Morris*, [1897] P. 40.]

¹ [The general doctrine of this Article is fully recognized in this country (Gr. Ev. i. §§ 127-140, 145 ; *Ellicott* v. *Pearl*, 10 Pet. 412 ; *Shuttle* v. *Thompson*, 15 Wall. 151 ; *McKinnon* v. *Bliss*, 21 N. Y. 206, 218 ; *People* v. *Velarde*, 59 Cal. 457 ; *Drury* v. *Midland R. Co.*, 127 Mass. 571 ; *Wooster* v. *Butler*, 13 Ct. 309 ; *Birmingham* v. *Anderson*, 40 Pa. 506 ; *Hampson* v. *Taylor*, 15 R. I. 83 ; *Young* v. *Kansas City, etc. R. Co.*, 39 Mo. App. 52 ; *Mullaney* v. *Duffy*, 145 Ill. 559). Thus the boundaries established by the United States surveys are provable by such evidence of common repute, when the monuments have disappeared (*Thoen* v. *Roche*, 57 Minn. 135). But in many States evidence is also received of the declarations of deceased persons as to the *boundaries of private estates ;* but the limitations of this doctrine are different in different States. In some States such declarations, if made by one in possession of land owned by him, while he was pointing out the boundaries on the land itself, are admissible, when nothing appears to show an interest to deceive or misrepresent ; the declarations are part of the *res gestæ* (*Long* v. *Colton*, 116 Mass. 414 ; *Robinson* v. *Dewhurst*, 68 F. R. 336 ; *Royal* v. *Chandler*, 83 Me. 150). In other States the declarations of deceased surveyors, made while they were surveying the land, or of other deceased persons having special means of knowledge of the facts stated, made while they were pointing out or describing the boundaries, are deemed competent, if no interest to misrepresent appears (*Kramer* v. *Goodlander*, 98 Pa. 366 ; *Clement* v. *Packer*, 125 U. S. 309 ; *Lemmon* v. *Hartsook*, 80 Mo. 13 ; *Powers* v. *Silsby*, 41 Vt. 288 ; *Smith* v. *Forrest*, 49 N. H. 230 ; *Kinney* v. *Farnsworth*, 17 Ct. 355 ; *Fry* v. *Stowers*, 92 Va. 13 ; *Bethea* v. *Byrd*, 95 N. C. 309 ; contra, *Chapman* v. *Twitchell*, 37 Me. 59 ; cf. *Jackson* v. *McCall*, 10 Johns. 377) ; though such declarations

matter of public or general interest may be inferred, are deemed to be irrelevant.[1]

A right is public if it is common to all her Majesty's subjects,[2] and declarations as to public rights are relevant whoever made them.

A right or custom is general if it is common to any considerable number of persons, as the inhabitants of a parish, or the tenants of a manor.

Declarations as to general rights are deemed to be relevant only when they were made by persons who are shown, to the satisfaction of the judge, or who appear from the circumstances of their statement, to have had competent means of knowledge.

Such declarations may be made in any form and manner.

Illustrations.

(a) The question is, whether a road is public.

A statement by A (deceased) that it is public is deemed to be relevant.[3]

---

relate to "particular facts" showing boundaries, they are still held admissible in many of these States (Id.; *Hunnicutt* v. *Peyton*, 102 U.S. 333). So ancient deeds, wills, and other solemn instruments are sometimes deemed competent to prove matters of a private nature, though evidence of verbal declarations would be excluded (*Oldtown* v. *Shapleigh*, 33 Me. 278; *Greenfield* v. *Camden*, 74 Me. 56; *Ward* v. *Oxford*, 8 Pick. 476; see *Wright* v. *Boston*, 126 Mass. 161).

When private and public boundaries coincide, evidence of reputation as to the latter will avail to prove the former. *Curtis* v. *Aaronson*, 49 N. J. L. 68, 76; *Mullaney* v. *Duffy*, 145 Ill. 559.]

[1] [*Hall* v. *Mayo*, 97 Mass. 416; *S. W. School Dist.* v. *Williams*, 48 Ct. 504; *Fraser* v. *Hunter*, 5 Cr. C. C. 470. So declarations concerning *private rights* are, in general, deemed to be irrelevant (Id.; *Boston, etc. Co.* v. *Hanlon*, 132 Mass. 483; *Curtis* v. *Aaronson*, 49 N. J. L. 68); but see last note as to private boundaries.]

[2] [Or in this country, to all the citizens of the State; the "whoever" which follows would apply to any such citizen. Gr. Ev. i. § 128.]

[3] *Crease* v. *Barrett*, per Parke, B., 1 C. M. & R. 929.

A statement by A (deceased) that he planted a willow (still standing) to show where the boundary of the road had been when he was a boy is deemed to be irrelevant.[1]

(*ab*) [The question is, whether certain fences and trees have been placed by A on his own land or within the limits of the public highway.

Old men who lived in the vicinity of the highway fifty years or more ago may be allowed to state where the line of the highway was reputed to be when they were young men.

Extracts from ancient records of the town, showing the boundaries of the highway when laid out, are deemed to be relevant.][2]

(*b*) The following are instances of the manner in which declarations as to matters of public and general interest may be made:—They may be made in

Maps prepared by, or by the direction of, persons interested in the matter;[3]

Copies of court rolls;[4]

Deeds and leases between private persons;[5]

Verdicts, judgments, decrees, and orders of courts, and similar bodies,[6] if final.[7]

ARTICLE 31.*

DECLARATIONS AS TO PEDIGREE.

A declaration is deemed to be relevant (subject to the conditions hereinafter mentioned), if it relates to the existence of any relationship between persons, whether

---

* See Note XXI. [Appendix].

[1] *R.* v. *Bliss,* 7 A. & E. 550.

[2] [*State* v. *Vale Mills,* 63 N. H. 4.]

[3] Implied in *Hammond* v. *Bradstreet,* 10 Ex. 390, and *Pipe* v. *Fulcher,* 1 E. & E. 111. In each of these cases the map was rejected as not properly qualified. [Cf. *McCausland* v. *Fleming,* 63 Pa. 36; *Smith* v. *Forrest,* 49 N. H. 230; see p. 115, *post,* note 2.]

[4] *Crease* v. *Barrett,* 1 C. M. & R. 928.

[5] *Plaxton* v. *Dare,* 10 B. & C. 17; [*Drury* v. *Midland R. Co.,* 127 Mass. 571.]

[6] *Duke of Newcastle* v. *Broxtowe,* 4 B. & Ad. 273; [*Willey* v. *Portsmouth,* 35 N. H. 303.]

[7] *Pim* v. *Currell,* 6 M. & W. 234, 266.

living or dead, or to the birth, marriage, or death of
any person, by which such relationship was constituted,
or to the time or place at which any such fact occurred,
or to any fact immediately connected with its occurrence.[1]

Such declarations may express either the personal
knowledge of the declarant, or information given to him
by other persons qualified to be declarants, but not information collected by him from persons not qualified to
be declarants.[2] They may be made in any form and in

---

[1] Illustration (a). [*Eisenlord* v. *Clum*, 126 N. Y. 552; *Jackson* v.
King, 5 Cow. 237; *Haddock* v. *B. & M. R. Co.*, 3 Allen, 298; *Fulker-
son* v. *Holmes*, 117 U. S. 389; *Pickens's Estate*, 163 Pa. 14; *Shorten* v.
Judd, 56 Kan. 43; *Robbs' Estate*, 37 S. Car. 19; *Jackson* v. *Jackson*, 80
Md. 176; *Weaver* v. *Leiman*, 52 Md. 708; *Van Sickle* v. *Gibson*, 40
Mich. 170; *Cuddy* v. *Brown*, 78 Ill. 415; *Morrill* v. *Foster*, 33 N. H.
379; *Eaton* v. *Tallmadge*, 24 Wis. 217; *Dawson* v. *Mayall*, 45 Minn.
408. The declarant must be dead (Id.; *Mooers* v. *Bunker*, 29 N. H. 420).
But such evidence is not generally received in this country to show
the *place*, though it is deemed competent to show the *time*, of birth,
marriage, or death (*Adams* v. *Swansea*, 116 Mass. 591, 596; *McCarty*
v. *Terry*, 7 Lans. 236; *Union* v. *Plainfield*, 39 Ct. 563; *Greenfield* v.
Camden, 74 Me. 56; *Tyler* v. *Flanders*, 57 N. H. 618; *Swink* v. *French*,
11 Lea, 78; but see *Byers* v. *Wallace*, 87 Tex. 503, 511; *Wise* v.
Wynn, 59 Miss. 588; *Jackson* v. *Jackson*, 80 Md. 176). A person's
age may be a question of pedigree (*Watson* v. *Brewster*, 1 Pa. 381;
Conn. Life Ins. Co. v. *Schwenk*, 94 U. S. 593, 598), and he may testify
to his own age, stating what he learned thereon from deceased parents,
from family tradition, etc. (*State* v. *Marshall*, 137 Mo. 463; *Comm.* v.
Stevenson, 142 Mass. 466; *State* v. *McClain*, 49 Kan. 730; *Morrison*
v. *Emsley*, 53 Mich. 564; *People* v. *Ratz*, 115 Cal. 132; *Holton* v. *Man-
teuffel*, 51 Minn. 185; *Stevenson* v. *Kaiser*, 29 N. Y. S. 1122); sometimes his testimony has been received, though his parents were still
living (*West Virginia* v. *Cain*, 9 W. Va. 559; *Pearce* v. *Kyzer*, 16 Lea,
521; cf. *Kreitz* v. *Behrensmeyer*, 125 Ill. 141). The personal appearance of the person whose age is in question may also be considered
by the jury. *Hermann* v. *State*, 73 Wis. 248; *Comm.* v. *Phillips*, 162
Mass. 504.]

[2] *Davies* v. *Lowndes*, 6 M. & G. 527. [*Jewell's Lessee* v. *Jewell*,
1 How. (U. S.) 219, 231; *Eisenlord* v. *Clum*, 126 N. Y. 552, 565.]

any document or upon anything in which statements as to relationship are commonly made.[1]

The conditions above referred to are as follows—

(1) Such declarations are deemed to be relevant only in cases in which the pedigree to which they relate is in issue, and not to cases in which it is only relevant to the issue ;[2]

(2) They must be made by a declarant shown to be legitimately related by blood to the person to whom they relate ; or by the husband or wife of such a person.[3]

---

[1] Illustration (c).

[2] Illustration (b). [*Comm.* v. *Felch*, 132 Mass. 22 ; but see *North Brookfield* v. *Warren*, 16 Gray, 174. Thus birth, marriage, and death cannot be proved by such evidence in cases in which pedigree is not in issue. *Blaisdell* v. *Bickum*, 139 Mass. 250 ; *Eisenlord* v. *Clum*, 126 N. Y. 552, 566 ; *Ross* v. *Loomis*, 64 Ia. 432.]

[3] *Shrewsbury Peerage Case*, 7 H. L. C. 26. For Scotch law, see *Lauderdale Peerage Case*, 10 App. Cas. 692 ; also *Lovat Peerage Case*, Id. 763. In *In re Turner, Glenister* v. *Harding*, 29 Ch. Div. 985, a declaration by a deceased reputed father of his daughter's illegitimacy was admitted on grounds not very clear to me, and on the authority of two Nisi Prius cases, *Morris* v. *Davies*, 3 C. & P. 215, and 1 Mo. & Rô. 269. See note to Art. 34. [The rule generally stated in American cases is that the pedigree of a person may be shown by the declarations of deceased persons related to him by blood or marriage (Gr. Ev. i. § 103 ; *Northrop* v. *Hale*, 76 Me. 306 ; *Haddock* v. *B. & M. R. Co.*, 3 Allen, 298 ; *Sitler* v. *Gehr*, 105 Pa: 577 ; *Conn. Life Ins. Co.* v. *Schwenk*, 94 U. S. 593, 598). But whether all relatives by marriage, both near and remote, are competent to make such declarations is undetermined (see *People* v. *Fulton Fire Ins. Co.*, 25 Wend. 205). In *Jewell's Lessee* v. *Jewell*, 1 How. (U. S.) 219, the declarations of a deceased husband, that the parents of his wife were not married, were received. So the declarations or conduct of deceased persons may be shown to prove their children or grandchildren illegitimate (*Haddock* v. *B. & M. R. Co.*, 3 Allen, 298 ; but see *Flora* v. *Anderson*, 75 F. R. 217), or to prove legitimacy (*Kenyon* v. *Ashbridge*, 35 Pa. 157 ; cf. *Alexander* v. *Chamberlain*, 1 T. & C. 600). The declarations of a deceased woman have been received to show her sister's son to be illegitimate (*Northrop* v. *Hale*, 76 Me. 306). But the relationship of the declarant must in any case

(3) They must be made before the question in relation to which they are to be proved has arisen; but they do not cease to be deemed to be relevant because they were made for the purpose of preventing the question from arising.[1]

This condition applies also to statements as to public and general rights or customs and matters of public and general interest.

Illustrations.

(*a*) The question is, which of three sons (Fortunatus, Stephanus, and Achaicus) born at a birth is the eldest.

The fact that the father said that Achaicus was the youngest, and he took their names from St. Paul's Epistles (see 1 Cor. xvi. 17), and the fact that a relation present at the birth said that she tied a string round the second child's arm to distinguish it, are relevant.[2]

(*b*) The question is, whether A, sued for the price of horses and pleading infancy, was on a given day an infant or not.

The fact that his father stated in an affidavit in a chancery suit, to

---

be shown by other evidence than the declarations themselves (*Blackburn* v. *Crawfords*, 3 Wall. 175; *Lamoreaux* v. *Att'y General*, 89 Mich. 146; *Thompson* v. *Woolf*, 8 Or. 454); it is said, however, that only slight proof of such relationship will be required (*Fulkerson* v. *Holmes*, 117 U. S. 389; see *Northrop* v. *Hale*, 76 Me. 306, 309).

The declarations of deceased neighbors, acquaintances, servants, or other strangers are not competent evidence. *In re Seabury*, 1 App. Div. (N. Y.) 231; *Chapman* v. *Chapman*, 2 Ct. 347; *Carnes* v. *Crandall*, 10 Ia. 377; *De Haven* v. *De Haven*, 77 Ind. 236; and cases supra; contra, *Carter* v. *Montgomery*, 2 Tenn. Ch. 216.]

[1] *Berkeley Peerage Case*, 4 Camp. 401–417; and see *Lovat Peerage Case*, 10 App. Cas. 797. [The form in which this rule is usually stated is that the declarations must have been made *ante litem motam*, i. e., before a controversy arose about the matter. *People* v. *Fulton Fire Ins. Co.*, 25 Wend. 205; *Stein* v. *Bowman*, 13 Pet. 209; *Chapman* v. *Chapman*, 2 Ct. 347; *Northrop* v. *Hale*, 76 Me. 306; *Metheny* v. *Bohn*, 160 Ill. 263; *Comm.* v. *Felch*, 132 Mass. 23; *Barnum* v. *Barnum*, 42 Md. 251, 304; *Caujolle* v. *Ferrié*, 23 N. Y. 90, 104.]

[2] Vin. Abr. *tit.* Evidence, T. b. 91. The report calls the son Achicus.

which the plaintiff was not a party, that A was born on a certain day, is irrelevant.[1]

(c) The question is, whether one of the *cestuis que vie* in a lease for lives is living.

The fact that he was believed in his family to be dead is deemed to be irrelevant, as the question is not one of pedigree.[2]

(d) The following are instances of the ways in which statements as to pedigree may be made: By family conduct or correspondence; in books used as family registers; in deeds and wills; in inscriptions on tombstones, or portraits; in pedigrees, so far as they state the relationship of living persons known to the compiler.[3]

ARTICLE 32.*

EVIDENCE GIVEN IN FORMER PROCEEDING, WHEN RELEVANT.

Evidence given by a witness in a previous action is relevant for the purpose of proving the matter stated in a subsequent proceeding, or in a later stage of the same

---

* See Note XXII. [Appendix].

[1] *Guthrie* v. *Haines*, 13 Q. B. D. 818 (1884). In this case all the authorities on this point are fully considered.

[2] *Whittuck* v. *Walters*, 4 C. & P. 375. [For cases in which death has been deemed a question of pedigree, see *Cochrane* v. *Libby*, 18 Me. 39; *Webb* v. *Richardson*, 42 Vt. 465; *Clark* v. *Owens*, 18 N. Y. 434.]

[3] In 1 Ph. Ev. 203–215, and T. E. ss. 583–7, these and many other forms of statement of the same sort are mentioned; and see *Davies* v. *Lowndes*, 6 M. & G. 527. [See *Bussom* v. *Forsyth*, 32 N. J. Eq. 277, note. The following are instances: family conduct or reputation (*Eaton* v. *Tallmadge*, 24 Wis. 217; *Clark* v. *Owens*, 18 N. Y. 434; *Harland* v. *Eastman*, 107 Ill. 535; *Pickens's Estate*, 163 Pa. 14), at least, if the reputation be based upon declarations of deceased members of the family (*Hurlbut's Estate*, 68 Vt. 366); family Bible (*Greenleaf* v. *Dubuque, etc. R. Co.*, 30 Ia. 301; *Hunt* v. *Johnson*, 19 N. Y. 279, 286); will (*Pearson* v. *Pearson*, 46 Cal. 610); parchment pedigree and inscription on tombstone (*North Brookfield* v. *Warren*, 16 Gray, 171; *McClaskey* v. *Barr*, 54 F. R. 781); a soldier's private record book of pedigree (*Hunt* v. *Order of Chosen Friends*, 64 Mich. 671); deeds (*Scharff* v. *Keener*, 64 Pa. 376; *Fulkerson* v. *Holmes*, 117 U. S. 389). The persons executing such instruments must have been relatives (*Sitler* v. *Gehr*, 105 Pa. 577); as to the testimony of a witness who

proceeding, when the witness is dead,[1] or is mad,[2] or so ill that he will probably never be able to travel,[3] or is kept out of the way by the adverse party,[4] or in civil, but not, it seems, in criminal, cases, is out of the jurisdiction of the court,[5] or, perhaps, in civil, but not in criminal, cases, when he cannot be found.[6]

---

derives his information from documents, etc., of these kinds, see *Eastman* v. *Martin*, 19 N. H. 152.]

[1] *Mayor of Doncaster* v. *Day*, 3 Tau. 262.

[2] *R.* v. *Eriswell*, 3 T. R. 720.

[3] *R.* v. *Hogg*, 6 C. & P. 176.

[4] *R.* v. *Scaife*, 17 Q. B. 238, 243.

[5] *Fry* v. *Wood*, 1 Atk. 444; *R.* v. *Scaife*, 17 Q. B. 243.

[6] Godbolt, p. 326, case 418; *R.* v. *Scaife*, 17 Q. B. 243. [The death of the witness will in all States admit his former testimony. Insanity, also, is generally deemed a sufficient ground (*Whitaker* v. *Marsh*, 62 N. H. 477; *Stein* v. *Swensen*, 46 Minn. 360; *Howard* v. *Patrick*, 38 Mich. 795; *Morehouse* v. *Morehouse*, 17 Abb. N. C. 407). As to other disabilities, there is much difference of doctrine. Thus, in *civil cases*, the New York rule is that absence from the jurisdiction, or the fact that the witness cannot be found, is not enough (*Weeks* v. *Lowerre*, 8 Barb. 530; *Mutual Life Ins. Co.* v. *Anthony*, 50 Hun, 101). In Pennsylvania such evidence is received, if the witness has died, has become insane, is sick and unable to attend, has lost his memory through disease or old age, is out of the jurisdiction, cannot be found, or has become incompetent to testify by reason of the death of the opposite party to the suit (*Walbridge* v. *Knipper*, 96 Pa. 48; *Ballman* v. *Heron*, 169 Pa. 510; *Thornton* v. *Britton*, 144 Pa. 126). In Illinois, death, insanity, or the keeping of the witness away by the adverse party, is sufficient (*Stout* v. *Cook*, 47 Ill. 530; cf. *Cassaday* v. *Trustees*, 105 Ill. 560). Absence from the jurisdiction is held sufficient in California, Nebraska, Michigan, and Iowa (*Benson* v. *Shotwell*, 103 Cal. 163; *Young* v. *Sage*, 42 Neb. 38; *Hudson* v. *Roos*, 76 Mich. 173; cf. *Kellogg* v. *Secord*, 42 Mich. 318; *Fleming* v. *Shenandoah*, 71 Ia. 456; cf. *Bank of Monroe* v. *Gifford*, 79 Ia. 300); but not in New Jersey (*Berney* v. *Mitchell*, 34 N. J. L. 337, and that, too, even though he cannot be found, Id.); nor in Mississippi (*Gastrell* v. *Phillips*, 64 Miss. 473); in Minnesota, if a witness *resides* beyond the jurisdiction of the court, his former testimony may be proved (*Minneapolis Mill Co.* v. *Minn. etc. R. Co.*, 51 Minn. 304; S. P. *Dunbar* v. *McGill*, 69 Mich. 297). Sickness which renders the witness unable to attend is sometimes held sufficient (*Chase* v. *Springvale Mills Co.*, 75 Me. 156; *Scoville* v. *Hannibal. etc. R Co.*, 94 Mo.

Provided in all cases—

(1) That the person against whom the evidence is to

84; cf. *Central R. Co.* v. *Murray*, 97 Ga. 326; *Berney* v. *Mitchell*, 34 N. J. L. 337, 341).

In *criminal cases*, death of the witness is deemed sufficient (*Mattox* v. *U. S.*, 156 U. S. 237; *Bass* v. *State*, 136 Ind. 165; *State* v. *Elliott*, 90 Mo. 350; *State* v. *George*, 60 Minn. 503; *Barnett* v. *People*, 54 Ill. 325; *People* v. *Dowdigan*, 67 Mich. 95; *Jackson* v. *State*, 81 Wis. 127; *State* v. *Fitzgerald*, 63 Ia. 268); but not his absence from the jurisdiction (*U. S.* v. *Angell*, 11 F. R. 34; *Brogy* v. *Comm.*, 10 Gratt. 722; *People* v. *Newman*, 5 Hill, 295; *People* v. *Gordon*, 99 Cal. 227; *Pittman* v. *State*, 92 Ga. 480; *Owens* v. *State*, 63 Miss. 450; contra, *McNamara* v. *State*, 60 Ark. 400; *Thompson* v. *State*, 106 Ala. 67, if the absence be permanent or indefinite); nor his illness (*Comm.* v. *McKenna*, 158 Mass. 207; *State* v. *Staples*, 47 N. H. 113). But if the witness is wrongfully kept away by the defendant, the former evidence against such defendant has been received (*Reynolds* v. *U. S.*, 98 U. S. 145; *State* v. *Houser*, 26 Mo. 431; contra, *Bergen* v. *State*, 17 Ill. 426). And now, in some States, by statute, depositions given on a preliminary examination before a magistrate may be read in evidence on the trial, if the witness is dead, or insane, or cannot with due diligence be found (*People* v. *Fish*, 125 N. Y. 137; *People* v. *Gardner*, 98 Cal. 127; *State* v. *King*, 86 N. C. 603; cf. *Mattox* v. *U. S.*, 156 U. S. 237; the rule in Pennsylvania is broader still, *Comm.* v. *Cleary*, 148 Pa. 26). The constitutional provision that the defendant shall be confronted with the witnesses against him is generally held not to exclude this kind of evidence (*People* v. *Sligh*, 48 Mich. 54; see all the cases in this paragraph).

The former testimony may be proved by any witness who heard and remembers it, if he can state the substance of the whole of it (*Woods* v. *Keyes*, 14 Allen, 236; *Hepler* v. *Mt. Carmel Bk.*, 97 Pa. 420; *Harrison* v. *Charlton*, 42 Ia. 573; *Black* v. *Woodrow*, 39 Md. 194; *German Nat. Bk.* v. *Leonard*, 40 Neb. 677; *Emery* v. *Fowler*, 39 Me. 326). He need only state the substance of such testimony, not its precise language; nor need his language be even substantially the same (Gr. Ev. i. § 165; *Ruch* v. *Rock Island*, 97 U. S. 693; *Hepler* v. *Mt. Carmel Bk.*, 97 Pa. 420; *U. S.* v. *Macomb*, 5 McL. 286; *State* v. *Able*, 65 Mo. 357; *Summons* v. *State*, 5 O. St. 325; *Lime Rock Bk.* v. *Hewett*, 52 Me. 531; *State* v. *O'Brien*, 81 Ia. 88). But in Massachusetts substantially the original language must be given (*Costigan* v. *Lunt*, 127 Mass. 354). The New York cases seem to support the former rule, but they do not appear to be entirely in accord (*Crawford* v. *Loper*,

be given had the right and opportunity to cross-examine the declarant when he was examined as a witness;[1]

(2) That the questions in issue were substantially the same in the first as in the second proceeding;[1]

---

25 Barb. 449; *Martin v. Cope*, 3 Abb. Dec. 182; *Clark v. Vorce*, 15 Wend. 193; *Wilbur v. Selden*, 6 Cow. 162). In *McIntyre v. N. Y. C. R. Co.*, 37 N. Y. 287, 291, a witness, who took minutes of the deceased witness's former testimony, said:—"I designed to take the substance of the testimony as given by the witness, and presume I have; I have no recollection of the testimony aside from what I have here; should judge that it was not possible for me to take the whole testimony *verbatim*; did not aim to take more than the substance." On this basis the testimony of the deceased witness was allowed to be proved.

Such former testimony may be proved by a stenographer from memory (*Moore v. Moore*, 39 Ia. 461), or by using his minutes to refresh recollection (*Sage v. State*, 127 Ind. 15; *State v. George*, 60 Minn. 503); by a juror who heard it (*Hutchings v. Corgan*, 59 Ill. 70); by an attorney (*Earl v. Tupper*, 45 Vt. 275; *Costigan v. Lunt*, 127 Mass. 354, who may refresh his recollection by his minutes, Id.); by the judge's minutes, duly authenticated by him as to completeness and accuracy (*Martin v. Cope*, 3 Abb. Dec. 182; *Whitcher v. Morey*, 39 Vt. 459); by the minutes of stenographers, counsel, masters in chancery, etc., if they are duly shown to have been taken correctly (*Lueigert v. Volker*, 153 Ill. 385; *Labar v. Crane*, 56 Mich. 585; *Jackson v. State*, 81 Wis. 127; *Quinn v. Halbert*, 57 Vt. 178; *Rhine v. Robinson*, 27 Pa. 30; *Yale v. Comstock*, 112 Mass. 267); by a bill of exceptions or "case," duly authenticated as containing the evidence fully and accurately (*Davis v. Kline*, 96 Mo. 401; *Slingerland v. Slingerland*, 46 Minn. 100; *Wilson v. Noonan*, 35 Wis. 321; cf. *Solomon R. Co. v. Jones*, 34 Kan. 443; contra, *Stern v. People*, 102 Ill. 540); and by other like methods.

These rules apply also to the former testimony of a deceased *party*. But by statute in some States, if this testimony is not proved on the second trial, the surviving party cannot be a witness to testify against the decedent's representatives (*Emerson v. Bleakley*, 2 Abb. Dec. 22; *Bradley v. Mirick*, 91 N. Y. 293; *Stewart v. First Nat. Bk.*, 43 Mich. 257; see *Blair v. Ellsworth*, 55 Vt. 415).

Former testimony given before arbitrators may be proved. *Walbridge v. Knipper*, 96 Pa. 48; *Bailey v. Woods*, 17 N. H. 365; contra, *Jessup v. Cook*, 6 N. J. L. 434; cf. *Jackson v. Bailey*, 2 Johns. 17.]

[1] [See p. 111, note 1, and cases cited.]

Provided also—

(3) That the proceeding, if civil, was between the same parties or their representatives in interest;[1]

(4) That, in criminal cases, the same person is accused upon the same facts.[2]

If evidence is reduced to the form of a deposition, the provisions of Article 90 apply to the proof of the fact that it was given.[3]

The conditions under which depositions may be used as evidence are stated in Articles 140–142.

---

[1] *Doe* v. *Tatham*, 1 A. & E. 319; *Doe* v. *Derby*, 1 A. & E. 783, 785, 789. See, as a late illustration, as to privies in estate, *Llanover* v. *Homfray*, 19 Ch. D. 224. In this case the first set of proceedings was between lords of the same manor and tenants of the same manor as the parties to the second suit. [*Osborn* v. *Pell*, 5 Den. 370; *Jackson* v. *Crissey*, 3 Wend. 251; *Chase* v. *Springvale Mills Co.*, 75 Me. 156; *Walbridge* v. *Knipper*, 96 Pa. 48, 51; *Marshall* v. *Hancock*, 80 Cal. 82; *Lane* v. *Brainerd*, 30 Ct. 565; *Orr* v. *Hadley*, 36 N. H. 575; and cases *supra*. It is enough that the *opportunity* for cross-examination exist, though it is not exercised (*Bradley* v. *Mirick*, 91 N. Y. 293). Privies in blood, in law, or in estate, are "representatives in interest" within this rule (*Jackson* v. *Lawson*, 15 Johns. 539; *Yale* v. *Comstock*, 112 Mass. 267). So the plaintiffs in one suit may be defendants in the other. And if the parties to the second suit were all parties to the first, the evidence is admissible, though there were additional parties to the first suit (*Allen* v. *Chouteau*, 102 Mo. 309); *aliter*, if new parties are introduced into the second suit (*Orr* v. *Hadley*, 36 N. H. 575). The testimony of a deceased witness is, however, inadmissible, unless he would, if living, have been a competent witness in the second suit (*Eaton* v. *Alger*, 47 N. Y. 345). The testimony of a witness given at a coroner's inquest is not admissible in an action to recover damages for causing the death of the deceased, though the witness has since died (*Cook* v. *N. Y. Central R. Co.*, 5 Lans. 401; *Pittsburgh, etc. R. Co.* v. *McGrath*, 115 Ill. 172; cf. *McLain* v. *Comm.*, 99 Pa. 86; *U. S. Life Ins. Co.* v. *Vocke*, 129 Ill. 557). The inquest is not an action or judicial proceeding between the parties.]

[2] *Beeston's Case*, Dears. 405. [See the criminal cases cited in note on p. 109, *ante.*]

[3] [See *Chase* v. *Springvale Mills Co.*, 75 Me. 156; *People* v. *Fish*, 125 N. Y. 136.]

SECTION II.

STATEMENTS IN BOOKS, DOCUMENTS, AND RECORDS, WHEN RELEVANT.

ARTICLE 33.

RECITALS OF PUBLIC FACTS IN STATUTES AND PROCLAMATIONS.[1]

When any act of state or any fact of a public nature is in issue or is, or is deemed to be, relevant to the issue, any statement of it made in a recital contained in any public Act of Parliament, or in any royal proclamation or speech of the Sovereign in opening Parliament, or in any address to the Crown of either House of Parliament. is deemed to be a relevant fact.[2]

ARTICLE 34.

RELEVANCY OF ENTRY IN PUBLIC RECORD MADE IN PERFORM-
ANCE OF DUTY.

An entry in any record, official book, or register kept in any of Her Majesty's dominions[3] or at sea, or in any

---

[1] [This Article may be adapted to American law by making it read as follows : When any act of state or any fact of a public nature is in issue, or is, or is deemed to be, relevant to the issue, any statement of it made in a recital contained in any public statute, or in any proclamation of the Executive, or in state papers communicated by the Executive to the Legislature, or published under public authority, or in legislative journals or resolutions, is deemed to be a relevant fact (Gr. Ev. i. § 491 ; *McKinnon* v. *Bliss*, 21 N. Y. 206 ; *Radcliff* v. *United Ins. Co.*, 7 Johns. 38, 51 ; *Root* v. *King*, 7 Cow. 613 ; *Spangler* v. *Jacoby*, 14 Ill. 297 ; *Whiton* v. *Albany, etc., Ins. Co.*, 109 Mass. 24, and cases cited ; *Worcester* v. *Northborough*, 140 Mass. 397 ; *Clemens* v. *Meyer*, 44 La. Ann. 390 ; see *Armstrong* v. *U. S.*, 13 Wall. 154).   So of recitals in the official precept of a governor (*Comm.* v. *Hall*, 9 Gray, 262).   As to the effect of recitals in private statutes, see *McKinnon* v. *Bliss*, supra.]

[2] *R.* v. *Francklin*, 17 S. T. 636 ; *R.* v. *Sutton*, 4 M. & S. 532.

[3] [For this country this should read, " in any State or Territory or the District of Columbia."]

foreign country, stating, for the purpose of being referred
to by the public, a fact in issue or relevant or deemed to
be relevant thereto, and made in proper time by any
person in the discharge of any duty imposed upon him by
the law of the place in which such record, book, or register
is kept, is itself deemed to be a relevant fact.[1]

---

[1] *Sturla* v. *Freccia*, 5 App. Cas. 623 ; see especially pp. 633-4 and
643-4 ; *Lyell* v. *Kennedy*, 14 App. Cas. 437 ; T. E. (from Greenleaf)
ss. 1429, 1432. See also *Queen's Proctor* v. *Fry*, L. R. 4 P. D. 230.   In
In re Turner, Glenister v. *Harding*, 29 Ch. D. 990, Chitty, J., in a pedigree case, held, though with some hesitation, and though it was not
necessary to the decision of the case, that a statement of age in a bap-
tismal register, made under 52 Geo. III. c. 146, might be looked at in a
question of legitimacy.   His authorities were *Morris* v. *Davies*, 3 C.
& P. 215, and *Cope* v. *Cope*, 1 M. & R. 269.   These are only Nisi Prius
decisions, though spoken of by Chitty, J., as binding on him.   See note
to Article 31.   [Gr. Ev. i. §§ 483-485, 493-495 ; *Evanston* v. *Gunn*, 99
U. S. 660 ; *Sandy White* v. *United States*, 164 U. S. 100 ; *Gurney* v.
Howe, 9 Gray, 404 ; *Pells* v. *Webquish*, 129 Mass. 469 ; *Galt* v. *Gallo-
way*, 4 Pet. 332 ; *Cassaday* v. *Trustees*, 105 Ill. 560 ; *Bell* v. *Kendrick*,
25 Fla. 778 ; *Succession of Justus*, 48 La. Ann. 1096 ; *Jacobi* v. *Order
of Germania*, 73 Hun, 602 ; *Bissell* v. *Hamblin*, 6 Duer, 512 ; *People*
v. *Zeyst*, 23 N. Y. 140 ; cf. *Tessmann* v. *United Friends*, 103 Mich. 185 ;
see Art. 27, Illustration (*e*), *ante*.   Thus records of the weather kept
by officers of the United States Signal Service are admissible (*Evanston* v. *Gunn*, supra ; *Chicago, etc. R. Co.* v. *Trayes*, 17 Ill. App. 136 ;
cf. *People* v. *Dow*, 64 Mich. 717).
  This rule is limited to such statements in official documents as the
officers make in the regular course of official duty (Id.; *United States*
v. *Corwin*, 129 U. S. 381 ; *Rindge* v. *Walker*, 61 N. H. 58 ; *Erwin* v.
English, 61 Ct. 502).
  The *books of a private corporation* are of the nature of public books
as between the members (Gr. Ev. i. § 493).   When they are duly kept in
the regular course of business, they are, in general, competent to show
the acts and proceedings of the corporation (*Wetherbee* v. *Baker*,
35 N. J. Eq. 501 ; *Ten Eyck* v. *Railroad Co.*, 74 Mich. 226 ; *Hubbell* v.
Meigs, 50 N. Y. 480 ; *Turnpike Co.* v. *M'Kean*, 10 Johns. 154 ; see
Angell & Ames on Corp. §§ 679, 681).   So they are evidence in favor
of the corporation, to show that it was properly organized (*McFarlan*
v. *Triton Ins. Co.*, 4 Den. 392).   But they are not generally competent
evidence in favor of the corporation against a stranger (*Graville* v.

ARTICLE 35.

RELEVANCY OF STATEMENTS IN WORKS OF HISTORY, MAPS, CHARTS, AND PLANS.

Statements as to matters of general public history made in accredited historical books are deemed to be relevant, when the occurrence of any such matter is in issue or is, or is deemed to be, relevant to the issue ; but statements in such works as to private rights or customs are deemed to be irrelevant.[1]

(*Submitted*) Statements of facts in issue, or relevant or deemed to be relevant to the issue, made in published maps or charts generally offered for public sale as to matters of public notoriety, such as the relative position of towns and countries, and such as are usually represented or stated in such maps or charts, are themselves

---

N. Y. C. R. Co., 34 Hun, 224 ; *Railroad Co.* v. *Cunnington*, 39 O. St. 327 ; *Chase* v. *Sycamore, etc. R. Co.*, 38 Ill. 215); nor even against a member or director, of his contracts or private dealings with the company, for in that respect he is to be deemed a stranger (*Haynes* v. *Brown*, 36 N. H. 545 ; *Rudd* v. *Robinson*, 126 N. Y. 113).

The stock books of a corporation are *prima facie* evidence to show who are its stockholders (*Turnbull* v. *Payson*, 95 U. S. 418 ; *Vanderwerken* v. *Glenn*, 85 Va. 9 ; *Lehman* v. *Glenn*, 87 Ala. 618). The right of a stockholder to inspect the books may be enforced by *mandamus* in proper cases (*Phœnix Iron Co.* v. *Commonwealth*, 113 Pa. 563 ; *People* v. *Pacific Mail Co.*, 50 Barb. 280).

As to entries in other books of a private or *quasi*-official character, see Art. 27, *ante.*]

[1] See cases in 2 Ph. Ev. 155-6, and *Read* v. *Bishop of Lincoln*, [1892] A. C. 644, at pp. 652-4. [*McKinnon* v. *Bliss*, 21 N. Y. 206, 216; *Bogardus* v. *Trinity Church*, 4 Sandf. Ch. 633; *Crill* v. *Rome*, 47 How. Pr. 400 ; *Morris* v. *Harmer*, 7 Pet. 554 ; *State* v. *Wagner*, 61 Me. 178, 188 ; *Spalding* v. *Hedges*, 2 Pa. 240, 243. These cases favor the view that if the author is living, he should be called as a witness to be examined as to the sources and accuracy of his knowledge. Mere local histories are not admitted in evidence. *Roe* v. *Strong*, 107 N. Y. 350.]

deemed to be relevant facts;[1] but such statements are irrelevant[2] if they relate to matters of private concern or

---

[1] In *R.* v. *Orton*, maps of Australia were given in evidence to show the situation of various places at which the defendant said he had lived.

[2] *E.g.*, a line in a tithe commutation map, purporting to denote the boundaries of A's property, is irrelevant in a question between A and B as to the position of the boundaries: *Wilberforce* v. *Hearfield*, 5 Ch. Div. 709, and see *Hammond* v. ——, 10 Ex. 390. [As a general rule, maps, surveys, and plans of land are not competent evidence, unless their accuracy is shown by other evidence in the case (*Johnston* v. *Jones*, 1 Black, 209; *Donohue* v. *Whitney*, 133 N. Y. 178; *Comm.* v. *Switzer*, 134 Pa. 383; *Burwell* v. *Sneed*, 104 N. C. 118; *Wilkinson* v. *State*, 106 Ala. 23; *Rowland* v. *McCown*, 20 Or. 538; *Whitehouse* v. *Bickford*, 29 N. H. 471), as *e. g.*, by the testimony of the surveyors who prepared them (*Curtiss* v. *Ayrault*, 3 Hun, 487). But a map of public land, made by a public surveyor, and duly certified, and filed in a public office, as prescribed by statute, is admissible *per se* (*People* v. *Denison*, 17 Wend. 312; S. P. *Comm.* v. *King*, 150 Mass. 221; *Henry* v. *Dulle*, 74 Mo. 443; *Galvin* v. *Palmer*, 113 Cal. 46). Ancient maps, duly authenticated as genuine, are admissible, to show matters of public and general right (*Lawrence* v. *Tennant*, 64 N. H. 532; *McCausland* v. *Fleming*, 63 Pa. 36; cf. *Missouri* v. *Kentucky*, 11 Wall. 395; see Art. 30, *ante*); or, in some States, to establish private boundaries (*Gibson* v. *Poor*, 21 N. H. 440; *Whitman* v. *Shaw*, 166 Mass. 451) But an ancient map of partition, showing the division of land among private owners, is not evidence of title (*Jackson* v. *Witter*, 2 Johns. 180).

Where a plan or map of land is prepared, and is referred to in making conveyances of such land, it is evidence to show boundary or location, or to explain the contract (*Clark* v. *N. Y. Life Ins. Co.*, 64 N. Y. 33; *Kingsland* v. *Chittenden*, 6 Lans. 15; *Crawford* v. *Loper*, 25 Barb. 449). So in dedicating land to the public (*Derby* v. *Alling*, 40 Ct. 410). But if made by a stranger without authority, it cannot be received to vary or contradict a title under a previous deed (*Marble* v. *McMinn*, 57 Barb. 610; cf. *Jackson* v. *Frost*, 5 Cow. 346). Sometimes maps are admissible by statute, as *e. g.*, maps of the public canals of New York (*Carpenter* v. *Cohoes*, 81 N. Y. 21).

Some other rules as to the admissibility of books, papers, etc., may here be noticed. Thus it is generally held that a medical or other scientific treatise is not competent evidence to prove the truth of matters stated therein (*Comm.* v. *Sturtivant*, 117 Mass. 122; *Harris*

matters not likely to be accurately stated in such documents.

---

v. *Panama R. Co.*, 3 Bos. 7; *Fox* v. *Peninsular, etc. Works*, 84 Mich. 676; *Gallagher* v. *Market St. R. Co.*, 67 Cal. 13; *Epps* v. *State*, 102 Ind. 539; *Boyle* v. *State*, 57 Wis. 472; contra, *Bales* v. *State*, 63 Ala. 30; *Burg* v. *Chicago, etc. R. Co.*, 90 Ia. 106 [by statute]); nor can such books be read in argument to the jury (*Washburn* v. *Cuddihy*, 8 Gray, 430; *Boyle* v. *State*, supra; *People* v. *Wheeler*, 60 Cal. 581; but see *Richmond's Appeal*, 59 Ct. 226), nor given in evidence to sustain or contradict the opinion of a witness (*Davis* v. *State*, 38 Md. 15; *Knoll* v. *State*, 55 Wis. 249); nor is it proper to examine a witness in such a way as to get the contents of such books before the jury (*Waterman* v. *Chicago, etc. R. Co.*, 82 Wis. 613; *Lilley* v. *Parkinson*, 91 Cal. 655; *Marshall* v. *Brown*, 50 Mich. 148). But such a book may be read to discredit a witness when he has referred to it as supporting his statements (*Pinney* v. *Cahill*, 48 Mich. 584; *Ripon* v. *Bittel*, 30 Wis. 614; *N. J. Zinc, etc. Co.* v. *Lehigh, etc. Zinc Co.*, 59 N. J. L. 189; *Bloomington* v. *Shrock*, 110 Ill. 219; *Hess* v. *Lowrey*, 122 Ind. 225). An engraving in a medical book is not competent evidence (*Ordway* v. *Haynes*, 50 N. H. 159). So counsel should not in general be allowed to read to the jury extracts from other books or from newspapers (*Baldwin* v. *Bricker*, 86 Ind. 221; *Williams* v. *Brooklyn Elev. R. Co.*, 126 N. Y. 96). The reading of law books by counsel to the jury is sanctioned in some States (*N. & W. R. Co.* v. *Harman's Admr.*, 83 Va. 553; *Hannah* v. *State*, 11 Lea, 201), prohibited in others (*Yarbrough* v. *State*, 105 Ala. 45; *Lendberg* v. *Iron Mining Co.*, 75 Mich. 84; *Steffenson* v. *Chicago, etc. R. Co.*, 48 Minn. 285), but in many States is subject to the discretion of the trial court, which may permit or refuse or limit the privilege (*Comm.* v. *Hill*, 145 Mass. 305; *State* v. *Fitzgerald*, 130 Mo. 407; *Gregory* v. *Ohio Riv. R. Co.*, 37 W. Va. 606; *Blum* v. *Jones*, 86 Tex. 492; *People* v. *Anderson*, 44 Cal. 65; *Curtis* v. *State*, 36 Ark. 284; cf. *Williams* v. *Brooklyn Elev. R. Co.*, 126 N. Y. 96). In some States, moreover, where the jury are, in criminal cases, judges of the law as well as of the facts, such reading of law books is matter of right in criminal cases, but not permissible in civil cases (*Wohlford* v. *People*, 148 Ill. 296; *Stout* v. *State*, 96 Ind. 407; *Johnson* v. *Culver*, 116 Ind. 278; *State* v. *Whitmore*, 53 Kan. 343; *Hudson* v. *Hudson*, 90 Ga. 582; *Powell* v. *State*, 65 Ga. 707).

A price current list, if shown by extrinsic evidence to be reliable, is competent to prove market value (*Cliquot's Champagne*, 3 Wall. 114; *Whelan* v. *Lynch*, 60 N. Y. 469; *Seligman* v. *Rogers*, 113 Mo. 642; see *Whitney* v. *Thacher*, 117 Mass. 523; *Peter* v. *Thickstun*, 51 Mich.

ARTICLES 36, 37, 38.

ENTRIES IN BANKERS' BOOKS.[1]

ARTICLE 39.*

JUDGMENT.

The word "judgment" in Articles 40–47 means any final judgment, order, or decree of any court.

The provisions of Articles 40–45, inclusive, are all subject to the provisions of Article 46.

ARTICLE 40.

ALL JUDGMENTS CONCLUSIVE PROOF OF THEIR LEGAL EFFECT.

All judgments whatever are conclusive proof as against all persons of the existence of that state of things which

---

* See Note XXIII. [Appendix].

589); standard life and annuity tables, as the Northampton or Carlisle tables, to show expectancy of life (*Vicksburg, etc. R. Co.* v. *Putnam*, 118 U. S. 545 ; *Sauter* v. *N. Y. C. R. Co.*, 66 N. Y. 50; *Steinbrunner* v. *Pittsburgh, etc. R. Co.*, 146 Pa. 504 ; *Denman* v. *Johnston*, 85 Mich. 387 ; *Joliet* v. *Blower*, 155 Ill. 414); an almanac to show time of sunrise, etc. (*State* v. *Morris*, 47 Ct. 179; *Munshower* v. *State*, 55 Md. 11). So market reports have been received (*Aulls* v. *Young*, 98 Mich. 231 ; cf. *Vogt* v. *Cope*, 66 Cal. 31), and a weather record kept at a State asylum (*De Armond* v. *Neasmith*, 32 Mich. 231). But a gazetteer is not admissible to prove relative distances of places (*Spalding* v. *Hedges*, 2 Pa. 240), nor an encyclopædia to prove facts of recent occurrence stated therein (*Whiton* v. *Albany, etc. Ins. Co.*, 109 Mass. 24 ; cf. *Worden* v. *Humeston, etc. R. Co.*, 76 Ia. 310); nor are law reports of formerly decided cases competent to prove the facts of those cases (*Mackay* v. *Easton*, 19 Wall. 619), nor to prove a local custom of trade.   *Iron Cliffs Co.* v. *Buhl*, 42 Mich. 86.]

[1] [Articles 36, 37, and 38 state the provisions of special English statutes relating to entries in bankers' books As they are peculiar to English law, they are not retained here in the text, but will be found in the Appendix, Note XLIX. As to the admissibility of corporation books in this country, see Articles 27 and 34, *ante*, and notes.]

they actually effect, when the existence of the state of things so effected is a fact in issue or is, or is deemed to be, relevant to the issue.[1] The existence of the judgment effecting it may be proved in the manner prescribed in Part II.

Illustrations.

(a) The question is, whether A has been damaged by the negligence of his servant B in injuring C's horse.

A judgment in an action, in which C recovered damages against A, is conclusive proof as against B, that C did recover damages against A in that action.[2]

(b) The question is, whether A, a shipowner, is entitled to recover as for a loss by capture against B, an underwriter.

A judgment of a competent French prize court, condemning the ship and cargo as prize, is conclusive proof that the ship and cargo were lost to A by capture.[3]

(c) The question is, whether A can recover damages from B for a malicious prosecution.

The judgment of a court by which A was acquitted is conclusive proof that A was acquitted by that court.[4]

(d) A, as executor to B, sues C for a debt due from C to B.

---

[1] [Gr. Ev. i. §§ 527, 538, 539; *Dorrell* v. *State*, 83 Ind. 357; *Chamberlain* v. *Carlisle*, 26 N. H. 540; *Wadsworth* v. *Sharpsteen*, 8 N. Y. 388; *Spencer* v. *Dearth*, 43 Vt. 98, 105; *Harrington* v. *Wadsworth*, 63 N. H. 400; *Aron* v. *Chaffe*, 72 Miss. 159; *Smith* v. *Chapin*, 31 Ct. 530. Thus when a judgment forms a muniment of title or a link in a chain of title, it is competent evidence, not only as against parties and privies, but also as against strangers. *Gage* v. *Goudy*, 141 Ill. 215; *Murray* v. *Deyo*, 10 Hun, 3; *Railroad Equipment Co.* v. *Blair*, 145 N. Y. 607.]

[2] *Green* v. *New River Company*, 4 T. R. 590. See Article 44, Illustration (a). [See *Kip* v. *Brigham*, 7 Johns. 168; *Dubois* v. *Hermance*, 56 N. Y. 673; *Masser* v. *Strickland*, 17 S. & R. 354; and *post*, Art. 44, Illustration (ab).]

[3] Involved in *Geyer* v. *Aguilar*, 7 T. R. 681; [cf. *Rose* v. *Himely*, 4 Cr. 241.]

[4] *Leggatt* v. *Tollervey*, 14 Ex. 301; and see *Caddy* v. *Barlow*, 1 Man. & R. 277. [See *Sayles* v. *Briggs*, 4 Met. 421; *Burt* v. *Place*, 4 Wend. 591.]

The grant of probate to A is conclusive proof as against C, that A is B's executor.[1]

(e) A is deprived of his living by the sentence of an ecclesiastical court.

The sentence is conclusive proof of the fact of deprivation in all cases.[2]

(f) A and B are divorced *a vinculo matrimonii* by a sentence of the Divorce Court.

The sentence is conclusive proof of the divorce in all cases.[3]

---

[1] *Allan* v. *Dundas*, 3 T. R. 125–130. In this case the will to which probate had been obtained was forged. [*Kelly* v. *West*, 80 N. Y. 139; N. Y. Code Civ. Pro. § 2591; *Emery* v. *Hildreth*, 2 Gray, 228; *Day* v. *Floyd*, 130 Mass. 488; *Mutual Ins. Co.* v. *Tisdale*, 91 U. S. 238, 243; *Steen* v. *Bennett*, 24 Vt. 303; *Quidort* v. *Pergeaux*, 18 N. J. Eq. 472. So as to guardian (*Farrar* v. *Olmstead*, 24 Vt. 123); or receiver (*Whittlesey* v. *Frantz*, 74 N. Y. 456); or trustee (*Bassett* v. *Crafts*, 129 Mass. 513). But the grant of administration upon the estate of a living person is wholly void for lack of jurisdiction (*Stevenson* v. *Superior Ct.*, 62 Cal. 60; *Jochumsen* v. *Suffolk Sav. Bk.*, 3 Allen, 87; *Melia* v. *Simmons*, 45 Wis. 334; *Springer* v. *Shavender*, 118 N. C. 33; *Thomas* v. *People*, 107 Ill. 517; *Devlin* v. *Comm.*, 101 Pa. 273; *Lavin* v. *Emigrant Sav. Bk.*, 18 Blatch. 1, 36; cf. *Plume* v. *Howard Sav. Inst.*, 46 N. J. L. 211). But in New York, by statute, the determination by the surrogate of the fact of death is deemed conclusive, so far as to render the acts of the administrator valid until his authority is revoked (*Roderigas* v. *East River Sav. Inst.*, 63 N. Y. 460); but this power of the surrogate does not extend to his clerk (S. C. 76 N. Y. 316; cf. *Bolton* v. *Schriever*, 135 N. Y. 65; *Davis* v. *Greve*, 32 La. Ann. 420). The U. S. Supreme Court, however, holds that a State law declaring a judicial determination that a man is dead conclusive upon him, though he was not served with process, and vesting his property in his administrator, is void, as depriving him of his property without due process of law. *Scott* v. *McNeal*, 154 U. S. 34.]

[2] Judgment of Lord Holt in *Philips* v. *Bury*, 2 T. R. 346, 351; [cf. *Bouldin* v. *Alexander*, 15 Wall. 131.]

[3] Assumed in *Needham* v. *Bremner*, L. R. 1 C. P. 582. [*Hood* v. *Hood*, 110 Mass. 463; *Burlen* v. *Shannon*, 3 Gray, 387; *Hunt* v. *Hunt*, 72 N. Y. 217; *In re Eickhoff*, 101 Cal. 600; as to impeaching the judgment for lack of jurisdiction, see *People* v. *Baker*, 76 N. Y. 78; *Adams* v. *Adams*, 154 Mass. 290.]

(*g*) [The question is, whether A, an alien born, is a citizen of the United States.

The record of a judgment of a competent court admitting him to become a citizen and reciting the facts which entitled him to such judgment is conclusive proof of his citizenship.][1]

ARTICLE 41.

JUDGMENTS CONCLUSIVE AS BETWEEN PARTIES AND PRIVIES OF FACTS FORMING GROUND OF JUDGMENT.

Every judgment is conclusive proof as against parties and privies of facts directly in issue in the case, actually decided by the court, and appearing[2] from the judgment

---

[1] [*McCarthy* v. *Marsh*, 5 N. Y. 263; *Mutual Ins. Co.* v. *Tisdale*, 91 U. S. 238, 245; *People* v. *McGowan*, 77 Ill. 644; *State* v. *Macdonald*, 24 Minn. 48; see *Behrensmeyer* v. *Kreitz*, 135 Ill. 591, 630.]

[2] [Gr. Ev. i. § 528 *et seq.*; *Shaw* v. *Broadbent*, 129 N. Y. 114; *Marsteller* v. *Marsteller*, 132 Pa. 517; *Orthwein* v. *Thomas*, 127 Ill. 554; *Sanderson* v. *Peabody*, 58 N. H. 116. But it is generally held in this country that a judgment is conclusive between parties and privies as to facts actually decided, whether these do or do not appear upon the record; such as do not so appear may be shown by parol evidence to have been litigated and determined (*Campbell* v. *Rankin*, 99 U. S. 261; *Bowe* v. *Wilkins*, 105 N. Y. 322; *Stone* v. *St. Louis Stamping Co.*, 155 Mass. 267; *Title Co.* v. *Shallcross*, 147 Pa. 485; *Harding* v. *Bader*, 75 Mich. 323; *Palmer* v. *Sanger*, 143 Ill. 34; *Perkins* v. *Brazos*, 66 Ct. 248; *State* v. *Waterman*, 87 Ia. 255; see Art. 44, Illustration (*cc*)). But such evidence must not contradict the record (*Wilson's Excr.* v. *Deen*, 121 U. S. 525; *Lorillard* v. *Clyde*, 122 N. Y. 41; *Embden* v. *Lisherness*, 89 Me. 578). A judgment binds one who is a real party in interest, even if he is not a party of record (*Marsh* v. *Smith*, 73 Ia. 295; *Cheney* v. *Patton*, 144 Ill. 373; *Claflin* v. *Fletcher*, 10 Biss. 281).

A judgment is said to be conclusive not only as to matters which *were*, but also as to those which, under the issues, *might have been*, litigated and determined in the action (*Pray* v. *Hegeman*, 98 N. Y. 351; *Huntley* v. *Holt*, 59 Ct. 102; *Wright* v. *Anderson*, 117 Ind. 315; *Bassett* v. *Ct. Riv. R. Co.*, 150 Mass. 178; *Diamond State Iron Co.* v. *Rarig*, 93 Va. 595; *Petersine* v. *Thomas*, 28 O. St. 596). Thus, if part of a single cause of action be sued on and judgment recovered, it bars

itself to be the ground on which it was based; unless

---

an action for the residue (Illustrations (*e*), (*g*), (*h*); *Secor* v. *Sturgis*, 16 N. Y. 548; *Baird* v. *U. S.*, 96 U. S. 430; *Bennett* v. *Hood*, 1 Allen, 47; *Buck* v. *Wilson*, 113 Pa. 423). So a judgment is conclusive as to the grounds of recovery or defence which, under the issues, might have been but were not presented (Illustration (*f*); *Beloit* v. *Morgan*, 7 Wall. 619; *Harmon* v. *Auditor*, 123 Ill. 122; *Lieb* v. *Lichtenstein*, 121 Ind. 483); if, therefore, judgment goes against a defendant, this will bar any subsequent action by him, based on a ground of defence which he might have interposed in the former suit (Illustrations (*i*), (*j*); *White* v. *Merritt*, 7 N. Y. 352; *Homer* v. *Fish*, 1 Pick. 435; *Gleason* v. *Knapp*, 56 Mich. 291; *Johnson Co.* v. *Wharton*, 152 U. S. 252; *Malloney* v. *Horan*, 49 N. Y. 111; *Reich* v. *Cochran*, 151 N. Y. 122). But matters of set-off and recoupment (and sometimes other matters), though not set up by the defendant in actions where they might be so pleaded, may still be sued on independently, unless a recovery upon them would be inconsistent with what was decided by the former judgment (*Brown* v. *Gallaudet*, 80 N. Y. 413; *Malloney* v. *Horan*, 49 N. Y. 111; *Yates* v. *Fassett*, 5 Den. 21; *Bascom* v. *Manning*, 52 N. H. 132; *Fiske* v. *Steele*, 152 Mass. 260; *Mimnaugh* v. *Partlin*, 67 Mich. 391); if, however, such matters are pleaded and determined by way of counterclaim, the judgment will bar any subsequent action upon them (*Howe* v. *Lewis*, 121 Ind. 110; *Patrick* v. *Shaffer*, 94 N. Y. 423).

When a second suit is upon a *different cause of action*, though between the same parties, the former judgment is a bar only as to the matters which *actually were*, and not as to those which *might have been*, litigated and determined (*Nesbitt* v. *Riverside Dist.*, 144 U. S. 610; *Foye* v. *Patch*, 132 Mass. 105; *Metcalf* v. *Gilmore*, 63 N. H. 174; *City of Paterson* v. *Baker*, 51 N. J. Eq. 49; *Bond* v. *Markstrum*, 102 Mich. 11; *Hixson* v. *Ogg*, 53 O. St. 361; *Wright* v. *Griffey*, 147 Ill. 496).

Some additional rules of importance concerning judgments are the following: (*a*) A judgment, in order to conclude parties and privies, must be a final decision on the merits (Gr. Ev. i. §§ 529, 530; *Webb* v. *Buckelew*, 82 N. Y. 555). Thus a judgment of nonsuit or of dismissal of the complaint in an action at law does not bar another action (*Smith* v. *McNeal*, 109 U. S. 426; *Wheeler* v. *Ruckman*, 51 N. Y. 391), though a dismissal in equity on the merits will have that effect (*Lyon* v. *Perin Mfg. Co.*, 125 U. S. 698; *Edgar* v. *Buck*, 65 Mich. 356; *aliter*, if not on the merits, *Hughes* v. *U. S.*, 4 Wall. 232; *Henninger* v. *Heald*, 51 N. J. Eq. 74; see N. Y. Code Civ. Pro. § 1209). So if there be a dis-

evidence was admitted in the action in which the judg*

---

continuance (*Loeb* v. *Willis*, 100 N. Y. 231), or the action be prematurely brought (*Rose* v. *Hawley*, 141 N. Y. 366 ; *Brackett* v. *People*, 115 Ill. 29), or a plea in abatement be sustained (*Atkins* v. *Anderson*, 63 Ia. 139), judgment for such causes is no bar. A verdict without judgment entered is no bar (*Springer* v. *Bien*, 128 N. Y. 99 ; *Smith* v. *McCool*, 16 Wall. 560). (*b*) Judgment on demurrer, rendered for defendant on the merits, is a bar to another action on substantially the same complaint ; but not to an action on a new complaint founded on the same transaction but containing new or amended averments so as to present a good cause of action (*Gould* v. *Evansville R. Co.*, 91 U. S. 533 ; *Wiggins Co.* v. *Ohio, etc. R. Co.*, 142 U. S. 396 ; *Rodman* v. *Mich. Cent. R. Co.*, 59 Mich. 395 ; *Stowell* v. *Chamberlain*, 60 N. Y. 272 ; *Detrick* v. *Sharrar*, 95 Pa. 521 ; but see *Lamb* v. *McConkey*, 76 Ia. 47). (*c*) Judgment by confession or default is a bar (*Town* v. *Smith*, 14 Mich. 348 ; *Goebel* v. *Iffla*, 111 N. Y. 170 ; *Last Chance Mining Co.* v. *Tyler Co.*, 157 U. S. 683 ; *Spring Run Co.* v. *Tosier*, 102 Pa. 342); so is judgment by *retraxit* (*U. S.* v. *Parker*, 120 U. S. 89), and judgment entered upon an offer made by the adverse party and accepted (*Shepherd* v. *Moodhe*, 150 N. Y. 183). (*d*) An interlocutory order is not, in general, conclusive between parties (*Webb* v. *Buckelew*, 82 N. Y. 555 ; *Riggs* v. *Pursell*, 74 N. Y. 380 ; *Sels* v. *Presburger*, 49 N. J. L. 396 ; *Allison* v. *Whittier*, 101 N. C. 490 ; *Heidel* v. *Benedict*, 61 Minn. 170 ; *Miami Nat. Bk.* v. *Barkalow*, 53 Kan. 68 ; but see *Commrs. of Wilson Co.* v. *McIntosh*, 30 Kan. 234); *aliter*, as to final orders on the merits in special proceedings, where there are opposing parties who have full opportunity to be heard (Id.; *Culrose* v. *Gibbons*, 130 N. Y. 447 ; *Spitley* v. *Frost*, 15 F. R. 299 ; cf. *Frauenthal's Appeal*, 100 Pa. 290). (*e*) A judgment of a court of competent jurisdiction, whether of law, equity, admiralty, etc., will bar an action on the same ground in another court whose jurisdiction is of a different nature (*Westcott* v. *Edmunds*, 68 Pa. 34 ; *Powers* v. *Chelsea Sav. Bk.*, 129 Mass. 44 ; *Goodrich* v. *City*, 5 Wall. 566 ; *People* v. *Rickert*, 159 Ill. 496). Thus if one sues on a contract at law as it is, and judgment is rendered against him, he cannot afterwards sue in equity to reform the contract (*Steinbach* v. *Relief Ins. Co.*, 77 N. Y. 498).

Special rules apply to particular actions or proceedings : (*a*) In an action of ejectment, at common law, one judgment does not bar repeated actions between the same parties (*Small* v. *Mitchell*, 143 U. S. 99 ; *Stevens* v. *Hughes*, 31 Pa. 381, 384 ; *Sutton* v. *Dameron*, 100 Mo. 141); but by statute in some States concurrent judgments in *two* successive actions will be a bar (*Blanchard* v. *Brown*, 3 Wall. 245 ; N.

ment was delivered which is excluded in the action in which that judgment is intended to be proved.[1]

Illustrations.

(a) The question is, whether C, a pauper, is settled in parish A or parish B.

D is the mother and E the father of C. D, E, and several of their children were removed from A to B before the question as to C's settlement arose, by an order unappealed against, which order described D as the wife of E.

The statement in the order that D was the wife of E is conclusive as between A and B.[2]

(b) A and B each claim administration to the goods of C, deceased.

Administration is granted to B, the judgment declaring that, as far as appears by the evidence, B has proved himself next of kin.

Afterwards there is a suit between A and B for the distribution of the effects of C. The declaration in the first suit is in the second suit conclusive proof as against A that B is nearer of kin to C than A.[3]

Y. Code Civ. Pro. § 1525; *Britton* v. *Thornton*, 112 U. S. 526), while in other States *one* judgment is a bar (*Sturdy* v. *Jackaway*, 4 Wall. 174). (b) A judgment for damages for a nuisance or trespass will not bar an action for a continuance of the injury; but if the act complained of is *permanent* in its nature, prospective damages are recoverable in the first action, and the first judgment will therefore be a bar (*Schlitz Brewing Co.* v. *Compton*, 142 Ill. 511; *Uline* v. *N. Y. Cent. R. Co.*, 101 N. Y. 98; *Bixer* v. *Ottumwa Co.*, 70 Ia. 145). (c) A decision upon one writ of *habeas corpus*, refusing to discharge a prisoner, does not bar the issuing of another writ by another court or officer (*Bradley* v. *Beetle*, 153 Mass. 154; *In re Snell*, 31 Minn. 110; *People* v. *Brady*, 56 N.Y. 182); *aliter*, as to a decision discharging the prisoner on the same state of facts (*Weir* v. *Marley*, 99 Mo. 484; *McConologue's Case*, 107 Mass. 154), and as to a decision determining the right to the custody of an infant child. *Mercein* v. *People*, 25 Wend. 64; *State* v. *Bechdel*, 37 Minn. 360.]

[1] *R.* v. *Hutchins*, 5 Q. B. D. 353, supplies a recent illustration of this principle. [Cf. *Putnam* v. *Clark*, 34 N. J. Eq. 532; *Maybee* v. *Avery*, 18 Johns. 352; *Quinn* v. *Quinn*, 16 Vt. 426.]

[2] *R.* v. *Hartington Middle Quarter*, 4 E. & B. 780; and see *Flitters* v. *Allfrey*, L. R. 10 C. P. 29; and contrast *Dover* v. *Child*, 1 Ex. D. 172; [see *Bethlehem* v. *Watertown*, 47 Ct. 237.]

[3] *Barrs* v. *Jackson*, 1 Phill. 582, 587, 588; [see *Caujolle* v. *Ferrié*, 13 Wall. 465; *White* v. *Weatherbee*, 126 Mass. 450.]

(c) A company sues A for unpaid premium and calls. A special case being stated in the Court of Common Pleas, A obtains judgment on the ground that he never was a shareholder.

The company being wound up in the Court of Chancery, A applies for the repayment of the sum he had paid for premium and calls. The decision that he never was a shareholder is conclusive as between him and the company that he never was a shareholder, and he is therefore entitled to recover the sums he paid.[1]

(d) A obtains a decree of judicial separation from her husband B, on the ground of cruelty and desertion, proved by her own evidence.

Afterwards B sues A for dissolution of marriage on the ground of adultery, in which suit neither B nor A can give evidence. A charges B with cruelty and desertion. The decree in the first suit is deemed to be irrelevant in the second.[2]

(e) [A sues B to recover damages for the conversion of some bed-quilts and obtains judgment.

This judgment defeats a recovery in a subsequent action for the conversion of a bed which was taken by B at the same time with the quilts.][3]

(f) [A sues B for the conversion of a derrick and by mistake omits to allege and claim certain special damages which resulted from the conversion. He recovers judgment for the value of the derrick.

This judgment bars a subsequent action by A to recover these special damages.][4]

(g) [B owes A, upon a running account for meat bought from time to time during ten months, $160. A sues B for $100 and recovers judgment.

This judgment bars a subsequent action by A for the remaining $60.][5]

---

[1] *Bank of Hindustan, etc., Allison's Case*, L. R. 9 Ch. App. 24.

[2] *Stoate* v. *Stoate*, 2 S. & T. 223 ; both would now be competent witnesses in each suit. [See *Woodruff* v. *Woodruff*, 11 Me. 475 ; *Bradley* v. *Bradley*, id. 367]

[3] [*Farrington* v. *Payne*, 15 Johns. 432 ; S. P. *McCaffrey* v. *Carter*, 125 Mass. 330 ; *Funk* v. *Funk*, 35 Mo. App. 246 ; cf. *Brunsden* v. *Humphrey*, 14 Q. B. D. 141 ; *Bliss* v. *N. Y. Cent. R. Co.*, 160 Mass. 447, 455.]

[4] [*Sullivan* v. *Baxter*, 150 Mass. 261.]

[5] [*Memmer* v. *Carey*, 30 Minn. 458 ; *Coal Co.* v. *Brick Co.*, 52 Kan. 747 ; *Stevens* v. *Lockwood*, 13 Wend. 644 ; contra, *Badger* v. *Titcomb*, 15 Pick. 409 ; cf. *Secor* v. *Sturgis*, 16 N. Y. 548.]

(*h*) [B, A's tenant, has agreed to pay rent monthly in advance. When twenty-five months' rent is in arrear, A brings one action against B for the rent of the first twenty-four months, and another action for that of the last month. This action for a month's rent is tried first and A recovers judgment.

This judgment bars the maintenance of the action for the twenty-four months' rent.][1]

(*i*) [A, a physician, sues B, his patient, in a justice's court to recover the value of his medical services, and upon B's default to appear and contest the action, recovers judgment.

B afterwards sues A in a superior court to recover damages for malpractice in rendering said services. The former judgment is conclusive in bar of the action. The alleged malpractice being inconsistent with the claim that the physician's services were of any value, it follows that the former judgment, determining that they did have value, bars the action for malpractice. B might have proved the malpractice in the first suit to prevent the recovery of judgment by the physician.][2]

(*j*) [A sues B on a promissory note, and the suit not being defended, enters judgment for its full face value, without crediting B with a payment already made thereon. This judgment bars a subsequent action by B to recover the amount of said payment.][3]

(*k*) [A sues B, his wife, for divorce on the ground of desertion. Upon a prior petition by B against A for separate maintenance, it was decreed that B's living apart from A was for justifiable cause.

This decree bars the action for divorce.][4]

[1] [*Burritt* v. *Belfy*, 47 Ct. 323; see *Whitaker* v. *Hawley*, 30 Kan. 317; *Reformed Dutch Church* v. *Brown*, 54 Barb. 191. The authorities are not in accord as to whether a judgment for an instalment of interest upon a note, after the principal is due, bars a subsequent action for the principal. *Dulaney* v. *Payne*, 101 Ill. 325.]

[2] [*Blair* v. *Bartlett*, 75 N. Y. 150; *Bell* v. *Merrifield*, 109 N. Y. 202, 210; S. P. *Dunham* v. *Bower*, 77 N. Y. 76; contra, *Ressequie* v. *Byers*, 52 Wis. 650; *Sykes* v. *Bonner*, 1 Cinc. (O.) 464; see *Goble* v. *Dillon*, 86 Ind. 327; *Lawson* v. *Conaway*, 37 W. Va. 159; *Howell* v. *Goodrich*, 69 Ill. 556; *Haynes* v. *Ordway*, 58 N. H. 167; *Schopen* v. *Baldwin*, 83 Hun, 234.]

[3] [*Binck* v. *Wood*, 43 Barb. 315; *Greenabaum* v. *Elliott*, 60 Mo. 25; *Fuller* v. *Shattuck*, 13 Gray, 70; *Litch* v. *Clinch*, 136 Ill. 410; but see *Lent* v. *N. Y. & M. R. Co.*, 130 N. Y. 504.]

[4] [*Miller* v. *Miller*, 150 Mass. 111.]

(*l*) [An assignee in bankruptcy sued several defendants to determine the title to certain goods, and it was adjudged that the title was in him. One of these defendants, who claimed title in himself and had put it in issue in this suit, afterwards sued another of them to recover the same goods.

The judgment in the first suit is conclusive against the right to recover in the second.][1]

(*m*) [A sues B for the conversion of goods which are a part of those included in a certain bill of sale given by C to B, and A recovers judgment on the ground that the bill of sale is fraudulent and void. B afterwards sues A for the residue of the goods covered by the bill of sale.

The former judgment is deemed conclusive upon the question of fraud, and defeats B's recovery.][2]

(*n*) [A sues B to recover the price of goods sold and obtains judgment.

Afterwards A sues B to recover damages for fraud in obtaining a credit for the goods. The former judgment defeats recovery.][3]

ARTICLE 42.

STATEMENTS IN JUDGMENTS IRRELEVANT AS BETWEEN STRANGERS, EXCEPT IN ADMIRALTY CASES.

Statements contained in judgments as to the facts upon which the judgment is based are deemed to be irrelevant as between strangers, or as between a party or privy and a stranger,[4] except[5] in the case of judgments of courts of

---

[1] [*Tuska* v. *O'Brien*, 68 N. Y. 446.]

[2] [*Doty* v. *Brown*, 4 N. Y. 71; see *Wilson's Excr.* v. *Deen*, 121 U. S. 525 ; *Strauss* v. *Meertief*, 64 Ala. 299.]

[3] [*Caylus* v. *N. Y. etc. R. Co.*, 76 N. Y. 609. It is a general rule that a prior recovery will bar a subsequent action for the same claim, though the forms of action be entirely different. Gr. Ev. i. §§ 532, 533 ; *Walsh* v. *Chesapeake, etc. R. Co.*, 59 Md. 423 ; *Rendall* v. *School Dist.*, 75 Me. 358 ; *Bradley* v. *Brigham*, 149 Mass. 141.]

[4] [*Campbell* v. *Hall*, 16 N. Y. 575 ; *Railroad Co.* v. *Nat. Bk.*, 102 U. S. 14 ; *Jones* v. *Vert*, 121 Ind. 140 ; *Wing* v. *Bishop*, 3 Allen, 456.]

[5] [This exception is treated by Lord Eldon as an objectionable anomaly in *Lothian* v. *Henderson*, 3 B. & P. 545. See, too, *Castrique* v.

admiralty condemning a ship as prize.[1] In such cases the judgment is conclusive proof as against all persons of the fact on which the condemnation proceeded, where such fact is plainly stated upon the face of the sentence.

Illustrations.

(a) The question between A and B is, whether certain lands in Kent had been disgavelled. A special verdict on a feigned issue between C and D (strangers to A and B), finding that in the 2d Edw. VI. a disgavelling act was passed in words set out in the verdict, is deemed to be irrelevant.[2]

Imrie, L. R. 4 E. & I. App. 434-5. [See *Brigham* v. *Fayerweather,* 140 Mass. 411.]

[1] [A judgment of a court of admiralty condemning a ship as prize, or of any competent court condemning property under laws of forfeiture, belongs to the class of judgments commonly called judgments *in rem.* It is a general rule that such judgments are conclusive, not only as to parties and privies, but even as to all the world (*Gelston* v. *Hoyt,* 13 Johns. 561, 3 Wheat. 246 ; *Shores* v. *Hooper,* 153 Mass. 228, 233 ; *Brigham* v. *Fayerweather,* 140 Mass. 411, 413 ; *Risley* v. *Phenix Bk.,* 83 N. Y. 318, 332). Decisions as to personal status, viz., marriage, divorce, bastardy, etc., are often included in the same category (Gr. Ev. i. §§ 525, 541-546; *McClurg* v. *Terry,* 21 N. J. Eq. 225 ; see Art. 40, Illustration (*f*), *ante*). But an adjudication as to personal status may, in some cases, only be effectual within the limits of the State in which the decision is rendered (*People* v. *Baker,* 76 N. Y. 78 ; Wh. Ev. ii. §§ 815-818; cf. Bishop, M. D. & S. ii. §§ 150-158). So attachment suits against non-residents are in the nature of actions *in rem,* the property attached being the *res* (*Pennoyer* v. *Neff,* 95 U. S. 714 ; *McKinney* v. *Collins,* 88 N. Y. 216). This general doctrine as to judgments *in rem* is virtually included in Article 40, *supra.* See Appendix, Note XXIII.

The English rule stated in this Article, that the judgment of condemnation is conclusive, not only as to title but also as to the grounds of condemnation stated therein, is upheld also in some American courts (*Croudson* v. *Leonard,* 4 Cr. 434 ; *Baxter* v. *New Eng. Ins. Co.,* 6 Mass. 277; see *Cushing* v. *Laird,* 107 U. S. 69, 80 ; *Brigham* v. *Fayerweather,* 140 Mass. 411, 413). But in New York it is only *prima facie* evidence of such facts, and in a collateral action such evidence may be rebutted. *Durant* v. *Abendroth,* 97 N. Y. 132, 141.]

[2] *Doe* v. *Brydges,* 6 M. & G. 282.

(*b*) The question is, whether A committed bigamy by marrying B during the lifetime of her former husband C.

A decree in a suit of jactitation of marriage, forbidding C to claim to be the husband of A, on the ground that he was not her husband, is deemed to be irrelevant.[1]

(*c*) The question is, whether A, a shipowner, has broken a warranty to B, an underwriter, that the cargo of the ship whose freight was insured by A was neutral property.

The sentence of a French prize court condemning ship and cargo, on the ground that the cargo was enemy's property, is conclusive proof in favor of B that the cargo was enemy's property, (though on the facts the court thought it was not).[2]

(*d*) [The question is, whether A or C is rightfully entitled to hold a public office.

A judgment in a previous action between A and B to determine the title to the same office, in which it was declared that A had the rightful title, is deemed to be irrelevant as against C.][3]

ARTICLE 43.

EFFECT OF JUDGMENT NOT PLEADED AS AN ESTOPPEL.

If a judgment is not pleaded by way of estoppel, it is as between parties and privies deemed to be a relevant fact, whenever any matter which was or might have been decided[4] in the action in which it was given is in issue, or is or is deemed to be relevant to the issue, in any subsequent proceeding.

Such a judgment is conclusive proof of the facts which it decides, or might have decided,[4] if the party who gives evidence of it had no opportunity of pleading it as an estoppel.[5]

---

[1] *Duchess of Kingston's Case*, 2 S. L. C. 760; [see *Williams* v. *Williams*, 3 Barb. Ch. 628.]

[2] *Geyer* v. *Aguilar*, 7 T. R. 681 ; [see p. 127, note 1, *ante*.]

[3] [*People* v. *Murray*, 73 N. Y. 535.]

[4] [That a judgment is conclusive as to what "might have been decided," see p. 120, note 2, *ante*.]

[5] [It is held in a number of the States of this country that a judg-

Illustrations.

(*a*) A sues B for deepening the channel of a stream, whereby the flow of water to A's mill was diminished.

A verdict recovered by B in a previous action for substantially the same cause, and which might have been pleaded as an estoppel, is deemed to be relevant, but not conclusive in B's favor.[1]

(*b*) A sues B for breaking and entering A's land, and building thereon a wall and a cornice. B pleads that the land was his, and obtains a verdict in his favor on that plea.

Afterward B's devisee sues A's wife (who on the trial admitted that she claimed through A) for pulling down the wall and cornice. As the first judgment could not be pleaded as an estoppel (the wife's right not appearing on the pleadings), it is conclusive in B's favor that the land was his.[2]

---

ment is equally conclusive when given in evidence, as if pleaded, even though there was an opportunity to plead it (*Chamberlain* v. *Carlisle*, 26 N. H. 540; *Westcott* v. *Edmunds*, 68 Pa. 34; *Trayhern* v. *Colburn*, 66 Md. 277; *So. Pac. R. Co.* v. *U. S.*, 168 U. S. 1; see *Foye* v. *Patch*, 132 Mass. 105; *Blain* v. *Blain*, 45 Vt. 538; *Sheldon* v. *Patterson*, 55 Ill. 507); so also as to a foreign judgment (*Whiting* v. *Burger*, 78 Me. 287). But in many States a statutory rule requires that special defences (under which the defence of "estoppel by former recovery" is ordinarily included) be specially pleaded, if there is an opportunity so to do, in order that evidence thereof shall be admissible; when so pleaded and proved the judgment is conclusive; so also if it is proved in cases where there was no opportunity to plead it (*Fanning* v. *Hibernia Ins. Co.*, 37 O. St. 344; *Meiss* v. *Gill*, 44 O. St. 253; *Piercy* v. *Sabin*, 10 Cal. 22; *Wixson* v. *Devine*, 67 Cal. 341; *Howe* v. *Minnesota Milk Co.*, 44 Minn. 460; *Bays* v. *Trulson*, 25 Or. 109; *Brazill* v. *Isham*, 12 N. Y. 9; *Gregory* v. *Kenyon*, 34 Neb. 640; *Porter* v. *Leache*, 56 Mich. 40). But where a judgment is sought to be used, not by way of estoppel or bar to the action, but as evidence of a material fact in issue, it may be given in evidence without being specially pleaded. *Krekeler* v. *Ritter*, 62 N. Y. 372; *Swank* v. *St. Paul R. Co.*, 61 Minn. 423.]

[1] *Vooght* v. *Winch*, 2 B. & A. 662; and see *Feversham* v. *Emerson*, 11 Ex. 391. [See *Plate* v. *N. Y. C. R. Co.*, 37 N. Y. 472; *Bowyer* v. *Schofield*, 1 Abb. Dec. 177; *Newell* v. *Carpenter*, 118 Mass. 411.]

[2] *Whitaker* v. *Jackson*, 2 H. & C. 92ᶜ This had previously been doubted. See 2 Ph. Ev. 24, note 4.

ARTICLE 44.

JUDGMENTS GENERALLY DEEMED TO BE IRRELEVANT AS BETWEEN STRANGERS.

Judgments are not deemed to be relevant as rendering probable facts which may be inferred from their existence, but which they neither state nor decide—

as between strangers;[1]

as between parties and privies in suits where the issue is different, even though they relate to the same occurrence or subject-matter;[2]

or in favor of strangers against parties or privies.[3]

---

[1] [Gr. Ev. i. §§ 522, 523; *Bartlett* v. *Boston Gas Co.*, 122 Mass. 209; *Schrauth* v. *Dry Dock Bk.*, 86 N. Y. 390; see p. 126, note 4, *ante*.]

[2] [Gr. Ev. i. §§ 532, 533; *Bell* v. *Merrifield*, 109 N. Y. 202; *Coleman's Appeal*, 62 Pa. 252; *Russell* v. *Place*, 94 U. S. 606; *Norton* v. *Huxley*, 13 Gray, 285; see Illustrations (*ca*), (*cb*). So a judgment is not binding on the parties as to matters not passed upon, though they are stated in the complaint (*Sweet* v. *Tuttle*, 14 N. Y. 465), or are given in evidence (see Illustration (*cc*); *Belden* v. *State*, 103 N. Y. 1), or are improperly set up by way of counterclaim (*People* v. *Denison*, 84 N. Y. 272); nor as to matters which the judgment does affirm, but which are immaterial to the issue and not actually in controversy (*Whitney* v. *Marshall*, 138 Ind. 472; *House* v. *Lockwood*, 137 N. Y. 259; *Concha* v. *Concha*, 11 App. Cas. 541; *Munday* v. *Vail*, 34 N. J. L. 418); nor as to matters which are only incidentally cognizable, or to be inferred by argument from the judgment (Gr. Ev. i. § 528; *Hopkins* v. *Lee*, 6 Wheat. 109; *Schwan* v. *Kelly*, 173 Pa. 65; *Kitson* v. *Farwell*, 132 Ill. 327; *Burlen* v. *Shannon*, 99 Mass. 200); nor is a judgment against a party as an individual binding on him in a suit wherein he appears in a representative capacity (*Collins* v. *Hydorn*, 135 N. Y. 320; *Lander* v. *Arno*, 65 Me. 26). A party sought to be bound by a former judgment must have been a party to both actions *in the same character or capacity* (*State* v. *Branch*, 134 Mo. 592; *Fuller* v. *Metropolitan Ins. Co.*, 68 Ct. 55; *Kitts* v. *Willson*, 140 Ind. 604). A judgment against an administrator in one State is no evidence of debt in a subsequent action in another State against an administrator of the same decedent. *Johnson* v. *Powers*, 139 U. S. 156; *McGarvey* v. *Darnall*, 134 Ill. 367.]

[3] [*Burdick* v. *Norwich*, 49 Ct. 225: *Bissell* v. *Kellogg*, 65 N. Y. 432;

But a judgment is deemed to be relevant as between strangers:

(1) if it is an admission,[1] or

(2) if it relates to a matter of public or general interest, so as to be a statement under Article 30.[2]

Illustrations.

(*a*) The question is, whether A has sustained loss by the negligence of B, his servant, who has injured C's horse.

A judgment recovered by C against A for the injury, though conclusive as against B as to the fact that C recovered a sum of money from A, is deemed to be irrelevant to the question whether this was caused by B's negligence.[3]

(*ab*) [B unlawfully creates an obstruction in the street of a city, and A, being injured thereby, sues the city for damages. The city gives notice to B to defend the action, and that he will be liable for the

---

Stamp v. *Franklin*, 144 N. Y. 607; see *Phillips* v. *Jamieson*, 51 Mich. 153. But a judgment against one of two or more *joint tortfeasors*, if followed by satisfaction (not otherwise), is available to bar a suit against another (*Knapp* v. *Roche*, 94 N. Y. 329; *Roodhouse* v. *Christian*, 158 Ill. 137; *The Beaconsfield*, 158 U. S. 303; *Cleveland* v. *Bangor*, 87 Me. 259; *Savage* v. *Stevens*, 128 Mass. 254; *Seither* v. *Phila. Traction Co.*, 125 Pa. 397); and the rule is the same as to a judgment against one of two or more persons *jointly and severally liable on contract* (*Sawyer* v. *White*, 19 Vt. 40); but judgment against one of two or more *joint contractors* bars an action against the others, unless they were out of the jurisdiction so that they could not be served with process. *Kingsley* v. *Davis*, 104 Mass. 178; *Russell* v. *McCall*, 141 N. Y. 437, 450; *Yoho* v. *McGovern*, 42 O. St. 11; *Kendall* v. *Hamilton*, 4 App. Cas. 504; cf. *Wegg Prosser* v. *Evans*, [1895] 1 Q. B. 108.]

[1] [Gr. Ev. i. § 527 *a*; *Rudolph* v. *Landwerlen*, 92 Ind. 34; *St. Louis Ins. Co.* v. *Cravens*, 69 Mo. 72; *Parks* v. *Mosher*, 71 Me. 304, holding it open to explanation; see *Clark* v. *Dillon*, 97 N. Y. 370.]

[2] [See *Patterson* v. *Gaines*, 6 How. (U. S.) 550, 599; *People* v. *Buckland*, 13 Wend. 594.]

[3] *Green* v. *New River Company*, 4 T. R. 589. [*Bank of Oswego* v. *Babcock*, 5 Hill, 152; *Grand Trunk R. Co.* v. *Latham*, 63 Me. 177; *Oceanic Nav. Co.* v. *Compania*, 134 N. Y. 461: *Drummond* v *Prestman*, 12 Wheat. 515; see next note.]

amount recovered. B does not defend the action, and A recovers judgment.

In a suit afterwards brought by the city against B for indemnity, the prior judgment is conclusive evidence against B of the city's liability to A, of the amount of damages recoverable, and that the injury was not caused by any default on A's part ; but is not competent to prove that the injury was caused by B's negligence, which must therefore be shown.][1]

[1] [*City of Rochester* v. *Montgomery*, 72 N. Y. 65 ; *Robbins* v. *Chicago*, 4 Wall. 657, 2 Black, 418 ; *Brookville* v. *Arthurs*, 130 Pa. 501; *St. Joseph* v. *Union R. Co.*, 116 Mo. 636 ; *Boston* v. *Worthington*, 10 Gray, 496 ; cf. *Mayor* v. *Brady*, 151 N Y. 611 ; *Portland* v. *Richardson*, 54 Me. 46. The notice need not be express (*Village of Port Jervis* v. *First Nat. Bk.*, 96 N. Y. 550).

The same principle applies in other cases where one party is primarily liable, but has a remedy over against another to obtain indemnity (*Heiser* v. *Hatch*, 86 N. Y. 614 ; *Carleton* v. *Lombard*, 149 N. Y. 137, 152 ; *Hoppaugh* v. *McGrath*, 53 N. J. L. 81 ; *Davis* v. *Smith*, 79 Me. 351 ; *Chicago, etc. R. Co.* v. *Packet Co.*, 70 Ill. 217). As a general rule, a judgment against a principal is not binding upon his surety (though it may be used to prove the fact of its recovery), unless the latter agreed to indemnify against the results of the suit, or unless he had notice and opportunity to defend (*Thomas* v. *Hubbell*, 15 N. Y. 405 ; *Grommes* v. *St. Paul Trust Co.*, 147 Ill. 634 ; *Ball* v. *Chancellor*, 47 N. J. L. 125 ; cf. *Giltinan* v. *Strong*, 64 Pa. 242). But sureties upon official bonds, as administrators' bonds, sheriffs' bonds, etc., are often held concluded by such judgments (in the absence of fraud or collusion), though they had no notice, such being deemed the obligation of their contracts (*Harrison* v. *Clark*, 87 N. Y. 572 ; *Wheeler* v. *Sweet*, 137 N. Y. 435 ; *Tute* v. *James*, 50 Vt. 124 ; *McMicken* v. *Comm.*, 58 Pa. 213; *Stovall* v. *Banks*, 10 Wall. 583 ; *Nevitt* v. *Woodburn*, 160 Ill. 203; *Tracy* v. *Goodwin*, 5 Allen, 409 ; cf. *New Haven* v. *Chidsey*, 68 Ct. 397). In some States, however, a judgment against a principal in an official bond is only *prima facie* evidence against the sureties (*Beauchaine* v. *McKinnon*, 55 Minn. 318; *Norris* v. *Mersereau*, 74 Mich. 687; *Stephens* v. *Shafer*, 48 Wis. 54 ; cf. *Moses* v. *United States*, 166 U. S. 571). As to the different kinds of indemnity contracts and the necessity of giving notice, see *Bridgeport Ins. Co.* v. *Wilson*, 34 N. Y. 275, 280 ; cf. *Konitzky* v. *Meyer*, 49 N. Y. 571.

A judgment recovered by the holder of a bill or note against an indorser does not, unless it has been satisfied, bar an action against the acceptor or maker. *Gilmore* v. *Carr*, 2 Mass. 171; *Railroad Co.* v. *Nat. Bk.*, 102 U. S. 14.]

(b) The question whether a bill of exchange is forged arises in an action on the bill. The fact that A was convicted of forging the bill is deemed to be irrelevant.[1]

(c) A collision takes place between two ships, A and B, each of which is damaged by the other.

The owner of A sues the owner of B, and recovers damages on the ground that the collision was the fault of B's captain. This judgment is not conclusive in an action by the owner of B against the owner of A, for the damage done to B.[2] (Semble, it is deemed to be irrelevant.)[3]

(ca) [A recovers damages from B for a wrongful dismissal from B's employment before the term of service had expired.

This judgment does not preclude a recovery by A in a subsequent action of the sum due for wages during the time he was actually employed, and payable before the dismissal.][4]

(cb) [The will of A is duly admitted to probate by a surrogate's court having competent jurisdiction.

A's widow afterwards brings action for the admeasurement of her dower.

The surrogate's record of probate of A's will is not deemed to be relevant to prove A's death.][5]

(cc) [A sues B to recover the value of board furnished to B's wife, and recovers judgment; but the judgment does not state whether it is rendered (1) because B's wife had left him on account of his cruelty, or (2) because she was absent from him on his credit by his consent. Evidence to support both grounds was given on the trial.

A afterwards sues B to recover board for a subsequent period, and

---

[1] Per Blackburn, J., in *Castrique* v. *Imrie*, L. R. 4 E. & I. App. 434. [Gr. Ev. i. § 537 ; *Corbley* v. *Wilson*, 71 Ill. 209 ; *People* v. *Kenyon*, 93 Mich. 19 ; *State* v. *Bradnack*, 69 Ct. 212 ; see *Mutual Ins. Co.* v. *Tisdale*, 91 U. S. 238, 244 ; *Willson* v. *Manhattan R. Co.*, 2 Misc. 127, 144 N. Y. 632 ; *Harger* v. *Thomas*, 44 Pa. 128.]

[2] *The Calypso*, 1 Swab. Ad. 28.

[3] On the general principle in *Duchess of Kingston's Case*, 2 S. L. C. 813.

[4] [*Perry* v. *Dickerson*, 85 N. Y. 345 ; cf. *Olmstead* v. *Bach*, 78 Md. 132.]

[5] [*Carroll* v. *Carroll*, 60 N. Y. 121 ; S. P. *Mutual Ins. Co.* v. *Tisdale*, 91 U. S. 238 ; cf. *Matter of Patteson*, 146 N. Y. 327 ; *Pick* v. *Strong*, 26 Minn. 303 ; *Kearney* v. *Denn*, 15 Wall. 51 : *Brigham* v. *Fayerweather*, 140 Mass. 411.][1]

sues now expressly on the ground that B's wife had left him for his cruelty. The former judgment is conclusive evidence that B's wife was absent from him during the prior period for *some* justifiable cause, but not that that cause was his cruelty, unless the jury find, from parol evidence submitted to show what was proved in the former trial, that the former jury gave their verdict on the ground of cruelty.][1]

(*d*) A is prosecuted and convicted as a principal felon.

B is afterwards prosecuted as an accessory to the felony committed by A.

The judgment against A is deemed to be irrelevant as against B, though A's guilt must be proved as against B.[2]

(*e*) A sues B, a carrier, for goods delivered by A to B.

A judgment recovered by B against a person to whom he had delivered the goods, is deemed to be relevant as an admission by B that he had them.[3]

(*f*) A sues B for trespass on land.

A judgment, convicting A for a nuisance by obstructing a highway on the place said to have been trespassed on, is (at least) deemed to be relevant to the question whether the place was a public highway (and is possibly conclusive).[4]

ARTICLE 45.

JUDGMENTS CONCLUSIVE IN FAVOR OF JUDGE.

When any action is brought against any person for anything done by him in a judicial capacity, the judgment delivered, and the proceedings antecedent thereto,

---

[1] [*Burlen* v. *Shannon*, 14 Gray, 433 ; cf. *Lewis* v. *Ocean Nav. Co.*, 125 N. Y. 341.]

[2] *Semble* from *R.* v. *Turner*, 1 Moo. C. C. 347. [In this country it is generally held that the judgment against A is admissible in such a case, and is *prima facie* evidence of A's guilt, but not conclusive. B may, therefore, controvert it. *Levy* v. *People*, 80 N. Y. 327 ; *State* v. *Mosley*, 31 Kan. 355 ; *Anderson* v. *State*, 63 Ga. 675 ; *State* v. *Gleim*, 17 Mont. 17 ; Bishop, New Cr. Pro. ii. § 12 ; cf. *Comm.* v. *Elisha*, 3 Gray, 460 ; *Jones* v. *People*, 20 Hun, 545, 81 N. Y. 637.]

[3] Buller, N. P. 242, *b*.

[4] *Petrie* v. *Nuttall*, 11 Ex. 569.

are conclusive proof of the facts therein stated, whether
they are or are not necessary to give the defendant jurisdiction, if, assuming them to be true, they show that he
had jurisdiction.

Illustration.

A sues B (a justice of the peace) for taking from him a vessel and
500 lbs. of gunpowder thereon.   B produces a conviction before himself of A for having gunpowder in a boat on the Thames (against 2
Geo. III. c. 28).

The conviction is conclusive proof for B, that the thing called a boat
was a boat.[1]

ARTICLE 46.

FRAUD, COLLUSION, OR WANT OF JURISDICTION MAY BE PROVED.

Whenever any judgment is offered as evidence under
any of the Articles hereinbefore contained, the party

---

[1] *Brittain* v. *Kinnaird,* 1 B. & B. 432. [*People* v. *House of Mercy,*
133 N. Y. 207; *People* v. *N. Y. Protectory,* 106 N. Y. 604; see *Harman*
v. *Brotherson,* 1 Den. 537; *People* v. *Collins,* 19 Wend. 56, 62; *Wells*
v. *Stevens,* 2 Gray, 115, 119. It is stated as a general rule (not limited
to actions against judges) that when the jurisdiction of a court depends
upon a fact which the court is required to ascertain and determine in
its decision, such decision is final, until reversed or vacated in a direct
proceeding for that purpose (*Otis* v. *The Rio Grande,* 1 Woods, 279;
Colton v. *Beardsley,* 38 Barb. 29, 51; *Ex parte Sternes,* 77 Cal. 156;
Dyckman v. *Mayor of N. Y.,* 5 N. Y. 434, 440; see *Austin* v. *Vrooman,*
128 N. Y. 229; *Bolton* v. *Shriever,* 135 N. Y. 65), and will protect all
persons acting upon it in good faith. But in other cases in which some
fact must exist to give jurisdiction, a court or judicial officer cannot
acquire jurisdiction simply by deciding that such fact exists; the
proceeding is a nullity, and its invalidity may be shown in a collateral
proceeding (*Roderigas* v. *East River Sav. Inst.,* 63 N. Y. 460, 464;
Scott v. *McNeal,* 154 U. S. 34; *People* v. *Bd. of Health,* 140 N. Y. 1;
Miller v. *Amsterdam,* 149 N. Y. 288; see *McLean* v. *Jephson,* 123
N. Y. 142). The distinction between the two classes of cases is considered in *People's Sav. Bk.* v. *Wilcox,* 15 R. I. 258, and *Noble* v.
Union Riv. R. Co., 147 U. S. 165, 173.]

against whom it is so offered may prove that the court
which gave it had no jurisdiction,[1] or that it has been

[1] [On the ground that "a record imports absolute verity," it is a generally received common law doctrine in this country that while the
judgment of a domestic court of general jurisdiction, acting in the
scope of its general powers, may be avoided by a party or privy in a
collateral proceeding for lack of jurisdiction *apparent on the face of
the record itself*, yet that it cannot be so impeached *when the recitals
of the record show that the court had jurisdiction* (*Blaisdell* v. *Pray*,
68 Me. 269; *Finneran* v. *Leonard*, 7 Allen, 54; *Culver's Appeal*, 48
Ct. 165, 173; *McCahill* v. *Equitable Assur. Soc.*, 26 N. J. Eq. 531;
Frankel v. *Satterfield*, 9 Houst. 201; *Adams* v. *Cowles*, 95 Mo. 501;
Sandwich Co. v. *Earl*, 56 Minn. 390; *Hill* v. *City Cab Co.*, 79 Cal. 188;
People v. *Seelye*, 146 Ill. 189; *Harman* v. *Moore*, 112 Ind. 221; *Wall*
v. *Wall*, 123 Pa 545); nor when the record fails to recite facts show-
ing jurisdiction, for then, as to such courts, jurisdiction is presumed
(*Galpin* v. *Page*, 18 Wall. 350; *Bateman* v. *Miller*, 118 Ind. 345;
McClanahan v. *West*, 100 Mo. 309; *In re Eickhoff*, 101 Cal. 600).
But there has been much diversity of opinion as to the doctrine that
such a record cannot be impeached collaterally when its recitals
show jurisdiction or are silent on the point (*Ferguson* v. *Crawford*, 70
N. Y. 253, 86 N. Y. 609; *Martin* v. *Gray*, 19 Kan. 458; *In re Watson*,
30 Kan. 753; *Frankel* v. *Satterfield*, supra). Judgments of inferior
courts, or of courts of limited jurisdiction, or even of courts of general
jurisdiction acting in the exercise of special statutory powers not according to the course of the common law, may, however, be attacked
collaterally, as a general rule, for lack of jurisdiction; the jurisdiction
of such courts is not presumed, but must be affirmatively made to
appear (Id.; *Coit* v. *Haven*, 30 Ct. 190; *Galpin* v. *Page*, supra; *People*
v. *Warden*, 100 N. Y. 20; *Fahey* v. *Mottu*, 67 Md. 250; *Richardson*
v. *Seevers*, 84 Va. 259; *Furgeson* v. *Jones*, 17 Or. 204; *Smith* v. *Claus-
meier*, 136 Ind. 120; *State* v. *Mobile, etc. R. Co.*, 108 Ala. 31; but see
Hahn v. *Kelly*, 34 Cal. 391). The States differ, however, to some
extent, in classifying courts as superior or inferior under these rules.
Thus generally a court of a justice of the peace is ranked as an inferior
court (*Turner* v. *Roby*, 3 N. Y. 193; *Fahey* v. *Mottu*, 67 Md. 250; *Clay-
born* v. *Tompkins*, 141 Ind. 19), but in some States it is classed with
the superior courts (*Hendrick* v. *Whittemore*, 105 Mass. 23, 28). So
probate courts or orphans' courts are of limited jurisdiction in some
States (*Fowle* v. *Coe*, 63 Me. 245; *People's Sav. Bk.* v. *Wilcox*, 15
R. I. 258; *Sears* v. *Terry*, 26 Ct. 273; cf. *Smith* v. *Wildman*, 178 Pa.
245), but in others of superior jurisdiction (*Macey* v. *Stark*, 116 Mo.

reversed,[1] or, if he is a stranger to it, that it was obtained by any fraud or collusion,[2] to which neither he nor any person to whom he is privy was a party.[3]

If an action is brought in an English court to enforce the judgment of a foreign court, and probably if an action

---

481; *State* v. *Mobile, etc. R. Co.*, 108 Ala. 29, 39; *Bolton* v. *Schriever*, 135 N. Y. 65; *Clark* v. *Costello*, 59 N. J. L. 234).

These rules as to questioning jurisdiction are subject to the limitation set forth in Article 45, note 1 (*Noble* v. *Union Riv. R. Co.*, 147 U. S. 165).

In some States, however, in which equitable defences are allowed in legal actions, fraud in acquiring jurisdiction may be interposed as a defence against the judgments of even the higher courts, notwithstanding this contradicts the record (*Ferguson* v. *Crawford*, supra; *Clark* v. *Little*, 41 Ia. 497; *Hogg* v. *Link*, 90 Ind. 346; see *Morrill* v. *Morrill*, 20 Or. 96).

As to all courts, it is a general rule that their judgments cannot be impeached collaterally by parties or privies for *error* or *irregularity*. *Comstock* v. *Crawford*, 3 Wall. 396; *Weiss* v. *Guerineau*, 109 Ind. 438; *Caulfield* v. *Sullivan*, 85 N. Y. 153.]

[1] [*Smith* v. *Frankfield*, 77 N. Y. 414; *Clodfelter* v. *Hulett*, 92 Ind. 426. While an appeal from a judgment is pending, the judgment still operates as an estoppel (*Parkhurst* v. *Berdell*, 110 N. Y. 386; *Smith* v. *Schreiner*, 86 Wis. 19; *Moore* v. *Williams*, 132 Ill. 589). But in some States the contrary rule prevails. *Harris* v. *Barnhart*, 97 Cal. 546; *Sherman* v. *Dilley*, 3 Nev. 21.]

[2] [A stranger but not a party, may avoid a judgment collaterally for fraud (*Ogle* v. *Baker*, 137 Pa. 378; *In re Burdick*, 162 Ill. 48; *Davis* v. *Davis*, 61 Me. 395). So a stranger may impeach a judgment collaterally for lack of jurisdiction (*Buffum* v. *Ramsdell*, 55 Me. 252; *Fall River* v. *Riley*, 140 Mass. 488). But as a party may in a proper case bring suit in equity to avoid a judgment procured by fraud (*Marshall* v. *Holmes*, 141 U. S. 589; *Mayor* v. *Brady*, 115 N. Y. 599), so in some States he may set up such fraud as an equitable defence (*Mandeville* v. *Reynolds*, 68 N. Y. 543-546; *Ferguson* v. *Crawford*, 70 N. Y. 253; *Stowell* v. *Eldred*, 26 Wis. 504; *Hallack* v. *Loft*, 19 Col. 74; see *Duringer* v. *Moschino*, 93 Ind. 495). And when the fraud is in acquiring jurisdiction, the rules in note 1, p. 136, *supra*, apply; see *Bolling* v. *Speller*, 96 Ala. 269.]

[3] Cases collected in T. E. ss. 1524-1525, s. 1530. See, too, 2 Ph. Ev. 35, and *Ochsenbein* v. *Papelier*, L. R. 8 Ch. 695.

is brought in an English court to enforce the judgment
of another English court, any such matter as aforesaid
may be proved by the defendant, even if the matter
alleged as fraud was alleged by way of defence in the
foreign court and was not believed by them to exist.[1]

Illustration.

(a) [Judgment is rendered against A in a common law action for
damages in a domestic court of general jurisdiction. He has never
been served with process in the action nor has he authorized any
attorney to appear for him and thus give the court jurisdiction over
his person. In fact, however, B, a duly admitted attorney of the court,
has appeared for A in the action and the recitals of the record show
such appearance. A cannot impeach the judgment collaterally on
the ground that B had no authority to appear for him. He may, however, attack the judgment by a direct proceeding for that purpose, as
by a motion in the original action to vacate it.][2]

ARTICLE 47.

FOREIGN JUDGMENTS.

The provisions of Articles 40–46 apply to such of the
judgments of courts of foreign countries as can by law

---

[1] *Aboulof* v. *Oppenheimer*, 10 Q. B. D. 295. [It was held in this
case that fraud in procuring a judgment in a foreign court was a good
defence to an action upon the judgment, though the fact whether such
fraud existed had been investigated in the foreign court. To the same
effect is *Vadala* v. *Lawes*, 25 Q. B. D. 310. As to the American law
on this question, see Art. 47, note.]

[2] [*Vilas* v. *Plattsburgh, etc. R. Co.*, 123 N. Y. 440; *Mutual Life Ins.
Co.* v. *Pinner*, 43 N. J. Eq. 52; *Bradley* v. *Welch*, 100 Mo. 258; *Cor-
bitt* v. *Timmerman*, 95 Mich. 581; *Reynolds* v. *Fleming*, 30 Kan. 106;
Cleveland v. *Hopkins*, 55 Wis. 387; *Denton* v. *Roddy*, 34 Ark. 642.
By some authorities, also, an action for damages will lie against the
attorney, if any loss has been sustained by his unauthorized act
(*Everett* v. *Warner Bk.*, 58 N. H. 340; *Hackett* v. *McMillan*, 112
N. C. 513). In *Ferguson* v. *Crawford*, 70 N. Y. 253, where there was

be enforced in this country, and so far as they can be so enforced.[1]

what purported to be an attorney's appearance, but this was a forgery, this fraud was held available by way of equitable defence to impeach the judgment. Some States allow judgments entered upon an unauthorized appearance to be collaterally attacked. *Bruschke* v. *N. Chicago Verein*, 145 Ill. 433; cf. *Shelton* v. *Tiffin*, 6 How. (U. S.) 163.]

[1] The cases on this subject are collected in the note on the *Duchess of Kingston's Case*, 2 S. L. C. 813–845. A list of the cases will be found in R. N. P. 221–3. The last leading cases on the subject are *Godard* v. *Gray*, L. R. 6 Q. B. 139, and *Castrique* v. *Imrie*, L. R. 4 E. & I. App. 414. See, too, *Schisby* v. *Westenholz*, L. R. 6 Q. B. 155 ; *Rousillon* v. *Rousillon*, 14 Ch. D. 370 ; and *Nouvion* v. *Freeman*, 15 App. Cas. 1.

[The *judgments of sister States* are in this country ranked as foreign judgments within this rule. The U. S. Constitution (Art. 4, § 1) declares that "full faith and credit shall be given in each State to the public acts, records, and judicial proceedings of every other State," and Congress has enacted that "the said records shall have such faith and credit given to them in every court within the United States as they have by law or usage in the courts of the State from which they are taken " (U. S. Rev. St. § 905 ; see *Huntington* v. *Attrill*, 146 U. S. 657 ; *Harrington* v. *Harrington*, 154 Mass. 517 ; *Dow* v. *Blake*, 148 Ill. 76 ; *Fairchild* v. *Fairchild*, 53 N. J. Eq. 678). Nevertheless, such judgments may be avoided collaterally for lack of jurisdiction, even in contradiction of recitals in the record showing jurisdiction (*Thompson* v. *Whitman*, 18 Wall. 457 ; *Graham* v. *Spencer*, 14 F. R. 603 ; *Gregory* v. *Gregory*, 78 Me. 187 ; *Cross* v. *Cross*, 108 N. Y. 628 ; *Royal Arcanum* v. *Carley*, 52 N. J. Eq. 642 ; *Price* v. *Schaeffler*, 161 Pa. 530 ; *Greensweig* v. *Sterlinger*, 103 Cal. 278 ; *Napton* v. *Leaton*, 71 Mo. 358 ; *People* v. *Dawell*, 25 Mich. 247 ; *Pennywit* v. *Foote*, 27 O. St. 600 ; *Gilman* v. *Gilman*, 126 Mass. 26); so they may be avoided for fraud in acquiring jurisdiction over the person (*Stanton* v. *Crosby*, 9 Hun, 370 ; *Toof* v. *Fooley*, 87 Ia. 8 ; cf. *Brown* v. *Eaton*, 98 Ind. 591). So fraud otherwise committed in procuring the judgment (if the party was debarred, without fault on his part, from availing himself of such fraud as a defence in the original suit), would be a sufficient ground in equity to have the judgment set aside (*Doughty* v. *Doughty*, 27 N. J. Eq. 315 ; *Payne* v. *O'Shea*, 84 Mo. 129 ; cf. *Davis* v. *Cornue*, 151 N. Y. 172), and may be set up in some States as an equitable defence to the judgment (*Dobson* v. *Pearce*, 12 N. Y. 156 ; *Rogers* v. *Gwinn*, 21 Ia. 58 ; *Keeler* v. *Elston*, 22 Neb. 310 ; see *Hunt* v. *Hunt*, 72 N. Y. 217). Except in equity, however, fraud in obtaining such a judgment is not

a sufficient defence to an action upon it (*Simmons* v. *Saul*, 138 U. S.
439, 459 ; *Allison* v. *Chapman*, 19 F. R. 488 ; see *Mooney* v. *Hinds*,
160 Mass. 469; *Ambler* v. *Whipple*, 139 Ill. 311). Such judgments are,
moreover, not impeachable upon the merits for *error* or for *irregularity* (*Pringle* v. *Woodworth*, 90 N. Y. 502 ; *Christmas* v. *Russell*, 5
Wall. 290; *Harryman* v. *Roberts*, 52 Md. 64 ; *National Bk.* v. *Wallis*,
59 N. J. L. 46 ; see *Nichols* v. *Nichols*, 25 N. J. Eq. 60).

Similar principles apply to *foreign judgments*. They may be im-
peached for lack of jurisdiction, but are generally held to be conclusive upon the merits (*Ritchie* v. *McMullen*, 159 U. S. 235 ; *Dunstan* v.
Higgins, 138 N. Y. 20; *Shepard* v. *Wright*, 113 N. Y. 582; *Lazier* v.
Westcott, 26 N. Y. 146; *Fisher* v. *Fielding*, 67 Ct. 91; *McEwan* v.
Zimmer, 38 Mich. 765; *Smith* v. *Grady*, 68 Wis. 215; *Bischoff* v.
Wetherel, 9 Wall. 812 ; *Roth* v. *Roth*, 104 Ill. 35). It is also generally
declared that they are impeachable for fraud (see cases *supra ; Baker*
v. *Palmer*, 83 Ill. 568), but for what forms of fraud or under what cir-
cumstances is wholly unsettled in this country (*Hilton* v. *Guyot*, 159
U. S. 113, 206, 207). An important decision of the U. S. Supreme Court
holds, however, that a judgment rendered in a foreign country, as
France, which does not regard our own judgments as conclusive, will
not be deemed conclusive in our courts, but only *prima facie* evidence
of the justice of the claim upon which the judgment was recovered
(*Hilton* v. *Guyot*, supra).

As to the effect of a judgment in another State obtained by default
upon service of process by publication on a non-resident or foreign
corporation and an attachment of defendant's property, see *Pennoyer*
v. *Neff*, 95 U. S. 714; *Fitzsimons* v. *Marks*, 66 Barb. 333; *Gilman* v.
Gilman, 126 Mass. 26. Such judgment only avails as *quasi in rem* to
reach the *property attached*, but is not valid, either in the State where
rendered or in other States, as a judgment *in personam* (Id.; *St. Clair*
v. *Cox*, 106 U. S. 350; *National Bk.* v. *Peabody*, 55 Vt. 492; *Needham*
v. *Thayer*, 147 Mass. 536; *Eastman* v. *Dearborn*, 63 N. H. 364; *Ward* v.
Boyce, 152 N. Y. 191); see generally as to judgments *in rem. Durant*
t. Abendroth, 97 N. Y. 132.]

CHAPTER V.*

OPINIONS, WHEN RELEVANT AND WHEN NOT.

ARTICLE 48.

OPINION GENERALLY IRRELEVANT.

THE fact that any person is of opinion that a fact in issue, or relevant or deemed to be relevant to the issue, does or does not exist is deemed to be irrelevant to the existence of such fact,[1] except in the cases specified in this chapter.[2]

---

* See Note XXIV. [Appendix].

[1] [It is a general rule that witnesses must give evidence of *facts*, not of *opinions* (*Conn. Ins. Co.* v. *Lathrop*, 111 U. S. 612, 618; *Graham* v. *Pa. Co.*, 139 Pa. 149; *Coates* v. *Burlington, etc. R. Co.*, 62 Ia. 486; *Chamberlain* v. *Platt*, 68 Ct. 126; *Teerpenning* v. *Corn Ex. Ins. Co.*, 43 N. Y. 279). This is especially true of opinions relating directly to the questions of law or fact at issue in the action. These are questions to be determined by court or jury from the *facts* in evidence. Id.; *Buffum* v. *Jones*, 144 Mass. 29; *Cannon* v. *People*, 141 Ill. 270; *Insley* v. *Shire*, 54 Kan. 793 ; see Illustrations (*b*) and (*c*).]

[2] [Besides the exceptions stated by the author, the following are recognized: (1) The subscribing witnesses to a will may state their opinions as to the testator's sanity at the time of executing the will (*Egbert* v. *Egbert*, 78 Pa. 326; *Williams* v. *Spencer*, 150 Mass. 346; *Hewlett* v. *Wood*, 55 N. Y. 634). (2) In many States, witnesses who are not experts may state their opinion as to a person's sanity or insanity, in connection with a statement of the facts within their personal knowledge and observation, upon which that opinion is based (*Conn. Ins. Co.* v. *Lathrop*, 111 U. S. 612; *Hardy* v. *Merrill*, 56 N. H. 227; *Foster's Excrs.* v. *Dickerson*, 64 Vt. 233; *Kimberly's Appeal*, 68 Ct. 428; *Gens* v. *State*, 58 N. J. L. 482; *Elcessor* v. *Elcessor*, 146 Pa. 359; *Stumph* v. *Muller*, 142 Ind. 442; *Denning* v. *Butcher*, 91 Ia. 425; *N. Y. etc. R. Co.* v. *Luebeck*, 157 Ill. 595; *Holland* v. *Zollner*, 102 Cal. 633; *Chase* v. *Winans*, 59 Md. 475; *Fishburne* v. *Ferguson*, 84 Va. 87; *Newcomb* v. *Newcomb*, 96 Ky. 120; *Prentis* v. *Bates*, 93 Mich. 234;

Illustrations.

(a) The question is, whether A, a deceased testator, was sane or not when he made his will. His friends' opinions as to his sanity, as ex-

---

State v. *Williamson*, 106 Mo. 162 ; *Baughman* v. *Baughman*, 32 Kan. 538). In New York this is not permissible, but the witness may testify to acts and declarations known or observed by him, and characterize them as rational or irrational acts or declarations (*Holcomb* v. *Holcomb*, 95 N. Y. 316 ; *People* v. *Strait*, 148 N. Y. 566). And so in Massachusetts testimony of opinion as to general soundness or unsoundness of mind is not received from non-experts, but still it has been held permissible to ask such a witness whether he ever observed any fact which led him to infer that there was any derangement of intellect, or whether a person had failed mentally within a given time (*May* v. *Bradlee*, 127 Mass. 414 ; *Clark* v. *Clark*, 168 Mass. 523). (3) So generally the opinions of non-experts, when based upon facts known and observed by them, are admissible as to many matters upon which men in general, without expert training, are competent to form a reliable opinion. An important reason for this rule is that if only the facts upon which such opinions were based could be stated to the jury, such facts could not usually be described so perfectly as to enable the jury to form a just and satisfactory conclusion from them (*Koccis* v. *State*, 56 N. J. L. 44 ; *Shelby* v. *Clagett*, 46 O. St. 549 ; *Laughlin* v. *Street R. Co.*, 62 Mich. 220 ; *State* v. *Rainsbarger*, 71 Ia. 746). Such testimony of opinion is received as to a person's identity (*State* v. *Dickson*, 78 Mo. 438 ; *People* v. *Rolfe*, 61 Cal. 540) ; a person's age (*Comm.* v. *O'Brien*, 134 Mass. 198 ; *Elsner* v. *Supreme Lodge*, 98 Mo. 640) ; a person's appearance or state of health (*Carthage Turnpike Co.* v. *Andrews*, 102 Ind. 138 ; *Chicago R. Co.* v. *Van Vleck*, 143 Ill. 480; *Smalley* v. *Appleton*, 70 Wis. 340) ; whether a person was drunk or sober (*Felska* v. *N. Y. C. R. Co.*, 152 N. Y. 339 ; *Cook* v. *Ins. Co.*, 84 Mich. 12 ; *Castner* v. *Sliker*, 33 N. J. L. 507) ; sick or well (*Elliott* v. *Van Buren*, 33 Mich. 49 ; *Robinson* v. *Exempt Fire Co.*, 103 Cal. 1 ; *Higbie* v. *Life Ins. Co.*, 53 N. Y. 603 ; but not as to the nature of a sickness, *Shawneetown* v. *Mason*, 82 Ill. 337) ; nervous, or calm, or excited, or angry (*Dimick* v. *Downs*, 82 Ill. 570 ; *White* v. *Beatty*, 64 Ia. 333) ; that a person had good eyesight (*Adams* v. *People*, 63 N. Y. 621) ; that a horse was frightened or tired (*Darling* v. *Westmoreland*, 52 N. H. 401 ; *State* v. *Ward*, 61 Vt. 153) ; that a highway was in good repair or was dangerous (*Kelleher* v. *Keokuk*, 60 Ia. 473 ; *Ryan* v. *Bristol*, 63 Ct. 26) ; and many like matters. See many illustrations given in *Sydleman* v. *Beckwith*, 43 Ct. 9 ; *Hardy* v. *Merrill*, 56 N. H. 227; *Comm.* v. *Sturtivant*, 117 Mass. 122; *McKillop* v. *Duluth R. Co.*, 53 Minn. 532 ; see Illustrations (*d*) and (*e*).]

pressed by the letters which they addressed to him in his lifetime, are deemed to be irrelevant.[1]

(b) [An action is brought to recover damages for a tort or breach of contract, or compensation is sought for land taken by eminent domain. The opinions of witnesses as to the amount of damage sustained by the plaintiff from the act complained of are deemed to be irrelevant. The jury are to estimate the damages from the *facts* proved.][2]

---

[1] *Wright* v. *Doe* d. *Tatham*, 7 A. & E. 313; [as to this case, see *Conn. Ins. Co.* v. *Lathrop*, 111 U. S. 612, 622; *People* v. *Montgomery*, 13 Abb. Pr. (N. S.) 207, 249.]

[2] [*Morehouse* v. *Mathews*, 2 N. Y. 514; *Roberts* v. *N. Y. El. R. Co.*, 128 N. Y. 455; *Bain* v. *Cushman*, 60 Vt. 343; *Railway Co.* v. *Gardner*, 45 O. St. 309; *Hartley* v. *Keokuk, etc. R. Co.*, 85 Ia. 455; *Spencer* v. *Metropolitan R. Co.*, 120 Mo. 154; *Atchison, etc. R. Co.* v. *Wilkinson*, 55 Kan. 83; *Jameson* v. *Kent*, 42 Neb. 412; but in some States such testimony is admissible (*Chicago, etc. R. Co.* v. *Nix*, 137 Ill. 141; *Portland, etc. R. Co.* v. *Deering*, 78 Me. 61; *Shattuck* v. *Stoneham R. Co.*, 6 Allen, 115).

It is a general rule, however, that evidence of opinion as to the *value* of houses, lands, chattels, medical, legal, or other services, etc., will be received from persons having special knowledge and experience concerning such matters (*Hills* v. *Home Ins. Co.*, 129 Mass. 345; *Shea* v. *Hudson*, 165 Mass. 43; *Montana R. Co.* v. *Warren*, 137 U. S. 348; *McElheny* v. *Bridge Co.*, 153 Pa. 108; *Wallace* v. *Schaub*, 81 Md. 594; *Louisville, etc. R. Co.* v. *Wallace*, 136 Ill. 87; *Edgecomb* v. *Buckhout*, 146 N. Y. 332; *Whiton* v. *Snyder*, 88 N. Y. 299; *Reynolds* v. *Robinson*, 64 N. Y. 589). This is in the nature of expert testimony, though it is not necessary that a witness as to the value of property should be a skilled expert, in the strict sense of that term (*Kelley* v. *Richardson*, 69 Mich. 430; *Erickson* v. *Drazkowski*, 94 id. 551; *Latham* v. *Brown*, 48 Kan. 190); thus not only real estate brokers or appraisers, but also other persons conversant with land values in a certain locality, may testify as to the value of a particular lot or farm there situated (*Clark* v. *Baird*, 9 N. Y. 183; *Blake* v. *Griswold*, 103 N. Y. 429; *Lyman* v. *Boston*, 164 Mass. 99; *Lee* v. *Springfield Co.*, 176 Pa. 223; *Mayor of Baltimore* v. *Smith*, 80 Md. 458; *Pike* v. *Chicago*, 155 Ill. 656; *Kansas City R. Co.* v. *Ehret*, 41 Kan. 22; but see *Laing* v. *United N. J. R. Co.*, 54 N. J. L. 576). But such opinion evidence is not necessarily controlling upon the judgment of the jury (*Head* v. *Hargrave*, 105 U. S. 45).

Evidence of opinion has been received as to the value of land both

(*c*) [The question is, which of two deeds conveys a greater right. A witness cannot be examined as to his opinion upon this point.][1]

(*d*) [In an action for breach of promise of marriage, the question is whether the plaintiff was sincerely attached to the defendant.

Witnesses who lived with the plaintiff during the courtship and observed her deportment may give in evidence their opinions upon this question.][2]

(*e*) [The question is, upon a trial for murder, whether certain hairs are human hairs and like the hair of the deceased.

Witnesses, who knew the deceased, may state their opinions on this point, though they are not experts.][3]

ARTICLE 49.

OPINIONS OF EXPERTS ON POINTS OF SCIENCE OR ART.

When there is a question as to any point of science or art, the opinions upon that point of persons specially skilled in any such matter are deemed to be relevant facts.

Such persons are hereinafter called experts.

The words "science or art" include all subjects on which a course of special study or experience is necessary to the formation of an opinion,[4] and amongst others the examination of handwriting.

---

before and after an injury thereto, or before and after a part thereof has been taken by eminent domain (*Sexton* v. *N. Bridgewater*, 116 Mass. 200; *Carter* v. *Thurston*, 58 N. H. 104; *Lewis* v. *Springfield Co.*, 176 Pa. 230). This is not only allowed in States which receive opinion evidence as to damages (Id.; *Snow* v. *B. & M. R. Co.*, 65 Me. 230), but also in States which reject such evidence. *Yost* v. *Conroy*, 92 Ind. 464; *Cleveland, etc. R. Co.* v. *Ball*, 5 O. St. 568; *Roberts* v. *N. Y. El. R. Co.*, 128 N. Y. 455, 467.]

[1] [*Bennett* v. *Clemence*, 6 Allen, 10.]

[2] [*McKee* v. *Nelson*, 4 Cow. 355; see *Vanderpool* v. *Richardson*, 52 Mich. 336; *State* v. *Stackhouse*, 24 Kan. 445.]

[3] [*Comm.* v. *Dorsey*, 103 Mass. 412.]

[4] 1 S. L. C. 555, 7th ed. (note to *Carter* v. *Boehm*); 28 Vict. c. 18, s. 18. [Gr. Ev. i. § 440; *Spring Co.* v. *Edgar*, 99 U. S. 645, 657; *Jones* v.

When there is a question as to a foreign law, the opinions of experts who in their profession are acquainted with such law are the only admissible evidence thereof, though such experts may produce to the court books which they declare to be works of authority upon the foreign law in question, which books the court, having received all necessary explanations from the expert, may construe for itself.[1]

Tucker, 41 N. H. 546; *Coyle* v. *Comm.*, 104 Pa. 117; *Muldowney* v. *Ill. Cent. R. Co.*, 36 Ia. 462; *Ferguson* v. *Hubbell*, 97 N. Y. 507. An expert may not only testify to opinions, but may state general facts which are the result of scientific knowledge (*Emerson* v. *Lowell Gas Co.*, 6 Allen, 146); or may testify as to the natural and reasonably probable future consequences of a certain state of facts concerning which his special knowledge qualifies him to judge (*Strohm* v. *N. Y. etc. R. Co.*, 96 N. Y. 305; *Louisville, etc. R. Co.* v. *Lucas*, 119 Ind. 583; *Clason* v. *Milwaukee*, 30 Wis. 316; cf. *Turner* v. *Newburgh*, 109 N. Y. 301). But the opinions of experts are not admissible upon matters of common knowledge; as these are within common observation and experience, the jurors are deemed qualified to judge without expert aid (*Ferguson* v. *Hubbell*, supra; *Milwaukee R. Co.* v. *Kellogg*, 94 U. S. 469; *N. J. Traction Co.* v. *Brabban*, 57 N. J. L. 691; *Hughes* v. *Richter*, 161 Ill. 409; *Stumore* v. *Shaw*, 68 Md. 11; *Dooner* v. *Canal Co.*, 164 Pa. 17; *Knoll* v. *State*, 55 Wis. 249; see Illustrations *g* and *h*). Nor, in general, is expert testimony received as to the very point in issue in the case (Illustration (*j*); *Seymour* v. *Fellows*, 77 N. Y. 180; *Buxton* v. *Somerset Works*, 121 Mass. 446; *Noonan* v. *State*, 55 Wis. 258; *Ill. Cent. R. Co.* v. *People*, 143 Ill. 434); though this is sometimes permissible, when the jury need such aid to properly decide the question. *Transportation Line* v. *Hope*, 95 U. S. 297; *Van Wycklen* v. *Brooklyn*, 118 N. Y. 424; *Quinn* v. *N. Y. etc. R. Co.*, 56 Ct. 44.]

[1] *Baron de Bode's Case*, 8 Q. B. 250–267; *Di Sora* v. *Phillipps*, 10 H. L. 624; *Castrique* v. *Imrie*, L. R. 4 E. & I. App. 434; see, too, *Picton's Case*, 30 S. T. 510–511. [That the *unwritten* or common law of other States or countries may be proved by expert testimony is well settled in this country (*Mowry* v. *Chase*, 100 Mass. 79; *Ennis* v. *Smith*, 14 How. (U. S.) 400; *Jenne* v. *Harrisville*, 63 N. H. 405; *In re Roberts' Will*, 8 Pai. 446), and is often declared in statutes, which also generally provide that in proving the common law of another State or Territory in the United States, the books of reports of cases may be given

It is the duty of the judge to decide, subject to the opinion of the court above, whether the skill of any person in the matter on which evidence of his opinion is

---

in evidence (see *e.g.*, N. Y. Code Civ. Pro. § 942 ; Maine Rev. St. c. 82, ss. 108, 109; Mass. Pub. St. c. 169, ss. 72, 73; 1 N. J. Rev. p. 381; 2 How. St. (Mich.) §§ 7508, 7509). Sometimes the latter provision is also extended to the law of foreign countries (Id.; see *The Pawashick*, 2 Lowell, 142).

In proof of foreign *written* law, expert evidence is deemed admissible in some States, either with or without a copy of such law (*Barrows v. Downs*, 9 R. I. 446; *Hall v. Costello*, 48 N. H. 176 ; see *Hennessy v. Farrelly*, 13 Daly, 468); but sometimes statutes provide that such evidence may be rejected, unless accompanied by such a copy (*Pierce v. Indseth*, 106 U. S. 546 ; see statutes *supra*). But other modes of proof are also in common use, as by an officially printed volume of the law or a duly authenticated copy (see Art. 84, *post*). This is the generally established mode of proving the statute law of Congress or of the sister States (see Art. 81, *post*). An expert or other credible witness may testify as to the official or authoritative character of the printed volume, etc. (*Pacific Gas Co.* v. *Wheelock*, 80 N. Y. 278; *Hynes* v. *McDermott*, 82 N. Y. 41, 54 ; *Spaulding* v. *Vincent*, 24 Vt. 501; *Dundee Mortgage Co.* v. *Cooper*, 26 F. R. 665). The construction of a statute of another State by the courts of that State may be shown by expert testimony or by the law reports of that State or by both (*Bollinger* v. *Gallagher*, 163 Pa. 245, 170 Pa. 84).

The expert is usually a lawyer of the State or country whose law is to be proved, but the testimony of other persons acquainted with the law may be received in proper cases (*Vander Donct* v. *Thellusson*, 8 C. B. 812; *Pickard v. Bailey*, 26 N. H. 152; *American Life Ins. Co.* v. *Rosenagle*, 77 Pa. 507).

Evidence of the foreign law must be first introduced in the trial court, not in the appellate court. The question what the foreign law is is usually deemed a question of fact, unless it involves merely the construction of a written statute or judicial opinion, when it is a question of law (*Hanley* v. *Donoghue*, 116 U. S. 1; *Ufford* v. *Spaulding*, 156 Mass. 65; *Molson's Bk.* v. *Boardman*, 47 Hun, 135; *Alexander* v. *Pennsylvania Co.*, 48 O. St. 623). In the absence of proof of the foreign law or that of another State, the law of the *forum* is applied (*McIntyre* v. *B. & M. R. Co.*, 163 Mass. 189 ; *Musser* v. *Stauffer*, 178 Pa. 99; *Slaughter* v. *Bernards*, 88 Wis. 111). In this country, when the law of a sister State is not proved, it is the *common law* of the *forum*,

offered is sufficient to entitle him to be considered as an expert.[1]

The opinion of an expert as to the existence of the

---

and not the *statute law*, which is generally held applicable (*Carpenter* v. *Grand Trunk R. Co.*, 72 Me. 388; *O'Reilly* v. *N. Y. etc. R. Co.*, 16 R. I. 389; *Kelley* v. *Kelley*, 161 Mass. 111; *Lane* v. *Wheelwright*, 69 Hun, 180, 143 N. Y. 634; *Jackson* v. *Pittsburgh, etc. R. Co.*, 140 Ind. 241; *Rice* v. *Rankans*, 101 Mich. 380, note; *Mohr* v. *Miesen*, 47 Minn. 228; *Burdict* v. *Mo. Pac. R. Co.*, 123 Mo. 221; *Kahl* v. *Memphis, etc. R. Co.*, 95 Ala. 337; *Thorn* v. *Weatherly*, 50 Ark. 237; *Pattillo* v. *Alexander*, 96 Ga. 60; see *Harris* v. *White*, 81 N. Y. 532, 544), except when the sister State (as *e. g.*, Texas) derived its system of law from some other source than the English law, in which case the general law of the *forum*, both written and unwritten, is applied (*Hurley* v. *Mo. Pac. R. Co.*, 57 Mo. App. 675; *Buchanan* v. *Hubbard*, 119 Ind. 187; *Brown* v. *Wright*, 58 Ark. 20; *Davison* v. *Gibson*, 56 F. R. 443; so as to a foreign country, *Savage* v. *O'Neil*, 44 N. Y. 298). In some States, however, the general law of the *forum* is applied in all cases when the law of the other State or country is not proved. *Cavallaro* v. *Texas, etc. R. Co.*, 110 Cal. 348; *Bennett* v. *Cadwell's Excr.*, 70 Pa. 253; *Neese* v. *Farmers' Ins. Co.*, 55 Ia. 604; *Smith* v. *Mason*, 44 Neb. 611; see p. 163, note 2, *post*.]

[1] *Bristow* v. *Sequeville*, 6 Ex. 275; *Rowley* v. *L. & N. W. Railway*, L. R, 8 Ex. 221; *In the Goods of Bonelli*, L. R. 1 P. D. 69; and see *In the Goods of Dost Aly Khan*, 6 P. D. 6. [*Slocovich* v. *Orient Ins. Co.*, 108 N. Y. 56; *Stillwell, etc. Co.* v. *Phelps*, 130 U. S. 520; *Struthers* v. *Phila. etc. R. Co.*, 174 Pa. 291; *Perkins* v. *Stickney*, 132 Mass. 217. The decision of the trial judge on this point will be deemed conclusive, unless clearly shown to be erroneous (Id.; *Marston* v. *Dingley*, 88 Me. 546; *N. J. Zinc Co.* v. *Lehigh Zinc Co.*, 59 N. J. L. 189; *Stevens* v. *Minneapolis*, 42 Minn. 136). The witness need not be still in the practice of his profession, etc. (*Roberts* v. *Johnson*, 58 N. Y. 613; cf. *Seckinger* v. *Mfg. Co.*, 129 Mo. 590).

The opinion of an expert is admissible though he has no personal knowledge of the facts of the case. But in the question asking his opinion, the facts, as counsel claim them to exist, should then be stated in *hypothetical form;* and in framing the question, counsel may assume such a state of facts as the evidence fairly tends to justify (*Stearns* v. *Field*, 90 N. Y. 640; *Jewett* v. *Brooks*, 134 Mass. 505; *Barber's Appeal*, 63 Ct. 393; *Meeker* v. *Meeker*, 74 Ia. 352; *Hicks* v. *Citizens' R. Co.*, 124 Mo. 115); but in cross-examination counsel need

facts on which his opinion is to be given is irrelevant, unless he perceived them himself.[1]

Illustrations.

(*a*) The question is, whether the death of A was caused by poison.

The opinions of experts as to the symptoms produced by the poison by which A is supposed to have died, are deemed to be relevant.[2]

---

not be so restricted (*People* v. *Augsbury*, 97 N. Y. 501). This rule that a hypothetical question must be asked applies even though the witness has heard the evidence of the facts as given by prior witnesses, if the facts are controverted or doubtful (*Guiterman* v. *Liverpool, etc. St. Co.*, 83 N. Y. 358 ; *People* v. *McElvaine*, 121 N. Y. 250 ; *Dexter* v. *Hall*, 15 Wall. 9 ; *Coyle* v. *Comm.*, 104 Pa. 117 ; *Stoddard* v. *Winchester*, 157 Mass. 567 ; *Pyle* v. *Pyle*, 158 Ill. 289 ; *Bennett* v. *State*, 57 Wis. 69). But in some cases, as where the facts are not in dispute, or the evidence heard is clear and plain and not difficult to bear in mind, the expert, having heard the evidence in the case, may be asked his opinion thereon, without a full hypothetical statement of the facts (*Seymour* v. *Fellows*, 77 N. Y. 178 ; *People* v. *Theobald*, 92 Hun, 182 ; *State* v. *Watson*, 81 Ia. 380 ; *Gates* v. *Fleischer*, 67 Wis. 504 ; *Hunt* v. *Lowell Gas Co.*, 8 Allen, 169 ; *State* v. *Klinger*, 46 Mo. 224 ; *State* v. *Hayden*, 51 Vt. 296). And where the expert bases his opinion upon his knowledge of the facts, a hypothetical case need not be stated (*Mercer* v. *Vose*, 67 N. Y. 56 ; *Niendorff* v. *Manhattan R. Co.*, 4 App. Div. (N. Y.) 46 ; *Bellefontaine, etc. R. Co.* v. *Bailey*, 11 O. St. 333). A medical expert may testify as to the mental condition of a person who has been his patient, or whom he has personally examined, without first disclosing the facts on which his opinion is based. *People* v. *Youngs*, 151 N. Y. 210 ; *Crockett* v. *Davis*, 81 Md. 134 ; cf. *People* v. *Nino*, 149 N. Y. 317.]

[1] 1 Ph. Ev. 507 ; T. E. s. 1278. [*Carpenter* v. *Eastern Trans. Co.*, 71 N. Y. 574. So his opinion is not received as to the effect of the evidence in establishing controverted facts (*Hunt* v. *Lowell Gas Co.*, 8 Allen, 169 ; *People* v. *Barber*, 115 N. Y. 475 ; see *Priest* v. *Groton*, 103 Mass. 530). Nor is a witness's opinion received as to a matter of legal or moral obligation. Gr. Ev. i. § 441 ; *Milwaukee, etc., R. Co.* v. *Kellogg*, 99 U. S. 469, 473 ; *Seliger* v. *Bastian*, 66 Wis. 521 ; *McKean* v. *R. Co.*, 55 Ia. 192 ; cf. *Cochrane* v. *Little*, 71 Md. 323 ; *Monroe* v. *Lattin*, 25 Kan. 351.]

[2] *R.* v. *Palmer* (*passim*). See my History of Crim. Law, iii. 389 [*Stephens* v. *People*, 4 Park. Cr. 396.]

(b) The question is, whether A, at the time of doing a certain act, was, by reason of unsoundness of mind, incapable of knowing the nature of the act, or that he was doing what was either wrong or contrary to law.

The opinions of experts upon the question whether the symptoms exhibited by A commonly show unsoundness of mind, and whether such unsoundness of mind usually renders persons incapable of knowing the nature of the acts which they do, or of knowing that what they do is either wrong or contrary to law, are deemed to be relevant.[1]

(c) The question is, whether a certain document was written by A. Another document is produced which is proved or admitted to have been written by A.

The opinions of experts on the question whether the two documents were written by the same person, or by different persons, are deemed to be relevant.[2]

(d) The opinions of experts on the questions, whether, in Illustration (a), A's death was in fact attended by certain symptoms; whether, in Illustration (b), the symptoms from which they infer that A was of unsound mind existed; whether, in Illustration (c), either or both of the documents were written by A, are deemed to be irrelevant.[3]

(e) [The question is, whether certain blood-stains have been caused by human blood or by the blood of animals.

The opinion of an expert that some of the stains are of the one sort and some of the other is deemed to be relevant.[4]

But a non-expert may give evidence that stains recently made are caused by blood.][5]

(f) [The question is, whether certain circumstances affecting property insured are material to the risk.

---

[1] *R.* v. *Dove* (*passim*). History Crim. Law, iii. 426. [See *People* v. *Tuczkewitz*, 149 N. Y. 240; *U. S.* v. *Guiteau*, 1 Mackey, 498; *State* v. *Hayden*, 51 Vt. 296.]

[2] 28 Vict. c. 18, s. 8; [see Art. 52, and note; *Ludlow* v. *Warshing*, 108 N. Y. 520.]

[3] [But that an expert may testify that the disputed document was written by A, see *Costello* v. *Crowell*, 133 Mass. 352; see Art. 52.]

[4] [*Linsday* v. *People*, 63 N. Y. 143, 147, 156.]

[5] [*Greenfield* v. *People*, 85 N. Y. 75; *State* v. *Welch*, 36 W. Va. 690; *State* v. *Robinson*, 117 Mo. 649. In *McLain* v. *Comm.*, 99 Pa. 86, it was even held that a non-expert might testify that stains were made by human blood, and that, too, though the stains were not freshly made.]

The opinions of experts upon the materiality of these circumstances are deemed to be relevant, except in cases where the question is within the scope of common knowledge and observation, so that jurors may be deemed capable of determining it without expert aid.][1]

(*g*) [The question is, whether a railway train stopped long enough at a station to enable passengers to get off.

The opinion of an expert upon this question is deemed to be irrelevant.][1]

(*h*) [The question is, on a trial for murder, whether a certain piece of paper has the appearance of wadding shot from a gun.

The opinion of an expert upon this point is deemed to be irrelevant.][1]

(*i*) [The question is, whether B, who, while engaged in constructing a railroad, built brush fires, took proper precautions to prevent their spreading to the adjacent land of A. X, a railroad engineer, experienced in railroad construction, is called as an expert to testify on this question. His testimony is inadmissible, since this is a matter which men of ordinary experience and intelligence could determine without such aid.][1]

(*j*) [A, an employee in B's machine shop, was injured by the breaking of a belt used to move machinery. The belt was fastened with a belt-fastener which gave way. A sued B for damages for this injury, alleging negligence. At the trial experts in the use of belts and fasteners were asked to state their opinion as to the safety and fitness of the kind of belt-fastener which caused A's injury. This evidence was deemed to be irrelevant. The main question at issue was, whether the fastener was suitable and safe, and this should be determined by the jury, not by the opinions of experts.][1]

---

[1] [*Cornish* v. *Farm, etc. Ins. Co.*, 74 N. Y. 295; *Schenck* v. *Mercer Co. Ins. Co.*, 24 N. J. L. 447; *Russell* v. *Cedar Ins. Co.*, 78 Ia. 215; *Franklin Ins. Co.* v. *Gruver*, 100 Pa. 266. But the cases are not entirely agreed as to what questions are appropriate for expert testimony under this rule; see *Luce* v. *Dorchester Ins. Co.*, 105 Mass. 297; *Thayer* v. *Providence Ins. Co.*, 70 Me. 531; Kent's Comm., iii. 285.]

[1] [*Keller* v. *N. Y. C. R. Co.*, 2 Abb. Dec. 480; *Madden* v. *Mo. Pac. R. Co.*, 50 Mo. App. 666; cf. *O'Neil* v. *Dry Dock, etc. R. Co.*, 129 N. Y. 125; *Inland Coasting Co.* v. *Tolson*, 139 U. S. 551.]

[1] [*Manke* v. *People*, 17 Hun, 410, 78 N. Y. 611.]

[1] [*Pulsifer* v. *Berry*, 87 Me. 405; *Ferguson* v. *Hubbell*, 97 N. Y. 507.]

[1] [*Harley* v. *Buffalo Car Co*, 142 N. Y. 31.]

ARTICLE 50.*

FACTS BEARING UPON OPINIONS OF EXPERTS.

Facts, not otherwise relevant, have in some cases been permitted to be proved, as supporting or being inconsistent with the opinions of experts.[1]

Illustrations.

(a) The question was, whether A was poisoned by a certain poison.

The fact that other persons, who were poisoned by that poison, exhibited certain symptoms alleged to be the symptoms of that poison, was deemed to be relevant.[2]

(b) The question is, whether an obstruction to a harbor is caused by a certain bank. An expert gives his opinion that it is not.

The fact that other harbors similarly situated in other respects, but where there were no such banks,[3] began to be obstructed at about the same time, is deemed to be relevant.

ARTICLE 51.

OPINION AS TO HANDWRITING, WHEN DEEMED TO BE RELEVANT.

When there is a question as to the person by whom any document was written or signed, the opinion of any per-

---

*I have altered the wording of this Article, so as to make it less absolute than it was in earlier editions. The admission of such evidence is rare and exceptional, and must obviously be kept within narrow limits. At the time of Palmer's trial only two or three cases of poisoning by strychnine had occurred.

---

[1] [Comm. v. Leach, 156 Mass. 99; Lincoln v. Taunton Mf'g Co., 9 Allen, 181; Tilton v. Miller, 66 Pa. 388; cf. Doyle v. N. Y. Infirmary, 80 N. Y. 631; Olmsted v. Gere, 100 Pa. 127.]

[2] R. v. Palmer, printed trial, p. 124, etc. History Crim. Law, iii. 389. In this case (tried in 1856) evidence was given of the symptoms attending the deaths of Agnes Senet, poisoned by strychnine in 1845, Mrs. Serjeantson Smith, similarly poisoned in 1848, and Mrs. Dove, murdered by the same poison subsequently to the death of Cook, for whose murder Palmer was tried.

[3] Folkes v. Chadd, 3 Doug. 157; [cf. Hawks v. Charlemont, 110 Mass. 110.]

son acquainted with the handwriting of the supposed
writer that it was or was not written or signed by him, is
deemed to be a relevant fact.[1]

A person is deemed to be acquainted with the handwriting of another person when he has at any time seen
that person write,[2] or when he has received documents
purporting to be written by that person in answer to
documents written by himself or under his authority, and
addressed to that person,[3] or when, in the ordinary course
of business, documents purporting to be written by that
person have been habitually submitted to him.[4]

---

[1] [For a valuable article on this subject, see Am. Law Rev. xvi. 569.]

[2] [*Comm.* v. *Hall*, 164 Mass. 152; *State* v. *Harvey*, 131 Mo. 339;
Karr v. *State*, 106 Ala. 1; *State* v. *Farrington*, 90 Ia. 673. Having
seen him write once is enough; this affects the weight, not the competency, of the testimony (*Hammond* v. *Varian*, 54 N. Y. 398; *Comm.*
v. *Nefus*, 135 Mass. 533; *McNair* v. *Comm.*, 26 Pa. 388; *State* v. *Stair*,
87 Mo. 268; *Diggin's Estate*, 68 Vt. 198). So a person's mark, having
some distinctive peculiarity, may be proved in this way (*Strong's
Excrs.* v. *Brewer*, 17 Ala. 706; *Fogg* v. *Dennis*, 3 Humph. 47; *Jackson* v. *Van Dusen*, 5 Johns. 144; *George* v. *Surrey*, 1 M. & M. 516;
contra, *Shinkle* v. *Crock*, 17 Pa. 159). But a person who sees another
write, or examines his handwriting, expressly for the purpose of being
able to testify, is, in general, an incompetent witness (*Reese* v. *Reese*,
90 Pa. 89; *Board of Trustees* v. *Misenheimer*, 78 Ill. 22; *Hynes* v. *Mc-
Dermott*, 82 N. Y. 41, 53). A witness may testify as to handwriting
who cannot read or write himself. *Foye* v. *Patch*, 132 Mass. 105.]

[3] [*Chaffee* v. *Taylor*, 3 Allen, 598; *Clark* v. *Freeman*, 25 Pa. 133;
Thomas v. *State*, 103 Ind. 419; *Riggs* v. *Powell*, 142 Ill. 453; *Cunningham* v. *Hudson River Bk.*, 21 Wend. 557; *Empire Mf'g Co.* v.
Stuart, 46 Mich. 482. So if the witness has received letters or other
writings of a person, who has afterwards, by words or acts, acknowledged their genuineness (Gr. Ev. i. § 577; *Johnson* v. *Daverne*, 19
Johns. 134; *Snyder* v. *McKeever*, 10 Ill. App. 188; *Flowers* v. *Fletcher*,
40 W. Va. 103; *Pinkham* v. *Cockell*, 77 Mich. 265, 272; *Violet* v. *Rose*,
39 Neb. 660; *White* v. *Tolliver*, 110 Ala. 300); but not if he has only
seen letters to strangers, purporting to be those of the person in question. *Phila. etc. R. Co.* v. *Hickman*, 28 Pa. 318; *Gibson* v. *Trow-
bridge Co.*, 96 Ala. 357; *Nunes* v. *Perry*, 113 Mass. 274.]

[4] See Illustration. [*Berg* v. *Peterson*, 49 Minn. 420; *Titford* v. *Knott*,

Illustration.

The question is, whether a given letter is in the handwriting of A, a merchant in Calcutta.

B is a merchant in London, who has written letters addressed to A, and received in answer letters purporting to be written by him.   C is B's clerk, whose duty it was to examine and file B's correspondence. D is B's broker, to whom B habitually submitted the letters purporting to be written by A for the purpose of advising with him thereon.

The opinions of B, C, and D on the question whether the letter is in the handwriting of A are relevant, though neither B, C, nor D ever saw A write.[1]

The opinion of E, who saw A write once twenty years ago, is also relevant.[2]

ARTICLE 52.

COMPARISON OF HANDWRITINGS.

Comparison of a disputed handwriting with any writing proved to the satisfaction of the judge to be genuine is permitted to be made by witnesses, and such writings, and the evidence of witnesses respecting the same, may be submitted to the court and jury as evidence of the genuineness or otherwise of the writing in dispute.   This paragraph applies to all courts of judicature, criminal

---

2 Johns. Cas. 211 ; *Comm.* v. *Smith,* 6 S. & R. 568.   Thus public officers who have seen many official documents filed in their office, having the signature of a certain justice, may testify as to an alleged signature of his (*Rogers* v. *Ritter,* 12 Wall. 317 ; *Amherst Bk.* v. *Root,* 2 Met. 522 ; *Burdell* v. *Taylor,* 89 Cal. 613).   As to signatures upon ancient writings, a person may testify who has gained his knowledge by inspecting other ancient authentic documents bearing the same signature.   *Jackson* v. *Brooks,* 8 Wend. 426, 15 id. 111.]

[1] *Doe* v. *Suckermore,* 5 A. & E. 705 (Coleridge, J.) ; 730 (Patteson, J.) ; 739-40 (Denman, C. J.).

[2] *R.* v. *Horne Tooke,* 25 S. T. 71-2.   [In *Wilson* v. *Van Leer,* 127 Pa. 371, the witness had seen the person whose signature was in question write his name twice, thirty-two years before ; and once, twenty-three years before ; see also *Brachman* v. *Hall,* 1 Disney, 539.]

or civil, and to all persons having by law, or by consent
of parties, authority to hear, receive, and examine evidence.[1]

---

[1] 17 & 18 Vict. c. 125, s. 27 ; 28 Vict. c. 18, s. 8. [There are diverse
rules on this subject in different States. A rule substantially like the
English rule prevails in all the New England States, in New York,
New Jersey, Maryland, Virginia, Kentucky, Tennessee, Mississippi,
Ohio, Iowa, Kansas, California, Colorado, Oregon, and Nebraska
(*State* v. *Thompson*, 80 Me. 194; *State* v. *Hastings*, 53 N. H. 452;
Rowell v. *Fuller*, 59 Vt. 688 ; *Costelo* v. *Crowell*, 139 Mass. 588 ; Pub.
St. R. I. c. 214, s. 542 ; *State* v. *Griswold*, 67 Ct. 290; *People* v. *Corey*,
148 N. Y. 476 ; Laws of 1888, N. Y. c. 555 ; N. J. Rev. p. 381 ; Laws of
Md. 1888, c. 545; *Hanriot* v. *Sherwood*, 82 Va. 1 ; *Andrews* v.
Hayden's Adm'r, 88 Ky. 455; *Powers* v. *McKenzie*, 90 Tenn. 167;
Wilson v. *Beauchamp*, 50 Miss. 24; *Koons* v. *State*, 36 O. St. 195;
Sankey v. *Cook*, 82 Ia. 125 ; *State* v. *Zimmerman*, 47 Kan. 242 ; *Mar-
shall* v. *Hancock*, 80 Cal. 82 ; Laws of 1893, Col. c. 88; *Holmes* v.
Goldsmith, 147 U. S. 150; *First Nat. Bk.* v. *Carson*, 48 Neb. 764).
But in many States, collateral and irrelevant writings cannot be
introduced for comparison (*Snider* v. *Burks*, 84 Ala. 53 ; *People* v.
Parker, 67 Mich. 222 ; *State* v. *Thompson*, 132 Mo. 301; *Himrod* v.
Gilman, 147 Ill. 293 ; *Hasleton* v. *Union Bank*, 32 Wis. 34 ; cf. *State*
v. *Koontz*, 31 W. Va. 127 ; *Tunstall* v. *Cobb*, 109 N. C. 316 ; *Smyth* v.
Caswell, 67 Tex. 567); so in the Federal courts (*Stokes* v. *U. S.*, 157 U.S.
187); generally, however, in these States genuine writings which are
properly in evidence in the case for other purposes may be used for
comparison by the jury, and in a number of them such comparison
may be made by experts to aid the jury (Id.; see *Kirksey* v. *Kirksey*,
41 Ala. 626 ; *Vinton* v. *Peck*, 14 Mich. 287 ; *Williams* v. *Conger*, 125
U. S. 397). In Indiana and Minnesota comparison may be made with
writings already in evidence in the case and also, by experts with
other writings which, though not relevant, are admitted to be genuine
(*McDonald* v. *McDonald*, 142 Ind. 55, 69; *Morrison* v. *Porter*, 35
Minn. 425; cf. *Dietz* v. *Fourth Nat. Bk.*, 69 Mich. 287). In Pennsylvania comparison with writings proved to be genuine may be made
by the jury as corroborative evidence, but not by experts (*Rockey's
Estate*, 155 Pa. 453). See this general subject fully treated in Am.
Law Rev. xvii. 21 ; Gr. Ev. i. §§ 576–582.

A person's signature or other writing made by him in court at the
trial will not generally be allowed to be used for comparison (*Comm.* v.
Allen, 128 Mass. 46; *Hickory* v. *U. S.*, 151 U. S. 303; *Gilbert* v. *Simpson*,
6 Daly, 29; *Williams* v. *State*, 61 Ala. 33). But this is sometimes per-

Article 53.

OPINION AS TO EXISTENCE OF MARRIAGE, WHEN RELEVANT.

When there is a question whether two persons are or are not married, the facts that they cohabited and were treated by others as man and wife are deemed to be relevant facts, and to raise a presumption that they were lawfully married, and that any act necessary to the validity of any form of marriage which may have passed between them was done; but such facts are not sufficient to prove a marriage in a prosecution for bigamy or in proceedings for a divorce, or in a petition for damages against an adulterer.[1]

---

mitted upon cross-examination of the person whose signature, etc., is in question, or when the writing is made at the request of the opposite party who offers it for comparison (*Chandler* v. *LeBarron*, 45 Me. 534; *People* v. *De Kroyft*, 49 Hun, 71; *U. S.* v. *Mullaney*, 32 F. R. 370; *Bradford* v. *People*, 22 Col. 157; *King* v. *Donahue*, 110 Mass. 155). Nor may a person's signature, counterfeited by another, be submitted to expert witnesses on cross-examination, to test their capacity as experts or their knowledge of the person's handwriting (*Gaunt* v. *Harkness*, 53 Kan. 405; *Rose* v. *First Nat. Bk.*, 91 Mo. 399).

Letterpress copies cannot be used for comparison (*Cohen* v. *Teller*, 93 Pa. 123; *Comm.* v. *Eastman*, 1 Cush. 189). But photographic copies may be, when the originals are also before the court (*Hynes* v. *McDermott*, 82 N. Y. 41; *Marcy* v. *Barnes*, 16 Gray, 161; but see *Tome* v. *Parkersburgh, etc. R. Co.*, 39 Md. 36).

Experts in handwriting may also testify to other matters; as *e. g.*, whether a writing is forged or altered, when a writing was probably made, whether all its parts are in the same handwriting, what certain words, difficult to decipher, really are, etc. *Travis* v. *Brown*, 43 Pa. 9; *Withee* v. *Rowe*, 45 Me. 571; *Dresler* v. *Hard*, 127 N. Y. 235; *Pearson* v. *Hardin*, 95 Mich. 360; *Eisfield* v. *Dill*, 71 Ia. 442.]

[1] *Morris* v. *Miller*, 4 Burr. 2057; *Birt* v. *Barlow*, 1 Doug. 170; and see *Catherwood* v. *Caslon*, 13 M. & W. 261. Compare *R.* v. *Mainwaring*, D. & B. 132. See, too, *De Thoren* v. *A. G.*, 1 App. Cas. 686; *Piers* v. *Piers*, 2 H. & C. 331. Some of the references in the report of *De Thoren* v. *A. G.* are incorrect. This Article was not expressed strongly enough in the former editions. [*Gall* v. *Gall*, 114

ARTICLE 54.

Whenever the opinion of any living person is deemed to be relevant, the grounds on which such opinion is based are also deemed to be relevant.[1]

Illustration.

An expert may give an account of experiments performed by him for the purpose of forming his opinion.[2]

N. Y. 109; *Greenawalt* v. *McEnelley*, 85 Pa. 352; *Maryland* v. *Baldwin*, 112 U. S. 490; *Wallace's Case*, 49 N. J. Eq. 530; *Peet* v. *Peet*, 52 Mich. 464; *White* v. *White*, 82 Cal. 427; *Jackson* v. *Jackson*, 80 Md. 176, 82 Md. 17; Mass. Pub. St. c. 145, s. 31. Cohabitation and repute do not, however, constitute marriage; they are only evidence of marriage, and the presumption of marriage arising therefrom may be rebutted (*Collins* v. *Voorhees*, 47 N. J. Eq. 555; *Grimm's Estate*, 131 Pa. 199; *Clayton* v. *Wardell*, 4 N. Y. 230).

Such evidence of repute, etc., has been deemed sufficient to prove a marriage in bastardy proceedings (*State* v. *Worthingham*, 23 Minn. 528), but not in criminal prosecutions for bigamy, incest, adultery, loose and lascivious cohabitation, nor in actions for criminal conversation (*Hayes* v. *People*, 25 N. Y. 390; *Green* v. *State*, 21 Fla. 403; *State* v. *Roswell*, 6 Ct. 446; *State* v. *Hodgskins*, 19 Me. 155; *Dann* v. *Kingdom*, 1 T. & C. 492; *Comm.* v. *Littlejohn*, 15 Mass. 163; *Hutchins* v. *Kimmell*, 31 Mich. 126; *Hiler* v. *People*, 156 Ill. 511; cf. *State* v. *Sherwood*, 68 Vt. 414; *State* v. *Cooper*, 103 Mo. 266). But in some States it is deemed sufficient in divorce suits (Bishop, M. D. & S. ii. §§ 746–758; see *Collins* v. *Collins*, 80 N. Y. 10).

A marriage may generally be proved by admissions either in civil or criminal cases (*Miles* v. *State*, 103 U. S. 304; *Womack* v. *Tankersley*, 78 Va. 242; *State* v. *Wylde*, 110 N. C. 500; but see *Eisenlord* v. *Clum*, 126 N. Y. 552, 562); especially is this true if evidence of cohabitation and repute be superadded. Id.; *State* v. *Hughes*, 35 Kan. 626.]

[1] [Thus the expert may state his reasons for his opinion. *Hawkins* v. *Fall River*, 119 Mass. 94; *Steam Mill Co.* v. *Water Power Co.*, 78 Me. 274.]

[2] [*Eidt* v. *Cutter*, 127 Mass. 522; *Sullivan* v. *Comm.*, 93 Pa. 284; *Moore* v. *State*, 96 Tenn. 209; *Linsday* v. *People*, 63 N. Y. 143, 156; *People* v. *Morrigan*, 29 Mich. 5. So an expert may be permitted to

perform experiments before the jury, or make illustrations on a blackboard, to explain his testimony (*Leonard* v. *Southern Pac. Co.*, 21 Or. 555; *McKay* v. *Lasher*, 121 N. Y. 477; *Pennsylvania Coal Co.* v. *Kelly*, 156 Ill. 9). Evidence of experiments may, however, be rejected unless they were performed under conditions like those existing in the case on trial (*Comm.* v. *Piper*, 120 Mass. 185 ; *People* v. *Slack*, 90 Mich. 448 ; *State* v. *Fletcher*, 24 Or. 295). Experiments performed by jurors, away from the court-room, have been held sufficient ground for a new trial. *People* v. *Conkling*, 111 Cal. 616.]

CHAPTER VI.*

CHARACTER, WHEN DEEMED TO BE RELEVANT AND WHEN NOT.

ARTICLE 55.

CHARACTER GENERALLY IRRELEVANT.

THE fact that a person is of a particular character is deemed to be irrelevant to any inquiry respecting his conduct, except in the cases mentioned in this chapter.

ARTICLE 56.

EVIDENCE OF CHARACTER IN CRIMINAL CASES.

In criminal proceedings, the fact that the person accused has a good character, is deemed to be relevant;[1] but the fact that he has a bad character is deemed to be

---

* See Note XXV. [Appendix].

[1] [*Edgington* v. *U. S.*, 164 U. S. 361; *People* v. *Sweeney*, 133 N. Y. 609; *Comm.* v. *Cleary*, 135 Pa. 64; *People* v. *Harrison*, 93 Mich. 594; *Jackson* v. *State*, 81 Wis. 127. It is generally held that the proof must be of good character in respect to the trait involved in the charge (*People* v. *Fair*, 43 Cal. 137; *Comm.* v. *Nagle*, 157 Mass. 554; *Kahlenbeck* v. *State*, 119 Ind. 118; *Griffin* v. *State*, 14 O. St. 55; *State* v. *King*, 78 Mo. 555; see *Cancemi* v. *People*, 16 N. Y. 501; Gr. Ev. iii. § 25). Such evidence is now generally received, whether the evidence to show the prisoner's guilt be direct or circumstantial; even when it is direct, evidence of good character may affect its credibility, or tend to create a doubt as to guilt (Id.; *Remsen* v. *People*, 43 N. Y. 6; *People* v. *Jassino*, 100 Mich. 536; *State* v. *Keefe*, 54 Kan. 197; *Comm.* v. *Leonard*, 140 Mass. 473; *State* v. *Howell*, 100 Mo. 628; *State* v. *Rodman*, 62 Ia. 456). If defendant fails to offer evidence of his good character, no presumption arises that he is guilty of the offence charged or that he is of bad character. *People* v. *Evans*, 72 Mich. 367.]

irrelevant, unless it is itself a fact in issue, or unless evidence has been given that he has a good character, in which case evidence that he has a bad character is admissible.[1]

[2] In this Article the word "character" means reputation as distinguished from disposition, and evidence may be given only of general reputation and not of particular acts by which reputation or disposition is shown.[3]

ARTICLE 57.

CHARACTER AS AFFECTING DAMAGES.[4]

In civil cases, the fact that a person's general reputation is bad may, it seems, be given in evidence in reduction of damages; but evidence of rumors that his reputation was bad, and evidence of particular facts

---

[1] [*People* v. *White*, 14 Wend. 111 ; *State* v. *Lapage*, 57 N. H. 245 ; *State* v. *Hull*, 18 R. I. 207 ; *People* v. *Fair*, 43 Cal. 137. But when defendant becomes a witness in his own behalf, he may be impeached like any other witness by proof of bad character (*State* v. *Nelson*, 98 Mo. 414 ; see *post*, Art. 133, note). For additional rules in criminal cases, see Art. 134, *post; Art. 7, note 3, ante.*]

[2] [Just before this last paragraph, Mr. Stephen inserts in this Article certain special statutory rules of the English law. They will be found in the Appendix, Note L.]

[3] *R.* v. *Rowton*, 1 L. & C. 520. [*Comm.* v. *O'Brien*, 119 Mass. 342 ; *Snyder* v. *Comm.*, 85 Pa. 519 ; *People* v. *Sharp*, 107 N. Y. 427, 457 ; *State* v. *Lapage*, 57 N. H. 245 ; *McQueen* v. *State*, 108 Ala. 54 ; *Berneker* v. *State*, 40 Neb. 810. The reputation of a person must be that in his own community (*Conkey* v. *People*, 1 Abb. Dec. 418 ; *Carthaus* v. *State*, 78 Wis. 560). In Iowa and Minnesota, however, evidence of "disposition" is received, as well as of "general reputation." *State* v. *Sterrett*, 68 Ia. 76 ; *State* v. *Lee*, 22 Minn. 407.] *R.* v. *Turberfield*, 1 L. & C. 495, is a case in which the character of a prisoner became incidentally relevant to a certain limited extent.

[4] [Mr. Stephen ends this Article with a paragraph stating a peculiar rule of the English law in regard to actions for libel and slander. It will be found in the Appendix, Note L.]

showing that his disposition was bad, cannot be given in
evidence.[1]

---

[1] *Scott* v. *Sampson*, 8 Q. B. D. 491, in which all the older cases are
minutely examined in the judgment of Cave, J. [This rule is expressed
too broadly by Mr. Stephen. The case of *Scott* v. *Sampson*, upon
which it is based, does not state it as applicable to *all civil cases*, but
only to actions for *libel* or *slander*.

Evidence of a party's character is generally incompetent in civil
actions (Gr. Ev. i. § 55 ; *Fakey* v. *Crotty*, 63 Mich. 383 ; *Vawter* v.
Hults, 112 Mo. 633 ; *American Ins. Co.* v. *Hazen*, 110 Pa. 530). Thus
in an action for assault and battery, the defendant cannot prove the
plaintiff's bad character (*Corning* v. *Corning*, 6 N. Y. 97 ; *Bruce* v.
Priest, 5 Allen, 100), nor his own good character (*Day* v. *Ross*, 154
Mass. 13 ; *Elliott* v. *Russell*, 92 Ind. 526); nor can the plaintiff's bad
repute be shown in an action for the seduction of his daughter (*Dain*
v. *Wyckoff*, 18 N. Y. 45); nor that of a party to a note in an action
thereon (*Battles* v. *Laudenslager*, 84 Pa. 446); nor the character of
either party for care and prudence in an action for negligence (*Mc-
Donald* v. *Savoy*, 110 Mass. 49 ; *Chase* v. *Me. Cent. R. Co.*, 77 Me. 62 ;
Holtzman v. *Hoy*, 118 Ill. 534 ; *Hall* v. *Rankin*, 87 Ia. 261). So in an
action against a master for the negligence of his servant, evidence of
the servant's good or bad reputation as to carefulness is excluded
(*Malcolm* v. *Fuller*, 152 Mass. 160 ; *Williams* v. *Edmunds*, 75 Mich.
92), unless the question is as to the master's negligence in employing
an incompetent servant (*Monahan* v. *Worcester*, 150 Mass. 439 ; *Lake
Shore, etc. R. Co.* v. *Stupak*, 123 Ind. 210 ; cf. *Park* v. *N. Y. C. R. Co.*,
155 N. Y. 215 ; see Art. 10, Illustration (*g*), *ante*). So evidence of the
defendant's good character is not admissible in his behalf in a civil
action, even though he be charged with fraud (*Gough* v. *St. John*, 16
Wend. 646 ; *Boardman* v. *Woodman*, 47 N. H. 120 ; *Simpson* v.
Westenberger, 28 Kan. 756 ; *Leinkauf* v. *Brinker*, 62 Miss. 255 ; contra,
Werts v. *Spearman*, 22 S. Car. 200); nor can the good character of a
party to a civil action be shown to rebut a charge of crime made
against him therein by the other party (*Stone* v. *Hawkeye Ins. Co.*, 68
Ia. 737 ; *Gebhart* v. *Burkett*, 57 Ind. 378 ; but see *Lamagdelaine* v.
Tremblay, 162 Mass. 339 ; as to libel and slander cases, see cases
infra). Nor generally can the good character of any party or person
interested in the action be shown, except in answer to evidence from
the other side attacking his character (*Pratt* v. *Andrews*, 4 N. Y. 493 ;
see *Young* v. *Johnson*, 123 N. Y. 226 ; *Mosley* v. *Ins. Co.*, 55 Vt. 142).

In some cases the question of character is involved in the nature of
the action, and evidence of general reputation is received. Thus in

actions for libel or slander, evidence may be given of the plaintiff's general bad reputation, in mitigation of damages (*Hamer* v. *McFarlin*, 4 Den. 509; *Drown* v. *Allen*, 91 Pa. 393; *Bathrick* v. *Detroit Post Co.*, 50 Mich. 629; *Nellis* v. *Cramer*, 86 Wis. 337); but not that reports were in circulation charging him with the act imputed (*Kennedy* v. *Gifford*, 19 Wend. 296; *Pease* v. *Shippen*, 80 Pa. 513; *Mahoney* v. *Belford*, 132 Mass. 393; *Sickra* v. *Small*, 87 Me. 493; *Hanners* v. *McClelland*, 74 Ia. 318; contra, *Case* v. *Marks*, 20 Ct. 248), at least if the defendant did not know of such reports when he made the charge (*Hatfield* v. *Lasher*, 81 N. Y. 246; *Lathrop* v. *Adams*, 133 Mass. 471; *Larrabee* v. *Minn. Tribune Co.*, 36 Minn. 141; cf. *Hoboken Printing Co.* v. *Kahn*, 58 N. J. L. 359); nor can particular acts of misconduct be proved (*McLaughlin* v. *Cowley*, 131 Mass. 70; *Hallowell* v. *Guntle*, 82 Ind. 554); nor can the defendant prove his own bad character (*Hastings* v. *Stetson*, 130 Mass. 76). In actions for libel and slander, as in other civil actions, the plaintiff cannot give evidence of his own good character until it has been assailed by the other side (*Hitchcock* v. *Moore*, 70 Mich. 112; *Chubb* v. *Gsell*, 34 Pa. 114; *Blakeslee* v. *Hughes*, 50 O. St. 490; *Cooper* v. *Phipps*, 24 Or. 357); but some States admit such evidence (*Adams* v. *Lawson*, 17 Gratt. 250; *Shroyer* v. *Miller*, 3 W. Va. 158), others admit it when the defendant has charged the plaintiff with crime (*Downey* v. *Dillon*, 52 Ind. 442; see *Howland* v. *Blake Mfg. Co.*, 156 Mass. 543, 568), and it has also been admitted when plaintiff's character has been expressly put in issue by the pleadings (*Stafford* v. *Morning Journal Ass'n*, 142 N. Y. 598; contra, *Lotto* v. *Davenport*, 50 Minn. 99). In actions for malicious prosecution, plaintiff's general bad repute may be shown to reduce the damages (*Gregory* v. *Chambers*, 78 Mo. 294; *Rosenkrans* v. *Barker*, 115 Ill. 331; *O'Brien* v. *Frasier*, 47 N. J. L. 349); and sometimes such evidence is received as affecting the existence of probable cause (*McIntire* v. *Levering*, 148 Mass. 546; *Woodworth* v. *Mills*, 61 Wis. 44; as to an action for false imprisonment, see *Amer. Express Co.* v. *Patterson*, 73 Ind. 430). In actions for criminal conversation, seduction, breach of promise of marriage, and indecent assault, the woman's bad reputation for chastity may be proved (*Sanborn* v. *Neilson*, 4 N. H. 501; *Van Storch* v. *Griffin*, 71 Pa. 240; *White* v. *Murtland*, 71 Ill. 250; *Hogan* v. *Cregan*, 6 Rob. 138; *Mitchell* v. *Work*, 13 R. I. 645; as to proof of specific acts of unchastity in such cases, see Id.; Art 134, note, *post*; Gr. Ev. ii. §§ 56 and 579). As to proving the character of a witness, see Art. 133, *post*.

"Character" in this Article and note means general reputation (except as otherwise stated) and cannot be shown by proof of specific acts (*Miller* v. *Curtis*, 158 Mass. 127, 131). Usually the reputation proved concerns the particular trait involved in the cause of action

(*Warner* v. *Lockerby*, 31 Minn. 421 ; *Maxwell* v. *Kennedy*, 50 Wis.
645 ; see, generally, the cases in this note), but sometimes evidence of
general moral character is also received. *Clark* v. *Brown*, 116 Mass.
504, slander case ; *Duval* v. *Davey*, 32 O. St. 604, 612 ; *Post Pub'g
Co.* v. *Hallam*, 59 F. R. 530 ; *Sickra* v. *Small*, 87 Me. 493 ; see *Root*
v. *King*, 7 Cow. 613, 4 Wend. 113.]

PART II.

ON PROOF.

CHAPTER VII.

FACTS PROVED OTHERWISE THAN BY EVIDENCE—JUDICIAL NOTICE.

ARTICLE 58.*

OF WHAT FACTS THE COURT TAKES JUDICIAL NOTICE.

IT is the duty of all judges to take judicial notice of the following facts:—

---

* See Note XXVI. [Appendix].

[It is the duty of courts in this country to take judicial notice of the following facts:

(1) The common law and public statute law of their own State,[1] but not the law of any other State or country;[2] but

---

[1] [*Shaw* v. *Tobias*, 3 N. Y. 188; *Unity* v. *Burrage*, 103 U. S. 447. So of the law merchant (*Reed* v. *Wilson*, 41 N. J. L. 29); of the charter of a municipal corporation, being a public statute (*Stier* v. *Oskaloosa*, 41 Ia. 353; *Kansas City* v. *Vineyard*, 128 Mo. 75; *Winooski* v. *Gokey*, 49 Vt. 282; in some States all acts of incorporation are public laws, Mass. Pub. St. c. 169, s. 68; *State* v. *McAllister*, 24 Me. 139); of the laws of the antecedent government, when there has been a union or division of states or countries (*U. S.* v. *Perot*, 98 U. S. 428; *Stokes* v. *Macken*, 62 Barb. 145); but not of private statutes (*Timlow* v. *P. & R. R. Co.*, 99 Pa. 284), unless, as often now happens, a special law authorizes it (*Railroad Co.* v. *Bank of Ashland*, 12 Wall. 226; *Case* v. *Kelly*, 133 U. S. 21); nor of municipal ordinances (*Porter* v. *Waring*, 69 N. Y. 250 *Central Sav. Bk.* v. *Baltimore*, 71 Md. 515; *St. Louis* v. *Roche*, 128 Mo. 541), except in the courts of the municipality. *Ex parte Davis*, 115 Cal. 445; *Foley* v. *State*, 42 Neb. 233; cf. *Hankinson* v. *Trenton*, 51 N. J. L. 495.]

[2] [*Liverpool Steam Co.* v. *Phenix Ins. Co.*, 129 U. S. 397; *Monroe* v.

(1) All unwritten laws, rules, and principles having the force of law administered by any court sitting under the authority of Her Majesty and her successors in England or Ireland, whatever may be the nature of the jurisdiction thereof.[1]

(2) All public Acts of Parliament,[1] and all Acts of Parliament whatever, passed since February 4, 1851, unless the contrary is expressly provided in any such Act.[2]

---

[1] Ph. Ev. 460-1 ; T. E. s. 4, and see 36 & 37 Vict. c. 66 (Judicature Act of 1873), s. 25.

[2] 13 & 14 Vict. c. 21, ss. 7, 8, and see (for date) caption of session of 14 & 15 Vict.

---

the Federal courts, in the exercise of their original jurisdiction, take notice of the public laws of the several States when such laws are properly applicable to cases heard before them,[1] and, in like manner, general acts of Congress will be noticed in State courts.[2]

(2) The existence of the legislature, the time and place of

Douglas, 5 N. Y. 447 ; see p. 145, note 1, *ante*. But in a few States of this country it has been held that in giving full faith and credit to the public acts and records of another State (see Art. 47, note, *ante*), judicial notice will be taken of the law of that State (*Paine* v. *Ins. Co.*, 11 R. I. 411; *Ohio* v. *Hinchman*, 27 Pa. 479 ; cf. *Carpenter* v. *Dexter*, 8 Wall. 513; *Wilson* v. *Phœnix Mfg. Co.*, 40 W. Va. 413). The great weight of authority, however, is to the contrary. *Hanley* v. *Donoghue*, 116 U. S. 1, 5 ; *Sammis* v. *Wightman*, 31 Fla. 10 ; *Osborn* v. *Blackburn*, 78 Wis. 209.]

[1] [*Lamar* v. *Micou*, 114 U. S. 218. But the U. S. Supreme Court, upon writ of error to the highest court of a State, does not take judicial notice of the law of another State, not proved in that court and made part of the record sent up, unless by the local law that court takes judicial notice of it. *Liverpool Steam Co.* v. *Phenix Ins. Co.*, 129 U. S. 397, 445 ; *Lloyd* v. *Matthews*, 155 U. S. 222 ; see last note.]

[2] [*Kessel* v. *Albetis*, 56 Barb. 362 ; *Bird* v. *Comm.*, 21 Gratt. 800 ; *Schwerdtle* v. *Placer Co.*, 108 Cal. 589. So of the decisions of the U. S. Supreme Court, construing acts of Congress. *Southern Pac. R. Co.* v. *Painter*, 113 Cal. 247.]

(3) The general course of proceeding and privileges of Parliament and of each House thereof, and the date and place of their sittings, but not transactions in their journals.[1]

[1] Ph. Ev. 460; T. E. s. 5.

its sessions, its usual course of proceeding, and the privileges of its members,[1] but not the transactions in its journals.[2]

(3) General customs observed in the transaction of business.[3]

[1] [Gr. Ev. i. § 6; *Coleman* v. *Dobbins*, 8 Ind. 156, 162. Thus the courts will notice which of two bodies of men is the rightful legislature, when each claims the right (Opinion of Justices, 70 Me. 609). The doings of the executive and legislative departments of the government will be noticed. Id.; *Prince* v. *Skillin*, 71 Me. 361; *Mullan* v. *State*, 114 Cal. 578; cf. *In re Gunn*, 50 Kan. 155.]

[2] [*Grob* v. *Cushman*, 45 Ill. 119; *Burt* v. *Winona, etc. R. Co.*, 31 Minn. 472. This rule is chiefly applied in holding that the courts will not take notice of such journals in order to impeach the validity of an enrolled act of the legislature, which has been officially attested by the presiding officers of both houses and approved by the executive (*Harwood* v. *Wentworth*, 162 U. S. 547; *Ex parte Wren*, 63 Miss. 512; *Carr* v. *Coke*, 116 N. C. 223; *State* v. *Denny*, 118 Ind. 449, 455; *Weeks* v. *Smith*, 81 Me. 538). In many States, however, judicial notice will be taken of the journals, under such circumstances, to determine whether the statute was duly passed by the legislature (*Rode* v. *Phelps*, 80 Mich. 598; *Moog* v. *Randolph*, 77 Ala. 597; *McDonald* v. *State*, 80 Wis. 407; *State* v. *Hocker*, 36 Fla. 358; *Robertson* v. *People*, 20 Col. 279; cf. *Rumsey* v. *N. Y. etc. R. Co.*, 130 N. Y. 88; *Division of Howard Co.*, 15 Kan. 194; see cases collected in *Field* v. *Clark*, 143 U. S. 649, 661). It is held also in some cases that the journals may be judicially noticed for other purposes. *Edgar* v. *Board of Commrs.*, 70 Ind. 331; *Ill. Cent. R. Co.* v. *Wren*, 43 Ill. 77.]

[3] [*Cameron* v. *Blackman*, 39 Mich. 108; *Atchison, etc. R. Co.* v. *Headland*, 18 Col. 477; *Nash* v. *Classen*, 163 Ill. 409; *Merchants' Nat. Bank* v. *Hall*, 83 N. Y. 338. In this last case, the court took notice of the practice of banks to grant renewals of obligations upon payment of a new discount. So the general mode of doing banking business, banking hours, etc., are noticed. *State* v. *Arnold*, 140 Ind. 628; *Hutchinson* v. *Manhattan Co.*, 150 N. Y. 250; *American Nat. Bank* v. *Bushey*, 45 Mich. 135.]

(4) All general customs which have been held to have
the force of law in any division of the High Court of Justice or by any of the superior courts of law or equity,
and all customs which have been duly certified to and
recorded in any such court.[1]

(5) The course of proceeding and all rules of practice

---

[1] The old rule was that each court took notice of customs held by or
certified to it to have the force of law. It is submitted that the effect
of the Judicature Act, which fuses all the courts together, must be to
produce the result stated in the text. As to the old law, see *Piper* v.
Chappell, 14 M. & W. 649-50. *Ex parte Powell, In re Matthews,* 1
Ch. D. 505-7, contains some remarks by Lord Justice Mellish as to
proving customs till they come by degrees to be judicially noticed.

---

(4) The course of proceeding and all rules of practice in
force in the court itself ;[1] its own record books and entries
therein ;[2] the other courts established by law in the same
State, their judges, extent of jurisdiction and course of proceeding ;[3] but appellate courts will not take judicial notice

---

[1] [Wh. Ev. i. § 324. The terms of court are noticed (*Kidder* v. *Blaisdell*, 45 Me. 461 ; *Rodgers* v. *State*, 50 Ala. 102) ; but not the pendency
of another action in the same or another court. *Eyster* v. *Gaff*, 91 U.
S. 521 ; *State* v. *Wilson*, 39 Mo. App. 114.]

[2] [*Fellers* v. *Lee*, 2 Barb. 488 ; *Robinson* v. *Brown*, 82 Ill. 279 ; *Denney* v. *State*, 144 Ind. 504 ; *Hallenbach* v. *Schnabel*, 101 Cal. 312. A
court will take notice of its own orders or prior proceedings in the
same case (*State* v. *Ulrich*, 110 Mo. 350 ; *Jordan* v. *Circuit Ct.*, 69 Ia.
177 ; *State* v. *Stevens*, 56 Kan. 720 ; cf. *Garretson* v. *Ferrall*, 92 Ia.
728) ; but not of a former judgment or decree between the same parties in the same or another court. *Ralphs* v. *Hensler*, 97 Cal. 296 ;
McCormick v. *Herndon*, 67 Wis. 648 ; *Schuler* v. *Israel*, 120 U. S. 506,
509 ; *Enix* v. *Miller*, 54 Ia. 551.]

[3] [*Vahle* v. *Brackenseik*, 145 Ill. 231 ; *State* v. *Wright*, 16 R. I. 518 ;
State v. *Higgins*, 124 Mo. 640 ; *Hatcher* v. *Rocheleau*, 18 N. Y. 86, 90 ;
Kennedy v. *Comm.*, 78 Ky. 447 ; *Kilpatrick* v. *Comm.*, 31 Pa. 198. This
last case holds that the superior courts will take notice who are the
judges of the inferior State tribunals,—which by common law was a
doubtful question (see Gr. Ev. i. § 6, note). The fact that a judge
has resigned is judicially noticed. *People* v. *McConnell*, 155 Ill. 192.]

in force in the Supreme Court of Justice. Courts of a limited or inferior jurisdiction take judicial notice of their own course of procedure and rules of practice, but not of those of other courts of the same kind, nor does the Supreme Court of Justice take judicial notice of the course of procedure and rules of practice of such courts.[1]

(6) The accession and (*semble*) the sign manual of Her Majesty and her successors.[2]

(7) The existence and title of every State and Sovereign recognized by Her Majesty and her successors.[3]

---

[1] 1 Ph. Ev. 462-3 ; T. E. s. 19.   [2] 1 Ph. Ev. 458 ; T. E. ss. 16, 12.
[3] 1 Ph. Ev. 460 ; T. E. s. 3.

---

of the rules of practice in inferior courts when reviewing their judgments or decrees.[1]

(5) The official *status* and signatures of officers of the court, as attorneys, clerks of court, etc.[2]

(6) The political constitution of their own government; the accession of the President of the United States or of the executive of the State, and their signatures;[3] the official *status* of the chief public officers of the United States or of the State, as *e. g.*, cabinet officers, foreign ministers, sen-

---

[1] [*Knarr* v. *Conaway*, 42 Ind. 260; *Anderson* v. *McCormick*, 129 Ill. 308 ; *Cutter* v. *Caruthers*, 48 Cal. 178 ; *Cherry* v. *Baker*, 17 Md. 75 ; *Kindel* v. *Le Bert*, 23 Col. 385: but see *Oliver* v. *Palmer*, 11 G. & J. 426. The Federal courts take judicial notice of the rules and regulations of the Department of the Interior and other departments. *Caha* v. *U. S.*, 152 U. S. 211.]

[2] [*Mackinnon* v. *Barnes*, 66 Barb. 91; *Hammann* v. *Mink*, 99 Ind. 279; *Buell* v. *State*, 72 Ind. 523 ; *Ferris* v. *Commercial Nat. Bk.*, 158 Ill. 237 ; *State* v. *Barrett*, 40 Minn. 65 (deputy clerk); *State* v. *Kinney*, 81 Mo. 101 ; *State* v. *Myers*, 85 Tenn. 203 ; *Avery* v. *Maude*, 112 Cal. 565. Thus the signature of an attorney, admitting service of papers, will be noticed. *Ripley* v. *Burgess*, 2 Hill, 360.]

[3] [*Yount* v. *Howell*, 14 Cal. 465 ; *Wells* v. *Company*, 47 N. H. 235; *State* v. *Williams*, 5 Wis. 308.]

(8) The accession to office, names, titles, functions, and when attached to any decree, order, certificate, or other judicial or official documents, the signatures of all the judges of the Supreme Court of Justice.[1]

(9) The Great Seal, the Privy Seal, the seals of the Superior Courts of Justice,[2] and all seals which any court is

---

[1] 1 Ph. Ev. 462; T. E. s. 19; and as to latter part, 8 & 9 Vict. c. 113, s. 2, as modified by 36 & 37 Vict. c. 66, s. 76 (Judicature Act of 1873).

[2] The Judicature Acts confer no seal on the Supreme or High Court or its divisions. .

---

ators, and the like,[1]—also of sheriffs and marshals (and their signatures),[2] but not of their deputies.[3]

(7) The existence and title of every State and sovereign recognized by the national government;[4] also their public seals when attached to public acts, decrees, judgments or other official documents.[5]

(8) The law of nations;[6] foreign admiralty and maritime

---

[1] [*State* v. *Myers*, 85 Tenn. 203, 208 ; *York, etc. R. Co.* v. *Winans*, 17 How. (U. S.) 30 ; see *Brown* v. *Piper*, 91 U. S. 37, 42. The signatures of heads of departments will be noticed. *Comm.* v. *Dunlop*, 89 Va. 431.]

[2] [*Thompson* v. *Haskell*, 21 Ill. 215 ; *Ingram* v. *State*, 27 Ala. 17. Some cases say that notice will be taken of all county officers (*Farley* v. *McConnell*, 7 Lans. 428 ; *Himmelmann* v. *Hoadley*, 44 Cal. 213), at least if the court sits therein (*Thielmann* v. *Burg*, 73 Ill. 293). Thus it has been noticed who are notaries public of the county in which the court is held (*Hertig* v. *People*, 159 Ill. 237). So notice has been taken of justices and aldermen (*Fox* v. *Comm.*, 81* Pa. 511), and as to who were elected officers at a general election. *State* v. *Seibert*, 130 Mo. 202.]

[3] [Gr. Ev. i. § 6 ; *Ward* v. *Henry*, 19 Wis. 76 ; *contra*, under a statute, *Burke* v. *Lacock*, 41 Minn. 250, 255.]

[4] [*Jones* v. *U. S.*, 137 U. S. 202. The recognition must be by the executive branch of the government, before the courts will take such judicial notice. *Gelston* v. *Hoyt*, 13 Johns. 561, 587, 3 Wheat. 249.]

[5] [*Lazier* v. *Westcott*, 26 N. Y. 146 ; *Griswold* v. *Pitcairn*, 2 Ct. 85 ; *Coit* v. *Milliken*, 1 Den. 376.]

[6] [*The Scotia*, 14 Wall. 170.

authorized to use by any act of Parliament,[1] certain other
seals mentioned in acts of Parliament,[1] the seal of the

---

[1] *Doe* v. *Edwards*, 9 A. & E. 555.   See a list in T. E. s. 6.

---

courts and their seals ;[1] the seals of notaries public ;[2] the
seals of their own State and of the United States, and of the
courts thereof which have seals ;[3] but not the seals of foreign
municipal courts or of foreign officers.[4]

(9) Public proclamations by the executive branch of the
government, as of war, peace, amnesty, etc. ;[5] treaties made
with foreign countries ;[6] executive decrees or messages of a
public nature and ordinances of state ;[7] days of general
political elections.[8]

(10) The extent of territory included within their own State
or within the national domain ;[9] the civil divisions of the

---

[1] [*Thompson* v. *Stewart*, 3 Ct. 171 ; *Mumford* v. *Bowne*, Anth. N. P.
56.]

[2] [*Pierce* v. *Indseth*, 106 U. S. 546 ; *Johnson* v. *Brown*, 154 Mass. 105 ;
Barkydt v. *Alexander*, 59 Mo. App. 188.]

[3] [*Robinson* v. *Gilman*, 20 Me. 299 ; *Delafield* v. *Hand*, 3 Johns. 310,
314 ; *Williams* v. *Wilkes*, 14 Pa. 228.   The seal of a Federal court will
be noticed in other Federal courts and in State courts.   *Turnbull* v.
Payson, 95 U. S. 418 ; *Adams* v. *Way*, 33 Ct. 419.]

[4] [*Delafield* v. *Hand*, supra ; *Vandervoort* v. *Smith*, 2 Cai. 155 ;
Church v. *Hubbart*, 2 Cr. 187.   These rules are sometimes modified
by statutory provisions, providing how foreign records shall be proved.
See N. Y. Code Civ. Pro. §§ 952–956 ; *Hinton* v. *Life Ins. Co.*, 116 N. C.
22.]

[5] [*Armstrong* v. *U. S.*, 13 Wall. 154.]

[6] [*U. S.* v. *Rauscher*, 119 U. S. 407 ; *People* v. *Stout*, 81 Hun, 336.]

[7] [*Wells* v. *Mo. Pac, R. Co.*, 110 Mo. 286 ; *Turner's Admr.* v. *Patton*,
49 Ala. 406, 410 ; but not the orders of a military commander (*Burke*
v. *Miltenberger*, 19 Wall. 519), unless they have become matters of
public history (*Holmes* v. *Kring*, 93 Mo. 452 ; *Lanfear* v. *Mestier*, 18
La. Ann. 497); nor executive acts of a private nature, affecting persons not citizens.   *Dole* v. *Wilson*, 16 Minn. 525.]

[8] [*Mills* v. *Green*, 159 U. S. 651 ; *State* v. *Minnick*, 15 Ia. 123 ; *Copeland* v. *State*, 126 Ind. 51 ; *Jackson Co.* v. *Arnold*, 135 Mo. 207.]

[9] [*Jones* v. *U. S.*, 137 U. S. 202 ; *State* v. *Wagner*, 61 Me. 178 ; *State*
v. *Dunwell*, 3 R. I. 127.]

Corporation of London,[1] and the seal of any notary public in the Queen's dominions.[2]

(10) The extent of the territories under the dominion of Her Majesty and her successors; the territorial and

---

[1] 1 Ph. Ev. 464 ; T. E. s. 6.
[2] *Cole* v. *Sherard*, 11 Ex. 482. As to foreign notaries, see *Earl's Trust*, 4 K. & J. 300.

---

country or State, as into States, counties, cities, towns, etc.;[1] the relative positions of such divisions in the State, as that a city or town is in a certain county ;[2] the chief geographical features of the State ;[3] the existence of war against the United States ;[4] other public matters directly concerning the general government of the State or country ;[5] the existence

---

[1] [*Comm.* v. *Desmond*, 103 Mass. 445 ; *Chapman* v. *Wilber*, 6 Hill, 475 ; *Rogers* v. *Cady*, 104 Cal. 288 ; *Pitts* v. *Lewis*, 81 Ia. 51 ; *People* v. *Waller*, 70 Mich. 237 ; *State* v. *Cunningham*, 81 Wis. 440.]

[2] [*People* v. *Suppiger*, 103 Ill. 434 ; *State* v. *Powers*, 25 Ct. 48 ; *State* v. *Reader*, 60 Ia. 527 ; *Bryan* v. *Scholl*, 109 Ind. 367 ; *People* v. *Wood*, 131 N. Y. 617. So notice is taken that a certain town is or is not within a certain distance of the place of trial or the seat of government (*Hinckley* v. *Beckwith*, 23 Wis. 328 ; *Benson* v. *Clark*, 151 Ill. 495 ; *Hoyt* v. *Russell*, 117 U. S. 401). Such local divisions may be determined by public statutes and be noticed for that reason. *Bronson* v. *Gleason*, 7 Barb. 472 ; *Kansas City, etc. R. Co.* v. *Burge*, 40 Kan. 736.]

[3] [*Winnipiseogee Lake Co.* v. *Young*, 40 N. H. 420 ; *State* v. *Thompson*, 85 Me. 189 ; *People* v. *Brooks*, 101 Mich. 98 ; Note to 10 Abb. N. C. 117. The population of the State or its counties, etc., as shown by the census is noticed (*State* v. *Wofford*, 121 Mo. 61 ; *Denney* v. *State*, 144 Ind 503 ; *People* v. *McKane*, 80 Hun, 322, 143 N. Y. 455 ; *Worcester Nat. Bk.* v. *Cheney*, 94 Ill. 430); the boundaries of a State or county (*State* v. *Pennington*, 124 Mo. 388); what rivers in the State are navigable (*Wood* v. *Fowler*, 26 Kan. 682 ; *Comm.* v. *King*, 150 Mass. 221); but not the width of streets or sidewalks in a city (*Porter* v. *Waring*, 69 N. Y. 250). The distance between great cities in different States has been noticed. *Pearce* v. *Langfit*, 101 Pa. 507 ; but see *Goodwin* v. *Appleton*, 22 Me. 453.]

[4] [*Swinnerton* v. *Columbian Ins. Co.*, 37 N. Y. 174.]

[5] [Opinion of Justices, 70 Me. 609 ; *People* v. *Snyder*, 41 N. Y. 397.]

political divisions of England and Ireland, but not their geographical position or the situation of particular places ; the commencement, continuance, and termination of war between Her Majesty and any other Sovereign ; and all

---

of foreign countries and that they have a government and courts and a system of law like our own.[1] The Federal courts take notice of the ports of the United States in which the tide ebbs and flows, and of the boundaries of the several States and judicial districts.[2]

(11) Matters which must have happened according to the ordinary course of nature ;[3] natural and artificial divisions of time ;[4] the ordinary meaning of English words and common abbreviations ;[5] legal weights and measures and moneys

---

[1] [*Lasier* v. *Westcott*, 26 N. Y. 148 ; *Morse* v. *Hewett*, 28 Mich. 481.]

[2] [Gr. Ev. i. § 6 ; *Thorson* v. *Peterson*, 9 F. R. 517. So of internal revenue districts. *U. S.* v. *Jackson*, 104 U. S. 41.]

[3] [*Wood* v. *Ins. Co.*, 46 N. Y. 421, 426 ; *Dixon* v. *Niccolls*, 39 Ill. 372 ; as the time when the sun or moon rises or sets on a certain day (*People* v. *Mayer*, 113 Cal. 618 ; *State* v. *Morris*, 47 Ct. 179 ; *Case* v. *Perew*, 46 Hun, 57); and the succession of the seasons. *Ross* v. *Boswell*, 60 Ind. 235 ; *Garth* v. *Caldwell*, 72 Mo. 622.]

[4] [Wh. Ev. i. § 335. Thus notice is taken of the coincidence of days of the week with days of the month, as *e.g.*, upon what day a particular date falls (*Phila. etc. R. Co.* v. *Lehman*, 56 Md. 209 ; *Bank* v. *Kingsley*, 84 Me. 111 ; *Roberts* v. *Farmers'*, *etc. Bk.*, 136 Ind. 154 ; *Mechanics' Bank* v. *Gibson*, 7 Wend. 460), and, in general, of the calendar. *State* v. *Harris*, 121 Mo. 445.]

[5] [*Nix* v. *Hedden*, 149 U. S. 304 (meaning of "fruit" and "vegetable"); *Toplits* v. *Hedden*, 146 U. S. 252, 257 ("bonnets"); *Cook* v. *State*, 110 Ala. 40 ("oleomargarine"); *Comm.* v. *Marzynski*, 149 Mass. 68 (that "cigars" are not drugs); *State* v. *Intoxicating Liquors*, 73 Me. 278 ("C. O. D."); *Moseley* v. *Mastin*, 37 Ala. 216 ("admr."); *South Mo. Co.* v. *Jeffries*, 40 Mo. App. 360. So of the meaning of current expressions which every one understands (*Bailey* v. *Kalamazoo Pub'g Co.*, 40 Mich. 251 ; but see *Baltimore* v. *State*, 15 Md. 376, 484); but not of uncommon or extraordinary meanings given to English words in particular localities (*People* v. *Gastro*, 75 Mich. 127). In *Accola* v. *Chicago, etc. R. Co.*, 70 Ia. 185, the court would not notice the meaning of the abbreviation, "C., B. & Q. R. Co.," used in a pleading.]

other public matters directly concerning the general government of Her Majesty's dominions.[1]

(11) The ordinary course of nature, natural and arti-ficial divisions of time, the meaning of English words.[2]

---

[1] 1 Ph. Ev. 466, 460, 458 ; and T. E. ss. 15–16.
[2] 1 Ph. Ev. 465–6 ; T. E. s. 14.

---

of the country ;[1] matters of general public history,[2] but not those of mere private or local history ;[3] other matters of such general and public notoriety that every one may fairly be presumed to be acquainted with them.[4]

---

[1] [Gr. Ev. i. § 5 ; *Johnston* v. *Hedden*, 2 Johns. Cas. 274.]

[2] [*Thomas* v. *Stigers*, 5 Pa. 480 ; *Mode* v. *Beasley*, 143 Ind. 306 ; *Bissing* v. *Smith*, 85 Hun, 564; *Mayor of N. Y.* v. *Sands*, 105 N. Y. 210, 217; *Howard* v. *Moot*, 64 N. Y. 262 ; as *e. g.*, the civil war in this country, 1861-65, and its duration. *Cross* v. *Sabin*, 13 F. R. 308 ; *Turner's Admr.* v. *Patton*, 49 Ala. 406 ; *Swinnerton* v. *Columbian Ins. Co.*, 37 N. Y. 174.]

[3] [*McKinnon* v. *Bliss*, 21 N. Y. 206.]

[4] [*King* v. *Gallun*, 109 U. S. 99 ; *Gilbert* v. *Flint, etc. R. Co.*, 51 Mich. 488 ; *Menominee Co.* v. *Milwaukee, etc. R. Co.*, 91 Wis. 447 ; *State* v. *Me. Cent. R. Co.*, 86 Me. 309 ; as *e. g.*, the ordinary duration of human life (*Johnson* v. *Hudson R. R. Co.*, 6 Duer, 634); the average height of the human body (*Hunter* v. *N. Y. etc. R. Co.*, 116 N. Y. 615); the usual length of time for a voyage across the Atlantic (*Oppenheim* v. *Wolf*, 3 Sandf. Ch. 571); the usual time to run trains between prominent cities (*Pearce* v. *Langfit*, 101 Pa. 507 ; contra, *Wiggins* v. *Burkham*, 10 Wall. 129); the practice of checking baggage in this country (*Isaacson* v. *N. Y. C. R. Co.*, 94 N. Y. 278); the nature and properties of such things as natural or artificial gas, electricity, gun-powder, kerosene, tobacco and the like (*Jamieson* v. *Ind. Nat. Gas Co.*, 128 Ind. 555 ; *In re Jacobs*, 98 N. Y. 98, 113 ; *State* v. *Hays*, 78 Mo. 307 ; *State* v. *Johnson*, 118 Mo. 491 ; *Crawfordsville* v. *Braden*, 130 Ind. 149); that whiskey, brandy, gin, ale, and strong beer are intoxicating (*Blatz* v. *Rohrbach*, 116 N. Y. 450 ; *Thomas* v. *Comm.*, 90 Va. 92 ; *Eagan* v. *State*, 53 Ind. 162); but not that all malt liquors are intoxicating. Id.; *Schlicht* v. *State*, 56 Ind. 188 ; but see *Briffit* v. *State*, 58 Wis. 39.]

(12) All other matters which they are directed by any statute to notice.[1]

---

[1] *E. g.*, the Articles of War.   See sec. 1 of the Mutiny Act.

---

(12) Matters of general knowledge and experience within their jurisdiction ;[1] and matters which they are directed by any statute to notice.]

ARTICLE 59.

AS TO PROOF OF SUCH FACTS.

No evidence of any fact of which the court will take judicial notice need be given by the party alleging its existence;[2] but the judge, upon being called upon to take judicial notice thereof, may, if he is unacquainted with such fact, refer to any person or to any document or book of reference for his satisfaction in relation thereto, or may refuse to take judicial notice thereof unless and until the party calling upon him to take such notice produces any such document or book of reference.[3]

---

[1] [*Howard* v. *Moot*, 64 N. Y. 262, 271 ; *Hilliker* v. *Coleman*, 73 Mich. 170 ; *People* v. *Powers*, 147 N. Y. 104, 110 ; Opinion of Justices, 70 Me. 609 ; as *e. g.*, the result of an election affecting the organization of a county (*Andrews* v. *Knox Co.*, 70 Ill. 65 ; *Thomas* v. *Comm.*, 90 Va. 92 ; but see *Whitman* v. *State*, 80 Md. 410); the effect of elevated railroads upon the business of the streets through which they run. *Bookman* v. *N. Y. El. R. Co.*, 137 N. Y. 302.]

[2] [In *Hoyt* v. *Russell*, 117 U. S. 401, judgment was reversed because the court below required proof of a fact of which it was bound to take judicial notice.   Cf. *State* v. *Main*, 69 Ct. 123, 136.]

[3] T. E. (from Greenleaf) s. 20.   *E. g.*, a judge will refer in case of need to an almanac, or to a printed copy of the statutes, or write to the Foreign Office, to know whether a State had been recognized. [Gr. Ev. i. § 6 ; *Nix* v. *Hedden*, 149 U. S. 304 ; *Jones* v. *U. S.*, 137 U. S. 202 ; *Walton* v. *Stafford*, 14 App. Div. (N. Y.) 310 ; *Vahle* v. *Brackenseik*, 145 Ill. 236 ; *Bowen* v. *Mo. Pac. R. Co.*, 118 Mo. 541 ; *Heffernan* v. *Harvey*, 41 W. Va. 766 ; *Wilson* v. *Van Leer*, 127 Pa. 372 ; *Hall* v.

ARTICLE 60.

EVIDENCE NEED NOT BE GIVEN OF FACTS ADMITTED.

No fact need be proved in any proceeding which the
parties thereto or their agents agree to admit at the hearing, or which they have admitted before the hearing and
with reference thereto, or by their pleadings.[1] Provided
that in a trial for felony the prisoner can make no admissions so as to dispense with proof, though a confession
may be proved as against him, subject to the rules stated
in Articles 21–24.[2]

Brown, 58 N. H. 95 ; *State* v. *Wagner*, 61 Me. 178 ; *State* v. *Morris*,
47 Ct. 179 ; *State* v. *Clare*, 5 Ia. 509. Counsel should cite statutes and
decisions to the court, even though the court is bound to judicially
notice them (*State* v. *Farlee*, 74 Ia. 451). But a judge is not to take
judicial notice of matters merely because he in fact knows them.
Lenahan v. *People*, 5 T. & C. 265.]

[1] Rules of Supreme Court, Order xxxii. [*Coffin* v. *Hydraulic Co.*,
136 N. Y. 655 ; *Waldron* v. *Waldron*, 156 U. S. 361 ; *McGowan* v.
McDonald, 111 Cal. 57 ; *State* v. *Brooks*, 99 Mo. 137 ; *Atkinson* v.
Linden Co., 138 Ill. 187 ; *Burke* v. *Mascarich*, 81 Cal. 302 ; *Musselman*
v. *Wise*, 84 Ind. 248. So evidence offered by a party contradicting
his admissions in the pleadings is not competent (*Getty* v. *Hamlin*,
46 Hun, 1), and a finding or judgment contrary to such admissions
is error (*Reinhart* v. *Lugo*, 75 Cal. 639 ; *Paige* v. *Willett*, 38 N. Y. 28).

A demurrer admits facts well pleaded, but only for the purposes of
the argument on the demurrer ; it is not evidence of such facts on the
trial of the issue of fact (*State's Att'y* v. *Branford*, 59 Ct. 402 ; cf.
Gray v. *Gray*, 143 N. Y. 354), unless the party demurring obtains
leave to withdraw his demurrer from the record and goes to trial
without having done so. *Cutler* v. *Wright*, 22 N. Y. 472.] The fact
that a document is admitted does not make it relevant and is not
equivalent to putting it in evidence. *Watson* v. *Rodwell*, 11 Ch. D.
150, per James, L. J.

[2] 1 Ph. Ev. 391, n. 6. In *R.* v. *Thornhill*, 8 C. & P. 575, Lord Abinger
acted upon this rule in a trial for perjury. [In this case Lord Abinger
rejected evidence of admissions made by defendant's counsel before
the trial, but said that admissions made *at the trial* might be allowed.
See Gr. Ev. iii. § 39.]

CHAPTER VIII.

OF ORAL EVIDENCE.

ARTICLE 61.

PROOF OF FACTS BY ORAL EVIDENCE.

ALL facts may be proved by oral evidence subject to the provisions as to the proof of documents contained in Chapters IX., X., XI., and XII.

ARTICLE 62.*

ORAL EVIDENCE MUST BE DIRECT.

Oral evidence must in all cases whatever be direct; that is to say —

If it refers to a fact alleged to have been seen, it must be the evidence of a witness who says he saw it;

If it refers to a fact alleged to have been heard, it must be the evidence of a witness who says he heard it;

If it refers to a fact alleged to have been perceived by any other sense or in any other manner, it must be the evidence of a witness who says he perceived it by that sense or in that manner; [1]

---

* See Note XXVII. [Appendix].

[1] [See *Teerpenning* v. *Corn Ex. Ins. Co.*, 43 N. Y. 279; *People* v. *Chin Hane*, 108 Cal. 597; *Simpson* v. *Smith*, 27 Kan. 565, 570; *Rea* v. *Harrington*, 58 Vt. 181; *Fassin* v. *Hubbard*, 55 N. Y. 465. A witness may testify as to a communication received through the telephone (*Wolfe* v. *Mo. Pac. R. Co.*, 97 Mo. 473; *Oskamp* v. *Gadsden*, 35 Neb. 7; *Miles* v. *Andrew*, 153 Ill. 262); but identification of the speaker, as *e. g.*, by the sound of his voice, may be necessary (*People*

If it refers to an opinion, or to the grounds on which
that opinion is held, it must be the evidence of the person
who holds that opinion on those grounds.

---

v. *McKane*, 143 N. Y. 455, 474). A witness may testify to his *impression*, if this is based upon his own recollection of facts which he saw, heard, perceived, etc., and not upon hearsay or inference (Gr. Ev. i. § 440; *Blake* v. *People*, 73 N. Y. 586; *Humphries* v. *Parker*, 52 Me. 502; *Whitman* v. *Morey*, 63 N. H. 448, 457; *State* v. *Ward*, 61 Vt. 153; *Dexter* v. *Harrison*, 146 Ill. 169; *Lovejoy* v. *Howe*, 55 Minn. 353; *Ala. Southern R. Co.* v. *Hill*, 93 Ala. 515; *Tait* v. *Hall*, 71 Cal. 149; *Duvall's Excr.* v. *Darby*, 38 Pa. 56). So testimony as to what the witness "understood" or "supposed" has been received, when it really expresses his knowledge and recollection of what was said or done or agreed upon, etc. (*Fiske* v. *Gowing*, 61 N. H. 431; *Leach* v. *Bancroft*, Id. 411; *Ganser* v. *Fireman's Ins. Co.*, 38 Minn. 74; *Moody* v. *Davis*, 10 Ga. 403); but usually such evidence is inadmissible, as constituting only hearsay or opinion (*Fosdick* v. *Van Arsdale*, 74 Mich. 303; *Kingsbury* v. *Moses*, 45 N. H. 222; *Mather* v. *Parsons*, 32 Hun, 338; *Crowell* v. *Western Res. Bk.*, 3 O. St. 406). So evidence of one's intent, understanding, etc., is not received to show or vary the meaning of a written instrument, nor can one's undisclosed intent at the time of making a contract be proved to bind the other party (*Rickerson* v. *Hartford Ins. Co.*, 149 N. Y. 307; *Bartley* v. *Phillips*, 179 Pa. 175). A witness may testify to *his own intent* or *motive* or *belief*, when that is material in the case (*Bayliss* v. *Cockcroft*, 81 N. Y. 363; *Wallace* v. *U. S.*, 162 U. S. 466, 477; *Brown* v. *Mass. Ins. Co.*, 151 Mass. 127; *Phelps* v. *George's, etc. R. Co.*, 60 Md. 536; *Wohlford* v. *People*, 148 Ill. 296; *Ross* v. *State*, 116 Ind. 495; *Angell* v. *Pickard*, 61 Mich. 561; *Plank* v. *Grimm*, 62 Wis. 251; contra, *Ala. Fertilizing Co.* v. *Reynolds*, 79 Ala. 497), but not to the intent or motive of another person (*Mfrs. & Traders' Bk.* v. *Koch*, 105 N. Y. 630; *Cihak* v. *Klekr*, 117 Ill. 643; *Garrett* v. *Trabue*, 82 Ala. 227). So a witness may not testify to a *conclusion of law* (Wh. Ev. i. §§ 507, 509; *Nicolay* v. *Unger*, 80 N. Y. 54; *Ward* v. *Kilpatrick*, 85 N. Y. 413; *Providence Tool Co.* v. *U. S. Mf'g. Co.*, 120 Mass. 35; *Fisher* v. *Green*, 142 Ill. 80; *Young* v. *Newark Ins. Co.*, 59 Ct. 41; *Gabbey* v. *Forgens*, 38 Kan. 62).

Objects which have a material bearing on the case may be shown to the jury, and thus have the effect of evidence; as the weapon or instrument used to commit a crime, bloody garments, a person's injured limb, etc. (Wh. Ev. i. §§ 345-347; *People* v. *Gonzales*, 35 N. Y. 49; *King* v. *N. Y. C. R. Co.*, 72 N. Y. 607; *Louisville, etc. R. Co.* v. *Wood*, 113 Ind. 544; *Lanark* v. *Dougherty*, 153 Ill. 163; *Langworthy* v. *Green*, 95

Mich. 93; *State* v. *Ward*, 61 Vt. 153); but if such an exhibition would be indecent or offensive, it may be denied (*Knowles* v. *Crampton*, 55 Ct. 336). So the jury may be permitted to view the *locus in quo* (*Vane* v. *Evanston*, 150 Ill. 616). A person may be produced before a jury to enable them to judge as to his being a minor (*Comm.* v. *Emmons*, 98 Mass. 6; *Herrman* v. *State*, 73 Wis. 248; N. Y. Pen. Code, § 19; contra, *Louisville*, *etc. R. Co.* v. *Wood*, 113 Ind. 544, 550); and a witness under examination or one present in court as a party may be required by the court to uncover his or her face or to stand up to be identified (*Rice* v. *Rice*, 47 N. J. Eq. 559; *People* v. *Goldenson*, 76 Cal. 328; *People* v. *Gardner*, 144 N.Y. 119; *Williams* v. *State*, 98 Ala. 52). So photographs or drawings of persons or places, if properly verified as being accurate, may be introduced in evidence (*Udderzook's Case*, 76 Pa. 340; *Cowley* v. *People*, 83 N. Y. 464; *Comm.* v. *Robertson*, 162 Mass. 90; *Wilson* v. *U. S.*, 162 U. S. 613; *Cleveland, etc. R. Co.* v. *Monaghan*, 140 Ill. 475; *Leidlein* v. *Meyer*, 95 Mich. 586; *People* v. *Johnson*, 140 N. Y. 350; cf. *Gilbert* v. *West End R. Co.*, 160 Mass. 403). But whether a person suing for personal injuries can be required by the court to submit to an examination by physicians is a matter upon which the authorities are conflicting; that he can, see *Atchison, etc. R. Co.* v. *Thul*, 29 Kan. 466; *Turnpike Co.* v. *Baily*, 37 O. St. 104; *White* v. *Milwaukee R. Co.*, 61 Wis. 536; *Schroeder* v. *Railroad Co.*, 47 Ia. 375; *Railway Co.* v. *Dobbins*, 60 Ark. 481; *Fullerton* v. *Fordyce*, 121 Mo. 1; *Graves* v. *Battle Creek*, 95 Mich. 266; N. Y. Code Civ. Pro. § 873; that he cannot, *Union Pac. R. Co.* v. *Botsford*, 141 U. S. 250; *Peoria, etc. R. Co.* v. *Rice*, 144 Ill. 229; *Pennsylvania Co.* v. *Newmeyer*, 129 Ind. 401. In suits for divorce because of impotence, it is well settled that the court has the power. Bishop, M. D. & S. ii. §§ 1298–1315; *Anonymous*, 89 Ala. 291; *Cahn* v. *Cahn*, 21 Misc. 506; cf. *McGuff* v. *State*, 88 Ala. 147.]

CHAPTER IX.

OF DOCUMENTARY EVIDENCE—PRIMARY AND SECONDARY, AND ATTESTED DOCUMENTS.

ARTICLE 63.

PROOF OF CONTENTS OF DOCUMENTS.

THE contents of documents may be proved either by primary or by secondary evidence.

ARTICLE 64.

PRIMARY EVIDENCE.

Primary evidence means the document itself produced for the inspection of the court, accompanied by the production of an attesting witness in cases in which an attesting witness must be called under the provisions of Articles 66 and 67 ; or an admission of its contents proved to have been made by a person whose admissions are relevant under Articles 15–20.[1]

---

[1] *Slatterie* v. *Pooley*, 6 M. & W. 664. [This doctrine that the contents of a document may be proved by a party's admissions is accepted in several States (*Loomis* v. *Wadhams*, 8 Gray, 557 ; *Edgar* v. *Richardson*, 33 O. St. 581; *Taylor* v. *Peck*, 21 Gratt. 11; *Edwards* v. *Tracy*, 62 Pa. 374 ; *Blackington* v. *Rockland*, 66 Me. 332 ; *Hoefling* v. *Hambleton*, 84 Tex. 517 ; *Morey* v. *Hoyt*, 62 Ct. 542 ; cf. *Morrill* v. *Robinson*, 71 Me. 24). But in New York and New Jersey it is rejected (*Sherman* v. *People*, 13 Hun, 575 ; *Cumberland Ins. Co.* v. *Giltinan*, 48 N. J. L. 495), though such evidence is receivable if the document is lost or destroyed. *Mundeville* v. *Reynolds*, 68 N. Y. 528, 537 ; *Corbin* v. *Jackson*, 14 Wend. 619 ; see Gr. Ev. i. § 96; Wh. Ev. ii. §§ 1091–1093.]

Where a document is executed in several parts, each part is primary evidence of the document ; [1]

Where a document is executed in counterpart, each counterpart being executed by one or some of the parties only, each counterpart is primary evidence as against the parties executing it. [2]

Where a number of documents are all made by printing, lithography, or photography, or any other process of such a nature as in itself to secure uniformity in the copies, each is primary evidence of the contents of the rest ; [3] but where they are all copies of a common original,

---

[1] [Each of several duplicate originals is primary evidence (*Lewis* v. *Payn*, 8 Cow. 71; *Hubbard* v. *Russell*, 24 Barb. 404; *Totten* v. *Bucy*, 57 Md. 446 ; *Gardner* v. *Eberhart*, 82 Ill. 316 ; cf. *Crossman* v. *Crossman*, 95 N. Y. 145 ; see p. 191, note 1, *post*). So a copy may, under special circumstances, be deemed primary evidence. *Carroll* v. *Peake*, 1 Pet. 18 ; *Aultman* v. *Ritter*, 81 Wis. 395.]

[2] *Roe* d. *West* v. *Davis*, 7 Ea. 362. [*Loring* v. *Whittemore*, 13 Gray, 228 ; *Nicoll* v. *Burke*, 8 Abb. N. C. 213 ; *Cleveland, etc. R. Co.* v. *Perkins*, 17 Mich. 296 ; *Anglo-Amer. Co.* v. *Cannon*, 31 F. R. 313. It is not usual now to execute instruments in counterpart. *Roland* v. *Pinckney*, 8 Misc. 458.]

[3] *R.* v. *Watson*, 2 Stark. 129. This case was decided long before the invention of photography ; but the judgments delivered by the court (Ellenborough, C. J., and Abbott, Bayley, and Holroyd, JJ.) establish the principle stated in the text. [Wh. Ev. i. §§ 70, 92 ; see *Huff* v. *Bennett*, 4 Sandf. 120 ; *Simmons* v. *Holster*, 13 Minn. 249.

When a telegram is to be proved, the primary evidence, in controversies between the sender and the company, is the original message delivered to the company for transmission (*W. U. Tel. Co.* v. *Hopkins*, 49 Ind. 223; but see *Conyers* v. *Postal Tel. Co.*, 92 Ga. 619); and the same is true when the question is whether the alleged sender of a dispatch did actually send it, or authorize it to be sent (*Oregon Steamship Co.* v. *Otis*, 100 N. Y. 446). But when a contract is made by telegrams, and the sender takes the initiative by sending the offer, thus making the company his agent to transmit the message, the primary evidence to prove the contract is the message of the sender as delivered to the receiver and the answering message of the receiver as delivered by him to the office for transmission (*Durkee* v. *Vt. R. Co.*, 29 Vt. 127 ;

no one of them is primary evidence of the contents of the original.[1]

ARTICLE 65.

PROOF OF DOCUMENTS BY PRIMARY EVIDENCE.

The contents of documents must, except in the cases mentioned in Article 71, be proved by primary evidence;[2] and in the cases mentioned in Article 66 by calling an attesting witness.[3]

ARTICLE 66.*

PROOF OF EXECUTION OF DOCUMENT REQUIRED BY LAW TO BE ATTESTED.

If a document is required by law to be attested,[4] it may not be used as evidence (except in the cases mentioned

---

* See Note XXVIII. [Appendix].

Howley v. *Whipple*, 48 N. H. 487; *Nickerson* v. *Spindell*, 164 Mass. 25; *Ayer* v. *Tel. Co.*, 79 Me. 493, 500; *Saveland* v. *Green*, 40 Wis. 431; cf. *Smith* v. *Easton*, 54 Md. 138; *Trevor* v. *Wood*, 36 N. Y. 307; see cases collected in 14 Abb. N. C. 394). So in other cases where the sender takes the initiative in sending directions by telegraph, or an offer or request, the message received by the addressee is primary evidence (*Anheuser-Busch Ass'n* v. *Hutmacher*, 127 Ill. 652; *Magie* v. *Herman*, 50 Minn. 424; cf. *Comm.* v. *Jeffries*, 7 Allen, 548). But when the sendee employs the telegraph company, the primary evidence is the message delivered to the operator. Id.]

[1] *Noden* v. *Murray*, 3 Camp. 224. [Letter-press copies of documents are secondary evidence (*Foot* v. *Bentley*, 44 N. Y. 166; *State* v. *Halstead*, 73 Ia. 376; *McDowell* v. *Ætna Ins. Co.*, 164 Mass. 444; *King* v. *Worthington*, 73 Ill. 161). So of photographic copies. *Duffin* v. *People*, 107 Ill. 113; *Maclean* v. *Scripps*, 52 Mich. 214; *White Co.* v. *Gordon*, 124 Ind. 495.]

[2] [Gr. Ev. i. §§ 82–88; Wh. Ev. i. §§ 60–160; *Kain* v. *Larkin*, 131 N. Y. 300, 311; *Woods* v. *Burke*, 67 Mich. 674; *Martin* v. *McCray*, 171 Pa. 575.]

[3] [One who subscribes an instrument as a witness, but without the knowledge or consent of the parties, is not to be deemed an attesting witness. Gr. Ev. i. § 569 a; *Sherwood* v. *Pratt*, 63 Barb. 137; *Huston* v. *Ticknor*, 99 Pa. 231.]

[4] [See Art. 69, note.]

or referred to in the next Article) if there be an attesting witness alive, sane, and subject to the process of the court, until one attesting witness at least has been called for the purpose of proving its execution.[1]

If it be shown that no such attesting witness is alive or can be found, it must be proved that the attestation of one attesting witness at least is in his handwriting, and that the signature of the person executing the document is in the handwriting of that person.[2]

---

[1] [Gr. Ev. i. § 569 ; Wh. Ev. i. §§ 723-725 ; *Henry* v. *Bishop,* 2 Wend. 575 ; *International, etc. R. Co.* v. *McRae,* 82 Tex. 614 ; *Barry* v. *Ryan,* 4 Gray, 523. Only one witness need testify, though there be two or more (*O'Sullivan* v. *Overton,* 56 Ct. 102 ; *White* v. *Wood,* 8 Cush. 413 ; *Melcher* v. *Flanders,* 40 N. H. 139). But the absence of all must be accounted for, before evidence of handwriting will be admitted. *Jackson* v. *Gager,* 5 Cow. 383 ; *Tams* v. *Hitner,* 9 Pa. 441 ; *Turner* v. *Green,* 2 Cr. C. C. 202.]

[2] [The same general rule is established by statute in some States in regard to deeds (Mass. Pub. St. c. 120, ss. 8, 10 ; Maine Rev. St. c. 73, s. 19 ; Vt. Rev. St. ss. 1938, 1943). But generally in this country it is sufficient to prove the signature either of a witness or of the party, without proving both (*Borst* v. *Empie,* 5 N. Y. 33). Proof of the signature of one witness is sufficient proof of execution (*Stebbins* v. *Duncan,* 108 U. S. 32 ; *Gelott* v. *Goodspeed,* 8 Cush. 411 ; *Van Rensselaer* v. *Jones,* 2 Barb. 643); but proof of the party's identity may be needed besides, in cases of doubt or suspected fraud (Id.; *Brown* v. *Kimball,* 25 Wend. 259); and the signatures of other witnesses or of the party may, of course, always be proved, in addition to that of one witness (*Jackson* v. *Chamberlain,* 8 Wend. 620; *Servis* v. *Nelson,* 14 N. J. Eq. 94). In New York and some other States the signature of a witness must always be proved, if practicable, before that of a party can be (*Willson* v. *Betts,* 4 Den. 201; *Stebbins* v. *Duncan,* 108 U. S. 32; see *McVicker* v. *Conkle,* 96 Ga. 584, criticising the rule); but if the witness's handwriting cannot be proved, then the party's should be (*Jackson* v. *Waldron,* 13 Wend. 178 ; *Lessee of Clarke* v. *Courtney,* 5 Pet. 319). But in a number of the States the writing of the party may be proved without proving that of a witness (*Jones* v. *Roberts,* 65 Me. 273 ; *Cox* v. *Davis,* 17 Ala. 714 ; *Landers* v. *Bolton,* 26 Cal. 393; *Wellford* v. *Eakin,* 1 Cr. C. C 264); that the handwriting of either or both may be proved, see *Snider* v. *Burks,* 84 Ala. 53, 56 ;

The rule extends to cases in which—
the document has been burnt,[1] or canceled,[2] [or lost];[3]

Gelott v. *Goodspeed*, 8 Cush. 411 ; cf. *Troeder* v. *Hyams*, 153 Mass. 536.

Besides death or insanity (*Neely* v. *Neely*, 17 Pa. 227 ; *McKay* v. *Lasher*, 121 N. Y. 477), absence of witnesses from the State will let in proof of handwriting ; it is not necessary to send a commission to take their depositions (*Trustees of Charities* v. *Connolly*, 157 Mass. 272 ; *Hanrick* v. *Patrick*, 119 U. S. 156; *Grogan* v. *U. S. Industrial Ins. Co.*, 90 Hun, 521 ; *Lush* v. *Druse*, 4 Wend. 313; *N. J. Zinc Co.* v. *Lehigh Zinc Co.*, 59 N. J. L. 189 ; *Gallagher* v. *London Assur. Corp.*, 149 Pa. 25 ; *Ballinger* v. *Davis*, 29 Ia. 512). So handwriting may be proved when no witness can be found after diligent search, or none who is competent to testify (Gr. Ev. i. § 572 ; *Pelletreau* v. *Jackson*, 11 Wend. 110 ; *Woodman* v. *Segar*, 25 Me. 90).

Special statutes in some States require proof of certain documents by more than one witness, as *e. g.*, proof of a *will* by both or all the subscribing witnesses upon an application for the admission of the will to probate (N. Y. Code Civ. Pro. § 2618 ; Ohio R. S. s. 5926; Ill. R. S. c. 148, ss. 2 & 6). But in other proceedings than those for probate, the testimony of one subscribing witness to the will may be sufficient (*Upton* v. *Bernstein*, 76 Hun, 516). In several States a will may be proved, upon an application for probate, by one witness, if the probate is not contested (Mass. Pub. St. c. 129, s. 1 ; R. S. of N. H. c. 187, s. 6 ; Wis. R. S. ii. p. 2014). If any witness or witnesses to a will are dead, insane, absent, etc., proof of handwriting may be given ; by some statutes the signature of the testator must be proved as well as that of the witness or witnesses. Id.; N. Y. Code Civ. Pro. § 2620 ; *Denny* v. *Pinney*, 60 Vt. 524 ; cf. *Collyer* v. *Collyer*, 4 Dem. 53.]

[1] *Gillies* v. *Smither*, 2 Stark. 528. [But where the instrument which was burned was a deed which had been duly acknowledged, it was held not necessary to call the subscribing witness to prove its execution. *Simmons* v. *Haven*, 101 N. Y. 427 ; see Art. 67, *post*, note 4.]

[2] *Breton* v. *Cope*, Pea. R. 43.

[3] [*Hewitt* v. *Morris*, 5 J. & Sp. 18; *Kelsey* v. *Hanmer*, 18 Ct. 311; *Porter* v. *Wilson*, 13 Pa. 641; *Wells* v. *Jackson Iron Co.*, 48 N. H. 491; cf. *Jackson* v. *Frier*, 16 Johns. 193 ; *Moore* v. *Livingston*, 28 Barb. 543 ; *Kimball* v. *Morrill*, 4 Me. 368. If, however, by reason of the loss, it cannot be ascertained who were the subscribing witnesses, other evidence is admissible. *Jackson* v. *Vail*, 7 Wend. 125 ; *Davis* v. *Spooner*, 3 Pick. 284.]

the subscribing witness is blind ;[1]

the person by whom the document was executed is prepared to testify to his own execution of it ;[2]

the person seeking to prove the document is prepared
to prove an admission of its execution by the person who
executed it, even if he is a party to the cause,[3] unless such
admission be made for the purpose of, or has reference to
the cause.[4]

ARTICLE 67.*

CASES IN WHICH ATTESTING WITNESS NEED NOT BE CALLED.

In the following cases, and in the case mentioned in
Article 88, but in no others, a person seeking to prove the
execution of a document required by law to be attested is

---

* See Note XXVIII. [Appendix].

[1] *Cronk* v. *Frith*, 9 C. & P. 197; [see *Cheeney* v. *Arnold*, 18 Barb.
434.]

[2] *R.* v. *Harringworth*, 4 M. & S. 353. [This is true, though parties
are now competent to testify. *Brigham* v. *Palmer*, 3 Allen, 450;
Jones v. *Underwood*, 28 Barb. 481 ; *Weigand* v. *Sichel*, 4 Abb. Dec.
592; *Fletcher* v. *Perry*, 97 Ga. 368; *Russell* v. *Walker*, 73 Ala. 315;
Hess v. *Griggs*, 43 Mich. 397; cf. *Rayburn* v. *Mason Lumber Co.*, 57
Mich. 273 ; contra, *Bowling* v. *Hax*, 55 Mo. 446; *Garrett* v. *Hanshue*,
53 O. St. 482.]

[3] *Call* v. *Dunning*, 4 Ea. 53. See, too, *Whyman* v. *Garth*, 8 Ex.
803; *Randall* v. *Lynch*, 2 Camp. 357. [*Fox* v. *Riel*, 3 Johns. 477;
Smith v. *Carolin*, 1 Cr. C. C. 99; *Richmond, etc. R. Co.* v. *Jones*, 92
Ala 218; *Kinney* v. *Flynn*, 2 R. I. 319; *Warner* v. *B. & O. R. Co.*,
31 O. St. 265. But a contrary rule became established in New York
as to negotiable paper (see *Jones* v. *Underwood*, 28 Barb. 483; S. P.
Williams v. *Floyd*, 11 Pa. 499; but see Art. 69, *post*, note 2).

If the witnesses are dead, and the document lost or canceled, so
that handwriting cannot be proved, evidence of admissions is receivable (*Jackson* v. *Vail*, 7 Wend. 125; *Kingwood* v. *Bethlehem*, 13
N. J. L. 221; *Elliott* v. *Dyche*, 78 Ala. 150). So if the witnesses' testimony is insufficient. *Frost* v. *Deering*, 21 Me. 156.]

[4] [Gr. Ev. i. §§ 569, 572 ; *Blake* v. *Sawin*, 10 Allen, 340; *Jones* v.
Henry, 84 N. C. 320. Such admissions may be made in the pleadings

not bound to call for that purpose either the party who executed the deed or any attesting witness, or to prove the handwriting of any such party or attesting witness—

(1) When he is entitled to give secondary evidence of the contents of the document under Article 71 (a);[1]

(2) When his opponent produces it when called upon, and claims an interest under it in reference to the subject-matter of the suit;[2]

(3) When the person against whom the document is sought to be proved is a public officer bound by law to procure its due execution, and who has dealt with it as a document duly executed.[3] [4]

(*Robert* v. *Good*, 36 N. Y. 408 ; *Thorpe* v. *Keokuk Coal Co.*, 48 N. Y. 253). So both parties may waive proof by witness. *Forsythe* v. *Hardin*, 62 Ill. 206.]

[1] *Cooke* v. *Tanswell*, 8 Tau. 450 ; *Poole* v. *Warren*, 8 A. & E. 588. [*Rawley* v. *Doe*, 6 Blackf. (Ind.) 143. In *Bright* v. *Young*, 15 Ala. 112, which was a case of this kind, the subscribing witness was examined, but failed to prove the execution of the instrument with any degree of certainty, and it was held that circumstantial evidence was then receivable to show its execution and identity. See *Jackson* v. *Woolsey*, 11 Johns. 446.]

[2] *Pearce* v. *Hooper*, 3 Tau. 60 ; *Rearden* v. *Minter*, 5 M. & G. 204. [Gr. Ev. i. § 571; *Jackson* v. *Kingsley*, 17 Johns. 158 ; *McGregor* v. *Wait*, 10 Gray, 72 ; *Woodstock Iron Co.* v. *Reed*, 84 Ala. 493 ; see *Balliett* v. *Fink*, 28 Pa. 266 ; *Adams* v. *O'Connor*, 100 Mass. 515.] As to the sort of interest necessary to bring a case within this exception, see *Collins* v. *Bayntun*, 1 Q. B. 118.

[3] *Plumer* v. *Briscoe*, 11 Q. B. 46 ; [*Scott* v. *Waithman*, 3 Stark. 168 ; Gr. Ev. i. §§ 571, 573 ; see *Battle* v. *Baird*, 118 N. C. 854 ; *McVicker* v. *Conkle*, 96 Ga. 584, 585.] *Bailey* v. *Bidwell*, 13 M. & W. 73, would perhaps justify a slight enlargement of the exception, but the circumstances of the case were very péculiar. Mr. Taylor (ss. 1650-1) considers it doubtful whether the rule extends to instruments executed by corporations, or to deeds enrolled under the provisions of any act of Parliament, but his authorities hardly seem to support his view; at all events, as to deeds by corporations.

[4] [The following are additional exceptions :
(a) It is a rule in some States that proof by a subscribing witness is

ARTICLE 68.

PROOF WHEN ATTESTING WITNESS DENIES THE EXECUTION.

If the attesting witness denies or does not recollect the execution of the document, its execution may be proved by other evidence.[1]

ARTICLE 69.

PROOF OF DOCUMENT NOT REQUIRED BY LAW TO BE ATTESTED.

An attested document not required by law to be attested may in all cases whatever, civil or criminal, be proved as if it was unattested.[2]

---

not required when the instrument is not directly in issue, but only comes incidentally or collaterally in question (Gr. Ev. i. § 573 *b*; Wh. Ev. i. § 724; *Kitchen* v. *Smith*, 101 Pa. 452; *Ayers* v. *Hewett*, 19 Me. 281; *Rand* v. *Dodge*, 17 N. H. 343, 357; *Curtis* v. *Belknap*, 21 Vt. 433; *Steiner Bros.* v. *Tranum*, 98 Ala. 315; see *Comm.* v. *Castles*, 9 Gray, 121; *Smith* v. *N. Y. C. R. Co.*, 4 Abb. Dec. 262; *post*, p. 190, note).

(*b*) In many States recorded deeds and other instruments may be proved by duly authenticated copies, without calling any subscribing witness; or the deed, etc., as acknowledged or proved and certified, so as to be recorded, may be given in evidence. But the rules vary in different States. See *Gragg* v. *Learned*, 109 Mass. 167; *Sudlow* v. *Warshing*, 108 N. Y. 520; *Brown* v. *Oldham*, 123 Mo. 621; N. Y. Code Civ. Pro. §§ 935–937; Maine Rev. St. c. 82. s. 110; Wh. Ev. i. § 740.]

[1] "Where an attesting witness has denied all knowledge of the matter, the case stands as if there were no attesting witness." *Talbot* v. *Hodson*, 7 Tau. 251, 254. [*Hamsher* v. *Kline*, 57 Pa. 397; *Matter of Cottrell*, 95 N. Y. 329; *Patterson* v. *Tucker*, 9 N. J. L. 322; *Barnewall* v. *Murrell*, 108 Ala. 366; *Thomas* v. *Le Baron*, 8 Met. 355; *Webb* v. *Dye*, 18 W. Va. 376; cf. *Tompson* v. *Fisher*, 123 Mass. 559. So generally if the witness's testimony is inadequate to prove execution. *Harrington* v. *Gable*, 81 Pa. 406; *Frost* v. *Deering*, 21 Me. 156.]

[2] 17 & 18 Vict. c. 125, s. 26; 28 & 29 Vict. c. 18, ss. 1, 7. [Similar statutes are in force in some States of this country (Laws of 1883, N. Y. c. 195; Pub. St. R. I. c. 214, s. 41; 3 How. St. (Mich.) § 7531, *a*;

ARTICLE 70.

SECONDARY EVIDENCE.

Secondary evidence means—

(1) Examined copies, exemplifications, office copies, and certified copies :[1]

(2) Other copies made from the original and proved to be correct :[2]

(3) Counterparts of documents as against the parties who did not execute them :[3]

(4) Oral accounts of the contents of a document given by some person who has himself seen it.[4]

ARTICLE 71.

CASES IN WHICH SECONDARY EVIDENCE RELATING TO DOCUMENTS MAY BE GIVEN.

Secondary evidence may be given of the contents of a document in the following cases :—

Laws of Md. of 1888, c. 545 ; cf. Ill. Rev. St. p. 543, s. 51 (ed. 1883); *Medary* v. *Cathers*, 161 Pa. 87). But by the common-law rule, which still generally prevails, if a document is actually attested, though the law does not require its attestation, its execution must be proved by the attesting witness, or as otherwise prescribed in Art. 66 (*Giannone* v. *Fleetwood*, 93 Ga. 491).

As to the proof of unattested documents, see *Nichols* v. *Allen*, 112 Mass. 23 ; *St. John* v. *Amer. Ins. Co.*, 2 Duer, 419 ; *Seibold* v. *Rogers*, 110 Ala. 438 ; *Pullen* v. *Hutchinson*, 25 Me. 249.]

[1] See Chapter X.

[2] [See p. 180, note 1. A copy of a copy is sometimes admissible. *Cameron* v. *Peck*, 37 Ct. 555 ; *Winn* v. *Patterson*, 9 Pet. 663.]

[3] *Munn* v. *Godbold*, 3 Bing. 292. [*Loring* v. *Whittemore*, 13 Gray, 228 ; see p. 179, note 2.]

[4] [The witness must be able to prove the substance of the contents of

(*a*) When the original is shown or appears to be in the possession or power of the adverse party,

and when, after the notice mentioned in Article 72, he does not produce it ;[1]

(*b*) When the original is shown or appears to be in the possession or power of a stranger not legally bound to produce it, and who refuses to produce it after being served with a *subpœna duces tecum*, or after having been sworn as a witness and asked for the document and having admitted that it is in court ;[2]

---

the document. *Edwards* v. *Noyes*, 65 N. Y. 125 ; *Richard's Appeal*, 122 Pa. 547 ; *Mayor of Baltimore* v. *War*, 77 Md. 593 ; *Camden* v. *Belgrade*, 78 Me. 204.]

[1] *R.* v. *Watson*, 2 T. R. 201. *Entick* v. *Carrington*, 19 S. T. 1073, is cited by Mr. Phillips as an authority for this proposition. I do not think it supports it, but it shows the necessity for the rule, as at common law no power existed to compel the production of documents. [*Comm.* v. *Shurn*, 145 Mass. 150 ; *Dunbar* v. *U. S.*, 156 U. S. 185 ; *Bishop* v. *Amer. Preservers' Co.*, 157 Ill. 284 ; *Carland* v. *Cunningham*, 37 Pa. 228 ; *Keagle* v. *Pessell*, 91 Mich. 618 ; *Gaffer* v. *Amer. Mortgage Co.*, 77 Ia. 736 ; *Golden* v. *Conner*, 89 Ala. 598 ; see Art. 72, *post*. The party refusing to produce on notice incurs the penalty of having all inferences from the secondary evidence, if such evidence be imperfect, vague, or uncertain, taken most strongly against himself (*Cahen* v. *Continental Ins. Co.*, 69 N. Y. 300 ; *Cartier* v. *Troy Lumber Co.*, 138 Ill. 533 ; *McGuiness* v. *School District*, 39 Minn. 499).

Notice need not be given to a party who has admitted that the original document is lost or destroyed. *R.* v. *Haworth*, 4 C. & P. 254 ; *Barmby* v. *Plummer*, 29 Neb. 64 ; but see *Burlington Lumber Co.* v. *Whitebreast Co.*, 66 Ia. 292.]

[2] *Mills* v. *Oddy*, 6 C. & P. 732 ; *Marston* v. *Downes*, 1 A. & E. 31. [As where an attorney refuses to produce a document of his client (*Brandt* v. *Klein*, 17 Johns. 335 ; *Hubbell* v. *Judd, etc. Oil Co.*, 19 Alb. L. J. 97 ; *Stokoe* v. *St. Paul, etc. R. Co.*, 40 Minn. 545 ; see Arts. 115, 118, 119, *post*) ; or a witness refuses, because the document will criminate him (*State* v. *Gurnee*, 14 Kan. 111) ; or the document is a public one on file in a public office and so not required to be produced. *Corbett* v. *Gibson*, 16 Blatch. 334 ; cf. *In re Hirsch*, 74 F. R. 928 ; see p. 193, note 1, *post*.]

(c) When the original has been destroyed or lost, and proper search has been made for it ;[1]

(d) When the original is of such a nature as not to be easily movable,[2] or is in a country from which it is not permitted to be removed ;[3]

---

[1] 1 Ph. Ev. 452; 2 Ph. Ev. 281; T. E. (from Greenleaf) s. 399. [*Mandeville* v. *Reynolds*, 68 N. Y. 528 ; *Stebbins* v. *Duncan*, 108 U. S. 32; *McConnell* v. *Wildes*, 153 Mass. 487 ; *Gorgas* v. *Hertz*, 150 Pa. 538. Diligent search must ordinarily be shown, exhausting all reasonable means of discovery (*Simpson* v. *Dall*, 3 Wall. 460 ; *Johnson* v. *Arnwine*, 42 N. J. L. 451; *Kearney* v. *Mayor of N. Y.*, 92 N. Y. 617 ; *Darrow* v. *Pierce*, 91 Mich. 63; *Mullanphy Bk.* v. *Schott*, 135 Ill. 655; *McCollister* v. *Yard*, 90 Ia. 621). But the less the importance of the instrument, the less the diligence required (*American Ins. Co.* v. *Rosenagle*, 77 Pa. 507 ; *Hatch* v. *Carpenter*, 9 Gray, 271). Proof of the existence and genuineness of the lost instrument is required, in order that secondary evidence may be admissible. *Nichols* v. *Kingdom Iron Co.*, 56 N. Y. 618; *Gunther* v. *Bennett*, 72 Md. 384 ; *Krise* v. *Neason*, 66 Pa. 253.] The loss may be proved by an admission of the party or his attorney (*R.* v. *Haworth*, 4 C. & P. 254 ; [*Pentecost* v. *State*, 107 Ala. 81]).

[A party who has voluntarily destroyed a document cannot give secondary evidence of its contents, unless he shows his act to have been with innocent intent. *Potter* v. *Adams*, 125 Mo. 118 ; *Steele* v. *Lord*, 70 N. Y. 280 ; *Bagley* v. *McMickle*, 9 Cal. 430 ; *Jones* v. *Knauss*, 31 N. J. Eq. 609 ; *Joannes* v. *Bennett*, 5 Allen, 169.]

[2] *Mortimer* v. *McCallan*, 6 M. & W. 67, 68, (this was the case of a libel written on a wall); *Bruce* v. *Nicolopulo*, 11 Ex. 133, (the case of a placard posted on a wall). [Gr. Ev. i. § 94 ; *North Brookfield* v. *Warren*, 16 Gray, 171, (inscription on a tombstone); *Stearns* v. *Doe*, 12 Gray, 482, (name of a vessel); cf. *Cozzens* v. *Higgins*, 1 Abb. Dec. 451, (photograph of a place ; see Art. 62, *ante*, and note).]

[3] *Alivon* v. *Furnival*, 1 C. M. & R. 277, 291-2. [*Mauri* v. *Heffernan*, 13 Johns. 58. So if the original is in the possession of a person in another State or country, so that its production cannot be compelled (*Elwell* v. *Mersick*, 50 Ct. 272 ; *Tucker* v. *Woolsey*, 6 Lans. 482; *Stevens* v. *Miles*, 142 Mass. 571 ; *Knickerbocker* v. *Wilcox*, 83 Mich. 200; *Beattie* v. *Hilliard*, 55 N. H. 428 ; *Fosdick* v. *Van Horn*, 40 O. St. 459; *Burton* v. *Driggs*, 20 Wall. 125, 134 ; *Memphis, etc. R. Co.* v. *Hembree*, 84 Ala. 182 ; *Zellerbach* v. *Allenberg*, 99 Cal. 57 ; *Otto* v. *Trump*,

(*e*) When the original is a public document; [1]

(*f*) [When the party has been deprived of the original by fraud, so that it cannot be procured.] [2]

(*g*) When the original is a document for the proof of which special provision is made by any act of Parliament, or any law in force for the time being; [3] or

(*h*) When the originals consist of numerous documents which cannot conveniently be examined in court, and the fact to be proved is the general result [4] of the whole col-

---

115 Pa. 425, 430). These cases do not declare it necessary to take his deposition, but in some cases his deposition has been taken, and secondary evidence of the document received because he would not give up the original (*Bullis* v. *Easton*, 96 Ia. 513; *Deitz* v. *Regnier*, 27 Kan. 94; *L'Herbette* v. *Pittsfield Nat. Bk.*, 162 Mass. 137; in these foregoing cases he gave a copy which was used; *Forrest* v. *Forrest*, 6 Duer, 102, 137; *Fisher* v. *Greene*, 95 Ill. 94). Some cases, however, hold that mere absence of the document from the State is not enough, but that the deposition of the witness should be taken or some proper effort made to obtain the original. *Wiseman* v. *N. P. R. Co.*, 20 Or. 425; *Wood* v. *Cullen*, 13 Minn. 394; *Shaw* v. *Mason*, 10 Kan. 184; see *Knowlton* v. *Knowlton*, 84 Me. 283; *Thomson-Houston Electric Co.* v. *Palmer*, 52 Minn. 174.]

[1] See Chapter X.; [including public records; see Gr. Ev. i. § 91.]

[2] [*Grimes* v. *Kimball*, 3 Allen, 518; *Nealley* v. *Greenough*, 25 N. H. 325; *Mitchell* v. *Jacobs*, 17 Ill. 235; see *Marlow* v. *Marlow*, 77 Ill. 633.

This paragraph is substituted for one which is peculiar to English law. It will be found in the Appendix, Note XLIX.]

[3] See Chapter X. [Many such statutes are in force in this country.]

[4] *Roberts* v. *Doxen*, Peake, 116; *Meyer* v. *Sefton*, 2 Stark. 276. The books, etc., should in such a case be ready to be produced if required. *Johnson* v. *Kershaw*, 1 De G. & S. 264. [Gr. Ev. i. § 93; Wh. Ev. i. § 80; *Burton* v. *Driggs*, 20 Wall. 125; *Von Sachs* v. *Krets*, 72 N. Y. 548; *Boston & W. R. Co.* v. *Dana*, 1 Gray, 83; *Chicago, etc. R. Co.* v. *Wolcott*, 141 Ind. 267; *State* v. *Findley*, 101 Mo. 217; *Wolford* v. *Farnham*, 47 Minn. 95.]

lection; provided that that result is capable of being ascertained by calculation.[1]

---

[1] [Besides the cases here stated, another has been asserted, viz., that parol evidence of the contents of documents may be given, when they do not form the foundation of the cause, but merely relate to some collateral fact (*M'Fadden* v. *Kingsbury*, 11 Wend. 667 ; *Roosevelt* v. *Eckard*, 17 Abb. N. C. 58 ; *Maxwell* v. *Hofheimer*, 81 Hun, 551 ; *Coonrod* v. *Madden*, 126 Ind. 197 ; *Rodgers* v. *Crook*, 97 Ala. 722 ; *Faulcon* v. *Johnston*, 102 N. C. 264 ; cf. *Daniels* v. *Smith*, 130 N. Y. 696 ; *Phinney* v. *Holt*, 50 Me. 570). This doctrine has been criticised (Ph. Ev. Amer. Ed., ii. *513 ; *Jones* v. *Underwood*, 28 Barb. 481), but there is now much weighty authority in its support.

So the contents of a document, as a notice, placard, inscription, etc., may be proved by parol, as a means of describing the place where it hangs, of identifying the object to which it is attached, of showing the nature and purpose of a display or exhibition in which it is carried, etc. (*Comm.* v. *Brown*, 124 Mass. 318 ; *Comm.* v. *Morrell*, 99 id. 542 ; *R.* v. *Hunt*, 3 B. & Ald. 566). Parol evidence has also been received of the contents of a document which was a transient casual paper, not likely to be preserved, or when such contents were referred to incidentally or by way of inducement or recital, etc. (*State* v. *Credle*, 91 N. C. 640 ; *People* v. *Jones*, 106 N. Y. 523, 526 ; *Chrysler* v. *Renois*, 43 N. Y. 209 ; *N. J. Zinc Co.* v. *Lehigh Zinc Co.*, 59 N. J. L. 189, 193 ; *Massey* v. *Farmers' Nat. Bk.*, 113 Ill. 334).

A document may also be so far collateral to the question in issue, though relating to the same subject-matter, that its production is not required, nor proof of its contents necessary. In such a case parol evidence is receivable of the transaction to which it relates ; as *e. g.*, where a contract is made by parol, but a written memorandum of its terms is made at the same time ; the writing may; however, be competent evidence to corroborate the oral testimony (*Lathrop* v. *Bramhall*, 64 N. Y. 365 ; *Thomas* v. *Nelson*, 69 N. Y. 118 ; *Mobile, etc. R. Co.* v. *Jurey*, 111 U. S. 584 ; *Freeman* v. *Bartlett*, 47 N. J. L. 33 ; *Adams* v. *Sullivan*, 100 Ind. 8). So the existence of a fact or a state of facts, as a tenancy, a partnership, etc., may be proved by parol evidence, though it was created by the use of a document (*Hammon* v. *Sexton*, 69 Ind. 37 ; *Uhl* v. *Moorhous*, 137 Ind. 445 ; *Gallagher* v. *London Assur. Corp.*, 149 Pa. 25 ; *State* v. *Grant*, 104 N. C. 908 ; *East* v. *Pace*, 57 Ala. 521), or though a writing was made as some record or memorial thereof (*Hewitt* v. *State*, 121 Ind. 245 ; *Comm.* v. *Dill*, 156 Mass. 226 ; cf. *Comm.* v. *Stevens*, 155 id. 291). So the payment of a debt may be proved by parol, without producing the written receipt

Subject to the provisions hereinafter contained, any secondary evidence of a document is admissible.[1]

In case (*h*) evidence may be given as to the general result of the documents by any person who has examined them, and who is skilled in the examination of such documents.

Questions as to the existence of facts rendering secondary evidence of the contents of documents admissible are to be decided by the judge, unless in deciding such a question the judge would in effect decide the matter in issue.[2]

(*Kingsbury* v. *Moses*, 45 N. H. 222); so oftentimes of written proposals, notices, demands, etc. (Gr. Ev. i. §§ 89, 90 ; Wh. Ev. i. §§ 64, 77 ; *Jones* v. *Call*, 93 N. C. 170 ; *Mich. Land, etc. Co.* v. *Republic T'p*, 65 Mich. 628). So collateral facts about a document may be proved by parol (*Winslow* v. *State*, 76 Ala. 42 ; see p. 224, note 3, *post*).

As to proof of a person's holding a public office, see Art. 90, *post*, last paragraph.]

[1] If a counterpart is known to exist, it is the safest course to produce or account for it (*Munn* v. *Godbold*, 3 Bing. 297 ; *R.* v. *Castleton*, 7 T. R. 236).

[It is the English doctrine that there are no degrees in secondary evidence, and a party may introduce any form thereof (as *e. g.*, oral testimony instead of a copy), if the original cannot be had. Some American States adopt the same doctrine (*Comm.* v. *Smith*, 151 Mass. 491 ; *Magie* v. *Herman*, 50 Minn. 424 ; *Eslow* v. *Mitchell*, 26 Mich. 500 ; *Carpenter* v. *Dame*, 10 Ind. 125). But generally in this country a party must produce the best form of secondary evidence that is or appears to be procurable by him, as *e. g.*, a copy instead of oral testimony (*Cornett* v. *Williams*, 20 Wall. 226 ; *Reddington* v. *Gilman*, 1 Bos. 235 ; *Lazzaro* v. *Maugham*, 10 Misc. 230 ; *Mandeville* v. *Reynolds*, 68 N. Y. 528, 533 ; *Stevenson* v. *Hoy*, 43 Pa. 191 ; *Illinois Land Co.* v. *Bonner*, 75 Ill. 315 ; *Harvey* v. *Thorpe*, 28 Ala. 250 ; *Higgins* v. *Reed*, 8 Ia. 298 ; *Ford* v. *Cunningham*, 87 Cal. 209).

As to counterparts, see *Poignand* v. *Smith*, 8 Pick. 272 ; *Riggs* v. *Tayloe*, 9 Wheat. 483 ; Art. 64, *ante*. Of duplicate originals, all must be shown to be lost, destroyed, etc., before secondary evidence will be received. *Dyer* v. *Fredericks*, 63 Me. 173, 592 ; *McMakin* v. *Weston*, 64 Ind. 270 ; *Ala. Southern R. Co.* v. *Mt. Vernon Co.*, 84 Ala. 173.]

[2] [*Mason* v. *Libbey*, 90 N. Y. 683 ; *Elwell* v. *Mersick*, 50 Ct. 272.]

ARTICLE 72.*

RULES AS TO NOTICE TO PRODUCE.

Secondary evidence of the contents of the documents referred to in Article 71 (*a*) may not be given, unless the party proposing to give such secondary evidence has,

if the original is in the possession or under the control of the adverse party, given him such notice to produce it as the court regards as reasonably sufficient to enable it to be procured;[1] or has,

if the original is in the possession of a stranger to the

---

*See Note XXIX. [Appendix].

[1] *Dwyer* v. *Collins*, 7 Ex. 648. [*Foster* v. *Newbrough*, 58 N. Y. 481; *Draper* v. *Hatfield*, 124 Mass. 53; *People* v. *Walker*, 38 Mich. 159; *Dunbar* v. *U. S.*, 156 U. S. 185; *Mayor of Baltimore* v. *War*, 77 Md. 593, 603; *Trelever* v. *Northern Pac. R. Co.*, 89 Wis. 598; *Eilbert* v. *Finkbeiner*, 68 Pa. 243. Notice is not required unless the original is in the party's possession or control (*Roberts* v. *Spencer*, 123 Mass. 397; *Baker* v. *Pike*, 33 Me. 213; *Shepard* v. *Giddings*, 22 Ct. 282). The notice may be given to the party's attorney (*Brown* v. *Littlefield*, 7 Wend. 454; *Den* v. *M'Allister*, 7 N. J. L. 46). The notice must be given a sufficient time beforehand (*Bourne* v. *Buffington*, 125 Mass. 481; *U. S.* v. *Duff*, 6 F. R. 45; *DeWitt* v. *Prescott*, 51 Mich. 298; *McPherson* v. *Rathbone*, 7 Wend. 216; *Utica Ins. Co.* v. *Cadwell*, 3 Wend. 296); if the time allowed be unreasonably short, secondary evidence will not be admissible (Id.; *Mortlock* v. *Williams*, 76 Mich. 568; *Dade* v. *Ætna Ins. Co.*, 54 Minn. 336). The notice must also definitely describe the document required (*Walden* v. *Davison*, 11 Wend. 65; *Arnstine* v. *Treat*, 71 Mich. 561; *McDowell* v. *Ætna Ins. Co.*, 164 Mass. 444; see Gr. Ev. i. § 563; Art. 71, *ante;* Arts. 138, 139, *post*). Whether sufficient notice has been given is a question for the court to determine (*Comm.* v. *Sullivan*, 156 Mass. 229; *Hanselman* v. *Doyle*, 90 Mich. 142).

In the Federal courts, the production of books and writings by a party may also be required under a special statute in actions at law (U. S. Rev. St. § 724; *Lowenstein* v. *Carey*, 12 F. R. 811, and note; *Exchange Nat. Bk.* v. *Washita Co.*, 61 id. 190). Statutes in many States also allow discovery and inspection of documents before trial. N. Y. Code Civ. Pro. §§ 803–809; Mass. Pub. St. c. 167, ss. 49–60; Laws

action, served him with a *subpœna duces tecum* requiring
its production ; [1]

if a stranger so served does not produce the document,
and has no lawful justification for refusing or omitting to
do so, his omission does not entitle the party who served
him with the *subpœna* to give secondary evidence of the
contents of the document.[2]

Such notice is not required in order to render secondary
evidence admissible in any of the following cases—

(1) When the document to be proved is itself a notice ; [3]

---

of Me. of 1893, c. 217; *Pynchon* v. *Day*, 118 Ill. 9; *Arnold* v. *Paw-
tuxet Co.*, 18 R. I. 189.]

[1] *Newton* v. *Chaplin*, 10 C. B. 56-69. [*Aikin* v. *Martin*, 11 Pai. 499;
Lane v. *Cole*, 12 Barb. 680; *Baker* v. *Pike*, 33 Me. 213; *In re Shep-
hard*, 3 F. R. 12. So on examinations before masters and commissioners in Federal practice (*Erie R. Co.* v. *Heath*, 8 Blatch. 413 ; *U. S.*
v. *Tilden*, 10 Ben. 566). Such a subpœna may be served on a party,
now that parties are competent witnesses (*Shelp* v. *Morrison*, 13 Hun,
110 ; *Murray* v. *Elston*, 23 N. J. Eq. 212 ; *Cummer* v. *Kent Judge*, 38
Mich. 351; but see *Campbell* v. *Johnston*, 3 Del. Ch. 94), or on a corporation, by serving the proper officer (*Johnson Steel Rail Co.* v.
North Branch Co., 48 F. R. 195 ; *Ex parte Brown*, 72 Mo. 83 (telegrams); *U. S.* v. *Babcock*, 3 Dill. 566 (telegrams); N. Y. Code Civ. Pro.
§ 868 ; *In re Sykes*, 10 Ben. 162). The writ should describe documents
definitely (*State* v. *Davis*, 117 Mo. 614 ; *U. S.* v. *Hunter*, 15 F. R. 712 ;
Ex parte Jaynes, 70 Cal. 638), and is compulsory, unless it is set aside,
or the witness is privileged (*Bonesteel* v. *Lynde*, 8 How. Pr. 226, 352 ;
Corbett v. *Gibson*, 16 Blatch. 334 ; *In re Hirsch*, 74 F. R. 928 ; *Johnson* v. *Donaldson*, 3 F. R. 22 ; see Art. 71 (*b*), *ante;* Arts. 118-120,
post). A *subpœna duces tecum* may only be used to compel the production of documents, books, drawings, and the like, but not of such
objects as iron plates, patterns for stove castings, etc. *Johnson Steel
Rail Co.* v. *North Branch Co.*, 48 F. R. 191.]

[2] *R.* v. *Llanfaethly*, 2 E. & B. 940. [The recusant witness may be
sued for damages (*Lane* v. *Cole*, 12 Barb. 680), punished for contempt
(*Holly Mfg. Co.* v. *Venner*, 74 Hun, 458, 143 N. Y. 639), and is generally subject also to a statutory penalty. When he is a party, his pleading has sometimes been stricken out. *Shelp* v. *Morrison*, 13 Hun, 110.]

[3] [*Quinley* v. *Atkins*, 9 Gray, 370 ; *Michigan, etc. Land Co.* v. *Republic Township*, 65 Mich. 628 ; *Pensacola, etc. R. Co.* v. *Brayton*, 34

(2) When the action is founded upon the assumption that the document is in the possession or power of the adverse party and requires its production; [1]

(3) When it appears or is proved that the adverse party has obtained possession of the original from a person subpœnaed to produce it; [2]

(4) When the adverse party or his agent has the original in court.[3] [4]

Fla. 471; *Edwards* v. *Bonneau*, 1 Sandf. 610; *Gethin* v. *Walker*, 59 Cal. 502; *Morrow* v. *Comm.*, 48 Pa. 305; *Central Bk.* v. *Allen*, 16 Me. 41.]

[1] *How* v. *Hall*, 14 Ea. 247. In an action on a bond, no notice to produce the bond is required. See other illustrations in 2 Ph. Ev. 373; T. E. s. 422. [*Lawson* v. *Bachman*, 81 N. Y. 616; *Morrill* v. *B. & M. R. Co.*, 58 N. H. 68; *Dana* v. *Conant*, 30 Vt. 246; *Railway Co.* v. *Cronin*, 38 O. St. 122; as *e. g.*, in an action of trover for the document (*Hotchkiss* v. *Mosher*, 48 N. Y. 478). The rule applies also in criminal cases, as *e. g.*, where the defendant was charged by the indictment with fraudulently possessing himself of certain documents. *State* v. *Mayberry*, 48 Me. 218; cf. *People* v. *Swetland*, 77 Mich. 53.]

[2] *Leeds* v. *Cook*, 4 Esp. 256. [*Gray* v. *Kernahan*, 2 Mill (S. Car.) 65; cf. *Bonesteel* v. *Lynde*, 8 How. Pr. 226, 352. So where a party tore off a part of a document with intent to destroy, notice to produce the portion he took was held unnecessary. *Scott* v. *Pentz*, 5 Sandf. 572.]

[3] Formerly doubted, see 2 Ph. Ev. 278, but so held in *Dwyer* v. *Collins*, 7 Ex. 639. [A verbal notice in court is in this case sufficient to let in secondary evidence (*Overlock* v. *Hall*, 81 Me. 348; *Field* v. *Zemansky*, 9 Ill. App. 479; *Winslow* v. *State*, 92 Ala. 78; *Downer* v. *Button*, 26 N. H. 338, 343; *Chadwick* v. *U. S.*, 3 F. R. 750; *Kerr* v. *McGuire*, 28 N. Y. 446; see *Atwell* v. *Miller*, 6 Md. 10; *Barton* v. *Kane*, 17 Wis. 37; *Dole* v. *Belden*, 1 N. Y. S. 667); but some early cases are to the contrary (*Watkins* v. *Pintard*, 1 N. J. L. (Coxe) 378; *Milliken* v. *Barr*, 7 Pa. 23). The court may compel a witness to produce a document which he has in court. *Boynton* v. *Boynton*, 25 How. Pr. 490, 41 N. Y. 619; *Shelp* v. *Morrison*, 13 Hun, 110, 113; *McGregor* v. *Wait*, 10 Gray, 72.]

[4] [Additional rules are as follows:

(*a*) A duplicate original may be given in evidence, without giving notice to produce the other (Gr. Ev. i. § 561; *Totten* v. *Bucy*, 57 Md. 446; *Westbrook* v. *Fulton*, 79 Ala. 510; see Art. 64, *ante*).

(*b*) Absence of the party having the document from the State is no excuse for not giving notice, if he can be found (*Carland* v. *Cunning-ham*, 37 Pa. 228 ; *Dade* v. *Ætna Ins. Co.*, 54 Minn. 336). *Aliter*, if a *stranger* out of the State have the document (*Stirling* v. *Buckingham*, 46 Ct. 461; see *Burton* v. *Driggs*, 20 Wall. 125, 134.; Art. 71 (*d*), *ante*).

(*c*) In States where the contents of an instrument may be proved by parol, because it is only collaterally in question, notice to produce the instrument is not necessary. *Coonrod* v. *Madden*, 126 Ind. 197 ; *Askew* v. *Steiner*, 76 Ala. 218, 221; see *ante*, p. 190, note.]

CHAPTER X.

PROOF OF PUBLIC DOCUMENTS.

ARTICLE 73.

PROOF OF PUBLIC DOCUMENTS.

WHEN a statement made in any public document, register, or record, judicial or otherwise, or in any pleading or deposition kept therewith is in issue, or is relevant to the issue in any proceeding, the fact that that statement is contained in that document, may be proved in any of the ways mentioned in this chapter.[1]

ARTICLE 74.

PRODUCTION OF DOCUMENT ITSELF.

The contents of any public document whatever may be proved by producing the document itself for inspection from proper custody, and identifying it as being what it professes to be.[2]

---

[1] See Articles 34 and 90.

[2] [Gr. Ev. i. §§ 479, 482-484; Wh. Ev. i. §§ 635-660; Arts. 33 and 34 *ante*, and cases cited; *Evanston* v. *Gunn*, 99 U. S. 660; *Taylor* v. *Adams*, 115 Ill. 570; *Phelps* v. *Hunt*, 43 Ct. 194. A printed report of a decision is not competent original evidence of a judgment (*Donellan* v. *Hardy*, 57 Ind. 393), unless the original record has been destroyed (*Frost* v. *Frost*, 21 S. Car. 501). If a public record be lost, its contents may be proved by the testimony of a witness, no better evidence being available. *Richard's Appeal*, 122 Pa. 547.]

ARTICLE 75.*

EXAMINED COPIES.

The contents of any public document whatever may in all cases be proved by an examined copy.[1]

An examined copy is a copy proved by oral evidence to have been examined with the original and to correspond therewith.[2]   The examination may be made either by one person reading both the original and the copy, or by two persons, one reading the original and the other the copy, and it is not necessary (except in peerage cases[3]) that each should alternately read both.[4]

ARTICLE 76.†

[GENERAL RECORDS OF THE NATION OR STATE.]

[Copies of any documents, records, books, or papers in any of the executive departments of the United States Government, authenticated under the seals of such departments, respectively, are admitted in evidence equally with the originals ; and the same is true of copies of doc-

---

* See Note XXX. [Appendix]; also *Doe* v. *Ross*, 7 M. & W. 106.
† [For original Article, see Note LI. Appendix.]
[1] [Gr. Ev. i. §§ 485, 508; *State* v. *Loughlin*, 66 N. H. 266.]
[2] [Gr. Ev. i. § 508 ; *State* v. *Lynde*, 77 Me. 561; *State* v. *Spaulding*, 60 Vt. 228 ; *Hill* v. *Packard*, 5 Wend. 376, 387; *Amer. Life Ins. Co.* v. *Rosenagle*, 77 Pa. 507 ; see N. Y. Code Civ. Pro. § 962.   It is also called a "sworn copy" (Id.; Gr. Ev. i. §§ 485, 501 ; *Hubbell* v. *Meigs*, 50 N. Y. 480, 492; *Moore* v. *Gaus Mfg. Co.*, 113 Mo. 98; *State* v. *Clothier*, 30 N. J. L. 351).   An examined copy must be made by comparison with the original document, not by comparison with some other copy. *Lasater* v. *Van Hook*, 77 Tex. 650.]
[3] *Slane Peerage Case*, 5 C. & F. 42.
[4] 2 Ph. Ev. 200, 231; T. E. ss. 1379, 1389; R. N. P. 113. [*Kellogg* v. *Kellogg*, 6 Barb. 116; see *Krise* v. *Neason*, 66 Pa. 253.]

uments in various public offices, certified by the proper public officer and authenticated under his seal of office.[1]

A similar rule as to the proof in State courts of public documents in State offices is commonly established by statutes of the States, respectively.][2]

ARTICLE 77.*

EXEMPLIFICATIONS.

An exemplification is a copy of a record set out either under the Great Seal or under the Seal of a court.[3]

A copy made by an officer of the court, bound by law to make it, is equivalent to an exemplification, though it is sometimes called an office copy.[4]

---

* See Note XXXI. [Appendix].

[1] [U. S. Rev. St. ss. 882–898 ; *Ballew* v. *U. S.*, 160 U. S. 191 ; decisions collected in Bump's Federal Procedure, pp. 552–562, and Foster's Fed. Pr. 1, § 268, 2d ed.]

[2] [See N. Y. Code Civ. Pro. §§ 933, 957, 958 ; Mass. Pub. St. c. 169, s. 70. So statutes may provide that documents in U. S. offices may be so proved in State courts. N. Y. Code Civ. Pro. §§ 943, 944.]

[3] [The term applies primarily to domestic *judicial* records, and is here defined from that point of view (Gr. Ev. i. §§ 488, 501 ; Wh. Ev. i. § 95 ; *Traction Co.* v. *Board of Works*, 57 N. J. L. 315, 316 ; *Patterson* v. *Winn*, 5 Pet. 233). But it is often now applied both to domestic and to foreign records, laws, and documents, whether judicial or non-judicial. *Lincoln* v. *Battelle*, 6 Wend. 475 ; *Ropes* v. *Kemps*, 38 Fla. 233 ; *Lasier* v. *Westcott*, 26 N. Y. 146 ; *Watson* v. *Walker*, 23 N. H. 471 ; *Spaulding* v. *Vincent*, 24 Vt. 501.]

[4] [*Traction Co.* v. *Board of Works*, 57 N. J. L. 316. This rule applies to all courts within the same jurisdiction (Gr. Ev. i. § 507). Copies of public records, whether judicial or otherwise, made by a public officer authorized by law to make them, are also often termed "office copies," as *e. g.*, copies of recorded deeds (*Gragg* v. *Learned*, 109 Mass. 167 ; *Elwell* v. *Cunningham*, 74 Me. 127). They are also called "certified copies" (*Samuels* v. *Borrowscale*, 104 Mass. 207). They are declared admissible in many cases in courts of the same jurisdiction without further authentication. The officer may be required to attach his seal of office, if he has one. See Art. 79.]

An exemplification is equivalent to the original document exemplified.[1]

ARTICLE 78.*

COPIES EQUIVALENT TO EXEMPLIFICATIONS.

A copy made by an officer of the court, who is authorized to make it by a rule of court, but not required by law to make it, is regarded as equivalent to an exemplification in the same cause and court, but in other causes or courts it is not admissible unless it can be proved as an examined copy.[2]

ARTICLE 79.

CERTIFIED COPIES.

It is provided by many statutes that various certificates, official and public documents, documents and proceedings of corporations, and of joint stock and other companies, and certified copies of documents, by-laws, entries in registers and other books, shall be receivable in evidence of certain particulars in courts of justice, provided they are respectively authenticated in the manner prescribed by such statutes.[3]

---

* See Note XXXI. [Appendix].

[1] [This is spoken of domestic records, etc.; foreign records may need additional authentication. Gr. Ev. i. § 501; Art. 84, *post.*]

[2] [Gr. Ev. i. § 507; Wh. Ev. i. §§ 104, 105; *Kellogg* v. *Kellogg*, 6 Barb. 116, 130; *Traction Co.* v. *Board of Works*, 57 N. J. L. 313, 316. These are called "office copies" (Id.). But certified copies authorized by statute (or "office copies" in the broader sense of the term; see preceding Article) are now commonly used in their place, being admissible in all domestic courts.]

[3] 8 & 9 Vict. c. 113, preamble. Many such statutes are specified in T. E. s. 1440 and following sections. See, too, R. N. P. 114-5. [See, *e. g.*, U. S. Rev. St. ss. 882-900; N. Y. Code Civ. Pro. §§ 921-924, 928-941, 943-947, 957-962; *Northumberland Co.* v. *Zimmerman*, 75 Pa. 26;

Whenever, by virtue of any such provision, any such
certificate or certified copy as aforesaid is receivable in
proof of any particular in any court of justice, it is admissible as evidence if it purports to be authenticated in the
manner prescribed by law without proof of any stamp,
seal, or signature required for its authentication or of the
official character of the person who appears to have signed
it.[1]

Whenever any book or other document is of such a public nature as to be admissible in evidence on its mere production from the proper custody, and no statute exists

---

Elwood v. *Flannigan,* 104 U. S. 562; *Gethin* v. *Walker,* 59 Cal. 502;
Preston v. *Evans,* 56 Md. 476. In some States such copies may be used
by virtue of immemorial usage (*Chamberlin* v. *Ball,* 15 Gray, 352).
But it is sometimes provided, as in New York, that the common-law
methods of proof may be used, as well as the special statutory methods
(Code Civ. Pro. § 962).

Certificates or certified copies are not admissible in evidence unless
authorized by law, and then only as to matters which the officer is
required or authorized to certify. *Water Comm'rs* v. *Lansing,* 45
N. Y. 19; *Parr* v. *Greenbush,* 72 N. Y. 463; *Wayland* v. *Ware,* 109
Mass. 248; *Jay* v. *East Livermore,* 56 Me. 107; *Francis* v. *Newark,*
58 N. J. L. 522; *People* v. *Lee,* 112 Ill. 113.]

[1] Ibid., s. 1. I believe the above to be the effect of the provision,
but the language is greatly condensed. Some words at the end of the
section are regarded as unmeaning by several text-writers. See, *e. g.,*
R. N. P. 116; 2 Ph. Ev. 241; T. E. s. 7, note 1. Mr. Taylor says that
the concluding words of the section were introduced into the act while
passing through the House of Commons. He adds, they appear to
have been copied from 1 & 2 Vict. c. 94, s. 13 (see Art. 76) "by some
honorable member who did not know distinctly what he was about."
They certainly add nothing to the sense. [S. P. *Thurman* v. *Cameron,*
24 Wend. 87; *Trustees of Canandarqua Academy* v. *McKechnie,* 19
Hun, 62, 90 N. Y. 618; *Keichline* v. *Keichline,* 54 Pa. 75; *Kingman* v.
Cowles, 103 Mass. 283; *Harris* v. *Doe,* 4 Blackf. 369; *Galvin* v. *Palmer,*
113 Cal. 46; *Bixby* v. *Carskaddon,* 55 Ia. 533. Such copies or certificates are, however, generally deemed only presumptive or *prima facie*
evidence, open to rebuttal. Id.; see N. Y. Code Civ. Pro. §§ 921-924,
928, 936.]

which renders its contents provable by means of a copy, any copy thereof or extract therefrom is admissible in proof of its contents,[1] provided it purport to be signed and certified as a true copy or extract by the officer to whose custody the original is intrusted.[2][3]

Article 80.[*]

[DOCUMENTS AND RECORDS OF THE SEVERAL STATES ADMISSIBLE THROUGHOUT THE UNITED STATES.][4]

[The records and judicial proceedings of the courts of any State or Territory or of any country subject to the jurisdiction of the United States, shall be proved or ad-

---

[*] [For the original Article, see Note LI. Appendix.]

[1] The words "provided it be proved to be an examined copy or extract or," occur in the act, but are here omitted because their effect is given in Article 75.

[2] 14 & 15 Vict. c. 99, s. 14. [Some American decisions have maintained this rule as a common-law principle (Gr. Ev. i. § 485; *U. S.* v. *Percheman,* 7 Pet. 51; *People* v. *Lee,* 112 Ill. 113); but the weight of authority is that certified copies of public documents are not admissible unless authorized by statute (*Traction Co.* v. *Board of Works,* 57 N. J. L. 313; *Selden* v. *Canal Co.,* 29 N. Y. 634; see, also, cases cited in note 1, p. 200, *ante*). But the use of certified copies is now so generally authorized by statute that this question as to the common-law doctrine has become of little practical importance.]

[3] [At this point Mr. Stephen adds the English statutory rule that "every such officer must furnish such certified copy or extract to any person applying at a reasonable time for the same, upon payment of a reasonable sum for the same, not exceeding fourpence for every folio of ninety words. 14 & 15 Vict. c. 99. s. 14." So in this country it is a general rule that when the use of certified copies is authorized by statute, the proper officer must give such a copy on payment of his legal fees for the same. U. S. Rev. St. ss. 213, 460, 461, 828, 892, 4194, 4195; N. Y. Code Civ. Pro. § 961.]

[4] [The acts of Congress herein stated were enacted under the authority of the constitutional provision declaring that " full faith and credit

mitted in any other court within the United States, by the
attestation of the clerk, and the seal of the court annexed,
if there be a seal, together with a certificate of the judge,
chief justice, or presiding magistrate, that the said attestation is in due form.[1] And the said records and judicial
proceedings, so authenticated, shall have such faith and
credit given to them in every court within the United

---

shall be given in each State to the public acts, records, and judicial
proceedings of every other State.   And the Congress may, by
general laws, prescribe the manner in which such acts, records, and
proceedings shall be proved, and the effect thereof." U. S. Constitution, Art. iv. § 1.]

[1] [As to the construction of this provision, see Gr. Ev. i. §§ 504–506;
Wh. Ev. i. §§ 96–103; *First Nat. Bk.* v. *Crosby,* 179 Pa. 63. The
authorities are fully collected in Bump's Fed. Pro. pp. 566–616. The
attestation must be made by the *clerk* of the court; that of a deputy
clerk is not sufficient (*Morris* v. *Patchin,* 24 N. Y. 394); if the court
has ceased to exist and its records have been transferred to another
court, the clerk of the latter should attest (*Folsom* v. *Blood,* 58 N. H.
11). If the court has no seal, this fact should be stated. The certificate
must be added by the judge of the court, if there be only one, but,
when there are more than one, by the *chief* or *presiding* judge of the
court, if any judge bears such title (*Van Storch* v. *Griffin,* 71 Pa. 240;
People v. *Smith,* 121 N. Y. 578; *Andrews* v. *Flack,* 88 Ala. 294; *Barlow* v. *Steel,* 65 Mo. 611); this certificate must be that the attestation
is in *due form* (*i. e.,* in the form required in the State whence the
record comes); if the judge certifies, not this fact but some other, the
certificate is insufficient (*Craig* v. *Brown,* 1 Pet. C. C. 352; *Morris*
v. *Patchin,* supra; see *Burnell* v. *Weld,* 76 N. Y. 103). If the judge
is also clerk of the court, he must attest and certify in each capacity
(*Keith Bros.* v. *Stiles,* 92 Wis. 15). This statute does not apply to the
Federal courts, but their records, when certified by the clerk of the
court under its seal, are admissible in State courts and Federal courts
alike (*Turnbull* v. *Payson,* 95 U. S. 418). Nor does it apply, as is
generally held, to courts of inferior jurisdiction, as courts of justices
of the peace (*Farnsworth* v. *Briggs,* 6 N. H. 561; *Ransom* v. *Wheeler,*
12 Abb. Pr. 139; *Case* v. *Huey,* 26 Kan. 553; *Snyder* v. *Wise,* 10 Pa.
157). The mode of proving their dockets and judgments is that prescribed by the laws of the several States, or by common law. See
N. Y. Code Civ. Pro. §§ 948–951; Gr. Ev. i. § 505; *Case* v. *Huey,* supra]

States as they have by law or usage in the courts of the
State from which they are taken.[1]

All records and exemplifications of books, which may
be kept in any public office of any State or Territory, or
of any country subject to the jurisdiction of the United
States, not appertaining to a court, shall be proved or admitted in any court or office in any other State or Territory, or in any such country, by the attestation of the
keeper of the said records or books, and the seal of his
office annexed, if there be a seal, together with a certificate of the presiding justice of the court of the county,
parish, or district, in which said office may be kept, or of
the governor, or secretary of state, the chancellor or
keeper of the great seal of the State or Territory, or
country, that the said attestation is in due form, and by
the proper officers. If the said certificate is given by the
presiding justice of a court, it shall be further authenticated by the clerk or prothonotary of the said court, who
shall certify, under his hand and the seal of his office,
that the said presiding justice is duly commissioned and
qualified; or, if given by such governor, secretary, chancellor or keeper of the great seal, it shall be under the
great seal of the State, Territory, or country aforesaid in
which it is made. And the said records and exemplifications, so authenticated, shall have such faith and credit
given to them in every court and office within the United
States as they have by law or usage in the courts or offices of the State, Territory, or country as aforesaid, from
which they are taken.[2]

But these provisions do not preclude the several States

---

[1] [U. S. Rev. St. s. 905 ; as to the effect of such records, see *ante*,
Art. 47, note.]

[2] [U. S. Rev. St. s. 906; *Chase* v. *Caryl*, 57 N. J. L. 545; Bump's
Fed. Pro. p. 618 ; as to the scope of this section, see *Snyder* v. *Wise*,
10 Pa. 157 158.]

from establishing other modes of proving in their own courts the records of other States.] [1]

ARTICLE 81.*

[OFFICIALLY PRINTED COPIES.]

[The Revised Statutes of the United States, printed under the direction of the Secretary of State at the government printing-office and embracing the statutes of the United States general and permanent in their nature, in force on December 1, 1873, as revised and consolidated, and including also the amendatory acts passed by Congress between that date and the year 1878, shall be legal evidence of the laws therein contained, in all the courts of the United States and of the several States and Territories, but shall not preclude reference to, nor control, in case of any discrepancy, the effect of any original act as passed by Congress since December 1, 1873. And copies of the acts of Congress, printed as aforesaid at the close of each session of Congress, shall be legal evidence of the laws and treaties therein contained, in said courts.[2]

---

* [For the original Article, see Note LI. Appendix.]

[1] [*Kingman* v. *Cowles*, 103 Mass. 283 ; *In re Ellis' Estate*, 55 Minn. 401 ; *Garden City Co.* v. *Miller*, 157 Ill. 225 ; *Otto* v. *Trump*, 115 Pa. 425 ; *Hawes* v. *State*, 88 Ala. 37 ; Gr. Ev. i. §§ 489, 505. Some States have adopted special statutes of this kind (Id.; Mass. Pub. St. c. 169, s. 67); but usually the modes prescribed by the acts of Congress are followed. The common-law methods, as by exemplified or examined copy, may also be used. *Otto* v. *Trump*, supra ; *Dean* v. *Chapin*, 22 Mich. 275.]

[2] [U. S. Rev. St. (ed. 1878), Appendix, pp. 1090-1092 ; so as to the supplement to the Revised Statutes (21 Stat. L. 308 ; see *Wright* v. *U. S.*, 15 Ct. of Cl. 80). The acts of Congress were formerly published by Little and Brown, of Boston, and it is provided also that their edition shall be evidence of the laws and treaties therein contained (U. S. Rev. St. § 908). If there is any variance between an act of

It is common for State statutes to provide that the statute law of that State, and of other States and Territories, and of the United States, may be read in evidence in its courts from a printed book, paper, or other publication, duly published under official authority and direction.][1]

Article 82.*

[PROOF OF THE STATUTES OF ANY STATE OR TERRITORY.]

[The acts of the legislature of any State or Territory, or of any country subject to the jurisdiction of the United States, shall be authenticated by having the seals of such State, Territory, or country affixed thereto, and shall then

---

*[For the original Article, see Note LI. Appendix.]
Congress, as found in the printed volume of statutes, and the original, as enrolled and deposited with the Secretary of State, the latter must prevail (*McLaughlin* v. *Menotti*, 105 Cal. 572), and the same rule holds good as to State statutes. *Bruce* v. *State*, 48 Neb. 570.]

[1] [*Harryman* v. *Roberts*, 52 Md. 64 ; *Tenant* v. *Tenant*, 110 Pa. 478; *Bride* v. *Clark*, 161 Mass. 130; *People* v. *McQuaid*, 85 Mich. 123; *Eagan* v. *Connelly*, 107 Ill. 458; *Falls* v. *U. S. Savings, etc. Co.*, 97 Ala. 417 ; *Leach* v. *Linde*, 70 Hun, 145, 142 N. Y. 628; *Glenn* v. *Hunt*, 120 Mo. 330; *Rogero* v. *Zippel*, 33 Fla. 625 ; see Mass. Pub. St. c. 169, ss. 69, 71; N. Y. Code Civ. Pro. §§ 932, 942, extending the same rule to printed copies of any proclamation, edict, decree, or ordinance, by the executive power of any other State or country. If the official publication of the law of another State or country be not of recent date, still it will be presumed to contain the existing law, in the absence of evidence to the contrary (*In re Huss*, 126 N. Y. 537 ; *People* v. *Calder*, 30 Mich. 85).
In some States where no statutes exist authorizing the statute law of other States to be read from a printed volume, this has yet been allowed by the courts (Gr. Ev. i. §§ 480, 489). The common-law mode of proof is by exemplification under the great seal, or by examined copy, and this may still be used (Id.). The evidence of experts may also be received (see p. 145, *ante*, note 1). As to the cases in which statutes are judicially noticed, see Art. 58 (1), *ante*.]

be admitted in evidence in every other court within the United States.[1]

But this provision does not preclude the several States from establishing other modes of proving in their own courts the written law of other States.][2]

ARTICLE 83.*

[The contents of State papers, public documents, and legislative journals, printed by the official printer under the authority of Congress or a State legislature respectively (or of the proper branch thereof),[3] may be proved by the production of such a printed copy, as well as by the production of the originals.[4] Executive proclamations and acts of state may be proved by an officially printed copy.[5]

Extracts from the journals of the Senate of the United States, or of the House of Representatives and of the

---

* [For the original Article, see Note LI. Appendix.]

[1] [U. S. Rev. St. s. 905; Bump's Fed. Pro. p. 566; *Grant* v. *Coal Co.*, 80 Pa. 208; *U. S.* v. *Amedy*, 11 Wheat. 392; cf. *McClerkin* v. *State*, 105 Ala. 107.]

[2] [Gr. Ev. i. § 489; *Ansley* v. *Meikle*, 81 Ind. 260; as to the other modes of proof allowed, see Art. 81 and notes; also Art. 49, *ante*, and note 1 on p. 145; this last Article also shows the mode of proving the common law of other States.]

[3] [*Whiton* v. *Albany, etc. Ins. Co.*, 109 Mass. 24.]

[4] [Gr. Ev. i. § 479; *Watkins* v. *Holman*, 16 Pet. 25; *Bryan* v. *Forsyth*, 19 How. (U. S.) 334; *Gregg* v. *Forsyth*, 24 Id. 179; *Clemens* v. *Meyer*, 44 La. Ann. 390; *Milford* v. *Greenbush*, 77 Me. 330; *Lincoln* v. *Haugan*, 45 Minn. 451; *Root* v. *King*, 7 Cow. 613; *Post* v. *Supervisors*, 105 U. S. 667; cf. *Marks* v. *Orth*, 121 Ind. 10.]

[5] [Gr. Ev. i. §§ 479, 492; *Lurton* v. *Gilliam*, 2 Ill. (1 Scam.) 577; but proclamations are, in general, judicially noticed; see *ante*, Art. 58.

There is a statute in New York as to the proof of executive decrees and proclamations of other States and countries; see *ante*, p. 205, note 1.]

executive journal of the Senate when the injunction of
secrecy is removed, certified by the secretary of the Senate or by the clerk of the House of Representatives, shall
be admitted as evidence in the courts of the United States,
and shall have the same force and effect as the originals
would have, if produced and authenticated in court.] [1]

ARTICLE 84.*

[FOREIGN WRITTEN LAWS, ACTS OF STATE, RECORDS, ETC.]

[Foreign written laws, acts of state, and judicial records
may be proved by an exemplification of a copy under the
great seal of the state, or by a copy proved to be a true
copy by a witness who has examined and compared it
with the original, or by a certificate of an officer properly
authorized by law to give a copy, which certificate must
itself be duly authenticated.[2] Moreover, in some juris-
dictions, a foreign written law may be proved by the
statute book containing it, officially published by the government which made the law, either with or without the
testimony of experts.] [3]

---

* [For the original Article, see Note LI. Appendix.]

[1] [U. S. Rev. St. s. 895. For a like rule in State courts, see *Post* v.
Supervisors, 105 U. S. 667; cf. *Southwark Bk.* v. *Comm.*, 26 Pa. 446;
see *ante*, p. 165, note 2.]

[2] [These are the recognized common-law methods. Gr. Ev. i. §§ 488,
514; *Church* v. *Hubbart*, 2 Cr. 187; *Lincoln* v. *Battelle*, 6 Wend. 475;
Watson v. *Walker*, 23 N. H. 471; *Gunn* v. *Peakes*, 36 Minn. 177;
Jacobi v. *Order of Germania*, 73 Hun, 602; cf. *Tessmann* v. *United
Friends*, 103 Mich. 185.]

[3] [This is provided in some States by statute (Mass. Pub. St. c. 169,
s. 73; Maine Rev. St. c. 82, s. 109; N. Y. Code Civ. Pro. § 942; Laws
of N. J. of 1893, c. 38; see *In re Huss*, 126 N. Y. 537; p. 145, note 1,
ante), but is declared in *Ennis* v. *Smith*, 14 How. (U. S.) 401, as a
common-law doctrine; but see *Hynes* v. *McDermott*, 82 N. Y. 41, 56.
Sometimes expert testimony is received without a printed copy of the

law; see Art. 49, *ante*, and note 1 on p. 145, which also states the mode of proving a foreign unwritten law. As to proof of the statutes of sister States, see Articles 81 and 82, *ante*, and notes.

Special State statutes are also in force, establishing modes of proving foreign records, etc. (*Dunstan* v. *Higgins*, 138 N. Y. 70; *Wickersham* v. *Johnston*, 104 Cal. 407; *Fisher* v. *Fielding*, 67 Ct. 94; N. Y. Code Civ. Pro. §§ 952–956). But these are not generally made exclusive of common-law methods. Id. § 962.]

CHAPTER XI.

PRESUMPTIONS AS TO DOCUMENTS.

ARTICLE 85.

PRESUMPTION AS TO DATE OF A DOCUMENT.

WHEN any document bearing a date has been proved, it is presumed to have been made on the day on which it bears date,[1] and if more documents than one bear date on the same day, they are presumed to have been executed in the order necessary to effect the object for which they were executed,[2] but independent proof of the correctness of the date will be required if the circumstances are such that collusion as to the date might be practised, and would, if practised, injure any person, or defeat the objects of any law.[3]

---

[1] [Gr. Ev. i. § 40, n.; Wh. Ev. ii. § 977 ; *Livingston* v. *Arnoux*, 56 N. Y. 507, 519 ; *Smith* v. *Porter*, 10 Gray, 66 ; *Pringle* v. *Pringle*, 59 Pa. 281. So a deed, found in the hands of the grantee, is presumed to have been delivered on the day of its date (*People* v. *Snyder*, 41 N. Y. 397 ; *Scobey* v. *Walker*, 114 Ind. 254); but this is not true of forged instruments (*Remington Co.* v. *O'Dougherty*, 81 N. Y. 474). The presumption as to all instruments may be rebutted by proof of the real date of execution. *Parke* v. *Neeley*, 90 Pa. 52 ; *Germania Bank* v. *Distler*, 67 Barb. 333, 64 N. Y. 642 ; *Knisely* v. *Sampson*, 100 Ill. 573.]

[2] [*Dudley* v. *Cadwell*, 19 Ct. 218; *Jones* v. *Phelps*, 2 Barb Ch. 440; see *Gilman* v. *Moody*, 43 N. H. 239. So it is a general principle that two or more instruments of the same date, between the same parties, and relating to the same subject-matter, form parts of the same agreement or transaction. *Mott* v. *Richtmyer*, 57 N. Y. 49, 65; *Hagerty* v. *White*, 69 Wis. 317.]

[3] 1 Ph. Ev. 482–3; T. E. s. 137; Best, s. 403; [see *Philpot* v. *Gruninger*, 14 Wall. 570.]

Illustrations.

(*a*) An instrument admitting a debt, and dated before the act of bankruptcy, is produced by a bankrupt's assignees, to prove the petitioning creditor's debt. Further evidence of the date of the transaction is required in order to guard against collusion between the assignees and the bankrupt, to the prejudice of creditors whose claims date from the interval between the act of bankruptcy and the adjudication.[1]

(*b*) In a petition for damages on the ground of adultery letters are produced between the husband and wife, dated before the alleged adultery, and showing that they were then on affectionate terms. Further evidence of the date is required to prevent collusion to the prejudice of the person petitioned against.[2]

ARTICLE 86.

PRESUMPTION AS TO STAMP OF A DOCUMENT.[3]

When any document is not produced after due notice to produce, and after being called for, it is presumed to have been duly stamped,[4] unless it be shown to have remained unstamped for some time after its execution.[5]

---

[1] *Anderson* v. *Weston*, 6 Bing. N. C. 302 ; *Sinclair* v. *Baggallay*, 4 M. & W. 318.

[2] *Houlston* v. *Smith*, 2 C. & P. 24. [Gr. Ev. i. § 102, ii. § 57 ; *Fratini* v. *Caslini*, 66 Vt. 273 ; see Art. 11, Illustration (*k*), *ante*.]

[3] [The general abolition in this country, until recently, of laws requiring stamps upon written instruments has caused a dearth of modern decisions upon this subject. Analogous decisions of interest under the former law requiring revenue stamps are *Van Rensellaer* v. *Vickery*, 3 Lans. 57 ; *Long* v. *Spencer*, 78 Pa. 303 ; for a case in which stamps were used as seals, see *Van Bokkelen* v. *Taylor*, 62 N. Y. 105.]

[4] *Closmadeuc* v. *Carrel*, 18 C. B. 44. In this case the growth of the rule is traced, and other cases are referred to, in the judgment of Cresswell, J.

[5] *Marine Investment Co.* v. *Haviside*, L. R. 5 E. & I. App. 624.

ARTICLE 87.

PRESUMPTION AS TO SEALING AND DELIVERY OF DEEDS.

When any document purporting to be and stamped as a deed, appears or is proved to be or to have been signed and duly attested, it is presumed to have been sealed and delivered, although no impression of a seal appears thereon.[1]

[1] *Hall* v. *Bainbridge*, 12 Q. B. 699-710; *Re Sandilands*, L. R. 6 C. P. 411. [These cases, so far as they support this Article, are based upon the English rule, that neither an impression upon wax or other tenacious substance, nor a scroll or other mark, is necessary to constitute a seal; (thus in *Re Sandilands* it was declared that sealing might be done with the end of a ruler or anything else and that there need be no visible impression). But in this country, except in States which have abolished the use of seals, the general rule is that no deed or other specialty is complete without a seal in one or the other of these forms, though in many States a mere scroll or similar device, and in some a mere flourish or dash, if intended as a seal, is deemed sufficient (*Hacker's Appeal*, 121 Pa. 192; *Lorah* v. *Nissley*, 156 Pa. 329; *Osborn* v. *Kistler*, 35 O. St. 99; *Deininger* v. *McConnell*, 41 Ill. 227; cf. *Jacksonville, etc. R. Co.* v. *Hooper*, 160 U. S. 514). If, therefore, an instrument has no seal upon it, in the form recognized as valid in the particular State, the fact that it purports to be sealed, and is attested as such, is not sufficient to make it a deed (*Chilton* v. *People*, 66 Ill. 501; *State* v. *Humbird*, 54 Md. 327; *State* v. *Thompson*, 49 Mo. 188; *Taylor* v. *Glaser*, 2 S. & R. 502; *Boothbay* v. *Giles*, 68 Me. 160; *Cadell* v. *Allen*, 99 N. C. 542; cf. *Rensens* v. *Staples*, 52 F. R. 91). But where a deed is proved by the public records, and no seal has been recorded, the fact that the instrument purports to have been sealed and is so attested will raise the presumption of a seal upon the original (*Flowery Co.* v. *Bonanza Co.*, 16 Nev. 302; *Starkweather* v. *Martin*, 28 Mich. 471; *McCoy* v. *Cassidy*, 96 Mo. 429; *Le Franc* v. *Richmond*, 5 Sawy. 601; cf. *Todd* v. *Union Dime Inst.*, 118 N. Y. 337; *Rensens* v. *Lawson*, 91 Va. 226; *Heath* v. *Cotton Mills*, 115 N. C. 202; *Beardsley* v. *Day*, 52 Minn. 451; contra, *Switzer* v. *Knapps*, 10 Ia. 72; *Williams* v. *Bass*, 22 Vt. 352). If a seal is omitted by mistake, equity will cause the omission to be supplied or will assume that the instrument is sealed (*Harding* v. *Jewell*, 73 Me. 426; *Probate Ct.* v. *May*, 52 Vt. 182; *Barnard* v. *Gantz*, 140 N. Y. 249; *Henkleman* v. *Peterson*, 154 Ill. 419).

If an instrument, when given in evidence, bears a seal, this is pre-

ARTICLE 88.

PRESUMPTION AS TO DOCUMENTS THIRTY YEARS OLD.

Where any document purporting or proved to be thirty years old is produced from any custody which the judge in the particular case considers proper, it is presumed that the signature and every other part of such document which purports to be in the handwriting of any particular

---

sumed to be the seal of the party signing (*Mill Dam Foundery* v. *Hovey*, 21 Pick. 417, 428; *Trustees of Canandarqua Academy* v. *Mc-Kechnie*, 90 N. Y. 618); and upon proof of the signature, it may be presumed that the instrument was regularly sealed and delivered, especially if there be a recital stating the fact of sealing; such recital is, however, by the weight of authority, held unnecessary, though it may be material to show that a particular device was intended as a seal (*Merritt* v. *Cornell*, 1 E. D. Sm. 335; *Miller* v. *Binder*, 28 Pa. 489; *Bradford* v. *Randall*, 5 Pick. 496; *Trasher* v. *Everhart*, 3 G. & J. 234; *Force* v. *Craig*, 7 N. J. L. 272; *Anthony* v. *Harrison*, 14 Hun, 200, 74 N. Y. 613; cf. *Corlies* v. *Van Note*, 16 N. J. L., 324; but see *Clegg* v. *Lemessurier*, 15 Gratt. 108). But the presumption is rebuttable (*Koehler* v. *Black River Co.*, 2 Black, 715). Still the fact that an instrument bears a seal and also purports to be sealed is evidence for the jury that it was sealed when signed, though the obligor denies this (*Brolley* v. *Lapham*, 13 Gray, 294; *State* v. *Peck*, 53 Me. 284, 286); and the obligor may even be estopped to deny the seal, if the obligee has acted in good faith upon the instrument as being duly sealed (*Metropolitan Ins. Co.* v. *Bender*, 124 N. Y. 47; but see *Barnet* v. *Abbott*, 53 Vt. 120).

In a number of the States, by statute, the use of seals by private persons is now unnecessary, as *e. g.*, Ohio, Indiana, Iowa, Kansas, Nebraska, Tennessee, etc.

When a deed with the regular evidence of its execution upon its face is found in the hands of the grantee, it is presumed to have been duly delivered (*Butrick* v. *Tilton*, 141 Mass. 93; *Strough* v. *Wilder*, 119 N. Y. 530; *Harshbarger* v. *Carroll*, 163 Ill. 636); so if it is upon record duly acknowledged and attested (*Munoz* v. *Wilson*, 111 N. Y. 295; *Johnson* v. *Seidel*, 150 Pa. 397; *Stevens* v. *Castel*, 63 Mich. 111, collecting also the cases which hold differently). But these presumptions are also rebuttable. Id.; *Black* v. *Sharkey*, 104 Cal. 279; *Townsend* v. *R·ckham*, 143 N. Y. 516; see Washb. R. P. iii. 312 (5th ed.).]

person is in that person's handwriting, and, in the case of
a document executed or attested, that it was duly executed
and attested, by the persons by whom it purports to be
executed and attested;[1] and the attestation or execution
need not be proved, even if the attesting witness is alive
and in court.[2]

Documents are said to be in proper custody if they are
in the place in which, and under the care of the person
with whom, they would naturally be; but no custody is
improper if it is proved to have had a legitimate origin,

---

[1] 2 Ph. Ev. 245-8; Starkie, 521-6; T. E. s. 74 and ss. 593-601; Best,
s. 220. [Wh. Ev. i. §§ 194-199, 703, 732; Gr. Ev. i. §§ 21, 142-144, 570;
Applegate v. *Lexington, etc. Mining Co.,* 117 U. S. 255; *Dodge* v. *Gal-
latin,* 130 N. Y. 118; *Bell* v. *Brewster,* 44 O. St. 690; *Fowler* v. *Scott,*
64 Wis. 509; *Geer* v. *Lumber Co.,* 134 Mo. 85; *Scharff* v. *Keener,* 64
Pa. 376; *Goodwin* v. *Jack,* 62 Me. 414. The age of a will under this
rule is reckoned from the testator's death (*Staring* v. *Bowen,* 6 Barb.
109). If material and suspicious alterations appear upon the instrument, they should be explained by the party offering it in evidence
(*Rodriguez* v. *Haynes,* 76 Tex. 225; *Wisdom* v. *Reeves,* 110 Ala. 418;
Herrick v. *Malin,* 22 Wend. 388). It has been a mooted question,
whether, if the document were a conveyance of land, it would be
necessary to prove, besides its age and its production from the proper
custody, that there had been possession of the land under it and in
accordance with its terms. The better opinion is that evidence of
possession is not strictly necessary, but other corroborative evidence
may be received to establish the genuineness of the instrument (*Ha-
vens* v. *Sea Shore Co.,* 47 N. J. Eq. 365; *Nowlin* v. *Burwell,* 75 Va.
551; *Applegate* v. *Lexington, etc. Mining Co.,* supra; *Long* v. *Mc-
Dow,* 87 Mo. 197; *Whitman* v. *Heneberry,* 73 Ill. 109; *Walker* v.
Walker, 67 Pa. 185; *Boston* v. *Richardson,* 105 Mass. 351; *Clark* v.
Owens, 18 N. Y. 434; *Enders* v. *Sternbergh,* 2 Abb. Dec. 31; see Gr.
Ev. i. § 144, n.). But evidence of possession is the best means of cor-
roboration, and should be produced when practicable (*Willson* v.
Betts, 4 Den. 201). Unless there be some satisfactory corroboration,
the execution of the document must be proved; its age alone is not
enough to authenticate it. *Jackson* v. *Luquere,* 5 Cow. 221; *Martin* v.
Rector, 24 Hun, 27.]

[2] [*Jackson* v. *Christman,* 4 Wend. 277; *McReynolds* v. *Longenberger,*
57 Pa. 13.]

or if the circumstances of the particular case are such as
to render such an origin probable.[1]

ARTICLE 89.

PRESUMPTION AS TO ALTERATIONS.

No person producing any document which upon its
face appears to have been altered in a material part can
claim under it the enforcement of any right created by it,
unless the alteration was made before the completion of
the document or with the consent of the party to be
charged under it or his representative in interest.[2]

---

[1] [*Whitman* v. *Shaw*, 166 Mass. 451, 460; *Nowlin* v. *Burwell*, 75 Va.
551; *Beard* v. *Ryan*, 78 Ala. 37 ; and see other cases in notes 1 and 2,
supra, on p. 213.]

[2] [Gr. Ev. i. § 565 ; *Angle* v. *Life Ins. Co.*, 92 U. S. 330; *Drum* v.
Drum, 133 Mass. 566 ; *Hunt* v. *Gray*, 35 N. J. L. 227 ; *Russell* v. *Reed*,
36 Minn. 376. A material alteration made by a party intentionally
after execution avoids the instrument, though it be innocently made
(*Booth* v. *Powers*, 56 N. Y. 22 ; *Eckert* v. *Pickel*, 59 Ia. 545 ; *Craighead* v. *McLoney*, 99 Pa. 211); but then, in the case of a contract, a
recovery may be had on the original consideration (Id.; *Miller* v.
Stark, 148 Pa. 164), though the rule is otherwise, if the alteration be
fraudulent (*Meyer* v. *Huneke*, 55 N. Y. 412 ; *Warder* v. *Willyard*, 46
Minn. 531). Some authorities, however, hold that a material alteration, if made innocently or to correct a mistake, does not vitiate the
instrument (*Foote* v. *Hambrick*, 70 Miss. 157 ; *Croswell* v. *Labree*, 81
Me. 44). A negotiable instrument, materially altered by a party, is
void even in the hands of an innocent purchaser for value (*Benedict*
v. *Cowden*, 49 N. Y. 396; *Charlton* v. *Reed*, 61 Ia. 166; *Gettysburg
Nat. Bk.* v. *Chisolm*, 169 Pa. 564 ; *Newman* v. *King*, 54 O. St. 273 ;
Angle v. *Life Ins. Co.*, supra). Alterations in a deed of land, however, will not divest the title conveyed by it, though they will, if
material, avoid the covenants (Gr. Ev. i. § 265 ; *Herrick* v. *Malin*, 22
Wend. 388 ; *Woods* v. *Hilderbrand*, 46 Mo. 284 ; *Wallace* v. *Harm-
stad*, 15 Pa. 462 ; cf. *Potter* v. *Adams*, 125 Mo. 118).

Alterations before execution should be noted in the attestation
clause (Gr. Ev. i. § 564). Alterations by consent of parties do not
avoid the instrument (*Penny* v. *Corwithe*, 18 Johns. 499 ; *Taddiken* v.

This rule extends to cases in which the alteration was
made by a stranger, whilst the document was in the
custody of the person producing it, but without his
knowledge or leave.[1]

Alterations and interlineations appearing on the face
of a deed are, in the absence of all evidence relating to
them, presumed to have been made before the deed was
completed.[2]

Cantrell, 69 N. Y. 597), though they may have that effect as to sureties,
if made without their consent. *Paine* v. *Jones*, 76 N. Y. 274 ; *Eckert*
v. *Louis*, 84 Ind. 99 ; *Thompson* v. *Massie*, 41 O. St. 307.]

[1] *Pigot's Case*, 11 Rep. 47 ; *Davidson* v. *Cooper*, 11 M. & W. 778 ;
13 M. & W. 343 ; *Aldous* v. *Cornwell*, L. R. 3 Q. B. 573. This qualifies
one of the resolutions in *Pigot's Case*. The judgment reviews a great
number of authorities on the subject. [It is the general rule in this
country, however, that unauthorized alterations by a stranger, even
though material, do not affect the validity of the document (*Drum* v.
Drum, 133 Mass. 566 ; *Hunt* v. *Gray*, 35 N. J. L. 227 ; *Bigelow* v.
Stilphens, 35 Vt. 521 ; *Waring* v. *Smyth*, 2 Barb. Ch. 119 ; *Mix* v.
Royal Ins. Co., 169 Pa. 639 ; *Sewing Machine Co.* v. *Dakin*, 86 Mich.
581 ; *Ames* v. *Brown*, 22 Minn. 257 ; *Orlando* v. *Gooding*, 34 Fla. 244 ;
cf. *Gleason* v. *Hamilton*, 138 N. Y. 353), and the fact that the document is in the party's custody at the time seems to make no difference
(Id.; see *Nickerson* v. *Swett*, 135 Mass. 514 ; *Kingan* v. *Silvers Co.*,
13 Ind. App. 80). The stranger's act is called a "spoliation," rather
than an alteration. Gr. Ev. i. § 566 ; *John* v. *Hatfield*, 84 Ind. 75 ;
State v. *McGonigle*, 101 Mo. 353.]

[2] *Doe* v. *Catomore*, 16 Q. B. 745. [The American rule differs from
the English in many States, though there is much diversity of doctrine
in the different States. It is generally agreed, however, that if a
material alteration appear upon the face of a document, and be
suspicious in its character and beneficial to the party claiming the
enforcement of a right under the document, the burden of proof is
upon such party to show that the alteration was made before or at
the time of execution, or is for other reasons proper or excusable ;
and if evidence be adduced to explain any material alteration, it is
submitted to the jury, who are to determine as a question of fact,
when, by whom, and for what reason the alteration was made (*Nat.
Ulster Co. Bk.* v. *Madden*, 114 N. Y. 280 (note); *Smith* v. *McGowan*, 3
Barb. 404 (deed) ; *Smith* v. *U. S.*, 2 Wall. 219, 232 (bond); *Citizens'
Nat. Bk.* v. *Williams*, 174 Pa. 66 (note); *Robinson* v. *Myers*, 67 Pa. 9

Alterations and interlineations appearing on the face
of a will are, in the absence of all evidence relating to

(deed); *Wilson* v. *Hotchkiss' Estate*, 81 Mich. 172 (note); *Comstock*
v. *Smith*, 26 Mich. 306 (covenant in deed); *Ely* v. *Ely*, 6 Gray, 439
(mortgage); *Drum* v. *Drum*, 133 Mass. 566 (note); *Dodge* v. *Haskell*,
69 Me. 429 (note); *Hodnett* v. *Pace*, 84 Va. 873 (note); *Hill* v. *Nelms*,
86 Ala. 442 (mortgage); *Stillwell* v. *Patton*, 108 Mo. 352 (note); *Sisson*
v. *Pearson*, 44 Ill. App. 81 (deed)).   But if the alteration be not suspicious, such explanatory evidence is not required (Id.; *Zimmerman*
v. *Camp*, 155 Pa. 152; *Brand* v. *Johnrowe*, 60 Mich. 210; *Paramore*
v. *Lindsey*, 63 Mo. 63); and the same is true if the alteration be not
apparent; if in such a case the opposing party alleges a wrongful
alteration, the burden of proving it is on him (*Williamsburgh Bk.* v.
Solon, 136 N. Y. 465; *Insurance Co.* v. *Brim*, 111 Ind. 281).
    In some States maintaining the above rule, it is held that if the
party who is bound to explain a suspicious material alteration offers no
evidence for the purpose, the document may be rejected by the court
as inadmissible in evidence (*Burgwin* v. *Bishop*, 91 Pa. 336 (lease);
Hartley v. *Corboy*, 150 Pa. 23 (note); *Collins* v. *Ball*, 82 Tex. 259
(deed); *Tillou* v. *Clinton, etc. Ins. Co.*, 7 Barb. 564 (written consent);
but see *Maybee* v. *Sniffen*, 2 E. D. Sm. 1 (release); this is the English rule of *Knight* v. *Clements*, 8 A. & E. 215). In other States the
document, upon proof of execution, is submitted to the jury in all
cases of alteration, with or without explanatory evidence *aliunde*,
so that they may determine from its inspection, etc., when, and for
what purpose, the alteration was made (*Hoey* v. *Jarman*, 39 N. J. L.
523, 40 id. 379 (specialty); *Cole* v. *Hills*, 44 N. H. 227 (note); *Stayner*
v. *Joyce*, 120 Ind. 99 (note); *Goodin* v. *Plugge*, 47 Neb. 284 (note);
Dodge v. *Haskell*, supra); but the jury must be satisfied by a preponderance of evidence that any material alteration was rightfully
made, and in the absence of evidence to show this, a verdict against
the validity of the instrument will be sustainable, or may be directed
(Id.; *Putnam* v. *Clark*, 33 N. J. Eq. 338, 343). Under both these
theories, it is sometimes said that there is a presumption of *fact* that
a material alteration, not sufficiently explained, was made *after
execution*. It is denied, however, that there is any presumption of
law as to the time of alteration, in such a case, though such a doctrine
has been often asserted (*Ely* v. *Ely*, *Comstock* v. *Smith*, supra;
Closson v. *Morrison*, 47 N. H. 482, 487; *Jordan* v. *Stewart*, 23 Pa.
244, 249).
    In a number of the States the foregoing rules do not prevail, but
the presumption is that an unexplained alteration of an instrument

them, presumed to have been made after the execution of the will.[1]

There is no presumption as to the time when alterations and interlineations, appearing on the face of writings not under seal, were made,[2] except that it is presumed that they were so made that the making would not constitute an offence.[3]

An alteration is said to be material when, if it had been

---

was made *before* or *at the time of execution* (*Neil* v. *Case*, 25 Kan. 510 (note); *Beaman* v. *Russell*, 20 Vt. 205 (note); *Franklin* v. *Baker*, 48 O. St. 296 (note); *Wilson* v. *Hayes*, 40 Minn. 531 (note); *Little* v. *Herndon*, 10 Wall. 26 (asserting this as to *deeds*, following the English rule); cf. *Hayden* v. *Goodnow*, 39 Ct. 164). Under this doctrine the instrument is admissible in evidence, though no explanatory evidence is offered ; if, however, such evidence is introduced, the question as to the time and purpose of the alteration is for the jury (Id.).

There are other theories, also, on this vexed subject. Thus by some authorities there is a presumption of law that suspicious alterations were made after execution, but other alterations before (*Cox* v. *Palmer*, 1 McCrary, 431 (mortgage); *Orlando* v. *Gooding*, 34 Fla. 244), while others assert that an apparent alteration raises no presumption either way (*Hagan* v. *Merchants' etc. Ins. Co.*, 81 Ia. 321 (insurance policy); see *Wilson* v. *Hayes*, supra).

In general, each State, as the cases hitherto cited indicate, applies one and the same rule to deeds, bills and notes, written contracts of any kind, and other like documents. As to wills, see next note.]

[1] *Simmons* v. *Rudall*, 1 Sim. (N. S.) 136. [*Wetmore* v. *Carryl*, 5 Redf. 544 ; *Toebbe* v. *Williams*, 80 Ky. 661 ; contra, *Wikoff's Case*, 15 Pa. 281 ; see *In re Voorhees*, 6 Dem. 162 ; *Linnard's Appeal*, 93 Pa. 313 ; *Haynes* v. *Haynes*, 33 O. St. 598. When alterations are made after execution, it is generally held that the will must be reëxecuted ; if not, the will stands as it read before such alteration (*Gardner* v. *Gardiner*, 65 N. H. 230 ; *Simrell's Estate*, 154 Pa. 604 ; *Lovell* v. *Quitman*, 88 N. Y. 377 ; *Eschbach* v. *Collins*, 61 Md. 478 ; *Giffin* v. *Brooks*, 48 O. St. 211 ; *Hesterberg* v. *Clark*, 166 Ill. 241), except in cases where the alteration is by cancellation or obliteration, revoking the will in whole or in part.   *Townshend* v. *Howard*, 86 Me. 285 ; *Bigelow* v. *Gillott*, 123 Mass. 102.]

[2] *Knight* v. *Clements*, 8 A. & E. 215 ; [see p. 215, note 2, *supra*.]

[3] *R.* v. *Gordon*, Dears. 592 ; [see *Jordan* v. *Stewart*, 23 Pa. 244.]

made with the consent of the party charged, it would
have affected his interest or varied his obligations in any
way whatever.[1]

An alteration which in no way affects the rights of the
parties or the legal effect of the instrument, is immaterial.[2]

---

[1] [*Craighead* v. *McLoney*, 99 Pa. 211; *Booth* v. *Powers*, 56 N. Y. 22;
Murray v. *Klinzing*, 64 Ct. 78; *Wood* v. *Steele*, 6 Wall. 80. Whether
an alteration is material or not, is a question for the court. Id.; *Belfast Bk.* v. *Harriman*, 68 Me. 522; *Keens' Excr.* v. *Monroe*, 75 Va.
424.]

[2] This appears to be the result of many cases referred to in T. E. ss.
1619–20; see also the judgments in *Davidson* v. *Cooper* and *Aldous* v.
Cornwell, referred to above. [Immaterial alterations by a party or
stranger do not avoid an instrument (*Casoni* v. *Jerome*, 58 N. Y. 315;
Robertson v. *Hay*, 91 Pa. 242; *Cushing* v. *Field*, 70 Me. 50; *Prudden*
v. *Nester*, 103 Mich. 540; *Ryan* v. *First Nat. Bk.*, 148 Ill. 349; *Mersman* v. *Werges*, 112 U. S. 139; *Vose* v. *Dolan*, 108 Mass. 155; *Derby* v.
Thrall, 44 Vt. 413), even though they are made by a party with
fraudulent intent (*Fuller* v. *Green*, 64 Wis. 159; *Moye* v. *Herndon*, 30
Miss. 116; *Robinson* v. *Phœnix Ins. Co.*, 25 Ia. 430); but in some
States immaterial alterations by a party do avoid an instrument
(*Jones* v. *Crowley*, 57 N. J. L. 222; *Kingston Bk.* v. *Bosserman*, 52
Mo. App. 269; see Gr. Ev. i. § 568; cf. *Comm.* v. *Emigrant Sav. Bk.*,
98 Mass. 12).

If blank spaces are left in a negotiable bill or note so that it is
incomplete, any *bona fide* holder may fill them up, and the instrument
will be valid in the hands of an innocent purchaser for value (*Weyerhauser* v. *Dun*, 100 N. Y. 150; *Bank* v. *Sargent*, 85 Me. 349; *Brown*
v. *First Nat. Bk.*, 115 Ind. 572; *Angle* v. *Life Ins. Co.*, 92 U. S. 330;
Garrard v. *Lewis*, 10 Q. B. D. 30). But unwritten spaces in a *complete*
note or bill cannot be so filled (*McGrath* v. *Clark*, 56 N. Y. 34; *Bruce*
v. *Westcott*, 3 Barb. 374; *De Pauw* v. *Bank*, 126 Ind. 553; *Knoxville
Nat. Bk.* v. *Clark*, 51 Ia. 264; *Simmons* v. *Atkinson*, 69 Miss. 862;
Burrows v. *Klunk*, 70 Md. 451; *Greenfield Sav. Bk.* v. *Stowell*, 123
Mass. 196). But there are cases to the contrary, which are collected
in this last decision. As to filling blanks in deeds or bonds, see
Washb. R. P. iii. 252–256 (5th ed.); *Bell* v. *Kennedy*, 100 Pa. 215;
Chicago v. *Gage*, 95 Ill. 593; *State* v. *Mathews*, 44 Kan. 596; *Allen* v.
Withrow, 110 U. S. 119; *Brim* v. *Fleming*, 135 Mo. 597; *Lafferty* v.
Lafferty, 42 W. Va. 783.]

CHAPTER XII.

*OF THE EXCLUSION OF ORAL BY DOCUMENTARY
EVIDENCE, AND OF THE MODIFICATION AND
INTERPRETATION OF DOCUMENTARY BY ORAL
EVIDENCE.*

Article 90.*

**EVIDENCE OF TERMS OF CONTRACTS, GRANTS, AND OTHER DIS-
POSITIONS OF PROPERTY REDUCED TO A DOCUMENTARY FORM.**

WHEN any judgment of any court or any other judicial or
official proceeding, or any contract or grant, or any other
disposition of property, has been reduced to the form of
a document or series of documents, no evidence may be
given of such judgment or proceeding, or of the terms
of such contract, grant, or other disposition of property,
except the document itself, or secondary evidence of its
contents in cases in which secondary evidence is admissible under the provisions hereinbefore contained.[1] Nor
may the contents of any such document be contradicted,
altered, added to, or varied by oral evidence.[2]

---

* See Note XXXII. [Appendix].

[1] Illustrations (*a*) and (*b*). See *ante*, Arts.63–84. [Contemporaneous
writings between the same parties, relating to the same subject-matter, are admissible in evidence (Gr. Ev. i. § 283; *Wilson* v. *Randall*,
67 N. Y. 338; *McNamara* v. *Gargett*, 68 Mich. 454; *Windmill Co.* v.
Piercy, 41 Kan. 763); but neither of them can be varied by parol evidence (*Myers* v. *Munson*, 65 Ia 423). So writings referred to in another instrument are admissible with such instrument. *Maxted* v.
Seymour, 56 Mich. 129; *Amos* v. *Amos*, 117 Ind. 19.]

[2] [Gr. Ev. i. §§ 275–282; Wh. Ev. ii. §§ 920–927. This rule of the
English courts is well established in this country. It excludes (subject to the modifying rules hereinafter stated) evidence of prior, contemporaneous, or subsequent oral declarations or stipulations of the

Provided that any of the following matters may be
proved :—

(1) Fraud, intimidation, illegality, want of due execution, want of capacity in any contracting party, the fact
that it is wrongly dated,[1] want or failure of consideration,
or mistake in fact or law, or any other matter which, if
proved, would produce any effect upon the validity of
any document, or of any part of it, or which would entitle
any person to any judgment, decree, or order relating
thereto.[2]

---

parties (*Mott* v. *Richtmyer*, 57 N. Y. 49; *Seitz* v. *Brewers' Co.*, 141
U. S. 510; *Wodock* v. *Robinson*, 148 Pa. 503; *Johnson* v. *Glover*, 121
Ill. 283; *Caulfield* v. *Hermann*, 64 Ct. 325; *Tuttle* v. *Burgett*, 53 O. St.
498; *Boyd* v. *Paul*, 125 Mo. 9; *Black* v. *Bachelder*, 120 Mass. 171;
Naumberg v. *Young*, 44 N. J. L. 331). But in Pennsylvania it is applied with less stringency than in other States (*Greenawalt* v. *Kohne*,
85 Pa. 369). The rule as to *wills* is the same as in respect to other
instruments. Parol evidence is not received of the testator's oral
declarations of intention, except in the special cases stated in the
next Article (*Williams* v. *Freeman*, 83 N. Y. 561; *Warren* v. *Gregg*,
116 Mass. 304; *Mackie* v. *Story*, 93 U. S. 589; *Hoitt* v. *Hoitt*, 63 N. H.
475; *Hawke* v. *Chicago, etc. R. Co.*, 165 Ill. 561). The general rule
for all instruments is simply this:—*Ascertain the intention of the
party or parties from the instrument itself*, not from parol evidence
independent of the instrument (*Waters* v. *Bishop*, 122 Ind. 516; *Eyer*
v. *Beck*, 70 Mich. 179). But, as is shown by this Article and the next,
parol evidence of various kinds is admissible *to enable one to find the
intent in the instrument*. *House* v. *Walch*, 144 N. Y. 418.]

[1] *Reffell* v. *Reffell*, L. R. 1 P. & D. 139. [*Kincaid* v. *Archibald*, 73
N. Y 189; *Battles* v. *Fobes*, 21 Pick. 239; *Pigott* v. *O'Halloran*, 37
Minn. 415. But when the parties to a contract have made the date a
material part thereof, as when the time of performance is fixed with
reference to it, parol evidence is not admissible to change it. *Bar-
low* v. *Buckingham*, 68 Ia. 169; *Joseph* v. *Bigelow*, 4 Cush. 82.] Mr.
Starkie extends this to mistakes in some other formal particulars. 3
Stark. Ev. 787-8.

[2] Illustration (*c*). [Gr. Ev. i. §§ 284, 285; Wh. Ev. ii. §§ 930-935,
1009, 1054; *Trambly* v. *Ricard*, 130 Mass. 259 (fraud); *Mayer* v.
Dean, 115 N. Y. 556 (fraud); *Paine* v. *Upton*, 87 N. Y. 327 (fraud,
accident, and mistake); *Haughwout* v. *Garrison*, 69 N. Y. 339

(2) The existence of any separate oral agreement as to any matter on which a document is silent, and which is not inconsistent with its terms, if from the circumstances of the case the court infers that the parties did not intend

---

(usury); *Sherman* v. *Wilder*, 106 Mass. 537 (illegality); *Anthony* v. *Harrison*, 14 Hun, 198, 74 N. Y. 613; *Baird* v. *Baird*, 145 N. Y. 659; *Fire Ins. Ass'n* v. *Wickham*, 141 U. S. 564 (want of consideration). So parol evidence is admissible to show the real consideration of a contract or deed, though different from that expressed, or an additional consideration, not inconsistent with that expressed (*Hebbard* v. *Haughian*, 70 N. Y. 54; *Burnham* v. *Dorr*, 72 Me. 198; *Snow* v. *Alley*, 156 Mass. 193; *Silvers* v. *Potter*, 48 N. J. Eq. 539; *Koch* v. *Roth*, 150 Ill. 212; cf. *Emmett* v. *Penoyer*, 151 N. Y. 564; but see *Simanovich* v. *Wood*, 145 Mass. 180; *Conant* v. *Nat. State Bk.*, 121 Ind. 323; *Davis* v. *Gann*, 63 Mo. App. 425); to show a deed to be a mortgage (*Hassam* v. *Barrett*, 115 Mass. 256; *Barry* v. *Hamburg Ins. Co.*, 110 N. Y. 1; *German Ins. Co.* v. *Gibe*, 162 Ill. 251; *McMillan* v. *Bissell*, 63 Mich. 66; *Peugh* v. *Davis*, 96 U. S. 332; this is only true in *equity* in most States); to show a bill of sale of goods to be a chattel mortgage (*Marsh* v. *McNair*, 99 N. Y. 174, 178; *Susman* v. *Whyard*, 149 N. Y. 127; *Morgan's Assignees* v. *Shinn*, 15 Wall. 105; *Booth* v. *Robinson*, 55 Md. 419; this also, in most States, is in *equity*, but not at *law*, *Philbrook* v. *Eaton*, 134 Mass. 398); to establish a trust in personal property, or a constructive or resulting trust in land, though a deed or other writing has purported to carry an absolute title (*Minchin* v. *Minchin*, 157 Mass. 265; *Ducie* v. *Ford*, 138 U. S. 587; *Parker* v. *Snyder*, 31 N. J. Eq. 164; cf. *Zimmerman* v. *Barber*, 176 Pa. 1); to show that a deed was intended as an advancement (*Palmer* v. *Culbertson*, 143 N. Y. 213); to show that the signer of an unsealed non-negotiable instrument signed as agent, not as principal (*Brady* v. *Nally*, 151 N. Y. 258, 262; *Barbie* v. *Goodale*, 28 Or. 465; *Lerned* v. *Johns*, 9 Allen, 419; contra in N. J., *Schenck* v. *Spring Lake Co.*, 47 N. J. Eq. 44; as to *sealed* instruments, see *Henricus* v. *Englert*, 137 N. Y. 488); to show the true relations of the parties signing an instrument as between themselves, as that they are co-sureties though they signed as makers, and *vice versa*, etc. (*Mansfield* v. *Edwards*, 136 Mass. 15; *Paul* v. *Rider*, 58 N. H. 119; *Hubbard* v. *Gurney*, 64 N. Y. 457; *Kiel* v. *Choate*, 92 Wis. 517; *Farwell* v. *Ensign*, 66 Mich. 600); to show that a writing purporting to be a contract was not intended as such (*Grierson* v. *Mason*, 60 N. Y. 394; cf. *Michels* v. *Olmstead*, 157 U. S. 198); to show which of two contemporaneous writings expresses the real intention

the document to be a complete and final statement of the whole of the transaction between them.[1]

(3) The existence of any separate oral agreement, constituting a condition precedent to the attaching of any obligation under any such contract, grant, or disposition of property.[2]

---

of the parties (*Payson* v. *Lamson*, 134 Mass. 593). So a receipt may be contradicted or explained by parol, except in so far as it constitutes or contains a contract, as, *e. g.*, in the case of a bill of lading (*Macdonald* v. *Dana*, 154 Mass. 152; *Ryan* v. *Ward*, 48 N. Y. 204; *Goodwin* v. *Goodwin*, 59 N. H. 548; *Chapin* v. *Chicago, etc. R. Co.*, 79 Ia. 582; *Swain* v. *Frasier*, 35 N. J. Eq. 326); so as to a written license or admission (*Fargis* v. *Walton*, 107 N. Y. 398; *Smith* v. *Mayfield*, 163 Ill. 447); and there are many other like cases.]

[1] Illustrations (*d*), (*e*), and (*ee*). [Gr. Ev. i. § 284 *a*; *Thomas* v. *Scutt*, 127 N. Y. 133; *Graffam* v. *Pierce*, 143 Mass. 386; *Stahelin* v. *Lowle*, 87 Mich. 124; *Hand* v. *Ryan Co.*, 63 Minn. 539; *Platt* v. *Ætna Ins. Co.*, 153 Ill. 113, 121; *Greening* v. *Steele*, 122 Mo. 287; *Sivers* v. *Sivers*, 97 Cal. 518; *Naumberg* v. *Young*, 44 N. J. L. 331. Thus, *e. g.*, an independent collateral agreement may be shown by parol (*Van Brunt* v. *Day*, 81 N. Y. 251; *Backus* v. *Sternberg*, 59 Minn. 403; *Neal* v. *Flint*, 88 Me. 73; *Ayer* v. *Bell Mfg. Co.*, 147 Mass. 46). But the rule in the text does not apply when it appears from inspection of the instrument that it was intended to express the full and complete intentions of the parties (*Eighmie* v. *Taylor*, 98 N. Y. 288; *Seitz* v. *Brewers' Co.*, 141 U. S. 510; *Dickson* v. *Hartman Mfg. Co.*, 179 Pa. 343; *Averill* v. *Sawyer*, 62 Ct. 560); nor does it apply to contracts which are required by the Statute of Frauds to be in writing. *Ringer* v. *Holtzclaw*, 112 Mo. 519.]

[2] Illustrations (*f*) and (*g*). [*Wilson* v. *Powers*, 131 Mass. 539; *McFarland* v. *Sikes*, 54 Ct. 250; *Reynolds* v. *Robinson*, 110 N. Y. 654; *Higgins* v. *Ridgway*, 153 N. Y. 130; *Burke* v. *Delaney*, 153 U. S. 228; *Smith* v. *Mussetter*, 58 Minn. 159; cf. *McCormick Co.* v. *Wilson*, 39 Minn. 467. Generally, however, in this country a condition attached to the delivery of an instrument under seal, or at least of a conveyance of land, to the obligee or grantee, whereby it is to take effect only upon the happening of a contingent event, cannot be shown by parol (*Newman* v. *Baker*, 10 App. D. C. 187; *Blewitt* v. *Boorum*, 142 N. Y. 357); but in other respects specialties and deeds are subject to this rule, as well as instruments not under seal (*Wendlinger* v. *Smith*, 75 Va. 309; *Brackett* v. *Barney*, 28 N. Y. 333; *State* v. *Wallis*,

(4) The existence of any distinct subsequent oral agreement to rescind or modify any such contract, grant, or disposition of property, provided that such agreement is not invalid under the Statute of Frauds, or otherwise.[1]

(5) Any usage or custom by which incidents not expressly mentioned in any contract are annexed to contracts of that description; unless the annexing of such

---

57 Ark. 73; *Keener* v. *Crago*, 81 * Pa. 166; *Harrison* v. *Morton*, 83 Md. 456). It has been held, however, not applicable to *wills* (*Sewell* v. *Slingluff*, 57 Md. 537).

But conditions other than such "conditions precedent" as the text describes cannot be engrafted upon a writing by parol evidence (*Wilson* v. *Deen*, 74 N. Y. 531; *Allen* v. *Furbish*, 4 Gray, 504; *Holzworth* v. *Koch*, 26 O. St. 33); in Pennsylvania, however, a less stringent rule prevails, and parol evidence is received of oral promises or conditions on the faith of which a written contract has been executed. *Cullmans* v. *Lindsay*, 114 Pa. 170.]

[1] Illustration (*h*). [Gr. Ev. i. §§ 302-304; *Teal* v. *Bilby*, 123 U. S. 578; *Hastings* v. *Lovejoy*, 140 Mass. 261; *West Haven Co.* v. *Redfield*, 58 Ct. 39; *Nicoll* v. *Burke*, 78 N. Y. 580; *Church* v. *Florence Iron Works*, 45 N. J. L. 129; *Holloway* v. *Frick*, 149 Pa. 178. Generally the subsequent agreement requires a new consideration (*Malone* v. *Dougherty*, 79 Pa. 46; *Stewart* v. *Keteltas*, 36 N. Y. 388, 392; *Barton* v. *Gray*, 57 Mich. 622; *Carruthers* v. *McMurray*, 75 Ia. 173), but the original consideration may be deemed sufficient (*Lynch* v. *McHenry*, 75 Wis. 631; cf. *Anderson* v. *Moore*, 145 Ill. 61). So in case of a parol waiver or a parol extension of time for performance, no consideration is generally required (*Stevens* v. *Taylor*, 58 Ia. 664; *Mead* v. *Parker*, 111 N. Y. 259; *Thomson* v. *Poor*, 147 N. Y. 402; *Cobbs* v. *Fire Ass'n*, 68 Mich. 463). As to the modification by parol of a contract under seal, see *Canal Co.* v. *Ray*, 101 U. S. 522; *Quigley* v. *De Haas*, 98 Pa. 292; *McCreery* v. *Day*, 119 N. Y. 1; *Herzog* v. *Sawyer*, 61 Md. 344; *Blagborne* v. *Hunger*, 101 Mich. 375; *Alschuler* v. *Schiff*, 164 Ill. 298.

The authorities are conflicting as to whether a contract within the Statute of Frauds can be varied by a subsequent parol agreement. *Cummings* v. *Arnold*, 3 Met. 486; *Negley* v. *Jeffers*, 28 O. St. 90; *Hill* v. *Blake*, 97 N. Y. 216; *Thomson* v. *Poor*, 147 N. Y. 402, 408; *Swain* v. *Seamens*, 9 Wall. 254, 272; *Packer* v. *Steward*, 34 Vt. 127, 130; *Williams* v. *Flood*, 63 Mich. 487; *Burns* v. *Fidelity Co.*, 52 Minn. 31; see *Long* v. *Hartwell*, 34 N. J. L. 116; Reed on St. of Frauds, ii. § 473.]

incident to such contract would be repugnant to or inconsistent with the express terms of the contract.[1]

Oral evidence of a transaction is not excluded by the
fact that a documentary memorandum of it was made, if
such memorandum was not intended to have legal effect
as a contract, or other disposition of property.[2]

Oral evidence of the existence of a legal relation is not
excluded by the fact that it has been created by a document, when the fact to be proved is the existence of the
relationship itself, and not the terms on which it was
established or is carried on.[3]

---

[1] Illustration (*ha*); *Wigglesworth* v. *Dallison*, and note thereto,
S. L. C. 598–628. A late case is *Johnson* v. *Raylton*, 7 Q. B. D. 438, in
which it was held that evidence was admissible of a custom that in a
contract with a manufacturer for iron plates he warranted them to be
of his own make. [Gr. Ev. i. §§ 294, 295; *Walls* v. *Bailey*, 49 N. Y.
464; *Page* v. *Cole*, 120 Mass. 37; *Robinson* v. *U. S.*, 13 Wall. 363;
Patterson v. *Crowther*, 70 Md. 124; *Pennell* v. *Transportation Co.*,
94 Mich. 247. But evidence of usage will not be received to defeat
a settled rule of law or the plain meaning of a statute. *Barnard* v.
Kellogg, 10 Wall. 383; *Corn Exch. Bk.* v. *Nassau Bk.*, 91 N. Y. 74;
Suburban Elec. Co. v. *Elizabeth*, 59 N. J. L. 134; cf. *Armstrong* v.
Granite Co., 147 N. Y. 495.]

[2] Illustration (*i*). [*Brigg* v. *Hilton*, 99 N. Y. 517; *Lathrop* v. *Bramhall*, 64 N. Y. 365; *Perrine* v. *Cooley's Excrs.*, 39 N. J. L. 449; *Irwin*
v. *Thompson*, 27 Kan. 643; *Grant* v. *Frost*, 80 Me. 202; *Kreuzberger*
v. *Wingfield*, 96 Cal. 251; see *ante*, p. 190, note 1.]

[3] Illustration (*j*). [Thus the existence of a partnership or corporation
may be proved by parol (*Widdifield* v. *Widdifield*, 2 Binn. 245; *Cutler*
v. *Thomas*, 25 Vt. 73; *State* v. *Grant*, 104 N. C. 908; see p. 190, note 1,
ante); or the fact of a tenancy in land (*Hammon* v. *Sexton*, 69 Ia. 37); or
the ownership of property (*Gallagher* v. *London Assur. Co.*, 149 Pa. 25;
cf. *Uhl* v. *Moorhous*, 137 Ind. 445). So various collateral facts about an
instrument may be proved by parol; as *e. g.*, the purpose or object
for which it was given (*Hutchins* v. *Hebbard*, 34 N. Y. 24; *Bunker* v.
Barron, 79 Me. 62; *Bruce* v. *Slemp*, 82 Va. 352); the reason why it was
not indorsed (*Bank* v. *Kennedy*, 17 Wall. 19); the fact that notes were
sent to a banking-house for collection (*Cecil Bk.* v. *Snively*, 23 Md. 253);
and many like cases. See *Brick* v. *Brick*, 98 U. S. 514; *Buchanon* v.
Adams, 49 N. J. L. 636; *Shoenberger* v. *Hackman*, 37 Pa. 87.]

The fact that a person holds a public office need not be proved by the production of his written or sealed appointment thereto, if he is shown to have acted on it.[1]

Illustrations.

(a) A policy of insurance is effected on goods "in ships from Surinam to London." The goods are shipped in a particular ship, which is lost.

The fact that that particular ship was orally excepted from the policy cannot be proved.[2]

(b) An estate called Gotton Farm is conveyed by a deed which describes it as consisting of the particulars described in the first division of a schedule and delineated in a plan on the margin of the schedule.

Evidence cannot be given to show that a close not mentioned in the schedule or delineated in the plan was always treated as part of Gotton Farm, and was intended to be conveyed by the deed.[3]

(c) A institutes a suit against B for the specific performance of a contract, and also prays that the contract may be reformed as to one of its provisions, as that provision was inserted in it by mistake.

A may prove that such a mistake was made as would entitle him to have the contract reformed.[4]

(d) A lets land to B, and they agree that a lease shall be given by A to B.

Before the lease is given, B tells A that he will not sign it unless A promises to destroy the rabbits. A does promise. The lease is afterwards granted, and reserves sporting rights to A, but does not mention

[1] See authorities collected in 1 Ph. Ev. 449-50; T. E. s. 139. [Gr. Ev. i. §§ 83, 92; *Comm.* v. *Kane,* 108 Mass. 423; *Colton* v. *Beardsley,* 38 Barb. 29; *State* v. *Row,* 81 Ia. 138; *Ritchie* v. *Widdemer,* 59 N. J. L. 290; *Lucier* v. *Pierce,* 60 N. H. 13; *Golder* v. *Bressler,* 105 Ill. 419, 428; cf. *Short* v. *Symmes,* 150 Mass. 298.]

[2] *Weston* v. *Eames,* 1 Tau. 115.

[3] *Barton* v. *Dawes,* 10 C. B. 261-265.

[4] Story's Equity Jurisprudence, chap. v. ss. 153-162. [Gr. Ev. i. § 296 a; *Thompson* v. *Phenix Ins. Co.,* 136 U. S. 287; *Goode* v. *Riley,* 153 Mass. 585; *Park Bros.* v. *Blodgett Co.,* 64 Ct. 28; *Christopher St. R. Co.* v. *23d St. R. Co.,* 149 N. Y. 58; *N. & W. Branch R. Co.* v. *Swank,* 105 Pa. 555; but equity will not reform a *will. Sherwood* v. *Sherwood,* 45 Wis. 357; *Sturgis* v. *Work,* 122 Ind. 134.]

the destruction of the rabbits. B may prove A's verbal agreement as to the rabbits.[1]

(*e*) A & B agree verbally that B shall take up an acceptance of A's, and that thereupon A and B shall make a written agreement for the sale of certain furniture by A to B. B does not take up the acceptance A may prove the verbal agreement that he should do so.[2]

(*ee*) [A makes an oral assignment to B for a valid consideration of a portion of a debt due to A by a bank, and at the same time gives to B a check to enable him to draw the amount assigned. The check is not the contract between the parties and does not render parol evidence of the agreement inadmissible:][3]

(*f*) A & B enter into a written agreement for the sale of an interest in a patent, and at the same time agree verbally that the agreement shall not come into force unless C approves of it. C does not approve. The party interested may show this.[4]

(*g*) A, a farmer, agrees in writing to transfer to B, another farmer, a farm which A holds of C. It is verbally agreed that the agreement is to be conditional on C's consent. B sues A for not transferring the farm. A may prove the condition as to C's consent and the fact that he does not consent.[5]

(*h*) A agrees in writing to sell B 14 lots of freehold land and make a good title to each of them. Afterwards B consents to take one lot though the title is bad. Apart from the Statute of Frauds this agreement might be proved.[6]

---

[1] *Morgan* v. *Griffiths*, L. R. 6 Ex. 70 ; and see *Angell* v. *Duke*, L. R. 10 Q. B. 174. [Cf. *Willis* v. *Hulbert*, 117 Mass. 151 ; *Lewis* v. *Seabury*, 74 N. Y. 409 ; *Dodge* v. *Zimmer*, 110 N. Y. 49 ; *Bradstreet* v. *Rich*, 72 Me. 233. *Morgan* v. *Griffiths* is disapproved in *Naumberg* v. *Young*, 44 N. J. L. 331.]

[2] *Lindley* v. *Lacey*, 17 C. B. (N. S.) 578 ; [see *Engelhorn* v. *Reitlinger*, 122 N. Y. 80.]

[3] [*Risley* v. *Phenix Bank*, 83 N. Y. 318 ; cf. *Ludeke* v. *Sutherland*, 87 Ill. 481.]

[4] *Pym* v. *Campbell*, 6 E. & B. 370. [See *Ware* v. *Allen*, 128 U. S. 590 ; *Faunce* v. *Life Ins. Co.*, 101 Mass. 279 ; *Seymour* v. *Cowing*, 4 Abb. Dec. 200 ; *Whitford* v. *Laidler*, 94 N. Y. 145 ; *Miller* v. *Gambie*, 4 Barb. 146.]

[5] *Wallis* v. *Littell*, 11 C. B. (N. S.) 369 ; [see *Schmittler* v. *Simon*, 114 N. Y. 184.]

[6] *Goss* v. *Lord Nugent*, 5 B. & Ad. 58, 65 ; [see *Wiggin* v. *Goodrich*, 63 Me. 389.]

(*ha*) [A written contract is made between A and B whereby the former is engaged as manager of the latter's theatre "at a weekly salary of $40 per week." A claims payment at this rate for every week in the year. Evidence of a custom in the theatrical profession to pay wages only for the weeks in the theatrical season, and not for all the weeks of the year, is admissible.] [1]

(*i*) A sells B a horse, and orally warrants him quiet in harness. A also gives B a paper in these words: "Bought of A a horse for 7*l.* 2*s.* 6*d.*"

B may prove the oral warranty.[2]

(*j*) The question is, whether A gained a settlement by occupying and paying rent for a tenement. The facts of occupation and payment of rent may be proved by oral evidence, although the contract is in writing.[3]

ARTICLE 91.[*]

WHAT EVIDENCE MAY BE GIVEN FOR THE INTERPRETATION OF DOCUMENTS.

(1) Putting a construction upon a document means ascertaining the meaning of the signs or words made upon it, and their relation to facts.[4]

---

* See Note XXXIII. [Appendix].

[1] [*Leavitt* v. *Kennicott*, 157 Ill. 235; *Grant* v. *Maddox*, 15 M. & W. 737.]

[2] *Allen* v. *Pink*, 4 M. & W. 140.   [*Filkins* v. *Whyland*, 24 N. Y. 338; *Dunham* v. *Barnes*, 9 Allen, 352.]

[3] *R.* v. *Hull*, 7 B. & C. 611.

[4] [Usually it is for the court and not for the jury to construe a document; but where its language is ambiguous or equivocal or technical, or the special circumstances of the case affect its meaning, or the facts attending its execution need to be ascertained, etc., the question becomes a mixed one of law and fact, and may as such be submitted to the jury (*Kenyon* v. *Knights Templar Ass'n*, 122 N. Y. 247; *Jordan* v. *Patterson*, 67 Ct. 473; *Shafer* v. *Senseman*, 125 Pa. 310; *Tompkins* v. *Gardner Co.*, 69 Mich. 59; *Hamilton* v. *Liverpool Ins. Co.*, 136 U. S. 242); so where a contract rests partly in writing and partly in parol, the jury determine what the contract is (*Roberts* v. *Bonaparte*, 73 Md. 191). If printed and written parts of a document conflict with each

(2) In order to ascertain the meaning of the signs and words made upon a document, oral evidence may be given of the meaning of illegible or not commonly intelligible characters, of foreign, obsolete, technical, local, and provincial expressions, of abbreviations, and of common words which, from the context, appear to have been used in a peculiar sense;[1] but evidence may not be given to show that common words, the meaning of which is plain, and which do not appear from the context to have been used in a peculiar sense, were in fact so used.[2]

(3) If the words of a document are so defective or ambiguous as to be unmeaning, no evidence can be given to show what the author of the document intended to say.[3]

other, the written parts prevail (*Clark* v. *Woodruff*, 83 N. Y. 518; *Haws* v. *Insurance Co.*, 130 Pa. 113; *Summers* v. *Hibbard*, 153 Ill. 102). When a written contract is ambiguous, the practical construction given to it by the parties may be considered, and is of much weight. *Dist. of Columbia* v. *Gallaher*, 124 U. S. 505; *Hosmer* v. *McDonald*, 80 Wis. 54.]

[1] Illustrations (*a*), (*b*), (*c*). [Gr. Ev. i. §§ 280, 292; *Houghton* v. *Watertown Ins. Co.*, 131 Mass. 300; *Hatch* v. *Douglas*, 48 Ct. 116; *Atkinson* v. *Truesdell*, 127 N. Y. 230; *Conestoga Co.* v. *Finke*, 144 Pa. 159; *McDonough* v. *Jolly*, 165 Pa. 542; *Elgin* v. *Joslyn*, 136 Ill. 525; *Converse* v. *Wead*, 142 Ill. 132; *Walrath* v. *Whittekind*, 26 Kan. 482. So where an instrument appears to be incomplete, or where words and phrases used are ambiguous or unintelligible, parol proof is admissible to supplement the incomplete term, and to explain what is obscure or doubtful. *Emmett* v. *Penoyer*, 151 N. Y. 564; *Quick* v. *Glass*, 128 Mo. 320.]

[2] Illustration (*d*). [*Collender* v. *Dinsmore*, 55 N. Y. 200; *Gray* v. *Shepard*, 147 N. Y. 177; *Moran* v. *Prather*, 23 Wall. 492; *Odiorne* v. *Marine Ins. Co.*, 101 Mass. 551. Such words are to be understood in their plain and ordinary sense. Id.; *Holston Co.* v. *Campbell*, 89 Va. 396; *Hunt* v. *Gray*, 76 Ia. 268.]

[3] Illustrations (*e*) and (*f*). [*Kelley* v. *Kelley*, 25 Pa. 460; *Palmer* v. *Albee*, 50 Ia. 429; cf. *Wootton* v. *Redd's Excrs.*, 12 Gratt. 196. This is often called a case of "patent ambiguity," but the better term for it is "uncertainty." The same terms are also applied when the meaning of a document remains uncertain, even after evidence of "sur-

(4) In order to ascertain the relation of the words of a document to facts, every fact may be proved to which it refers, or may probably have been intended to refer,[1] or which identifies any person or thing mentioned in it.[2] Such facts are hereinafter called the "circumstances of the case."[3]

(5) If the words of a document have a proper legal meaning, and also a less proper meaning, they must be deemed to have their proper legal meaning, unless such a construction would be unmeaning in reference to the

rounding circumstances " and other permissible explanatory evidence (see paragraphs 2 and 4 in this Article) have been received (Gr. Ev. i. § 300 ; *Kretschmer* v. *Hard*, 18 Col. 223).   But a patent ambiguity may not be resolved by parol evidence of other kinds, as *e. g.*, by evidence of a testator's parol statements of intention as to the meaning of his will.   *Lewis* v. *Douglas*, 14 R. I. 604 ; *Senger* v. *Senger*, 81 Va. 687 ; *Taylor* v. *Maris*, 90 N. C. 614.]

[1] See all the Illustrations.

[2] Illustration (*g*).   [Gr. Ev. i. §§ 286–290 ; *Coleman* v. *Manhattan Co.*, 94 N. Y. 229 ; *Reed* v. *Ins. Co.*, 95 U. S. 23 ; *Bond's Appeal*, 31 Ct. 183 ; *Stoops* v. *Smith*, 100 Mass. 63 ; *Gilmor's Estate*, 154 Pa. 523 ; *Perry* v. *Bowman*, 151 Ill. 25 ; *Andrews* v. *Dyer*, 81 Me. 104.   This evidence of the " circumstances of the case " or (as they are more commonly called) "surrounding circumstances" is received, to put the court in the position of the parties at the time when the instrument was drawn and thus enable it to comprehend their intentions (Id.; *Bingel* v. *Volz*, 142 Ill. 214 ; *Barnard* v. *Barlow*, 50 N. J. Eq. 131). But such evidence is not received to alter or modify the plain language of an instrument, nor when the meaning of the instrument is clear without it (*Brawley* v. *U. S.*, 96 U. S. 168 ; *Veazie* v. *Forsaith*, 76 Me. 172 ; *Humphreys* v. *N. Y. etc. R. Co.*, 121 N. Y. 435 ; *Fruin* v. *Crystal R. Co.*, 89 Mo. 397 ; *Fowler* v. *Black*, 136 Ill. 363).

Under this rule, proof may be given that the maker of the instrument habitually applied a nickname or peculiar designation used therein to a particular person or thing.   *Boggs* v. *Taylor*, 26 O. St. 604 ; *Ryerss* v. *Wheeler*, 22 Wend. 148 ; *Lanning* v. *Sisters of St. Francis*, 35 N. J. Eq. 392, note ; see Illustrations (*e*) and (*gg*).]

[3] As to proving facts showing the knowledge of the writer, and for an instance of a document which is not admissible for that purpose, see *Adie* v. *Clark*, 3 Ch. D. 134, 142.

circumstances of the case, in which case they may be interpreted according to their less proper meaning.[1]

(6) If the document has one distinct meaning in reference to the circumstances of the case, it must be construed accordingly, and evidence to show that the author intended to express some other meaning is not admissible.[2]

(7) If the document applies in part but not with accuracy or not completely to the circumstances of the case, the court may draw inferences from those circumstances as to the meaning of the document, whether there is more than one, or only one thing or person to whom or to which the inaccurate description may apply. In such cases no evidence can be given of statements made by the author of the document as to his intentions in reference to the matter to which the document relates, though evidence may be given as to his circumstances, and to his habitual use of language or names for particular persons or things.[3]

---

[1] Illustration (*h*). [*Cromer* v. *Pinckney*, 3 Barb Ch. 466 ; *Daugherty* v. *Rogers*, 119 Ind. 254 ; *In re Fish*, [1894] 2 Ch. 83 ; cf. *DeKay* v. *Irving*, 5 Den. 646.]

[2] Illustration (*i*). [*American Bible Soc.* v. *Pratt*, 9 Allen, 109 ; *Best* v. *Hammond*, 55 Pa. 409 ; *Drew* v. *Swift*, 46 N. Y. 204 ; *Jackson* v. *Sill*, 11 Johns. 201 ; *Cotton* v. *Smithwick*, 66 Me. 360 ; *Jackson* v. *Alsop*, 67 Ct. 249 ; *Dunham* v. *Averill*, 45 Ct. 61 ; *Fitzpatrick* v. *Fitzpatrick*, 36 Ia. 674 ; *Kurtz* v. *Hibner*, 55 Ill. 514 ; *In re Seal*, [1894] 1 Ch. 316. The meaning of plain language in a will must be followed, though it make the will void. *Van Nostrand* v. *Moore*, 52 N. Y. 12.]

[3] Illustrations (*k*), (*l*), (*m*). [*Morse* v. *Stearns*, 131 Mass. 389 ; *Hinckley* v. *Thatcher*, 139 Mass. 477 ; *Fairfield* v. *Lawson*, 50 Ct. 501 ; *St. Luke's Home* v. *Ass'n for Females*, 52 N. Y. 191 ; *Griscom* v. *Evens*, 40 N. J. L. 402, 42 id. 579 ; *Button* v. *Amer. Tract Soc.*, 23 Vt. 336 ; *Appeal of Washington and Lee Univ.*, 111 Pa. 572 ; *Halliday* v. *Hess*, 83 Ill. 588. This rule illustrates the well-known maxim, *Falsa demonstratio non nocet, cum de corpore constat*, i. e., a false description works no harm, when the matter of substance remains. The false part of the description is rejected, and if sufficient remains to identify

(8) If the language of the document, though plain in itself, applies equally well to more objects than one, evidence may be given both of the circumstances of the case and of statements made by any party to the document as to his intentions in reference to the matter to which the document relates.[1]

(9) If the document is of such a nature that the court will presume that it was executed with any other than its apparent intention, evidence may be given to show that it was in fact executed with its apparent intention.[2]

---

a particular person or thing, effect can be given to the instrument; otherwise it is void for uncertainty (Id.; Gr. Ev. i. §§ 291, 301 ; see Illustration (*ii*); *Muldoon* v. *Deline*, 135 N. Y. 150; *Decker* v. *Decker*, 121 Ill. 341 ; *Eckford* v. *Eckford*, 91 Ia. 54). Evidence of "surrounding circumstances" may serve to correct a mistake in description (*Patch* v. *White*, 117 U. S. 210 ; *Hawkins* v. *Garland*, 76 Va. 149). The expression "latent ambiguity" is sometimes applied to cases falling under this paragraph, since the ambiguity is developed by evidence extrinsic to the instrument. Id.; *Thornell* v. *Brockton*, 141 Mass. 151 ; *Whitcomb* v. *Rodman*, 156 Ill. 116 ; *Covert* v. *Sebern*, 73 Ia. 564.]

[1] Illustrations (*n*), (*o*). [Gr. Ev. i. §§ 289, 290, 297, 298 ; *St. Luke's Home* v. *Ass'n for Females*, 52 N. Y. 191, 198; *Trustees* v. *Colegrove*, 4 Hun, 362; *Griscom* v. *Evens*, supra ; *Bodman* v. *Amer. Tract Soc.*, 9 Allen, 447; *Fairfield* v. *Lawson*, 50 Ct. 501 ; *Goff* v. *Roberts*, 72 Mo. 570; *Pfeifer* v. *Nat. Ins. Co.*, 62 Minn. 536 ; *Morgan* v. *Burrows*, 45 Wis. 211. These are also (and more commonly than the cases referred to in the preceding note) called cases of "latent ambiguity," but the more appropriate name is "equivocation" (Gr. Ev. i. § 289; *Tucker* v. *Seamen's Aid Society*, 7 Met. 188, 206; *Bradley* v. *Rees*, 113 Ill. 327). This form of latent ambiguity may be explained by evidence of *parol statements of intention*, as well as by proof of "*surrounding circumstances;*" still the "surrounding circumstances" are often found to suffice as a means of determining the meaning of the document. *Gilmer* v. *Stone*, 120 U. S. 586; *Skinner* v. *Harrison T'p*, 116 Ind. 139; *Putnam* v. *Bond*, 100 Mass. 58; *Ayers* v. *Weed*, 16 Ct. 291 ; *Tilton* v. *Amer. Bible Soc.*, 60 N. H. 377 ; *Tyler* v. *Fickett*, 73 Me. 410; *Sargent* v. *Adams*, 3 Gray, 72.]

[2] Illustration (*p*). [This is called evidence "to rebut an equity" (*i.e.*, an equitable presumption), and *oral statements of intention* are

Illustrations.

(*a*) A lease contains a covenant as to "ten thousand" rabbits. Oral evidence to show that a thousand meant, in relation to rabbits, 1200, is admissible.[1]

(*b*) A sells to B "1170 bales of gambier." Oral evidence is admissible to show that a "bale" of gambier is a package compressed and weighing 2 cwt.[2]

(*c*) A, a sculptor, leaves to B "all the marble in the yard, the tools in the shop, bankers, mod tools for carving." Evidence to show whether "mod" meant models, moulds, or modeling-tools, and to show what bankers are, may be given.[3]

(*d*) Evidence may not be given to show that the word "boats," in a policy of insurance, means "boats not slung on the outside of the ship on the quarter."[4]

(*e*) A leaves an estate to K, L, M, etc., by a will dated before 1838. Eight years afterwards A declares that by these letters he meant particular persons. Evidence of this declaration is not admissible. Proof that A was in the habit of calling a particular person M would have been admissible.[5]

(*f*) A leaves a legacy to ——. Evidence to show how the blank was intended to be filled is not admissible.[6]

---

provable for the purpose. Gr. Ev. i. § 296 ; *Van Houten* v. *Post*, 33 N. J. Eq. 344 ; *Reynolds* v. *Robinson*, 82 N. Y. 103, 107 ; *Richardson* v. *Eveland*, 126 Ill. 37 ; *Bank* v. *Fordyce*, 9 Pa. 275 ; cf. *Phillips* v. *McCombs*, 53 N. Y. 494.]

[1] *Smith* v. *Wilson*, 3 B. & Ad. 728. [See *Soutier* v. *Kellerman*, 18 Mo. 509 ; *Brown* v. *Brown*, 8 Met. 576. But except in special cases like these where words have a peculiar meaning by local custom, usages of business, etc., the meaning of ordinary words cannot be varied. *Butler* v. *Gale*, 27 Vt. 739 ; *Mann* v. *Mann*, 14 Johns. 1.]

[2] *Gorrissen* v. *Perrin*, 2 C. B. (N. S.) 681. [See *Miller* v. *Stevens*, 100 Mass. 518 (meaning of "barrels"); *Confederate Note Case*, 19 Wall. 548 (of "dollars"); *Carey* v. *Bright*, 58 Pa. 70 (of "collieries"); *People* v. *Borda*, 105 Cal. 636 (of "corral"); *Dana* v. *Fiedler*, 12 N. Y. 40 ; *McDonough* v. *Jolly*, 165 Pa. 542.]

[3] *Goblet* v. *Beechy*, 3 Sim. 24 ; 2 R. & M. 624. [See *Ryerss* v. *Wheeler*, 22 Wend. 148, 153.]

[4] *Blackett* v. *Royal Exchange Co* , 2 C. & J. 244.

[5] *Clayton* v. *Lord Nugent*, 13 M. & W. 200 ; see 205-6. [See *Beatty* v. *Trustees*, 39 N. J. Eq. 452.]

[6] *Baylis* v. *A. G.*, 2 Atk. 239. [See *Crooks* v. *Whitford*, 47 Mich. 283;

(g) Property was conveyed in trust in 1704 for the support of "Godly preachers of Christ's holy Gospel." Evidence may be given to show what class of ministers were at the time known by that name.[1]

(gg) [A leaves a legacy in his will to "The Home of the Friendless in New York." There is no institution of that name, but the legacy is claimed by the "American Female Guardian Society." Evidence may be given that this society has been commonly designated by the name used in the will, both by its officers and friends and by the testator, and that upon its circulars and business signs a name almost identical has been used.][2]

(h) A leaves property to his "children." If he has both legitimate and illegitimate children, the whole of the property will go to the legitimate children. If he has only illegitimate children, the property may go to them, if he cannot have intended to give it to unborn legitimate children.[3]

(i) A testator leaves all his estates in the county of Limerick and city of Limerick to A. He had no estates in the county of Limerick, but he had estates in the county of Clare, of which the will did not dispose. Evidence cannot be given to show that the words "of Clare" had been erased from the draft by mistake, and so omitted from the will as executed.[4]

(ii) [A testator devises to X "all that my farm called Trogues-farm,

---

Wallize v. *Wallize*, 55 Pa. 242; *Lefevre* v. *Lefevre*, 59 N. Y. 434, 441; *Vandervoort* v. *Dewey*, 42 Hun, 68; cf. *Crocker* v. *Crocker*, 5 Hun, 587.] In *In re Bacon's Will, Camp* v. *Coe*, 31 Ch. D. 460, blanks were left in a will, and parol evidence was admitted to rebut any presumption arising from them against the *prima facie* claim of the executor to the residue undisposed of.

[1] *Shore* v. *Wilson*, 9 C. & F. 365, 565–6. [See *Robertson* v. *Bullions*, 11 N. Y. 243, 259; *Hinckley* v. *Thatcher*, 139 Mass. 477, 480; *Goddard* v. *Foster*, 17 Wall. 143.]

[2] [*Lefevre* v. *Lefevre*, 59 N. Y. 434; see *Sutton* v. *Bowker*, 5 Gray, 416; *Wood* v. *Hammond*, 16 R. I. 98; *Missionary Soc.* v. *Mead*, 131 Ill. 338.]

[3] Wig. Ext. Ev. pp. 18 and 19, and note of cases. [*Appel* v. *Byers*, 98 Pa. 479; *Brower* v. *Bowers*, 1 Abb. Dec. 214; *Hill* v. *Crook*, L. R. 6 H. L. 265; see *Gelston* v. *Shields*, 16 Hun, 143, 78 N. Y. 275. So the word "children" does not include grandchildren, except when there are no children, in the usual sense of the word. *Mowatt* v. *Carow*, 7 Pai. 328; *West* v. *Rassman*, 135 Ind. 278.]

[4] *Miller* v. *Travers*, 8 Bing. 244. [See *Tucker* v. *Seamen's Aid Soc.*,

now in the occupation of C." Evidence of "surrounding circumstances" being received showed that the testator owned a farm called by this name, but that only part of it was in the occupation of C. The last part of the description being inaccurate was therefore rejected, and it was held that the *whole* of Trogues-farm passed to the devisee, thus satisfying the word "all" in the first part of the description.][1]

(*j*) A leaves a legacy to "Mrs. and Miss Bowden." No such persons were living at the time when the legacy was made, but Mrs. Washburne, whose maiden name had been Bowden, was living, and had a daughter, and the testatrix used to call them Bowden. Evidence of these facts was admitted.[2]

(*k*) A devises land to John Hiscocks, the eldest son of John Hiscocks. John Hiscocks had two sons, Simon, his eldest, and John, his second son, who, however, was the eldest son by a second marriage. The circumstances of the family, but not the testator's declarations of intention, may be proved in order to show which of the two was intended.[3]

(*l*) A devises property to Elizabeth, the natural daughter of B. B has a natural son John, and a legitimate daughter Elizabeth. The court may infer from the circumstances under which the natural child was born, and from the testator's relationship to the putative father, that he meant to provide for John.[4]

(*m*) A leaves a legacy to his niece, Elizabeth Stringer. At the date of the will he had no such niece, but he had a great-great-niece named Elizabeth Jane Stringer. The court may infer from these circumstances that Elizabeth Jane Stringer was intended; but they may not refer to instructions given by the testator to his solicitor, showing that the legacy was meant for a niece, Elizabeth Stringer, who had died

---

7 Met. 188 ; *Dunham* v. *Averill*, 45 Ct. 61; *Sturgis* v. *Work*, 122 Ind. 134.]

[1] [*Goodtitle* v. *Southern*, 1 M. & S. 299 ; approved in *Slingsby* v. *Grainger*, 8 H. L. C. 273, 282. S. P. *Winkley* v. *Kaime*, 32 N. H. 268 ; *Fitzpatrick* v. *Fitzpatrick*, 36 Ia. 674.]

[2] *Lee* v. *Pain*, 4 Hare, 251-3 ; [Gr. Ev. i. § 291.]

[3] *Doe* v. *Hiscocks*, 5 M. & W. 363. [*In re Taylor*, 34 Ch. D. 255 ; *In re Chappell*, [1894] P. 98 ; see *Smith* v. *Smith*, 1 Edw. Ch. 189, 4 Pai. 271; *Connolly* v. *Pardon*, 1 Pai. 291; *Thayer* v. *Boston*, 15 Gray, 347.]

[4] *Ryall* v. *Hannam*, 10 Beav. 536.

before the date of the will, and that it was put into the will by a mistake on the part of the solicitor.[1]

(*n*) A devises one house to George Gord, the son of George Gord, another to George Gord, the son of John Gord, and the third to George Gord, the son of Gord. Evidence both of the circumstances and of the testator's statements of intention may be given to show which of the two George Gords he meant.[2]

(*o*) A appointed " Percival —, of Brighton, Esquire, the father," one of his executors. Evidence of surrounding circumstances may be given to show who was meant, and (probably) evidence of statements of intention.[3]

(*p*) A leaves two legacies of the same amount to B, assigning the same motive for each legacy, one being given in his will, the other in a codicil. The court presumes that they are not meant to be cumulative, but the legatee may show, either by proof of surrounding circumstances, or of declarations by the testator, that they were.[4]

ARTICLE 92.*

CASES TO WHICH ARTICLES 90 AND 91 DO NOT APPLY.

Articles 90 and 91 apply only to parties to documents, and their representatives in interest, and only to cases in which some civil right or civil liability dependent upon

---

* See Note XXXIV. [Appendix].

[1] *Stringer* v. *Gardiner,* 27 Beav. 35 ; 4 De G. & J. 468 ; [cf. *Gallup* v. *Wright,* 61 How. Pr. 286.]

[2] *Doe* v. *Needs,* 2 M. & W. 129. [There were only *two* George Gords to claim the third devise, viz., those who were named as the recipients of the first and second devises. Hence this became a case of " equivocation," admitting evidence of statements of intention.]

[3] *In the Goods of de Rosaz,* L. R. 2 P. D. 66. [Mr. Stephen's statement, that " probably evidence of statements of intention " might have been given in this case, hardly seems warranted by the decision. No such evidence was received, and, on principle, it does not seem competent. There was only one person to whom the description accurately applied.]

[4] Per Leach, V. C., in *Hurst* v. *Leach,* 5 Madd. 351, 360-1. The rule in this case was vindicated, and a number of other cases both before and after it were elaborately considered by Lord St. Leonards,

the terms of a document is in question. Any person other than a party to a document or his representative in interest may, notwithstanding the existence of any document, prove any fact which he is otherwise entitled to prove;[1] and any party to any document or any representative in interest of any such party may prove any such fact for any purpose other than that of varying or altering any right or liability depending upon the terms of the document.[2]

Illustrations.

a) The question is, whether A, a pauper, is settled in the parish of Cheadle. A deed of conveyance to which A was a party is produced, purporting to convey land to A for a valuable consideration. The parish appealing against the order was allowed to call A as a witness to prove that no consideration passed.[3]

(*b*) The question is, whether A obtained money from B under false pretences. The money was obtained as a premium for executing a deed of partnership, which deed stated a consideration other than the one which constituted the false pretence. B may give evidence of the false pretence, although he executed the deed mis-stating the consideration for the premium.[4]

---

when Chancellor of Ireland, in *Hall* v. *Hall*, 1 Dru. & War. 94, 111-133. See, too, *Jenner* v. *Hinch*, L. R. 5 P. D. 106. [See p. 231, note 2, *ante*, and cases cited.]

[1] [Gr. Ev. i. § 279; *Wilson* v. *Sullivan*, 58 N. H. 260; *Burnham* v. *Dorr*, 72 Me. 198; *Fonda* v. *Burton*, 63 Vt. 355; *Hankinson* v. *Vantine*, 152 N. Y. 20; *First Nat. Bk.* v. *Dunn*, 55 N. J. L. 404; *Bruce* v. *Roper Co.*, 87 Va. 381; *Needles* v. *Hanifan*, 11 Ill. App. 303; *Pfeifer* v. *Nat. Ins. Co.*, 62 Minn. 536, 538; *Burns* v. *Thompson*, 91 Ind. 146. In a suit between a party to an instrument and a stranger to it, either of them may prove facts by parol evidence differing from the contents of the instrument; so also may strangers to the instrument, in a suit between themselves (*Lowell Mfg. Co.* v. *Safeguard Ins. Co.*, 88 N. Y. 591; *Clapp* v. *Banking Co.*, 50 O. St. 528; *Dunn* v. *Price*, 112 Cal. 46). And even in a controversy between the parties, the rule prohibiting parol evidence may be waived. *Brady* v. *Nally*, 151 N. Y. 258.]

[2] [See Illustration (*b*).]

[3] *R.* v. *Cheadle*, 3 B. & Ad. 833.

[4] *R.* v. *Adamson*, 2 Moody, 286.

PART III.

PRODUCTION AND EFFECT OF EVIDENCE.

CHAPTER XIII.*

BURDEN OF PROOF.

ARTICLE 93.†

HE WHO AFFIRMS MUST PROVE.

WHOEVER desires any court to give judgment as to any legal right or liability dependent on the existence or non-existence of facts which he asserts or denies to exist, must prove that those facts do or do not exist.[1]

ARTICLE 94.†

PRESUMPTION OF INNOCENCE.

If the commission of a crime is directly in issue in any proceeding, criminal or civil, it must be proved beyond reasonable doubt.[2]

---

*See Note XXXV. [Appendix].   † See Note XXXVI. [Appendix].

[1] 1 Ph. Ev. 552; T. E. (from Greenleaf) s. 337; Best, ss. 265–6; Starkie, 585–6. [Gr. Ev. i. § 74; Wh. Ev. i. §§ 353–357; *Sawyer* v. *Child*, 68 Vt. 365; *Willett* v. *Rich*, 142 Mass. 356.]

[2] [In respect to *trials for crime* this rule is well settled (*Miles* v. *U. S.*, 103 U. S. 304; *People* v. *Downs*, 123 N. Y. 558; *Gardner* v. *State*, 55 N. J. L. 17; *Nevling* v. *Comm.*, 98 Pa. 322). "Beyond reasonable doubt" is sometimes defined to mean the same as "to a moral certainty"

The burden of proving that any person has been guilty

(*Comm.* v. *Costley*, 118 Mass. 1; *Morgan* v. *State*, 48 O. St. 371; *People* v. *Paulsell*, 115 Cal. 6; *Carr* v. *State*, 23 Neb. 749); sometimes as requiring evidence so convincing that reasonable men would unhesitatingly be governed by it in their most important and serious interests (*Hopt* v. *Utah*, 120 U. S. 430; *Siberry* v. *State*, 133 Ind. 677; *Fletcher* v. *State*, 90 Ga. 468); and other definitions are given, not always harmonious (*People* v. *Barker*, 153 N. Y. 111; *Comm.* v. *Mudgett*, 174 Pa. 211; *Little* v. *People*, 157 Ill. 153; *People* v. *Ezzo*, 104 Mich. 341; *State* v. *Rounds*, 76 Me. 123; *Comm.* v. *Leach*, 160 Mass. 542). Every constituent element of the crime must be proved beyond reasonable doubt, but this is not required as to each evidentiary fact (*Wade* v. *State*, 71 Ind. 535; *Jamison* v. *People*, 145 Ill. 357; *People* v. *Fairchild*, 48 Mich. 31; *Kallock* v. *State*, 88 Wis. 663; *Porterfield* v. *Comm.*, 91 Va. 801; *Clare* v. *People*, 9 Col. 122; cf. *State* v. *Magoon*, 68 Vt. 289). The court should, if requested, charge the jury that the law presumes a person accused of crime to be innocent, as well as instruct them that guilt must be proved beyond reasonable doubt (*Coffin* v. *U. S.*, 156 U. S. 432; *Newsom* v. *State*, 107 Ala. 133; cf. *State* v. *Smith*, 65 Ct. 283).

In *civil cases*, on the contrary, it is the rule that only a preponderance of evidence is required to sustain a verdict (*Seybolt* v. *N. Y. etc. R. Co.*, 95 N. Y. 562; *Taylor* v. *Felsing*, 164 Ill. 331; *Hall* v. *Wolff*, 61 Ia. 559; *Strand* v. *Chicago, etc. R. Co.*, 67 Mich. 380), and this rule applies both to a plaintiff in proving his cause of action (*Farmers' L. & T. Co.* v. *Siefke*, 144 N. Y. 355) and to a defendant in establishing his defence (*Ætna Life Ins. Co.* v. *Ward*, 140 U. S. 76; *Phenix Ins. Co.* v. *Pickel*, 119 Ind. 155). If the evidence on the two sides is in equipoise, the verdict should be against the party having the general burden of proof upon the issue (*Broult* v. *Hanson*, 158 Mass. 17; *Whitlatch* v. *Fidelity, etc. Co.*, 149 N. Y. 45; *Birmingham Union R. Co.* v. *Hall*, 90 Ala. 8; *Rogers* v. *Wallace*, 10 Or. 387; *Gage* v. *Railway Co's*, 88 Tenn. 724). Preponderance of evidence does not consist merely in having a greater number of witnesses, for "witnesses are to be weighed and not counted" (*Fengar* v. *Brown*, 57 Ct. 60; *State* v. *Musick*, 71 Mo. 401; *Grant* v. *McPherson*, 104 Cal. 165; cf. *Kelley* v. *Brown*, 18 R. I. 41); still if opposing witnesses are of equal credit, excess in number may count for much with the court or jury (*Kentner* v. *Kline*, 41 N. J. Eq. 422; *Lillibridge* v. *Barber*, 55 Ct. 366; *Peters* v. *Canfield*, 74 Mich. 498; but see *Thomas* v. *Paul*, 87 Wis. 607; *Braunschweiger* v. *Waits*, 179 Pa. 47).

There is much conflict of opinion in this country as to which of these

of a crime or wrongful act is on the person who asserts it,

rules applies in *civil cases, where the commission of a crime is in issue.* A few States have adopted the general English rule (*Grimes* v. *Hilliary*, 150 Ill. 141; *Williams* v. *Dickenson*, 28 Fla. 90); but in most States only a preponderance of evidence is generally required to prove the crime (*People* v. *Briggs*, 114 N. Y. 56; *Baird* v. *Abbey*, 73 Mich. 347; *Thoreson* v. *Northwestern Ins. Co.*, 29 Minn. 107; *Continental Ins. Co.* v. *Jachnichen*, 110 Ind. 59; *U. S. Express Co.* v. *Jenkins*, 73 Wis. 471; *Coit* v. *Churchill*, 61 Ia. 296; *Smith* v. *Burrus*, 106 Mo. 94). Thus in actions for libel or slander, where the defendant pleads a "justification," viz., that the charge of crime he made against the plaintiff was true, proof beyond a reasonable doubt is required in some States to support this plea (*Fowler* v. *Wallace*, 131 Ind. 347; *Burckhalter* v. *Coward*, 16 S. Car. 435; *Merk* v. *Gelzhaeuser*, 50 Cal. 631); but in most States only a preponderance of evidence is required (*Bell* v. *McGuinness*, 40 O. St. 204; *Ellis* v. *Buzzell*, 60 Me. 209; *Folsom* v. *Brawn*, 25 N. H. 114; *Currier* v. *Richardson*, 63 Vt. 617; *Lewis* v. *Shull*, 67 Hun, 543; *McBee* v. *Fulton*, 47 Md. 403; *Atlanta Journal* v. *Mayson*, 92 Ga. 640; Ill. Rev. St. c. 126, s. 3; *Peoples* v. *Evening News*, 51 Mich. 11; *Kidd* v. *Fleek*, 47 Wis. 443; *Riley* v. *Morton*, 65 Ia. 306; *Edwards* v. *Knapp*, 97 Mo. 432). In insurance cases, similar to Illustration (*a*), the great weight of authority is against the English rule, and requires only a preponderance of evidence (*Blaeser* v. *Milwaukee Ins. Co.*, 37 Wis. 31; *Kane* v. *Hibernia Ins. Co.*, 39 N. J. L. 697; *Rothschild* v. *Amer. Ins. Co.*, 62 Mo. 356; *Behrens* v. *Germania Ins. Co.*, 58 Ia. 26; *Johnson* v. *Agr. Ins. Co.*, 25 Hun, 251, and see 114 N. Y. 56; *Schmidt* v. *N. Y. etc. Ins. Co.*, 1 Gray, 529, see 15 Gray, 413; *Somerset Co. Ins. Co.* v. *Usaw*, 112 Pa. 80; *Hall* v. *Matthews*, 118 Ind. 527; *Monaghan* v. *Agr. Ins. Co.*, 53 Mich. 238); but in a few States the English rule is followed (*Germania Ins. Co.* v. *Klewer*, 129 Ill. 599; *Schultz* v. *Pacific Ins. Co.*, 14 Fla. 73). In many other civil cases involving a charge of crime, the rule of preponderance has been applied (*Roberge* v. *Burnham*, 124 Mass. 277 (action for sale of liquor to minor); *Mead* v. *Husted*, 52 Ct. 53, *Kendig* v. *Overhulser*, 58 Ia. 195 (action for setting property on fire); *Munson* v. *Atwood*, 30 Ct. 102 (action for damages, under statute, for stealing cattle); *Poertner* v. *Poertner*, 66 Wis. 644 (action for divorce on ground of adultery, which is a crime in Wisconsin; S. P. *Lindley* v. *Lindley*, 68 Vt. 421; *Nelson* v. *Pierce*, 18 R. I. 539; cf. *Allen* v. *Allen*, 101 N. Y. 658); so fraud in a civil action requires only preponderance of evidence, even though it also amounts to a crime (*Jones* v. *Greaves*, 26 O. St. 2; *Hough* v. *Dickinson*, 58 Mich. 89; *Turner* v. *Hardin*, 80 Ia. 691; *Bullard* v.

whether the commission of such act is or is not directly in
issue in the action.[1]

Creditors, 56 Cal. 600); so, in most States, as to proof of bastardy in
proceedings against the putative father (*Semon* v. *People*, 42 Mich. 141;
State v. *Severson*, 78 Ia. 653; *Reynolds* v. *State*, 115 Ind. 421; *Johnson*
v. *People*, 140 Ill. 350; contra, *Van Tassel* v. *State*, 59 Wis. 351).

There are some issues in civil actions or proceedings which require
more than a mere preponderance of evidence to maintain them. The
rule, as variously stàted, declares that the evidence must be "clear,
unequivocal and convincing," "clear, precise and indubitable," "full,
clear and satisfactory," "clear and conclusive," etc. Such an amount
or weight of evidence is required to prove a deed to be a mortgage
(*Cadman* v. *Peter*, 118 U. S. 73; *Wilson* v. *Parshall*, 129 N. Y. 223;
Fisher v. *Witham*, 132 Pa. 488; *Cake* v. *Shull*, 45 N. J. Eq. 208; *Blake*
v. *Taylor*, 142 Ill. 482; *Tilden* v. *Streeter*, 45 Mich. 533); to reform a
deed or other written instrument (*Simmons Creek Coal Co.* v. *Doran*,
142 U. S. 417; *Schwass* v. *Hershey*, 125 Ill. 653; *Phœnix Ins. Co.* v.
Ryland, 69 Md. 437; *Turner* v. *Shaw*, 96 Mo. 22; *Boyertown Nat. Bk.*
v. *Hartman*, 147 Pa. 558; *Christopher St. R. Co.* v. *23d St. R. Co.*, 149
N. Y. 51; *Green* v. *Stone*, 54 N. J. Eq. 387; *Pulaski Iron Co.* v. *Palmer*,
89 Va 384); to establish a resulting trust (*Burdett* v. *May*, 100 Mo. 13;
Towle v. *Wadsworth*, 147 Ill. 80; *Murphy* v. *Hanscome*, 76 Ia. 192; cf.
Allen v. *Withrow*, 110 U. S. 119); to set aside a written instrument
for fraud or mistake (*U. S.* v. *Budd*, 144 U. S. 154; *Cummins* v. *Hurl-
butt*, 92 Pa. 165); to establish a gift *causa mortis* (*Devlin* v. *Greenwich Sav. Bk.*, 125 N. Y. 756; *Barnum* v. *Reed*, 136 Ill. 388); to sustain the defence of usury (*Rosenstein* v. *Fox*, 150 N. Y. 354, 364; *Taylor* v. *Morris*, 22 N. J. Eq. 606; *Poppleton* v. *Nelson*, 12 Or. 349); to
impeach the certificate of acknowledgment in a deed (*Ford* v. *Osborne*, 45 O. St. 1; *Griffin* v. *Griffin*, 125 Ill. 430; *Albany Co. Sav. Bk.*
v. *McCarty*, 149 N. Y. 71; *Young* v. *Duvall*, 109 U. S. 573; *Lewars* v.
Weaver, 121 Pa. 268). It is sometimes said that the evidence in these
cases must be convincing "beyond reasonable doubt" (*First Presb.
Church* v. *Logan*, 77 Ia. 326; *Bodwell* v. *Heaton*, 40 Kan. 36; *Stockbridge Iron Co.* v. *Hudson Iron Co.*, 102 Mass. 45; *Hupsch* v. *Resch*,
45 N. J. Eq. 657; *Strauch* v. *Hathaway*, 101 Ill. 11), but this has been
held too extreme (*Southard* v. *Curley*, 134 N. Y. 148). Evidence to
show a statute to be unconstitutional should be beyond reasonable
doubt. *People* v. *Supervisors*, 147 N. Y. 1.]

[1] [Gr. Ev. i. §§ 35, 78–80; *Whitney Arms Co.* v. *Barlow*, 68 N. Y. 34;
Slocovich v. *Orient Ins. Co.*, 108 N. Y. 56; *Davis* v. *Davis*, 123 Mass.
590. This rule will, in general, make it necessary to prove a *negative*

Illustrations.

(*a*) A sues B on a policy of fire insurance. B pleads that A burned down the house insured. B must prove his plea as fully as if A were being prosecuted for arson.[1]

(*b*) A sues B for damage done to A's ship by inflammable matter loaded thereon by B without notice to A's captain. A must prove the absence of notice.[2]

(*c*) The question in 1819 is, whether A is settled in the parish of a man to whom she was married in 1813. It is proved that in 1812 she was married to another person, who enlisted soon afterwards, went abroad on service, and had not been heard of afterwards. The burden of proving that the first husband was alive at the time of the second marriage is on the person who asserts it.[3]

---

proposition, if that is a constituent element of the crime or wrongful act. *Colorado Coal Co.* v. *U. S.*, 123 U.'S. 307 ; see Illustration (*b*).]

[1] *Thurtell* v. *Beaumont*, 1 Bing. 339; [generally denied in this country; see note on p. 239, *supra*, and 10 Am. Law Rev. 642, 17 Am. Law Reg. N. S. 302 ; *Welch* v. *Jugenheimer*, 56 Ia. 11.]

[2] *Williams* v. *East India Co.*, 3 Ea. 102, 108-9. [*Harris* v. *White*, 81 N. Y. 532, 547 ; cf. *Boston, etc. R. Co.* v. *Shanly*, 107 Mass. 568.]

[3] *R.* v. *Twyning*, 2 B. & A. 386. [The ground of this decision was that the law presumes against the commission of crime. The woman was, therefore, presumed innocent of bigamy, though the second marriage was only a year after the first and though it would ordinarily be presumed that the first husband was still living (see Art. 99; also Art. 95, Illustration *i*). The presumption of life yielded to the presumption of innocence and the person asserting her guilt of bigamy had, consequently, the burden of *proving* that the first husband was alive. So in this country it is held that the law, in cases like this, in a general way prefers the presumption of innocence to that of the continuance of life (Bishop, M. D. & S. i. § 953; Gr. Ev. i. § 35 ; *Nesbit* v. *Nesbit*, 3 Dem. 329; *Johnson* v. *Johnson*, 114 Ill. 611; *Wilkie* v. *Collins*, 48 Miss. 511; *Hunter* v. *Hunter*, 111 Cal. 261; *Squire* v. *State*, 46 Ind. 459, see 86 Ind. 75; *Murray* v. *Murray*, 6 Or. 17; *Dixon* v. *People*, 18 Mich. 84; *Kelly* v. *Drew*, 12 Allen, 107 ; cf. *Hyde Park* v. *Canton*, 130 Mass. 505; *Dunlop* v. *U. S.*, 165 U. S. 486, 503 ; *Howard* v. *State*, 75 Ala. 27 ; *People* v. *Strassman*, 112 Cal. 683). So a divorce from a prior marriage has been presumed in order to sustain the validity of a second marriage. *Schmisseur* v. *Beatrie*, 147 Ill. 210 ; *Boulden* v. *McIntire*, 119 Ind. 574 ; *Erwin* v. *English*, 61 Ct. 502 ; *In re Edwards*, 58 Ia. 431; cf. *Barnes* v. *Barnes*, 90 Ia. 282 ; *Castor* v. *Davis*, 120 Ind. 231; *Randlett* v. *Rice*, 141 Mass. 385.]

ARTICLE 95.

ON WHOM THE GENERAL BURDEN OF PROOF LIES.

The burden of proof in any proceeding lies at first on that party against whom the judgment of the court would be given if no evidence at all were produced on either side, regard being had to any presumption which may appear upon the pleadings.[1] As the proceeding goes on, the burden of proof may be shifted from the party on

---

[1] 1 Ph. Ev. 552; T. E. ss. 338-9; Starkie, 586-7 & 748; Best, s. 263; and see *Abrath* v. *N. E. Ry.*, 11 Q. B. D. 440, especially the judgment of Bowen, L. J., 455-462. [Gr. Ev. i. §§ 74-82; *Veiths* v. *Hagge*, 8 Ia. 163; *Wilder* v. *Cowles*, 100 Mass. 487, 490; *Heinemann* v. *Heard*, 62 N. Y. 448; *Jones* v. *Jones*, 137 N. Y. 610; *Judge of Probate* v. *Stone*, 44 N. H. 593; *Lindley* v. *Sullivan*, 133 Ind. 588; *McReynolds* v. *Burlington, etc. R. Co.*, 106 Ill. 152; *Ky. Mfg. Co.* v. *Louisville*, 97 Ky. 548. If the defendant in an action pleads a traverse or denial (either with or without pleas by way of confession and avoidance, counterclaims, etc.), and thus denies the whole or any material part of the plaintiff's claim, the plaintiff has the burden of proof at first, for he must prove what is denied in order to establish his cause of action ; and this is true whether any material averment thus denied is affirmative or negative in form (*Roberts* v. *Chittenden*, 88 N. Y. 33; *Lake Ontario Bk.* v. *Judson*, 122 N. Y. 278; *Schutz* v. *Jordan*, 141 U. S. 213; *Rahm* v. *Deeg*, 121 Ind. 283; *Carpenter* v. *First Nat. Bk.*, 119 Ill. 352; *Boston Relief Co.* v. *Burnett*, 1 Allen, 410; *Button* v. *Frink*, 51 Ct. 342; see Art. 96, Illustration *c*). But where the defendant so pleads (as by confession and avoidance or other affirmative defence, without a denial) as to admit *all* the allegations of the complaint or declaration which are essential to the cause of action, the burden of proof lies upon him, the issue then being upon such matter of defence (*Murray* v. *N. Y. Life Ins. Co.*, 85 N. Y. 236; *Conselyea* v. *Swift*, 103 N. Y. 604; *Kent* v. *Mason*, 79 Ill. 540; *Phenix Ins. Co.* v. *Pickel*, 119 Ind. 156; *Bixby* v. *Carskaddon*, 70 Ia. 726; *Clark* v. *Murphy*, 164 Mass. 490); if, however, the action is for *unliquidated damages* and the defendant pleads only an affirmative defence, it is held in a number of our States that the plaintiff, if he seeks substantial damages, has the burden of proof and the right to begin, since the amount recoverable is not admitted upon the pleadings, and

whom it rested at first by his proving facts which raise a
presumption in his favor.[1]

---

the plaintiff must therefore prove his damages (*Johnson* v. *Josephs,*
75 Me. 544; *Dille* v. *Lovell,* 37 O. St. 415; *Wausau Boom Co.* v.
Dunbar, 75 Wis. 133; *Young* v. *Highland,* 9 Gratt. 16; *Tallmadge*
v. *Press Pub'g Co.,* 14 N. Y. S. 331; but see *McCoy* v. *McCoy,* 106
Ind. 492). The party having the right to begin has also, in general,
the right to close the case (see all the cases *supra*), but in some States
the court may, in its discretion, vary this order, if the other side is not
prejudiced thereby (*Carpenter* v. *First Nat. Bk.,* 119 Ill. 352). In
Massachusetts it is a general rule that the right to open and close belongs to the plaintiff. *Dorr* v. *Tremont Nat. Bk.,* 128 Mass. 349, 358.]

[1] [The general burden of proof upon the main issue does not really
shift from the party upon whom it rests at the beginning, but remains
upon him throughout the trial (Gr. Ev. i. 74, n.; *Heinemann* v. *Heard,*
62 N. Y. 448; *Farmers' L. & T. Co.* v. *Siefke,* 144 N. Y. 355; *Tarbox* v.
Eastern Steamboat Co., 50 Me. 339; *Phipps* v. *Mahon,* 141 Mass. 471;
Atkinson v. *Goodrich Transp. Co.,* 69 Wis. 5; *Scott* v. *Wood,* 81 Cal. 398;
Central Bridge Corp. v. *Butler,* 2 Gray, 132). In criminal cases it remains on the government throughout the trial (*Lilienthal's Tobacco* v.
U. S., 97 U. S. 237, 266; *Tiffany* v. *Comm.,* 121 Pa. 165; *People* v. *Mc-
Whorter,* 93 Mich. 641; *People* v. *Ribolski,* 89 Cal. 493; *State* v. *Wingo,*
66 Mo. 181; *O'Connell* v. *People,* 87 N. Y. 377). But after such party has
given evidence, which, in the absence of further proof, would be sufficient to entitle him to recover, the other party will then need to give
evidence in rebuttal or defence, whereupon the former may need to
furnish additional evidence to complete the requisite proof of his allegations. And this successive transfer from one party to the other of
the obligation to submit evidence is what is often called the "shifting
of the burden," though in fact what really takes place is rather a shifting of the weight of evidence as the trial progresses (*Lamb* v. *Camden,
etc. R. Co.,* 46 N. Y. 271; *Pease* v. *Cole,* 53 Ct. 53; *Burnham* v. *Allen,* 1
Gray, 496; *Agnew* v. *U. S.,* 165 U. S. 36; *Clark* v. *Hills,* 67 Tex. 141).

Sometimes, upon the principle, *res ipsa loquitur*, the party holding
the affirmative upon the issue can establish a sufficient *prima facie*
case by showing the mere occurrence of acts which raise a presumption in his favor (Illustration (*j*); *Gleeson* v. *Va. R. Co.,* 140 U. S. 435;
Houston v. *Brush,* 66 Vt. 331; *Graham* v. *Badger,* 164 Mass. 42; *Len-
non* v. *Rawitzer,* 57 Ct. 583; *Volkmar* v. *Manhattan R. Co.,* 134 N. Y.
418; *Excelsior Elec. Co.* v. *Sweet,* 57 N. J. L. 224; *Shafer* v. *Lacock,*
168 Pa. 496; *Howser* v. *Cumberland, etc. R. Co.,* 80 Md. 146; *Och* v.
Mo. etc. R. Co., 130 Mo. 27). But ordinarily he must give sufficient

Where there are conflicting presumptions, the case is the same as if there were conflicting evidence.[1]

Illustrations.

(a) It appears upon the pleadings that A is indorsee of a bill of exchange. The presumption is that the indorsement was for value, and the party interested in denying this must prove it.[2]

(ab) [A, the indorsee of a negotiable instrument, produces it in evidence in an action against the maker. The presumption is that he acquired it *bona fide* for value before maturity. The defendant may then prove that the instrument had been lost or stolen before A acquired it, or that there was fraud or illegality in its inception. The burden then falls upon A to prove that he obtained the instrument for value before maturity and in good faith, without knowledge or notice of the facts impeaching its validity.][3]

(b) A, a married woman, is accused of theft and pleads not guilty.

The burden of proof is on the prosecution. She is shown to have been in possession of the stolen goods soon after the theft. The burden of proof is shifted to A. She shows that she stole them in the

---

evidence to prove all the material allegations of his case, regard being had to the different degrees of proof required in civil and criminal cases. *Comm.* v. *McKie,* 1 Gray, 61 ; *Cosulich* v. *Standard Oil Co.,* 122 N. Y. 118 ; *Bahr* v. *Lombard,* 53 N. J. L. 233 ; *Mixter* v. *Imperial Coal Co.,* 152 Pa. 395 ; *Hart* v. *Washington Club,* 157 Ill. 9 ; *Dowell* v. *Guthrie,* 116 Mo. 646.]

[1] See Illustration (*i*).

[2] *Mills* v. *Barber,* 1 M. & W. 425. [*Harger* v. *Worrall,* 69 N. Y. 370 ; *Gray's Admr.* v. *Bk. of Kentucky,* 29 Pa. 365 ; *Estabrook* v. *Boyle,* 1 Allen, 412 ; cf. *Smith* v. *Sac Co.,* 11 Wall. 139.]

[3] [*Canajoharie Nat. Bk.* v. *Diefendorf,* 123 N. Y. 191 ; *Smith* v. *Livingston,* 111 Mass. 342 ; *Lerch Hardware Co.* v. *First Nat. Bk.,* 109 Pa. 240 ; *McCorker* v. *Banks,* 84 Md. 292 ; *Giberson* v. *Jolley,* 120 Ind. 301 ; *Horrigan* v. *Wyman,* 90 Mich. 121 ; *Bank of Montreal* v. *Richter,* 55 Minn. 362 ; *Campbell* v. *Hoff,* 129 Mo. 317 ; cf. *Amer. Ex. Nat. Bk.* v. *N. Y. Belting Co,* 148 N. Y. 698. This is the generally accepted rule, though a few authorities state that ultimately the burden is on defendant to show that plaintiff had notice of impeaching facts, instead of on plaintiff to show that he had no notice. *Todd* v *Wich Bros.,* 36 O. St. 370, 390 ; *Kellogg* v. *Curtis,* 69 Me. 212.]

presence of her husband. The burden of proving that she was not coerced by him is shifted on to the prosecutor.[1]

(c) A is indicted for bigamy. On proof by the prosecution of the first marriage, A proves that at the time he was a minor. This throws on the prosecution the burden of proving the consent of A's parents.[2]

(cc) [A, the owner of goods, sues B, a bailee, to whom he has entrusted them, for the value of the goods, on the ground that they have been lost or injured through B's neglect. A establishes a *prima facie* case of negligence by proving the bailment of his goods and that B, upon due demand made by A for their delivery, refused to restore them. The duty then resting on B to explain the loss or destruction, he shows that the goods were taken by thieves or were destroyed by fire. It then devolves upon A to prove that such theft or fire was the result of defendant's negligence.][3]

---

[1] 1 Russ. Cri. 33 ; 2 id. 337. [The old rule that the recent exclusive possession of stolen goods raises a *legal* presumption of guilt, is still maintained in Missouri (*State* v. *Jennings*, 81 Mo. 185 ; *State* v. *Warford*, 106 Mo. 55). But the rule now generally established in this country is that such possession only raises a presumption of *fact*, or affords *prima facie* evidence of guilt, to be considered by the jury, and juries are instructed that if the possession is not satisfactorily explained, they *may* infer guilt or *are authorised* to find guilt (*Wilson* v. *U. S.*, 162 U. S. 613 ; *Comm.* v. *McGorty*, 114 Mass. 299 ; *Stover* v. *People*, 56 N. Y. 315 ; *People* v. *Weldon*, 111 N. Y. 569 ; *Blaker* v. *State*, 130 Ind. 203 ; *Keating* v. *People*, 160 Ill. 480 ; *State* v. *Richart*, 57 Ia. 245 ; *State* v. *Hoffman*, 53 Kan. 700 ; *Porterfield* v. *Comm.*, 91 Va. 801 ; *Orr* v. *State*, 107 Ala. 35 ; *Griffin* v. *State*, 86 Ga. 257 ; *Bellamy* v. *State*, 35 Fla. 242 ; *Harper* v. *State*, 71 Miss. 202). Upon either theory the burden is on the defendant to explain his possession. Some cases regard the recent possession as simply evidence for the jury *tending* to show guilt (*State* v. *Hodge*, 50 N. H. 510 ; *People* v. *Abbott*, 101 Cal. 645). Similar rules are generally applied in trials for burglary, arson and like offences, but in some States such evidence is not deemed *prima facie* evidence of burglary as it is of larceny (*State* v. *Jennings*, 79 Ia. 513 ; *People* v. *Wood*, 99 Mich. 620 ; *Gravely* v. *Comm.*, 86 Va. 396).

As to presumed coercion of wife by husband, see Art. 101, note.]

[2] *R.* v. *Butler*, 1 R. & R. 61. [The English Marriage Act, then in force, provided that the marriage of a minor, without the consent of parents, should be "null and void."]

[3] [*Claflin* v. *Meyer*, 75 N. Y. 260 ; *Stewart* v. *Stone*, 127 N. Y. 500 ;

... or the ground of the ... proponent to establish a ... This he may do ... the testator duly ... evidence being aided ... then upon the ... of unsound mind. ... during the trial. The genera. ... on both sides has ... the ... should not be

... 80 Me. 600: ... removed in a ... *C. R. I. &* ... due to his ... *Shields.* Minn. 142: ... similar rules apply to ... Pa. 170: *Ellsworth* v. ... *Bockl* v. ... *Downer*, 11 ... as modified by ... *Rees*, 82 Hun, 49: ... *Merrill*, 56 N. H. ... Some States, however, hold ... but is solely a matter for ... 22 Me. 360: 10 *McMecken* ... on *Robinson*, 12 Minn. 371: ... in the production, 12 Vt. 658). ... sufficient *prima facie* case (*Grubbs* v. ... *Wilton*, 38 Md. 115: *McCulloch* ... in Illinois, if the evidence on ... is equally balanced, the pre- ... be proponent and the will is adm-

(ce) [A is indicted for a crime and pleads not guilty. The burden is upon the prosecution to prove that he committed the act charged. He then gives evidence to show that he was insane when the act was committed. The prosecution may then give evidence to prove that he was sane, and if the entire evidence does not satisfy the jury of his sanity beyond a reasonable doubt, A must be acquitted.][1]

---

to probate; the burden of proof on the whole case is, therefore, said to lie upon the contestant (*Graybeal* v. *Gardner*, 146 Ill. 337; see *Barber's Appeal*, 63 Ct. 393).

The burden of proof as to *undue influence* is generally held to lie upon the contestant, after it has been made to appear that the will was duly executed by a person of competent understanding (*Baldwin* v. *Parker*, 99 Mass. 79; *Will of Martin*, 98 N. Y. 193; *Dumont* v. *Dumont*, 46 N. J. Eq. 223; *Webber* v. *Sullivan*, 58 Ia. 260; *Armstrong* v. *Armstrong*, 63 Wis. 162; *Morton* v. *Heidorn*, 135 Mo. 608; *Prentis* v. *Bates*, 93 Mich. 234, 245; *McMechen* v. *McMechen*, 17 W. Va. 683; cf. *Freeman* v. *Hamilton*, 74 Ga. 317). But when the contestant has given evidence sufficient to establish undue influence, the burden of rebutting it lies on the proponent (*Matter of Green*, 67 Hun, 527; *Loder* v. *Whelpley*, 110 N. Y. 239, 250; *Denning* v. *Butcher*, 91 Ia. 425, 440). A New York statute provides that, in order that a will may be admitted to probate, it must appear to the surrogate that it was duly executed and that the testator was competent to make a will and *not under restraint* (Code Civ. Pro. § 2623; see *Matter of Mabie*, 5 Misc. 179).

The existence of a special confidential relation between the testator and a beneficiary under the will may cast the burden, as to undue influence or coercion, upon the proponent. *Will of Smith*, 95 N. Y. 516; *Richmond's Appeal*, 59 Ct. 226; *Miller's Estate*, 179 Pa. 645; *Henry* v. *Hall*, 106 Ala. 84; cf. *Denning* v. *Butcher*, 91 Ia. 425; see Art. 97 A.]

[1] [*Walker* v. *People*, 88 N. Y. 81; *People* v. *Nino*, 149 N. Y. 317; *Davis* v. *U. S.*, 160 U. S. 469; *State* v. *Bartlett*, 43 N. H. 224; *Comm.* v. *Pomeroy* (Mass.) cited in 160 U. S. 483; *Plummer* v. *State*, 135 Ind. 308; *Lilly* v. *People*, 148 Ill. 467; *Revoir* v. *State*, 82 Wis. 295; *State* v. *Nixon*, 32 Kan. 205; *Furst* v. *State*, 31 Neb. 403; *Armstrong* v. *State*, 30 Fla. 170; *Ford* v. *State*, 73 Miss. 734; *King* v. *State*, 91 Tenn. 617; cf. *State* v. *Schweitzer*, 57 Ct. 532. But in most of the States it is the rule that the defendant, to be acquitted, must prove his insanity by a preponderance of evidence (*State* v. *Lawrence*, 57 Me. 574; *Graves* v. *State*, 45 N. J. L. 203 & 347; *Comm.* v. *Bezek*, 168 Pa. 603; *Kelch* v. *State*, 55 O. St. 146; *State* v. *Trout*, 74 Ia. 545; *State* v.

(*d*) A deed of gift is shown to have been made by a client to his solicitor. The burden of proving that the transaction was in good faith is on the solicitor.[1]

Grear, 29 Minn. 221; *State* v. *Lewis,* 20 Nev. 333; *People* v. *Ward,* 105 Cal. 335; *State* v. *Wright,* 134 Mo. 404; *Bolling* v. *State,* 54 Ark. 588; *Moore* v. *Comm.,* 92 Ky. 630; *Dejarnette* v. *Comm.,* 75 Va. 867; *State* v. *Alexander,* 30 S. Car. 74; *Maxwell* v. *State,* 89 Ala. 150; *Keener* v. *State,* 97 Ga. 388; *Boren* v. *State,* 32 Tex. Cr. 637. In a few States he is required to prove his insanity beyond a reasonable doubt (*State* v. *Hansen,* 25 Or. 391; *State* v. *Clements,* 47 La. Ann. 1088).

As to the defence of *alibi,* the burden is also on the defendant to produce evidence to prove it. In most States, if upon such evidence, either by itself (*Howard* v. *State,* 50 Ind. 190; *Walters* v. *State,* 39 O. St. 216; *Bennett* v. *State,* 30 Tex. App. 341), or in connection with the other evidence in the case, the jury have, at the end of the trial, a reasonable doubt of guilt, they should acquit (*Carlton* v. *People,* 150 Ill. 181; *Comm.* v. *Choate,* 105 Mass. 451; *State* v. *Harvey,* 131 Mo. 339; *People* v. *Fong Ah Sing,* 64 Cal. 253; *Ware* v. *State,* 59 Ark. 379; *Murphy* v. *State,* 31 Fla. 166; *State* v. *Conway,* 55 Kan. 323; *State* v. *Stone,* 117 N. Y. 480). In a few States the defendant, to be acquitted, must prove the *alibi* by a preponderance of evidence (*State* v. *Beasley,* 84 Ia. 83; *State* v. *Jackson,* 36 S. Car. 487). In still other States the rule is that defendant's evidence as to this defence should preponderate, but if it does not, and yet, with the other evidence in the case, it leaves a reasonable doubt of guilt, there should be an acquittal (*State* v. *Ward,* 61 Vt. 153; *Miles* v. *State,* 93 Ga. 117; *Rudy* v. *Comm.,* 128 Pa. 500; *State* v. *Freeman,* 100 N. C. 429; *Prince* v. *State,* 100 Ala. 144).

So as to evidence to show *self-defence,* the accused is entitled to the benefit of a reasonable doubt (*Plummer* v. *State,* 135 Ind. 308; *State* v. *Donahoe,* 78 Ia. 486; *Hubbard* v. *State,* 37 Fla. 156; *People* v. *Coughlin,* 65 Mich. 704; *People* v. *Riordan,* 117 N. Y. 71; *Tiffany* v. *Comm.,* 121 Pa. 165; *Miller* v. *State,* 107 Ala. 40; *State* v. *Wingo,* 66 Mo. 181); but in a few States such evidence, adduced by the defendant, must preponderate (*State* v. *Jones,* 20 W. Va. 764; *Weaver* v. *State,* 24 O. St. 584).

In some States it is held that upon *all* matters of defence, the accused is entitled to the benefit of a reasonable doubt. *People* v. *Riordan,* 117 N. Y. 71; *Gravely* v. *State,* 38 Neb. 873; *People* v. *Boling,* 83 Cal. 380; *State* v. *Schweitzer,* 57 Ct. 532; *People* v. *Coughlin,* 65 Mich. 704.]

[1] 1 Story, Eq. Juris., s. 310, n. 1, quoting *Hunter* v. *Atkins,* 3 M. &

(*e*) It is shown that a hedge stands on A's land. The burden of proving that the ditch adjacent to it is not A's also is on the person who denies that the ditch belongs to A.[1]

(*f*) A proves that he received the rent of land. The presumption is that he is owner in fee simple, and the burden of proof is on the person who denies it.[2]

(*g*) A finds a jewel mounted in a socket, and gives it to B to look at. B keeps it, and refuses to produce it on notice, but returns the socket. The burden of proving that it is not as valuable a stone of the kind as would go in the socket is on B.[3]

(*h*) A sues B on a policy of insurance, and shows that the vessel insured went to sea, and that after a reasonable time no tidings of her have been received, but that her loss has been rumored. The burden of proving that she has not foundered is on B.[4]

(*i*) Z in 1864 married A. In 1868 he was convicted of bigamy in having in 1868 married B during the life of A. In 1879 he married C. In 1880, C being alive, he married D, and was prosecuted for bigamy in marrying D in the lifetime of C. The prisoner on his second trial proved the first conviction, thereby proving that A was living in 1868. No further evidence was given. A's being alive in 1868 raises a presumption that she was living in 1879. Z's marriage to C in 1879, being presumably innocent, raises a presumption that A was then dead. The inference [*i. e.*, whether A was alive when Z married C] ought to have been left to the jury.[5]

(*j*) [While A was passing along the street in front of the shop of B, a dealer in flour, a barrel of flour fell from an upper window of the shop and striking A knocked him down and injured him. In an action

K. 113. [*Whitehead* v. *Kennedy*, 69 N. Y. 462; *Dunn* v. *Record*, 63 Me. 17; *Cuthbertson's Appeal*, 97 Pa. 163; see Art. 97 A, *post.*]

[1] *Guy* v. *West*, Selw. N. P. 1297.

[2] *Doe* v. *Coulthred*, 7 A. & E. 235. [*Burt* v. *Panjaud*, 99 U. S. 180; cf. *Linthicum* v. *Ray*, 9 Wall. 241.]

[3] *Armoury* v. *Delamirie*, 1 S. L. C. 357. [Gr. Ev. i. § 37; *Clark* v. *Miller*, 4 Wend. 628; *McCown* v. *Quigley*, 147 Pa. 307; but see *Berney* v. *Dinsmore*, 141 Mass. 42.]

[4] *Koster* v. *Reed*, 6 B. & C. 19. [See *Gordon* v. *Bowne*, 2 Johns. 150; *Berwind* v. *Greenwich Ins. Co.*, 114 N. Y. 231.]

[5] *R.* v. *Willshire*, 6 Q. B. D. 366. [See *Comm.* v. *McGrath*, 140 Mass. 296; *Parker* v. *State*, 77 Ala. 47; *State* v. *Plym*, 43 Minn. 385; *Williams* v. *Williams*, 63 Wis. 58; Art. 94, *ante*, Illustration (*c*); p 262, *post*, note.]

by A against B, A proved only the fact of the injury, and this was held sufficient to establish a *prima facie* case of negligence against B, so that A might recover in the absence of opposing evidence.][1]

ARTICLE 96.

BURDEN OF PROOF AS TO PARTICULAR FACT.

The burden of proof as to any particular fact lies on that person who wishes the court to believe in its existence, unless it is provided by any law that the burden of proving that fact shall lie on any particular person;[2] but the burden may in the course of a case be shifted from one

---

[1] [*Byrne* v. *Boadle*, 2 H. & C. 722 ; see *Scott* v. *London, etc. Docks Co.*, 3 id. 596 (fall of bags of sugar from warehouse); *Kearney* v. *London, etc. R. Co.*, L. R. 5 Q. B. 411, 6 id. 759 (fall of brick from bridge over highway); *Hogan* v. *Manhattan R. Co.*, 149 N. Y. 23 (fall of piece of iron from elevated railway); *Mullen* v. *St. John*, 57 N. Y. 567 (fall of building into highway); *Breen* v. *N. Y. C. R. Co.*, 109 N. Y. 297 (injury to passenger by swinging door on train); *Uggla* v. *West End R. Co.*, 160 Mass. 351 (fall of electric railway apparatus); *Sheridan* v. *Foley*, 58 N. J. L. 230 (fall of bricks from scaffold or hod); *Treadwell* v. *Whittier*, 80 Cal. 574 (fall of elevator); cf. *Huey* v. *Gahlenbeck*, 121 Pa. 238. The maxim *res ipsa loquitur* is frequently applied to cases of injury by carriers, especially railroad companies, to goods or passengers, as by collision, derailment of cars, etc. (*Buck* v. *Pa. R. Co.*, 150 Pa. 170; *Bush* v. *Barrett*, 96 Cal. 203; *Montgomery, etc. R. Co.* v. *Mallett*, 92 Ala. 209; Hutchinson on Carriers, 2d ed. §§ 798-801). Oftentimes they are made subject to this rule by statute. *Louisville, etc. R. Co.* v. *Spencer*, 149 Ill. 97; *Chicago, etc. R. Co.* v. *McBride*, 54 Kan. 172.]

[2] For instances of such provisions see T. E. ss. 345-6. [*Perley* v. *Perley*, 144 Mass. 104; *Farmers' L. & T. Co.* v. *Siefke*, 144 N. Y. 354; *Phenix Ins. Co.* v. *Pickel*, 119 Ind. 155. Thus the defendant must prove any affirmative defences which he sets up, as payment, usury, fraud, illegality, etc. (*Noble* v. *Fagnant*, 162 Mass. 275; *Spencer* v. *Citizens' Ins. Co.*, 142 N. Y. 505; *Rosenstein* v. *Fox*, 150 N. Y. 354, 364; *Haughwout* v. *Garrison*, 69 N. Y. 339; *Godfrey* v. *Crisler*, 121 Ind. 203; *Ætna Life Ins. Co.* v. *Ward*, 140 U. S. 76.]

side to the other, and in considering the amount of evidence necessary to shift the burden of proof, the court has regard to the opportunities of knowledge with respect to the fact to be proved which may be possessed by the parties respectively.[1]

Illustrations.

(a) A prosecutes B for theft, and wishes the court to believe that B admitted the theft to C. A must prove the admission.

B wishes the court to believe that, at the time in question, he was elsewhere. He must prove it.[2]

(aa) [A sues B for negligence causing damage. The burden of proving B's negligence rests upon A, but A need not prove the absence on his own part of contributory negligence; such negligence of A is to be proved by B as matter of defence, unless, indeed, it has been already sufficiently disclosed by A's evidence.][3]

(b) A, a shipowner, sues B, an underwriter, on a policy of insurance

---

[1] [*Harris* v. *White*, 81 N. Y. 532, 547, 548; *Selma, etc. R. Co.* v. *U. S.*, 139 U. S. 560; *Greeley* v. *Passaic*, 42 N. J. L. 87; *State* v. *Hathaway*, 115 Mo. 36; *Robinson* v. *Robinson*, 51 Ill. App. 317. Thus it is held that in proceedings against a person who has been selling liquor, exercising a trade or profession, or doing other acts, without having the license prescribed by law, the burden is on him to prove that he has a license, not on the prosecutor to prove the want of a license. *U. S.* v. *Nelson*, 29 F. R. 202; *State* v. *Nulty*, 57 Vt. 543; Mass. Pub. St. c. 214, s. 12; *Comm.* v. *Towle*, 138 Mass. 490; *State* v. *Higgins*, 13 R. I. 330; *People* v. *Maxwell*, 83 Hun, 157; *People* v. *Fulda*, 52 Hun, 65; *Plainfield* v. *Watson*, 57 N. J. L. 525; *People* v. *Nedrow*, 16 Ill. App. 192; *State* v. *Ahern*, 54 Minn. 195; *St Louis* v. *Weitzel*, 130 Mo. 600; *Evans* v. *State*, 54 Ark. 227; *State* v. *Emery*, 98 N. C. 668; *Information ag'st Oliver*, 21 S. Car. 318; cf. *People* v. *Cannon*, 139 N. Y. 32, 46; contra, *Hepler* v. *State*, 58 Wis. 46; *State* v. *Kuhuke*, 26 Kan. 405.]

[2] [See p. 248, note.]

[3] [This is the rule in a majority of the States (*Indianapolis, etc. R. Co.* v. *Horst*, 93 U. S. 291; *N. J. Exp. Co.* v. *Nichols*, 33 N. J. L. 434; *Sopherstein* v. *Bertels*, 178 Pa. 401; *State* v. *Balt. & P. R. Co.*, 58 Md. 482; *Gill* v. *Homrighousen*, 79 Wis. 634; *Lorimer* v. *St. Paul Ry. Co.*, 48 Minn. 391; *St. Louis, etc. R. Co.* v. *Weaver*, 35 Kan. 412; *Omaha R. Co.* v. *Martin*, 48 Neb. 66; *MacDougall* v. *Central R. Co.*, 63 Cal. 431; *Moffatt* v. *Tenney*, 17 Col. 189; *Ford* v. *Umatilla Co.*, 15 Or. 313;

on a ship. B alleges that A knew of and concealed from B material
facts. B must give enough evidence to throw upon A the burden of
disproving his knowledge; but slight evidence will suffice for this
purpose.[1]

(c) In an action for malicious prosecution the plaintiff must prove
(1) his innocence; (2) want of reasonable and probable cause for the
prosecution; (3) malice or indirect motive; and he must prove all
that is necessary to establish each proposition sufficiently to throw the
burden of disproving that proposition on the other side.[2]

(d) In actions for penalties under the old game laws, though the
plaintiff had to aver that the defendant was not duly qualified, and
was obliged to give general evidence that he was not, the burden of
proving any definite qualification was on the defendant.[3]

Gordon v. *Richmond*, 83 Va. 436; *Comer* v. *Coal, etc. Co.*, 34 W. Va.
533; *Jordan* v. *Asheville*, 112 N. C. 743; *Donahue* v. *Railroad Co.*,
32 S. Car. 299; *Cahill* v. *Cincinnati R. Co.*, 92 Ky. 345; *Stewart* v.
Nashville, 96 Tenn. 50; *Jones* v. *Malvern Co.*, 58 Ark. 125; *Hudson* v.
Wabash, etc. Ry. Co., 101 Mo. 13; *McDonald* v. *Montgomery R. Co.*,
110 Ala. 162; *Gulf, etc. R. Co.* v. *Shieder*, 88 Tex. 152). But in some
States A must prove B's negligence and that he was not himself guilty
of contributory negligence. *Benson* v. *Titcomb*, 72 Me. 31; *Bovee* v.
Danville, 53 Vt. 183; *Mayo* v. *B. & M. R. Co.*, 104 Mass. 137; *Ryan*
v. *Bristol*, 63 Ct. 26; *Whalen* v. *Citizens' Gas Co.*, 151 N.Y. 70; *Thomas*
v. *Hoosier Co.*, 140 Ind. 518; *Chicago, etc. R. Co.* v. *Levy*, 160 Ill. 355;
Denman v. *Johnston*, 85 Mich. 387; *Gamble* v. *Mullin*, 74 Ia. 99.]

[1] *Elkin* v. *Janson*, 13 M. & W. 655. See, especially, the judgment of
Alderson, B., 663-6. [See *Insurance Co.* v. *Folsom*, 18 Wall. 237;
Fiske v. *New Eng. Ins. Co.*, 15 Pick. 310; *Livingston* v. *Delafield*, 3
Cai. 49. It is a general rule that in proving a negative averment,
plenary proof is not required. Gr. Ev. i. § 78; *State* v. *Foster*, 23 N.
H. 348; *Schmisseur* v. *Beatrie*, 147 Ill. 210; but see *Colorado Coal
Co.* v. *U. S.*, 123 U. S. 307, 318.]

[2] *Abrath* v. *North Eastern Ry.*, 11 Q. B. D. 441. [*Good* v. *French*,
115 Mass. 201; *Anderson* v. *How*, 116 N. Y. 336; *McClafferty* v. *Philp*,
151 Pa. 86. Plaintiff's innocence is shown by proving the termination
of the alleged malicious proceeding in his favor. *O'Brien* v. *Barry*,
106 Mass. 300; *Robbins* v. *Robbins*, 133 N. Y. 597.]

[3] 1 Ph. Ev. 556, and cases there quoted. The illustration is founded
more particularly on *R.* v. *Jarvis*, in a note to *R.* v. *Stone*, 1 Ea. 639,
where Lord Mansfield's language appears to imply what is stated
above. [See *Potter* v. *Deyo*, 19 Wend. 361; *Bliss* v. *Brainard*, 41
N. H. 256.]

ARTICLE 97.

BURDEN OF PROVING FACT TO BE PROVED TO MAKE EVIDENCE ADMISSIBLE.

The burden of proving any fact necessary to be proved in order to enable any person to give evidence of any other fact is on the person who wishes to give such evidence.

Illustrations.

(*a*) A wishes to prove a dying declaration by B.

A must prove B's death, and the fact that he had given up all hope of life when he made the statement.[1]

(*b*) A wishes to prove, by secondary evidence, the contents of a lost · document.

A must prove that the document has been lost.[2]

ARTICLE 97 A.

BURDEN OF PROOF WHEN PARTIES STAND IN A FIDUCIARY RELATION.

When persons stand in a relation to each other of such a nature that the one reposes confidence in the other, or is placed by circumstances under his authority, control or influence, when the question is as to the validity of any transaction between them from which the person in whom confidence is reposed or in whom authority or influence is vested derives advantage, the burden of proving that the confidence, authority or influence was not abused, and that the transaction was in good faith and valid, is on the person in whom such confidence or authority or influence is vested, and the nature and amount of the evidence re-

---

[1] [See Art. 26, *ante.*]

[2] [See Art. 71, *ante; Grimes* v *Hilliary,* 150 Ill. 141; *Hansen* v. *Amer. Ins. Co.,* 57 Ia. 741.]

quired for this purpose depends upon the nature of the
confidence or authority, and on the character of the transaction.[1]

---

[1] See Story's Equity, § 307 and following ; also Taylor on Evidence,
s. 129 and following. The illustrations of the principle are innumerable and very various. [See Pomeroy's Eq. Jur., §§ 943-963. Such
confidential relations exist between trustee and *cestui que trust*, attorney and client, physician and patient, priest and penitent, parent and
child, guardian and ward, husband and wife, partner and co-partner,
principal and surety, principal and agent, and generally where persons are associated together in some special relation of trust and confidence. The trustee, attorney, etc., must prove that in dealings with
the other, beneficial to himself, he took no advantage but exercised
entire good faith (*Darlington's Estate*, 147 Pa. 624 ; *Barnard* v. *Gantz*,
140 N. Y. 249 ; *Roby* v. *Colehour*, 135 Ill. 300). For cases of attorney
and client, see *Morrison* v. *Smith*, 130 Ill. 305 ; *Porter* v. *Bergen*, 54
N. J. Eq. 405 ; *Burnham* v. *Heselton*, 82 Me. 495 ; *Whipple* v. *Barton*,
63 N. H. 613 ; *Tancre* v. *Reynolds*, 35 Minn. 476 ; Art. 95, *ante*, Illustration (*d*) ; of parent and child, *White* v. *Ross*, 160 Ill. 56 ; *Clark* v.
Clark, 174 Pa. 309 ; of guardian and ward, *Gillett* v. *Wiley*, 126 Ill. 310 ;
McConkey v. *Cockey*, 69 Md. 286 ; of priest and confiding parishioner,
Pironi v. *Corrigan*, 47 N. J. Eq. 135 ; *Marx* v. *McGlynn*, 88 N. Y. 357 ;
of physician and patient, *Bogie* v. *Nolan*, 96 Mo. 86 ; of business adviser and aged or feeble-minded person relying upon him, *Green* v.
Roworth, 113 N. Y. 462 ; *Zimmerman* v. *Bitner*, 79 Md. 115 ; *Gates* v.
Cornett, 72 Mich. 420 ; *Mott* v. *Mott*, 49 N. J. Eq. 192 ; *Hall* v. *Knap-
penberger*, 97 Mo. 509 ; *Stepp* v. *Frampton*, 179 Pa. 284.]

CHAPTER XIV.

*ON PRESUMPTIONS AND ESTOPPELS.**

Article 98.

PRESUMPTION OF LEGITIMACY.

The fact that any person was born during the continuance of a valid marriage between his mother and any man, or within such a time after the dissolution thereof and before the celebration of another valid marriage, that his mother's husband could have been his father, is conclusive proof that he is the legitimate child of his mother's husband, unless it can be shown

either that his mother and her husband had no access to each other at any time when he could have been begotten, regard being had both to the date of the birth and to the physical condition of the husband,

or that the circumstances of their access (if any) were such as to render it highly improbable that sexual intercourse took place between them when it occurred.[1]

---

* See Note XXXV. [Appendix].

[1] [The presumption of legitimacy, it is said, "can only be rebutted by the most satisfactory and convincing proof that the husband was not the father of the child," or, as a number of the cases express it, "by proof beyond a reasonable doubt " (Gr. Ev. i. § 28, ii. §§ 150-153 ; *Cross* v. *Cross*, 3 Pai. 139 ; *Van Aernam* v. *Van Aernam*, 1 Barb. Ch. 375 ; *Phillips* v. *Allen*, 2 Allen, 453 ; *Egbert* v. *Greenwalt*, 44 Mich. 245 ; *Patterson* v. *Gaines*, 6 How. (U. S.) 550 ; *Scanlon* v. *Walshe*, 8· Md. 118 ; *State* v. *Lavin*, 80 Ia. 555 ; *Bullock* v. *Knox*, 96 Ala. 195 *Grant* v. *Mitchell*, 83 Me. 23 ; *Wilson* v. *Babb*, 18 S. Car. 59; *Scott* v. *Hillenberg*, 85 Va. 245 ; *Watts* v. *Owens*, 62 Wis. 512 ; *Goss* v. *Froman*, 89 Ky. 318 ; *Pittsford* v. *Chittenden*, 58 Vt. 49; see N. Y. Rev. St. i. 642). Legitimacy will be presumed, even in the absence of proof

Neither the mother nor the husband is a competent witness[1] as to the fact of their having or not having had sexual intercourse with each other,[2] nor are any declarations by them upon that subject deemed to be relevant facts when the legitimacy of the woman's child is in question,[3] whether the mother or her husband can be called as a witness or not, provided that in applications for affiliation orders when proof has been given of the non-access of the husband at any time when his wife's child could have been begotten, the wife may give evidence[4] as to the person by whom it was begotten.[5]   Letters

---

that the child's parents were married; such former marriage will be assumed until contrary proof is given. *Matter of Matthews*, 153 N. Y. 443.]

[1] [*Boykin v. Boykin*, 70 N. C. 262; *People v. Court of Sessions*, 45 Hun, 54; *Abington v. Duxbury*, 105 Mass. 287; *Tioga Co. v. South Creek T'p*, 75 Pa. 433; *Mink v. State*, 60 Wis. 583; *Burnaby v. Baillie*, 42 Ch. D. 282. But in cases between third parties husband and wife may testify as to the time of their marriage, the time of a child's birth, and any other independent facts affecting the question of legitimacy. *Janes's Estate*, 147 Pa. 527.]

[2] [Here Mr. Stephen inserts a special statutory qualification of the English law (32 & 33 Vict. c. 68, s. 3), viz.,—"unless the proceedings in the course of which the question arises are proceedings instituted in consequence of adultery."]

[3] [*Hemmenway v. Towner*, 1 Allen, 209; *Shuman v. Shuman*, 83 Wis. 250; *Dennison v. Page*, 29 Pa. 420; *Bowles v. Bingham*, 2 Munf. 442. But their conduct and declarations, forming part of the *res gestæ*, and thus tending to show what relations they maintained towards each other, their recognition of the child's illegitimacy, etc., may be proved (*Aylesford Peerage Case*, 11 App. Cas. 1; *Goss v. Froman*, 89 Ky. 318; see *Janes's Estate*, 147 Pa. 527, 531); and the same has been held as to the declarations of the wife's alleged paramour that the child was his. *Burnaby v. Baillie*, 42 Ch. D. 282; but see *Grant v. Mitchell*, 83 Me. 23; *Montgomery v. Montgomery*, 3 Barb. Ch. 132; *Scanlon v. Walshe*, 81 Md. 118.]

[4] [Gr. Ev. i. § 344; *State v. McDowell*, 101 N. C. 734; *People v. Overseers, etc.*, 15 Barb. 286; *Comm. v. Shepherd*, 6 Binn. 283; cf. *Cuppy v. State*, 24 Ind. 389; *Bowers v. Wood*, 143 Mass. 182.]

[5] *R v. Luffe*, 8 Ea. 207; *Cope v. Cope*, 1 Mo. & Ro. 272-4; *Legge v.*

written by the mother may, as part of the *res gestæ*, be admissible evidence to show illegitimacy, though the mother could not be called as a witness to prove the statements contained in such letters.[1]

ARTICLE 99.

PRESUMPTION OF DEATH FROM SEVEN YEARS' ABSENCE.

A person shown not to have been heard of for seven years by those (if any) who if he had been alive would naturally have heard of him, is presumed to be dead, unless the circumstances of the case are such as to account for his not being heard of without assuming his death; but there is no presumption as to the time when he died, and the burden of proving his death at any particular time is upon the person who asserts it.[2]

Edmonds, 25 L. J. Eq. 125, see p. 135; *R.* v. *Mansfield*, 1 Q. B. 444; *Morris* v. *Davies*, 3 C. & P. 215. See, as an illustration of these principles, *Hawes* v. *Draeger*, 23 Ch. D. 173. [These cases are cited by Mr. Stephen as authorities upon this whole Article.] I am not aware of any decision as to the paternity of a child born say six months after the death of one husband, and three months after the mother's marriage to another husband. Amongst common soldiers in India such a question might easily arise. The rule in European regiments is that a widow not remarried within the year (it used to be six months) must leave the regiment: the result was and is that widowhoods are usually very short. [In a recent American case it appeared that a child was born seven months after the mother was divorced from her first husband and four months and twenty-one days after her marriage to a second husband. The child being fully developed at birth was held to be the offspring of the first husband. *Shuman* v. *Hurd*, 79 Wis. 656; *Shuman* v. *Shuman*, 83 Wis. 250; cf. *Drennan* v. *Douglas*, 102 Ill. 341.]

[1] *Aylesford Peerage Case*, 11 App. Cas. 1, in which the general rule stated above is considered and affirmed. [See note 3, *supra.*]

[2] *McMahon* v. *McElroy*, 5 Ir. Rep. Eq. 1; *Hopewell* v. *De Pinna*, 2 Camp. 113; *Nepean* v. *Doe*, 2 S. L. C. 562, 681; *Nepean* v. *Knight*, 2 M. & W. 894, 912; *R.* v. *Lumley*, L. R. 1 C. C. R. 196; and see the caution of Lord Denman in *R.* v. *Harborne*, 2 A. & E. 544. All the cases are

There is no presumption as to the age at which a person died who is shown to have been alive at a given time, or as to the order in which two or more persons died who are shown to have died in the same accident, shipwreck, or battle.[1]

---

collected and considered in *In re Phené's Trust*, L. R. 5 Ch. App. 139. The doctrine is also much discussed in *Prudential Assurance Company v. Edmonds*, 2 App. Cas. 487. The principle is stated to the same effect as in the text in *Re Corbishley's Trusts*, 14 Ch. D. 846. [Gr. Ev. i. § 41; *Davie v. Briggs*, 97 U. S. 628; *Johnson v. Merithew*, 80 Me. 111; *Winship v. Conner*, 42 N. H. 341; *Stockbridge's Case*, 145 Mass. 517; *O'Gara v. Eisenlohr*, 38 N. Y. 296; *Hoyt v. Newbold*, 45 N. J. L. 219; *Cooper v. Cooper*, 86 Ind. 75; *State v. Henke*, 58 Ia. 457; *Flood v. Growney*, 126 Mo. 262; *Shriver v. State*, 65 Md. 278; *University v. Harrison*, 90 N. C. 385; *Shown v. McMackin*, 9 Lea, 601; cf. *In re Taylor*, 20 N. Y. S. 960. Some American cases hold that the absent person, unheard from, is presumed to have lived *till the end of the seven years* (*Excrs. of Clarke v. Canfield*, 15 N. J. Eq. 119; *Mutual Ben. Co.'s Petition*, 174 Pa. 1; *Schaub v. Griffin*, 84 Md. 557; *Reedy v. Nullizen*, 155 Ill. 636); but others support the English rule stated in this Article (*Davie v. Briggs*, 97 U. S. 628; *McCartee v. Camel*, 1 Barb. Ch. 455; *Evans v. Stewart*, 81 Va. 724; *Whiteley v. Equitable Assur. Soc.*, 72 Wis. 170; cf. *Corley v. Holloway*, 22 S. Car. 380).

From special circumstances justifying such a conclusion, the jury may infer death from an absence of less than seven years; thus, *e. g.*, death was inferred after six months in regard to a person who had sailed on a voyage usually taking 25 to 40 days, no tidings of the vessel having been received. *Johnson v. Merithew*, 80 Me. 111; see *Waite v. Coaracy*, 45 Minn. 159; *Matter of Stewart*, 1 Connol. 86; *Cox v. Ellsworth*, 18 Neb. 664; *Hancock v. Amer. Life Ins. Co.*, 62 Mo. 26.

[1] *Wing v. Angrave*, 8 H. L. C. 183, 198; and see authorities in last note. [Gr. Ev. i. §§ 29, 30; *Newell v. Nichols*, 75 N. Y. 78; *Russell v Hallett*, 23 Kan. 276; *Coye v. Leach*, 8 Met. 371; *Paden v. Briscoe*, 81 Tex. 563; see *Fuller v. Linzee*, 135 Mass. 468. The question of survivorship is wholly one of fact, depending upon evidence, and the burden of proof lies upon him who asserts that one person survived the other. In the absence of evidence, property rights are disposed of as if all died at the same time (Id.; *Johnson v. Merithew*, 80 Me. 111; *Ehle's Will*, 73 Wis. 445).

In California and Louisiana there are special legal presumptions as to survivorship, depending on the age and sex of the persons who

Article 100.

PRESUMPTION OF LOST GRANT.[1]

When it has been shown that any person has, for a long period of time, exercised any proprietary right which might have had a lawful origin by grant or license from the Crown or from a private person, and the exercise of which might and naturally would have been prevented by the persons interested if it had not had a lawful origin, there is a presumption that such right had a lawful origin and that it was created by a proper instrument which has been lost.[2]

Illustrations.

(*a*) The question is, whether B is entitled to recover from A the possession of lands which A's father and mother successively occupied from 1754 to 1792 or 1793, and which B had occupied (without title) from 1793 to 1809. The lands formed originally an encroachment on the Forest of Dean.

The undisturbed occupation for thirty-nine years raises a presumption of a grant from the Crown to A's father.[3]

---

perished. Cal. Code Civ. Pro. § 1963, subd. 40; *Hollister* v. *Cordero*, 76 Cal. 649; La. Civ. Code, Art. 938.]

[1] The subject of the doctrine of lost grants is much considered in *Angus* v. *Dalton*, 3 Q. B. D. 84, 6 App. Cas. 740. [See *Lehigh R. Co.* v. *McFarlan*, 43 N. J. L. 605; *McRoberts* v. *Bergman*, 132 N. Y.73.]

[2] [Gr. Ev. i. §§ 46, 47; *Jackson* v. *McCall*, 10 Johns. 377; *Fletcher* v. *Fuller*, 120 U. S. 534; *Roe* v. *Strong*, 119 N. Y. 316; *Texas Mex. Ry. Co.* v. *Uribe*, 85 Tex. 386; *Carter* v. *Fishing Co.*, 77 Pa. 310; *Oaksmith's Lessee* v. *Johnston*, 92 U. S. 343. It is said in this last case that in this country there can seldom be occasion to presume a grant from the government, except in cases of very ancient possessions running back to colonial days, since, from the beginning of the century, a record has been preserved of all such grants. See *Mission of the I. V.* v. *Cronin*, 143 N. Y. 524.]

[3] *Goodtitle* v. *Baldwin*, 11 Ea. 488. The presumption was rebutted in this case by an express provision of 20 Ch. II. c. 3, avoiding grants of the Forest of Dean. See also *Doe* d. *Devine* v. *Wilson*, 10 Moo. P. C. 502.

(*b*) A fishing mill dam was erected more than 110 years before 1861 in the River Derwent, in Cumberland (not being navigable at that place), and was used for more than sixty years before 1861 in the manner in which it was used in 1861. This raises a presumption that all the upper proprietors whose rights were injuriously affected by the dam had granted a right to erect it.[1]

(*c*) A borough corporation proved a prescriptive right to a several oyster fishery in a navigable tidal river. The free inhabitants of ancient tenements in the borough proved that from time immemorial and claiming as of right they had dredged for oysters, within the limits of the fishery, from February 2 to Easter Eve in each year. The court presumed a grant from the Crown to the corporation before legal memory of a several fishery, with a condition in it that the free inhabitants of ancient tenements in the borough should enjoy such a right.[2]

(*d*) A builds a windmill near B's land in 1829, and enjoys a free current of air to it over B's land as of right, and without interruption till 1860. This enjoyment raises no presumption of a grant by B of a right to such a current of air, as it would not be natural for B to interrupt it.[3]

(*e*) No length of enjoyment (by means of a deep well), of water percolating through underground undefined passages, raises a presumption of a grant from the owners of the ground under which the water so percolates of a right to the water.[4]

---

[1] *Leconfield* v. *Lonsdale*, L. R. 5 C. P. 657.

[2] *Goodman* v. *Mayor of Saltash*, 6 App. Cas. 633 (see especially 650). Lord Blackburn dissented on the ground that such a grant would not have been legal (pp. 651–662). See same case in 6 Q. B. D. 106, and 5 C. P. D. 431, both of which were reversed.

[3] *Webb* v. *Bird*, 13 C. B. (N. S) 841. [As to the reasons upon which this and the following decision are to be supported, see *Dalton* v. *Angus*, 6 App. Cas. 796, 798, 824. As the English doctrine that a right to light and air can be gained by prescription is generally discarded in this country, the decision in *Webb* v. *Bird* would apply here *a fortiori*. See *Parker* v. *Foote*, 19 Wend. 309; *Gilmore* v. *Driscoll*, 122 Mass. 199, 207.]

[4] *Chasemore* v. *Richards* 7 H. L. C. 349. [*Mayor of Bradford* v. *Pickles*, [1895] A. C. 587; *Chatfield* v. *Wilson*, 28 Vt. 49; *Wilson* v. *New Bedford*, 108 Mass. 265; *Frazier* v. *Brown*, 12 O. St. 294; *Roath* v. *Driscoll*, 20 Ct. 533; *Wheatly* v. *Baugh*, 25 Pa. 528; *Ellis* v. *Duncan*, 21 Barb. 230, 29 N. Y. 466; see *Phelps* v. *Nowlen*, 72 N. Y. 39.]

ARTICLE 101.*

PRESUMPTION OF REGULARITY AND OF DEEDS TO COMPLETE TITLE.

When any judicial or official act is shown to have been done in a manner substantially regular, it is presumed that formal requisites for its validity were complied with.[1]

When a person in possession of any property is shown to be entitled to the beneficial ownership thereof, there is a presumption* that every instrument has been executed which it was the legal duty of his trustees to execute in order to perfect his title.*

---

* See Note XXXVII. [Appendix], and *Macdougall v. Purrier*, 3 Bligh, N. S. 433. *R. v. Cresswell*, 1 Q. B. D. (C. C. R.) 446, is a recent illustration of the effect of this presumption.

---

[1] [*Wood v. Morehouse*, 45 N. Y. 368; *State v. Potter*, 52 Vt. 33; *Mc-Murray's Heirs v. Erie*, 59 Pa. 223; *Nofire v. U. S.*, 164 U. S. 657; *Platt v. Grover*, 136 Mass. 115; *Brownell v. Palmer*, 22 Ct. 107, 119. The maxim in such cases is *Omnia præsumuntur rite esse acta* (Id.; *Schell's Excrs. v. Fauche*, 138 U. S. 562). Thus it is presumed that public officers perform their duty and do not exceed their lawful authority; also that corporations act within their lawful powers, etc. (Id. *Hogue v. Corbitt*, 156 Ill. 540; *State v. Williams*, 99 Mo. 291; *Swarthout v. Ranier*, 143 N. Y. 499, 504; *Sinclair v. Learned*, 51 Mich. 335; *Kent v. Quicksilver Mining Co.*, 78 N. Y. 159, 183; cf. *Murphy v. Chase*, 103 Pa. 260; Gr. Ev. i. §§ 38, n., 40, n.). As to similar presumptions from lapse of time, see Gr. Ev. i. § 20; *Hilton v. Bender*, 69 N. Y. 75.]

* *Doe* d. *Hammond v. Cooke*, 6 Bing. 174, 179. [*Jackson v. Cole*, 4 Cow. 587; *Jackson v. Moore*, 13 Johns. 513; *Lincoln v. French*, 105 N. Y. 614; Perry on Trusts, i. § 349, 4th ed.]

* [Other important presumptions are: (1) That a previously existing personal relation or state of things continues to exist, until the contrary is shown, as *e. g.*, a relation between parties (*Eames v. Eames*, 41 N. H. 177); a law (*Matter of Huss*, 126 N. Y. 537); residence (*Greenfield v. Camden*, 74 Me. 56; *Nixon v Palmer*, 10 Barb. 175); character (*Graham v. Chrystal*, 2 Abb. Dec. 263); habits and personal appearance (*Marston v. Dingley*, 88 Me. 546); insanity, if it be of a fixed and

ARTICLE 102.*

ESTOPPEL BY CONDUCT.

When one person by anything which he does or says, or abstains from doing or saying, intentionally causes ᴏ. permits another person to believe a thing to be true, and to act upon such belief otherwise than but for that belief

---

* See Note XXXVIII. [Appendix].

permanent character, and not simply temporary or occasional (*Taylor* v. *Pegram*, 151 Ill. 107; *Wright* v. *Wright*, 139 Mass. 177; *Wallis* v. *Luhring*, 134 Ind. 447; *People* v. *Lane*, 101 Cal. 513; *State* v. *Hayward*, 62 Minn. 474); status (*Kidder* v. *Stevens*, 60 Cal. 414); and many other matters (Gr. Ev. i. § 41; *Cohoes* v. *D. & H. Canal Co.*, 134 N. Y. 397). The presumption is rebuttable. Its force and duration will be affected by the transient or permanent nature of the subject-matter (*Donahue* v. *Coleman*, 49 Ct. 464; *High* v. *Bk. of Commerce*, 103 Cal. 525, and cases *supra*). It has also been often held that there is a legal presumption that life continues (within the usual limits of human existence) until the contrary is shown, or until the presumption of death attaches under the rule stated in Article 99 (*Stevens* v. *McNamara*, 36 Me. 176; *Shriver* v. *State*, 65 Md. 278; *Montgomery* v. *Bevans*, 1 Sawy. 653); but the modern English and some American authorities regard it as a presumption of fact, to be weighed by the jury with all the evidence in the case bearing upon the probability that life still continues (*In re Phené's Trusts*, L. R. 5 Ch. App. 139; *State* v. *Plym*, 43 Minn. 385; *Comm.* v. *McGrath*, 140 Mass. 296; *Whiteley* v. *Equitable Assur. Soc.*, 72 Wis. 170; see Art. 95, Illustration (*i*), *ante*).

(2) That the regular course of business in a public office or in the course of trade or conduct of affairs is followed (Gr. Ev. i. §§ 38, 40); as *e. g.*, that letters properly mailed reach their destination (see Art. 13, *ante; Austin* v. *Holland*, 69 N. Y. 571); that a bill or note found after circulation in the hands of the acceptor or maker has been paid (*Grimes* v. *Hilliary*, 150 Ill. 141; *Connelly* v. *McKean*, 64 Pa. 113); that a person having the possession of property is the owner (*Rawley* v. *Brown*, 71 N. Y. 85; *Anderson* v. *McCormick*, 129 Ill. 308; *Trevorrow* v. *Trevorrow*, 65 Mich. 234; *McClellan* v. *St. Paul, etc. R. Co.*, 58 Minn. 104). These are disputable presumptions, and are often called presumptions of fact (Id.).

(3) That a man intends the natural and probable consequences of his

he would have acted, neither the person first mentioned nor his representative in interest is allowed, in any suit or proceeding between himself and such person or his

acts (*Filkins* v. *People*, 69 N. Y. 101 ; *State* v. *Patterson*, 116 Mo. 513). The presumption is rebuttable (*Roberts* v. *Buckley*, 145 N. Y. 215).

(4) That, in trials for homicide, malice is to be presumed from the deliberate use of a deadly weapon against another, in the absence of evidence of explanatory circumstances (*Comm.* v. *Hawkins*, 3 Gray, 463 ; *Friederich* v. *People*, 147 Ill. 310 ; *State* v. *Hockett*, 70 Ia. 442 ; *State* v. *Musick*, 101 Mo. 260 ; *Hale* v. *Comm.*, 89 Va. 171, 178 ; *State* v. *Fuller*, 114 N. C. 885 ; *Robinson* v. *State*, 108 Ala. 14 ; *Hawthorne* v. *State*, 58 Miss. 778). The presumption is rebuttable (Id.; *Tiffany* v. *Comm.*, 121 Pa. 165 ; *People* v. *Wolf*, 95 Mich. 625). But in some States such killing with a deadly weapon is simply held to furnish presumptive evidence for the jury of an intent to kill (*Thomas* v. *People*, 67 N. Y. 218 ; *People* v. *Fish*, 125 N. Y. 136 ; *Newport* v. *State*, 140 Ind. 299 ; cf. *State* v. *Earnest*, 56 Kan. 31).

(5) That a wife committing a crime (except treason, murder, and perhaps robbery) in the presence of her husband, acts under his coercion. The presumption is disputable (*People* v. *Ryland*, 97 N. Y. 126 ; *Comm.* v. *Moore*, 162 Mass. 441 ; *State* v. *Shee*, 13 R. I. 535 ; *State* v. *Ma Foo*, 110 Mo. 7). In New York this presumption has been abolished (Penal Code, § 24).

(6) *Omnia præsumuntur contra spoliatorem ;* hence from the destruction, suppression or fabrication of evidence, unfavorable inferences may be drawn, to the disadvantage of the person committing such acts (*Allen* v. *U. S.*, 164 U. S. 492, 500 ; *Simes* v. *Rockwell*, 156 Mass. 373 ; *Eckel* v. *Eckel*, 49 N. J. Eq. 587 ; *Winchell* v. *Edwards*, 57 Ill. 41 ; *In re Lambie*, 97 Mich. 54 ; *Diamond* v. *Henderson*, 47 Wis. 172 ; *Pomeroy* v. *Benton*, 77 Mo. 86). The presumption may be rebutted (Id.; *Drosten* v. *Mueller*, 103 Mo. 624).

(7) From identity of name, identity of person is, in general, presumable (*Aultman* v. *Timm*, 93 Ind. 158 ; *Goodell* v. *Hibbard*, 32 Mich. 47 ; *People* v. *Riley*, 75 Cal. 98 ; cf. *Linck* v. *Litchfield*, 141 Ill. 469); but the contrary may be shown (Id.).

(8) A debt by record or specialty, if unclaimed or unrecognized for twenty years, is, though the Statute of Limitations does not include such debts, presumed to have been paid ; but the presumption may be rebutted (*Barker* v. *Jones*, 62 N. H. 497 ; *Fanton* v. *Middlebrook*, 50 Ct. 44 ; *Gregory* v. *Comm.*, 121 Pa. 611). In some States, however, such debts are now included within the Statute of Limitations. *Walker* v. *Robinson*, 136 Mass. 280 ; *Martin* v. *Stoddard*, 127 N. Y. 61.]

representative in interest, to deny the truth of that thing.[1]

When any person under a legal duty to any other person to conduct himself with reasonable caution in the transaction of any business neglects that duty, and when the person to whom the duty is owing alters his position for the worse because he is misled as to the conduct of the negligent person by a fraud, of which such neglect is in the natural course of things the proximate cause, the negligent person is not permitted to deny that he acted in the manner in which the other person was led by such fraud to believe him to act.[2]

Illustrations.

(a) A, the owner of machinery in B's possession, which is taken in execution by C, abstains from claiming it for some months, and converses with C's attorney without referring to his claim, and by these means impresses C with the belief that the machinery is B's. C sells the machinery. A is estopped from denying that it is B's.[3]

(b) A, a retiring partner of B, gives no notice to the customers of the firm that he is no longer B's partner. In an action by a customer, he cannot deny that he is B's partner.[4]

---

[1] [*Dickerson* v. *Colgrove*, 100 U. S. 578; *Morgan* v. *Railroad Co.*, 96 Id. 716; *Carroll* v. *M. & R. R. Corp.*, 111 Mass. 1; *Chase's Appeal*, 57 Ct. 236; *Andrews* v. *Ætna Ins. Co.*, 85 N. Y. 334; *Union Dime Sav. Inst.* v. *Wilmot*, 94 N. Y. 221; *Mutual Life Ins. Co.* v. *Norris*, 31 N. J. Eq. 583; *Slocumb* v. *Railroad Co.*, 57 Ia. 675; *Stevens* v. *Ludlum*, 46 Minn. 160; *Bates* v. *Swiger*, 40 W. Va. 421.]

[2] [*Putnam* v. *Sullivan*, 4 Mass. 45; *Chapman* v. *Rose*, 56 N. Y. 137; *Ruddell* v. *Fhalor*, 72 Ind. 533; *Ross* v. *Doland*, 29 O. St. 473; *Shirts* v. *Overjohn*, 60 Mo. 305; cf. *Nance* v. *Lary*, 5 Ala. 370; *Nat. Bk.* v. *Zeims*, 93 Ia. 140. An estoppel may be created by silence, when there is a duty and opportunity to speak. *Leather Mfrs. Bk.* v. *Holley*, 117 U. S. 96; *Thompson* v. *Simpson*, 128 N. Y. 270; *O'Mulcahy* v. *Holley*, 28 Minn. 31; *Allen* v. *Shaw*, 61 N. H. 95.]

[3] *Pickard* v. *Sears*, 6 A. & E. 469, 474. [See *Thompson* v. *Blanchard*, 4 N. Y. 303; *Fall Riv. Bk.* v. *Buffinton*, 97 Mass. 500; *Miles* v. *Lefi*, 60 Ia. 168; *Reiss* v. *Hanchett*, 141 Ill. 419; *Putnam* v. *Tyler*, 117 Pa. 570; cf. *Bray* v. *Flickinger*, 69 Ia. 167.]

[4] (Per Parke, B.) *Freeman* v. *Cooke*, 2 Ex. 661. [*Elmira, etc. Co.*

(c) A sues B for a wrongful imprisonment. The imprisonment was wrongful, if B had a certain original warrant; rightful, if he had only a copy. B had in fact a copy. He led A to believe that he had the original, though not with the intention that A should act otherwise than he actually did. B may show that he had only a copy and not the original.[1]

(d) A sells eighty quarters of barley to B, but does not specifically appropriate to B any quarters. B sells sixty of the eighty quarters to C. C informs A, who assents to the transfer. C being satisfied with this, says nothing further to B as to delivery. B becomes bankrupt. A cannot, in an action by C to recover the barley, deny that he holds for C on the ground that, for want of specific appropriation, no property passed to B.[2]

(e) A signs blank cheques and gives them to his wife to fill up as she wants money. A's wife fills up a cheque for £50 2s. so carelessly that room is left for the insertion of figures before the "50" and for the insertion of words before the "fifty." She then gives it to a clerk of A's to get it cashed. He writes 3 before "50" and "three hundred and" before "fifty." A's banker pays the cheque so altered in good faith. A cannot recover against the banker.[3]

---

v. *Harris*, 124 N. Y. 280; *Backus* v. *Taylor*, 84 Ind. 503; *Lovejoy* v. *Spafford*, 93 U. S. 430. So one who has permitted himself to be held out to the world as a partner in a firm is estopped from denying that he is one as against those who have dealt with the firm in the *bona fide* belief that he is a partner. *Fletcher* v. *Pullen*, 70 Md. 205; *Brown* v. *Grant*, 39 Minn. 404.]

[1] *Howard* v. *Hudson*, 2 E. & B. 1. [See *Audenried* v. *Betteley*, 3 Allen, 382.]

[2] *Knights* v. *Wiffen*, L. R. 5 Q. B. 660. [See Kent's Comm. iii. 85, note 1 (14th ed.); *Barnard* v. *Campbell*, 55 N. Y. 456; *Anderson* v. *Read*, 106 N. Y. 333, 353.]

[3] *Young* v. *Grote*, 4 Bing. 253. [This case has been much considered of late and its authority is carefully limited to its special facts (*Greenfield Sav. Bk.* v. *Stowell*, 123 Mass. 196; *Lehman* v. *Central R. Co.*, 12 F. R. 595; *McGrath* v. *Clark*, 56 N. Y. 34; *Holmes* v. *Trumper*, 22 Mich. 427; cf. *Leas* v. *Walls*, 101 Pa. 57; *Yocum* v. *Smith*, 63 Ill. 321; *Belknap* v. *Nat. Bk. of N. America*, 100 Mass. 376; *Crawford* v. *West Side Bk.*, 100 N. Y. 50). In a recent English case it is shown to be doubtful on what ground *Young* v. *Grote* was decided, whether on the theory of estoppel arising out of the special duty of a customer to protect his banker against danger from "raised" checks,

(*f*) A railway company negligently issues two delivery orders for the same wheat to A, who fraudulently raises money from B as upon two consignments of different lots of wheat. The railway is liable to B for the amount which A fraudulently obtained by the company's negligence.[1]

(*g*) A carelessly leaves his door unlocked, whereby his goods are stolen. He is not estopped from denying the title of an innocent purchaser from the thief.[2]

ARTICLE 103.

ESTOPPEL OF TENANT AND LICENSEE.

No tenant, and no person claiming through any tenant, of any land or hereditament of which he has been let into possession, or for which he has paid rent, is, till he has given up possession, permitted to deny that the landlord had, at the time when the tenant was let into possession or paid the rent, a title to such land or hereditament;[3]

---

or on the ground that any one who signs a blank check authorizes the person in whose hands it is to fill it up as his agent (*Scholfield* v. *Earl of Londesborough*, [1896] A. C. 514; see p. 218, n. 2, *ante*). In this recent case and in similar American cases the sum stated in a bill or note was increased by the filling in of unwritten spaces by a forger, but the acceptor or maker was held not liable. The proximate cause of loss to the purchaser of the bill or note was the forgery. *Burrows* v. *Klunk*, 70 Md. 451; *Knoxville Nat. Bk.* v. *Clark*, 51 Ia. 264; *Simmons* v. *Atkinson*, 69 Miss. 862; and cases *supra*.]

[1] *Coventry* v. *Gt. Eastern Ry. Co.*, 11 Q. B. D. 776.

[2] Per Blackburn, J., in *Swan* v. *N. B. Australasian Co.*, 2 H. & C. 181. See *Baxendale* v. *Bennett*, 3 Q. B. D. 525. The earlier cases on the subject are much discussed in *Jorden* v. *Money*, 5 H. & C. 209-16, 234-5. [Cf. *People* v. *Bank N. America*, 75 N. Y. 547; *Lowery* v. *Telegraph Co.*, 60 N. Y. 198; *Knox* v. *Eden Musée Co.*, 148 N. Y. 441; *Dist. of Columbia* v. *Cornell*, 130 U. S. 655; *Zell's Appeal*, 103 Pa. 344.]

[3] *Doe* v. *Barton*, 11 A. & E. 307; *Doe* v. *Smyth*, 4 M. & S. 347; *Doe* v. *Pegg*, 1 T. R. 760, note. [*Stott* v. *Rutherford*, 92 U. S. 107; *Prevot* v. *Lawrence*, 51 N. Y. 219; *Tilyou* v. *Reynolds*, 108 N. Y. 558; *Streeter* v. *Ilsley*, 147 Mass. 141; *Sexton* v. *Carley*, 147 Ill. 269; *Derrick* v. *Luddy*, 64 Vt. 462; Washb. R. P. i. 588-601, 5th ed.; cf. *Robertson* v.

and no person who came upon any land by the license of the person in possession thereof, is, whilst he remains on it, permitted to deny that such person had a title to such possession at the time when such license was given.[1]

ARTICLE 104.

ESTOPPEL OF ACCEPTOR OF BILL OF EXCHANGE.

No acceptor of a bill of exchange is permitted to deny the signature of the drawer or his capacity to draw, or if the bill is payable to the order of the drawer, his capacity to indorse the bill, though he may deny the fact of the indorsement;[2] nor if the bill be drawn by procuration, the authority of the agent, by whom it purports to be drawn, to draw in the name of the principal,[3] though he may deny his authority to indorse it.[4] If the bill is accepted in blank, the acceptor may not deny the fact that the drawer indorsed it.[5]

ARTICLE 105.

ESTOPPEL OF BAILEE, AGENT, AND LICENSEE.

No bailee, agent, or licensee is permitted to deny that the bailor, principal, or licensor, by whom any goods were

---

Pickrell, 109 U. S. 608. As to the limitations of the doctrine, see *Corrigan* v. *Chicago*, 144 Ill. 537.]

[1] *Doe* v. *Baytup*, 3 A. & E. 188. [*Glynn* v. *George*, 20 N. H. 114; *Hamilton, etc., Co.* v. *Railroad Co.*, 29 O. St. 341.]

[2] *Garland* v. *Jacomb*, L. R. 8 Ex. 216. [*White* v. *Continental Nat. Bk.*, 64 N. Y. 316; *Marine Nat. Bk.* v. *Nat. City Bk.*, 59 N. Y. 67; *Hoffman* v. *Bank of Milwaukee*, 12 Wall. 181; *National Bank* v. *Bangs*, 106 Mass. 441. See as to this whole Article, Daniel Neg. Inst. i. §§ 532–541.]

[3] *Sanderson* v. *Coleman*, 4 M. & G. 209.

[4] *Robinson* v. *Yarrow*, 7 Tau. 455.

[5] *L. & S. W. Bank* v. *Wentworth*, 5 Ex. D. 96. [In this case the

entrusted to any of them respectively, was entitled to those goods at the time when they were so entrusted.[1]

Provided that any such bailee, agent, or licensee, may show that he was compelled to deliver up any such goods to some person who had a right to them as against his bailor, principal, or licensor, or that his bailor, principal, or licensor, wrongfully and without notice to the bailee, agent, or licensee, obtained the goods from a third person who has claimed them from such bailee, agent, or licensee.[2]

Every bill of lading in the hands of a consignee or indorsee for valuable consideration, representing goods to have been shipped on board a vessel, is conclusive proof of that shipment as against the master or other person signing the same, notwithstanding that such goods or some part thereof may not have been so shipped, unless such holder of the bill of lading had actual notice at the time of receiving the same that the goods had not been in fact laden on board, provided that the master or other person so signing may exonerate himself in respect of such misrepresentation by showing that it was caused without any default on his part, and wholly by the fraud

---

drawer's signature and the indorsement were written upon the bill after it had been accepted in blank. "The blank acceptance is an acceptance of the bill which is afterwards put upon it." *Schultz* v. *Astley*, 2 Bing. N. C. 544; cf. *Weyerhauser* v. *Dun*, 100 N. Y. 150.]

[1] [*Sinclair* v. *Murphy*, 14 Mich. 392; *Osgood* v. *Nichols*, 5 Gray, 420; *Roberts* v. *Noyes*, 76 Me. 590; *Bricker* v. *Stroud*, 56 Mo. App. 183; cf. *Jackson* v. *Allen*, 120 Mass. 64, 79.]

[2] *Dixon* v. *Hammond*, 2 B. & A. 313; *Crossley* v. *Dixon*, 10 H. L. C. 293; *Gosling* v. *Birnie*, 7 Bing. 339; *Hardman* v. *Wilcock*, 9 Bing. 382; *Biddle* v. *Bond*, 34 L. J. Q. B. 137, [6 B. & S. 225]; *Wilson* v. *Anderton*, 1 B. & Ad. 450. As to carriers, see *Sheridan* v. *New Quay*, 4 C. B. (N. S.) 618. [*The Idaho*, 93 U. S. 575; *Western Trans. Co.* v. *Barber*, 56 N. Y. 544; *King* v. *Richards*, 6 Whart. 418; *Roberts* v. *Noyes*, 76 Me. 590; *Dusky* v. *Rudder*, 80 Mo. 400; *Singer Mfg. Co.* v. *King*, 14 R. I. 511.]

of the shipper or of the holder, or some person under
whom the holder holds.[1]

---

[1] 18 & 19 Vict. c. 111, s. 3. [But it is held that a *ship-owner* is not
estopped by the signature of a bill of lading by the master from showing that the goods or some of them were never actually put on board.
Brown v. *Powell Co.*, L. R. 10 C. P. 562; *Cox* v. *Bruce*, 18 Q. B. D.
147; see *McLean* v. *Fleming*, L. R. 2 Sc. App. 128.

The law of this country is not governed by statutes like the above.
The general rules here in force are stated in *Sears* v. *Wingate*, 3 Allen,
103: "(1) The receipt in a bill of lading is open to explanation between the master and the shipper of the goods. (2) The master is estopped, as against a consignee who is not a party to the contract and
as against an assignee of the bill of lading, when either has taken it
for a valuable consideration upon the faith of the acknowledgments
which it contains, to deny the truth of the statements to which he has
given credit by his signature, so far as those statements relate to matters which are or ought to be within his knowledge. (3) When the
master is acting within the limits of his authority, the owners are estopped in like manner with him; but it is not within the general scope
of the master's authority to sign bills of lading for any goods not actually received on board." There is, however, a noteworthy difference
of opinion in regard to the rule stated in this last sentence. In the
U. S. Supreme Court and in a number of the States this rule is adopted,
and it is held that if the master does sign a bill of lading for goods
not actually received on board, his act does not bind the owner of the
ship even in favor of an innocent purchaser (*Pollard* v. *Vinton*, 105
U. S. 7; *Nat. Bk. of Commerce* v. *Chicago, etc. R. Co.*, 44 Minn. 224;
Balt. & O. R. Co. v. *Wilkens*, 44 Md. 11; *Dean* v. *King*, 22 O. St.
118; *La. Nat. Bk.* v. *Laveille*, 52 Mo. 380). But in New York and
some other States, if the master acts within his apparent authority
in such a case, the owner is held bound by his act on the ground of
estoppel (*Bk. of Batavia* v. *N. Y. etc. R. Co.*, 106 N. Y. 195; *Brooke*
v. *N. Y. etc. R. Co.*, 108 Pa. 529; *Sioux City, etc. R. Co.* v. *First Nat.
Bk.*, 10 Neb. 556; *Sav. Bk.* v. *Atchison, etc. R. Co.*, 20 Kan. 519; cf.
Hanover Bk. v. *Amer. Dock Co.*, 148 N. Y. 612). These same rules
are applied to the bills of lading of railroad companies. Id.; *Fried-
lander* v. *Texas, etc. R. Co.*, 130 U. S. 416.]

CHAPTER XV.

OF THE COMPETENCY OF WITNESSES. *

ARTICLE 106.

WHO MAY TESTIFY.

ALL persons are competent to testify in all cases except
as hereinafter excepted.[1]

---

* See Note XXXIX. [Appendix].

[1] [The common law rules disqualifying *parties* and *persons interested
in the event of the suit* from being witnesses are now almost univer-
sally abolished (see N. Y. Code Civ. Pro. § 828; U. S. Rev. St. § 858;
Mass. Pub. St. c. 169, s. 18; and generally the statutes of the different
States), though the interest of a witness may still be shown to affect
his credibility (*Pennsylvania Co.* v. *Versten*, 140 Ill. 637; *Will of Snelling*, 136 N. Y. 515; *Norwood* v. *Andrews*, 71 Miss. 641). But there is
established by statute in the several States one important exception,
prohibiting a party or interested person from testifying in an action
against an executor or administrator concerning a transaction with the
decedent. These statutes differ in details, but their general features
may be well illustrated by the law of New York. This provides that,
in a civil action or special proceeding, a *party* or *person interested in
the event* (or a predecessor of such person) shall not be examined as
a witness *in his own behalf or interest* (or in behalf of his successor in
interest), against the *executor, administrator,* or *survivor* of a deceased
person, or the *committee* of a lunatic (or the successor in interest of
such decedent or lunatic), concerning *a personal transaction or communication* between the witness and the decedent or lunatic. Such testimony is, however, receivable if the executor, etc., is examined in his
own behalf, or if the former testimony of the decedent or lunatic concerning the same transaction, etc., is given in evidence (N. Y. Code
Civ. Pro. § 829; *Rogers* v. *Rogers*, 153 N. Y. 343). The intention of the
statute is that the surviving party to the transaction shall not have the
unfair advantage of giving his version of the matter when the other
party is prevented by death from being heard to contradict or explain

ARTICLE 107.

WHAT WITNESSES ARE INCOMPETENT.[1]

A witness is incompetent if in the opinion of the judge he is prevented by extreme youth, disease affecting his mind, or any other cause of the same kind, from recollecting the matter on which he is to testify, from understanding the questions put to him, from giving rational answers

---

it (*Card* v. *Card*, 39 N. Y. 317). Thus in an action by an attorney against the executor of a deceased person to recover for legal services rendered to the decedent, the plaintiff cannot be a witness and testify as to advice given by him to the decedent (*Brague* v. *Lord*, 67 N. Y. 495); so in proceedings for the probate of a will, a legatee under the will may not testify as to personal transactions with the testator (*Matter of Eysaman*, 113 N. Y. 62). "Personal transaction or communication" is defined in *Heyne* v. *Doerfler*, 124 N. Y. 505, and "interest" in *Connelly* v. *O'Connor*, 117 N. Y. 91; see also *Eisenlord* v. *Clum*, 126 N. Y. 552. A release of one's interest may make him a competent witness (*Matter of Wilson*, 103 N. Y. 374).

The law of Congress is that in an action by or against an executor, etc., neither party shall testify against the other as to transactions with the decedent, unless called to testify thereto by the opposite party or required to do so by the court (U. S. Rev. St. § 858; *Potter* v. *National Bank*, 102 U. S. 163). As to the law of other States, see Gr. Ev. i. § 329, 15th ed.; *English* v. *Porter*, 63 N. H. 206; *Rowland* v. *Phila. etc. R. Co.*, 63 Ct. 415; *Woolverton* v. *Van Syckel*, 57 N. J. L. 393; *Stauffer* v. *Ins. Ass'n*, 164 Pa. 205; *Thomas* v. *Miller*, 165 Pa. 216; *Webster* v. *Le Compte*, 74 Md. 249; *Barker* v. *Hebbard*, 81 Mich. 267; *Williams* v. *Edwards*, 94 Mo. 447.

There is a special rule in some States that a party to a negotiable instrument (as an indorser) cannot be a witness to prove that it was invalid in its inception (as for usury) to the prejudice of an innocent holder for value before maturity (*Smith* v. *McGlinchy*, 77 Me. 153; *Davis* v. *Brown*, 94 U. S. 423; *John's Admr.* v. *Pardee*, 109 Pa. 545; cf. *Jones* v. *Matthews*, 8 Lea, 84); but in most States such testimony is admissible. Gr. Ev. i. §§ 383-385; *Haines* v. *Dennett*, 11 N. H. 180; *Pecker* v. *Sawyer*, 24 Vt. 459; *Williams* v. *Walbridge*, 3 Wend. 415.]

[1] See Note XL. [Appendix]. A witness under sentence of death was said to be incompetent in *R.* v. *Webb*, 11 Cox, 133, *sed quære*.

·to those questions, or from knowing that he ought to speak the truth.[1]

A witness unable to speak or hear is not incompetent, but may give his evidence by writing or by signs, or in any other manner in which he can make it intelligible; but such writing must be written and such signs made in open court.[2] Evidence so given is deemed to be oral evidence.[3]

---

[1] [In the following cases children were deemed competent under this rule and were allowed to testify (*Wheeler* v. *U. S.,* 159 U. S. 523 (child five years of age); *Comm.* v. *Robinson*, 165 Mass. 426 (five years and nine months); *People* v. *Linzey*, 79 Hun, 23 (ten years); *Draper* v. *Draper*, 68 Ill. 17 (ten years); *McGuire* v. *People*, 44 Mich. 286 (six years); *State* v. *Juneau*, 88 Wis. 180 (five years); *State* v. *Levy*, 23 Minn. 104 (eight years); *State* v. *Doyle*, 107 Mo. 36 (nine years); *State* v. *Douglas*, 53 Kan. 669 (nine years); *McGuff* v. *State*, 88 Ala. 147 (seven years); see Illustrations (*a*) and (*b*)). In some States, by statute, children may be allowed to testify in special cases without taking an oath (N. Y. Code Cr. Pro., § 392; *Hughes* v. *Detroit, etc. R. Co.*, 65 Mich. 16; cf. *White* v. *Comm.*, 96 Ky. 180).

Persons of unsound mind may also testify, if they can appreciate the obligation of an oath and have sufficient understanding to give intelligent and reliable answers. The jury may consider their mental condition as affecting their credibility (Illustration (*c*); Gr. Ev. i. § 365; *District of Columbia* v. *Armes*, 107 U. S. 519; *People* v. *N. Y. Hospital*, 3 Abb. N. C. 229; *Livingston* v. *Kriersted*, 10 Johns. 362; *Pease* v. *Burrowes*, 86 Me. 153; *Kendall* v. *May*, 10 Allen, 59; *Holcomb* v. *Holcomb*, 28 Ct. 177; *Coleman* v. *Comm.*, 25 Gratt. 865; *Tucker* v. *Shaw*, 158 Ill. 326; *Bowdle* v. *Railway Co.*, 103 Mich. 272; *Cannaday* v. *Lynch*, 27 Minn. 435; *Worthington* v. *Mencer*, 96 Ala. 310). The same general rules apply to intoxicated persons. *Hartford* v. *Palmer*, 16 Johns. 143; *Gould* v. *Crawford*, 2 Pa. 89; cf. *State* v. *Costello*, 62 Ia. 404.]

[2] [Gr. Ev. i. § 366; Wh. Ev. i. §§ 406, 407; *Queen* v. *Halbert*, 55 Vt. 224, 57 Vt. 178; *Skaggs* v. *State*, 108 Ind. 53; *State* v. *Howard*, 118 Mo. 127; *State* v. *Weldon*, 39 S. Car. 318.]

[3] [Persons not believing in the existence of a God who will punish false swearing are also incompetent witnesses by common law (*Blair* v. *Seaver*, 26 Pa. 274; *People* v. *Matteson*, 2 Cow. 433; *Free* v. *Buckingham*, 59 N. H. 219; *Arnd* v. *Amling*, 53 Md. 192; *Clinton* v. *State*, 33 O. St. 27; *Attorney Gen'l* v. *Bradlaugh*, 14 Q. B. D. 667). But this

Illustrations.

(*a*) [Upon a criminal trial a girl thirteen years old was offered as a witness for the prosecution. The defendant objected to the administration of an oath to her, on the ground that she was ignorant of the nature and obligation of an oath. The judge asked her some questions, to which she replied that she understood that the oath was to tell the truth, and that she would be punished if she did not tell the truth after taking it, but that she did not know how or by whom she would

---

disqualification has been removed in many States or rendered less stringent (Gr. Ev. i. §§ 368–371; Wh. Ev. i. §§ 395, 396; *Percey* v. *Powers,* 51 N. J. L. 432; *Hronek* v. *People,* 134 Ill. 139; *Londener* v. *Lichtenheim,* 11 Mo. App. 385; *People* v. *Copsey,* 71 Cal. 548; *Bush* v. *Comm.,* 80 Ky. 244). But in some States, where atheism no longer disqualifies, it may nevertheless be shown to affect the witness's credit (*Stanbro* v. *Hopkins,* 28 Barb. 265; *Searcy* v. *Miller,* 57 Ia. 613). It is the general rule, however, that the witness must not himself be examined as to his religious belief (see all the cases; *Dedric* v. *Hopson,* 62 Ia. 562).

Infamous persons, *i. e.,* persons convicted of treason, felony, or the *crimen falsi,* are also incompetent witnesses at common law in the State of their conviction. The *crimen falsi* includes, in general, offences tending to pervert the administration of justice through falsehood and fraud, as *e. g.,* perjury, forgery, bribery of witnesses, etc. (Gr. Ev. i. §§ 372–376; Wh. Ev. i. § 397; *Schuylkill Co.* v. *Copley,* 67 Pa. 386; *State* v. *Randolph,* 24 Ct. 363; *Benton* v. *Comm.,* 89 Va. 570; *Sylvester* v. *State,* 71 Ala. 17; *State* v. *Mullen,* 33 La. Ann. 159). This disability may be removed by a reversal of the judgment or by a full pardon (*Boyd* v. *U. S.,* 142 U. S. 450; *Diehl* v. *Rodgers,* 169 Pa. 316; *Perkins* v. *Stevens,* 24 Pick. 277; *Werner* v. *State,* 44 Ark. 122; *Carr* v. *State,* 19 Tex. App. 635), though, in case of a pardon, it has been held that the conviction may still be shown to affect credibility (*Curtis* v. *Cochran,* 50 N. H. 242). Conviction of an infamous crime by courts in other States, it is generally held, does not disqualify (Gr. Ev. i. §§ 376–378; *Logan* v. *U. S.,* 144 U. S. 263; *Sims* v. *Sims,* 75 N. Y. 466; cf. *Pitner* v. *State,* 23 Tex. App. 366). Now, in most States, under modern statutes, infamy no longer disqualifies, though it may be proved to affect credibility (Wh. Ev. i. § 397; N. Y. Code Civ. Pro. § 832; Mass. Pub. St. c. 169, s. 19; *Quigley* v. *Turner,* 150 Mass. 108; *Card* v. *Foot,* 57 Ct. 427; *People* v. *O'Neil,* 109 N. Y. 251; *Matter of Noble,* 124 Ill. 266; *State* v. *Loehr,* 93 Mo. 103; *Sutton* v. *Fox,* 55 Wis. 531; see Art. 130, *post,* note). In some States, also, conviction for a non-infamous

be punished. As the district attorney did not care to call her then, the judge said he would postpone the decision of her competency, and she could be instructed if necessary. The next day she was offered again, and it appeared that in the meantime she had been instructed by a Christian minister. She testified that the minister told her that God would punish her if, after taking the oath, she testified what was not true, and that she did not know that before. The judge decided that she was a competent witness and her testimony was properly received.][1]

(*b*) [A girl nine years old was offered as a witness, and being questioned said that she did not know what the Bible was; had never been to church but once and that was to her mother's funeral; did not know what book it was she laid her hand on when sworn; had heard tell of God, but did not know who it was; and that, if she swore to a lie, she would be put in jail, but did not know that she would be punished in any other way. It was held that she was not a competent witness.][2]

(*c*) [Upon a trial for manslaughter for the killing of a lunatic patient in an insane asylum, A, another lunatic patient, was offered as a witness for the prosecution. Officers of the asylum testified that A was under a delusion that he had a number of spirits about him which were continually talking to him, but that they had found him perfectly rational except for this delusion, and that they believed him to be

---

crime may be shown to affect credibility (*State* v. *Watson*, 63 Me. 128; *Comm.* v. *Ford*, 146 Mass. 131; *People* v. *Burns*, 33 Hun, 296; *State* v. *Sauer*, 42 Minn. 258), but not in other States (*Card* v. *Foot*, 57 Ct. 427; *Coble* v. *State*, 31 O. St. 100; *Bartholomew* v. *People*, 104 Ill. 601 (criminal cases); *Hanners* v. *McClelland*, 74 Ia. 318; *State* v. *Donelly*, 130 Mo. 642). There are a few States, moreover, in which conviction for perjury or subornation of perjury is declared by statute to render a witness incompetent. Gr. Ev. i. § 372, note, 15th ed.]

[1] [*Comm.* v. *Lynes*, 142 Mass. 577; S. P. *Day* v. *Day*, 56 N. H. 316 (ten years old); *R.* v. *Baylis*, 4 Cox, 23. But the contrary rule has also been asserted, viz., that it is improper to privately instruct a child and thus render it a competent witness. *Taylor* v. *State*, 22 Tex. App. 529.]

[2] [*Carter* v. *State*, 63 Ala. 52; similar cases are *McKelton* v. *State*, 88 Ala. 181 (thirteen years old); *Beason* v. *State*, 72 Ala. 191 (eleven years); *Adams* v. *State*, 34 Fla. 185 (five years); *State* v. *Belton*, 24 S. Car. 185 (twelve years); *Holst* v. *State*, 23 Tex. App. 1 (seven years); *State* v. *Michael*, 37 W. Va. 565 (five years); *Jones* v. *People*, 6 Park. Cr. 126 (nine years).]

quite capable of giving an account of any transaction that happened
before his eyes. A, being then examined, said: "I am fully aware
that I have a spirit and twenty thousand of them; they are not all
mine. . . . Those ascend from my stomach to my head and also
those in my ears; the flesh creates spirits by the palpitation of the
nerves and the rheumatics; all are now in my body, and round my
head; they speak to me incessantly,—particularly at night; . . . they
are now speaking to me; they are not separate from me; but I can't
be a spirit, for I am flesh and blood. . . . I know what it is to
take an oath; my catechism taught me from my infancy when it is
lawful to swear; it is when God's honor, our own or our neighbor's
good, require it. . . . When I swear, I appeal to the Almighty; it is
perjury, the breaking a lawful oath or taking an unlawful one; he that
does it will go to hell for all eternity." He was then sworn, and gave
a perfectly connected and rational account of a transaction which he
reported himself to have witnessed. It was held on appeal that his
testimony was properly received.][1]

ARTICLE 108.*

COMPETENCY IN CRIMINAL CASES.

In criminal cases the accused person and his or her
wife or husband, and every person and the wife or husband of every person jointly indicted with him and tried
at the same time,[2] is incompetent[3] to testify.[4]

Provided that in any criminal proceeding against a

---

* See Note XLI. [Appendix].

[1] [R. v. Hill, 2 Den. C. C. 254; see District of Columbia v. Armes,
107 U. S. 519.]

[2] Not if they are tried separately; Winsor v. R., L. R. 1 Q B. 390;
Re Bradlaugh, 15 Cox, 217. [See p. 276, note.]

[3] R. v. Payne, L. R. 1 C. C. R. 349, and R. v. Thompson, Id. 377.

[4] [The general rules of the common law, stated in this Article, are
still in force in the different States, unless abolished or modified by
statute (Gr. Ev. i. §§ 330, 334-346, 362; Wh. Cr. Ev. §§ 390-402, 427;
Hiler v. People, 156 Ill. 511; Holley v. State, 105 Ala. 100; Holman v.
State, 72 Miss. 108; State v. Pain, 48 La. Ann. 311). But if a co-
defendant be discharged from the record, as by the entry of a nolle

husband or wife for any bodily injury or violence inflicted

---

prosequi, or by an acquittal, he may be a witness upon the trial of the others (Gr. Ev. i. § 363; Wh. Cr. Ev. § 445; *Linsday v. People*, 63 N. Y. 143; *Love v. People*, 160 Ill. 501; *State v. Walker*, 98 Mo. 95); so if he be convicted, or plead guilty, but be not yet sentenced (*State v. Minor*, 117 Mo. 302; *Brown v. Comm.*, 86 Va. 935; contra, *Kehoe v. Comm.*, 85 Pa. 127), or even after sentence, if he is not thereby rendered infamous (*State v. Jones*, 51 Me. 125); so if, though jointly indicted with the others, he is to have a separate trial (*Benson v. U. S.*, 146 U. S. 325; *Noyes v. State*, 41 N. J. L. 418; *State v. Bogue*, 52 Kan. 79; *Smith v. Comm.*, 90 Va. 759; *Allen v. State*, 10 O. St. 287; cf. *State v. Chiagk*, 92 Mo. 395; *People v. Van Alstine*, 57 Mich. 69; *Adams v. State*, 28 Fla. 511; contra, *Staup v. Comm.*, 74 Pa. 458).

Husband or wife may testify, by common law, as to assault and battery upon him or her by the other, or an attempt to murder, and the like (*People v. Northrup*, 50 Barb. 147; *State v. Pennington*, 124 Mo. 388; *Comm. v. Sapp*, 90 Ky. 580; *Johnson v. State*, 94 Ala. 53; for a further exception, see page 298, note 2). So if either spouse be a co-defendant with other persons and be discharged from the record, as by a *nolle prosequi*, a plea of guilty, etc., the other spouse is a competent witness on the trial of the rest (*Love v. People*, 160 Ill. 501; *State v. Miller*, 100 Mo. 606; *State v. Guest*, 100 N. C. 410; *Woods v. State*, 76 Ala. 35; *Carr v. State*, 42 Ark. 204).

But it is now provided by the laws of Congress and by the statutes of many States, that the defendant in a criminal case may be a witness in his own behalf, though the qualification is generally added that his failure to testify shall not create any presumption against him; so comment by the prosecuting officer upon such failure to testify is often prohibited by these statutes (Act of Congress, Mar. 16, 1878; N. Y. Code Cr. Pro. § 393; Mass. Pub. St. c. 169, s. 18, par. 3; Wh. Cr. Ev. §§ 428-436; *Wilson v. U. S.*, 149 U. S. 60; *Comm. v. Scott*, 123 Mass. 239; *People v. Hayes*, 140 N. Y. 484; *Showalter v. State*, 84 Ind. 562; *Watt v. People*, 126 Ill. 9; *People v. Sansome*, 98 Cal. 235; *Yarbrough v. State*, 70 Miss. 593); if, however, defendant does testify, the jury may consider his interest in the result of the trial as affecting his credibility (*Reagan v. U. S.*, 157 U. S. 301; *People v. Crowley*, 102 N. Y. 234; *Doyle v. People*, 147 Ill. 394; *State v. Pratt*, 121 Mo. 566). So by the statutes of some States, persons jointly indicted may be witnesses for or against each other (*People v. Dowling*, 84 N. Y. 478; *Comm. v. Brown*, 130 Mass. 279; *Conway v. State*, 118 Ind. 482; *State v. Smith*, 86 N. C. 705; *Kidwell v. Comm.*, 97 Ky. 538; Wh. Cr. Ev. § 445); or the husband or wife of the defendant may be

upon his or her wife or husband,[1] such wife or husband is
competent and compellable to testify.[2]

<h2 style="text-align:center">ARTICLE 109.</h2>

[HUSBAND AND WIFE IN CIVIL CASES—CASES OF ADULTERY.]

[In civil cases the lawful husband or wife of a party, or
of a person whose interests are directly involved in the
suit, is an incompetent witness by the common law.[3] And
even after the marriage is dissolved by the death of

---

a witness, except to disclose confidential communications (N. Y. Pen.
Code, § 715; Me. Rev. St. c. 134, s. 19; Md., Laws of 1888, c. 545, s. 3).
By some statutes husbands and wives may not testify against each
other in criminal cases except for a crime committed by one against
the other. Some States hold that not only criminal acts of violence,
but also adultery, bigamy, and incest are crimes against the other
(*State* v. *Chambers*, 87 Ia. 1; *Lord* v. *State*, 17 Neb. 526; cf. *Jordan*
v. *State*, 142 Ind. 422; *Dill* v. *People*, 19 Col. 469); but other decisions
are to the contrary (*Bassett* v. *U. S.*, 137 U. S. 496; *People* v.
Quanstrom, 93 Mich. 254; *McLean* v. *State*, 32 Tex. App. 521). Again,
in some States each spouse may be for certain purposes a witness, if
the other consent (*People* v. *Gordon*, 100 Mich. 518; *State* v. *Willis*,
119 Mo. 485), or is declared competent, but not compellable, to testify
against the other (*Comm.* v. *Moore*, 162 Mass. 441; *State* v. *McCord*,
8 Kan. 232); and there are also other special statutory rules. See the
statutes of the different States.]

[1] *Reeve* v. *Wood*, 5 B. & S. 364. Treason has been also supposed to
form an exception. See T. E. s. 1237.

[2] [At this point Mr. Stephen adds to this Article certain English
statutory qualifications, and also inserts Articles 108 A and 108 B, sum-
marizing the provisions of special English statutes, which provide
that accused persons, and their husbands or wives, may be witnesses in
trials for particular criminal offences. These provisions, as stated
by Mr. Stephen, will be found in the Appendix, Note LII.]

[3] [Gr. Ev. i. §§ 334-346; *Banister* v. *Ovit*, 64 Vt. 480; *Johnson* v.
Fry, 88 Va. 695; *Craig* v. *Miller*, 133 Ill. 300; *Carney* v. *Gleissner*,
58 Wis. 674; *Joice* v. *Branson*, 73 Mo. 28; *Leahy* v. *Leahy*, 97 Ky. 59.
So a wife cannot testify for or against a co-defendant tried with her
husband, where her testimony would concern her husband or affect

either party or by divorce, neither party thereto can testify as to the facts learned through the confidence of the marital relation, but may as to other facts.¹ These rules apply to proceedings instituted in consequence of adultery² as well as to other civil cases.]³

---

his interests (Gr. Ev. i. § 335; *Cornelius* v. *Hambay*, 150 Pa. 364). But in collateral proceedings, not immediately affecting their mutual interests, the testimony of husband or wife may be received, though tending indirectly to criminate the other. Gr. Ev. i. § 342; *Keep* v. *Griggs*, 12 Ill. App. 511; see *post*, page 298, note 2.]

¹ [*French* v. *Ware*, 65 Vt. 338; *Bigelow* v. *Sickles*, 75 Wis. 427; *Toovey* v. *Baxter*, 59 Mo. App. 470; *Lingreen* v. *Ill. Cent. R. Co.*, 61 Ill. App. 174; *Babcock* v. *Booth*, 2 Hill, 181; *Dickerman* v. *Graves*, 6 Cush. 308; *Robb's Appeal*, 98 Pa. 501; *Wottrich* v. *Freeman*, 71 N. Y. 601; Bishop, M. D. & S. ii. §§ 1662–1665; but see *Rea* v. *Tucker*, 51 Ill. 110; *Hanselman* v. *Dovel*, 102 Mich. 505; *Swan* v. *Housman*, 90 Va. 816. The same rule has been applied in criminal cases. *U. S.* v. *Guiteau*, 1 Mackey, 498; *Comm.* v. *Sapp*, 90 Ky. 580; cf. *Owen* v. *State*, 78 Ala. 425.]

² [Id. For a special rule in bastardy cases, see Art. 98, *ante*. The common law rules, stated in this Article, are still in force in the different States, unless changed by statute.]

³ [The original article of Mr. Stephen, stating the present English law, is as follows:

"COMPETENCY IN PROCEEDINGS RELATING TO ADULTERY.

"In proceedings instituted in consequence of adultery, the parties and their husbands and wives are competent witnesses, provided that no witness in any (such?) proceeding, whether a party to the suit or not, is liable to be asked or bound to answer any question tending to show that he or she has been guilty of adultery, unless such witness has already given evidence in the same proceeding in disproof of his or her alleged adultery. 32 & 33 Vict. c. 68, s. 3. (The word 'such' seems to have been omitted accidentally.)"

In this country also, by modern statutes, husband and wife are in many States allowed to testify for or against each other in civil actions, but special limitations are sometimes imposed in cases grounded upon adultery. Thus in New York, husband or wife cannot testify against the other in proceedings founded upon an allegation of adultery, except to prove the marriage or disprove the allegation of adultery; and in an action for criminal conversation plaintiff's wife cannot testify for him, but may for the defendant, except that she

ARTICLE 110.

COMMUNICATIONS DURING MARRIAGE.

No husband is compellable to disclose any communication made to him by his wife during the marriage, and no wife is compellable to disclose any communication made to her by her husband during the marriage.[1]

cannot disclose confidential communications between herself and her husband without his consent (Code Civ. Pro. § 831). In other cases they may testify, but neither can disclose confidential communications without the consent of the other, if living (Id. §§ 828, 831). Similar provisions are in force in several other States (Ind. Rev. St. §§ 505, 509; 3 How. St. (Mich.) § 7546; Wis. Rev. St. § 4072; Code of N. C. § 588). In New Jersey husband and wife may testify in civil actions generally, including proceedings for divorce on account of adultery, except as to confidential communications (N. J. Rev. i. p. 378; ii. p. 288; *Lippincott* v. *Wikoff*, 54 N. J. Eq. 107; cf. Br. Purd. Dig. (Pa.) 12th ed. i. p. 817). So in Massachusetts they may testify, except as to private conversations with each other (Pub. St. c. 169, § 18). It is a special provision of some statutes that either spouse, having acted as agent for the other, may testify as to such transactions as agent (*Pfeferle* v. *State*, 39 Kan. 128; *Reno* v. *Kingsbury*, 39 Mo. App. 240; Ill. Rev. St. c. 51, s. 5). So the right of either to testify is sometimes made to depend upon the other's consent (*Wolford* v. *Farnham*, 44 Minn. 159; 3 How. St. (Mich.) § 7546; Cal. Code Civ. Pro. § 1881). The statutes of the different States have many diverse provisions, and should be specially consulted (see *Spitz's Appeal*, 56 Ct. 184; *Bitner* v. *Boone*, 128 Pa. 567; *Reynolds* v. *Schaffer*, 91 Mich. 494; *Howard* v. *Brower*, 37 O. St. 402; Wh. Ev. i. § 431; Bishop, M. D. & S. ii. §§ 777–786). But statutes removing the disability of *parties* or *persons interested* to testify do not enable husband and wife to be witnesses; there must be special acts for this purpose. *Lucas* v. *Brooks*, 18 Wall. 436; Wh. Ev. i. § 430.]

[1] 16 & 17 Vict. c. 83, s. 3. It is doubtful whether this would apply to a widower or divorced person, questioned after the dissolution of the marriage as to what had been communicated to him whilst it lasted.

[So under modern statutes in this country, it is the general rule that confidential communications between husband and wife cannot be disclosed by either (see Art. 109, note). These do not include *all* communications made between husband and wife, but only "such as are

ARTICLE III.*

JUDGES AND ADVOCATES PRIVILEGED AS TO CERTAIN QUESTIONS.

It is doubtful whether a judge is compellable to testify as to anything which came to his knowledge in court as

---

*See Note XLII. [Appendix].

expressly made confidential, or such as are of a confidential nature or induced by the marital relation" (*Parkhurst* v. *Berdell*, 110 N. Y. 386; *Warner* v. *Press Co.*, 132 N. Y. 181; *Seitz* v. *Seitz*, 170 Pa. 71; *Schmied* v. *Frank*, 86 Ind. 250; cf. *Wood* v. *Chetwood*, 27 N. J. Eq. 311; *U. S.* v. *Guiteau*, 1 Mackey, 498). Some statutes omit the word "confidential," specifying only "communications" as privileged, including therefore those which are and those which are not confidential (*Campbell* v. *Chace*, 12 R. I. 333; *Leppla* v. *Tribune Co.*, 35 Minn. 310; *People* v. *Mullings*, 83 Cal. 138; *Comm.* v. *Sapp*, 90 Ky. 580; S. P. in Mass. as to "private" conversations, *Comm.* v. *Hayes*, 145 Mass. 289). "Communications" includes both oral and written statements (*People* v. *Hayes*, 140 N. Y. 484; *Orr* v. *Miller*, 98 Ind. 436), while "conversations" does not include writings (*Comm.* v. *Caponi*, 155 Mass. 534). When oral communications are overheard, the hearer (*Comm.* v. *Griffin*, 110 Mass. 181; *Gannon* v. *People*, 127 Ill. 507; *State* v. *Gray*, 55 Kan. 135) or the husband or wife (*Lyon* v. *Prouty*, 154 Mass. 488; *Sessions* v. *Trevitt*, 39 O. St. 259; contra, *Campbell* v. *Chace*, 12 R. I. 333; cf. *Hopkins* v. *Grimshaw*, 165 U. S. 342) may be required to disclose them. So written communications may be used as evidence, if they have been transferred to the hands of third persons, not agents or representatives of the recipient (*People* v. *Hayes*, 140 N. Y. 484; *State* v. *Buffington*, 20 Kan. 599; *State* v. *Hoyt*, 47 Ct. 518); but they are privileged, if in the possession of the recipient's attorney or executor (*Selden* v. *State*, 74 Wis. 271; *Bowman* v. *Patrick*, 32 F. R. 368; cf. *Brown* v. *Brown*, 53 Mo. App 453). The death of either spouse or a divorce does not destroy the privilege as to communications between husband and wife (*Hitchcock* v. *Moore*, 70 Mich. 112; *O'Bryan* v. *Allen*, 95 Mo. 68; *Hopkins* v. *Grimshaw*, 165 U. S. 342; *Stanley* v. *Montgomery*, 102 Ind. 102; *Goelz* v. *Goelz*, 157 Ill. 33). When a husband is made use of by others to perpetrate a fraud upon his wife, a court of equity may, in order to expose the fraud, permit both to testify to their conversations about the matter. *Moeckel* v. *Heim*, 134 Mo. 576.]

such judge.[1]   It seems that a barrister cannot be compelled

---

[1] *R.* v. *Gazard*, 8 C. & P. 595. [A judge sitting alone to try a cause cannot be a witness on the same trial ; nor when he sits with others and his presence is necessary to a duly organized court, can he properly testify in the cause on trial (*Dabney* v. *Mitchell*, 66 Ala. 495 ; *Rogers* v. *State*, 60 Ark. 76 ; *Baker* v. *Thompson*, 89 Ga. 486 ; *People* v. *Miller*, 2 Park. Cr. 197 ; see *McMillen* v. *Andrews*, 10 O. St. 112). But if he does testify when he sits with others, and no exception is taken thereto, the judgment of the court is not invalidated (*People* v. *Dohring*, 59 N. Y. 374 ; *Wright* v. *McCampbell*, 75 Tex. 644). These rules apply also to other judicial officers, as referees, etc. (*Morss* v. *Morss*, 11 Barb. 510 ; see Gr. Ev. i. §§ 249, 364). A judge's testimony as to the grounds of a former decision rendered by him has also been excluded (*Agan* v. *Hey*, 30 Hun, 591 ; but see *Supples* v. *Cannon*, 44 Ct. 430 ; *Taylor* v. *Larkin*, 12 Mo. 103 ; cf. *Barrett* v. *James*, 30 S. Car. 329 ; *Appeal of Allen*, 38 Atl. R. (Ct.), 701).

A justice may be a witness to verify his minutes or docket entries, in proving the testimony of a witness in a former case tried before him (*Huff* v. *Bennett*, 4 Sandf. 120, 6 N. Y. 337; *Spalding* v. *Lowe*, 56 Mich. 366; *Zitske* v. *Goldberg*, 38 Wis. 216; *Welcome* v. *Batchelder*, 23 Me. 85 ; *Schall* v. *Miller*, 5 Whart. 156 ; cf. *Corby* v. *Wright*, 9 Mo. App. 5); or in proving the proceedings before him or the judgment rendered (*Pollock* v. *Hoag*, 4 E. D. Sm. 473 ; *Boomer* v. *Laine*, 10 Wend. 526; *McGrath* v. *Seagrave*, 2 Allen, 443 ; *Hibbs* v. *Blair*, 14 Pa. 413); but his entries, not so verified, are not good evidence (*Schafer* v. *Schafer*, 93 Ind. 586; *State* v. *Whelehon*, 102 Mo. 17). So a justice may testify as to the identity of an issue on trial with one formerly tried before him, if his testimony does not contradict the record (*State* v. *Waterman*, 87 Ia. 255 ; *Black* v. *Miller*, 75 Mich. 323); or as to admissions or contradictory evidence in testimony previously given before him (*State* v. *Van Winkle*, 80 Ia. 15 ; *State* v. *Duffy*, 57 Ct. 525); or upon what papers process was issued by him (*Heyward's Case*, 1 Sandf. 701), or as to various collateral matters (*Highberger* v. *Stiffler*, 21 Md. 338; *Jackson* v. *Humphrey*, 1 Johns. 498).

Auditors, arbitrators, etc. may not give testimony to impeach their report or award (*Packard* v. *Reynolds*, 100 Mass. 153; *Schmidt* v. *Glade*, 126 Ill. 485; *Ellison* v. *Weathers*, 78 Mo. 115; see *Briggs* v. *Smith*, 20 Barb. 409; *aliter*, in cases of fraud, *Withington* v. *Warren*, 10 Met. 431 ; *Pulliam* v. *Pensoneau*, 33 Ill. 375). But they may testify as to matters openly occurring before them on the hearing, including admissions of a party, etc. (*Calvert* v. *Friebus*, 48 Md. 44 ; *Tobin* v. *Jones*, 143 Mass. 448; *Graham* v. *Graham*, 9 Pa. 254); or in support

to testify as to what he said in court in his character of a
barrister.[1]

ARTICLE 112.

EVIDENCE AS TO AFFAIRS OF STATE.

No one can be compelled to give evidence relating to
any affairs of state, or as to official communications between public officers upon public affairs, unless the officer
at the head of the department concerned permits him to
do so,[2] or to give evidence of what took place in either

---

or explanation of their award, or as to collateral facts (Gr. Ev. ii. § 78;
Wh. Ev. i. § 599; *Converse* v. *Colton*, 49 Pa. 346; *Hale* v. *Huse*, 10
Gray, 99; *Robinson* v. *Shanks*, 118 Ind. 125; *Duke of Buccleugh* v.
Metr. Bd. of Works, L. R. 5 E. & I. App. 418).

A quasi-judicial officer, as a merchant appraiser under tariff laws,
may not testify to his own neglect of duty (*Oelberman* v. *Merritt*, 19
F. R. 408). In some States, also, an officer who has taken an acknowledgment of a deed is not a competent witness to prove facts
impeaching his certificate. *Mutual Ins. Co.* v. *Corey*, 135 N. Y. 334;
Stone v. *Montgomery*, 35 Miss. 83.]

[1] *Curry* v. *Walter*, 1 Esp. 456. [A person is a competent witness in
a case in which he is acting as attorney or counsel; but the practice
is, in general, disapproved, and should only be resorted to in case of
necessity, as where it is requisite to prevent injustice (Gr. Ev. i. § 364;
French v. *Hall*, 119 U. S. 152; *Freeman* v. *Fogg*, 82 Me. 408; *Connolly* v. *Straw*, 53 Wis. 645; *Sebree* v. *Smith*, 2 Ida. 330; *Little* v.
McKeon, 1 Sandf. 607; *Follansbee* v. *Walker*, 72 Pa. 228; *Potter* v.
Ware, 1 Cush. 519; *Branson* v. *Caruthers*, 49 Cal. 374; *Morgan* v.
Roberts, 38 Ill. 65). The fact of his being attorney in the case, or that
his fee is contingent upon the result, goes to his credibility, not to his
competency (*Thon* v. *Rochester R. Co.*, 83 Hun, 443; *C. B. U. P. R.
Co.* v. *Andrews*, 41 Kan. 370; *Moats* v. *Rymer*, 18 W. Va. 642). So
the practice is discountenanced of a lawyer's being his own witness,
when he is acting as his own client. *Thresher* v. *Stonington Bk.*, 68
Ct. 201.]

[2] *Beatson* v. *Skene*, 5 H. & N. 838. [Cf. *Hennessy* v. *Wright*, 21 Q. B.
D. 509. So in this country, the President, the governors of the several

House of Parliament, without the leave of the House, though he may state that a particular person acted as Speaker.[1]

ARTICLE 113.

INFORMATION AS TO COMMISSION OF OFFENCES.

In cases in which the government is immediately concerned no witness can be compelled to answer any question, the answer to which would tend to discover the names of persons by or to whom information was given as to the commission of offences.[2]

In ordinary criminal prosecutions it is for the judge to decide whether the permission of any such question would or would not, under the circumstances of the particular case, be injurious to the administration of justice.[3]

States, and their cabinet officers, are not bound to produce papers or disclose information committed to them, in a judicial inquiry, when *in their own judgment* the disclosure would on public grounds be inexpedient (Gr. Ev. i. § 251; *Appeal of Hartranft*, 85 Pa. 433; *Thompson* v. *German, etc. R. Co.*, 22 N. J. Eq. 111; cf. *Totten* v. *U. S.*, 92 U. S. 105). Nor without permission of government can other persons be compelled to make such disclosures (see *Worthington* v. *Scribner*, 109 Mass. 487).

A foreign ambassador in the United States is not bound to obey a *subpœna*, and the same rule is sometimes, by treaty, made applicable to foreign consuls. *In re Dillon*, 7 Sawy. 561; *U. S.* v. *Trumbull*, 48 F. R. 94.]

[1] *Chubb* v. *Salomons*, 3 C. & K. 77; *Plunkett* v. *Cobbett*, 5 Esp. 136.

[2] [At this point Mr. Stephen adds a special rule of the English law, not applicable here. It will be found in the Appendix, Note LII.]

[3] *R.* v. *Hardy*, 24 S. T. 811; *A. G.* v. *Bryant*, 15 M. & W. 169; *R.* v. *Richardson*, 3 F. & F. 693. [Gr. Ev. i. § 250; *Marks* v. *Beyfus*, 25 Q. B. D. 494; *U. S.* v. *Moses*, 4 Wash. C. C. 726; *Vogel* v. *Gruaz*, 110 U. S. 311; *People* v. *Laird*, 102 Mich. 135; *State* v. *Soper*, 16 Me. 293; *Worthington* v. *Scribner*, 109 Mass. 487. This last case maintains that the assent of the *government* is required before a witness can disclose such information, and *R.* v. *Richardson* is questioned.]

ARTICLE 114.

COMPETENCY OF JURORS.

A petty juror may not,[1] and it is doubtful whether a grand juror may, give evidence as to what passed be-

---

[1] *Vaise* v. *Delaval*, 1 T. R. 11; *Burgess* v. *Langley*, 5 M. & G. 722. [Gr. Ev. i. § 252 *a*; *Woodward* v. *Leavitt*, 107 Mass. 453; *Rowe* v. *Canney*, 139 Mass. 41; *Comm.* v. *White*, 147 Mass. 76; *Dalrymple* v. *Williams*, 63 N. Y. 361; *State* v. *Pike*, 65 Me. 111; *Hutchinson* v. *Consumers' Coal Co.*, 36 N. J. L. 24. It is a general rule, often applied upon motions for a new trial, that the affidavits or testimony of jurors are not admissible to impeach their own verdict, as *e. g.*, by showing their mistakes or misconduct, or their improper methods of reaching a verdict, or the motives which influenced them, or what was said or done in their deliberations, or that they misunderstood the instructions of the court or the effect of their verdict, etc. (*Bridgewater* v. *Plymouth*, 97 Mass. 382; *Williams* v. *Montgomery*, 60 N. Y. 648; *Meade* v. *Smith*, 16 Ct. 346; *Shepherd* v. *Camden*, 82 Me. 535; *Taylor* v. *Garnett*, 110 Ind. 166; *Sanitary District* v. *Cullerton*, 147 Ill. 385; *People* v. *Stimer*, 82 Mich. 17; *State* v. *Wood*, 124 Mo. 412; *People* v. *Kloss*, 115 Cal. 567; for a full collection of cases, see 24 Am. Dec. 475; 12 Id. 142); nor are statements of like character made by them out of court after the trial provable (*Comm.* v. *Meserve*, 156 Mass. 61; *Warren* v. *Spencer Co.*, 143 Mass. 155; *State* v. *Cooper*, 85 Mo. 256). But their testimony has been received to support or establish their verdict, which has been attacked or impeached by evidence *aliunde*, or to exculpate them from alleged misconduct (*Peck* v. *Brewer*, 48 Ill. 54; *People* v. *Hunt*, 59 Cal. 430; *Clement* v. *Spear*, 56 Vt. 401; *Chicago, etc. R. Co.* v. *McDaniel*, 134 Ind. 166; *State* v. *Rush*, 95 Mo. 199), though some authorities exclude even such evidence, when it discloses the conduct or grounds of action of the jurors in their deliberations (*Woodward* v. *Leavitt*, supra; *Mattox* v. *U. S.*, 146 U. S. 140; contra, *Knight* v. *Epson*, 62 N. H. 356; *Kennedy* v. *Kennedy*, 18 N. J. L. 450). Jurors may also give evidence in denial or explanation of acts or declarations made by them outside of the jury room, which are relied upon to show bias or prejudice (*Chemical Light Co.* v. *Howard*, 150 Mass. 495; *State* v. *Harrison*, 36 W. Va. 729); or to show the identity of the subject-matter in different actions, when this is not disclosed by the record (*Stapleton* v. *King*, 40 Ia. 278; *Follansbee* v. *Walker*, 74 Pa. 306; see *Packet Co.* v. *Sickles*, 5 Wall. 580); or to show a juror's

tween the jurymen in the discharge of their duties.[1] It is also doubtful whether a grand juror may give evidence as to what any witness said when examined before the grand jury.

Illustration.

[Upon a motion for a new trial, the moving party offers in evidence the affidavits of some of the jurors who sat upon the original trial that they arrived at their verdict by agreeing that each juror

---

acts while separated from his fellows, or that he was improperly approached outside of the jury room by a party or witness, etc.(*Heffron* v. *Gallupe*, 55 Me. 563; *Johnson* v. *Witt*, 138 Mass. 79); or to show that the verdict was wrongly announced in court by the foreman or was wrongly entered (*Peters* v. *Fogarty*, 55 N. J. L. 386; *Dalrymple* v.*Williams*, 63 N. Y. 361); or to show what testimony was given on a former trial (*Hewett* v. *Chapman*, 49 Mich. 4); and even in some States to impeach a verdict for grounds not essentially inherent therein (*Swails* v. *Cissna*, 61 Ia. 693; *Brothers* v. *Jasper*, 27 Kan. 770; *Harris* v. *State*, 24 Neb. 803; cf. *Mattox* v. *U. S.*, 146 U. S. 140). A juror may be a witness upon the same trial in which he is acting as juror. *Howser* v. *Comm.*, 51 Pa. 332; *People* v. *Dohring*, 59 N. Y. 374, 378; *Schmidt* v. *N. Y. etc. R. Co.*, 1 Gray, 529; *White* v. *State*, 73 Miss. 50; *State* v. *Vari*, 35 S. Car. 175; N. Y. Code Cr. Pro. § 413; cf. *Richards* v. *State*, 36 Neb. 17.]

[1] 1 Ph. Ev. 140; T. E. s. 863. [It is the general rule in this country that a grand juror cannot give such testimony as to their deliberations, proceedings, votes, etc. (Gr. Ev. i. § 252; Wh. Ev. i. § 601; *State* v. *Hamlin*, 47 Ct. 95; *People* v. *Hulbut*, 4 Den. 133; *State* v. *Davis*, 41 Ia. 311; *Loveland* v. *Cooley*, 59 Minn. 259; *State* v. *Comeau*, 48 La. Ann. 249; N. Y. Code Cr. Pro. § 265; Mass. Pub. St. c. 213, s. 13); nor can persons who were present in the grand jury room by lawful authority, as the prosecuting attorney, the clerk, etc (*Gitchell* v. *People*, 146 Ill. 175; *State* v. *Johnson*, 115 Mo. 480; but see *State* v. *Grady*, 84 Mo. 220). But grand jurors, it is now generally held, may testify whether a particular person did or did not give evidence before them (*Comm.* v. *Hill*, 11 Cush. 137; *People* v. *Northey*, 77 Cal. 619); or who was the prosecutor (*Huidekoper* v. *Cotton*, 3 Watts, 56); or, in impeachment of a witness's credibility, may disclose his testimony before them, in order to show that it differed from that given before the petty jury (*Comm.* v. *Mead*, 12 Gray, 167; *State* v. *Benner*, 64 Me. 267; *State* v. *Wood*, 53 N. H. 484; *Gordon* v. *Comm.*, 92 Pa. 216; *Burdick* v. *Hunt*,

should write down the sum which he wished to give as damages, that
the aggregate amount should be divided by twelve, and that the sum
so ascertained should be given as the amount of their verdict. Though
such a verdict is void, the affidavits of the jurors are not admissible
to show its invalidity.][1]

ARTICLE 115.*

PROFESSIONAL COMMUNICATIONS.

No legal adviser is permitted, whether during or after
the termination of his employment as such, unless with

---

* See Note XLIII. [Appendix].

43 Ind. 381; *Bressler* v. *People*, 117 Ill. 422; *State* v. *Thomas*, 99 Mo.
235; *State* v. *Brown*, 28 Or. 147; *Pellum* v. *State*, 89 Ala. 28; N. Y.
Code Cr. Pro. § 266); or to show a witness's perjury, confessions, or vol-
untary statements, made before the grand jury (Id.; *U. S.* v. *Negro
Charles*, 2 Cr. C. C. 76; *State* v. *Coffee*, 56 Ct. 399; *Izer* v. *State*, 77 Md.
110; *State* v. *Carroll*, 85 Ia. 1; *State* v. *Moran*, 15 Or. 262; *Comm.* v.
Scowden, 92 Ky. 120; *Jenkins* v. *State*, 35 Fla. 737; Bishop's New Cr.
Pro. §§ 857, 858); or, in an action for malicious prosecution, to disclose
the evidence given against plaintiff before the grand jury (*Hunter* v.
Randall, 69 Me. 183; contra, *Kennedy* v. *Holladay*, 105 Mo. 24; cf.
Owens v. *Owens*, 81 Md. 518). It is also held in some States that in a
direct proceeding to set aside or quash an indictment, the testimony
of the grand jurors will be received, that twelve of their number did
not concur in finding it (*Low's Case*, 4 Me. 439; *Territory* v. *Hart*, 7
Mont. 42 & 489; *People* v. *Shattuck*, 6 Abb. N. C. 33; and so as to other
grounds for quashing, see *U. S.* v. *Farrington*, 5 F. R. 343); but some
States refuse to adopt this rule (*Gitchell* v. *People*, 146 Ill. 175; *State*
v. *Grady*, 84 Mo. 220; see, as to a collateral proceeding, *People* v. *Hulbut*, supra; and see 16 Am. Dec. 281). Some States declare broadly
that the evidence of grand jurors is admissible wherever it is necessary, (without disclosing their deliberations or their votes), to uphold
public justice or protect private rights. *U. S.* v. *Farrington*, 5 F. R.
343; *Hunter* v. *Randall*, 69 Me. 183; *N. H. Ins. Co.* v. *Healey*, 151
Mass. 537; *State* v. *Coffee*, 56 Ct. 399.]

[1] [*Sawyer* v. *Hannibal, etc. R. Co.*, 37 Mo. 240; *Moses* v. *Cromwell*,
78 Va. 1; *Palmer* v. *People*, 138 Ill. 356; cf. *People* v. *Azoff*, 105
Cal. 632. But the officer in charge of the jury may testify that they
rendered such a "chance" or "quotient" verdict, as it is called

his client's express consent, to disclose any communication, oral or documentary, made to him as such legal adviser, by or on behalf of his client, during, in the course, and for the purpose of his employment, whether in reference to any matter as to which a dispute has arisen or otherwise, or to disclose any advice given by him to his client during, in the course, and for the purpose of such employment.   It is immaterial whether the client is or is not a party to the action in which the question is put to the legal adviser.[1]

(*Wright* v. *Abbott*, 160 Mass. 395; *Chicago, etc. R. Co.* v. *McDaniel*, 134 Ind. 166). By some decisions a verdict reached by this method is valid, if the jurors *did not agree beforehand* to be bound by the quotient, but left its adoption to subsequent deliberation.   *Luft* · *Lingane*, 17 R. I. 420; *Dana* v. *Tucker*, 4 Johns. 487; *Knight* v. *Epsot* 62 N. H. 356; see *Moses* v. *Central Pk. etc. R. Co.*, 3 Misc. 322.}

[1] [Gr. Ev. i. §§ 237–246; Wh. Ev. i. §§ 576–594; N. Y. Code Civ. Pro. §§ 835, 836; *Bacon* v. *Frisbie*, 80 N. Y. 394; *Root* v. *Wright*, 84 Id. 72; *Higbee* v. *Dresser*, 103 Mass. 523; *Conn. Life Ins. Co.* v. *Schaefer*, 94 U. S. 457; *Earle* v. *Grout*, 46 Vt. 113; *People* v. *Barker*, 56 Ill. 299; *Sweet* v. *Owens*, 109 Mo. 1; *McLellan* v. *Longfellow*, 32 Me. 494; cf. *Wade* v. *Ridley*, 87 Me. 368; *Blount* v. *Kimpton*, 155 Mass. 378. The privilege is that of the client alone, and if he voluntarily waives it, the attorney may testify; other persons have no right to insist upon it (*Hunt* v. *Blackburn*, 128 U. S. 464; *Passmore* v. *Passmore's Estate*, 50 Mich. 626). The client's waiver may in some cases be implied, as well as express, as *e. g.*, by failing to object on the trial to the attorney's testifying (*Sleeper* v. *Abbott*, 60 N. H. 162; *Hoyt* v. *Hoyt*, 112 N. Y. 493, 515). But the client's becoming himself a witness in the case in his own behalf does not amount to a waiver (*Montgomery* v. *Pickering*, 116 Mass. 227; see *Duttenhofer* v. *State*, 34 O. St. 91). If a testator has his attorney become a subscribing witness to his will, this is a waiver and the attorney may testify as to the execution of the will on the proceedings for probate (*Re Coleman*, 111 N. Y. 220; *Pence* v. *Waugh*, 135 Ind. 143; *Denning* v. *Butcher*, 91 Ia. 425; *McMaster* v. *Scriven*, 85 Wis. 162; *In re Mullin*, 110 Cal. 252).

In some cases, statements made to an attorney with a view to retaining him have been held privileged, though the relation was never in fact established.   *Sargent* v. *Hampden*, 38 Me. 581; *State* v. *Tally*, 102 Ala. 25; *Denver Tramway Co.* v. *Owens*, 20 Col. 107.]

This Article does not extend to—

(1) Any such communication as aforesaid made in furtherance of any criminal purpose, whether such purpose was at the time of the communication known to the professional adviser or not ; [1]

(2) Any fact observed by any legal adviser, in the course of his employment as such, showing that any crime or fraud has been committed since the commencement of his employment, whether his attention was directed to such fact by or on behalf of his client or not ; [2]

(3) Any fact with which such legal adviser became acquainted otherwise than in his character as such.[3] The

---

[1] *R.* v. *Cox & Railton*, 14 Q. B. D. 153. The judgment in this case is that of ten judges in the Court for Crown Cases Reserved, and examines minutely all the cases on the subject. These cases put the rule on the principle, that the furtherance of a criminal purpose can never be part of a legal adviser's business. As soon as a legal adviser knowingly takes part in preparing for a crime, he ceases to act as a lawyer and becomes a criminal,—a conspirator or accessory, as the case may be. [*People* v. *Blakeley*, 4 Park. Cr. 176 ; *People* v. *Van Alstine*, 57 Mich. 69 ; *State* v. *Kidd*, 89 Ia. 54 ; *Dudley* v. *Beck*, 3 Wis. 274 ; *Orman* v. *State*, 22 Tex. App. 604 ; cf. *State* v. *Barrows*, 52 Ct. 323. The English decisions include cases of *fraud* within this exception (*In re Postlethwaite*, 35 Ch. D. 722 ; *R.* v. *Cox & Railton*, supra), and recent American cases have adopted the same doctrine (*Matthews* v. *Hoagland*, 48 N. J. Eq. 455 ; *Hamil* v. *England*, 50 Mo. App. 338 ; see *Bank of Utica* v. *Mersereau*, 3 Barb. Ch. 528, 598). But an attorney cannot disclose statements made to him by his client about a crime committed by the latter, which were not made till after the crime was committed. *Alexander* v. *U. S.*, 138 U. S. 353.]

[2] [See Illustration (*a*).]

[3] [Gr. Ev. i. §§ 244, 245; Wh. Ev. i. §§ 588, 589; *State* v. *Fitzgerald*, 68 Vt. 125 ; as *e. g.*, communications made to him before he became legal adviser, or after the relation ceased (*Jennings* v. *Sturdevant*, 140 Ind. 641 ; *Theisen* v. *Dayton*, 82 Ia. 74 ; *Brady* v. *State*, 39 Neb. 529); or while he was acting in some other capacity than as attorney, as *e. g.*, as a friend, agent, etc. (*Coon* v. *Swan*, 30 Vt. 6 ; *Patten* v. *Glover*, 1 App. D. C. 466); so as to communications not relating to the professional employment (*Mowell* v. *Van Buren*, 77 Hun, 569; *Mc-Donald* v. *McDonald*, 142 Ind. 55 ; *State* v. *Mewherter*, 46 Ia. 88;

expression "legal adviser" includes barristers and solicitors,[1] their clerks,[2] and interpreters[2] between them and
their clients. It does not include officers of a corporation

Carroll v. *Sprague*, 59 Cal. 655 ; cf. *State* v. *Hedgepeth*, 125 Mo. 14).
So an attorney may be required to testify as to many collateral matters: as the name of his client (*Harriman* v. *Jones*, 58 N. H. 328), or
his residence (*Alden* v. *Goddard*, 73 Me. 345), or his signature (*Brown*
v. *Jewett*, 120 Mass. 215); or that in collecting a claim he acted for his
client (*Mulford* v. *Muller*, 3 Abb. Dec. 330); or the fact of his employment as attorney (*Hampton* v. *Boylan*, 46 Hun, 151; *Eickman* v. *Troll*,
29 Minn. 124); or that he has the client's papers in his hands (*Stokoe*
v. *St. Paul, etc. R. Co.*, 40 Minn. 545 ; see Art. 119); so as to communications which are not of a private or confidential nature, or which have
ceased to be such (*Snow* v. *Gould*, 74 Me. 540; *Rosseau* v. *Bleau*, 131
N. Y. 177; *Roper* v. *State*, 58 N. J. L. 420), or as to communications
made to him by persons other than his client (*Turner's Estate*, 167 Pa.
609; *State* v. *Hedgepeth*, 125 Mo. 14), and many like matters (see p.
290, note 2, *post;* *Comm.* v. *Goddard*, 14 Gray, 402 ; *Crosby* v. *Berger*,
11 Pai. 377; *Hughes* v. *Boone*, 102 N. C. 137).
A communication made to counsel by one party to a controversy
while the others are present is not privileged from disclosure in a subsequent suit between such parties themselves (*Hurlbut* v. *Hurlbut*,
128 N. Y. 420; *Goodwin Co.'s Appeal*, 117 Pa. 514 ; *Colt* v. *McConnell*,
116 Ind. 249; *Lynn* v. *Lyerle*, 113 Ill. 128; *Sparks* v. *Sparks*, 51 Kan.
195; *Cady* v. *Walker*, 62 Mich. 157; *Murphy* v. *Waterhouse*, 113 Cal.
467); so, where two persons employ an attorney in the same business,
as to communications made to him by either of them concerning such
business (*Gulick* v. *Gulick*, 39 N. J. Eq. 516; *Deip's Estate*, 163 Pa.
423; *In re Bauer*, 79 Cal. 304); but in an action between such persons
and a stranger, the communications are protected (Id.; *Root* v. *Wright*,
84 N. Y. 72).
It is held in some States that, after a testator's death, his attorney
may, in support of the will or to carry out the testator's intentions as
respects those claiming under him, testify as to directions, communications, etc. made by said testator. *Blackburn* v. *Crawfords*, 3 Wall.
175, 193; *Doherty* v. *O'Callaghan*, 157 Mass. 90; *In re Austin*, 42 Hun,
516; *Scott* v. *Harris*, 113 Ill. 447; *Thompson* v. *Ish*, 99 Mo. 160, 176;
Layman's Will, 40 Minn. 371; *Olmstead* v. *Webb*, 5 App. D. C. 38.]
[1] *Wilson* v. *Rastall*, 4 T. R. 753. As to interpreters, Id. 756. [All
attorneys and counselors are included in this country.]
[2] *Taylor* v. *Foster*, 2 C. & P. 195; *Foote* v. *Hayne*, 1 C. & P. 545.
Quære, whether licensed conveyancers are within the rule ? Parke, B.,

through whom the corporation has elected to make statements.[1]

Illustrations.

(a) A, being charged with embezzlement, retains B, a barrister, to defend him. In the course of the proceedings B observes that an entry has been made in A's account book, charging A with the sum said to have been embezzled, which entry was not in the book at the commencement of B's employment.

This being a fact observed by B in the course of his employment, showing that a fraud has been committed since the commencement of the proceedings, is not protected from disclosure in a subsequent action by A against the prosecutor in the original case for malicious prosecution.[2]

---

in *Turquand* v. *Knight*, 7 M. & W. 100, thought not. Special pleaders would seem to be on the same footing. [Gr. Ev. i. § 239. Communications to lawyers' clerks, agents, and interpreters are protected (*Sibley* v. *Waffle*, 16 N. Y. 180 ; *Jackson* v. *French*, 3 Wend. 337); but statements to an attorney's clerk by one who did not know him to be such, but who did know he was not a lawyer, have been held not privileged (*Hawes* v. *State*, 88 Ala. 37); so a law student to whom a communication is made, not being the clerk or agent of the attorney, may be required to testify as to such communication (*Barnes* v. *Harris*, 7 Cush. 576; *Schubkagel* v. *Dierstein*, 131 Pa. 46; *Holman* v. *Kimball*, 22 Vt. 555); and so may a person who overhears a client's statements to his lawyer (*Hoy* v. *Morris*, 13 Gray, 519; *Goddard* v. *Gardner*, 28 Ct. 172; *People* v. *Buchanan*, 145 N. Y. 1; *Tyler* v. *Hall*, 106 Mo. 313). A lawyer simply employed to draft deeds or other papers, without giving legal advice, is not generally within the rule of privilege. *Todd* v. *Munson*, 53 Ct. 579; *Childs* v. *Merrill*, 66 Vt. 302; *Hanlon* v. *Doherty*, 109 Ind. 37; *Stallings* v. *Hullum*, 79 Tex. 421; *Smith* v. *Long*, 106 Ill. 485; *Hatton* v. *Robinson*, 14 Pick. 416; but see *Linthicum* v. *Remington*, 5 Cr. C. C. 546; *Carter* v. *West*, 93 Ky. 211.]

[1] *Mayor of Swansea* v. *Quirk*, 5 C. P. D. 106; nor pursuivants of the Herald's College, *Slade* v. *Tucker*, 14 Ch. D. 824; [nor a solicitor of patents who is not an attorney at law (*Brungger* v. *Smith*, 49 F. R. 124); nor a person supposed to be a lawyer but who is not one in fact (*Barnes* v. *Harris*, 7 Cush. 576). But in *Benedict* v. *State*, 44 O. St. 679, communications to one whose regular business had been for years practising law before justices of the peace were held privileged, though he had not been admitted to the bar.]

[2] *Brown* v. *Foster*, 1 H. & N. 736. [This case was so decided be-

(*b*) If a legal adviser witnesses a deed, he must give evidence as to what happened at the time of its execution.[1]

(*c*) A retains B, an attorney, to prosecute C (whose property he had fraudulently acquired) for murder, and says, " It is not proper for me to appear in the prosecution for fear of its hurting me in the cause coming on between myself and him ; but I do not care if I give £10,000 to get him hanged, for then I shall be easy in my title and estate." This communication is not privileged.[2]

ARTICLE 116.

CONFIDENTIAL COMMUNICATIONS WITH LEGAL ADVISERS.

No one can be compelled to disclose to the court any communication between himself and his legal adviser, which his legal adviser could not disclose without his permission, although it may have been made before any dispute arose as to the matter referred to.[3]

---

cause the fact in question was not information communicated by the client, but knowledge which counsel acquired by his own observation. For a like rule, see *Patten* v. *Moor*, 29 N. H. 163; *Daniel* v. *Daniel*, 39 Pa. 191; *Hebbard* v. *Haughian*, 70 N. Y. 54; *Comm.* v. *Bacon*, 135 Mass. 521; *Swaim* v. *Humphreys*, 42 Ill. App. 370.]

  [1] *Crawcour* v. *Salter*, 18 Ch. D. 34.
  [2] *Annesley* v. *Anglesea*, 17 S. T. 1223-4.
  [3] *Minet* v. *Morgan*, L. R. 8 Ch. App. 361, reviewing all the cases, and adopting the explanation given in *Pearse* v. *Pearse*, 1 De G. & S. 18-31, of *Radcliffe* v. *Fursman*, 2 Br. P. C. 514. A recent illustration will be found in *Mayor of Bristol* v. *Cox*, 26 Ch. D. 678. [This rule applies though parties to actions are now competent witnesses (*Hemenway* v. *Smith*, 28 Vt. 701; *Barker* v. *Kuhn*, 38 Ia. 392; *Swenk* v. *People*, 20 Ill. App. 111; *Verdelli* v. *Gray's Harbor Co.*, 115 Cal. 517; *Duttenhofer* v. *State*, 34 O. St. 91). A party does not waive the privilege by voluntarily becoming a witness in his own behalf (Id.; *State* v. *White*, 19 Kan. 445; *Carnes* v. *Platt*, 15 Abb. Pr. (N. S.) 337; contra, *Inhab. of Woburn* v. *Henshaw*, 101 Mass. 193); but it is deemed a waiver, if he voluntarily testifies to confidential communications made by him to his attorney (*Oliver* v. *Pate*, 43 Ind. 132; cf. *State* v. *Tall*, 43 Minn. 273). So where an accomplice turns "State's evidence," he may be compelled to disclose communications to his

Illustration.

[In an action for the conversion of goods, plaintiff became a witness in his own behalf, and, having given his evidence in chief, he was asked on cross-examination as to statements made by him to his lawyer, on the day the goods were taken, as to trading the goods for a note and as to the validity of the note. Due objection being made, the witness was held not bound to answer the question.] [1]

ARTICLE 117.*

CLERGYMEN AND MEDICAL MEN.

Medical men [2] and (probably) clergymen may be compelled to disclose communications made to them in professional confidence. [3]

---

* See Note XLIV. [Appendix].

counsel as to the offence charged (*Jones* v. *State*, 65 Miss. 179; *People* v. *Gallagher*, 75 Mich. 512). But a party to an action cannot be compelled to testify as to knowledge, information, or belief, which he derived solely from privileged communications made to him by his attorney. *Lyell* v. *Kennedy*, L. R. 9 App. Cas. 81.]

[1] [*Bigler* v. *Reyher*, 43 Ind. 112. So a patient cannot be compelled to disclose communications made by him to his physician which the physician could not disclose. *Post* v. *State*, 14 Ind. App. 452; see next Article.]

[2] *Duchess of Kingston's Case*, 20 S. T. 572-3. As to clergymen, see Note XLIV. [Appendix].

[3] [This is the general rule of the common law (Gr. Ev. i. § 247). But in a number of the States of this country, a different rule has been established by statute. In New York, *e. g.*, it is provided that a clergyman shall not be allowed to disclose a confession made to him in his professional character, in the course of discipline enjoined by the rules or practice of his religious body (N. Y. Code Civ. Pro. § 833; see *People* v. *Gates*, 13 Wend. 311); and that a person duly authorized to practise physic or surgery shall not be allowed to disclose any information which he acquired in attending a patient in a professional capacity, and which was necessary to enable him to act in that capacity (Code Civ. Pro. § 834; see *People* v. *Schuyler*, 106 N. Y. 298; *People* v. *Murphy*, 101 N. Y. 126; *Fisher* v. *Fisher*, 129 N. Y. 654). But this privilege may be waived by the person confessing or by the

Article 118.

PRODUCTION OF TITLE-DEEDS OF WITNESS NOT A PARTY.

No witness who is not a party to a suit can be compelled to produce his title-deeds to any property,[1] or any

---

patient (Code Civ. Pro. § 836; as to what will be deemed a waiver,
see *Morris* v. *N. Y. etc. R. Co.*, 148 N. Y. 88 ; *Alberti* v. *N. Y. etc. R.
Co.*, 118 N. Y. 77 ; *McKinney* v. *Grand St. etc. R. Co.*, 104 N. Y. 352).
This rule as to physicians applies to "information" obtained by them,
in attending a patient, by their own observation or the statements of
others, as well as to communications from the patient himself (*Edington* v. *Life Ins. Co.*, 67 N. Y. 185 ; *Renihan* v. *Dennin*, 103 N. Y. 573 ;
S. P. *Heuston* v. *Simpson*, 115 Ind. 62 ; *Briesenmeister* v. *Knights*, 81
Mich. 525 ; *Gartside* v. *Conn. Ins. Co.*, 76 Mo. 446). But it does not
prevent a physician from testifying upon a trial for murder as to the
condition of the person injured whom he attended before death ensued
(*Pierson* v. *People*, 79 N. Y. 424 ; *People* v. *Harris*, 136 N. Y. 423 ; cf.
People v. *West*, 106 Cal. 89); nor, in some States, does it exclude the
testimony of physicians, in probate proceedings, to show the condition
of the decedent as bearing upon his testamentary capacity, his representatives waiving the privilege (*Fraser* v. *Jennison*, 42 Mich. 206 ;
Morris v. *Morris*, 119 Ind. 341 ; *Denning* v. *Butcher*, 91 Ia. 425 ;
Thompson v. *Ish*, 99 Mo. 160 ; N. Y. Code Civ. Pro. § 836 ; contra,
In re Flint, 100 Cal. 391).

Similar statutes have been passed in Michigan, Wisconsin, Indiana,
Iowa, Kansas, Missouri, California, Oregon, etc. See *Conn. Ins. Co.*
v. *Union Trust Co.*, 112 U. S. 250 ; *Gurley* v. *Park*, 135 Ind. 440 ; *Excelsior Ass'n* v. *Riddle*, 91 Ind. 84 ; *Kansas City, etc. R. Co.* v. *Murray*,
55 Kan. 336; *People* v. *Lane*, 101 Cal. 513 ; as to clergymen, see
Gillooley v. *State*, 58 Ind. 182 ; as to modes of waiver in regard to
physicians, see *Lane* v. *Boicourt*, 128 Ind. 420 ; *Penn. Ins. Co.* v. *Wiler*,
100 Ind. 92 ; *McConnell* v. *Osage*, 80 Ia. 293 ; *Mellor* v. *Mo. Pac. R.
Co.*, 105 Mo. 455 ; *Carrington* v. *St. Louis*, 89 Mo. 208 ; *In re Mullin*,
110 Cal. 252.]

[1] *Pickering* v. *Noyes*, 1 B. & C. 263 ; *Adams* v. *Lloyd*, 3 H. & N. 351.
[It is a rule of chancery practice that a party shall not be compelled
to make discovery of his title-deeds when they simply support his own
title, but only when they support the title of his adversary; and a similar rule applies to other documents (Story, Eq. Jur. ii. § 1490; *Thompson* v. *Engle*, 4 N. J. Eq. 271; *Cullison* v. *Bossom*, 1 Md. Ch. 95 ; *Adams*

document the production of which might tend to criminate him, or expose him to any penalty or forfeiture;[1] but

v. *Porter*, 1 Cush. 170; *Machine Co.* v. *Batchelder*, 68 Vt. 431). The
same rule has been applied in some States under modern statutes allowing the discovery and inspection of documents (*Meakings* v. *Cromwell*, 1 Sandf. 698; *Shoe & Leather Ass'n* v. *Bailey*, 17 J. & Sp. 385;
Stichter v. *Tillinghast*, 43 Hun, 95; *Lester* v. *People*, 150 Ill. 408; Mass.
Pub. St. c. 167, s. 56; *Wilson* v. *Webber*, 2 Gray, 558; *Wetherbee* v.
Winchester, 128 Mass. 293; N. H. Pub. St. c. 224, s. 14 (ed. 1891); but
see *Seligman* v. *Real Est. Trust Co.*, 20 Abb. N. C. 210; *Thebaud* v.
Hume, 15 N. Y. S. 664; *Herbage* v. *Utica*, 109 N. Y. 81).

A person not a party to an action may by *subpœna duces tecum* be required to produce his private papers in evidence that are relevant to
the issue, if they do not tend to criminate him or expose him to a penalty or forfeiture (Wh. Ev. i. § 537; *Burnham* v. *Morrissey*, 14 Gray,
226, 240; *In re Dunn*, 9 Mo. App. 255; *U. S.* v. *Tilden*, 10 Ben. 566;
cf. *Davenbagh* v. *M'Kinnie*, 5 Cow. 27 (deed); *Lane* v. *Cole*, 12 Barb.
680 (docket book); *Bonesteel* v. *Lynde*, 8 How. Pr. 226, 352 (*party*
subpœnaed to produce lease and inventory); *Wertheim* v. *Continental
R. Co.*, 15 F. R. 716 (corporate books); *Johnson Co.* v. *North Branch
Co.*, 48 F. R. 191 (drawings containing valuable trade secrets as to a
process of manufacture). But the court may relieve him from the
obligation of giving them in evidence (though he must bring them into
court), if this would be prejudicial to his rights and interests; of this
the court is to judge upon inspection (Gr. Ev. i. § 246; *Mitchell's Case*,
12 Abb. Pr. 249, 259; *In re O'Toole*, 1 Tucker, 39; *Bull* v. *Loveland*,
10 Pick. 9; so now as to a *party*, *Bonesteel* v. *Lynde*, 8 How. Pr. 226, 233;
Champlin v. *Stoddart*, 17 W. D. 76; cf. *Pynchon* v. *Day*, 18 Ill. App.
147; *Moats* v. *Rymer*, 18 W. Va. 642; *Robinson* v. *Phila. R. Co.*, 28 F. R.
340). Trade secrets have been protected from disclosure, when disclosure was not necessary for the determination of the matter before
the court. *Dobson* v. *Graham*, 49 F. R. 17; *Moxie Co.* v. *Beach*, 35
F. R. 465.]

[1] *Whitaker* v. *Izod*, 2 Tau. 115. [*Byass* v. *Sullivan*, 21 How. Pr. 50;
Lawson v. *Boyden*, 160 Ill. 613; *Boyle* v. *Smithman*, 146 Pa. 255; *Johnson* v. *Donaldson*, 18 Blatch. 287. The seizure or compulsory production of a man's private papers, to be used as evidence against him in
a prosecution for a crime, penalty, or forfeiture, is prohibited by the
U. S. Constitution (*Boyd* v. *U. S.*, 116 U. S. 616; cf. *State* v. *Griswold*,
67 Ct. 307), and also by State Constitutions (*Lester* v. *People*, 150 Ill.
408; cf. *People* v. *Spiegel*, 143 N. Y. 107; *State* v. *Pomeroy*, 130 Mo.
489; *State* v. *Davis*, 108 Mo. 666). In this last case, however, this rule

a witness is not entitled to refuse to produce a document in his possession only because its production may expose him to a civil action,[1] or because he has a lien[2] upon it.[3]

ARTICLE 119.

PRODUCTION OF DOCUMENTS WHICH ANOTHER PERSON, HAVING POSSESSION, COULD REFUSE TO PRODUCE.

No solicitor,[4] trustee, or mortgagee can be compelled to produce (except for the purpose of identification) documents in his possession as such, which his client, *cestui que trust*, or mortgagor would be entitled to refuse to produce if they were in his possession; nor can any one who is entitled to refuse to produce a document be compelled to give oral evidence of its contents.[5]

---

was held not applicable to physicians' prescriptions, which a State statute required druggists to preserve; this was because they were deemed, under the statute, to be public, and not private, papers.]

[1] *Doe* v. *Date*, 3 Q. B. 609, 618. [Wh. Ev. i. § 537; *Bull* v. *Loveland*, 10 Pick. 9.]

[2] *Hope* v. *Liddell*, 7 De G. M. & G. 331; *Hunter* v. *Leathley*, 10 B. & C. 858; *Brassington* v. *Brassington*, 1 Sim. & Stu. 455. It has been doubted whether production may not be refused on the ground of a lien as against the party requiring the production. This is suggested in *Brassington* v. *Brassington*, and was acted upon by Lord Denman in *Kemp* v. *King*, 2 Mo. & Ro. 437; but it seems to be opposed to *Hunter* v. *Leathley*, in which a broker who had a lien on a policy for premiums advanced was compelled to produce it in an action against the underwriter by the assured who had created the lien. See *Ley* v. *Barlow* (Judgt. of Parke, B.) 1 Ex. 801. [See *Morley* v. *Green*, 11 Pai. 240; *Bull* v. *Loveland*, 10 Pick. 9.]

[3] [Mr. Stephen ends Art. 118 as follows: "No bank is compellable to produce the books of such bank, except in the case provided for in Art. 37 (42 & 43 Vict. c. 11)." See Note XLIX., Appendix.]

[4] *Volant* v. *Soyer*, 13 C. B. 231; *Phelps* v. *Prew*, 3 E. & B. 431. [*Bursill* v. *Tanner*, 16 Q. B. D. 1.]

[5] *Davies* v. *Waters*, 9 M. & W. 608; *Few* v. *Guppy*, 13 Beav. 454. [Formerly when a party to a suit could not be required to give evidence, his legal adviser could likewise not be compelled to produce

ARTICLE 120.

WITNESS NOT TO BE COMPELLED TO CRIMINATE HIMSELF.

No one is bound to answer any question if the answer thereto would, in the opinion of the judge, have a tend-

---

in evidence a deed or other document entrusted to him by his client, nor to disclose its contents. Notice to produce might be given him (see Art. 72, *ante*), and he might be examined as to the existence of the paper, and as to its being in his possession, so as to enable the other party to give secondary evidence of its contents (Gr. Ev. i. § 241; *Mitchell's Case*, 12 Abb. Pr. 249, 258; *Coveney* v. *Tannahill*, 1 Hill, 33; *Durkee* v. *Leland*, 4 Vt. 612; *Lessee of Rhoades* v. *Selin*, 4 Wash. C. C. 715; *Stokoe* v. *St. Paul, etc. R. Co.*, 40 Minn. 545); and the same rule was applied to the agent of a party, as *e. g.*, an officer of a corporation (*Bank of Utica* v. *Hillard*, 5 Cow. 419; *Westcott* v. *Atlantic Co.*, 3 Met. 282). In equity, however, it has been the rule that a party might, in some cases, be required to make discovery of his deeds and papers (see p. 293, note 1, *ante*), and, therefore, that his attorney would, in such cases, be bound to produce them, if they were in the latter's possession (*Wakeman* v. *Bailey*, 3 Barb. Ch. 482). And now that by modern statutes parties may be subpœnaed (see Art. 72, *ante*), it is in like manner declared that whatever papers a party must produce, his attorney must produce if he has them (*Mitchell's Case*, supra; *Andrews* v. *Ohio, etc. R. Co.*, 14 Ind. 169; *In re Whitlock*, 15 N. Y. Civ. Pro. R. 204; *Harrisburgh Car Co.* v. *Sloan*, 120 Ind. 156; *Steed* v. *Cruise*, 70 Ga. 168; cf. *Moats* v. *Rymer*, 18 W. Va. 642; *Hoyt* v. *Jackson*, 3 Dem. 388; *Prelford's Appeal*, 48 Ct. 247); and so an officer of a corporation may be required to produce the corporate books and papers (*Wertheim* v. *Continental R. Co.*, 15 F. R. 716; see p. 193, note 1, *ante*). A client cannot combine with his attorney to keep papers from being produced by putting them in the latter's possession (*People* v. *Sheriff*, 29 Barb. 622; *Edison Electric Co.* v. *U. S. Electric Co.*, 44 F. R. 294; *Trustees* v. *Blount*, 70 Ga. 779). But papers which are professional communications are still protected (*Mitchell's Case*, supra; *Mallory* v. *Benjamin*, 9 How. Pr. 419; *Hubbell* v. *Judd Oil Co.*, 19 Alb. L. J. 97; *Arnold* v. *Chesebrough*, 41 F. R. 74; *Liggett* v. *Glenn*, 51 F. R. 381; *Davenport Co.* v. *Pa. R. Co.*, 166 Pa. 480; *Pearce* v. *Fosier*, 15 Q. B. D. 114; and see p. 293, note 1, *ante*). In a criminal case an attorney cannot be compelled by the prosecution to produce papers entrusted to him by

ency to expose the witness,[1] (or the wife or husband of

his client, to be used as evidence against the client (*Comm.* v. *Moyer*, 15 Phila. 397; *Anonymous*, 8 Mass. 370).

The agents of a telegraph company are bound to produce telegraphic messages upon a *subpœna duces tecum.* *Ex parte Brown*, 72 Mo. 83; *State* v. *Litchfield*, 58 Me. 267; *In re Storror*, 63 F. R. 564; cf. *Ex parte Jaynes*, 70 Cal. 638; see p. 193, note 1, *ante*.]

[1] *R.* v. *Boyes*, 1 B. & S. 330; followed and approved in *Ex parte Reynolds*, 20 Ch. D. 298, by the Court of Appeal. [Gr. Ev. i. §§ 451-453; Wh. Ev. i. §§ 533-541; N. Y. Code Civ. Pro. § 837; *People* v. *Forbes*, 143 N. Y. 219; *Comm.* v. *Trider*, 143 Mass. 180; *Eckstein's Petition*, 148 Pa. 509; *Temple* v. *Comm.*, 75 Va. 892. The rule applies though the testimony of the witness would only *tend* to criminate him or would only furnish a link in a chain of evidence which might lead to his conviction (Id.; Illustration (*a*); *State* v. *Simmons Co.*, 109 Mo. 118; *Stevens* v. *State*, 50 Kan. 712; *Ex parte Boscowitz*, 84 Ala. 463). The privilege is that of the witness and not of the party to the suit, and may be waived by the witness (*Cloyes* v. *Thayer*, 3 Hill, 564; *Comm.* v. *Shaw*, 4 Cush. 594; *State* v. *Wentworth*, 65 Me. 234; *Chesapeake Club* v. *State*, 63 Md. 446; *Samuel* v. *People*, 164 Ill. 379; *State* v. *Van Winkle*, 80 Ia. 15), and ceases to exist if a criminal prosecution against him is barred by the Statute of Limitations (Wh. Ev. i. § 540; *Childs* v. *Merrill*, 66 Vt. 302; *Lamson* v. *Boyden*, 160 Ill. 613; *Mahanke* v. *Cleland*, 76 Ia. 401; cf. *Southern Ry. News Co.* v. *Russell*, 91 Ga. 808), or if some statute, requiring criminating evidence to be given in certain cases, affords to the witness, in return, absolute immunity from prosecution (*Brown* v. *Walker*, 161 U. S. 591; *State* v. *Nowell*, 58 N. H. 314; *Emery's Case*, 107 Mass. 172; *People* v. *Forbes*, 143 N. Y. 219; *Ex parte Cohen*, 104 Cal. 524); the privilege is not lost, however, if the statute simply provides that the criminating evidence cannot afterwards be used against the witness (Id.; *Counselman* v. *Hitchcock*, 142 U. S. 547; *Kendrick* v. *Comm.*, 78 Va. 490; but see *People* v. *Kelley*, 24 N. Y. 74; *Comm.* v. *Bell*, 145 Pa. 374). The privilege is not always to be allowed when claimed, but only when it appears to the court from the nature of the examination that the witness is exposed to danger if he should be compelled to answer; but this appearing, he need not show how the answer will criminate him (*Ex parte Reynolds*, 20 Ch. D. 294; *Youngs* v. *Youngs*, 5 Redf. 505; *La Fontaine* v. *Underwriters*, 83 N. C. 132; see Illustration (*b*); *Friess* v. *N. Y. C. R. Co.*, 67 Hun, 205; *Lamb* v. *Munster*, 10 Q. B. D. 110). If the witness discloses without objection part of a transaction criminating him, it is the general American rule that he must disclose the whole (*Comm.* v. *Pratt*, 126 Mass. 462; *People* v. *Freshour*, 55 Cal. 375; *Coburn* v. *Odell*, 30 N. H. 540; *State* v. *Fay*, 43

the witness), to any criminal charge, or to any penalty or forfeiture[1] which the judge regards as reasonably likely to be preferred or sued for;[2] but no one is excused from

Ia. 651; *State* v. *Nichols*, 29 Minn. 357; see *Youngs* v. *Youngs*, supra; *Samuel* v. *People*, 164 Ill. 379), unless the partial disclosure is made under innocent mistake (*Mayo* v. *Mayo*, 119 Mass. 290). But in England a partial statement does not forfeit the privilege (*R.* v. *Garbett*, 1 Den. C. C. 236; S. P. *Chesapeake Club* v. *State*, 63 Md. 446). Testimony given under compulsion of the court, contrary to the privilege, cannot be used against the witness (*Horstman* v. *Kaufman*, 97 Pa. 147; see Art. 23, *ante*).

When a defendant, in a criminal trial, voluntarily becomes a witness in his own behalf, it is held in many States that he thereby waives his privilege as to criminating himself and may be cross-examined upon all facts relevant to the issue (*Comm.* v. *Nichols*, 114 Mass. 285; *State* v. *Ober*, 52 N. H. 459; *State* v. *Witham*, 72 Me. 531; *State* v. *Griswold*, 67 Ct. 307; *People* v. *Tice*, 131 N. Y. 651; *Disque* v. *State*, 49 N. J. L. 249; *Thomas* v. *State*, 103 Ind. 419; *State* v. *Wells*, 54 Kan. 161; *State* v. *Thomas*, 98 N. C. 599; *Thomas* v. *State*, 100 Ala. 53; see *Comm.* v. *Smith*, 163 Mass. 431; *Este* v. *Wilshire*, 44 O. St. 636). In some States, however, the cross-examination must relate to matters as to which he was examined in chief (*People* v. *Wong Ah Leong*, 99 Cal. 440; *State* v. *Graves*, 95 Mo. 510; see *Spies* v. *Illinois*, 123 U. S. 131; also, Articles 127 and 129, *post*).

Where a defendant, in a criminal trial, was required to stand up in court to be identified, this was held not to be a violation of the rule that no person shall be required to give evidence against himself in a criminal case. *People* v. *Gardner*, 144 N. Y. 119; but see *Cooper* v. *State*, 86 Ala. 610; cf. *O'Brien* v. *State*, 125 Ind. 38; *Williams* v. *State*, 98 Ala. 52; *Myers* v. *State*, 97 Ga. 99; see p. 177, note, *ante*.]

[1] [See page 294, note 1, *ante*.]

[2] As to husbands and wives, see 1 Hale, P. C. 301; *R.* v. *Cliviger*, 2 T. R. 263; *Cartwright* v. *Green*, 8 Ves. 405; *R.* v. *Bathwick*, 2 B. & Ad. 639; *R.* v. *All Saints, Worcester*, 6 M. & S. 194. These cases show that even under the old law which made the parties and their husbands and wives incompetent witnesses, a wife was not incompetent to prove matter which might tend to criminate her husband. *R.* v. *Cliviger* assumes that she was, and was to that extent overruled. As to the later law, see *R.* v. *Halliday*, Bell, 257. The cases, however, do not decide that if the wife claimed the privilege of not answering she would be compelled to do so, and to some extent they suggest that she would not. [See *State* v. *Briggs*, 9 R. I. 361; *State* v. *Bridg-*

answering any question only because the answer may
establish or tend to establish that he owes a debt, or is
otherwise liable to any civil suit, either at the instance of
the Crown or of any other person.[1]

Illustrations.

(a) [A, testifying before the grand jury in regard to a charge under
investigation by them whether certain persons had been guilty of
gambling by playing with cards for money, was asked, "Do you
know of any person playing at a game of cards for money in this
county within eighteen months past?" He answered, "I do." The
foreman then asked him, "Whom did you see playing?" He refused
to answer on the ground that he could not do so without giving
evidence against and tending to criminate himself. The court
adjudged him guilty of contempt for refusing to answer; but it was
held on appeal that he rightfully claimed his privilege; that, as he
himself had played in the game with the persons to whom his first
answer related, he could not disclose their names without thereby
furnishing a link in a chain of testimony tending to establish his own
guilt.][2]

(b) [A was indicted and put on trial for forgery of a promissory
note purporting to have been executed by B. The prosecuting
attorney called B as a witness, exhibited the note to him and asked
him if the name affixed was his signature. He declined to answer
because it might criminate himself, and the court excused him from
answering. The attorney then asked, "Have you ever seen this note
before?" He refused to answer for the same reason; but the court

---

man, 49 Vt. 202; *Royal Ins. Co.* v. *Noble,* 5 Abb. Pr. (N. S.) 54; *State*
v. *Wilson,* 31 N. J. L. 77; *Cornelius* v. *Hambay,* 150 Pa. 359; *State* v.
Welch, 26 Me. 30; *Comm.* v. *Sparks,* 7 Allen, 534; *Keep* v. *Griggs,*
12 Ill. App. 511; *State* v. *Vollander,* 57 Minn. 225; *People* v. *Langtree,*
64 Cal. 256; *Woods* v. *State,* 76 Ala. 35; p. 277, note 3, *ante.*]

[1] 46 Geo. III. c. 37. See *R.* v. *Scott,* 25 L. J. M. C. 128, 7 Cox, 164, and
subsequent cases as to bankrupts, and *Ex parte Scholfield,* 6 Ch. D.
230. *Quære,* Is he bound to produce a document criminating himself?
See *Webb* v. *East,* 5 Ex. D. 23 & 109. [Gr. Ev. i. § 452; N. Y. Code
Civ. Pro. § 837; *In re Kip,* 1 Pai. 601; *Bull* v. *Loveland,* 10 Pick. 9;
Lowney v. *Perham,* 20 Me. 235; *Lees* v. *U. S.,* 150 U. S. 476; *Gadsden*
v. *Woodward,* 103 N. Y. 242.]

[2] [*Minters* v. *People,* 139 Ill. 363; cf. *Ward* v. *State,* 2 Mo. 120; *People* v. *Forbes,* 143 N. Y. 219.]

ruled that he must answer, and he then replied, "Yes." The attorney
then asked, ".When?" and he again asserted a like claim of privilege.
The court again ruled that he must answer, and he then stated,when
he saw the note. On appeal it was held that the witness was not
entitled to a privilege as respects any of the questions asked, since
there was nothing in the circumstances of the case, or in the nature
of the questions, to suggest any reasonable apprehension of danger to
him from being compelled to answer. The very nature of the offence
charged against defendant negatived the idea of the witness's being
a party to it, and there was nothing in the character of the evidence
sought to be elicited from him that would reasonably suggest any real
or appreciable danger that it would or could tend to inculpate him in
any other offence.]¹

ARTICLE 121.

CORROBORATION, WHEN REQUIRED.²

When the only proof against a person charged with
a criminal offence is the evidence of an accomplice,

---

¹ [*State* v. *Thaden*, 43 Minn. 253, following the English rule. Some
American decisions state the rule in a different form, saying that "the
witness may be compelled to answer when he contumaciously refuses,
or when it is perfectly clear and plain that he is mistaken, or that the
answer cannot possibly injure him or tend in any degree to subject him
to the peril of prosecution. Where it is not so perfectly evident that
the answer called for cannot incriminate as to preclude all reasonable
doubt or fair argument, the privilege must be recognized and protected." *People* v. *Forbes*, 143 N. Y. 219; *Janvrin* v. *Scammon*, 29
N. H. 280.]

² [Mr. Stephen begins this Article with the following special
statutory rules of the English law, (adding also another rule, which will
be found in the Appendix, Note LIII.):—"No plaintiff in any action for
breach of promise of marriage can recover a verdict, unless his or
her testimony is corroborated by some other material evidence in
support of such promise (32 & 33 Vict. c. 68 s. 2). The fact that the
defendant did not answer letters affirming that he had promised to
marry the plaintiff is not such corroboration (*Wiedemann* v. *Walpole*,
[1891] 2 Q. B. 534).

" No order against any person alleged to be the father of a bastard
child can be made by any justices, or confirmed on appeal by any
Court of Quarter Session, unless the evidence of the mother of the
said bastard child is corroborated in some material particular to the

uncorroborated in any material particular, it is the duty
of the judge to warn the jury that it is unsafe to convict
any person upon such evidence, though they have a legal
right to do so.[1]

---

satisfaction of the said justices or court respectively (8 & 9 Vict. c.
10, s. 6 ; 35 & 36 Vict. c. 6, s. 4)."

Generally in this country the common-law rule applies in these cases
and no corroboration is required. It has been so held as to an action
for breach of promise of marriage (*Giese* v. *Schultz*, 65 Wis. 487 ; cf.
Homan v. *Earle*, 53 N. Y. 267), and as to bastardy proceedings (*State*
v. *Nichols*, 29 Minn. 357 ; *State* v. *McGlothlen*, 56 Ia. 544 ; *Olson* v.
Peterson, 33 Neb. 358 ; *People* v. *Lyon*, 83 Hun, 303 ; *State* v. *Tipton*,
15 Mont. 74 ; for a special rule in Massachusetts and Connecticut, see
Mass. Pub. St. c. 85, s. 16 ; *Leonard* v. *Bolton*, 148 Mass. 66 ; *Benton*
v. *Starr*, 58 Ct. 285).

In some analogous cases corroboration is required. Thus in New
York and some other States, seduction under promise of marriage is
declared to be a crime, but no conviction can be had on the testimony
of the female seduced, uncorroborated by other evidence (*People* v.
Kearney, 110 N. Y. 188 ; *Zabriskie* v. *State*, 43 N. J. L. 640 ; *Rice* v.
Comm., 100 Pa. 28 ; *State* v. *McCaskey*, 104 Mo. 644 ; *State* v. *Lockerby*,
50 Minn. 363 ; *State* v. *Smith*, 84 Ia. 522 ; *La Rosae* v. *State*, 132 Ind.
219 ; *Mill's Case*, 93 Va. 815); so in some States as to criminal prosecutions for abduction, rape, and like offences (N. Y. Pen. Code, § 283;
People v. *Plath*, 100 N. Y. 590; *State* v. *Keith*, 47 Minn. 559; *State* v.
Grossheim, 79 Ia. 75); in a number of the States, however, no corroboration is required in trials for rape (*State* v. *Dusenberry*, 112 Mo.
277 ; *State* v. *Juneau*, 88 Wis. 180; *State* v. *Connelly*, 57 Minn. 482;
Barnett v. *State*, 83 Ala. 40).

So in some States it is a general rule not to grant a divorce upon the
uncorroborated testimony of the complainant (*Robbins* v. *Robbins*, 100
Mass. 150; *McShane* v. *McShane*, 45 N. J. Eq. 341; *Cooper* v. *Cooper*,
88 Cal. 45 ; *Lewis* v. *Lewis*, 75 Ia. 200 ; *Rie* v. *Rie*, 34 Ark. 37 ; contra,
Flattery v. *Flattery*, 88 Pa. 27; *Sylvis* v. *Sylvis*, 11 Col. 319), or upon the
uncorroborated confessions of the defendant (*Summerbell* v. *Summerbell*, 37 N. J. Eq. 603; *Madge* v. *Madge*, 42 Hun, 524 ; Cal. Civ. Code,
§ 130; cf. N. Y. Code Civ. Pro. § 1753); so, in actions for divorce, the
evidence of prostitutes and private detectives has been held to need
corroboration (*Moller* v. *Moller*, 115 N. Y. 466; *McCarthy* v. *McCarthy*, 143 N. Y. 235; *McGrail* v. *McGrail*, 48 N. J. Eq. 532).

For other cases, in which corroboration is required, see Article 122.]
[1] 1 Ph. Ev. 93–101; T. E. ss. 887–891; 3 Russ. Cri. 600–611. [Gr. Ev.

ARTICLE 121 A.

CLAIM ON ESTATE OF DECEASED PERSON.

Claims upon the estates of deceased persons, whether founded upon an allegation of debt or of gift, ought not to be maintained upon the uncorroborated testimony of

---

i. §§ 45, 380-382; *State* v. *Woolard*, 111 Mo. 248; *State* v. *Patterson*, 52 Kan. 335.   It is held, however, in many States to be a *rule of practice* to warn the jury, not a *rule of law*, and to be discretionary with the court (*Comm.* v. *Wilson*, 152 Mass. 12; *Comm.* v. *Bishop*, 165 Mass. 148; *Collins* v. *State*, 98 Ill. 584; *Cheatham* v. *State*, 67 Miss. 335; *State* v. *Barber*, 113 N. C. 711; *State* v. *Kibling*, 63 Vt. 636; *Ingalls* v. *State*, 48 Wis. 647).   Whether such warning be given or not, however, the jury may convict on the uncorroborated testimony of the accomplice, if they are convinced by it beyond a reasonable doubt that the defendant is guilty (Id.; *Cox* v. *Comm.*, 125 Pa. 94; *Hoyt* v. *People*, 140 Ill. 588; *Ayers* v. *State*, 88 Ind. 275; *State* v. *Maney*, 54 Ct. 178; *People* v. *Gallagher*, 75 Mich. 512; *State* v. *Dana*, 59 Vt. 614; *Lamb* v. *State*, 40 Neb. 312; *Campbell* v. *People*, 159 Ill. 9).   Evidence is deemed properly corroborative which tends to connect the accused with the commission of the crime (*Comm.* v. *Holmes*, 127 Mass. 424; *State* v. *Maney*, 54 Ct. 178; *State* v. *Donnelly*, 130 Mo. 642; *Hester* v. *Comm.*, 85 Pa. 139; *Robison* v. *State*, 16 Lea, 146); but some cases say that the corroboration must be as to some material part of the accomplice's testimony or as to some material fact (*State* v. *Patterson*, 52 Kan. 335; *State* v. *Dana*, 59 Vt. 614; *U. S.* v. *Howell*, 56 F. R. 20).

In a number of the States it is provided by statute that no conviction can be had on the testimony of an accomplice, unless there be corroborative evidence tending to connect the defendant with the commission of the crime (*People* v. *Elliott*, 106 N. Y. 288; *People* v. *Mayhew*, 150 N. Y. 346; *State* v. *Van Winkle*, 80 Ia. 15; *Malachi* v. *State*, 89 Ala. 134; *State* v. *Vaughan*, 58 Ark. 353; *State* v. *Jarvis*, 18 Or. 360; *People* v. *Armstrong*, 114 Cal. 570).

Persons who, as detectives, informers, and the like, engage with criminals in their wrongful designs and acts, with the honest purpose of exposing them and bringing them to justice, are not accomplices, within the above rules, and their testimony does not need corroboration, unless otherwise open to question (Gr. Ev. i. § 382; *State* v. *McKean*, 36 Ia. 343; *People* v. *Bolanger*, 71 Cal. 17; *Comm.* v. *Hollister*, 157 Pa. 13; *State* v. *Hoxsie*, 15 R. I. 1; *Comm.* v. *Ingersoll*, 145 Mass.

the claimant, unless circumstances appear or are proved which make the claim antecedently probable, or throw the burden of disproving it on the representatives of the deceased.

Illustrations.

(a) A, a widow, swore that her deceased husband gave her plate, etc., in his house, but no circumstances corroborated her allegation. Her claim was rejected.[1]

(b) A, a widow, claimed the rectification of a settlement drawn by her husband the night before their marriage, and giving him advantages which, as she swore, she did not mean to give him, and were not explained to her by him. Her claim was admitted though uncorroborated.[2]

ARTICLE 122.

NUMBER OF WITNESSES.

In trials for high treason, or misprision of treason, no one can be indicted, tried, or attainted (unless he pleads guilty) except upon the oath of two lawful witnesses,

---

231); so persons forced into criminal acts are not accomplices (*People v. Miller,* 66 Cal. 468; cf. *U. S. v. Thompson,* 31 F. R. 331).

Upon the maxim *falsus in uno, falsus in omnibus,* the testimony of a witness who has wilfully and knowingly sworn falsely as to a material point *may* be disregarded by the jury unless corroborated (*State v. Martin,* 124 Mo. 514; *City of Sandwich v. Dolan,* 141 Ill. 430; *People v. Clark,* 84 Cal. 573; *Judge v. Jordan,* 81 Ia. 519; *Cole v. Lake Shore, etc. R. Co.,* 95 Mich. 77; *Schmitt v. Milwaukee R. Co.,* 89 Wis. 195; *Moett v. People,* 85 N. Y. 373; *Lemmon v. Moore,* 94 Ind. 40). But it is not a rule of law that they *must* so disregard it (Id.; *Comm. v. Billings,* 97 Mass. 405; *Hoge v. People,* 117 Ill. 35; *Hillman v. Schwenk,* 68 Mich. 293; *Ala. etc. R. Co. v. Frazier,* 93 Ala. 45; *Bonnie v. Earll,* 12 Mont. 239; but see *People v. Paulsell,* 115 Cal. 6). The rule applies to *parties,* when they testify, as well as to other witnesses. *People v. Petmecky,* 99 N. Y. 415; *Siebert v. People,* 143 Ill. 571.]

[1] *Finch v. Finch,* 23 Ch. D. 267. [See *Devlin v. Greenwich Sav. Bk.,* 125 N. Y. 756; *Dilts v. Stevenson,* 17 N. J. Eq. 407; *Hatch v. Atkinson,* 56 Me. 324.]

[2] *Lovesy v. Smith,* 15 Ch. D. 655. *In re Garnett, Gandy v. Macaulay,*

either both of them to the same overt act, or one of them
to one and another of them to another overt act of the
same treason.[1] If two or more distinct treasons of divers
heads or kinds are alleged in one indictment, one witness
produced to prove one of the said treasons and another
witness produced to prove another of the said treasons
are not to be deemed to be two witnesses to the same
treason[2] within the meaning of this Article.[3]

If upon a trial for perjury the only evidence against
the defendant is the oath of one witness contradicting
the oath on which perjury is assigned,[4] and if no cir-

---

31 Ch. D. 1, is a similar case. In *In re Hodgson, Beckett* v. *Ramsdale*,
31 Ch. D. p. 183, the language of Hannen, J., in words somewhat re-
laxes the rule, but not, I think, in substance. [The ground of the
decision in *Lovesy* v. *Smith* was that the husband should have explained to the wife, in the clearest terms, the provision in his favor,
and that as the settlement, on its face, was not such as the court
would have sanctioned in the absence of agreement, the burden of
proof was on the husband's representatives. Cf. *Farmer's Excr.* v.
Farmer, 39 N. J. Eq. 211.]

[1] [The law of this country is somewhat different, the U. S. Constitution (Art. 3, s. 3) providing that "no person shall be convicted of
treason unless on the testimony of two witnesses to the *same overt
act*, or on confession in open court." A similar provision is found in
many of the State Constitutions as to treason against the State. Gr.
Ev. i. § 255.]

[2] 7 & 8 Will. III. c. 3, ss. 2, 4. [Gr. Ev. i. § 256.]

[3] [At this point Mr. Stephen adds the following special rule of the
English law: " This provision does not apply to cases of high treason
in compassing or imagining the Queen's death, in which the overt act
or overt acts of such treason alleged in the indictment are assas-
sination or killing of the Queen, or any direct attempt against her life,
or any direct attempt against her person, whereby her life may be
endangered, or her person suffer bodily harm, or to misprision of such
treason. 39 & 40 Geo. III. c. 93."]

[4] 3 Russ. on Crimes, 77–86. [Perjury may be proved by the testimony of two witnesses, or by that of one witness supplemented by
evidence of corroborating circumstances; but not by the uncorroborated testimony of one witness (Gr Ev. i. §§ 257–259; *Williams* v.

cumstances are. proved which corroborate such witness, the defendant is entitled to be acquitted.[1]

Comm., 91 Pa. 493; *People* v. *Wells*, 103 Cal. 631; *State* v. *Hawkins* 115 N. C. 712; *U. S.* v. *Hall*, 44 F. R. 864; *State* v. *Jean*, 42 La. Ann 946; *Thomas* v. *State*, 51 Ark. 138; *Brookin* v. *State*, 27 Tex. App. 701; *People* v. *Stone*, 32 Hun, 41; *State* v. *Heed*, 57 Mo. 252; *Comm.* v. *Parker*, 2 Cush. 212); so documentary evidence alone may suffice to prove perjury (*U. S.* v. *Wood*, 14 Pet. 430). But proof that the accused, on two different occasions, swore to contradictory statements is not sufficient. *Freeman* v. *State*, 19 Fla. 552; *U. S.* v. *Mayer*, Deady, 127.]

[1] [It is a chancery rule that where a bill is so framed as to compel an answer on oath and such answer denies the allegations of the bill, the uncorroborated evidence of one witness in support of the bill will not be sufficient basis for a decree (Gr. Ev. i. § 260; *Morris* v. *White*, 36 N. J. Eq. 324; *Jones* v. *Abraham*, 75 Va. 466; *Smith* v. *Ewing*, 151 Pa. 256; *Southern Development Co.* v. *Silva*, 125 U. S. 247; *Deimel* v. *Brown*, 136 Ill. 586; cf. *Shackelford* v. *Brown*, 72 Miss. 380). But in New York and some other States this rule no longer exists (*Stilwell* v. *Carpenter*, 62 N. Y. 639; *Quertermous* v. *Taylor*, 62 Ark. 598).

After some doubt, it is now held that a usage of business may be established by the testimony of one witness. *Robinson* v. *U. S.*, 13 Wall. 363; *Bissell* v. *Campbell*, 54 N. Y. 353; *Jones* v. *Hoey*, 128 Mass. 585; *Adams* v. *Pittsburgh Ins. Co.*, 95 Pa. 348; *Wootters* v. *Kauffman*, 67 Tex. 488.]

CHAPTER XVI.

OF TAKING ORAL EVIDENCE, AND OF THE EXAMINATION OF WITNESSES.

ARTICLE 123.

EVIDENCE TO BE UPON OATH, EXCEPT IN CERTAIN CASES.

ALL oral evidence given in any proceeding must be given upon oath, except as is stated in this and the following Article.[1]

Every person objecting to being sworn, and stating, as the ground of such objection, either that he has no religious belief, or that the taking of an oath is contrary to his religious belief, may make his solemn affirmation, which is of the same force and effect as if he had taken the oath, and if, having made such affirmation, he wilfully and corruptly gives false evidence, he is liable to be punished as for perjury.

Such affirmation must be as follows:—

"I, A. B., do solemnly, sincerely, and truly declare and affirm,"

and then proceed with the words of the oath prescribed by law, omitting any words of imprecation or calling to witness.[2]

------

[1] [The "following Article" (Art. 123 A) contains a special statutory rule of the English law. It will be found in the Appendix, Note LIII.]

[2] 51 & 52 Vict. c. 46, the Oaths Act, 1888, which repeals the previous enactments on the subject. [Provisions similar to those set forth in

Where an oath has been duly administered and taken, the fact that the person to whom the same was administered had, at the time of taking such oath, no religious belief, does not for any purpose affect the validity of such oath.[1]

ARTICLE 124.

FORM OF OATHS; BY WHOM THEY MAY BE ADMINISTERED.

Oaths are binding which are administered in such form and with such ceremonies as the person sworn declares to be binding.[2]

---

this Article have been generally adopted in this country by statute. Thus it is provided in the U. S. Revised Statutes (s. 1) that "the requirement of an 'oath' shall be deemed complied with by making affirmation in judicial form." So in New York, a solemn declaration or affirmation, in the following form, is administered to a person who declares that he has conscientious scruples against taking an oath: "You do solemnly, sincerely, and truly, declare and affirm," etc. (Code Civ. Pro. § 847). Other States have like provisions. Under such laws a wilful false oath or affirmation constitutes perjury. Id. § 851; U. S. Rev. St. s. 5392.]

[1] 51 & 52 Vict. c. 46, s. 3.
[2] 1 & 2 Vict. c. 105. For the old law, see *Omichund* v. *Barker*, 1 S. L. C. 455. [See *Attorney General* v. *Bradlaugh*, 14 Q. B. D. 667. By the regular common-law form, the oath is administered upon the Gospels, the witness kissing the book, the usual formula repeated to him being, "You do swear that," etc.————"So help you God." But often, nowadays, the witness, instead of kissing the book, simply raises his hand while taking the oath. But the rule stated in this Article is everywhere accepted (*McKinney* v. *People*, 7 Ill. 540; *Green* v. *State*, 71 Ga. 487; *Comm.* v. *Buzzell*, 16 Pick. 153). Thus a Mohammedan may be sworn on the Koran, a Brahmin or a Chinaman by the peculiar methods used in their countries, etc. (*People* v. *Jackson*, 3 Park. Cr. 590; *State* v. *Chiagk*, 92 Mo. 395; *Central, etc. R. Co.* v. *Rockafellow*, 17 Ill. 541; *Bow* v. *People*, 160 Ill. 438; *Newman* v. *Newman*, 7 N. J. Eq. 26). But if such persons take the usual form of oath without objection, they are liable for perjury, if

Any person to whom an oath is administered, who so desires, may be sworn with uplifted hand in the form and manner usual in Scotland.[1]

Every person now or hereafter having power by law or by consent of parties to hear, receive, and examine evidence, is empowered to administer an oath to all such witnesses as are lawfully called before him.[2]

ARTICLE 125.

HOW ORAL EVIDENCE MAY BE TAKEN.

Oral evidence may be taken[3] (according to the law relating to civil and criminal procedure)—

In open court upon a final or preliminary hearing;[4]

---

they wilfully swear falsely (Gr. Ev. i. § 371; *Comm.* v. *Jarboe*, 89 Ky. 143).

In many States, these general rules, more or less modified, are prescribed by statute (see N. Y. Code Civ. Pro. §§ 845-851 ; Mass. Pub. St. c. 169, ss. 13-18; Me. R. S. c. 82, s. 103; Ill. R. S. c. 101 ; 2 How. St. (Mich.) ss. 7537-7539). If an oath be administered *substantially* in the form prescribed by statute, it is valid, and the witness will be guilty of perjury if he wilfully swears falsely. *State* v. *Mason*, 90 N. C. 676 ; *State* v. *Dayton*, 23 N. J. L. 49 ; see *People* v. *Cook*, 8 N. Y. 67, 84.]

[1] 51 & 52 Vict. c. 46, s. 5. [See p. 307, note 2, *ante.*]

[2] 14 & 15 Vict. c. 99, s. 16. [Similar statutes are generally in force in this country. See U. S. Rev. St. ss. 101, 183, 474, 1778, etc.; N. Y. Code Civ. Pro. § 843; Mass. Pub. St. c. 169, ss. 7, 12.]

[3] As to civil procedure, see Order xxxvii. to Judicature Act of 1875 ; Wilson, pp. 264-7. As to criminal procedure, see 11 & 12 Vict. c. 42, for preliminary procedure, and the rest of this chapter for final hearings.

[4] [As to preliminary hearings in *criminal cases*, there are statutes in force in the several States of this country, providing for an examination before a magistrate into the circumstances of a charge against an accused person, and the prisoner may be examined, as well as witnesses for and against him (Bishop's New Cr. Pro. §§ 225-239; N. Y. Code Cr. Pro. §§ 188-221; see Art. 23, *ante*, and notes). So in *civil cases*, statutes in some States provide for the examination before trial of the

Or out of court for future use in court—
(*a*) upon affidavit,
(*b*) under a commission,[1]

---

parties to a cause, or of other persons whose testimony is material and necessary and may otherwise be lost (see N. Y. Code Civ. Pro. §§ 870–886; Mass. Pub. St. c. 167, ss. 49–60); but the examination of a *party* to an action before trial is not permissible in actions at law in the Federal courts. *Ex parte* Fisk, 113 U. S. 713.]

[1] The law as to commissions to take evidence is as follows : The root of it is 13 Geo. III. c. 63. Section 40 of this Act provides for the issue of a commission to the Supreme Court of Calcutta (which was first established by that Act) and the corresponding authorities at Madras and Bombay to take evidence in cases of charges of misdemeanor brought against governors, etc., in India in the Court of Queen's Bench. S. 42 applies to parliamentary proceedings, and s. 44 to civil cases in India. These provisions have been extended to all the colonies by 1 Will. IV. c. 22, and so far as they relate to civil proceedings to the world at large. 3 & 4 Vict. c. 105, gives a similar power to the courts at Dublin. See as to cases in which commissions will not be granted, *In re Boyse*, *Crofton* v. *Crofton*, 20 Ch. D. 760; and *Berdan* v. *Greenwood*, Id., in note, 764; also *Langer* v. *Tate*, 24 Ch. D. 322; *Lawson* v. *Vacuum Brake Co.*, 27 Ch. D. 137.

[There are statutes in the several States of this country, providing for the issuing of commissions by a court or judge, by which commissioners are appointed to take the depositions of witnesses in other States or countries, for use in the particular State issuing the commission. The courts of the foreign jurisdiction will usually aid such commissioners in obtaining the desired testimony, by compelling witnesses to come before them, etc., either upon principles of comity, or in accordance with their own local statutes making this their duty. Another mode of obtaining such evidence is by the issuing of "letters rogatory," which are in the form of a letter missive from a domestic to a foreign court, requesting it to procure and return the desired testimony, under promise of a like favor when required (Gr. Ev. i. § 320). Sometimes foreign courts will comply with such a request, but will not aid commissioners, and then the use of letters rogatory is necessary; but the usual practice is to issue a commission. See U. S. Rev. St. ss. 863–876: N. Y. Code Civ. Pro. §§ 887–920; Mass. Pub. St. c. 169, ss. 23–64 ; 2 How. St. (Mich.) ss. 7433–7447; *Anonymous*, 59 N. Y. 313; *Stein* v. *Bowman*, 13 Pet. 209; *Cortes Co.* v. *Tannhauser*, 18 F. R. 667.]

(c) [1] before any officer of the court or any other person
or persons, appointed for that purpose by the
court or a judge [under due legal authority, or .
designated by statute, or selected by agreement
of the parties.] [2]

Oral evidence taken in open court must be taken
according to the rules contained in this chapter relating
to the examination of witnesses.

Oral evidence taken under a commission must be
taken in the manner prescribed by the terms of the commission. [3]

Oral evidence taken under a commission must be taken
in the same manner as if it were taken in open court; [4]
but the examiner has no right to decide on the validity
of objections taken to particular questions, but must

---

[1] [This paragraph is somewhat changed from the original, and the
next one in the original is wholly omitted here, since they relate to
the special provisions of English statutes. The original paragraphs
will be found in the Appendix, Note LIII.]

[2] [Commonly in this country, by the provisions of statutes or of rules
of court, persons called variously referees, auditors, commissioners,
examiners, etc., may be appointed by a judge or court to take testimony and report it for the information of the court; or such persons
may be appointed by the court or selected by the parties to act as
judges in hearing and deciding causes (see N. Y. Code Civ. Pro.
§§ 827, 1011-1026; Mass. Pub. St. c. 159, s. 51; *Holmes* v. *Turner's Falls
Co.*, 150 Mass. 535; *Howe Machine Co.* v. *Edwards*, 15 Blatch. 402);
masters in chancery perform similar duties. So statutes providing
for the taking of testimony in special cases may designate by official
name the persons before whom it may be taken. N. Y. Code Civ. Pro.
§ 899; U. S. Rev. St. s. 863; Laws of N. J. 1893, c. 100.]

[3] T. E. s. 491. [The mode of taking depositions is often prescribed by
statute or by rules of court; it is sometimes provided that such regulations shall be annexed to the depositions (see U. S. Rev. St. ss. 863-
868; Rules of the Federal Courts; N. Y. Code Civ. Pro. §§ 900-909).
It is a general rule that such regulations must be carefully and pre-
cisely followed.]

[4] T. E. s. 1283. [See last note.]

record the questions, the fact that they were objected to, and the answers given.[1]

If secondary evidence of the contents of any document is not objected to on the taking of a commission, it cannot be objected to afterwards.[2]

Oral evidence given on affidavit must be confined to such facts as the witness is able of his own knowledge to prove,[3] except on interlocutory motions, on which statements as to his belief and the grounds thereof may be admitted.[4] The costs of every affidavit unnecessarily setting forth matters of hearsay or argumentative mat-

---

[1] [So it is held in New York that a referee appointed to take evidence should take all that is offered, and has no power to pass upon objections, such power belonging to the court (*Scott* v. *Williams*, 14 Abb. Pr. 70; *Fox* v. *Moyer*, 54 N. Y. 125). A similar rule is adopted in the equity practice of the Federal courts as to the taking of testimony by examiners (Rule 67 of the Equity Rules, U. S. Courts, 144 U. S. 689). And other States have similar practice (*Brotherton* v. *Brotherton*, 14 Neb. 186; *Estate of Howell*, 14 Phila. 329; *Elyton Co.* v. *Denny*, 108 Ala. 553; cf. *Jones* v. *Keen*, 115 Mass. 170). But referees, etc., who have power to hear and determine issues, may decide upon objections to testimony. *Cincinnati* v. *Cameron*, 33 O. St. 336; *Lathrop* v. *Bramhall*, 64 N. Y. 365; N. Y. Code Civ. Pro. § 1018.]

[2] *Hawksley* v. *Bradshaw*, 5 Q. B. D. 22. [See p. 312, note 2, *post.*]

[3] Judicature Act, 1875, Order xxxvii. 4.

[4] [So in New York and some other States, affidavits upon interlocutory motions may contain statements upon information and belief, but the sources of such information and the grounds of such belief should also be stated, and the reasons why the affidavit of a person having knowledge of the matter cannot be procured should usually appear (*Howe Co.* v. *Pettibone*, 74 N. Y. 68; *Buell* v. *Van Camp*, 119 N. Y. 160; *Bennett* v. *Edwards*, 27 Hun, 352; *Clement* v. *Bullens*, 159 Mass. 193; *Peebles* v. *Foote*, 83 N. C. 102; *Mitchell* v. *Pitts*, 61 Ala. 219). But affidavits merely stating belief, or information and belief, have, in many cases, been held insufficient (*Hadley* v. *Watson*, 143 Mass. 27; *Taylor* v. *Wright*, 121 Ill. 455; *Inglis* v. *Schreiner*, 58 N. J. L. 120; *Hackett* v. *Judge, etc.*, 36 Mich. 334; *Murphy* v. *Purdy*, 13 Minn. 422; *Garner* v. *White*, 23 O. St. 192; *Thompson* v. *Higginbotham*, 18 Kan. 42).

Ex parte affidavits are evidence only when made so by some statute

ter, or copies of or extracts from documents, must be paid by the party filing them.[1]

[2] When a deposition, or the return to a commission, or an affidavit, or evidence taken before an examiner, is used in any court as evidence of the matter stated therein, the party against whom it is read may object to the reading of anything therein contained on any ground on which he might have objected to its being stated by a

---

(*People* v. *Walsh*, 87 N. Y. 481 ; *Bookman* v. *Stegman*, 105 N. Y. 621). As to the difference between an affidavit and a deposition, see *Stimpson* v. *Brooks*, 3 Blatch. 456.]

[1] [An attorney who draws an affidavit is liable for costs if it contains irrelevant and scandalous matter, which is stricken out on motion. *McVey* v. *Cantrell*, 8 Hun, 522 ; cf. *Pitcher* v. *Clark*, 2 Wend. 631.]

[2] T. E. s. 491. *Hutchinson* v. *Bernard*, 2 Mo. & Ro. 1. [It is a general rule in this country that, if opportunity exists for so doing, objections to a deposition in respect to matters of form, or on the ground that it was irregularly or improperly taken, or that fraud was practised, etc., should be raised when the interrogatories are framed, or upon the examination of the witness under the commission, or upon a motion to suppress the deposition ; but objections to the competency of the witness, or to the relevancy or competency of any question or answer, may be made when the deposition is read in evidence (*York Co.* v. *Central R. Co.*, 3 Wall. 107 ; *Howard* v. *Stillwell, etc. Co.*, 139 U. S. 199 ; N. Y. Code Civ. Pro. §§ 910, 911 ; *Newton* v. *Porter*, 69 N. Y. 133 ; *Atlantic Ins. Co.* v. *Fitzpatrick*, 2 Gray, 279 ; *Leavitt* v. *Baker*, 82 Me. 26 ; *Pence* v. *Waugh*, 135 Ind. 143 ; *Stowell* v. *Moore*, 89 Ill. 563 ; *Horseman* v. *Todhunter*, 12 Ia. 230 ; *Barnum* v. *Barnum*, 42 Md. 251). Objections to questions as leading relate to form, and should be taken before the trial (*Akers* v. *Demond*, 103 Mass. 318 ; *Hazlewood* v. *Heminway*, 3 T. & C. 787 ; *Crowell* v. *Western Reserve Bk.*, 3 O. St. 406 ; *Hill* v. *Canfield*, 63 Pa. 77 ; *Chambers* v. *Hunt*, 22 N. J. L. 552).

Answers in the deposition which are not responsive may be objected to on the trial by either party (*Lansing* v. *Coley*, 13 Abb. Pr. 272 ; *Greenman* v. *O'Connor*, 25 Mich. 30 ; *Kingsbury* v. *Moses*, 45 N. H. 222). And where a party uses a deposition taken by his opponent, he makes it his own, and such opponent has the same right of objection to the questions and answers as if the deposition had been taken by the party offering it (*Hatch* v. *Brown*, 63 Me. 410 ; *In re*

witness examined in open court, provided that no one is entitled to object to the reading of any answer to any question asked by his own representative on the execution of a commission to take evidence.

ARTICLE 126.*

EXAMINATION IN CHIEF, CROSS-EXAMINATION, AND RE-EXAMINATION.

Witnesses examined in open court must be first examined in chief, then cross-examined, and then re-examined.[1]

---

* See Note XLV. [Appendix].

Smith, 34 Minn. 436; see *Rucker* v. *Reid*, 36 Kan. 468; *Little* v. *Edwards*, 69 Md. 499); so he may contradict the witness as if the latter were the witness of the party reading the deposition (*Bloomington* v. *Osterle*, 139 Ill. 120).

Though a witness's deposition has been taken, yet if at the time of the trial he is present and is ready and able to testify, his personal testimony is, by the law of many States, deemed preferable, and the deposition is inadmissible (*Neilson* v. *Hartford St. R. Co.*, 67 Ct. 466; *Whitford* v. *Clark Co.*, 119 U. S. 522; *Hayward* v. *Barron*, 38 N. H. 366; contra, *Hedges* v. *Williams*, 33 Hun, 546; *Scott* v. *Indianapolis Wagon Works*, 48 Ind. 75.]

[1] [The court may, in its discretion, order witnesses to withdraw from the court-room, so that they may not hear each other's testimony (*Comm.* v. *Follansbee*, 155 Mass. 274; *People* v. *Burns*, 67 Mich. 537; *State* v. *Morgan*, 35 W. Va. 260). If any witness disobeys the order, this may be observed upon to the jury to affect his credibility, and he is punishable for contempt; but the court cannot refuse to allow him to be examined, unless his disobedience was by the procurement, connivance, or other fault of the party calling him, in which case it may refuse or permit examination; a party cannot, without fault on his own part, be deprived of the testimony of the witness (Gr. Ev. i. § 432; *Holder* v. *U. S.*, 150 U. S. 91; *Parker* v. *State*, 67 Md. 329; *State* v. *Thomas*, 111 Ind. 515; *State* v. *Gesell*, 124 Mo. 531; *State* v. *Falk*, 46 Kan. 498; *Dickson* v. *State*, 39 O. St. 73; *Hubbard* v. *Hubbard*, 7 Or. 42; *People* v. *Boscovitch*, 20 Cal. 436; *Comm.* v. *Brown*, 90 Va. 671; *Rooks* v. *State*, 65 Ga. 330; cf. *Pergason* v. *Etcherson*, 91 Ga. 785). In like manner, expert witnesses may be required to withdraw, though this is rarely done (*Vance* v. *State*, 56 Ark. 402; *Leache* v. *State*, 22

Whenever any witness has been examined in chief, or
has been intentionally sworn,[1] or has made a promise
and declaration as hereinbefore mentioned for the purpose of giving evidence,[2] the opposite party has a right

---

Tex. App. 279). But *parties* to actions, either civil or criminal, cannot
be excluded, even though they are to testify as witnesses (*McIntosh
v. McIntosh*, 79 Mich. 198; *Schneider v. Haas*, 14 Or. 174; *Bernheim
v. Dibrell*, 66 Miss. 199; *Garman v. State*, id. 196; *Richards v. State*,
91 Tenn. 723; cf. *French v. Sale*, 63 Miss. 386); nor can the guardian
of an infant party (*Cottrell v. Cottrell*, 81 Ind. 87); nor one having a
pecuniary interest in the suit (*Simon Gregory Co. v. McMahan*, 61
Mo. App. 499). Another method of excluding witnesses is to place
them under the charge of an officer of the court, to be kept by him out
of the court-room (*Hey's Case*, 32 Gratt. 946).

A party's failure to call a witness whom he might call does not generally raise a presumption that his testimony would be unfavorable to
such party, especially if such witness is equally accessible to both parties, or his testimony would be simply cumulative (*Scovill v. Baldwin*,
27 Ct. 316; *Bleecker v. Johnston*, 69 N. Y. 309; *State v. Fitzgerald*,
68 Vt. 125; *Coleman v. State*, 111 Ind. 563; *Cross v. Lake Shore, etc.
R. Co.*, 69 Mich. 363; *Kerstner v. Vorweg*, 130 Mo. 196; *Bates v. Morris*, 101 Ala. 282). But where the witness's testimony would be of vital
importance in the case (as *e. g.*, if he were the only eye-witness of the
facts), and, under the special circumstances of the case, the adverse
party has no legal right to call him, an unfavorable inference by the
jury is warranted (*People v. Hovey*, 92 N. Y. 554; *Comm. v. Weber*,
167 Pa. 153; *State v. Rodman*, 62 Ia. 456; *The Fred. M. Laurence*, 15
F. R. 635); and the same is true if a party fails to call a material witness who is within his control and whom he would naturally be expected to call to testify in his behalf (*Kirby v. Tallmadge*, 160 U. S.
379; *Comm. v. McCabe*, 163 Mass. 98; *State v. Hogan*, 67 Ct. 581;
Kenyon v. Kenyon, 88 Hun, 211; *Rice v. Comm.*, 102 Pa. 408; *People
v. Germaine*, 101 Mich. 485; cf. *Graves v. U. S.*, 150 U. S. 118; *People
v. Sharp*, 107 N. Y. 427, 465); so if a party fails to testify himself as to
vital facts peculiarly within his own knowledge. *Cole v. Lake Shore,
etc. R. Co.*, 81 Mich. 156.]

[1] See cases in T. E. s. 1238.

[2] [See Art. 123. As forms of affirmation different from the English
are allowed in this country, this clause will need variation to adapt it
to the local State law]

to cross-examine him;[1] but the opposite party is not entitled to cross-examine merely because a witness has been
called to produce a document on a *subpœna duces tecum,*
or in order to be identified.[2] After the cross-examination
is concluded, the party who called the witness has a right
to re-examine him.

The court may in all cases permit a witness to be
recalled either for further examination in chief or for
further cross-examination, and if it does so, the parties
have the right of further cross-examination and further
re-examination respectively.[3]   .

If a witness dies, or becomes incapable of being further

---

[1] [In a few States of this country, a similar rule prevails, and a witness called to testify merely as to the formal execution of a written
instrument, or as to other preliminary matter, etc., may be cross-
examined as to all matters material to the issue (*Blackington* v. *Johnson,* 126 Mass. 21; *Beal* v. *Nichols,* 2 Gray, 262; *Diel* v. *Stegner,* 56
Mo. App. 535 (in civil cases); *Hemminger* v. *Western Assurance Co.,* 95
Mich. 355; *Huntsville, etc. R. Co.* v. *Corpening,* 97 Ala. 681; *Perry* v.
Mulligan, 58 Ga. 479, 482; *King* v. *Atkins,* 33 La. Ann. 1057 (in civil
cases); *Kibler* v. *McIlwain,* 16 S. Car. 550). But in most States the
rule is adopted that the cross-examination must be limited to matters stated upon the direct examination. See next Article and note 1
on p. 317; Gr. Ev. i. §§ 445–447; Wh. Ev. i. § 529.]

[2] [See note to 15 F. R. 726; *Aikin* v. *Martin,* 11 Pai. 499. The
simple verification of a signature by a witness does not entitle the
adverse party to see the document or to cross-examine the witness
upon it, until it is offered in evidence. *Stiles* v. *Allen,* 5 Allen, 320;
Calderon v. *O'Donahue,* 47 F. R. 39; *Arnold* v. *Chesebrough,* 30 F.
R. 145.]

[3] [*Shepard* v. *Potter,* 4 Hill, 202; *Williams* v. *Sargeant,* 46 N. Y.
481; *Continental Ins. Co.* v. *Delpeuch,* 82 Pa. 225; *Comm.* v. *McGorty,*
114 Mass. 299; *Faust* v. *U. S.,* 163 U. S. 452; *Brown* v. *State,* 72 Md.
468; *Osborne* v. *O'Reilly,* 34 N. J. Eq. 60; *State* v. *Johnson,* 89 Ia. 1;
Rea v. *Wood,* 105 Cal. 314; *Cummings* v. *Taylor,* 24 Minn. 429. It is
a general rule that the order of proof is in the discretion of the trial
court. *Platner* v. *Platner,* 78 N. Y. 90; *Hess* v. *Wilcox,* 58 Ia. 380;
Thiede v. *Utah,* 159 U. S. 510; *State* v. *Murphy,* 118 Mo. 1.]

examined at any stage of his examination, the evidence given before he became incapable is good.[1]

If in the course of a trial a witness who was supposed to be competent appears to be incompetent, his evidence may be withdrawn from the jury, and the case may be left to their decision independently of it.[2]

---

[1] *R.* v. *Doolin,* 1 Jebb, C. C. 123. The judges compared the case to that of a dying declaration, which is admitted though there can be no cross-examination. [By the weight of authority in this country, if the death of a witness in a *common-law action* precludes his cross-examination, his testimony given on the direct examination is not admitted (*People* v. *Cole,* 43 N. Y. 508; S. C. 2 Lans. 370; *Pringle* v. *Pringle,* 59 Pa. 281; *Sperry* v. *Moore's Estate,* 42 Mich. 353; see *Curtice* v.*West,* 50 Hun, 47; cf. *People* v. *Severance,* 67 Hun, 182; *Lewis* v. *Eagle Ins. Co.,* 10 Gray, 508), unless the party having the right to cross-examine him had the opportunity of doing so before death occurred and did not choose to exercise it (*Bradley* v. *Mirick,* 91 N. Y. 293; *Celluloid Mfg. Co.* v. *Arlington Mfg. Co.,* 47 F. R. 4). Where, however, the witness's testimony is substantially complete, though the examination was not wholly finished, it will be received (*Fuller* v. *Rice,* 4 Gray, 343). Where the opportunity to cross-examine is lost by the misconduct of the witness, or through the fault of the party introducing him, or other like cause, his evidence in chief is rejected (*Hewlett* v. *Wood,* 67 N. Y. 394; *Matthews* v. *Matthews,* 53 Hun, 244; *The Jacob Brandow,* 33 F. R. 160).

The English rule, as stated by Mr. Stephen, has been said by some American decisions to be applicable in *equity cases* (Gr. Ev. i. § 554; *Gass* v. *Stinson,* 3 Sumn. 98; *Scott* v. *McCann,* 76 Md. 47); and there is some judicial expression in favor of applying it also to *common-law* actions (*Forrest* v.*Kissam,* 7 Hill, 463; see *Sturm* v. *Atlantic Ins. Co.,* 63 N. Y. 77, 87; the N. Y. cases contain contradictory expressions).

As to the effect of cross-examination being lost by the death of a *party,* see *Hay's Appeal,* 91 Pa. 265; *Comins* v. *Hetfield,* 12 Hun, 375, 80 N. Y. 261.]

[2] *R.* v. *Whitehead,* L. R. 1 C. C. R. 33. [Wh. Ev. i. § 393; Gr. Ev. i. §§ 421, 422; *Lester* v. *McDowell,* 18 Pa. 91; *State* v. *Damery,* 48 Me. 327; *Shurtleff* v. *Willard,* 19 Pick. 202; *Seeley* v. *Engell,* 13 N. Y. 542; *Loveridge* v. *Hill,* 96 N. Y. 222. But if the incompetency of the witness is known when he is called and sworn, objection should be made then, or it will ordinarily be deemed to be waived (*Benson* v. *U. S.,* 146 U. S. 325; *Monfort* v. *Rowland,* 38 N. J. Eq. 181; *Quin* v.

Article 127.

TO WHAT MATTERS CROSS-EXAMINATION AND RE-EXAMINATION MUST BE DIRECTED.

The examination and cross-examination must relate to facts in issue or relevant or deemed to be relevant thereto, but the cross-examination need not be confined to the facts to which the witness testified on his examination in chief.[1]

Lloyd, 41 N. Y. 349; *Donelson* v. *Taylor,* 8 Pick. 390; *Watson* v. *Riskamire,* 45 Ia. 231; *Atchison, etc. R. Co.* v. *Stanford,* 12 Kan. 354; *Hickman* v. *Green,* 123 Mo. 165; *Dickinson* v. *Buskie,* 59 Wis. 136; *Smith* v. *Profitt,* 82 Va. 832).

So incompetent or improper evidence may be stricken out or withdrawn from the jury after it has been admitted. *Stokes* v. *Johnson,* 57 N. Y. 673; *Wilson* v. *Kings Co.,* 114 N. Y. 487; *Beaudette* v. *Gagne,* 87 Me. 534; *Specht* v. *Howard,* 16 Wall. 564; *Selkirk* v. *Cobb,* 13 Gray, 313.]

[1] [See p. 315, note 1, *ante.* But it is the rule in most of the States of this country that the cross-examination must be limited to the matters stated in the examination in chief; if the party cross-examining inquires as to new matter, he makes the witness so far his own (*Houghton* v. *Jones,* 1 Wall. 702; *People* v. *Oyer & Term. Court,* 83 N. Y. 436; *Carey* v. *Hart,* 63 Vt. 424; *State* v. *Smith,* 49 Ct. 376; *Donnelly* v. *State,* 26 N. J. L. 463 & 601; *Sullivan* v. *Railroad Co.,* 175 Pa. 361; *Hunsinger* v. *Hofer,* 110 Ind. 390; *Rigdon* v. *Conley,* 141 Ill. 565; *Martin* v. *Capital Ins. Co.,* 85 Ia. 643; *Richards* v. *State,* 82 Wis. 172; *Hurlbut* v. *Hull,* 39 Neb. 892; *People* v. *Van Ewan,* 111 Cal. 144; *Miller* v. *Miller's Admr.,* 92 Va. 510; *Williams* v. *State,* 32 Fla. 315; *Austin* v. *State,* 14 Ark. 555; *State* v. *Wright,* 40 La. Ann. 589 (in criminal cases); as to the range of inquiry which this rule permits, see *Bohan* v. *Avoca Borough,* 154 Pa. 404; *Boyle* v. *State,* 105 Ind. 469; *Erie, etc. Dispatch* v. *Stanley,* 123 Ill. 158; *Glenn* v. *Gleason,* 61 Ia. 28; *Birdseye* v. *Butterfield,* 34 Wis. 52). The same rule applies to *parties* to actions, when they become witnesses (*Boyd* v. *Conshohocken Mills,* 149 Pa. 363; *Hansen* v. *Miller,* 145 Ill. 538; but see *Schultz* v. *Chicago, etc. R. Co.,* 67 Wis. 616). Some States have special statutes applying the rule to defendants as witnesses in *criminal cases* (*State* v. *Avery,* 113 Mo. 475; *People* v. *Wong Ah Leong,* 99 Cal. 440; cf. *State* v. *Saunders,* 14 Or. 300; see p. 298, note, *ante*). If

The re-examination must be directed to the explanation of matters referred to in cross-examination; and if new matter is, by permission of the court, introduced in re-examination, the adverse party may further cross-examine upon that matter.[1]

---

the bounds authorized by law for cross-examination are not exceeded, the witness is deemed to be continually that of the party introducing him, and the testimony which he gives, both upon the direct and the cross-examination, is treated as evidence given in behalf of such party (*Turnbull* v. *Richardson*, 69 Mich. 400; *Davis* v. *California Powder Works*, 84 Cal. 617; and see cases *supra*).

This rule does not limit cross-examination of the kind described in Art. 129. The rule there stated is commonly accepted doctrine. See *Rangley* v. *Wadsworth*, 99 N. Y. 61.]

[1] [Gr. Ev. i. § 467; *Gilbert* v. *Sage*, 5 Lans. 287, 57 N. Y. 639; *U. S.* v. *18 Barrels, etc.*, 8 Blatch. 475; *Somerville, etc. R. Co.* v. *Doughty*, 22 N. J. L. 495; *Farrell* v. *Boston*, 161 Mass. 106; *McElheny* v. *Pittsburgh, etc. R. Co.*, 147 Pa. 1; *Stoner* v. *Devilbiss*, 70 Md. 144; *Norwegian Plow Co.* v. *Hanthorn*, 71 Wis. 529. The general rule that the re-examination must relate to matters developed on the cross-examination is usually adhered to in practice, but still it is generally held that the trial court may, in its discretion, allow the re-examination to extend to other matters (*Kendall* v. *Weaver*, 1 Allen, 277; *Clark* v. *Vorce*, 15 Wend. 193; *Springfield* v. *Dalby*, 139 Ill. 34; *Blake* v. *Stump*, 73 Md. 160; *Schaser* v. *State*, 36 Wis. 429; see *People* v. *Buchanan*, 145 N. Y. 1; *Hemmens* v. *Bentley*, 32 Mich. 89). If part of a conversation or transaction be developed on the direct or cross-examination, the other party may, on the cross or re-direct, bring out such other parts of the same conversation or transaction as explain or qualify the portion already testified to, but he may not give evidence of distinct and independent statements or matters (*People* v. *Beach*, 87 N. Y. 508; *Nay* v. *Curley*, 113 N. Y. 575; *Ballew* v. *U. S.*, 160 U. S. 187, 193; *Dole* v. *Wooldredge*, 142 Mass. 161; *Scott* v. *People*, 141 Ill. 195; *Walsh* v. *Porterfield*, 87 Pa. 376; *Oakland Ice Co.* v. *Maxcy*, 74 Me. 294).

In some States it is held that if one party, without objection, introduces irrelevant evidence which is prejudicial to the other party, the latter may give evidence (even if this be also irrelevant) which goes directly to contradict it (*State* v. *Witham*, 72 Me. 531; *Mowry* v. *Smith*, 9 Allen, 67; *Furbush* v. *Goodwin*, 25 N. H. 425; *Perry* v. *Moore*, 66 Vt. 519; *Budd* v. *Meriden Elec. R. Co.*, 69 Ct. 272; *Mobile*,

ARTICLE 128.

LEADING QUESTIONS.

Questions suggesting the answer which the person putting the question wishes or expects to receive, or suggesting disputed facts as to which the witness is to testify, must not, if objected to by the adverse party, be asked in examination in chief, or in re-examination, except with the permission of the court, but such questions may be asked in cross-examination.[1]

---

etc. R. Co. v. *Ladd*, 92 Ala. 287; cf. *Perkins* v. *Hayward*, 124 Ind. 449; *Milbank* v. *Jones*, 141 N. Y. 340; *Gorsuch* v. *Rutledge*, 70 Md. 272).

The party who opens a case must, in general, introduce all the evidence to prove his side of the case before he closes; then after his adversary's evidence is given, he may give proof in reply or rebuttal. But it is in the discretion of the court to permit evidence to be given in reply which should properly have been given in chief. *Marshall* v. *Davies*, 78 N. Y. 414; *Young* v. *Edwards*, 72 Pa. 257; *Watkins* v. *Rist*, 68 Vt. 486; *McGowan* v. *Chicago, etc. R. Co.*, 91 Wis. 147; *Huntsman* v. *Nichols*, 116 Mass. 521; *Belden* v. *Allen*, 61 Ct. 173; *Goldsby* v. *U. S.*, 160 U. S. 70; *City of Sandwich* v. *Dolan*, 141 Ill. 430; *People* v. *Cox*, 70 Mich. 247; *Lurssen* v. *Lloyd*, 76 Md. 360; *Tierney* v. *Spiva*, 76 Mo. 279; *Graham* v. *Davis*, 4 O. St. 362.]

[1] [Gr. Ev. i. §§ 434, 435, 445; Wh. Ev. i. §§ 499–504. But such questions may be allowed to be put on the direct examination when the witness appears hostile to the party introducing him (*McBride* v. *Wallace*, 62 Mich. 451; *Bradshaw* v. *Combs*, 102 Ill. 428; *Whitman* v. *Morey*, 63 N. H. 448; *State* v. *Benner*, 64 Me. 267; *St. Clair* v. *U. S.*, 154 U. S. 150); or when the examination relates to items, dates, or numerous details, where the memory ordinarily needs suggestion (*Huckins* v. *People's Ins. Co.*, 31 N. H. 238; *Graves* v. *Merchants' Ins. Co.*, 82 Ia. 637); or when it is necessary to direct the witness's attention plainly to the subject-matter of his testimony, etc. (*People* v. *Mather*, 4 Wend. 229; *Union Pac. R. Co.* v. *O'Brien*, 49 F. R. 538; *Farmers' Ins. Co.* v. *Bair*, 87 Pa. 124). It is discretionary with the trial court whether such questions shall be permitted and judgment will not be reversed for permitting them, unless there be a plain abuse of discretion (*Vrooman* v. *Griffiths*, 1 Keyes, 53; *Northern Pac. R. Co.* v. *Urlin*, 158 U. S. 271; *Badder* v. *Keefer*, 91 Mich. 611; *Goudy* v.

ARTICLE 129.*

QUESTIONS LAWFUL IN CROSS-EXAMINATION.

When a witness is cross-examined, he may, in addition to the questions hereinbefore referred to, be asked any questions which tend—

(1) To test his accuracy, veracity, or credibility;[1] or

(2) To shake his credit, by injuring his character.

Witnesses have been compelled to answer such questions, though the matter suggested was irrelevant to the matter in issue, and though the answer was disgraceful to the witness; but it is submitted that the court has the right to exercise a discretion in such cases, and to refuse to compel such questions to be answered when the truth of the matter suggested would not in the opinion of the court affect the credibility of the witness as to the matter to which he is required to testify.[2]

---

* See Note XLVI. [Appendix].

Werbe, 117 Ind. 154; *Crean v. Hourigan*, 158 Ill. 301; *York v. Pease*, 2 Gray, 282). Leading questions are legitimate on cross-examination (*U. S. v. Dickinson*, 2 McL. 325; *Helfrich v. Stein*, 17 Pa. 143). A leading question is one which suggests to the witness, and leads him to make, the answer desired (*People v. Mather*, supra; *Coogler v. Rhodes*, 38 Fla. 240; *Harvey v. Osborn*, 55 Ind. 535; *People v. Parish*, 4 Den. 153).

In those States where a party by cross-examining a witness as to new matter makes the witness so far his own (see p. 317, note 1, *ante*), he has no legal right to ask leading questions as to such new matter. *People v. Oyer & Term. Court*, 83 N. Y. 436; *Harrison v. Rowan*, 3 Wash. C. C. 580.]

[1] [*State v. Duffy*, 57 Ct. 525; *Tudor Iron Works v. Weber*, 129 Ill. 535; *Wallace v. Wallace*, 62 Ia. 651; *McFadden v. Santa Anna, etc. R. Co.*, 87 Cal. 464; *Uniacke v. Chicago, etc. R. Co.*, 67 Wis. 108.]

[2] [*Muller v. St. Louis Hospital Ass'n*, 5 Mo. App. 390, 73 Mo. 242; *Carroll v. State*, 32 Tex. App. 431. It is a well-settled doctrine in this country that a witness may be cross-examined as to specific facts tending to disgrace or degrade him, for the purpose of impairing his credibility, though these facts are purely irrelevant and collateral to the

In the case provided for in Article 120, a witness cannot
be compelled to answer such a question.

Illustrations.

(a) The question was, whether A committed perjury in swearing that
he was R. T. B deposed that he made tattoo-marks on the arm of R. T.,
which at the time of the trial were not and never had been on the
arm of A. B was asked and was compelled to answer the question

---

main issue; also that the extent to which such questions may be
allowed is to be determined by the discretion of the trial court, which
commits no error unless it abuses its discretion ; that the witness may
claim the privilege of declining to answer, when the court allows such
questions, but that when answers are called for which are material to
the issue, there is no privilege (*Great Western Turnpike Co. v. Loomis,*
32 N. Y. 127 ; *People v. Oyer & Terminer Ct.,* 83 N. Y. 436 ; *Huoncker
v. Merkey,* 102 Pa. 462 ; *Gutterson v. Morse,* 58 N. H. 165 ; *Storm v.
U. S.,* 94 U. S. 76 ; *Smith v. State,* 64 Md. 25 ; *State v. Hack,* 118 Mo.
92 ; *Helwig v. Lascowski,* 82 Mich. 619 ; *Fries v. Brugler,* 12 N. J. L.
79 ; *Shelby v. Clagett,* 46 O. St. 549 ; *State v. Pfefferle,* 36 Kan. 90 ;
State v. Row, 81 Ia. 138 ; *South Bend v. Hardy,* 98 Ind. 577, fully dis-
cussing the subject ; but in California and Massachusetts irrelevant
questions to affect credibility are not permitted, *Barkley v. Copeland,*
86 Cal. 483 ; *Comm. v. Schaffner,* 146 Mass. 512). The exercise of discretion is also limited by the rule that the examination as to collateral
facts should be such in its nature as to affect the witness's credibility (Id.; *Langley v. Wadsworth,* 99 N. Y. 61 ; *People v. Williams,* 93
Mich. 625 ; *Hayward v. People,* 96 Ill. 492 ; *State v. Gleim,* 17 Mont.
17). In New York it is held that questions as to his having been *accused, indicted, arrested,* etc., for wrongful acts are, when properly
excepted to, improper, since these facts are consistent with innocence,
and, therefore, do not in reality affect credibility (*People v. Crapo,* 76
N. Y. 288 ; *Van Bokkelen v. Berdelle,* 130 N. Y. 141; so in Arkansas,
Bates v. State, 60 Ark. 450 ; cf. *Kitteringham v. Dance,* 58 Ia. 566). In
a number of the States, however, such questions are held permissible,
subject to the discretion of the court (see Illustration (*d*); *People v.
Foote,* 93 Mich. 38 ; *State v. Taylor,* 118 Mo. 153 ; *Burdette v. Comm.,*
93 Ky. 76 ; *Hill v. State,* 91 Tenn. 521 ; *State v. Murphy,* 45 La. Ann.
958 ; cf. *State v. Bacon,* 13 Or. 143 ; *Hill v. State,* 42 Neb. 503 ; *Sexton
v. State,* 33 Tex. App. 416). These general rules apply also to *parties*
to actions (including defendants in criminal cases), when they become
witnesses (*Sullivan v. O'Leary,* 146 Mass. 322 ; *People v. Webster,* 139

whether, many years after the alleged tattooing, and many years before the occasion on which he was examined, he committed adultery
with the wife of one of his friends.[1]

(*b*) [On the trial of A for stealing a horse, a witness B was asked on
cross-examination whether he did not live with a woman who kept
a house of ill-fame. The court against objection admitted the
question, but informed the witness that he could answer or not as
he chose.][2]

(*c*) [Upon the trial of A for an assault, he became himself a witness
and was asked on cross-examination whether he had not committed
an assault upon another person at another time. This was objected
to, but was held on appeal, to have been properly allowed by the trial
court within its discretion.][3]

(*d*) [Upon the trial of A for murder, he became himself a witness
and was asked on cross-examination whether he had not once been
arrested for an assault with intent to kill. The court against objection
admitted the question, and the witness then answered without claiming his privilege. This was held a proper exercise of the court's discretion.][4]

(*e*) [A witness was asked on cross-examination, "Have you ever been

---

N. Y. 73; *People* v. *Noelke*, 94 N. Y. 137; *Leland* v. *Knauth*, 47 Mich.
508; *State* v. *Wells*, 54 Kan. 161; see cases *supra* and the Illustrations;
also p. 298, note, *ante*).

So a witness may be cross-examined as to facts showing his *favor*
towards the party calling him, his own *interest* in the case, or his *bias*,
malice, *ill-will*, *prejudice*, etc., against the opposite party; here, also,
the judge's discretion governs the range of examination (Illustrations (*g*), (*h*), (*i*); *Wallace* v. *Taunton St. Ry.*, 119 Mass. 91; *Garnsey* v. *Rhodes*, 138 N. Y. 461; *Fitzpatrick* v. *Riley*, 163 Pa. 65; *County
Commrs.* v. *Minderlein*, 67 Md. 567; *Hinchcliffe* v. *Koontz*, 121 Ind.
422; *Electric Light Co.* v. *Grant*, 90 Mich. 469; *People* v. *Thomson*,
92 Cal. 506; see Article 130). So when a *party* to an action testifies,
he may be cross-examined in like manner. *Lamb* v. *Lamb*, 146 N. Y.
317; *Mears* v. *Cornwall*, 73 Mich. 78.]

[1] *R.* v. *Orton*. See summing-up of Cockburn, C. J., vol. ii. p. 719, etc.

[2] [*State* v. *Ward*, 49 Ct. 429. The witness, when he avails himself
of his privilege not to answer, is not obliged to explain why he declines
to answer. *Merluzzi* v. *Gleeson*, 59 Md. 214.]

[3] [*People* v. *Irving*, 95 N. Y. 541; see *People* v. *McCormick*, 135
N. Y. 663.]

[4] [*Hanoff* v. *State*, 37 O. St. 178; see p. 321, note, *supra*.]

in jail, and, if so, what were you sent there for?" Counsel objected to the question, but the trial court allowed it; and this ruling was held, on appeal, to have been proper.][1]

(*f*) [A witness was asked on cross-examination in a civil action as to his belief in spiritualism. It was a proper exercise of discretion not to allow the question.][2]

(*g*) [Upon a proceeding to admit a will to probate, a subscribing witness may be asked on cross-examination, in order to show his bias· or interest, whether a reward has not been promised to him for his testimony by one of the beneficiaries under the will.][3]

(*h*) [On a trial for murder, it was held proper for the prosecution to cross-examine one of the principal witnesses for the defendant in such a way as to show that such witness was devotedly attached to the defendant and was, at the time of the homicide, practically one of his household, and that their relations were intimate and confidential.][4]

(*i*) [A brought action against a horse-car company to recover damages for an alleged injury caused by being wrongfully thrown off a car platform by the conductor. B, a former car-driver of the company, who had been discharged, testified in A's favor that A was thrown off the car by the conductor. It was held that the defendant might so cross-examine B as to show his hostility to the defendant by bringing out the fact that he had tried to get other employees of the company to make false statements in order to fasten liability upon the company.][5]

ARTICLE 129 A.

JUDGE'S DISCRETION AS TO CROSS-EXAMINATION TO CREDIT.

The judge may in all cases disallow any questions put in cross-examination of any party or other witness which

---

[1] [*McLaughlin* v. *Mencke*, 80 Md. 83; see, to the same effect, *State* v. *Pratt*, 121 Mo. 566; *State* v. *Alexis*, 45 La. Ann. 973; *Real* v. *People*, 42 N. Y. 270. In these cases it is held not necessary to prove his conviction for the offence for which he was confined, by the record of conviction. Id.; *State* v. *Martin*, 124 Mo. 514; contra, *Comm.* v. *Sullivan*, 161 Mass. 59; see page 325, note 1, *post.*]

[2] [*Free* v. *Buckingham*, 59 N. H. 219.]

[3] [*Matter of Will of Snelling*, 136 N. Y. 515.]

[4] [*People* v. *Webster*, 139 N. Y. 73.]

[5] [*Schultz* v. *Third Ave. R. Co.*, 89 N. Y. 242.]

may appear to him (*i. e.*, the judge) to be vexatious and
not relevant to any matter proper to be inquired into in
the cause or matter.[1]

ARTICLE 130.

EXCLUSION OF EVIDENCE TO CONTRADICT ANSWERS TO QUESTIONS TESTING VERACITY.

When a witness under cross-examination has been
asked and has answered any question which is relevant
to the inquiry only in so far as it tends to shake his credit
by injuring his character, no evidence can be given to
contradict him,[2] except in the following cases:—

(1) If a witness is asked whether he has been previously
convicted of any felony or misdemeanor, and denies or

---

[1] Rules of Supreme Court, Order xxxvi., Rule 38. I leave Article 129 as it originally stood, because this Order is, after all, only an exception to the rule. " Him" must refer to the judge, as it would otherwise refer to the " party or other witness," which would be absurd [See p. 320, note 2. *ante ; La Beau* v. *People*, 34 N. Y. 223; *Langley* v. *Wadsworth*, 99 N. Y. 61 ; *Goins* v. *Moberly*, 127 Mo. 116. Even if a wide latitude be allowable in cross-examination, still the witness is entitled to be protected by the court from unnecessary insult and abuse by counsel. *Toledo, etc. R. Co.* v. *Williams*, 77 Ill. 354 ; *People* v. *Durrant*, 116 Cal. 179.]

[2] *A. G.* v. *Hitchcock*, 1 Ex. 91, 99–105. See, too, *Palmer* v. *Trower*, 8 Ex. 247. [Gr. Ev. i. § 449; *People* v. *Ware*, 29 Hun, 473, 92 N. Y. 653; *People* v. *Knapp*, 42 Mich. 267; *Elliott* v. *Boyles*, 31 Pa. 65. It is a general rule as to *all collateral and irrelevant inquiries*, whether relating to character or not, that the answers given cannot be contradicted ; the cross-examining counsel is bound by the answers given ; the reason of the rule is that time may not be taken up with immaterial issues. *People* v. *Murphy*, 135 N. Y. 450; *Pullen* v. *Pullen*, 43 N. J. Eq. 136; *Robbins* v. *Spencer*, 121 Ind. 594 ; *Alexander* v. *Kaiser*, 149 Mass. 321; *People* v. *Hillhouse*, 80 Mich. 580; *Swanson* v. *French*, 92 Ia. 195; *Buckley* v. *Silverberg*, 113 Cal. 673; *Hester* v. *Comm* , 85 Pa. 139; *Sloan* v. *Edwards*, 61 Md. 89; *Moore* v. *People*, 108 Ill. 484; *State* v. *Benner*, 64 Me. 267 ; see Illustrations (*a*) and (*b*).]

does not admit it, or refuses to answer, evidence may be given of his previous conviction thereof.[1]

(2) If a witness is asked any question tending to show that he is not impartial, and answers it by denying the facts suggested, he may be contradicted.[2]

---

[1] 28 & 29 Vict. c. 18, s. 6. [At common law, conviction for crime must be proved by the record thereof, or by a duly authenticated copy, (these being the best evidence), and not by cross-examination (Gr. Ev. i. §§ 375, 457; *Newcomb* v. *Griswold*, 24 N. Y. 298). And now that, as has been seen (see p. 273, note, *ante*), it is the rule in this country in most States that conviction for crime no longer disqualifies a witness but may be proved to affect his credibility, proof of conviction must still, in some of these States, be made by the record or a copy thereof (Mass. Pub. St. c. 169, s. 19; *Comm.* v. *Gorham*, 99 Mass. 420; Pub. St. N. H. c. 224, s. 26 (ed. 1891); *Simons* v. *People*, 150 Ill. 66 (criminal cases); *State* v. *Brent*, 100 Mo. 531; *Boyd* v. *State*, 94 Tenn. 505; *Murphy* v. *State*, 108 Ala. 10; cf *People* v. *Schenick*, 65 Cal. 625); in most of these States, however, either the record (or a copy) may be used, or the witness may be cross-examined as to his conviction (Ill. Rev. St. c. 51, s. 1 (civil cases); Neb. Code Civ. Pro. § 338; *State* v. *Elwood*, 17 R. I. 763; *Spiegel* v. *Hays*, 118 N. Y. 660; *State* v. *O'Brien*, 81 Ia. 93; *State* v. *Sauer*, 42 Minn. 258; *State* v. *Probasco*, 46 Kan. 310; *State* v. *Bacon*, 13 Or. 143; *People* v. *Crowley*, 100 Cal. 478; *Burdette* v. *Comm.*, 93 Ky. 76; *Driscoll* v. *People*, 47 Mich. 413); and in some of these latter States, if he denies that he was convicted, his answer may be contradicted (N. Y. Code Civ. Pr. § 832; N. J. Rev. p. 378, § 1, p. 379 § 9; Wis. Rev. St. s. 4073; St. of Minn. s. 6841 (ed. 1894); *Helwig* v. *Lascowski*, 82 Mich. 619). These general rules apply to *parties* to actions (including defendants in criminal cases), when they become witnesses. *People* v. *Noelke*, 94 N. Y. 137; *Bartholomew* v. *People*, 104 Ill. 601; *State* v. *Pfefferle*, 36 Kan. 90; *State* v. *Minor*, 117 Mo. 302; *State* v. *McGuire*, 15 R. I. 23; and cases *supra*.]

[2] *A. G.* v. *Hitchcock*, 1 Ex. 91, pp. 100, 105. [It is a well-settled rule that if a witness be cross-examined for the purpose of showing his *interest* in the case, or his *bias, favor, hostility, prejudice*, etc., towards either party (see p. 322, note, *ante*), and answers by a denial, he may be contradicted (Illustration (c); Gr. Ev. i. § 450; *Davis* v. *Roby*, 64 Me. 427; *Folsom* v. *Brawn*, 25 N. H. 114; *McGuire* v. *McDonald*, 99 Mass. 49; *Schults* v. *Third Av. R. Co.*, 89 N. Y. 242; *Kent* v. *State*, 42 O. St. 426; *Staser* v. *Hogan*, 120 Ind. 207; *Phenix* v. *Castner*, 108 Ill. 207; *Tolbert* v. *Burke*, 89 Mich. 132; *Schuster* v. *State*, 80 Wis. 107; *People*

Illustrations.

(*a*) [On the trial of A for murder, a female witness B is asked on cross-examination whether she did not take things not belonging to her when she left a place where she had been at service. She answers by a denial. This being a collateral inquiry, it cannot be shown by another witness that her answer is untrue.][1]

(*b*) [The question is, whether two persons were jointly interested in buying and selling *cattle*. One of them becomes a witness, and is questioned, on cross-examination, as to their being jointly interested in a particular purchase and sale of *horses*, which is a matter irrelevant to the issue on trial. He answers that they were. This answer cannot be contradicted.][2]

(*c*) [A witness called by A, in a suit between A and B, testifies, on cross-examination, that he has never threatened revenge against B. This being an inquiry as to bias or hostility of feeling, he may be contradicted on this point by other testimony.][3]

ARTICLE 131.*

STATEMENTS INCONSISTENT WITH PRESENT TESTIMONY MAY BE PROVED.

Every witness under cross-examination in any proceeding, civil or criminal, may be asked whether he has made any former statement relative to the subject-matter of the proceeding and inconsistent with his present testimony, the circumstances of the supposed statement being referred to sufficiently to designate the

---

* See Note XLVII. [Appendix].

v. *Murray*, 85 Cal. 350). In some States such a state of feeling on the part of the witness may be proved without previously cross-examining him in respect thereto (*New Portland* v. *Kingfield*, 55 Me. 172; *Day* v. *Stickney*, 14 Allen, 255; *People* v. *Brooks*, 131 N. Y. 321); but in other States the rule is otherwise. *Aneals* v. *People*, 134 Ill. 401, 414; *Martineau* v. *May*, 18 Wis. 54; *Langhorne* v. *Comm.*, 76 Va. 1012; *State* v. *Dickerson*, 98 N. C. 708.]

[1] [*Stokes* v. *People*, 53 N. Y. 164; see *People* v. *Greenwall*, 108 N. Y. 296.]

[2] [*Farnum* v. *Farnum*, 13 Gray, 508.]

[3] [*Collins* v. *Stephenson*, 8 Gray, 438.]

particular occasion, and if he does not distinctly admit
that he has made such a statement, proof may be given
that he did in fact make it.[1]

---

[1] [A similar rule is in force here in most States. It only applies when
the testimony of the adversary's witness, which is to be contradicted,
is *relevant* to the issue (Gr. Ev. i. § 462; *Ayers* v. *Watson*, 132 U. S.
394; *Ankersmit* v. *Tuch*, 114 N. Y. 51; *Lawler* v. *McPheeters*, 73 Ind.
577; *Atchison, etc. R. Co.* v. *Feehan*, 149 Ill. 202; *State* v. *McLaughlin*, 44 Ia. 82; *Rice* v. *Rice*, 104 Mich. 371; *Welch* v. *Abbot*, 72 Wis. 512;
Granning v. *Swenson*, 49 Minn. 381; *State* v. *Bartley*, 48 Kan. 421;
Thompson v. *Wertz*, 41 Neb. 31; *State* v. *Hunsaker*, 16 Or. 497; *Birch*
v. *Hall*, 99 Cal. 299; *Brown* v. *State*, 72 Md. 468; *N. Y. etc. R. Co.* v.
Kellam, 83 Va. 851; *State* v. *Goodwin*, 32 W. Va. 177; *Allison* v. *Coal
Co.*, 87 Tenn. 60; *Spohn* v. *Mo. Pac. R. Co.*, 122 Mo. 1; *Haley* v. *State*,
63 Ala. 83; *State* v. *Jones*, 44 La. Ann. 960). It is a general rule that
the time and place of the supposed statement and the persons to whom
or in whose presence it was made should be definitely presented to
the witness's attention by the question put to him in cross-examination
(see the cases *supra*); it is sufficient, however, if the particular occasion is designated with reasonable certainty, so that the witness can
be under no mistake concerning it (*Mayer* v. *Appel*, 13 Ill. App. 87;
Pendleton v. *Empire, etc. Co.*, 19 N. Y. 13; *Evansville, etc. R. Co.* v.
Montgomery, 85 Ind. 494; see Illustrations *a* and *b*). This is commonly
called "laying the foundation" for the introduction of the impeaching
evidence; the object is to give the witness an opportunity either to
deny having made the alleged statement, or, if he admits that he made
it, to explain the alleged inconsistency. If such opportunity be not
given, the evidence offered to show the contradiction is not admissible
(*McCulloch* v. *Dobson*, 133 N. Y. 114; *Richardson* v. *Kelly*, 85 Ill. 491;
Stone v. *Northwestern Sleigh Co.*, 70 Wis. 585; *State* v. *Cleary*, 40
Kan. 287; *Paterson* v. *State*, 83 Md. 194; see cases *supra*). Still if the
opportunity be not afforded *before* the impeaching evidence is given,
but the witness is recalled *afterwards* and a chance to explain is then
properly given to him, this, though irregular practice, obviates the
ground of objection (*People* v. *Weldon*, 111 N. Y. 569; *Esterly* v. *Ep-
pelsheimer*, 73 Ia. 260; *Rounsavell* v. *Pease*, 45 Wis. 506; *State* v.
Goodbier, 48 La. Ann. 770). If, however, the witness's absence or
death prevents his receiving any opportunity to explain, the impeaching evidence must be rejected (Illustrations (*c*) and (*d*); *Mattox* v.
U.S., 156 U. S. 237; *Hubbard* v. *Briggs*, 31 N. Y. 518, 536; *Runyan* v.
Price, 15 O. St. 1; *Eppert* v. *Hall*, 133 Ind. 417).

When the witness, the proper foundation being laid, *denies* having

The same course may be taken with a witness upon his examination in chief, if the judge is of opinion that

---

made the statement, the fact that he did make it may be afterwards proved by the persons who heard it; and the same is true if his answer is that he *does not recollect* making it (*Martin* v. *Towle*, 59 N. H. 31; *Kelly* v. *Cohoes Co.*, 8 App. Div. (N. Y.) 156; Ind. Rev. St. § 508; *Consol. Ice Machine Co.* v. *Keifer*, 134 Ill. 481; *Jensen* v. *Railroad Co.*, 102 Mich. 176; *Payne* v. *State*, 60 Ala. 80). But if he *admits* having made the statement, such evidence is not necessary and is excluded (*Atchison, etc. R. Co.* v. *Feehan*, 149 Ill. 202; *State* v. *Goodbier*, 48 La. Ann. 770). Stenographic minutes of a witness's alleged contradictory evidence on a former trial will not be admissible to impeach him, but the stenographer may be called as impeaching witness and use the minutes to refresh his memory (*Stayner* v. *Joyce*, 120 Ind. 99; *Toohey* v. *Plummer*, 69 Mich. 345; *State* v. *Adams*, 78 Ia. 292; cf. *Campbell* v. *Campbell*, 138 Ill. 612). If a witness's present testimony is as to matter of *opinion*, and such opinion evidence is competent in the case, the fact that he has previously expressed or testified to contrary opinions may be shown to impeach him (*Sanderson* v. *Nashua*, 44 N. H. 492; *Waterman* v. *Chicago, etc. R. Co.*, 82 Wis. 613). But testimony as to matters of *fact* cannot be impeached by proving the expression of opinions inconsistent therewith (Gr. Ev. i. § 449; *Holmes* v. *Anderson*, 18 Barb. 420; *Sloan* v. *Edwards*, 61 Md. 89; *Central R. Co.* v. *Allmon*, 147 Ill. 471; *McFadin* v. *Catron*, 120 Mo. 252). The question put to the impeaching witness should, in general, be in the same language, substantially, as was used in calling the attention of the impeached witness to his former statements (*Sloan* v. *N. Y. C. R. Co.*, 45 N. Y. 125; *Farmers' Ins. Co.* v. *Bair*, 87 Pa. 124; *Pence* v. *Waugh*, 135 Ind. 143; *Rice* v. *Rice*, 104 Mich. 371; *People* v. *Monella*, 99 Cal. 333; but see *Rucker* v. *State*, 71 Miss. 680). The contradictory statements proved for impeachment are legitimate for this purpose only; they are not evidence of the facts asserted therein (*Plyer* v. *German Amer. Ins. Co.*, 121 N. Y. 689; *Lundberg* v. *Northwestern Elev. Co.*, 42 Minn. 37; *Charlton* v. *Unis*, 4 Gratt. 58). After they have been proved, the witness may be allowed to testify in rebuttal, by way of explanation (*McMurrin* v. *Rigby*, 87 Ia. 18; *Waterman* v. *Chicago, etc. R. Co.*, 82 Wis. 613; cf. *Bressler* v. *People*, 117 Ill. 422); or other witnesses may be called to support his denial of having made the contradictory statements (*Bronson* v. *Leach*, 74 Mich. 713).

In some of the New England States, a witness's contradictory statements can be proved without first calling his attention to them on cross-examination (*Wilkins* v. *Babbershall*, 32 Me. 184; *Cook* v.

he is "adverse" (*i. e.*, hostile) to the party by whom he
was called, and permits the question.[1]

Brown, 34 N. H. 460; *Day* v. *Stickney*, 14 Allen, 255, 260; *Tomlinson*
v. *Derby*, 43 Ct. 562); but he may be recalled to explain the alleged
inconsistency (*State* v. *Reed*, 62 Me. 129; *Gould* v. *Norfolk Lead Co.*,
9 Cush. 338; *Hedge* v. *Clapp*, 22 Ct. 262; see *Harrison's Appeal*, 48
Ct. 202). In Pennsylvania and Vermont it rests in the discretion of
the trial court which order of examination shall be pursued (*Rothrock*
v. *Gallaher*, 91 Pa. 108; *State* v. *Glynn*, 51 Vt. 577).

   The general rules, stated in this note, apply to the impeachment of
a *party* to an action, when he becomes a witness (*Winchell* v. *Winchell*,
100 N. Y. 159; *Comm.* v. *Tolliver*, 119 Mass. 312; *Browning* v.
Gosnell, 91 Ia. 448; *Dunbar* v. *McGill*, 69 Mich. 297; *Kelsey* v.
Layne, 28 Kan. 218); but if his prior inconsistent statements constitute
admissions, relevant to the issue, they may be proved without first
calling his attention to them. *Brown* v. *Calumet Riv. R. Co.*, 125 Ill.
600; *Hunter* v. *Gibbs*, 79 Wis. 70; *Leroy, etc. R. Co.* v. *Butts*, 40 Kan.
159; *White* v. *White*, 82 Cal. 427.]

[1] [This is by an English statute (see Note XLVII., Appendix). But
it is a general rule of the common law that *a party cannot impeach his
own witness*, by proving either his general bad character or his former
statements inconsistent with his testimony (Gr. Ev. i. § 442; *Cox* v.
Eayres, 55 Vt. 24; *Adams* v. *Wheeler*, 97 Mass. 67; *Becker* v. *Koch*,
104 N. Y. 395), and this is still true in most States (Id.; *Hildreth* v.
Aldrich, 15 R. I. 163; *Wheeler* v. *Thomas*, 67 Ct. 577; *Pollock* v.
Pollock, 71 N. Y. 137; *Brewer* v. *Porch*, 17 N. J. L. 377; *Stearns* v.
Merchants' Bk., 53 Pa. 490; *Hall* v. *Chicago, etc. R. Co.*, 84 Ia. 311;
State v. *Burks*, 132 Mo. 363; *State* v. *Keefe*, 54 Kan. 197; *Dixon* v.
State, 86 Ga. 754; *Dunlap* v. *Richardson*, 63 Miss. 447). But he may
prove the true facts of the case by other witnesses, though this may
incidentally discredit the witness; for such facts are competent evi-
dence in the cause and are not proved for the direct and special pur-
pose of impeachment (*Coulter* v. *Amer. Exp. Co.*, 56 N. Y. 585;
First Nat. Bk. v. *Post*, 66 Vt. 237; *Pennsylvania R. Co.* v. *Fortney*, 90
Pa. 323; *East St. Louis R. Co.* v. *O'Hara*, 150 Ill. 580; *Smith* v.
Utesch, 85 Ia. 381; *Smith* v. *Ehanert*, 43 Wis. 181; *Wallach* v. *Wylie*,
28 Kan. 138; *Sewell* v. *Gardner*, 48 Md. 178; *Meyer Drug Co.* v. *Mc-
Mahan*, 50 Mo. App. 18; *Hollingsworth* v. *State*, 79 Ga. 605). The
rule prohibiting impeachment applies also to the case where a party
makes a witness his own by cross-examining him as to new matter
(*Fairchild* v. *Bascomb*, 35 Vt. 398; *Deere* v. *Bagley*, 80 Ia. 197;
Richards v. *State*, 82 Wis. 172; cf. *Artz* v. *Railroad Co.*, 44 Ia. 284;

It seems that the discretion of the judge cannot be reviewed afterwards.[1]

---

[1] *Rice* v. *Howard*, 16 Q. B. D. 681.

---

see p. 317, note 1, *ante*). So where a party calls the opposing party as a witness, he cannot impeach him, though he may prove the true facts by other witnesses (*Tarsney* v. *Turner*, 48 F. R. 818; *Good* v. *Knox*, 64 Vt. 97; *Rindskopf* v. *Kuder*, 145 Ill. 607; *Gardner* v. *Connelly*, 75 Ia. 205; *Schmidt* v. *Durnam*, 50 Minn. 96; *Claflin* v. *Dodson*, 111 Mo. 195; *Chester* v. *Wilhelm*, 111 N. C. 314; but see *Brubaker's Admr.* v. *Taylor*, 76 Pa. 83); even in the absence of such counter evidence, however, he is not bound by whatever testimony such other party (who is naturally an adverse witness) may give, but the credibility of this testimony in all its parts is for the jury (*Becker* v. *Koch*, 104 N. Y. 395; *Cross* v. *Cross*, 108 N. Y. 628; *Mitchell* v. *Sawyer*, 115 Ill. 650). Where a witness is one whom the law obliges the party to call, as the subscribing witness to a deed or will, he may impeach him by showing his contradictory statements (*Thornton's Excrs.* v. *Thornton's Heirs*, 39 Vt. 122; *Shorey* v. *Hussey*, 32 Me. 579; *Whitman* v. *Morey*, 63 N. H. 448; cf. *People* v. *Case*, 105 Mich. 92; *State* v. *Slack*, 69 Vt. 486; but see *Whitaker* v. *Salisbury*, 15 Pick. 534).

If a party is surprised by unexpectedly adverse testimony given by his own witness, in conflict with prior statements which the witness has made, he may be permitted to examine the witness himself as to his having made such statements, calling his attention definitely to the time, place, and occasion of making them, and thus make it apparent to the court that the witness disappoints him, and give the latter a chance to explain, if possible, the apparent inconsistency; in this way the party, if the witness gives no satisfactory explanation, may at least succeed in neutralizing the effect of his testimony (*Putnam* v. *U. S.*, 162 U. S. 697-707; *Hickory* v. *U. S.*, 151 U. S. 303; *Bullard* v. *Pearsall*, 53 N. Y. 230; *McNerney* v. *Reading*, 150 Pa. 611; *Humble* v. *Shoemaker*, 70 Ia. 223; *Johnson* v. *Leggett*, 28 Kan. 590; *White* v. *State*, 87 Ala. 24; *State* v. *Vickers*, 47 La. Ann. 1574; cf. *Fisher* v. *Hart*, 149 Pa. 232). If, however, the witness denies having made such statements, the party cannot impeach him by evidence of his general bad character, nor by evidence that he did in fact make the statements (*Hurley* v. *State*, 46 O. St. 320; *Hildreth* v. *Aldrich*, 15 R. I. 163; *Bullard* v. *Pearsall*, supra; *Stearns* v. *Merchants' Bk.*, 53 Pa. 490); in some States, however, the contradictory statements may be proved (*Hurlburt* v. *Bellows*, 50 N. H. 105; *Selover* v. *Bryant*, 54 Minn. 434; *State* v. *Sorter*, 52 Kan. 531; see *Smith* v.

Illustrations.

(*a*) [Upon a trial for murder the defendant's wife was called as a witness in his behalf and testified that on the night before the commission of the crime he came home at nine o'clock, sick at his stomach, and with a severe headache, that he undressed and went to bed and lay there for hours. On cross-examination her attention was called to a certain occasion on the day after the crime was committed, when she met the district-attorney with Mr. A and Mr. B, and she was asked, "Did you say then to the district-attorney, in the presence of A & B, that you had never seen anything strange or unusual in your husband's conduct, and that he came home the night before and went to bed and slept as usual?" She denied having said so. Mr. A was afterwards called as a witness, and his attention being called to the above interview, he was asked if she did then make the above statement. He answered that she did, and his testimony was held to be competent.][1]

(*b*) [In an action to recover damages for an injury to plaintiff by being run over by a horse-car, the question was controverted whether the driver was intoxicated at the time. He was called as a witness and testified that he was not intoxicated. On cross-examination he was asked, "Did you not, *after* the first trial of this case, at the back door of A's place, at 8th and Jefferson Streets, tell B & C, in a conversation there about this accident, that you did not deny being intoxicated at the time of the accident?" He answered, "No." Then B was called as a witness and asked, "Did the driver, shortly *before* the first trial of this case, at the back door of A's business place, at 8th and Jefferson Streets in a conversation about the injury to the plaintiff, say

---

Briscoe, 65 Md. 561 ; *Chism* v. *State,* 70 Miss. 742 ; *Nat. Syrup Co.* v. *Carlson,* 42 Ill. App. 178). The party may also, of course, prove the true facts of the case by other witnesses (Id.; *Hickory* v. *U. S.,* 151 U. S. 303; *State* v. *Knight,* 43 Me. 11, 134).

There are statutes in some States, as in England, permitting a party to impeach his own witness (Ind. Rev. St. s. 515 (ed. 1894); Mass. Pub. St. c. 169, s. 22 ; St. of Vt. s. 1247 (ed. of 1894); Cal. Code Civ. Pro. § 2049 ; Rev. St. Fla. s. 1101 ; Code of Ga. § 3869 (ed. of 1882); Mont. Code Civ. Pro. § 3377 ; see *Brooks* v. *Weeks,* 121 Mass. 433; *Blough* v. *Parry,* 144 Ind. 463; *State* v. *Steeves,* 29 Or. 85 ; *Adams* v. *State,* 34 Fla. 185). So, in some States, a party who calls the opposing party as a witness, may impeach him. Pub. St. N. H. c. 224, s. 15 (ed. 1891); *Crocker* v. *Agenbroad,* 122 Ind. 585.]

[1] [*People* v. *Schuyler,* 106 N. Y. 298.]

to you, in the presence of C, that he did not deny being intoxicated at the time of the accident?" B answered, "Yes." On appeal, the ruling of the trial court admitting B's testimony was held to be erroneous, since the driver had not been questioned about a conversation *before* the first trial, and therefore the proper foundation had not been laid.] [1]

(*c*) [In a civil action a deposition of A, who was absent at sea, was read in evidence by the plaintiff. The defendant then offered to prove by a witness B, that the latter had had a number of conversations with A several months after the deposition was taken, in which A made statements inconsistent with his testimony and said that what he had sworn to was false. The court would not receive B's testimony, because A had had no opportunity afforded to him to explain the alleged contradictions.] [2]

(*d*) [Upon a trial for murder A testified against the defendant. The defendant was convicted, but his conviction was reversed and a new trial was had. Meanwhile A had died, and the testimony which he gave on the former trial was read to the jury. The defendant's counsel then offered testimony to the effect that A, subsequently to the first trial, had stated that the evidence given by him on the first trial was false. This testimony was rejected.] [3]

ARTICLE 132.

CROSS-EXAMINATION AS TO PREVIOUS STATEMENTS IN WRITING.

A witness under cross-examination, (or a witness whom the judge under the provisions of Article 131 has permitted to be examined by the party who called him as to previous statements inconsistent with his present testimony), may be questioned as to previous statements made by him in writing, or reduced into writing, relative to the subject-matter of the cause, without such writing being shown to him (or being proved in the first instance); but if it is intended to contradict him by the writing, his attention must, before such contradictory proof can be

---

[1] [*Quincy Horse R. Co.* v. *Gnuse*, 137 Ill. 264.]
[2] [*Stacy* v. *Graham*, 14 N. Y. 492.]
[3] [*Craft* v. *Comm.*, 81 Ky. 250; *Ayers* v. *Watson*, 132 U. S. 394.]

given, be called to those parts of the writing which are
to be used for the purpose of contradicting him. The
judge may, at any time during the trial, require the
document to be produced for his inspection, and may
thereupon make such use of it for the purposes of the trial
as he thinks fit.[1]

---

[1] 17 & 18 Vict. c. 125, s. 24; and 28 Vict. c. 18, s. 5. I think the words
in parenthesis represent the meaning of the sections, but in terms they
apply only to witnesses under cross-examination—"Witnesses may be
cross-examined," etc. [The statutory rule of this Article is not followed in this country, but the former English rule, laid down in the
Queen's Case, 2 B. & B. 286. When it is sought on cross-examination
to impeach an adversary's witness by inconsistent statements previously made by such witness *in writing*, as in a letter, affidavit, or
other written instrument, the witness should not be asked whether in
such letter (or other writing) he made certain statements, which counsel suggests, but the proper practice is to first exhibit the writing to
him and ask him if he wrote it or signed it. If he assents, the writing
should itself be read in evidence as the best evidence of its contents
and before examining the witness in reference to its statements. The
court may in its discretion permit it to be put in evidence when the
witness admits it to be his writing, if cross-examining counsel wishes
then to question in regard to its contents; but the regular time for introducing it is when said counsel develops his own side of the case. After
the paper has been given in evidence, due opportunity is afforded to
the witness to explain the alleged inconsistency (Gr. Ev. i. §§ 463-465;
Romertze v. *East River Bk.*, 49 N. Y. 577; *Gaffney* v. *People*, 50 N. Y.
416; *Hosmer* v. *Groat*, 143 Mass. 16; *Morford* v. *Peck*, 46 Ct. 380;
Chicago R. Co. v. *McLaughlin*, 146 Ill. 353; *Chicago, etc. R. Co.* v.
Hastings, 136 Ill. 251; *Lightfoot* v. *People*, 16 Mich. 507; *Glenn* v.
Gleason, 61 Ia. 28; *O'Riley* v. *Clampt*, 53 Minn. 539; *State* v. *Stein*, 79
Mo. 330; *So. Kan. R. Co.* v. *Painter*, 53 Kan. 414; *Floyd* v. *State*, 82
Ala. 16; *State* v. *Callegari*, 41 La. Ann. 578). The whole instrument
should be read, or at least all of it which has any bearing upon the
matters concerning which the witness is examined (*Whitman* v. *Morey*,
63 N. H. 448; *Hamilton* v. *People*, 29 Mich. 195; *Wilkerson* v. *Eilers*,
114 Mo. 245). Sometimes, however, this regular order of examination
is not pursued, but the witness is cross-examined about the contents
of the writing though it has not been read in evidence; this may hap-
pen when counsel entitled to object to this irregular practice does not
do so in due time and on proper grounds, or when it appears that no

Illustration.

[In an action brought by A, who had been bookkeeper and cashier for B, against the latter to recover damages for a wrongful discharge, B pleaded that A had been rightfully discharged for misconduct, and called C, his chief clerk, as a witness to prove such misconduct. C testified that A had been absent at various times during business hours, sometimes being away nearly half a day at a time, that he was frequently late in the morning, and that, when his presence in the office was very much needed, he was frequently away on his own business and could not be found. On the cross-examination of C, a letter was produced and shown to him, and he admitted that he . wrote it. At the close of the defendant's evidence this letter was read in evidence by plaintiff's counsel. It was as follows : " *To whom it may concern :* A was in the employ of B, and I can bear testimony to his promptness and efficiency in his duties as bookkeeper and cashier. C." It was held on appeal that the letter was properly admitted to impeach C's testimony.][1]

ARTICLE 133.

IMPEACHING CREDIT OF WITNESS.

The credit of any witness may be impeached by the adverse party, by the evidence of persons who swear that they, from their knowledge of the witness, believe him to be unworthy of credit upon his oath.[2] Such per-

---

prejudice can be occasioned thereby. *Chicago, etc. R. Co.* v. *Artery,* 137 U. S. 507; *The Charles Morgan,* 115 U. S. 69; *Dunbar* v. *McGill,* 69 Mich. 297; *State* v. *Mathews,* 88 Mo. 121; *State* v. *West,* 95 Mo. 139.]

[1] [*Western Mfrs.' Ins. Co.* v. *Boughton,* 136 Ill. 317.]

[2] [It is a well-settled rule in this country that a witness of the adverse party may be impeached by evidence from other persons of his *bad general reputation* in his own community. The impeaching witnesses must come from this community, and in examining any one of them the form of inquiry usually is to ask (1) whether he knows the general reputation in that community of the witness in question ; then, if he assents, (2) what that reputation is, and, if he says it is not good, (3) whether from such knowledge he would believe such witness on his

sons may not upon their examination in chief give reasons for their belief, but they may be asked their reasons in

---

oath (Gr. Ev. i. § 461; *Brown* v. *U. S.*, 164 U. S. 221; *Carlson* v. *Winterson*, 147 N. Y. 652; *Bogle's Excrs.* v. *Kreitzer*, 46 Pa. 465; *Gifford* v. *People*, 148 Ill. 173; *Spies* v. *People*, 122 Ill. 9, 208; *Sloan* v. *Edwards*, 61 Md. 89, 103; in Massachusetts it is discretionary with the trial court whether the first question shall be asked, *Wetherbee* v. *Norris*, 103 Mass. 565). The inquiry must only be as to *general reputation*, not as to specific wrongful acts (*Comm.* v. *O'Brien*, 119 Mass. 342; *People* v. *Greenwall*, 108 N. Y. 296; *Drew* v. *State*, 124 Ind. 9, 17; *State* v. *Rogers*, 108 Mo. 202). The reputation asked about must be in most States for *truth and veracity* (*Sargent* v. *Wilson*, 59 N. H. 396; *Shaw* v. *Emery*, 42 Me. 59; *State* v. *Fournier*, 68 Vt. 262; *Quinsigamond Bk.* v. *Hobbs*, 11 Gray, 250; *State* v. *Randolph*, 24 Ct. 363; *Atwood* v. *Impson*, 20 N. J. Eq. 150; *Warner* v. *Lockerby*, 31 Minn. 421; *Hillis* v. *Wylie*, 26 O. St. 574; *U. S.* v. *Van Sickle*, 2 McL. 219; *Laclede Bk.* v. *Keeler*, 109 Ill. 385; *Bogle's Excrs.* v. *Kreitzer*, supra; *People* v. *Abbott*, 97 Mich. 484; *Wallis* v. *White*, 58 Wis. 26; *State* v. *Johnson*, 40 Kan. 266; *Wimer* v. *Smith*, 22 Or. 469; see *Teese* v. *Huntington*, 23 How. (U. S.) 2); but in some States the inquiry may be as to *general moral character* (*Watkins* v. *State*, 82 Ga. 231; *Merriman* v. *State*, 3 Lea, 393), or it is optional to inquire either as to general moral character, or as to truth and veracity, or as to both (*Dollner* v. *Lints*, 84 N. Y. 669; *Wright* v. *Paige*, 3 Keyes, 581; *Robbins* v. *Spencer*, 121 Ind. 594; *Griffith* v. *State*, 140 Ind. 163; *State* v. *Larson*, 85 Ind. 659; *State* v. *Potts*, 78 Ia. 656; *State* v. *Gesell*, 124 Mo. 531; *Lockard* v. *Comm.*, 87 Ky. 201; *McCutchen* v. *Loggins*, 109 Ala. 457; *State* v. *Spurling*, 118 N. C. 1250; *Hollingsworth* v. *State*, 53 Ark. 387); in California the question is as to truth, honesty, and integrity (*People* v. *Ryan*, 108 Cal. 581). In most States also the third question (as to belief on oath) is asked (*U. S.* v. *Van Sickle*, 2 McL. 219; *Lyman* v. *Philadelphia*, 56 Pa. 488; *Hamilton* v. *People*, 29 Mich. 173, 185; *Titus* v. *Ash*, 24 N. H. 319; *Knight* v. *House*, 29 Md. 194; *Wilson* v. *State*, 3 Wis. 798; *Hillis* v. *Wylie*, 26 O. St. 574; *State* v. *Johnson*, 40 Kan. 266; *Peck* v. *State*, 86 Tenn. 259; *Cole* v. *State*, 59 Ark. 50; *State* v. *Christian*, 44 La. Ann. 950; Ga. Code, § 3873); in New York and Illinois it is permissible, but not necessary (*People* v. *Mather*, 4 Wend. 229; *Wright* v. *Paige*, 3 Keyes, 581; *Laclede Bk.* v. *Keeler*, 109 Ill. 385; and see *People* v. *Tyler*, 35 Cal. 553); but in a few States it is not allowable (*Willard* v. *Goodenough*, 30 Vt. 393; *Walton* v. *State*, 88 Ind. 9; *State* v. *Rush*, 77 Mo. 519; cf. *King* v. *Ruckman*, 20 N. J. Eq. 316).

When a *party* to an action (including a defendant in a criminal

cross-examination, and their answers cannot be contradicted.[1]

No such evidence may be given by the party by whom any witness is called,[2] but when such evidence is given by the adverse party, the party who called the witness may give evidence in reply to show that the witness is worthy of credit.[3]

---

case) is a witness, he may be impeached like other witnesses by proof of his bad general reputation (*Foster* v. *Newbrough*, 58 N. Y. 481; *Keyes* v. *State*, 122 Ind. 527; *State* v. *Kirkpatrick*, 63 Ia. 554; *State* v. *Day*, 100 Mo. 242; *Lockard* v. *Comm.*, 87 Ky. 201; *Peck* v. *State*, 86 Tenn. 259; *People* v. *Hickman*, 113 Cal. 80).

The inquiry is generally as to the impeached witness's reputation at the time of the trial, but since reputation once established is presumed to continue (see Art. 101, note 3, *ante*), it may relate to his reputation before or after the trial, if the period is not too remote (*Dollner* v. *Lintz*, 84 N. Y. 669; *Graham* v. *Chrystal*, 2 Abb. Dec. 263; *Amidon* v. *Hosley*, 54 Vt. 25). An interval of weeks, or months, or even of several years has been held not too remote (Id.; *Sleeper* v. *Van Middlesworth*, 4 Den. 431; *Pape* v. *Wright*, 116 Ind. 502; *Davis* v. *Comm.*, 95 Ky. 19); but upon the question of years the authorities are not in accord (*Francis* v. *Franklin T'p*, 179 Pa. 203; *State* v. *Potts*, 78 Ia. 656; *Buse* v. *Page*, 32 Minn. 111; *Wood* v. *Matthews*, 73 Mo. 477; *State* v. *Parker*, 96 Mo. 382; *Yarbrough* v. *State*, 105 Ala. 43; *Watkins* v. *State*, 82 Ga. 231; *Cline* v. *State*, 51 Ark. 140). Reputation at a former place of residence may also be inquired into, if the time is not too remote. *Norwood* v. *Andrews*, 71 Miss. 641; *Coates* v. *Sulan*, 46 Kan. 341.]

[1] 2 Ph. Ev. 503-4; T. E. ss. 1324-5; see *R.* v. *Brown*, L. R. 1 C. C. R. 70. [An impeaching witness may be cross-examined as to his means of knowledge, the grounds of his unfavorable opinion, his bias against the impeached witness, etc. (*People* v. *Mather*, 4 Wend. 229, 258; *Gulerette* v. *McKinley*, 27 Hun, 320; *Bates* v. *Barber*, 4 Cush. 107; *Hepworth* v. *Henshall*, 153 Pa. 592; *Robbins* v. *Spencer*, 121 Ind. 594; cf. *Hollywood* v. *Reed*, 57 Mich. 234); or his own general reputation may be attacked (*Phillips* v. *Thorn*, 84 Ind. 84; *Starks* v. *People*, 5 Den. 106), or his contradictory statements proved (*State* v. *Lawlor*, 28 Minn. 216). So a sustaining witness may be cross-examined. *Stape* v. *People*, 85 N. Y. 390.]

[2] 17 & 18 Vict. c. 125, s. 2; and 28 Vict. c. 18, s. 3. [See p. 329, note 1, *ante*.]

[3] 2 Ph. Ev. 504; T. E. ss. 1324-5. See *R.* v. *Brown*, L. R. 1 C. C. R.

ARTICLE 134.

OFFENCES AGAINST WOMEN.

When a man is prosecuted for rape or an attempt to ravish, it may be shown that the woman against whom the offence was committed was of a generally immoral

---

70. [There are several modes of *sustaining the credit* of an impeached witness: (1) If his general reputation is impeached, other witnesses who know his reputation may be called to show that such reputation is good, and (in most States) that they would believe him on oath. They are examined in much the same way as impeaching witnesses (*Hamilton* v. *People*, 29 Mich. 173, 184; *Sloan* v. *Edwards*, 61 Md. 89; *State* v. *Nelson*, 58 Ia. 208; *Comm.* v. *Ingraham*, 7 Gray, 46; *Morss* v. *Palmer*, 15 Pa. 51; *Magee* v. *People*, 139 Ill. 138; *First Nat. Bk.* v.*Wolff*, 79 Cal. 69; *Stape* v. *People*, 85 N. Y. 390; see *Adams* v. *Greenwich Ins. Co.*, 70 N. Y. 166). The court may, in its discretion, limit the number of impeaching and of sustaining witnesses (*Bunnell* v. *Butler*, 23 Ct. 65; *Bissell* v. *Cornell*, 24 Wend. 354; *Hollywood* v. *Reed*, 57 Mich. 234).

(2) If the witness is impeached by evidence of his prior inconsistent statements (see Art. 131), he may in some States be sustained by evidence of his good general reputation for truth (*Sweet* v. *Skerman*, 21 Vt. 23; *Bd. of Commrs.* v. *O'Connor*, 137 Ind. 622; *Walker* v. *Phœnix Ins. Co.*, 62 Mo. App. 209; *Isler* v. *Dewey*, 71 N. C. 14; *Hodgkins* v. *State*, 89 Ga. 761, 765; *Holley* v. *State*, 105 Ala. 100; *Crook* v. *State*, 27 Tex. App. 198); but in other States this is not permitted (*Brown* v. *Mooers*, 6 Gray, 451; *Webb* v. *State*, 29 O. St. 351; *Werts* v. *May*, 21 Pa. 274; *Frost* v. *McCargar*, 29 Barb. 617; *People* v. *Olmstead*, 30 Mich. 431; *State* v. *Archer*, 73 Ia. 320; *Sheppard* v. *Yocum*, 10 Or. 402, citing other cases). Such evidence of good reputation has also been received in some States to sustain the credit of a witness who has been impeached by proof of his conviction for crime (*Gertz* v. *Fitchburg R. Co.*, 137 Mass. 77; *Webb* v. *State*, 29 O. St. 351; *People* v. *Amanacus*, 50 Cal. 233), or by proof that he has suborned or has attempted to suborn witnesses or to suppress testimony (*People* v. *Ah Fat*, 48 Cal. 61; *Lewis* v. *State*, 35 Ala. 380; see *Stevenson* v. *Gunning*, 64 Vt. 601, 609). It has also been held in a few cases that when, on the cross-examination of a witness, facts are brought out which discredit him, he may be sustained by proof of his good reputation (*Central R. Co.* v. *Dodd*, 83 Ga. 507; *Texas, etc. R. Co.* v. *Raney*, 86 Tex. 363; cf. *State* v. *Cherry*, 63 N. C. 493; *Paine* v. *Tilden*, 20

character, although she is not cross-examined on the subject.[1] The woman may in such a case be asked whether she has had connection with other men, but her answer cannot be contradicted.[2] She may also be asked

---

Vt. 554; *Coombes* v. *State,* 17 Tex. App. 258; *Walker* v. *Phœnix Ins. Co.,* 62 Mo. App. 209; but see *Harrington* v. *Lincoln,* 4 Gray, 563; *People* v. *Gay,* 7 N. Y. 378). It is well settled, however, that such evidence of good reputation is not received to sustain a witness, simply because the testimony of other witnesses has been in conflict with his own (*Stevenson* v. *Gunning,* 64 Vt. 601; *Atwood* v. *Dearborn,* 1 Allen, 483; *State* v. *Ward,* 49 Ct. 429; *Starks* v. *People,* 5 Den. 106; *Fitzgerald* v. *Goff,* 99 Ind. 28; *Tedens* v. *Schumers,* 112 Ill. 266; *Miller* v. *Western, etc. R. Co.,* 93 Ga. 480; *Mobile, etc. R. Co.* v. *Williams,* 54 Ala. 168; *Texas, etc. R. Co.* v. *Raney,* 86 Tex. 363; but see *Davis* v. *State,* 38 Md. 15; *State* v. *Desforges,* 48 La. Ann. 73); but in Virginia it is received, in whatever way a witness may be discredited (*George* v. *Pilcher,* 28 Gratt. 299; cf. *Coltraine* v. *Brown,* 71 N. C. 19).

(3) It is not in general permissible to support a witness by evidence that he has made former statements similar to his testimony (Gr. Ev. i. § 469; *Robb* v. *Hackley,* 23 Wend. 50; *Conrad* v. *Griffey,* 11 How. (U. S.) 480; *State* v. *Flint,* 60 Vt. 304; *Reed* v. *Spaulding,* 42 N. H. 114; *Crooks* v. *Bunn,* 136 Pa. 368; *State* v. *Porter,* 74 Ia. 623; *Hodges* v. *Bates,* 102 Ind. 494; *Mason* v. *Vestal,* 88 Cal. 396; *Jones* v. *State,* 107 Ala. 93; and cases *infra*). But when his testimony is charged to have been given under the influence of some improper or interested motive, or to be a recent fabrication, and in other like cases, it may be shown that he made similar statements before the motive existed, or before there could have been any inducement to fabricate (*Hewitt* v. *Corey,* 150 Mass. 445; *In re Hesdra,* 119 N. Y. 615; *Clever* v. *Hilberry,* 116 Pa. 431; *Stolp* v. *Blair,* 68 Ill. 541; *State* v. *Hendricks,* 32 Kan. 559; *Barkly* v. *Copeland,* 74 Cal. 1; *City Pass. R. Co.* v. *Knee,* 83 Md. 77; *Howard* v. *Comm.,* 81 Va. 488; *Yarbrough* v. *State,* 105 Ala. 43; *State* v. *Cady,* 46 La. Ann. 1346). In some States, however, such evidence is received to sustain the credibility of a witness, whenever he has been impeached by proof of his prior inconsistent statements (*Hobbs* v. *State,* 133 Ind. 404; *State* v. *Whelehon,* 102 Mo. 17; *Graham* v. *McReynolds,* 90 Tenn. 673; *State* v. *Fontenot,* 48 La. Ann. 283; *Goode* v. *State,* 32 Tex. App. 505); so in North Carolina, if he has been discredited in any way. *State* v. *Whitfield,* 92 N. C. 831.}

[1] *R.* v. *Clarke,* 2 Stark. 241.
[2] *R.* v. *Holmes,* L. R. 1 C. C. R. 334.

whether she has had connection on other occasions with
the prisoner, and if she denies it she may be contradicted.[1][2]

[1] *R.* v. *Martin,* 6 C. & P. 562, and remarks in *R.* v. *Holmes,* p. 337,
per Kelly, C. B. See also *R.* v. *Cockcroft,* 11 Cox, 410, and *R.* v.
Riley, 18 Q. B. D. 481.

[2] [The cases in this country are agreed that in a criminal prosecution for rape or an attempt to ravish, the woman's bad general
character for chastity may be proved by witnesses, and also that she
may be examined as to her previous connection with the prisoner
(Gr. Ev. iii. § 214; *Conkey* v. *People,* 1 Abb. Dec. 418; *Woods* v. *People,*
55 N. Y. 515; *State* v. *Forshner,* 43 N. H. 89; *O'Blenis* v. *State,* 47
N. J. L. 279; *Bedgood* v. *State,* 115 Ind. 275; and cases *infra*). But
they disagree as to whether particular acts of connection with other
men can be proved. In many States the right to prove such acts,
either by her own examination or by the evidence of witnesses, is
denied (*State* v. *Knapp,* 45 N. H. 148; *Comm.* v. *Harris,* 131 Mass.
336; *State* v. *Fitzsimon,* 18 R. I. 236; *McCombs* v. *State,* 8 O. St. 643;
Richie v. *State,* 58 Ind. 355; *People* v. *McLean,* 71 Mich. 309; *State* v.
White, 35 Mo. 500; *State* v. *Brown,* 55 Kan. 766; *State* v. *Turner,* 1
Houst. 76; *Shartzer* v. *State,* 63 Md. 149; *Rice* v. *State,* 35 Fla. 236;
Pefferling v. *State,* 40 Tex. 486; *State* v. *Campbell,* 20 Nev. 122);
but in a few States such proof is competent (*State* v. *Hollenbeck,* 67
Vt. 34, permitting it by cross-examination; *Benstine* v. *State,* 2 Lea,
169, holding both modes of proof allowable, and so *People* v. *Benson,*
6 Cal. 221; cf. *Shirwin* v. *People,* 69 Ill. 55); in New York the decisions upon this point are conflicting (*Woods* v. *People,* 55 N. Y. 515;
cf. *Brown* v. *State,* 72 Miss. 997). In trials for rape upon a woman
under the age of legal consent, evidence of her bad repute for chastity,
or of intercourse with other men, is, in general, not competent
(*People* v. *Glover,* 71 Mich. 303; *People* v. *Abbott,* 97 id. 484; *State* v.
Duffey, 128 Mo. 549; *People* v. *Johnson,* 106 Cal. 289; but see *People*
v. *Flaherty,* 79 Hun, 48).

In actions for *indecent assault,* evidence of the woman's bad general
repute for chastity is competent; so, in some States, of particular acts
of unchastity with other men (*Mitchell* v. *Work,* 13 R. I. 645; *Watry*
v. *Ferber,* 18 Wis. 525; *Gulerette* v. *McKinley,* 27 Hun, 320; cf. *Young*
v. *Johnson,* 123 N. Y. 226), but not in other States (*Gore* v. *Curtis,* 81
Me. 403; cf. *Miller* v. *Curtis,* 158 Mass. 127).

In actions for *seduction,* the woman's bad general character for
chastity may be shown (see p. 161, note, *ante*); but she cannot, in some
States, be cross-examined as to prior acts of intercourse with other

ARTICLE 135.

WHAT MATTERS MAY BE PROVED IN REFERENCE TO DECLARA-
TIONS RELEVANT UNDER ARTICLES 25 ·32.

Whenever any declaration or statement made by a
deceased person, relevant or deemed to be relevant under
Articles 25–32, both inclusive, or any deposition is proved,
all matters may be proved in order to contradict it, or in
order to impeach or confirm the credit of the person by
whom it was made, which might have been proved if that
person had been called as a witness, and had denied
upon cross-examination the truth of the matter suggested.[1]

men than the seducer (*Hoffman* v. *Kemerer*, 44 Pa. 453; *Doyle* v. *Jessup*, 29 Ill. 460; *Smith* v. *Yaryan*, 69 Ind. 445; cf. *Clifton* v. *Granger*,
86 Ia. 573), unless a child is born and its paternity is in question (see
Smith v. *Yaryan*). But some cases hold that such acts may be proved
by the testimony of the men themselves (Gr. Ev. ii. § 577; *White* v.
Murtland, 71 Ill. 250; cf. *Ford* v. *Jones*, 62 Barb. 484), or by cross-
examination of the woman as well as by the evidence of witnesses
(*Love* v. *Masoner*, 6 Baxt. 24; *Wandell* v. *Edwards*, 25 Hun, 498;
cf. *West* v. *Druff*, 55 Ia. 335; *Stewart* v. *Smith*, 92 Wis. 76; *Ayer* v.
Colgrove, 81 Hun, 322).

Upon an indictment for *adultery*, the woman's bad character for
chastity may be proved (*Comm.* v. *Gray*, 129 Mass. 474).

In *bastardy* proceedings, as the fact of paternity is in question, it
may be shown that the woman had intercourse with other men during
the time when the child could have been begotten, but not at other
times (*Knight* v. *Morse*, 54 Vt. 432; *Ronan* v. *Dugan*, 126 Mass. 176;
Benham v. *State*, 91 Ind. 82; *People* v. *Kaminsky*, 73 Mich. 637; *State*
v. *Lavin*, 80 Ia. 555; *Holcomb* v. *People*, 79 Ill. 409; *Swisher* v. *Malone*, 31 W. Va. 442; cf. *People* v. *Schildwachter*, 5 App. Div. (N. Y.)
288); her general character for chastity, however, is not in issue.
Bookhout v. *State*, 66 Wis. 415; *Parker* v. *Dudley*, 118 Mass. 602.]

[1] *R.* v. *Drummond*, 1 Leach, 338; *R.* v. *Pike*, 3 C. & P. 598. In these
cases dying declarations were excluded, because the persons by whom
they were made would have been incompetent as witnesses, but the
principle would obviously apply to all the cases in question. [Thus

ARTICLE 136.

REFRESHING MEMORY.

A witness may, while under examination, refresh his memory by referring to any writing made by himself at the time of the transaction concerning which he is questioned, or so soon afterwards that the judge considers it likely that the transaction was at that time fresh in his memory.

The witness may also refer to any such writing made by any other person, and read by the witness within the time aforesaid, if when he read it he knew it to be correct.[1]

---

when dying declarations are offered in evidence, it may be shown that the deceased declarant was an atheist, to affect his competency or credibility (*State* v. *Elliott*, 45 Ia. 486; *Goodall* v. *State*, 1 Or. 333; *People* v. *Chin Mook Sow*, 51 Cal. 597; see p. 272, n. 3, *ante*), or that his general reputation was bad (*Lester* v. *State*, 37 Fla. 382; *Redd* v. *State*, 99 Ga. 210); or his contradictory statements may be proved (*People* v. *Lawrence*, 21 Cal. 368; *Carver* v. *State*, 164 U. S. 697; *State* v. *Shaffer*, 23 Or. 555; *Battle* v. *State*, 74 Ga. 101; *Shell* v. *State*, 88 Ala. 14; *Morelock* v. *State*, 90 Tenn. 528; *State* v. *Lodge*, 9 Houst. 542; *Felder* v. *State*, 23 Tex. App. 477; cf. *Richards* v. *State*, 82 Wis. 172; *Comm.* v. *Cooper*, 5 Allen, 495; contra, *Wroe* v. *State*, 20 O. St. 460).

As to *depositions*, see Art. 131, *ante*, Illustration (*c*); *Keran* v. *Price's Excrs.*, 75 Va. 690; *Dabney* v. *Mitchell*, 66 Ala. 495; *Wallach* v. *Wylie*, 28 Kan. 138; *Webster* v. *Mann*, 56 Tex. 119.]

[1] 2 Ph. Ev. 480, etc.; T. E. ss. 1264-70; R. N. P. 194-5. [There are three cases of *refreshing memory*: (1) Where the witness, by referring to the writing, is enabled to actually recollect the facts and can testify in reality from memory. The writing may be the original one made by himself, while the facts were fresh in mind (*Chamberlin* v. *Ossipee*, 60 N. H. 212; *Morrison* v. *Chapin*, 97 Mass. 72; *Nat. Bk. of Dubois* v. *Nat. Bk. of Williamsport*, 114 Pa. 1; *Card* v. *Foot*, 56 Ct. 369; *Welcome* v. *Batchelder* 23 Me. 85; *Russell* v. *Hudson River R. Co.*, 17 N. Y. 134; *Mason* v. *Phelps*, 48 Mich. 126; *People* v. *Cotta*, 49 Cal. 166), or a copy thereof (*Hudnutt* v. *Comstock*, 50 Mich. 596; *Bonnet* v. *Glattfeldt*, 120 Ill. 166; *Lawson* v. *Glass*, 6 Col. 134; so as to copy of

An expert may refresh his memory by reference to professional treatises.[1]

---

copy, *Folsom* v. *Apple River Co.*, 41 Wis. 602; or a copy in a newspaper, *Comm.* v. *Ford*, 130 Mass. 64; *Clifford* v. *Drake*, 110 Ill. 135), or it may be a writing made by another person (*State* v. *Miller*, 53 Ia. 209; *Hill* v. *State*, 17 Wis. 675; *Robinson* v. *Mulder*, 81 Mich. 75; *Culver* v. *Scott Lumber Co.*, 53 Minn. 360; *Huff* v. *Bennett*, 6 N. Y. 337; *Paige* v. *Carter*, 64 Cal. 489). It is not the writing, but the recollection of the witness, that is the evidence in the case (*Comm.* v. *Jeffs*, 132 Mass. 5; *Bigelow* v. *Hall*, 91 N. Y. 145; *Calloway* v. *Varner*, 77 Ala. 541; and cases *supra*).

(2) Where the witness, after referring to the writing, does not recollect the facts, and yet remembers that he made or saw the writing when the facts were fresh in his mind, and that it then stated the facts correctly. The writing may have been made by himself (*Dugan* v. *Mahoney*, 11 Allen, 572; *Howard* v. *McDonough*, 77 N. Y. 592; *Adae* v. *Zangs*, 41 Ia. 536; *Downer* v. *Rowell*, 24 Vt. 343; *Kelsea* v. *Fletcher*, 48 N. H. 282; see *Costello* v. *Crowell*, 133 Mass. 352), or by another person (*Davis* v. *Field*, 56 Vt. 426; *Chamberlain* v. *Sands*, 27 Me. 458; *Billingslea* v. *Smith*, 77 Md. 504; *Coffin* v. *Vincent*, 12 Cush. 98). In some States the writing is itself evidence in special cases, but not in other States (see Art. 137, note 1, *post*).

An analogous case is where the facts are such as naturally escape the memory, as items, dates, names, numerous details, etc., and a witness is allowed to use a memorandum thereof as an aid in testifying, which he knows and testifies to have been correctly made (*Fletcher* v. *Powers*, 131 Mass. 333; *Brown* v. *Galesburg Brick Co.*, 132 Ill. 648; *Wise* v. *Phœnix Ins. Co.*, 101 N. Y. 637; *King* v. *Faber*, 51 Pa. 387; *Pinney* v. *Andrus*, 41 Vt. 631).

(3) Where the witness, after referring to the writing, neither recollects the facts, nor remembers having seen it before, and yet from seeing his handwriting therein (as in signature, contents, or both), is enabled to testify to its genuineness and correctness (Gr. Ev. i. § 437; *Martin* v. *Good*, 14 Md. 398; *Mathias* v. *O'Neil*, 94 Mo. 520; *Alvord* v. *Collin*, 20 Pick. 418; *Crittenden* v. *Rogers*, 8 Gray, 452; *Moots* v. *State*, 21 O. St. 653; cf. *Parsons* v. *Mfr's. Ins. Co.*, 16 Gray, 463; *Cole* v. *Jessup*, 10 N. Y. 96). As to the writing being evidence, see next Article, note.]

[1] *Sussex Peerage Case*, 11 C. & F. 114–17. [*People* v. *Wheeler*, 60 Cal. 581, 585; *Healy* v. *Visalia R. Co.*, 101 Cal. 585; *State* v. *Baldwin*, 36 Kan. 1, 17.]

ARTICLE 137.

RIGHT OF ADVERSE PARTY AS TO WRITING USED TO REFRESH MEMORY.

Any writing referred to under Article 136 must be produced and shown to the adverse party if he requires it; and such party may, if he pleases, cross-examine the witness thereupon.[1]

---

[1] See Cases in R. N. P. 195. [Gr. Ev. i. § 437; *Peck* v. *Valentine*, 94 N. Y. 571. This is the general rule both as to *Case* (1), stated in the preceding note (see p. 341, note 1, *ante; Comm.* v. *Jeffs*, 132 Mass. 5; *Peck* v. *Lake*, 3 Lans. 136; *Chute* v. *State*, 19 Minn. 271; *Duncan* v. *Seeley*, 34 Mich. 369; *Stanwood* v. *McLellan*, 48 Me. 275; *McKivitt* v. *Cone*, 30 Ia. 455), and also as to *Case* (2) (*Dugan* v. *Mahoney*, 11 Allen, 573; *Costello* v. *Crowell*, 133 Mass. 352; *Adae* v. *Zangs*, 41 Ia. 536; see *Davis* v. *Field*, 56 Vt. 426). The writing is not itself admitted in evidence (see cases cited; *Taylor* v. *Chicago, etc. R. Co.*, 80 Ia. 431). The object of cross-examination is to ascertain when and by whom the writing was made, whether it is such a writing as may properly be used for the purpose, whether the witness's memory is refreshed by every part of it, etc. (*Chute* v. *State*, 19 Minn. 271; *Comm.* v. *Burke*, 114 Mass. 261). It is in the discretion of the trial court at what stage of the trial this examination shall be made (see last case). So when the witness, under *Case* (1), refers to the writing out of court, it has been held matter of judicial discretion whether he shall produce it in court (*Comm.* v. *Lannan*, 13 Allen, 563; see *Peck* v. *Lake*, 3 Lans. 136; *Trustees* v. *Bledsoe*, 5 Ind. 133).

A different rule is applied in some States in the special case where the witness himself made the writing when the facts were fresh in his mind, and remembers that it was then correct, but cannot, upon now referring to it, testify to the facts from actual recollection; the original writing (but not a *copy*) is itself received in evidence, upon his authenticating its genuineness and correctness (*McCormick* v. *Pa. Cent. R. Co.*, 49 N. Y. 303, 315; *Kelsea* v. *Fletcher*, 48 N. H. 282; *Kent* v. *Mason*, 1 Ill. App. 466; *Curtis* v. *Bradley*, 65 Ct. 99; *Battles* v. *Tallman*, 96 Ala. 403; cf. *Bates* v. *Preble*, 151 U. S. 149; *Vicksburgh, etc. R. Co.* v. *O'Brien*, 119 U. S. 99; cf. *Imhoff* v. *Richards*, 48 Neb. 590). But the writing is not evidence, if the witness has present recollection (Id.; *People* v. *McLaughlin*, 150 N. Y. 365, 392; *Pinkham* v.

ARTICLE 138.

GIVING, AS EVIDENCE, DOCUMENT CALLED FOR AND PRODUCED ON NOTICE.

When a party calls for a document which he has given the other party notice to produce, and such document is produced to, and inspected by, the party calling for its production, he is bound to give it as evidence if the party producing it requires him to do so, and if it is or is deemed to be relevant.[1]

Benton, 62 N. H. 687; contra, *Owens* v. *State,* 67 Md. 307; cf. *Lapham* v. *Kelly,* 35 Vt. 195).

In *Case* (3) the writing should be produced in court to examine the witness upon (Gr. Ev. i. § 437; *Hall* v. *Ray,* 18 N. H. 126; *Martin* v. *Good,* 14 Md. 398), but is often put in evidence itself, under other rules of the law of evidence (*Moots* v. *State,* 21 O. St. 653; *Crittenden* v. *Rogers,* 8 Gray, 452).

A writing made so long after the transaction to which it relates that the facts cannot be deemed to have then been fresh in the witness's mind cannot be used to refresh his recollection (Gr. Ev. i. § 438; *Howell* v. *Carden,* 99 Ala. 100; *Jones* v. *State,* 54 O. St. 1; *Morris* v. *Lachman,* 68 Cal. 109; *Schuyler Nat. Bk.* v. *Bullong,* 24 Neb. 825); so if its accuracy is justly open to suspicion (*Lovell* v. *Wentworth,* 39 O. St. 614). Thus a writing made five months after the transaction and by request of a party was not allowed to be used (*Spring Garden Ins. Co.* v. *Evans,* 15 Md. 54; cf. *Swartz* v. *Chickering,* 58 Md. 290); so of one made twenty months afterwards (*Maxwell* v. *Wilkinson,* 113 U. S. 656); so a witness was not allowed to be referred to his own prior testimony of the same facts which had been given four months after the event. *Putnam* v. *U. S.,* 162 U. S. 687; cf. *People* v. *Palmer,* 105 Mich. 568.]

[1] *Wharam* v. *Routledge,* 1 Esp. 235; *Calvert* v. *Flower,* 7 C. & P. 386. [In some American States this rule is followed (Gr. Ev. i. § 563; *Ellison* v. *Cruser,* 40 N. J. L. 444; *Merrill* v. *Merrill,* 67 Me. 70; *Long* v. *Drew,* 114 Mass. 77; *Cushman* v. *Coleman,* 92 Ga. 772; *Wallar* v. *Stewart,* 4 Cr. C. C. 532; *Edison Light Co.* v. *U. S. Lighting Co.,* 45 F. R. 55; cf. *Western Union Tel. Co.* v. *Hines,* 96 Ga. 688; *Stitt* v. *Huidekopers,* 17 Wall. 385); but in others it is rejected. *Austin* v. *Thompson,* 45 N. H. 113; *Smith* v. *Rents,* 131 N. Y. 169; cf. *Summers* v. *M'Kim,* 12 S. & R. 405; *Rumsey* v. *Lovell,* Anth. N. P. 26.]

ARTICLE 139.

USING, AS EVIDENCE, A DOCUMENT, PRODUCTION OF WHICH WAS
REFUSED ON NOTICE.

When a party refuses to produce a document which he
has had notice to produce, he may not afterwards use the
document as evidence without the consent of the other
party.[1]

[1] *Doe* v. *Hodgson*, 12 A. & E. 135 ; but see remarks in 2 Ph. Ev. 270.
[*Gage* v. *Campbell*, 131 Mass. 566; *Kingman* v. *Tirrell*, 11 Allen, 97 ;
Mather v. *Eureka Co.*, 118 N. Y. 629; *McGuiness* v. *School District*,
39 Minn. 499; *Powell* v. *Pearlstine*, 43 S. Car. 403.]

CHAPTER XVII.

OF DEPOSITIONS.

ARTICLE 140.

DEPOSITIONS BEFORE MAGISTRATES.

A DEPOSITION taken under 11 & 12 Vict. c. 42, s. 17, may be produced and given in evidence at the trial of the person against whom it was taken,

if it is proved (to the satisfaction of the judge) that the witness is dead, or so ill as not to be able to travel (although there may be a prospect of his recovery); [1]

(or, if he is kept out of the way by the person accused,) [2]
or, (probably, if he is too mad to testify,) [3] and

if the deposition purports to be signed by the justice by or before whom it purports to have been taken ; and

if it is proved by the person who offers it as evidence that it was taken in the presence of the person accused, and that he, his counsel, or attorney, had a full opportunity of cross-examining the witness ;

Unless it is proved that the deposition was not in fact signed by the justice by whom it purports to be signed,

(or, that the statement was not taken upon oath ;

or (perhaps) that it was not read over to or signed by the witness). [4]

---

[1] *R.* v. *Stephenson,* L. & C. 165.
[2] *R.* v. *Scaife,* 17 Q. B. 773.
[3] Analogy of *R.* v. *Scaife.*
[4] I believe the above to be the effect of 11 & 12 Vict. c. 42, s. 17, as interpreted by the cases referred to, the effect of which is given by the words in parenthesis, also by common practice. Nothing can be more rambling or ill-arranged than the language of the section itself. See

If there is a prospect of the recovery of a witness proved to be too ill to travel, the judge is not obliged to receive the deposition, but may postpone the trial.[1]

ARTICLE 141.

DEPOSITIONS UNDER 30 & 31 VICT. C. 35, S. 6.

A deposition taken for the perpetuation of testimony in criminal cases,[2] under 30 & 31 Vict. c. 35, s. 6, may be produced and read as evidence, either for or against the accused, upon the trial of any offender or offence[3] to which it relates—

if the deponent is proved to be dead, or

if it is proved that there is no reasonable probability that the deponent will ever be able to travel or to give evidence, and

if the deposition purports to be signed by the justice by or before whom it purports to be taken, and

if it is proved to the satisfaction of the court that reasonable notice in writing[4] of the intention to take such deposition was served upon the person (whether prosecutor or accused) against whom it was proposed to be read, and

---

1 Ph. Ev. 87-100; T. E. s. 448, etc. [The depositions to which this Article relates are those taken upon a preliminary examination of a charge of crime before a committing magistrate. Similar rules are established in many States of this country. N. Y. Code Cr. Pro., § 8; *People* v. *Fish*, 125 N. Y. 136; *State* v. *George*, 60 Minn. 503; *State* v. *Elliott*, 90 Mo. 350; *People* v. *Ward*, 105 Cal. 652; *People* v. *Dowdigan*, 67 Mich. 95; *Brown* v. *Comm.*, 73 Pa. 321; *Lucas* v. *State*, 96 Ala. 51; *Pittman* v. *State*, 92 Ga. 480; *State* v. *Fitzgerald*, 63 Ia. 268; Bishop's New Cr. Pro. i. § 1197; see p. 109, note, *ante*.]

1 *R.* v. *Tait*, 2 F. & F. 553.

2 [Similar statutes providing for the taking of depositions in criminal cases are found in some States. See N. Y. Code Cr. Pro. §§ 8, 620-657; Mass. Pub. St. c. 212, ss. 40, 41; Ohio R. S. ss. 7293, 7294 (7th ed.); Bishop's New Cr. Pro. i. §§ 1194-1206.]

3 *Sic.*   4 *R.* v. *Shurmer*, 17 Q. B. D. 323.

that such person or his counsel or attorney had or might have had, if he had chosen to be present, full opportunity of cross-examining the deponent.[1]

ARTICLE 142.

DEPOSITIONS UNDER MERCHANT SHIPPING ACT, 1854.

[2] Whenever, in the course of any legal proceedings instituted in any part of her Majesty's dominions before any judge or magistrate or before any person authorized by law or by consent of parties to receive evidence, the testimony of any witness is required in relation to the subject-matter of such proceeding, any deposition that such witness may have previously made on oath in relation to the same subject-matter before any justice or magistrate in her Majesty's dominions, or any British consular officer elsewhere, is admissible in evidence, subject to the following restrictions :—

1. If such proceeding is instituted in the United Kingdom or British possessions, due proof must be given that such witness cannot be found in that kingdom or possession respectively.

---

[1] 30 & 31 Vict. c. 35, s. 6. The section is very long, and as the first part of it belongs rather to the subject of criminal procedure than to the subject of evidence, I have omitted it. The language is slightly altered. I have not referred to depositions taken before a coroner (see 7 Geo. IV. c. 64, s. 4), because the section says nothing about the conditions on which they may be given in evidence. Their relevancy, therefore, depends on the common law principles expressed in Article 32. They must be signed by the coroner; but these are matters not of evidence, but of criminal procedure. [See *McLain* v. *Comm.*, 99 Pa. 86.]

[2] 17 & 18 Vict. c. 104, s. 270. There are some other cases in which depositions are admissible by statute, but they hardly belong to the Law of Evidence.

2. If such deposition was made in the United Kingdom, it is not admissible in any proceeding instituted in the United Kingdom.

3. If the deposition was made in any British possession, it is not admissible in any proceeding instituted in the same British possession.

4. If the proceeding is criminal, the deposition is not admissible unless it was made in the presence of the person accused.

Every such deposition must be authenticated by the signature of the judge, magistrate, or consular officer before whom it was made. Such judge, magistrate, or consular officer must, when the deposition is taken in a criminal matter, certify (if the fact is so) that the accused was present at the taking thereof; but it is not necessary in any case to prove the signature or the official character of the person appearing to have signed any such deposition.

In any criminal proceeding the certificate aforesaid is (unless the contrary is proved) sufficient evidence of the accused having been present in manner thereby certified.

Nothing in this Article contained affects any provision by Parliament or by any local legislature as to the admissibility of depositions or the practice of any court according to which depositions not so authenticated are admissible as evidence.

CHAPTER XVIII.

OF IMPROPER ADMISSION AND REJECTION OF EVIDENCE.

ARTICLE 143.

A NEW trial will not be granted in any civil action on the ground of the improper admission or rejection of evidence, unless, in the opinion of the court to which the application is made, some substantial wrong or miscarriage has been thereby occasioned in the trial of the action.[1]

If in a criminal case evidence is improperly rejected or admitted, there is no remedy, unless the prisoner is convicted, and unless the judge, in his discretion, states a case for the Court for Crown Cases Reserved; but if that court is of opinion that any evidence was improperly admitted or rejected, it must set aside the conviction.[2]

---

[1] Rules of Supreme Court, Order xxxix. 6. [If error has been committed in admitting or rejecting evidence but can have wrought no prejudice, it is no ground for granting a new trial in a civil action. *McGean* v. *Manhattan R. Co.*, 117 N. Y. 219; *Hornbuckle* v. *Stafford*, 111 U. S. 389; *Gilbert* v. *Moline Co.*, 119 U. S. 491; *Bulkley* v. *Devine*, 127 Ill. 406; *Wing* v. *Chesterfield*, 116 Mass. 353; *Girard Ins. Co.* v. *Marr*, 46 Pa. 504; *Ham* v. *Wisconsin, etc. R. Co.*, 61 Ia. 716.]

[2] [*R.* v. *Gibson*, 18 Q. B. D. 537. In this country, it is a general rule in criminal cases that a new trial will not be granted for the erroneous admission or rejection of evidence, where it clearly appears that the defendant could not have been prejudiced thereby. *People* v. *Strait*, 154 N. Y. 165; *Gens* v. *State*, 59 N. J. L. 488; *Ryan* v. *State*, 83 Atl. R. (N. J.) 672; *Wallace* v. *People*, 159 Ill. 446; *State* v. *McCaffrey*, 63 Ia. 479; *People* v. *Marshall* 112 Cal. 422; Bishop's New Cr. Pro. i. § 1276.]

APPENDIX OF NOTES.

NOTE I.

(TO ARTICLE I.)

The definitions are simply explanations of the senses in which the words defined are used in this work. They will be found, however, if read in connection with my 'Introduction to the Indian Evidence Act,' to explain the manner in which it is arranged.

I use the word "presumption" in the sense of a presumption of law capable of being rebutted. A presumption of fact is simply an argument. A conclusive presumption I describe as conclusive proof. Hence the few presumptions of law which I have thought it necessary to notice are the only ones I have to deal with.

In earlier editions of this work I gave the following definition of relevancy:

"Facts, whether in issue or not, are relevant to each other when one is, or probably may be, or probably may have been—

the cause of the other;

the effect of the other;

an effect of the same cause;

a cause of the same effect:

or when the one shows that the other must or cannot have occurred, or probably does or did exist, or not;

or that any fact does or did exist, or not, which in the common course of events would either have caused or have been caused by the other;

provided that such facts do not fall within the exclusive rules contained in chapters iii., iv., v., vi.; or that they do fall within the exceptions to those rules contained in those chapters." [1]

This was taken (with some verbal alterations) from a pamphlet called 'The Theory of Relevancy for the purpose of Judicial Evidence, by George Clifford Whitworth, Bombay Civil Service. Bombay, 1875.'

The 7th section of the Indian Evidence Act is as follows: "Facts which are the occasion, cause or effect, immediate or otherwise, of relevant facts or facts in issue, or which constitute the state of things under which they happened, or which afforded an opportunity for their occurrence or transaction, are relevant."

The 11th section is as follows :—

"Facts not otherwise relevant are relevant;

"(1) If they are inconsistent with any fact in issue or relevant fact;

"(2) If by themselves, or in connection with other facts, they make

---

[1] [In the earlier editions Mr. Stephen also gave the following excellent illustrations of relevancy as thus defined:

"(a) A's death is caused by his taking poison. The administration of the poison is relevant to A's death as its cause. A's death is relevant to the poisoning as its effect.

"(b) A and B each eat from the same dish and each exhibit symptoms of the same poison. A's symptoms and B's symptoms are relevant to each other as effects of the same cause.

"(c) The question is, whether A died of the effects of a railway accident.

"Facts tending to show that his death was caused by inflammation of the membranes of the brain, which probably might be caused by the accident; and facts tending to show that his death was caused by typhoid fever, which would have nothing to do with the accident, are relevant to each other as possible causes of the same effect,— A's death." [See *Pitts* v. *State*, 43 Miss. 472; *Comm.* v. *Ryan*, 134 Mass. 223; *Knox* v. *Wheelock*, 54 Vt. 150; *State* v. *Lentz*, 45 Minn. 177.]

"(d) A is charged with committing a crime in London on a given day. The fact that on that day he was at Calcutta is relevant, as proving that he could not have committed the crime.

"(e) The question is, whether A committed a crime.

"The circumstances are such that it must have been committed

the existence or non-existence of any fact in issue, or relevant fact, highly probable or improbable."

In my 'Introduction to the Indian Evidence Act,' I examined at length the theory of judicial evidence, and tried to show that the theory of relevancy is only a particular case of the process of induction, and that it depends on the connection of events as cause and effect. This theory does not greatly differ from Bentham's, though he does not seem to me to have grasped it as distinctly as if he had lived to study Mill's Inductive Logic.

My theory was expressed too widely in certain parts, and not widely enough in others; and Mr. Whitworth's pamphlet appeared to me to have corrected and completed it in a judicious manner. I accordingly embodied his definition of relevancy, with some variations and additions, in the text of the first edition. The necessity of limiting in some such way the terms of the 11th section of the Indian Evidence Act may be inferred from a judgment by Mr. Justice West (of the High Court of Bombay), in the case of *R.* v. *Parbhudas and others*, printed in the 'Law Journal,' May 27, 1876. I have substituted the present definition for it, not because I think it wrong, but because I think it

---

either by A, B, or C. Every fact which shows this, and every fact which shows that neither B nor C committed it, or that either of them did or might have committed it, is relevant.

"(*f*) B, a person in possession of a large sum of money, is murdered and robbed. The question is, whether A murdered him. The fact that after the murder A was or was not possessed of a sum of money unaccounted for is relevant, as showing the existence or the absence of a fact which, in the common course of events, would be caused by A's committing the murder. A's knowledge that B was in possession of the money would be relevant as a fact, which, in the ordinary course of events, might cause or be one of the causes of the murder." [See *Comm.* v. *Sturtivant*, 117 Mass. 122; *Williams* v. *Comm.*, 29 Pa. 102; *Kennedy* v. *People*, 39 N. Y. 245.]

"(*g*) A is murdered in his own house at night. The absence of marks of violence to the house is relevant to the question, whether the murder was committed by a servant, because it shows the absence of an effect which would have been caused by its being committed by a stranger."]

gives rather the principle on which the rule depends than a convenient practical rule.

As to the coincidence of this theory with English law, I can only say that it will be found to supply a key which will explain all that is said on the subject of circumstantial evidence by the writers who have treated of that subject. Mr. Whitworth goes through the evidence given against the German, Müller, executed for murdering Mr. Briggs on the North London Railway, and shows how each item of it can be referred to one or the other of the heads of relevancy which he discusses.

The theory of relevancy thus expressed would, I believe, suffice to solve every question which can arise upon the subject; but the legal rules based upon an unconscious apprehension of the theory exceed it at some points and fall short of it at others.

NOTE II.

(TO ARTICLE 2.)

See 1 Ph. Ev. 493, &c.; Best, ss. 111 and 251; T. E. chap. ii. pt. ii.

For instances of relevant evidence held to be insufficient for the purpose for which it was tendered, on the ground of remoteness, see *R.* v. ———, 2 C. & P. 459; and *Mann* v. *Langton*, 3 A. & E. 699.

Mr. Taylor (s. 867) adopts from Professor Greenleaf the statement that "the law excludes on public grounds . . . evidence which is indecent or offensive to public morals, or injurious to the feelings of third persons." The authorities given for this are actions on wagers which the court refused to try, or in which they arrested judgment, because the wagers were in themselves impertinent and offensive, as, for instance, a wager as to the sex of the Chevalier D'Eon (*Da Costa* v. *Jones*, Cowp. 729). No action now lies upon a wager, and I can find no authority for the proposition advanced by Professor Greenleaf. I know of no case in which a fact in issue, or relevant to an issue, which the court is bound to try can be excluded merely because it would pain some one who is a stranger to the action. Indeed, in *Da Costa* v. *Jones*, Lord Mansfield said expressly, "Indecency of evidence is no objection to its being received where it is necessary to the decision of a civil or criminal right" (p. 734). (See Article 129, and Note XLVI.) [See *Melvin* v. *Melvin*, 58 N. H. 569; *Cothran* v. *Ellis*, 125 Ill 496.]

NOTE III.

(TO ARTICLE 4.)

On this subject see also 1 Ph. Ev. 157–164; T. E. ss. 527–532; Best, s. 508; 3 Russ. on Crimes, by Greaves, 161–7. (See, too, *The Queen's Case*, 2 B. & B. 309–10.)

The principle is substantially the same as that of principal and accessory, or principal and agent. When various persons conspire to commit an offence, each makes the rest his agents to carry the plan into execution. (See, too, Article 17, Note XI.)

NOTE IV.

(TO ARTICLE 5.)

The principle is fully explained and illustrated in *Malcolmson* v. *O'Dea*, 10 H. L. C. 593. See particularly the reply to the questions put by the House of Lords to the Judges, delivered by Willes, J., 611–622. [See *Boston* v. *Richardson*, 105 Mass. 351, 371.]

See also 1 Ph. Ev. 234–9; T. E. ss. 593–601; Best, s. 499.

Mr. Phillips and Mr. Taylor treat this principle as an exception to the rule excluding hearsay. They regard the statements contained in the title-deeds as written statements made by persons not called as witnesses. I think the deeds must be regarded as constituting the transactions which they effect; and in the case supposed in the text, those transactions are actually in issue. When it is asserted that land belongs to A, what is meant is, that A is entitled to it by a series of transactions of which his title-deeds are by law the exclusive evidence (see Article 40). The existence of the deeds is thus the very fact which is to be proved.

Mr. Best treats the case as one of "derivative evidence," an expression which does not appear to me felicitous.

NOTE V.

(TO ARTICLE 8.)

The items of evidence included in this Article are often referred to by the phrase "res gestæ," which seems to have come into use on account of its convenient obscurity. The doctrine of "res gestæ" was much discussed in the case of *Doe* v. *Tatham* (p. 79, &c.). In the course of the argument, Bosanquet, J., observed, "How do you translate res gestæ? gestæ, by whom?" Parke, B., afterward observed, "The acts by whomsoever done are res gestæ, if relevant to the matter in issue. But the question is, what are relevant?" (7 A. & E. 353.) In delivering his opinion to the House of Lords, the same Judge laid down the rule thus: "Where any facts are proper evidence upon an issue" (*i. e.*, when they are in issue, or relevant to the issue) "all oral or written declarations which can explain such facts may be received in evidence." (Same Case, 4 Bing. N. C. 548.) The question asked by Baron Parke goes to the root of the whole subject, and I have tried to answer it at length in the text, and to give it the prominence in the statement of the law which its importance deserves.

Besides the cases cited in the Illustrations, see cases as to statements accompanying acts collected in 1 Ph. Ev. 152–7, and T. E. ss. 521, 528. I have stated, in accordance with *R.* v. *Walker*, 2 M. & R. 212, that the particulars of a complaint are not admissible; but I have heard Willes, J., rule that they were on several occasions, vouching Parke, B., as his authority. *R.* v. *Walker* was decided by Parke, B., in 1839. Though he excluded the statement, he said, "The sense of the thing certainly is, that the jury should in the first instance know the nature of the complaint made by the prosecutrix, and all that she then said. But for reasons which I never could understand, the usage has obtained that the prosecutrix's counsel should only inquire generally whether a complaint was made by the prosecutrix of the prisoner's conduct towards her, leaving the prisoner's counsel to bring before the jury the particulars of that complaint by cross-examination."

Lord Bramwell was in the habit, during the latter part of his judicial career, of admitting the complaint itself, and other judges have
sometimes done the same. The practice is certainly in accordance
with common sense.

NOTE VI.

(TO ARTICLES 10, 11, 12.)

Article 10 is equivalent to the maxim, "Res inter alios acta alteri
nocere non debet," which is explained and commented on in Best, ss.
506-510 (though I should scarcely adopt his explanation of it), and by
Broom ('Maxims,' 954-968). The application of the maxim to the
Law of Evidence is obscure, because it does not show how unconnected transactions should be supposed to be relevant to each other.
The meaning of the rule must be inferred from the exceptions to it
stated in Articles 11 and 12, which show that it means, You are not to
draw inferences from one transaction to another which is not specifically connected with it merely because the two resemble each other.
They must be linked together by the chain of cause and effect in
some assignable way before you can draw your inference.

In its literal sense the maxim also fails, because it is not true that a
man cannot be affected by transactions to which he is not a party. Illustrations to the contrary are obvious and innumerable ; bankruptcy,
marriage, indeed every transaction of life, would supply them.

The exceptions to the rule given in Articles 11 and 12 are general-
ized from the cases referred to in the Illustrations. It is important to
observe that though the rule is expressed shortly, and is sparingly
illustrated, it is of very much greater importance and more frequent
application than the exceptions. It is indeed one of the most characteristic and distinctive parts of the English Law of Evidence, for
this is the rule which prevents a man charged with a particular offence from having either to submit to imputations which in many
cases would be fatal to him, or else to defend every action of his
whole life in order to explain his conduct on the particular occasion.
A statement of the Law of Evidence which did not give due promi-

nence to the four great exclusive rules of evidence of which this is one would neither represent the existing law fairly nor in my judgment improve it.

The exceptions to the rule apply more frequently to criminal than to civil proceedings, and in criminal cases the courts are always disinclined to run the risk of prejudicing the prisoner by permitting matters to be proved which tend to show in general that he is a bad man, and so likely to commit a crime. In each of the cases by which Article 12 is illustrated, the evidence admitted went to prove the true character of facts which, standing alone, might naturally have been accounted for on the supposition of accident,—a supposition which was rebutted by the repetition of similar occurrences. In the case of *R*. v. *Gray* (Illustration (*a*)), there were many other circumstances which would have been sufficient to prove the prisoner's guilt, apart from the previous fires. That part of the evidence, indeed, seemed to have little influence on the jury. *Garner's Case* (Illustration (*c*), note) was an extraordinary one, and its result was in every way unsatisfactory. Some account of this case will be found in the evidence given by me before the Commission on Capital Punishments which sat in 1866.

NOTE VII.

(TO ARTICLE 13.)

As to presumptions arising from the course of office or business, see Best, s. 403; 1 Ph. Ev. 480-4; T. E. s. 147. The presumption, "Omnia esse rite acta," also applies. See Broom's 'Maxims,' 942; Best, ss. 353-365; T. E. s. 124, &c.; 1 Ph. Ev. 480; and Stark. 757, 763.

NOTE VIII.

(TO ARTICLE 14.)

The unsatisfactory character of the definitions usually given of hearsay is well known. See Best, s. 495; T. E. ss. 507-510. The definition given by Mr. Phillips sufficiently exemplifies it : " When a witness, in the course of stating what has come under the cognizance of his own senses concerning a matter in dispute, *states the language of others which he has heard*, or produces papers which he identifies as being written by particular individuals, he offers what is called hearsay evidence. This matter may sometimes be the very matter in dispute," etc. (1 Ph. Ev. 143). If this definition is correct, the maxim, " Hearsay is no evidence," can only be saved from the charge of falsehood by exceptions which make nonsense of it. By attaching to it the meaning given in the text, it becomes both intelligible and true. There is no real difference between the fact that a man was heard to say this or that, and any other fact. Words spoken may convey a threat, supply the motive for a crime, constitute a contract, amount to slander, etc., etc.; and if relevant or in issue, on these or other grounds, they must be proved, like other facts, by the oath of some one who heard them. The important point to remember about them is that bare assertion must not, generally speaking, be regarded as relevant to the truth of the matter asserted.

The doctrine of hearsay evidence was fully discussed by many of the judges in the case of *Doe* d. *Wright* v. *Tatham* on the different occasions when that case came before the court (see 7 A. & E. 313-408; 4 Bing. N. C. 489-573). The question was whether letters addressed to a deceased testator, implying that the writers thought him sane, but not acted upon by him, could be regarded as relevant to his sanity, which was the point in issue. The case sets the stringency of the rule against hearsay in a light which is forcibly illustrated by a passage in the judgment of Baron Parke (7 A. & E. 385-8), to the following effect :—He treats the letters as "statements of the writers, not on oath, of the truth of the matter in question, with this in addition, that they have acted upon the statements on the faith of their being true by their sending the letters to the testator." He then goes through a variety of illustrations which had been suggested in argument, and shows that in no case ought such statements to be regarded as relevant to the truth of the matter stated, even when the circumstances were such as to give the strongest possible guarantee that such statements expressed the honest opinions of the persons who made them. Amongst others he mentions the following :—"The conduct of the family or relations of a testator taking the same precautions in his absence as if he were a lunatic ; his election in his absence to some high and responsible office ; the conduct of a physician who permitted a will to be executed by a sick testator ; the conduct of a deceased captain on a question of seaworthiness, who, after examining every part of a vessel, embarked in it with his family ; all these, when deliberately considered, are, with reference to the matter in issue in each case, mere instances of hearsay evidence,—mere statements, not on oath, but implied in or vouched by the actual conduct of persons by whose acts the litigant parties are not to be bound." All these matters are therefore to be treated as irrelevant to the questions at issue.

These observations make the rule quite distinct, but the reason suggested for it in the concluding words of the passage extracted appears to be weak. That passage implies that hearsay is excluded because no one "ought to be bound by the act of a stranger." That no one shall have power to make a contract for another, or commit a crime for which that other is to be responsible, without his authority, is obviously reasonable, but it is not so plain why A's conduct should not furnish good grounds for inference as to B's conduct, though it was not authorized by B. The importance of shortening proceedings, the importance of compelling people to procure the best evidence they can, and the importance of excluding opportunities of fraud, are considerations which probably justify the rule excluding hearsay ; but Baron Parke's illustrations of its operation clearly prove that in some cases it excludes the proof of matter which, but for it, would be regarded not only as relevant to particular facts, but as good grounds for believing in their existence.

NOTE IX.

(TO ARTICLE 15.)

This definition is intended to exclude admissions by pleading, admissions which, if so pleaded, amount to estoppels, and admissions made for the purposes of a cause by the parties or their solicitors. These subjects are usually treated of by writers on evidence; but they appear to me to belong to other departments of the law. The subject, including the matter which I omit, is treated at length in 1 Ph. Ev. 308–401, and T. E. ss. 653–788. A vast variety of cases upon admissions of every sort may be found by referring to Roscoe, N. P. (Index, under the word *Admissions.*) It may perhaps be well to observe that when an admission is contained in a document, or series of documents, or when it forms part of a discourse or conversation, so much and no more of the document, series of documents, discourse or conversation, must be proved as is necessary for the full understanding of the admission, but the judge or jury may of course attach degrees of credit to different parts of the matter proved. This rule is elaborately discussed and illustrated by Mr. Taylor, ss. 655–665. It has lost much of the importance which attached to it when parties to actions could not be witnesses, but could be compelled to make admissions by bills of discovery. The ingenuity of equity draughtsmen was under that system greatly exercised in drawing answers in such a form that it was impossible to read part of them without reading the whole, and the ingenuity of the court was at least as much exercised in countermining their ingenious devices. The power of administering interrogatories, and of examining the parties directly, has made great changes in these matters.

NOTE X.

(TO ARTICLE 16.)

As to admissions by parties, see *Moriarty* v. *L. C. & D. Railway*, L. R. 5 Q. B. 320, per Blackburn, J.; *Alner* v. *George*, 1 Camp. 392; *Bauerman* v. *Radenius*, 7 T. R. 663.

As to admissions by parties interested, see *Spargo* v. *Brown*, 9 B. & C. 938.

See also on the subject of this Article 1 Ph. Ev. 362-3, 369, 398; and T. E. ss. 669-671, 685, 687, 719; Roscoe, N. P. 71.

As to admissions by privies, see 1 Ph. Ev. 394-7, and T. E. (from Greenleaf), s. 712.

NOTE XI.

(TO ARTICLE 17.)

The subject of the relevancy of admissions by agents is rendered difficult by the vast variety of forms which agency assumes, and by the distinction between an agent for the purpose of making a statement and an agent for the purpose of transacting business. If A sends a message by B, B's words in delivering it are in effect A's; but B's statements in relation to the subject-matter of the message have, as such, no special value. A's own statements are valuable if they suggest an inference which he afterwards contests because they are against his interest; but when the agent's duty is done, he has no special interest in the matter.

The principle as to admissions by agents is stated and explained by Sir W. Grant in *Fairlie* v. *Hastings*, 10 Ves. 126-7.

NOTE XII.

(TO ARTICLE 18.)

See for a third exception (which could hardly occur now), *Clay* v. *Langslow*, M. & M. 45.

NOTE XIII.

(TO ARTICLE 19.)

This comes very near to the case of arbitration. See, as to irregular arbitrations of this kind, 1 Ph. Ev. 383; T. E. ss. 689-90.

NOTE XIV.

(TO ARTICLE 20.)

See more on this subject in 1 Ph. Ev. 326–8; T. E. ss. 702, 720–3; R. N. P. 66.

NOTE XV.

(TO ARTICLE 22.)

On the law as to confessions, see 1 Ph. Ev. 401–423; T. E. ss. 796–807, and s. 824; Best, ss. 551–574; Roscoe, Cr. Ev. 38–56; 3 Russ. on Crimes, by Greaves, 365–436. Joy on Confessions reduces the law on the subject to the shape of 13 propositions, the effect of all of which is given in the text in a different form.

Many cases have been decided as to the language which amounts to an inducement to confess (see Roscoe, Cr. Ev. 40–43, where most of them are collected). They are, however, for practical purposes, summed up in *R.* v. *Baldry*, 2 Den. C. C. 430, which is the authority for the last lines of the first paragraph of this Article.

NOTE XVI.

(TO ARTICLE 23.)

Cases are sometimes cited to show that if a person is examined as a witness on oath, his deposition cannot be used in evidence against him afterwards (see T. E. ss. 809 and 818, n. 6; also 3 Russ. on Crimes, by Greaves, 407, etc.). All these cases, however, relate to the examinations before magistrates of persons accused of crimes, under the statutes which were in force before 11 & 12 Vict. c. 42.

These statutes authorized the examination of prisoners, but not their examination upon oath. The 11 & 12 Vict. c. 42, prescribes the form of the only question which the magistrate can put to a prisoner; and since that enactment it is scarcely possible to suppose that any magistrate would put a prisoner upon his oath. The cases may therefore be regarded as obsolete.

NOTE XVII.

(TO ARTICLE 26.)

As to dying declarations, see 1 Ph. Ev. 239-252; T. E. ss. 644-652; Best, s. 505; Starkie, 32 & 38; 3 Russ. Cri. 250-272 (perhaps the fullest collection of the cases on the subject); Roscoe, Cri. Ev. 31, 32. *R.* v. *Baker*, 2 Mo. & Ro. 53, is a curious case on this subject. A and B were both poisoned by eating the same cake. C was tried for poisoning A. B's dying declaration that she made the cake in C's presence, and put nothing bad in it, was admitted as against C, on the ground that the whole formed one transaction. [See *Brown* v. *Comm.*, 73 Pa. 321; *State* v. *Westfall*, 49 Ia. 328 ; *State* v. *Bohan*, 15 Kan. 407.]

NOTE XVIII.

(TO ARTICLE 27.)

1 Ph. Ev. 280-300; T. E. ss. 630-643; Best, 501; R. N. P. 63; and see note to *Price* v. *Lord Torrington*, 2 S. L. C. 328. The last case on the subject is *Massey* v. *Allen*, 13 Ch. D. 558.

NOTE XIX.

(TO ARTICLE 28.)

The best statement of the law upon this subject will be found in *Higham* v. *Ridgway*, and the note thereto, 2 S. L. C. 318. See also 1 Ph. Ev. 252-280; T. E. ss. 602-629; Best, s. 500; R. N. P. 584.

A class of cases exists which I have not put into the form of an Article, partly because their occurrence since the commutation of tithes must be very rare, and partly because I find a great difficulty in understanding the place which the rule established by them ought to occupy in a systematic statement of the law. They are cases which lay down the rule that statements as to the receipts

of tithes and moduses made by deceased rectors and other ecclesiastical corporations sole are admissible in favor of their successors.
There is no doubt as to the rule (see, in particular, *Short* v. *Lee*, 2
Jac. & Wal. 464; and *Young* v. *Clare Hall*, 17 Q. B. 537). The
difficulty is to see why it was ever regarded as an exception. It
falls directly within the principle stated in the text, and would
appear to be an obvious illustration of it; but in many cases it has
been declared to be anomalous, inasmuch as it enables a predecessor
in title to make evidence in favor of his successor. This suggests
that Article 28 ought to be limited by a proviso that a declaration
against interest is not relevant if it was made by a predecessor in
title of the person who seeks to prove it, unless it is a declaration
by an ecclesiastical corporation sole, or a member of an ecclesiastical
corporation aggregate (see *Short* v. *Lee*), as to the receipt of a
tithe or modus.

Some countenance for such a proviso may be found in the terms
in which Bayley, J., states the rule in *Gleadow* v. *Atkin*, and in the
circumstance that when it first obtained currency the parties to an
action were not competent witnesses. But the rule as to the indorsement of notes, bonds, etc., is distinctly opposed to such a view.

NOTE XX.

(TO ARTICLE 30.)

Upon this subject, besides the authorities in the text, see 1 Ph. Ev.
169-197; T. E. ss. 543-569; Best, s. 497; R. N. P. 50-54 (the latest
collection of cases).

A great number of cases have been decided as to the particular
documents, etc., which fall within the rule given in the text. They
are collected in the works referred to above, but they appear to me
merely to illustrate one or other of the branches of the rule, and not
to extend or vary it. An award, *e. g.*, is not within the last branch of
Illustration (*b*), because it "is but the opinion of the arbitrator, not
upon his own knowledge" (*Evans* v. *Rees*, 10 A. & E. 155); but the

detailed application of such a rule as this is better learned by experience, applied to a firm grasp of principle, than by an attempt to
recollect innumerable cases.

The case of *Weeks* v. *Sparke* is remarkable for the light it throws
on the history of the Law of Evidence. It was decided in 1813, and
contains *inter alia* the following curious remarks by Lord Ellenborough. "It is stated to be the habit and practice of different circuits to admit this species of evidence upon such a question as the
present. That certainly cannot make the law, but it shows at least,
from the established practice of a large branch of the profession, and
of the judges who have presided at various times on those circuits,
what has been the prevailing opinion upon this subject amongst so
large a class of persons interested in the due administration of the
law. It is stated to have been the practice both of the Northern and
Western Circuits. My learned predecessor, Lord Kenyon, certainly
held a different opinion, the practice of the Oxford Circuit, of which
he was a member, being different." So in the *Berkeley Peerage Case*,
Lord Eldon said, "when it was proposed to read this deposition as a
declaration, the Attorney-General (Sir Vicary Gibbs) flatly objected to
it. *He spoke quite right as a Western Circuiteer*, of what he had
often heard laid down in the West, and never heard doubted" (4
Camp. 419, A. D. 1811). This shows how very modern much of the
Law of Evidence is. Le Blanc, J., in *Weeks* v. *Sparke*, says, that a
foundation must be laid for evidence of this sort "by acts of enjoy-
nent within living memory." This seems superfluous, as no jury
would ever find that a public right of way existed, which had not
been used in living memory, on the strength of a report that some
deceased person had said that there once was such a right.

NOTE XXI.

(TO ARTICLE 31.)

See 1 Ph. Ev. 197-233; T. E. ss. 571-592; Best, 633; R. N. P. 49-50.
The *Berkeley Peerage Case* (Answers of the Judges to the House of

Lords), 4 Camp. 401, which established the third condition given in the text; and *Davies* v. *Lowndes*, 6 M. & G. 471 (see more particularly pp. 525-9, in which the question of family pedigrees is fully discussed) are specially important on this subject.

As to declarations as to the place of births, etc., see *Shields* v. *Boucher*, 1 De G. & S. 49-58.

NOTE XXII.

(TO ARTICLE 32.)

See also 1 Ph. Ev. 306-8; T. E. ss. 434-447; Buller, N. P. 238, and following.

In reference to this subject it has been asked whether this principle applies indiscriminately to all kinds of evidence in all cases. Suppose a man were to be tried twice upon the same facts—*e. g.*, for robbery after an acquittal for murder, and suppose that in the interval between the two trials an important witness who had not been called before the magistrates were to die, might his evidence be read on the second trial from a reporter's short-hand notes? This case might easily have occurred if Orton had been put on his trial for forgery as well as for perjury. I should be disposed to think on principle that such evidence would be admissible, though I cannot cite any authority on the subject. The common-law principle on which depositions taken before magistrates and in Chancery proceedings were admitted seems to cover the case.

NOTE XXIII.

(TO ARTICLES 39-47.)

The law relating to the relevancy of judgments of Courts of Justice to the existence of the matters which they assert is made to appear extremely complicated by the manner in which it is usually dealt with. The method commonly employed is to mix up the question of the effect of judgments of various kinds with that of their admissibility, subjects which appear to belong to different branches of the law.

Thus the subject, as commonly treated, introduces into the Law of Evidence an attempt to distinguish between judgments *in rem*, and judgments *in personam* or *inter partes*, (terms adapted from, but not belonging to, Roman law, and never clearly defined in reference to our own or any other system); also the question of the effect of the pleas of *autrefois acquit*, and *autrefois convict*, which clearly belong not to evidence, but to criminal procedure; the question of estoppels, which belongs rather to the law of pleading than to that of evidence; and the question of the effect given to the judgments of foreign Courts of Justice, which would seem more properly to belong to private international law. These and other matters are treated of at great length in 2 Ph. Ev. 1-78, and T. E. ss. 1480-1534, and in the note to the *Duchess of Kingston's Case* in 2 S. L. C. 777-880. Best (ss. 588-595) treats the matter more concisely.

The text is confined to as complete a statement as I could make of the principles which regulate the relevancy of judgments considered as declarations proving the facts which they assert, whatever may be the effect or the use to be made of those facts when proved. Thus the leading principle stated in Article 40 is equally true of all judgments alike. Every judgment, whether it be *in rem* or *inter partes*, must and does prove what it actually effects, though the effects of different sorts of judgments differ as widely as the effects of different sorts of deeds.

There has been much controversy as to the extent to which effect ought to be given to the judgments of foreign courts in this country, and as to the cases in which the courts will refuse to act upon them; but as a mere question of evidence, they do not differ from English judgments. The cases on foreign judgments are collected in the note to the *Duchess of Kingston's Case*, 2 S. L. C. 813-845. There is a convenient list of the cases in R. N. P. 201-3. The cases of *Godard v. Gray*, L. R. 6 Q. B. 139, *Castrique v. Imrie*, L. R. 4 E. & I. App. 414, [and *Aboulof v. Oppenheimer*, 10 Q. B. D. 295], are the latest leading cases on the subject.

NOTE XXIV.

(TO CHAPTER V.)

On evidence of opinions, see 1 Ph. Ev. 520-8; T. E. ss. 1273-81; Best, ss. 511-17; R. N. P. 193-4. The leading case on the subject is *Doe* v. *Tatham*, 7 A. & E. 313; and 4 Bing. N. C. 489, referred to above in Note VIII. Baron Parke, in the extracts there given, treats an expression of opinion as hearsay, that is, as a statement affirming the truth of the subject-matter of the opinion.

NOTE XXV.

(TO CHAPTER VI.)

See 1 Ph. Ev. 502-8; T. E. ss. 325-336; Best, ss. 257-263; 3 Russ. Cri. 299-304. The subject is considered at length in *R.* v. *Rowton*, 1 L. & C. 520. One consequence of the view of the subject taken in that case is that a witness may with perfect truth swear that a man, who to his knowledge has been a receiver of stolen goods for years, has an excellent character for honesty, if he has had the good luck to conceal his crimes from his neighbors. It is the essence of successful hypocrisy to combine a good reputation with a bad disposition, and according to *R.* v. *Rowton*, the reputation is the important matter. The case is seldom if ever acted on in practice. The question always put to a witness to character is, What is the prisoner's character for honesty, morality, or humanity? as the case may be; nor is the witness ever warned that he is to confine his evidence to the prisoner's reputation. It would be no easy matter to make the common run of witnesses understand the distinction.

NOTE XXVI.

(TO ARTICLE 58.)

The list of matters judicially noticed in this Article is not intended to be quite complete. It is compiled from 1 Ph. Ev. 458-67, and

T. E. ss. 4-20, where the subject is gone into more minutely. A convenient list is also given in R. N. P. ss. 88-92, which is much to the
same effect. It may be doubted whether an absolutely complete list
could be formed, as it is practically impossible to enumerate everything which is so notorious in itself, or so distinctly recorded by public authority, that it would be superfluous to prove it. Paragraph (1)
is drawn with reference to the fusion of Law, Equity, Admiralty, and
Testamentary Jurisdiction effected by the Judicature Act.

NOTE XXVII.

(TO ARTICLE 62.)

Owing to the ambiguity of the word "evidence," which is sometimes used to signify the effect of a fact when proved, and sometimes
to signify the testimony by which a fact is proved, the expression
"hearsay is no evidence" has many meanings. Its common and most
important meaning is the one given in Article 14, which might be
otherwise expressed by saying that the connection between events,
and reports that they have happened, is generally so remote that it is
expedient to regard the existence of the reports as irrelevant to the
occurrence of the events, except in excepted cases. Article 62 expresses the same thing from a different point of view, and is subject
to no exceptions whatever. It asserts that whatever may be the relation of a fact to be proved to the fact in issue, it must, if proved by
oral evidence, be proved by direct evidence. For instance, if it were
to be proved under Article 31 that A, who died fifty years ago, said
that he had heard from his father B, who died 100 years ago, that A's
grandfather C had told B that D, C's elder brother, died without issue,
A's statement must be proved by some one who, with his own ears,
heard him make it. If (as in the case of verbal slander) the speaking
of the words was the very point in issue, they must be proved in pre-
cisely the same way. Cases in which evidence is given of character
and general opinion may perhaps seem to be exceptions to this rule,
but they are not so. When a man swears that another has a good

character, he means that he has heard many people, though he does not particularly recollect what people, speak well of him, though he does not recollect all that they said.

NOTE XXVIII.

(TO ARTICLES 66 & 67.)

This is probably the most ancient, and is, as far as it extends, the most inflexible of all the rules of evidence. The following characteristic observations by Lord Ellenborough occur in *R. v. Harringworth*, 4 M. & S. 353:

"The rule, therefore, is universal that you must first call the subscribing witness; and it is not to be varied in each particular case by trying whether, in its application, it may not be productive of some inconvenience, for then there would be no such thing as a general rule. *A lawyer who is well stored with these rules would be no better than any other man that is without them*, if by mere force of speculative reasoning it might be shown that the application of such and such a rule would be productive of such and such an inconvenience, and therefore ought not to prevail; but if any general rule ought to prevail, this is certainly one that is as fixed, formal, and universal as any that can be stated in a Court of Justice."

In *Whyman v. Garth*, 8 Ex. 807, Pollock, C. B., said, "The parties are supposed to have agreed *inter se* that the deed shall not be given in evidence without his" (the attesting witness) "being called to depose to the circumstances attending its execution."

In very ancient times, when the jury were witnesses as to matter of fact, the attesting witnesses to deeds (if a deed came in question) would seem to have been summoned with, and to have acted as a sort of assessors to, the jury. See as to this, Bracton, fo. 38 *a;* Fortescue *de Laudibus*, ch. xxxii. with Selden's note; and cases collected from the Year-books in Brooke's Abridgement, tit. *Testmoignes.*

For the present rule, and the exceptions to it, see 1 Ph. Ev. 242–261; T. E. ss. 1637–42; R. N. P. 147–50; Best, ss. 220, etc.

The old rule which applied to all attested documents was restricted to those required to be attested by law, by 17 & 18 Vict. c. 125, s. 26, and 28 & 29 Vict. c. 18, ss. 1 & 7.

NOTE XXIX.

(TO ARTICLE 72.)

For these rules in greater detail, see 1 Ph. Ev. 452–3, and 2 Ph. Ev. 272–289; T. E. ss. 419–426; R. N. P. 8 & 9.

The principle of all the rules is fully explained in the cases cited in the footnotes, more particularly in *Dwyer* v. *Collins*, 7 Ex. 639. In that case it is held that the object of notice to produce is "to enable the party to have the document in court, and if he does not, to enable his opponent to give parol evidence . . . to exclude the argument that the opponent has not taken all reasonable means to procure the original, which he must do before he can be permitted to make use of secondary evidence" (p. 647–8).

NOTE XXX.

(TO ARTICLE 75.)

Mr. Phillips (ii. 196) says, that upon a plea of *nul tiel* record, the original record must be produced if it is in the same court.

Mr. Taylor (s. 1379) says, that upon prosecutions for perjury assigned upon any judicial document the original must be produced. The authorities given seem to me hardly to bear out either of these statements. They show that the production of the original in such cases is the usual course, but not, I think, that it is necessary. The case of *Lady Dartmouth* v. *Roberts*, 16 Ea. 334, is too wide for the proposition for which it is cited. The matter, however, is of little practical importance.

NOTE XXXI.

(TO ARTICLES 77 & 78.)

The learning as to exemplifications and office-copies will be found in the following authorities: Gilbert's Law of Evidence, 11–20; Buller,

Nisi Prius, 228, and following; Starkie, 256-66 (fully and very conveniently); 2 Ph. Ev. 196-200; T. E. ss. 1380-4; R. N. P. 112-15. The second paragraph of Article 77 is founded on *Appleton* v. *Braybrook*, 6 M. & S. 39.

As to exemplifications not under the Great Seal, it is remarkable that the Judicature Acts give no Seal to the Supreme Court, or the High Court, or any of its divisions.

NOTE XXXII.

(TO ARTICLE 90.)

The distinction between this and the following Article is, that Article 90 defines the cases in which documents are exclusive evidence of the transactions which they embody, while Article 91 deals with the interpretation of documents by oral evidence. The two subjects are so closely connected together, that they are not usually treated as distinct; but they are so in fact. A and B make a contract of marine insurance on goods, and reduce it to writing. They verbally agree that the goods are not to be shipped in a particular ship, though the contract makes no such reservation. They leave unnoticed a condition usually understood in the business of insurance, and they make use of a technical expression, the meaning of which is not commonly known. The law does not permit oral evidence to be given of the exception as to the particular ship. It does permit oral evidence to be given to annex the condition; and thus far it decides that for one purpose the document shall, and that for another it shall not, be regarded as exclusive evidence of the terms of the actual agreement between the parties. It also allows the technical term to be explained, and in doing so it interprets the meaning of the document itself. The two operations are obviously different, and their proper performance depends upon different principles. The first depends upon the principle that the object of reducing transactions to a written form is to take security against bad faith or bad memory, for which reason a writing is presumed as a general rule to embody the

final and considered determination of the parties to it. The second
depends on a consideration of the imperfections of language, and of
the inadequate manner in which people adjust their words to the
facts to which they apply.

The rules themselves are not, I think, difficult either to state, to understand, or to remember ; but they are by no means easy to apply,
inasmuch as from the nature of the case an enormous number of transactions fall close on one side or the other of most of them. Hence
the exposition of these rules, and the abridgment of all the illustrations of them which have occurred in practice, occupy a very
large space in the different text writers. They will be found in 2
Ph. Ev. 332-424; T. E. ss. 1031-1110; Stark. 648-731; Best (very
shortly and imperfectly), ss. 226-229; R. N. P. (an immense list of
cases), 17-35.

As to paragraph (4), which is founded on the case of *Goss* v. *Lord
Nugent*, it is to be observed that the paragraph is purposely so drawn
as not to touch the question of the effect of the Statute of Frauds. It
was held in effect in *Goss* v. *Lord Nugent* that if by reason of the
Statute of Frauds the substituted contract could not be enforced, it
would not have the effect of waiving part of the original contract;
but it seems the better opinion that a verbal rescission of a contract
good under the Statute of Frauds would be good. See *Noble* v. *Ward*,
L. R. 2 Ex. 135, and Pollock on Contracts, 411, note (6). A contract
by deed can be released only by deed, and this case also would fall
within the proviso to paragraph (4).

The cases given in the Illustrations will be found to mark sufficiently
the various rules stated. As to paragraph (5) a very large collection
of cases will be found in the notes to *Wigglesworth* v. *Dallison*, 1 S.
L. C. 598-628, but the consideration of them appears to belong rather
to mercantile law than to the Law of Evidence. For instance, the
question what stipulations are consistent with, and what are contradictory to, the contract formed by subscribing a bill of exchange, or
the contract between an insurer and an underwriter, are not questions
of the Law of Evidence.

NOTE XXXIII.

(TO ARTICLE 91.)

Perhaps the subject-matter of this Article does not fall strictly within the Law of Evidence, but it is generally considered to do so; and as it has always been treated as a branch of the subject, I have thought it best to deal with it.

The general authorities for the propositions in the text are the same as those specified in the last note; but the great authority on the subject is the work of Vice-Chancellor Wigram on Extrinsic Evidence. Article 91, indeed, will be found, on examination, to differ from the six propositions of Vice-Chancellor Wigram only in its arrangement and form of expression, and in the fact that it is not restricted to wills. It will, I think, be found, on examination, that every case cited by the Vice-Chancellor might be used as an illustration of one or the other of the propositions contained in it.

It is difficult to justify the line drawn between the rule as to cases in which evidence of expressions of intention is admitted and cases in which it is rejected (paragraph 7, Illustrations (*k*), (*l*), and paragraph 8, Illustration (*n*)). When placed side by side, such cases as *Doe* v. *Hiscocks* (Illustration (*k*)) and *Doe* v. *Needs* (Illustration (*n*)) produce a singular effect. The vagueness of the distinction between them is indicated by the case of *Charter* v. *Charter*, L. R. 2 P. & D. 315. In this case the testator Forster Charter appointed "my son Forster Charter" his executor. He had two sons, William Forster Charter and Charles Charter, and many circumstances pointed to the conclusion that the person whom the testator wished to be his executor was Charles Charter. Lord Penzance not only admitted evidence of all the circumstances of the case, but expressed an opinion (p. 319) that, if it were necessary, evidence of declarations of intention might be admitted under the rule laid down by Lord Abinger in *Hiscocks* v. *Hiscocks*, because part of the language employed ("my son —— Charter") applied correctly to each son, and the remainder, "Forster," to neither. This mode of construing the rule would admit evidence of declarations of

intention both in cases falling under paragraph 8, and in cases falling
under paragraph 7, which is inconsistent not only with the reasoning
in the judgment, but with the actual decision in *Doe* v. *Hiscocks*. It is
also inconsistent with the principles of the judgment in the later case
of *Allgood* v. *Blake*, L. R. 8 Ex. 160, where the rule is stated by Blackburn, J., as follows:—"In construing a will, the court is entitled to
put itself in the position of the testator, and to consider all material
facts and circumstances known to the testator with reference to which
he is to be taken to have used the words in the will, and then to declare what is the intention evidenced by the words used with reference
to those facts and circumstances which were (or ought to have been) in
the mind of the testator when he used those words." After quoting
Wigram on Extrinsic Evidence, and *Doe* v. *Hiscocks*, he adds: "No
doubt, in many cases the testator has, for the moment, forgotten or
overlooked the material facts and circumstances which he well knew.
And the consequence sometimes is that he uses words which express
an intention which he would not have wished to express, and would
have altered if he had been reminded of the facts and circumstances.
But the court is to construe the will as made by the testator, not to
make a will for him; and therefore it is bound to execute his expressed intention, even if there is great reason to believe that he has
by blunder expressed what he did not mean." The part of Lord
Penzance's judgment above referred to was unanimously overruled in
the House of Lords; though the court, being equally divided as to
the construction of the will, refused to reverse the judgment, upon
the principle "*præsumitur pro negante.*"

Conclusive as the authorities upon the subject are, it may not, perhaps, be presumptuous to express a doubt whether the conflict between a natural wish to fulfill the intention which the testator would
have formed if he had recollected all the circumstances of the case;
the wish to avoid the evil of permitting written instruments to be
varied by oral evidence; and the wish to give effect to wills, has not
produced in practice an illogical compromise. The strictly logical
course, I think, would be either to admit declarations of intention

both in cases falling under paragraph 7, and in cases falling under paragraph 8, or to exclude such evidence in both classes of cases, and to hold void for uncertainty every bequest or devise which was shown to be uncertain in its application to facts.   Such a decision as that in *Stringer* v. *Gardiner*, the result of which was to give a legacy to a person whom the testator had no wish to benefit, and who was not either named or described in his will, appears to me to be a practical refutation of the principle or rule on which it is based.

Of course every document, whatever, must to some extent be interpreted by circumstances.   However accurate and detailed a description of things and persons may be, oral evidence is always wanted to show that persons and things answering the description exist; and therefore in every case whatever, every fact must be allowed to be proved to which the document does, or probably may, refer; but if more evidence than this is admitted, if the court may look at circumstances which affect the probability that the testator would form this intention or that, why should declarations of intention be excluded? If the question is, "What did the testator say?" why should the court look at the circumstances that he lived with Charles, and was on bad terms with William?   How can any amount of evidence to show that the testator intended to write "Charles" show that what he did write means "Charles"?   To say that "Forster" means "Charles" is like saying that "two" means "three."   If the question is, "What did the testator wish?" why should the court refuse to look at his declarations of intention?   And what third question can be asked?   The only one which can be suggested is, "What would the testator have meant if he had deliberately used unmeaning words?"   The only answer to this would be, he would have had no meaning, and would have said nothing, and his bequest should be *pro tanto* void.

NOTE XXXIV.

(TO ARTICLE 92.)

See 2 Ph. Ev. 364; Stark. 726; T. E. (from Greenleaf), s. 1051. Various cases are quoted by these writers in support of the first part of the proposition in the Article; but *R. v. Cheadle* is the only one which appears to me to come quite up to it. They are all settlement cases.

NOTE XXXV.

(TO CHAPTER XIII.)

In this and the following Chapter many matters usually introduced into treatises on evidence are omitted, because they appear to belong either to the subject of pleading, or to different branches of Substantive Law. For instance, the rules as to the burden of proof of negative averments in criminal cases (1 Ph. Ev. 555, etc.; 3 Russ. Cri. 276–9) belong rather to criminal procedure than to evidence. Again, in every branch of Substantive Law there are presumptions, more or less numerous and important, which can be understood only in connection with those branches of the law. Such are the presumptions as to the ownership of property, as to consideration for a bill of exchange, as to many of the incidents of the contract of insurance. Passing over all these, I have embodied in Chapter XIV. those presumptions only which bear upon the proof of facts likely to be proved on a great variety of different occasions, and those estoppels only which arise out of matters of fact, as distinguished from those which arise upon deeds or judgments.

NOTE XXXVI.

(TO ARTICLE 94.)

The presumption of innocence belongs principally to the Criminal Law, though it has, as the Illustrations show, a bearing on the proof of ordinary facts. The question, "What doubts are reasonable in criminal cases?" belongs to the Criminal Law.

NOTE XXXVII.

(TO ARTICLE 101.)

The first part of this Article is meant to give the effect of the presumption, *omnia esse rite acta*, 1 Ph. Ev. 480, etc.; T. E. ss. 124, etc.;

Best, s. 353, etc. This, like all presumptions, is a very vague and fluid rule at best, and is applied to a great variety of different subject-matters.

NOTE XXXVIII.

(TO ARTICLES 102–105.)

These Articles embody the principal cases of estoppels *in pais*, as distinguished from estoppels by deed and by record. As they may be applied in a great variety of ways and to infinitely various circumstances, the application of these rules has involved a good deal of detail. The rules themselves appear clearly enough on a careful examination of the cases. The latest and most extensive collection of cases is to be seen in 2 S. L. C. 851–880, where the cases referred to in the text and many others are abstracted. See, too, 1 Ph. Ev. 350–3; T. E. ss. 88–90, 776, 778; Best, s. 543.

Article 102 contains the rule in *Pickard* v. *Sears*, 6 A. & E. 474. as interpreted and limited by Parke, B., in *Freeman* v. *Cooke*, 6 Bing. 174, 179. The second paragraph of the Article is founded on the application of this rule to the case of a negligent act causing fraud. The rule, as expressed, is collected from a comparison of the following cases: *Bank of Ireland* v. *Evans*, 5 H. L. C. 389; *Swan* v. *British and Australasian Company*, which was before three courts, see 7 C. B. (N. S.) 448; 7 H. & N. 603; 2 H. & C. 175, where the judgment of the majority of the Court of Exchequer was reversed; and *Halifax Guardians* v. *Wheelwright*, L. R. 10 Ex. 183, in which all the cases are referred to. All of these refer to *Young* v. *Grote* (4 Bing. 253), and its authority has always been upheld, though not always on the same ground. The rules on this subject are stated in general terms in *Carr* v. *L. & N. W. Railway*, L. R. 10 C. P. 316–17.

It would be difficult to find a better illustration of the gradual way in which the judges construct rules of evidence, as circumstances require it, than is afforded by a study of these cases.

NOTE XXXIX.

(TO CHAPTER XV.)

The law as to the competency of witnesses was formerly the most, or nearly the most, important and extensive branch of the Law of Evidence. Indeed, rules as to the incompetency of witnesses, as to the proof of documents, and as to the proof of some particular issues, are nearly the only rules of evidence treated of in the older authorities. Great part of Bentham's ' Rationale of Judicial Evidence' is directed to an exposure of the fundamentally erroneous nature of the theory upon which these rules were founded; and his attack upon them has met with a success so nearly complete that it has itself become obsolete. The history of the subject is to be found in Mr. Best's work, book i. part i. ch. ii. ss. 132–188. See, too, T. E. ss. 1210–57, and R. N. P. 177–81. As to the old law, see 1 Ph. Ev. 1, 104.

NOTE XL.

(TO ARTICLE 107.)

The authorities for the first paragraph are given at great length in Best, ss. 146–165. See, too, T. E. s. 1240. As to paragraph 2, see Best, s. 148; 1 Ph. Ev. 7; 2 Ph. Ev. 457; T. E. s. 1241. The concluding words of the last paragraph are framed with reference to the alteration in the law as to the competency of witnesses made by 32 & 33 Vict. c. 68, s. 4.[1] The practice of insisting on a child's belief in punishment in a future state for lying, as a condition of the admissibility of its evidence, leads to anecdotes and to scenes little calculated to increase respect either for religion or for the administration of justice. The statute referred to would seem to render this unnecessary. If a person who deliberately and advisedly rejects all belief in God and a future state is a competent witness, *a fortiori*, a child who has received no instructions on the subject must be competent also.

---

[1] Now (1893) repealed by the Oaths Act, 1888

NOTE XLI.

(TO ARTICLE 108.)

At Common Law the parties and their husbands and wives were incompetent in all cases. This incompetency was removed as to the parties in civil, but not in criminal cases, by 14 & 15 Vict. c. 99, s. 2; and as to their husbands and wives, by 16 & 17 Vict. c. 83, ss. 1, 2. But sec. 2 expressly reserved the Common Law as to criminal cases and proceedings instituted in consequence of adultery.

The words relating to adultery were repealed by 32 & 33 Vict. c. 68, s. 3, which is the authority for Article 109.

Persons interested and persons who had been convicted of certain crimes were also incompetent witnesses, but their incompetency was removed by 6 & 7 Vict. c. 85.

The text thus represents the effect of the Common Law as varied by four distinct statutory enactments.

NOTE XLII.

(TO ARTICLE 111.)

The cases on which these Articles are founded are only Nisi Prius decisions; but as they are quoted by wr. ers of eminence (1 Ph. Ev. 139; T. E. s. 859), I have referred to them.

In the trial of Lord Thanet, for an attempt to rescue Arthur O'Connor, Sergeant Shepherd, one of the special commissioners, before whom the riot took place in court at Maidstone, gave evidence, *R.* v. *Lord Thanet,* 27 S. T. 836.

I have myself been called as a witness on a trial for perjury to prove what was said before me when sitting as an arbitrator. The trial took place before Mr. Justice Hayes at York, in 1869.

As to the case of an advocate giving evidence in the course of a trial in which he is professionally engaged, see several cases cited and discussed in Best, ss. 184-6.

In addition to those cases, reference may be made to the trial of

Horne Tooke for a libel in 1777, when he proposed to call the Attorney-General (Lord Thurlow), 20 S. T. 740. These cases do not appear to show more than that, as a rule, it is for obvious reasons improper that those who conduct a case as advocates should be called as witnesses in it. Cases, however, might occur in which it might be absolutely necessary to do so. For instance, a solicitor engaged as an advocate might, not at all improperly, be the attesting witness to a deed or will.

NOTE XLIII.

(TO ARTICLE 115.)

This Article sums up the rule as to professional communications, every part of which is explained at great length, and to much the same effect, in 1 Ph. Ev. 105-122; T. E. ss. 832-9; Best, s. 581. It is so well established and so plain in itself that it requires only negative illustrations. It is stated at length by Lord Brougham in *Greenough* v. *Gaskell*, 1 M. & K. 98. The last leading case on the subject is *R.* v. *Cox & Railton*, 14 Q. B. D. 153. Leges Henrici Primi, v. 17: "Caveat sacerdos ne de hiis qui ei confitentur peccata alicui recitet quod ei confessus est, non propinquis, non extraneis. Quod si fecerit deponetur et omnibus diebus vitæ suæ ignominiosus peregrinando pœniteat." 1 M. 508.

NOTE XLIV.

(TO ARTICLE 117.)

The question whether clergymen, and particularly whether Roman Catholic priests, can be compelled to disclose confessions made to them professionally, has never been solemnly decided in England, though it is stated by the text writers that they can. See 1 Ph. Ev. 109; T. E. ss. 837-8; R. N. P. 190; Starkie, 40. The question is discussed at some length in Best, ss. 583-4; and a pamphlet was written to maintain the existence of the privilege by Mr. Baddeley in 1865. Mr. Best shows clearly that none of the decided cases are directly in point, except *Butler* v. *Moore* (MacNally, 253-4), and possibly *R.* v. *Sparkes*, which was cited by Garrow in arguing *Du Barré* v. *Livette* before Lord Kenyon (1 Pea. 108). The report of his argument is in these words: "The prisoner, being a Papist, had made a confession before a Protestant clergyman of the crime for which he was indicted; and that confession was permitted to be given in evidence on the trial" (before Buller, J.), "and he was convicted and executed." The report is of no value, resting as it does on Peake's note of Garrow's statement of a case in which he was probably not personally concerned; and it does not appear how the objection was taken, or whether the matter was ever argued. Lord Kenyon, however, is said to have observed: "I should have paused before I admitted the evidence there admitted."

Mr. Baddeley's argument is in a few words, that the privilege must have been recognized when the Roman Catholic religion was established by law, and that it has never been taken away.

I think that the modern Law of Evidence is not so old as the Reformation, but has grown up by the practice of the courts, and by decisions in the course of the last two centuries. It came into existence at a time when exceptions in favor of auricular confessions to Roman Catholic priests were not likely to be made. The general rule is that every person must testify to what he knows. An exception to the general rule has been established in regard to legal advisers, but there is nothing to show that it extends to clergymen, and it is usually so stated as not to include them. This is the ground on which the Irish Master of the Rolls (Sir Michael Smith) decided the case of *Butler* v. *Moore*, in 1802 (MacNally, Ev. 253-4). It was a demurrer to a rule to administer interrogatories to a Roman Catholic priest as to matter which he said he knew, if at all, professionally only. The Judge said, "It was the undoubted legal constitutional right of every subject of the realm who has a cause depending, to call upon a fellow-subject to testify what he may know of the matters in issue; and every man is bound to make the discovery, unless specially exempted and protected by law. It was candidly admitted, that no special exemption could be shown in the present instance, and analogous cases and principles alone were relied upon." The analogy, however, was not considered sufficiently strong.

Several judges have, for obvious reasons, expressed the strongest disinclination to compel such a disclosure. Thus Best, C. J., said, "I, for one, will never compel a clergyman to disclose communications made to him by a prisoner; but if he chooses to disclose them I shall receive them in evidence" (*obiter*, in *Broad* v. *Pitt*, 3 C. & P. 518). Alderson, B., thought (rather it would seem as a matter of good feeling than as a matter of positive law) that such evidence should not be given. *R.* v. *Griffin*, 6 Cox, 219.

NOTE XLV.

(TO ARTICLES 126, 127, 128.)

These Articles relate to matters almost too familiar to require authority, as no one can watch the proceedings of any court of justice without seeing the rules laid down in them continually enforced. The subject is discussed at length in 2 Ph. Ev. pt. 2, chap. x. p. 456, etc.; T. E. s. 1258, etc.; see, too, Best, s. 631, etc. In respect to leading questions it is said, "It is entirely a question for the presiding judge whether or not the examination is being conducted fairly." R. N. P. 182.

NOTE XLVI.

(TO ARTICLE 129.)

This Article states a practice which is now common, and which never was more strikingly illustrated than in the case referred to in the Illustration. But the practice which it represents is modern; and I submit that it requires the qualification suggested in the text. I shall not believe, unless and until it is so decided upon solemn argument, that by the law of England a person who is called to prove a minor fact, not really disputed, in a case of little importance, thereby exposes himself to having every transaction of his past life, however private, inquired into by persons who may wish to serve the basest purposes of fraud or revenge by doing so. Suppose, for instance, a medical man were called to prove the fact that a slight wound had been inflicted, and been attended to by him, would it be lawful, under pretence of testing his credit, to compel him to answer upon oath a series of questions as to his private affairs, extending over many years, and tending to expose transactions of the most delicate and secret kind, in which the fortune and character of other persons might be involved? If this is the law, it should be altered. The following section of the Indian Evidence Act (1 of 1872) may perhaps be deserving of consideration. After authorizing, in sec. 147, questions as to the credit of the witness, the Act proceeds as follows in sec. 148 :—

" If any such question relates to a matter not relevant to the suit or proceeding, except so far as it affects the credit of the witness by injuring his character, the court shall decide whether or not the witness shall be compelled to answer it, and may, if it thinks fit, warn the witness that he is not obliged to answer it. In exercising this discretion, the court shall have regard to the following considerations :—

"(1) Such questions are proper if they are of such a nature that the truth of the imputation conveyed by them would seriously affect the opinion of the court as to the credibility of the witness on the matter to which he testifies.

"(2) Such questions are improper if the imputation which they convey relates to matters so remote in time or of such a character that the truth of the imputation would not affect, or would affect in a slight degree, the opinion of the court as to the credibility of the witness on the matter to which he testifies.

"(3) Such questions are improper if there is a great disproportion between the importance of the imputation made against the witness's character and the importance of his evidence."

Order xxxvi., Rule 38, expressly gives the judge a discretion which was much wanted, and which I believe he always possessed.

NOTE XLVII.

(TO ARTICLE 131.)

The words of the two sections of 17 & 18 Vict. c. 125, meant to be represented by this Article, are as follows :—

22. A party producing a witness shall not be allowed to impeach his credit by general evidence of bad character; but he may, in case the witness shall, in the opinion of the judge, prove adverse, contradict him by other evidence, or, by leave of the judge, prove that he has made at other times a statement inconsistent with his present testimony; but before such last-mentioned proof can be given, the circumstances of the supposed statement, sufficient to designate the particular occasion, must be mentioned to the witness, and he must be asked whether or not he has made such statement.

23. If a witness, upon cross-examination as to a former statement made by him relative to the subject-matter of the cause, and inconsistent with his present testimony, does not distinctly admit that he made such statement, proof may be given that he did in fact make it; but before such proof can be given, the circumstances of the supposed statement, sufficient to designate the particular occasion, must be mentioned to the witness, and he must be asked whether or not he has made such statement.

The sections are obviously ill-arranged; but apart from this, s. 22 is so worded as to suggest a doubt whether a party to an action has a right to contradict a witness called by himself whose testimony is adverse to his interests. The words "he may, in case the witness shall, in the opinion of the judge, prove adverse, contradict him by other evidence," suggest that he cannot do so unless the judge is of that opinion. This is not, and never was, the law. In *Greenough* v. *Eccles*, 5 C. B. (N. S.) p. 802, Williams, J., says: "The law was clear that you might not discredit your own witness by general evidence of bad character; but you might, nevertheless, contradict him by other evidence relevant to the issue;" and he adds (p. 803): "It is impossible to suppose that the Legislature could have really intended to impose any fetter whatever on the right of a party to contradict his own witness by other evidence relevant to the issue,—a right not only established by authority, but founded on the plainest good sense."

Lord Chief Justice Cockburn said of the 22nd section: "There has been a great blunder in the drawing of it, and on the part of those who adopted it." . . . "Perhaps the better course is to consider the second branch of the section as altogether superfluous and useless (p. 806)." On this authority I have omitted it.

For many years before the Common Law Procedure Act of 1854 it was held, in accordance with *Queen Caroline's Case* (2 B. & B. 286–291), that a witness could not be cross-examined as to statements made in writing, unless the writing had been first proved. The effect of this rule in criminal cases was that a witness could not be cross-examined as to what he had said before the magistrates without putting in his deposition, and this gave the prosecuting counsel the reply. Upon this subject rules of practice were issued by the judges in 1837, when the Prisoner's Counsel Act came into operation. The rules are published in 7 C. & P. 676. They would appear to have been superseded by the 28 Vict. c. 18.

NOTE XLVIII.

The Statute Law relating to the subject of evidence may be regarded either as voluminous or not, according to the view taken of the extent of the subject.

The number of statutes classified under the head "Evidence" in Chitty's Statutes is 35. The number referred to under that head in the Index to the Revised Statutes is 39. Many of these, however, relate only to the proof of particular documents, or matters of fact which may become material under special circumstances.

Of these I have noticed a few, which, for various reasons, appear important. Such are: 34 & 35 Vict. c. 112, s. 19 (see Article 11); 9 Geo. IV. c. 14, s. 1, amended by 19 & 20 Vict. c. 97, s. 13 (see Article 17); 9 Geo. IV. c. 14, s. 3; 3 & 4 Will. IV. c. 42 (see Article 28); 11 & 12 Vict. c. 42, s. 17 (Article 33); 30 & 31 Vict. c. 35, s. 6 (Article

34); 7 James I. c. 12 (Article 38); 7 & 8 Geo. IV. c. 28, s. 11, amended by 6 & 7 Will. IV. c. 111; 24 & 25 Vict. c. 96, s. 116; 24 & 25 Vict. c. 99, s. 37 (see Article 56); 8 & 9 Vict. c. 10, s. 6; 35 & 36 Vict. c. 6, s. 4 (Article 121); 7 & 8 Will. III. c. 3, ss. 2–4; 39 & 40 Geo. III. c. 93 (Article 122).

Many, again, refer to pleading and practice rather than evidence, in the sense in which I employ the word. Such are the Acts which enable evidence to be taken on commission if a witness is abroad, or relate to the administration of interrogatories.

Those which relate directly to the subject of evidence as defined in the Introduction, are the ten following Acts:—

1.

46 *Geo. III. c.* 37 (1 section; see Article 120). This Act qualifies the rule that a witness is not bound to answer questions which crimi-nate himself, by declaring that he is not excused from answering questions which fix him with a civil liability.

2.

6 & 7 *Vict. c.* 85. This Act abolishes incompetency from interest or crime (4 sections; see Article 106).

3.

8 & 9 *Vict. c.* 113: "An Act to facilitate the admission in evi-dence of certain official and other documents" (8 August, 1845; 7 sections).

S. 1, after preamble reciting that many documents are, by various Acts, rendered admissible in proof of certain particulars if authenti-cated in a certain way, enacts *inter alia* that proof that they were so authenticated shall not be required if they purport to be so authenti-cated. (Article 79.)

S. 2. Judicial notice to be taken of signatures of certain judges. (Article 58, latter part of clause 8.)

S. 3. Certain Acts of Parliament, proclamations, etc., may be proved by copies purporting to be Queen's printer's copies. (Article 81.)

S. 4. Penalty for forgery, etc. This is omitted as belonging to the Criminal Law.

Ss. 5, 6, 7. Local extent and commencement of Act.

4.

14 & 15 *Vict. c.* 99: "An Act to amend the Law of Evidence," 7th August, 1851 (20 sections):—

S. 1 repeals part of 6 & 7 Vict. c. 85, which restricted the operation of the Act.

S. 2 makes parties admissible witnesses, except in certain cases. (Effect given in Articles 106 & 108.)

S. 3. Persons accused of crime, and their husbands and wives, not to be competent. (Article 108.)

S. 4. The first three sections not to apply to proceedings instituted in consequence of adultery. Repealed by 32 & 33 Vict. c. 68. (Effect of repeal, and of s. 3 of the last-named Act given in Article 109.)

S. 5. None of the sections above mentioned to affect the Wills Act of 1838, 7 Will. IV. & 1 Vict. c. 26. (Omitted as part of the Law of Wills.)

S. 6. The Common Law Courts authorized to grant inspection of documents. (Omitted as part of the Law of Civil Procedure.)

S. 7. Mode of proving proclamations, treaties, etc. (Article 84.)

S. 8. Proof of qualification of apothecaries. (Omitted as part of the law relating to medical men.)

Ss. 9, 10, 11. Documents admissible either in England or in Ireland, or in the colonies, without proof of seal, etc., admissible in all. (Article 80.)

S. 12. Proof of registers of British ships. (Omitted as part of the law relating to shipping.)

S. 13. Proof of previous convictions. (Omitted as belonging to Criminal Procedure.)

S. 14. Certain documents provable by examined copies or copies purporting to be duly certified (Article 70. last paragraph.)

S. 15. Certifying false documents a misdemeanor. (Omitted as belonging to Criminal Law.)

S. 16. Who may administer oaths. (Article 125.)

S. 17. Penalties for forging certain documents. (Omitted as belonging to the Criminal Law.)

S. 18. Act not to extend to Scotland. (Omitted.)

S. 19. Meaning of the word "Colony." (Article 80, note 1.)

S. 20. Commencement of Act.

5.

17 & 18 *Vict. c.* 125. The Common Law Procedure Act of 1854 contained several sections which altered the Law of Evidence.

S. 22. How far a party may discredit his own witness. (Articles 131, 133; and see Note XLVII.)

S. 23. Proof of contradictory statements by a witness under cross-examination. (Article 131.)

S. 24. Cross-examination as to previous statements in writing. (Article 132.)

S. 25. Proof of previous conviction of a witness may be given. (Article 130 (1).)

S. 26. Attesting witnesses need not be called unless writing requires attestation by law. (Article 72.)

S. 27. Comparison of disputed handwritings. (Articles 49 and 52.)

After several Acts, giving relief to Quakers, Moravians, and Separatists, who objected to take an oath, a general measure was passed for the same purpose in 1861.

6.

24 & 25 *Vict. c.* 66 (1st August, 1861, 3 sections). (Repealed by the Oaths Act, 1888):—

S. 1. Persons refusing to be sworn from conscientious motives may make a declaration in a given form. (Article 123.)

S. 2. Falsehood upon such a declaration punishable as perjury. (Do.)

S. 3. Commencement of Act.

7.

28 *Vict. c.* 18 (9th May, 1865, 10 sections):—

S. 1. Sections 3—8 to apply to all courts and causes, criminal as well as civil.

S. 3. Re-enacts 17 & 18 Vict. c. 125, s. 22.

S. 4.	"	"	"	s. 23.
S. 5.	"	"	"	s. 24.
S. 6.	"	"	"	s. 25.
S. 7.	"	"	"	s. 26.
S. 8.	"	"	"	s. 27.

The effect of these sections is given in the Articles above referred to by not confining them to proceedings under the Common Law Procedure Act, 1854.

The rest of the Act refers to other subjects.

8.

31 & 32 *Vict. c.* 37 (25th June, 1868, 6 sections):—

S. 1. Short title.

S. 2. Certain documents may be proved in particular ways. (Art. 83, and for schedule referred to, see note to the Article.)

S. 3. The Act to be in force in the colonies. (Article 83.)

S. 4. Punishment of forgery. (Omitted as forming part of the Criminal Law.)

S. 5. Interpretation clauses embodied (where necessary) in Article 83.

S. 6. Act to be cumulative on Common Law. (Implied in Article 73.)

9.

32 & 33 *Vict. c.* 68 (9th August, 1869; 6 sections):—

S. 1. Repeals part of 14 & 15 Vict. c. 99, s. 4, and part of 16 & 17

Vict. c. 83, s. 2. (The effect of this repeal is given in Article 109; and see Note XLI.)

S. 2. Parties competent in actions for breach of promise of marriage, but must be corroborated. (See Articles 106 and 121.)

S. 3. Husbands and wives competent in proceedings in consequence of adultery, but not to be compelled to answer certain questions. (Article 109.)

S. 4. Atheists rendered competent witnesses. (Repealed by Oaths Act, 1888.)

S. 5. Short title.

S. 6. Act does not extend to Scotland.

10.

51 & 52 Vict. c. 46 (24th Dec., 1888; 7 sections) provides that every person objecting to being sworn and stating the ground of his objection to be his religious belief, or the want of any religious belief, may make an affirmation in the manner provided. (See Article 123.)

These are the only Acts which deal with the Law of Evidence as I have defined it. It will be observed that they relate to three subjects only,—the competency of witnesses, the proof of certain classes of documents, and certain details in the practice of examining witnesses. These details are provided for twice over, namely, once in 17 & 18 Vict. c. 125, ss. 22–27, both inclusive, which concern civil proceedings only; and again in 28 Vict. c. 18, ss. 3–8, which re-enacts these provisions in relation to proceedings of every kind.

Thus, when the Statute Law upon the subject of Evidence is sifted and put in its proper place as part of the general system, it appears to occupy a very subordinate position in it. The ten statutes above mentioned are the only ones which really form part of the Law of Evidence, and their effect is fully given in twenty[1] Articles of the Digest, some of which contain other matter besides.

---

[1] 1, 49, 52, 58, 72, 79, 80, 81, 83, 84, 106, 108, 109, 120, 121, 123, 125, 131, 132, 133.

[NOTE XLIX.]

[The following are the original Articles 36, 37, and 38 of Mr. Stephen, transferred from the body of the work :]

ARTICLE 36. ENTRIES IN BANKERS' BOOKS.

A copy of any entry in a banker's book must in all legal proceedings be received as *prima facie* evidence of such entry, and of the matters, transactions, and accounts therein recorded (even in favor of a party to a cause producing a copy of an entry in the book of his own bank.) [1]

Such copies may be given in evidence only on the condition stated in Article 71 (*f*).

The expression 'Bankers' books' includes ledgers, day books, cash books, account books, and all other books used in the ordinary business of the bank.

The word "Bank" is restricted to banks which have duly made a return to the Commissioners of Inland Revenue,

Savings banks certified under the Act relating to savings banks, and

Post-office savings banks.

The fact that any bank has duly made a return to the Commissioners of Inland Revenue may be proved in any legal proceeding by the production of a copy of its return verified by the affidavit of a partner or officer of the bank, or by the production of a copy of a newspaper purporting to contain a copy of such return published by the Commissioners of Inland Revenue.

The fact that any such savings bank is certified under the Act relating to savings banks may be proved by an office or examined copy of its certificate. The fact that any such bank is a post-office savings bank may be proved by a certificate purporting to be under the hand of Her Majesty's Postmaster-General or one of the secretaries of the Post-Office. [2]

---

[1] *Harding* v. *Williams*, 14 Ch. D. 197.
[2] 42 & 43 Vict. c. 2.

ARTICLE 37. BANKERS NOT COMPELLABLE TO PRODUCE THEIR BOOKS.

A bank or officer of a bank is not, in any legal proceeding to which the bank is not a party, compellable to produce any banker's book, or to appear as a witness to prove the matters, transactions, and accounts therein recorded, unless by order of a judge of the High Court made for special cause (or by a County Court Judge in respect of actions in his own court.)[1]

ARTICLE 38. JUDGE'S POWERS AS TO BANKERS' BOOKS.

On the application of any party to a legal proceeding, a court or judge may order that such party be at liberty to inspect and take copies of any entries in a banker's book for any of the purposes of such proceedings. Such order may be made either with or without summoning the bank, or any other party, and must be served on the bank three clear days (exclusive of Sundays and Bank holidays) before it is to be obeyed, unless the court otherwise directs.[2]

[Upon this subject of bankers' books, Mr. Stephen says in Art. 71 (*f*), that secondary evidence is admissible, "when the document is an entry in a banker's book, proof of which is admissible under Article 36." He also adds: "In case (*f*) the copies cannot be received as evidence unless it be first proved that the book in which the entries copied were made was at the time of making one of the ordinary books of the bank, and that the entry was made in the usual and ordinary course of business, and that the book is in the custody and control of the bank, which proof may be given orally or by affidavit by a partner or officer of the bank, and that the copy has been examined with the original entry and is correct, which proof must be given by some person who has examined the copy with the original entry, and may be given orally or by affidavit. 42 & 43 Vict. c. 11, ss. 3, 5."]

------

[1] 42 & 43 Vict. c. 11.
[2] 42 & 43 Vict. c. 11, s. 7. See *Davies* v. *White*, 53 L. J., Q. B. D. 275; *In re Marshfield, Marshfield* v. *Hutchings*, 32 Ch. D. 499; *Arnott* v. *Hayes*, 36 Ch. D. 731.

[NOTE L.]

[The following are the portions of Articles 56 and 57, transferred from the body of the work :][1]

ARTICLE 56 [in part].

When any person gives evidence of his good character who—

Being on his trial for any felony not punishable with death, has been previously convicted of felony ;[2]

Or who, being upon his trial for any offence punishable under the Larceny Act, 1861, has been previously convicted of any felony, misdemeanor, or offence punishable upon summary conviction ;[3]

Or who, being upon his trial for any offence against the Coinage Offences Act, 1861, or any former Act relating to the coin, has been previously convicted of any offence against any such Act ;[4]

The prosecutor may, in answer to such evidence of good character, give evidence of any such previous conviction, before the jury return their verdict for the offence for which the offender is being tried.[5]

ARTICLE 57 [in part].

In actions for libel and slander in which the defendant does not by his defence assert the truth of the statement complained of, the defendant is not entitled on the trial to give evidence in chief with a view to mitigation of damages, as to the circumstances under which the libel or slander was published, or as to the character of the plaintiff, without the leave of the judge, unless seven days at least before the trial he furnishes particulars to the plaintiff of the matters as to which he intends to give evidence.[6]

---

[1] [See p. 159, notes 2 and 4, *ante.*]

[2] 6 and 7 Will. IV. c. 111, referring to 7 & 8 Geo. IV. c. 28, s. 11. If "not punishable with death " means not so punishable at the time when 7 & 8 Geo. IV. c. 28 was passed (21 June, 1827), this narrows the effect of the Article considerably.

[3] 24 & 25 Vict. c. 96, s. 116.

[4] 24 & 25 Vict. c. 99, s. 37.

[5] See each of the Acts above referred to.

[6] Supreme Court Rules, Order xxxvi., Rule 37.

[NOTE LI.]

[The following are the original Articles 76, 80–84 of Mr. Stephen, transferred from the body of the work :]

ARTICLE 76. GENERAL RECORDS OF THE REALM.

Any record, under the charge and superintendence of the Master of the Rolls for the time being, may be proved by a copy certified as a true and authentic copy by the deputy keeper of the records or one of the assistant record keepers, and purporting to be sealed or stamped with the seal of the Record Office. (1 & 2 Vict. c. 94, ss. 1, 12, 13.)

ARTICLE 80. DOCUMENTS ADMISSIBLE THROUGHOUT THE QUEEN'S DOMINIONS.

If by any law in force for the time being any document is admissible in evidence of any particular, either in courts of justice in England and Wales, or in courts of justice in Ireland, without proof of the seal, or stamp, or signature authenticating the same, or of the judicial or official character of the person appearing to have signed the same, that document is also admissible in evidence to the same extent and for the same purpose, without such proof as aforesaid, in any court or before any judge in any part of the Queen's dominions except Scotland.[1]

ARTICLE 81. QUEEN'S PRINTERS' COPIES.

The contents of Acts of Parliament, not being public Acts, may be proved by copies thereof purporting to be printed by the Queen's printers;

The journals of either House of Parliament; and

---

[1] Consolidates 14 & 15 Vict. c. 99, ss. 9, 10, 11, 19. Sec. 9 provides that documents admissible in England shall be admissible in Ireland; sec. 10 is the converse of 9; sec. 11 enacts that documents admissible in either shall be admissible in the "British Colonies;" and sec. 19 defines the British Colonies as including India, the Channel Islands, the Isle of Man, and "all other possessions" of the British Crown, wheresoever and whatsoever. This cannot mean to include Scotland, though the literal sense of the words would perhaps extend to it.

Royal proclamations,   •

may be proved by copies thereof purporting to be printed by the printers to the Crown or by the printers to either House of Parliament.[1]

ARTICLE 82.   PROOF OF IRISH STATUTES.

The copy of the statutes of the kingdom of Ireland enacted by the Parliament of the same prior to the union of the kingdoms of Great Britain and Ireland, and printed and published by the printer duly authorized by King George III. or any of his predecessors, is conclusive evidence of the contents of such statutes.[2]

ARTICLE 83.   PROCLAMATIONS, ORDERS IN COUNCIL, ETC.

The contents of any proclamation, order, or regulation issued at any time by Her Majesty or by the Privy Council, and of any proclamation, order, or regulation issued at any time by or under the authority of any such department of the Government or officer as is mentioned in the first column of the note[3] hereto, may be proved in all or any of the modes hereinafter mentioned; that is to say—

(1) By the production of a copy of the Gazette purporting to contain such proclamation, order, or regulation:

(2) By the production of a copy of such proclamation, order, or

---

[1] 8 & 9 Vict. c. 113, s. 3.   Is there any difference between the Queen's printers and the printers to the Crown?

[2] 41 Geo. III. c. 90, s. 9.

[3]

COLUMN 1.	COLUMN 2.
Name of Department or Officer.	Names of Certifying Officers.
The Commissioners of the Treasury.	Any Commissioner, Secretary, or Assistant Secretary of the Treasury.
The Commissioners for executing the Office of Lord High Admiral.	Any of the Commissioners for executing the Office of Lord High Admiral or either of the Secretaries to the said Commissioners.
Secretaries of State.	Any Secretary or Under-Secretary of State.

regulation purporting to be printed by the Government printer, or, where the question arises in a court in any British colony or possession, of a copy purporting to be printed under the authority of the legislature of such British colony or possession :

(3) By the production, in the case of any proclamation, order, or regulation issued by Her Majesty or by the Privy Council, of a copy or extract purporting to be certified to be true by the Clerk of the Privy Council or by any one of the Lords or others of the Privy Council, and, in the case of any proclamation, order, or regulation issued by or under the authority of any of the said departments or officers, by the production of a copy or extract purporting to be certified to be true by the person or persons specified in the second column of the said note in connection with such department or officer.

Any copy or extract made under this provision may be in print or in writing, or partly in print and partly in writing.

No proof is required of the handwriting or official position of any person certifying, in pursuance of this provision, to the truth of any copy of or extract from any proclamation, order, or regulation.[1]

Subject to any law that may be from time to time made by the legislature of any British colony or possession, this provision is in force in every such colony and possession.[2]

Where any, enactment, whether passed before or after June, 1882,

Committee of Privy Council for Trade.	Any Member of the Committee of Privy Council for Trade or any Secretary or Assistant Secretary of the said Committee.
The Poor Law Board.	Any Commissioners of the Poor Law Board or any Secretary or Assistant Secretary of the said Board.
The Postmaster-General.	Any Secretary or Assistant Secretary of the Post-Office (33 & 34 Vict. c. 79, s. 21).

(Schedule to 31 & 32 Vict. c. 37.   See also 34 & 35 Vict. c. 70, s. 5.)
[1] 31 & 32 Vict. c. 37, s. 2.   [2] *Ibid.* s. 3.

provides that a copy of any Act of Parliament, proclamation, order, regulation, rule, warrant, circular, list, gazette, or document, shall be conclusive evidence, or be evidence, or have any other effect when purporting to be printed by the government printer, or the Queen's printer, or a printer authorized by her Majesty, or otherwise under her Majesty's authority, whatever may be the precise expression used, such copy shall also be conclusive evidence, or evidence, or have the said effect, as the case may be, if it purports to be printed under the superintendence or authority of her Majesty's Stationery Office.[1]

ARTICLE 84.

FOREIGN AND COLONIAL ACTS OF STATE, JUDGMENTS, ETC.

All proclamations, treaties, and other acts of state of any foreign state, or of any British colony, and all judgments, decrees, orders, and other judicial proceedings of any court of justice in any foreign state or in any British colony, and all affidavits, pleadings, and other legal documents filed or deposited in any such court, may be proved either by examined copies or by copies authenticated as hereinafter mentioned ; that is to say—

If the document sought to be proved be a proclamation, treaty, or other act of state, the authenticated copy to be admissible in evidence must purport to be sealed with the seal of the foreign state or British possession to which the original document belongs ;

And if the document sought to be proved be a judgment, decree, order, or other judicial proceeding of any foreign court, in any British possession, or an affidavit, pleading, or other legal document filed or deposited in any such court, the authenticated copy to be admissible in evidence must purport either to be sealed with the seal of the foreign or other court to which the original document belongs, or, in the event of such court having no seal, to be signed by the judge, or, if there be more than one judge, by any one of the judges of the

---

[1] 45 Vict. c. 9, s. 2. Documentary Evidence Act, 1882. Sect. 4 extends the Act of 1868 to Ireland.

said court, and such judge must attach to his signature a statement
in writing on the said copy that the court whereof he is a judge has
no seal;

If any of the aforesaid authenticated copies purports to be sealed or
signed as hereinbefore mentioned, it is admissible in evidence in
every case in which the original document could have been received
in evidence, without any proof of the seal where a seal is necessary,
or of the signature, or of the truth of the statement attached thereto,
where such signature and statement are necessary, or of the judicial
character of the person appearing to have made such signature and
statement.[1]

Colonial laws assented to by the governors of colonies, and bills reserved by the governors of such colonies for the signification of her
Majesty's pleasure, and the fact (as the case may be) that such law
has been duly and properly passed and assented to, or that such bill
has been duly and properly passed and presented to the governor,
may be proved (*prima facie*) by a copy certified by the clerk or
other proper officer of the legislative body of the colony to be a true
copy of any such law or bill. Any proclamation purporting to be
published by authority of the governor in any newspaper in the
colony to which such law or bill relates, and signifying her Majesty's
disallowance of any such colonial law, or her Majesty's assent to any
such reserved bill, is *prima facie* proof of such disallowance or
assent.[2]

[NOTE LII.]

[The following are portions of Article 108 and of Article 113, and
also (in full) Articles 108 A and 108 B, transferred from the body of the
work:][3]

---

[1] 14 & 15 Vict. c. 99, s. 7.
[2] 28 & 29 Vict. c. 63, s. 6. "Colony" in this paragraph means "all
her Majesty's possessions abroad" having a legislature, "except the
Channel Islands, the Isle of Man, and India." "Colony" in the rest
of the Article includes those places.
[3] [See p. 277, note 2, and p. 283, note 2, *ante.*]

ARTICLE 108 [in part].

In any such criminal proceeding against a husband or a wife, as is authorized by the Married Women's Property Act, 1882 (45 & 46 Vict. c. 75, ss. 12 and 16), the husband and wife respectively are competent and admissible witnesses, and except when defendant compellable to give evidence.[1]

The following proceedings at law are not criminal within the meaning of this Article :—

Trials of indictments for the non-repair of public highways or bridges, or for nuisances to any public highway, river, or bridge ;[2]

Proceedings instituted for the purpose of trying civil rights only ;[3]

Proceedings on the Revenue side of the Exchequer Division of the High Court of Justice.[3]

ARTICLE 108 A.

STATUTORY EXCEPTIONS TO ARTICLE 108.

By the statutes referred to in the first column of the schedule hereto, the persons and the wives and husbands of the persons accused of the offences specified in the second column are made competent witnesses upon their trials for such offences.

---

[1] 47 Vict. c. 14; and see the case of *R. v. Brittleton*, 12 Q. B. D. 266, which turns on the wording of the Act of 1882, and occasioned this enactment. The following doubt arises on the effect of this enactment. Does it mean (*a*) only that the wife is competent as against the husband, and the husband as against the wife, notwithstanding their marriage, or (*b*) that in such cases not only the prosecutor, though married to the prisoner, but the prisoner, though prisoner and though married, is to be competent, though the prisoner is not to be compellable? It is observable that the first "husband and wife" does not become "wife or husband" before the word "respectively," as would have been natural. It is also remarkable that in the Act of 1882 a criminal proceeding is described as "a remedy,"—a very peculiar phrase.

[2] 40 & 41 Vict. c. 14.   [3] 28 & 29 Vict. c. 104, s. 34.

THE SCHEDULE.

___

Indictable Offences.

38 & 39 VICT. C. 86, s. 11. Conspiracy and Protection of Property Act, 1875.	Sect. 4. Wilful and malicious breach of contract relating to gas or water. Sect. 5. Wilful and malicious breach of contract, involving injury to person or property. Sect. 6. Master neglecting to provide servant or apprentice with food, &c.
39 & 40 VICT. C. 80, ss. 3 & 4. Merchant Shipping Act, 1876.	Sect. 4. Sending an unseaworthy ship to sea. Master of a British ship knowingly taking an unseaworthy ship to sea.
40 & 41 VICT. C. 14. Amending Law of Evidence.	Sect. 1. Non-repair of any public highway or bridge, nuisances to public highways, rivers or bridges, and defendants to any indictment instituted for the purpose of trying a civil right only.
46 VICT. C. 83. The Explosive Substances Act, 1883.	Sect. 3. Possession of explosive substances under suspicious circumstances. (The prisoner is not a competent witness in a charge under s. 2 or s. 3)
46 & 47 VICT. C. 51, s. 53. Corrupt and Illegal Practices Prevention Act, 1883.	Any prosecution for any offence under this Act. (These offences may be summary.)

48 & 49 VICT. C. 69, s. 20. Criminal Law Amendment Act, 1885.	Makes parties and their wives competent witnesses in any of the following cases:
	  1. Offences under the Act itself: abusing girls under 16 or children: keeping brothels: indecent behavior in certain cases, &c.
	  2. 24 & 25 Vict. c. 100, s. 48, rape; s. 52, indecent assault; s. 53, abduction of heiress; s. 54, forcible abduction; s. 55, abduction of girl under 16.
	N. B.—An assault with intent to ravish is not within the Act.

50 & 51 VICT. C. 28, s. 10. Merchandise Marks Act, 1887.	Any offence against this Act. (These offences may be summary.)
50 & 51 VICT. C. 58, s. 62, SUB-S. (ii.). Coal Mines Regulation Act, 1887.	Any person charged with an offence under this Act may be sworn and examined as an ordinary witness in the case. (The Act does not mention the wives or husbands of persons charged. Offences under the Act may be summary.)
52 & 53 VICT. C. 44, s. 7. Prevention of Cruelty to and Protection of Children Act, 1889.	In any proceeding under this Act the person charged and the wife and husband are competent but not compellable witnesses, but the wife or husband "may be required to attend to give evidence." (These offences may be summary.)
55 VICT. C. 4, s. 6. Betting and Loans (Infants) Act, 1892.	Any offence under this Act. (These offences may be summary.)

SUMMARY OFFENCES.

35 & 36 *Vict. c.* 77, *s.* 34 (4) . .	Metalliferous Mines Regulation Act.
35 & 36 *Vict. c.* 94, *s.* 51 (4) . .	Licensing Act, 1872.
38 & 39 *Vict. c.* 63, *s.* 21	Sale of Food and Drugs Act, 1875.
38 & 39 *Vict. c.* 17, *s.* 87	Explosives Act, 1875. (These offences may be indictable.)

ARTICLE 108 B.

EFFECT OF EVIDENCE BY ACCUSED PERSON.

When a prisoner is indicted for more misdemeanors than one, and is a competent witness upon one count and not upon another, and gives evidence, he may be convicted upon a count upon which he is not a competent witness.[1]

ARTICLE 113 [in part].

A criminal prosecution by the Director of Public Prosecutions is a public prosecution, and the Director of Public Prosecutions cannot be required to say from whom he acquired information or what it was.[2]

[NOTE LIII.]

[The following are portions of Article 121 and of Article 125, and also (in full) Article 123 A, transferred from the body of the work :][3]

ARTICLE 121 [in part].

No person can be convicted of an offence against Section 4 of the Criminal Law Amendment Act, 1885, upon the unsworn evidence of a

---

[1] *R.* v. *Owen*, 20 Q. B. D. 829. The ground of this decision appears to have been that the prisoner's evidence, though inadmissible as evidence upon the count upon which he was convicted, might be regarded as a voluntary admission by him in the presence of the jury. See *R.* v. *Paul*, 25 Q. B. D. 202, in which *R.* v. *Owen* is considered and explained.

[2] *Marks* v. *Beyfus*, 25 Q B. D. 494.

[3] [See p. 300, note 2, p. 306, note 1, and p. 310, note 1, *ante.*]

child of tender years, unless such unsworn evidence is corroborated by material evidence implicating the accused.[1]

ARTICLE 123 A.

UNSWORN EVIDENCE OF YOUNG CHILD.

Where, upon the hearing of a charge under Section 4 of the Criminal Law Amendment Act, 1885, a child of tender years who is tendered as a witness does not, in the opinion of the court, understand the nature of an oath, the evidence of such child may be received, though not given upon oath, if, in the opinion of the court, such child is possessed of sufficient intelligence to justify the reception of the evidence, and understands the duty of speaking the truth ;[2]

Provided, that no person can be convicted in such a case unless such unsworn evidence is corroborated by other material evidence implicating the accused.[2]

Any witness whose evidence, not under oath, has been admitted as mentioned in this Article is liable to indictment and punishment for perjury in all respects as if he or she had been sworn.[3]

If evidence not under oath is given under the provisions stated in this Article, and the charge is one of felony, the prisoner may be convicted under section 9 of the Criminal Law Amendment Act, 1885, of an offence[3] in respect of which such unsworn evidence might not have been given.[4] If the charge is one of misdemeanor, the prisoner cannot be convicted of another misdemeanor, in respect of which such unsworn evidence might not have been given, if such other misdemeanor was charged in another count of the indictment.[5]

---

[1] 48 & 49 Vict. c. 69, s. 4. See Art. 123 A.

[2] 48 & 49 Vict. c. 69, s. 4. The offences under this section are, unlawfully and carnally knowing, and attempting unlawfully and carnally to know, any girl under thirteen.

[3] These offences are, any offence under ss. 3, 4, 5 of the Criminal Law Amendment Act, 1885, and indecent assault.

[4] *R.* v. *Wealand,* 20 Q. B. D. 827.

[5] *R.* v. *Paul,* 25 Q. B. D. 202. It has not been expressly decided whether, upon an indictment in one count under s. 4 for attempting

ARTICLE 125 [in part].

[The paragraphs omitted from the original Article (see p. 310, *ante*) are as follows:]

(*c*) Before any officer of the court or any other person or persons appointed for that purpose by the court or a judge under the Judicature Act, 1875, Order xxxvii. 5.

Oral evidence taken upon a preliminary hearing may, in the cases specified in 11 & 12 Vict. c. 42, s. 17, 30 & 31 Vict. c. 35, s. 6, and 17 & 18 Vict. c. 104, s. 270, be recorded in the form of a deposition, which deposition may be used as documentary evidence of the matter stated therein in the cases and on the conditions specified in Chapter XVII.

---

to have carnal knowledge of a girl under thirteen, where evidence has been given not upon oath, the prisoner may be convicted of indecent assault, but it seems to be the logical result of *R.* v. *Wealand* and *R.* v. *Paul* that he might.

INDEX.

Bond (*continued*).

official sureties on, when bound by judgment against principal, 132.

Book entries, in partnership books evidence against partner, 58.

made in course of business, admissibility of, 91–95.

entries by deceased notaries, clerks, bank tellers, attorneys, physicians, etc., 91.

handwriting of deceased person to be proved, 91.

entries of insane or absent witness, 91, 93.

books of original entry only admissible, 93.

effect of transcribing charges, 93.

made upon information given by others, 94.

made by party himself, competency of, 92.

how authenticated, 91.

in public books and records, relevancy of, 94, 112, 113.

in corporation books, 113, 114.

in bank-books, 117, 393.

Books, historical, medical, scientific, etc., as evidence, 114–116.

price current lists, annuity tables, almanac, gazetteer, etc., 116, 117.

reading law books and other books to jury, 116.

Boundaries, public and private, declarations concerning, 61, 101, 102.

of public highways, etc., 102, 103.

provable by ancient maps, 115.

of State or county, etc., judicially noticed, 170, 171.

Breach of promise of marriage, woman's bad character for chastity provable, 161.

corroboration of plaintiff's evidence, when required, 300, 301.

Bribing of witness to go away, when provable, 22.

of juror, when provable, 23.

Burden of proof :

rests on person asserting or denying a state of facts, 237, 250.

general burden on party against whom, in the absence of evidence, judgment would be given, 242.

or upon party against whom pleadings raise a presumption, 242, 248, 249.

is on plaintiff when his cause of action is denied, in whole or in part, 242.

even though his cause of action involves negative averments, 240, 241, 242.

as in an action for malicious prosecution, 252.

in proving a negative, plenary proof not required, 252.

is on defendant when he admits cause of action and sets up affirmative defence, 242.

(The numbers refer to pages.)

(The numbers refer to pages.)

Confession, judgment on is a bar, 122.
Confessions, defined, 75.
    how different from admissions, 75.
    by silent acquiescence 15, 25, 27, 75.
    caused by inducement, threat, or promise, effect of, 76–82.
    extrajudicial must be corroborated by proof of *corpus delict.*
        75, 79.
        aliter, as to judicial confession, 76.
            effect of plea of guilty, 76.
    whole confession to be brought out, 75.
    of co-conspirators, 15.
    of one of several defendants, effect of, 15, 76.
    admissibility of determined by judge, 77.
    when voluntary and when involuntary, 77–85.
    burden of proof as to confession being voluntary or involuntary, 77.
    grand jurors may testify as to confessions given before them, 286.
    effect of when made to person in authority, 77–82.
        to person not in authority, 79, 82.
        who is person in authority, 80.
    by prisoner in custody, 78.
    by accomplice who turns State's evidence, 78.
    effect of when made after impression of hope or fear is removed,
        80, 82.
    facts discovered by means of involuntary confessions, when prov-
        able, 80, 82.
    effect of when made under oath, 82–84, 298, 363.
        upon preliminary examination before committing magistrate,
        83, 85.
        at coroner's inquest, 84.
        before grand jury, 84.
    effect of when made under promise of secrecy, 84.
        or when obtained by deception, 84.
            or by religious exhortations, 79, 81.
            or by collateral inducements, 79, 82.
            or by violence of mob, 79.
        when made by drunken person, 85.
            by person asleep, 85.
            by person in prayer, 85.
        or when made in answer to questions, 85.
        or when made without warning being given of the conse-
        quences, 85.
Congress, acts of judicially noticed in State courts, 164.
    laws of, how proved, 204.

(The numbers refer to pages.)

(The numbers refer to pages.)

(The numbers refer to pages.)

Judgment (*continued*).

not binding on parties as to matters not passed upon, 130.

nor as to immaterial matters, 130.

nor as to matters incidentally cognizable, 130.

judgment against person in one capacity, not binding on him in another, 130.

judgment against one administrator not binding on another, 130.

effect of judgment against one tort-feasor, upon the others, 131.

of judgment against one co-contractor, 131.

of judgment against indorsee of bill or note, 132.

of judgment against principal, upon surety or indemnitor, 132.

of judgment against principal felon as respects accessory, 134.

effect of judgment as admission, 131, 134.

effect of, to prove matters of public and general right, 103, 131.

conclusive in favor of judge, 134, 135.

so as to jurisdictional facts which court has power to decide, 135.

impeachable for lack of jurisdiction, 135–138.

judgment of superior domestic court not impeachable collaterally, except when record shows lack of jurisdiction, 136.

in some cases, lack of jurisdiction available as equitable defence, 137.

judgment upon unauthorized appearance of attorney, effect of, 138.

judgments of inferior courts, etc., impeachable, 136.

impeachable by showing its reversal, 137.

effect of pending appeal from judgment, 137.

impeachable by stranger for fraud, 137.

by party for fraud, in equity, 137.

not impeachable for error or irregularity, 137.

foreign judgments and those of sister States, effect of, 138–140.

impeachable for lack of jurisdiction, fraud, etc., 139, 140.

proof of, 146, 207, 399.

Judicial confession. (See Confessions.)

Judicial notice, of what facts taken, 163–173.

taken of common and statute law, corporate charters, etc., 163, 164.

of the laws of antecedent government, 163.

Federal courts notice laws of States, 164.

State courts notice Acts of Congress, 164.

of the legislature, its sessions, etc., 164, 165.

of customs of business, and customs enforced by courts, 165, 166.

(The numbers refer to pages.)

(The numbers refer to pages.)

Jurisdiction (*continued*).
    power of court to determine its own, 135.
    of superior courts presumed, 136.
        aliter, of inferior courts, 137.
    of domestic courts judicially noticed, 166.
    ᴊ ors, may testify as to evidence in former proceeding, 110.
    bribing of, when provable, 23.
    decide as to sufficiency of evidence, 4.
    grand and petit, competency of as witnesses, 284-286.

Knowledge, provable by similar acts or declarations, 42, 48.

Land, application of presumption to question of ownership of, 10, 14.
    title to, how provable, 17.
    value of, how provable, 36, 37, 143.
    admissions concerning. (See Admissions.)
Landlord and tenant :
    landlord's admissions bind tenant, 60.
    tenant's admissions do not bind landlord, 60.
    landlord, by making repairs, admits it to be his duty, 58.
    tenant estopped to deny landlord's title, 266.
    admissions of tenant in common do not bind co-tenant, 69.
Larceny, presumption of guilt from possession of stolen goods, 245.
Lascivious cohabitation, in trials for, marriage not provable by co-
    habitation and repute, 156.
Latent ambiguity, parol evidence to explain. (See Ambiguity.)
Law, common and statute, of forum, judicially noticed, 163, 164.
    of nations, judicially noticed, 168.
    foreign, how proved, 145-147, 201-207.
Law books, reading of to jury, 116.
Law reports as evidence, 117.
Lawyers. (See Attorney ; Barrister.)
Leading questions, nature of, 319, 320.
    not permitted on the examination in chief or on re-examination, 319.
        except when witness is hostile, 319.
        or the examination relates to items, details, etc., 319.
        or when necessary to direct witness's attention to subject-
          matter, 319.
        or when court allows them, 319.
    permitted on cross-examination, 319, 320.
        but not in some States, when counsel inquires as to new mat-
          ter, 320.
    objections to leading questions in taking depositions should be
      taken before the trial, 312.

(The numbers refer to pages.)

(The numbers refer to pages.)

(The numbers refer to pages.)

(The numbers refer to pages.)

(The numbers refer to pages.)

(The numbers refer to pages.)

THE END.

Milton Keynes UK
Ingram Content Group UK Ltd.
UKHW022351041223
433798UK00005B/275